A
Meskwaki-English
and
English-Meskwaki
Dictionary

Based on
Early Twentieth-Century Writings
by Native Speakers

Ives Goddard and Lucy Thomason

Mundart Press

2014

A publication of the Recovering Voices Program of the Smithsonian
Institution, supported in part by a gift from the Shoniya Fund.

Publisher's Cataloging-in-Publication Data

Goddard, Ives, 1941-

    A Meskwaki-English and English-Meskwaki dictionary : based on early twentieth-century writings by
native speakers / Ives Goddard and Lucy Thomason. – Petoskey, MI : Mundart Press, 2014.

    p. ; cm.

    ISBN: 978-0-9903344-0-8

    "A publication of the Recovering Voices Program of the Smithsonian Institution, supported in part by a gift
from the Shoniya Fund."–Title page verso.
    Includes separate appendixes of terms for animals, birds, body parts, calendar, numbers and counting, and
relatives.
    Includes bibliography.
    Summary: This is a dictionary of the Meskwaki language, a member of the Algonquian language family
spoken in Tama County, Iowa. It is a preliminary documentation of the words of the older form of the
language used in writings by native speakers from the early twentieth century, including those of William
Jones and the collection of manuscripts written for Truman Michelson of the Bureau of American Ethnology.
The name Meskwaki (earlier spelled Mesquakie) replaces the historical name Fox. The full official name of
the people who speak Meskwaki is the Sac and Fox Tribe of the Mississippi in Iowa.–Publisher.

    1. Fox language–Dictionaries–English. 2. English language–Dictionaries–Fox. 3. Algonquian languages–
Dictionaries–English. 4. English language–Dictionaries– Algonquian. 5. Fox language–Iowa–Tama County.
6. Sac & Fox Tribe of the Mississippi in Iowa–Languages–Dictionaries. I. Thomason, Lucy Grey, 1968-.
II. Title.

PM1195.Z5 G63 2014   2014939268
497/.314–dc23   1405

Contents

Preface   v

Abbreviations   vi

Introduction   1

Meskwaki-English   13

English-Meskwaki   189

Appendixes

    1. Animals   396

    2. Birds   400

    3. Bodyparts   403

    4. Calendar   408

    5. Numbers and Counting   409

    6. Relatives   412

Preface

This dictionary has been made possible by the work of many people over many years. William Jones (1871-1909), as a graduate student under Franz Boas, wrote his texts from dictation by speakers in the Tama settlement who were not named, perhaps at their request. He was assisted in editing and translating them by his father Henry Clay Jones (1844-1912). Truman Michelson (1879-1938), working for the Bureau of Ethnology of the Smithsonian Institution, collected over 27,000 pages of Meskwaki texts written by Meskwaki speakers, beginning in 1911 and continuing for a number of years. Nearly half of these pages were written by Alfred Kiyana (Keahna) (1877-1918). Other major contributors among the more than 30 writers were Charley H. Chuck (1867-1940), Sakihtanohkweha (1875-1957), Sam Peters (1887-1960), Jim Peters (1866-1917), Bill Leaf (1884-1947), and Jack Bullard (1879-1927). Michelson was assisted by Edward Davenport, Harry Lincoln, Horace Poweshiek, George Black Cloud, and others. James A. Geary compiled a slip file of words on the basis of manuscript and published sources and fieldwork.

In our work in Tama we relied most extensively on the patient assistance of Adeline Wanatee (1910-1996) and Everett Kapayou (1933-2006) in pronouncing and explaining the words in the writings. Many others also helped at different times, and we are grateful to them all.

Washington, April 2014

Abbreviations

AI	animate intransitive (i.e., with animate subject) (see p. 4)
anim.	animate (see p. 3)
dim., dimin.	diminutive (see p. 10)
e.g.	for example
esp.	especially
etc.	and so forth
exc.	exclusive (see pp. 113, 380, 408)
i.e.	that is
II	inanimate intransitive (i.e., with inanimate subject) (see p. 4)
inan.	inanimate (see p. 3)
inc.	inclusive (see pp. 81, 380, 408)
lit.	literally
obv.	obviative
s.o.	animate object or possessor ('he' ('his'), 'she' ('her'), or animate 'it') (see p. 5)
TA	transitive animate (i.e., with animate primary object) (see p. 5)
TI	transitive inanimate (i.e., with inanimate primary object) (see p. 5)

For the use of the little equals sign or double hyphen (=), see p. 2. For the use of the curly braces ({...}), see p. 8.

Introduction

This is a dictionary of the Meskwaki language, a member of the Algonquian language family spoken in Tama County, Iowa. It is a preliminary documentation of the words of the older form of the language used in writings by native speakers from the early twentieth century. These writings include the published work of William Jones (1907, 1911, 1939), a one-quarter Meskwaki who had learned the language from his father and grandmother, and the large collection of manuscripts written by Meskwaki speakers in the local alphabetic syllabary for Truman Michelson of the Bureau of American Ethnology in 1911 and the years following, which are now in the National Anthropological Archives of the Smithsonian Institution (in Suitland, Maryland). The pronunciation and meaning of words from these sources were checked with Meskwaki speakers to the extent possible in the years 1990 to 2005. A small number of additional words obtained then that happened not to be used in the early writings have also been included. The verbs with **neshiwanât-** for 'to ruin' various things in various ways are taken from Michelson (1925:644). Some plant identifications are from Huron Smith (1928).

The name Meskwaki (earlier spelled Mesquakie) replaces the historical name Fox, which has been used in many publications. The full official name of the people who speak Meskwaki is the Sac and Fox Tribe of the Mississippi in Iowa. The Meskwaki language is very similar to Sauk, the heritage language of the Sac and Fox Nation of Oklahoma, and the two could be considered dialects of each other.

This dictionary derives from and essentially replaces *Leonard Bloomfield's Fox Lexicon: Critical Edition* (Goddard 1994), but the earlier book may still be useful for its references to specific source locations in published texts and for its appendix on verbal inflections.

The written materials on which this dictionary is based are for the most part traditional oral literature, including accounts of recent history, tales of the deeds of legendary heroes, and the myths about ancient times that Meskwakis call "winter stories." There are also descriptions of ceremonies and their origins, personal reminiscences, and other miscellaneous categories of writing. Because these texts were written a century ago and were mostly set in earlier times that even then were recalled only in tradition, many of the words given pertain to practices and ways of life that no longer exist. And in fact, a compilation of all the words in these writings would more than double the size of this book. At the same time, much of the vocabulary of the living Meskwaki language of the twenty-first century is not to be found here, including most of the borrowings and adaptations of English words that are now part of everyday discourse. This preliminary inventory of the language also does not include all the words that could be made by employing the exuberant powers of Meskwaki derivation, which combine meaningful elements in a myriad of ways and may create for many word stems numerous modified forms with different grammatical functions, often serially derived one from another.

Spelling and pronunciation. The spelling of Meskwaki words in this dictionary conforms to the conservative pronunciation that would have been generally used in the early twentieth century and is recalled as the correct or proper style of speech today. A practical orthography that makes all the functional distinctions of the language is used:

Meskwaki alphabet:

a, â, ch, e, ê, h, i, î, k, m, n, o, ô, p, s, sh, t, w, y

The letters **â, ê, î,** and **ô** spell the long vowels, which are distinct from the short vowels (**a, e, i, o**). They follow the corresponding short vowels in the alphabet. The digraphs **ch** and **sh**, pronounced as in English *ship* and *chip*, are treated as unit symbols; **sh** is alphabetized after **s**, not as a sequence of **s** + **h**.

Meskwaki **ch, k, p,** and **t** are roughly as in English except that they are not released with a puff of air. Also, Meskwaki **t** is pronounced further forward, behind the front teeth. Meskwaki **s** is regularly or occasionally pronounced like English "th" by some speakers. Meskwaki **h** is pronounced like English **h**—sometimes stronger, sometimes weaker—including when it precedes another consonant. The same **h** sound is always present before **s** and **sh** inside a word, but because this **h** is predictable and redundant it is not written.

The vowels are pronounced with the approximate values they usually have in languages other than English. The long vowels are noticeably longer than the corresponding shorts but not extremely long; they are also distinctly lower (pronounced with a slightly more open jaw) than the shorts. Ordinary words end in a short vowel, which is devoiced (whispered) at the end of an utterance or before a pause. (Interjections, in contrast, may end in a long vowel.) With normal intonation the strongest stress and highest pitch fall on the fourth syllable from the end, or on the second syllable from the end of a shorter word or a word in isolation. In faster and less deliberate styles of speech long vowels may be shortened before **h, s,** and **sh**, while retaining the open quality of a long vowel, and short vowels may become voiceless or even disappear entirely.

Four words, all interjections, have additional sounds. In **ehêhe** 'yes (answering a question)' and **ôhô!** 'Oh yes!' the long vowels are optionally nasalized. For **hâhâw** (the town crier's cry) and **hao, hawo** 'hello; yes (agreeing to a suggestion or request)' phonetic transcriptions are given in square brackets showing glottal stops (written with [ʔ]).

There are several kinds of distinctive sentence intonation that affect these generalizations. For example, with the interrogative intonation (used for questions that can be answered yes or no; marked with **?**) the overall pitch is higher and the main stressed syllable is the third from the end. (Questions made with interrogative words have normal intonation.) In one kind of emphatic intonation a final vowel may be stressed. The expressive negative intonation (used, for example, to give a sarcastic negative tone; indicated by **!?**) has raised overall pitch, primary high pitch and stress on the fourth syllable from the end, and secondary stress with mid pitch on the second syllable from the end. The stressed final vowels of interjections are indicated with **!** in the dictionary entries.

Words entered in the dictionary with an initial little equals sign or double hyphen (**=**) are enclitics, words that must attach to a preceding host and therefore cannot begin a sentence. The main stress falls on the syllable before an enclitic (or before the last of a series of enclitics), or on the second syllable before if a vowel **i** at the beginning of the enclitic has been elided (in which case this is indicated by an apostrophe: **'**). The little equals sign is also used after the aorist proclitic or loose prefix (**êh=**), the future proclitics (**wîh=, nîh=, kîh=**), and the word **o=** 'or', which are always phonetically linked to what follows.

In the technical alphabet used by linguists **ch** is written "č"; **sh** is written "š"; and the long vowels are written with a following raised dot: "a·", "e·", "i·", and "o·". Earlier linguistic sources use different conventions. In the traditional alphabetic syllabary in which the texts are written, **ch** is written like "tt"; **sh** is written like "d"; **kw** may be written like "g"; and vowel length and **h** are not indicated.

Word structure. Meskwaki words are formed in various ways and may be internally quite complex. A basic stem (a word without any inflections) may have one, two, or three components. The first or only component is an INITIAL:

ihkwêwa 'woman': stem **ihkwêw-**, consisting of the initial **ihkwêw-**

wahônwa '(wolf or dog) howls': stem **wahôn-**, consisting of the initial **wahôn-**

The component at the end of the stem (if there is more than one) is a FINAL:

mehtekwinâkani 'wooden bowl': stem **mehtekwinâkan-**, consisting of the initial **mehtekw-** 'wood' and the final **-inâkan** 'bowl'

pôninâkêwa 'stops singing': stem **pôninâkê-**, consisting of the initial **pôn-** 'cease' and the final **-inâkê** 'sing'

A component between an initial and a final is a MEDIAL.

sâkikâshinwa 'lies with a foot sticking out': stem **sâkikâshin-**, consisting of the initial **sâk-** 'partly visible', the medial **-ikâ-** 'foot', and the final **-ishin** 'lie' (here **-shin**)

Many components are themselves derived. The initial **mehtekw-** 'wood' is from (and identical to) the stem of the noun **mehtekwi** 'tree, stick, wood'. The final **-inâkan** 'bowl' is from **anâkani** 'bowl' (stem **anâkan-**). The medial **-ikâ-** 'foot' is from **nehkâchi** 'my foot' (stem **-hkât-**, as in **nehkâtani** 'my feet'). As these examples show, the process of derivation may involve changes in shape, such as the addition or subtraction of sounds.

Processes of SECONDARY DERIVATION make stems with changed or added functions or status from complete stems. When a secondary final is added to a stem there may be modifications of shape, and more than one may be added in sequence:

From **anepyêhamwa** 'he or she writes it' (stem **anepyêh-** 'write (it)'):

anepyêhikêwa 'he or she writes' (stem **anepyêh-** with added final **-ikê**, making a new stem **anepyêhikê-** 'write (something, things)')

anepyêhikawêwa 'he or she writes to him or her' (stem **anepyêhikê-** 'write' with added final **-aw**, making **anepyêhikaw-** 'write to')

From **apanêniwa** 'he or she smiles' (stem **apanêni-** 'smile'):

apanênemêwa 'he or she smiles at him or her' (stem **apanêni-** with added final **-em**, making **apanênem-** 'smile at')

apanênetîwaki 'they smile at each other' (stem **apanênem-** 'smile at' with added final **-etî**, making the reciprocal stem **apanênetî-** 'smile at each other')

Grammatical gender. The fundamental organizing principle of the Meskwaki language is the distinction between two grammatical genders, conventionally called the ANIMATE and the INANIMATE. Included in the animate gender (which may be thought of as the higher category) are not only human beings, animals and other autonomous creatures, and spirits, but a great many other things that are not autonomous or conscious and not thought to be so. Compare these examples:

Animate nouns: **neniwa** 'man', **mahkwa** 'bear', **ashkotênêsiwa** 'Fire Spirit', **anâkwa** 'star', **atâpyâna** 'wagon', **atâmina** 'corn', **wîsakâhkwa** 'white ash tree', **akôna** 'snow', **mehtêha** 'bow', **amehkwaya** 'beaver skin', **netenya** 'my shoulder', **kwananâhaki** 'tubular beads'

Inanimate nouns: **chîmâni** 'canoe', **wâpikoni** 'squash, pumpkin', **mehtekwi** 'tree, stick', **anîpi** 'American elm', **nepi** 'water', **pâshkesikani** 'gun', **mahkwayi** 'bearskin', **mêmêshâhi** 'large bead', **netôshkwani** 'my elbow', **kehkyêweni** 'old age', **pâhpâshânani** 'thin slices of dried meat'

As these examples show, it is easy to tell the gender of any noun. Every noun in the dictionary that ends in **-a** (or in **-ki** if it is plural) is animate. Every noun that ends in **-i** (or **-ni** if plural) is inanimate.

Nouns. Nouns may be inflected with endings that specify gender, number (singular or plural), and other categories.

An animate noun may have an OBVIATIVE suffix: **-ani** (or **-ni**) obviative singular, **-ahi** (or **-hi**) obviative plural. Generally speaking, an obviative is thematically subordinate to an animate noun or pronoun in the same context, but the use of obviatives in connected discourse is complex, subtle, and variable. Verbs may be inflected for obviative subjects of both genders.

The possessor of a noun is indicated by a prefix: **nîchâpa** 'doll', **nenîchâpa** 'my doll'; **chîmâni** 'canoe', **kechîmâni** 'your (singular) canoe'. In some cases there is also a suffix: **ochîmânwâwi** 'their canoe'; **kâshôha** 'cat', **nekâshôhema** 'my cat'. Some nouns are only used with a possessive prefix; these are given in the dictionary with the prefix **ne-** 'my' (or variant **n-**), if such a form was found, otherwise with **o-** 'his or her': **nehkâchi** 'my foot'; **ketânesa** 'your (singular) daughter'; **okotâkani** 'his or her throat'. For some nouns of this type there is also a form with the prefix **me-** (or **m-**) indicating that no possessor is specified: **mehkâchi** 'a foot'; **metêhi** 'a (human or animal) heart'. For other nouns that require a prefix, the form with **o-** can also be used when there is no possessor: **okotâkani** 'a throat'; **owîshi** 'his, her, or its head; a (human or animal) head'. Kinship terms fall into a third category, using derived forms to suppress reference to a possessor: **otânesemâwa** 'the daughter'.

An animate noun possessed by a third person is always obviative: **otânesani** 'his or her daughter (obviative)', **otânesahi** 'his or her daughters (obviative)' (compare **netânesa** 'my daughter', **netânesaki** 'my daughters').

The stem of a noun may be determined by removing the singular ending (**-a** or **-i**) and any possessive inflection; this is the base to which inflections for other grammatical categories are added. For example, the stem **chîmân-** 'canoe' combines with the locative suffix **-eki** ('in, at, on') in **chîmâneki** 'in the canoe', **nechîmâneki** 'in my canoe'.

Verbs. Verbs are highly inflected, with many different endings and a small number of prefixes. In addition to marking verbal modes, they show agreement with the nouns or pronouns that are associated with them as subjects and objects. They typically come in pairs, the selection being determined by gender.

For an INTRANSITIVE verb (one having a subject but no primary object) the stem variant used with an animate subject is an ANIMATE INTRANSITIVE verb (or AI), and the variant used with an inanimate subject is an INANIMATE INTRANSITIVE (or II). A simple intransitive verb is given in the dictionary like this, with the AI first:

 asâwesiwa, asâwâwi (animate, inanimate) is yellow

This can be understood in expanded form as:

 asâwesiwa AI '(animate) is yellow'; *i.e.,* 'he, she, or it (animate) is yellow'

 asâwâwi II '(inanimate) is yellow'; *i.e.,* 'it (inanimate) is yellow'

Note that, because the animate gender includes many things that are referred to in English as "it," to give **asâwesiwa** as meaning simply 'he or she is yellow' would not cover all of its uses, or even the most common ones. In this dictionary "he or she" and "his or her" are only used when the reference is exclusively to people or personified beings. If the subject of an AI verb corresponds to a possessor in the English translation it is glossed 'one's', and if it corresponds to the object of an English preposition it is glossed 'one':

> **kîhpochêwa** 'one's stomach is full'
> **kîkikanêwa** 'regains one's strength'
> **ayîhkwinehkêhokowa** 'one's arms get tired from one's load'
> **pôhkesowa** 'has a hole shot in one by a firearm'

The forms in the dictionary entries for intransitive verbs include the inflectional endings **-wa** and **-wi**. These endings specify the subjects as third person singular, animate and inanimate, in the independent indicative mode, which is used for simple statements. With the endings removed what remains is the STEMS: **asâwesi-** AI, **asâwâ-** II. Verb stems may be inflected with a great many different endings indicating various kinds of subjects and various modes. Although the stem of an intransitive verb may usually be found in this way by removing the ending **-wa** or **-wi** from the citation form given in the dictionary, there is one complication. Some third singular verbs ending in **-êwa** or **-êwi** have stems that end in **-ê**, but others have stems ending in **-â**, which appears before most endings and is replaced by **-a** at the end of the word (where long vowels are excluded by a general rule). In these stems the **-â** is automatically replaced by **-ê** in the third person forms of the independent modes:

> Stems in **-ê** (**kîwê-** AI 'turn back'; **châketê-** II 'burn up')
> > **kîwêwa** 'turns back': **kîwêwaki** 'they turn back', **kîwête** 'if he or she turns back',
> > > **êh=kîwêchi** '(and, that, when) he or she turned back', **kîwêno** 'turn back!'
> > **châketêwi** 'it burns up': **êh=châketêki** 'it burned up'
> Stems in **-â** (e.g. **pyâ-** AI 'come'; **achikâ-** II 'drip, leak')
> > **pyêwa** 'comes': **pyêwaki** 'they come'; but **pyâte** 'if he or she comes', **êh=pyâchi** 'he or
> > > she came', **pyâno** 'come!'
> > **achikêwi** 'it drips, leaks'; but **êh=achikâki** 'it dripped, leaked'

An intransitive verb inflected as **-êwa** AI or **-êwi** II can be recognized as having a stem in **-â** if it ends with one of the following finals: **-âhpawâ** AI 'dream', **-ehkâ** AI, II 'proceed, continue', **-eshkâ** AI, II 'move, become, change', **-âshkâ** AI, II 'fall, fly, rush', **-ekâ** AI 'dance', **-isâ** AI, II 'move quickly, fall, fly', **-îhtâ** AI 'dress', **-îhtâ** AI 'work, do'. In other cases the fact that the stem has **-â** is indicated in the dictionary by the inclusion of an inflected form that shows the **-â** (or word-final **-a**): **nepêwa** 'sleeps', **nenepa** 'I sleep'. (There are also some stems in **-â** that inflect as **-âwa** AI, almost all of them with **-kâpâ** AI 'stand', and there are a good many like **asâwâwi** II 'it is yellow' that inflect as **-âwi** II.)

If a verb is TRANSITIVE (having a subject and a PRIMARY OBJECT) it is the gender of the primary object that selects the stem variants. (In fact, a primary object is, by definition, one that determines the selection of a stem variant.) The variant used with an animate primary object is a TRANSITIVE ANIMATE verb (or TA), and the variant used with an inanimate primary object is a TRANSITIVE INANIMATE (or TI). A typical transitive verb is given like this, with the TA first:

> **âpihwêwa, âpihamwa** 'unties s.o., it'

This can be expanded as:

> **âpihwêwa** TA '(animate) unties s.o.'
> **âpihamwa** TI '(animate) unties it'

Even fuller translations would be these:

> **âpihwêwa** TA 'he or she unties him, her, or it (animate), or them (animate)'
> **âpihamwa** TI 'he or she unties it (inanimate) or them (inanimate)'

To simplify things, the dictionary adopts the convention of using "s.o." to indicate that the primary object is animate and "it" to indicate that it is inanimate. The abbreviation "s.o." may be read for convenience as "someone," as long as it is kept in mind that an animate "it" is also a possibility (where the meaning permits). If the object of a TA verb is a possessor it is glossed 'their':

> **âhtawânêwa** 'puts s.o. on their back'
> **pasekwîchisahêwa** 'jerks s.o. to their feet'

The forms given in the dictionary for TA verbs all include the independent indicative ending **-êwa**, which specifies that the object is animate (singular or plural) and the subject is third person animate singular. The matching TI verbs fall into three formal classes. Verbs like 'untie', with the ending **-amwa**, are in class 1. Class 2 has the ending **-ôwa** (always preceded by **t**), and class 3, which has very few members, has the same ending **-wa** as an AI. In all TI verbs these endings specify that the object is inanimate (singular or plural) and the subject is third person animate singular. Typical entries with class 2 and class 3 TIs are these:

> TA and class 2 TI: **akihêwa, akihtôwa** 'loses s.o., it'
> TA and class 3 TI: **nânêwa, nâtwa** 'goes after s.o., it; goes to get s.o., it'

The stem of a transitive verb may be found by removing the ending **-êwa** from the citation form of the TA or the ending **-amwa, -ôwa,** or **-wa** from the citation form of the TI:

> **âpihw-** TA, **âpih-** TI (class 1) 'to untie'
> **akih-** TA, **akiht-** TI (class 2) 'to lose'
> **nân-** TA, **nât-** TI (class 3) 'to go after, to go get'

There are two formal categories of transitive stems that end with **-n**. Stems that include the TA final **-en** (in the shape **-n** or **-en**) generally meaning 'act on by hand', which is matched by an identical TI stem of class 1, keep this shape in all forms. All other TA stems ending with **-n** replace this with **-sh** before endings that begin with **-i** or **-î**:

> **pemeni** 'take care of (animate)!' (stem **pemen-** TA, **pemen-** TI class 1)
> **nâshi** 'go after (animate)! go get (animate)!' (stem **nân-** TA, **nât-** TI class 3)

Transitive stems have many more inflectional endings than intransitives, indicating various combinations of subjects and objects in all the various modes.

Some verbs that are inflected like an AI are used with a SECONDARY OBJECT of either gender, either optionally or obligatorily. (A secondary object does not determine the selection of a stem variant.) In the translations of these verbs the object is given as "(it)" or more explicitly "(s.o., it)" or "(s.o.)," where appropriate:

> **wêpâhkêwa** 'throws (it)' (used for both 'throws s.o.' and 'throws it')
> **nâkatôsêwa** 'runs following (s.o., it)'
> **mayôhtâkêwa** 'makes (s.o.) weep for people'

Some TA verbs have both a primary object (specified by the inflection) and an implied secondary object, which is indicated in the translation in the same way as with AI verbs:

> **mînêwa** 'gives (it) to s.o.' (used for both 'gives s.o. to s.o.' and 'gives it to s.o.')
> **kemôtemêwa** 'steals (it) from s.o.'
> **nahênetamawêwa** 'thinks (s.o., it) fit for, of s.o.'
> **keteminamawêwa** 'blesses (s.o.) for s.o.'

In TA verbs of this type the secondary object corresponds to the English direct object, and the primary object corresponds to the English indirect object.

Particles. Particles are uninflected words with a wide range of meanings and functions, as reflected by their translations:

> Negative clause marker: **âkwi** 'not', **kâta** 'don't'
> Potential clause marker: **âmihtahi** 'would, etc.'
> Temporal clause marker: **nâhinâhi** 'time', **îninâhi** '(at) that time'
> Conjunction: **ôni** 'then, and then'

Specific time: **anâkowe** 'yesterday'

Relative time: **ashawaye** 'long ago'

Duration: **kenwêshi** 'for a long time'

Specific location: **chîkepyêki** 'at the edge of the water'

Relative location: **penôchi** 'far away'

Manner: **kekeni** 'quickly'

Degree: **atenâwi** 'less'

Kind: **âchipanakichi** 'all different kinds'

Qualifying: **kêkyâta** 'nearly'

Abstract logical status: **mêkwêhe** 'I believe'

Contextual logical status: **môhchi** 'even'

Higher predicate: **kênemâpi** 'I don't know'

Because particles lack distinctive shapes or meanings that identify them as such, they are expressly labeled as particles in the dictionary.

Pronouns. There are several somewhat miscellaneous types of pronouns. Emphatic pronouns express the categories of person for which verbs are inflected. The other pronouns are substitutes for or parasitic to a noun and draw their categorization for gender and number from the noun they refer to. Inanimate singulars may also be used for abstract concepts that do not correspond to any noun.

Emphatic pronoun: **nîna** 'I' (emphatic or contrastive)'; '(by) myself'

Demonstrative pronoun: **îna** 'that (animate)'

Indefinite pronoun: **owiyêha** 'someone, anyone'; **kêkôhi** 'something, anything'

Interrogative pronoun: **wênêha** 'who?', **wêkonêhi** 'what?'

Place-holder pronoun: **awahîma**, **awahîna** 'what's-his-name; the one called (so-and-so)'

Alternative pronoun: **kotaka** 'other (animate)'

The functional type of a pronoun is reflected in its translation.

Compounds. Compound words consist of two or more separate words but function as a single word in the sentence and for purposes of inflection (like a simple, non-compound word). A compound has a head word (which may be a noun, verb, or particle) preceded by a preword (a PRENOUN, PREVERB, or PREPARTICLE), or more than one preword. The spaces between the component words of a compound are written with a hyphen rather than a space:

Compound noun:

meškwi-êhêwa 'red swan' (prenoun **meškwi** 'red' + **êhêw-** 'swan')

nenôtêwi-asêmâwa 'Indian tobacco' (prenoun **nenôtêwi** '(of) Indian' + **asêmâwa** 'tobacco'; compare the noun **nenôtêwa** 'Indian')

Compound verb:

wêpi-mîshâtesiwa 'he or she set about putting on fancy clothing' (preverb **wêpi** 'begin' + **mîshâtesi-** AI 'dress up')

pyêchi-wîtêmêwa 'he or she is coming with him, her, or them' (preverb **pyêchi** 'coming' + **wîtêm-** TA 'accompany')

Particle compound:

mâwachi-menehta 'first of all' (preparticle **mâwachi** 'of all (superlative)' + **menehta** 'first')

nâmi-anâhkane 'under the mat' (preparticle **nâmi** 'under, inside' + **anâhkan-** 'mat' + **-e** particle final; compare the noun **anâhkani** 'mat')

7

nekoti-wâsêyâwe 'for one day' (preparticle **nekoti** 'one' + **wâsêyâw-** 'day' + **-e** particle final; compare the noun **wâsêyâwi** 'day')

The component words of a compound may be separated from each other by words that are not part of the compound, and in this case hyphens are used to flag the components as parts of the same compound word. Multiple preverbs are common, and multiple prenouns are occasionally found. A preword often has the same shape as a particle with the same or a similar meaning, but these classes of words are not interchangeable and their meanings may be distinct. For example, **nîshwi** as a particle or a preparticle means 'two', but as a preverb it means 'as a pair, both together'; it is not used as a prenoun. The particle and preverb **ashki** means 'first, for the first time', but the prenoun **ashki** means 'new'; there is no matching preparticle. For this reason prewords are explicitly labeled in the dictionary and distinguished from particles.

Relative roots. Relative roots are initials that ordinarily require that there be a separate word of a particular semantic category to fill out the meaning, which is otherwise unspecified. They can be described as bearing a valence for a particular kind of OBLIQUE COMPLEMENT (defined as being required by the verb but not a subject or an object). Translations include as a place-holder a characterization of the unspecified component of the oblique complement enclosed in curly braces ({...}), indicating that this is a variable and not the literal meaning. There are six common initials with this property, listed here with brief characterizations of the kinds of obliques they take:

ahkw- (~ **ahko-**, **ahkô-**) '{so} far, {so} long' (linear or temporal extent)

ahpîht- (~ **ahpîhch-**) 'to {such} a degree or extent' (age, speed, intensity, and the like)

in- (~ **ish-**, **ih-**) '{so}, {some} way, to {somewhere}' (manner or goal)

ot- (~ **och-**, **os-**) 'from {something, somewhere}, because of {something}, toward {some direction}, through {some hole}, oriented {so}' (source, point of origin, reason, or direction)

tan- (~ **tash-**, **tah-**) '{somewhere}' (location)

tasw- (~ **taso-**, **tasô-**) '{so much, so many}' (number or amount)

A number of stems function as if they contained a virtual relative root, for example the following:

With virtual **in-** '{so}, {some} way, to {somewhere}':

iwa 'says {so}'

inêwa, **itamwa** 'says {so} to s.o., it'

ihêwa 'goes to {somewhere}'

pyêchihêwa 'comes {some} way'

With virtual **tan-** '{somewhere}':

positional verbs (those for sitting, standing, and lying)

verbs of having and being derived from noun stems

asêwa, **ahtôwa** 'places, puts s.o., it {somewhere}'

awiwa 'is {somewhere}, lives {somewhere}'

kîwitêwa 'stays (around) {somewhere}'

nepêwa 'sleeps {somewhere}'

With virtual **tasw-** '{so much, so many}':

tashiwa, **tasenwi** 'is {so much, so many}'

To various degrees, and often idiomatically, stems with relative roots or virtual relative roots are also used without an oblique complement:

ahkwahkamikatwi 'the world ends'

ahpîhchi 'as one goes along, in the meantime, constantly' (preverb, particle)
tashi 'engaged in' (preverb)
asêwa, **ahtôwa** 'has s.o., it'
kîwitêwa 'stays (around), remains'
nepêwa 'sleeps'
otâshkêwa 'falls off'

Reduplication. There are two general patterns of reduplication, a process that adds one or two syllables to the beginning of stems. One-syllable reduplication indicates repetition or plurality. Two-syllable reduplication typically indicates that an action is repeated, either on the same or different occasions, but it is sometimes used for actions that continue without sharp internal segmentation. These functions are somewhat imprecise, however, and intergrade.

Typically in one-syllable reduplication the initial consonant is copied and followed by a particular vowel, sometimes with additional modification:

nâkwêwaki 'they depart': **nânâkwêwaki** 'they depart to separate destinations'
nekotenwi 'once': **nênekotenwi** 'once each, once each time'
mâne 'many': **mamâne** 'many each'
takwi 'both or all together': **tahtakwi** 'all together, collectively'
pemwêwa 'shoots (at) s.o.': **pîpemwêwa** 'shoots repeatedly (at) s.o.'
pôhkeshamwa 'cuts a hole in it': **pôhpôhkeshamwa** 'cuts holes in it'
kehchi 'great' (prenoun): **kekyêhchi** 'great (plural)' (prenoun)
nemasowa 'stands': **nenyêmasowa** '(just) stands there'
kohkishinwa 'turns over': **kokwêhkishinwa** 'turns over repeatedly'
meshâwi 'it is big': **mêmêshâwani** 'they (inanimate) are big'
kenwâwi 'it is long': **kakânwâwani** 'they (inanimate) are long'

If there is no initial consonant, a **y** is inserted after an added vowel:

âteshi 'in a separate place': **âyâteshi** 'separately from each other'
anehkîhi 'a little': **âyânehkîhi** 'a little each'

There are also some irregular patterns:

taswi '{so many}, {so much}': **âyâtaswi** '{so many} each, {so much} each'

In two-syllable reduplication the entire first syllable with the consonant or consonant sequence that follows it is copied, and this is followed by the second vowel of the stem (shortened if it is long) or by short **a** as a default:

nepêwa 'sleeps': **nepenepêwa** 'is sleeping {somewhere}, sleeps and sleeps'
kîsâtesowa 'is seriously wounded by gunshot': **kîsakîsâtesowaki** 'they are seriously wounded by gunshot'
manesêwa 'gathers firewood': **manamanesêwaki** 'they (always) gather firewood'

If the stem has no initial consonant, an **h** is inserted:

apiwa 'sits': **apihapiwa** '(just) sits there'
opyêni 'slowly': **opyehopyêni** and **opahopyêni** 'taking one's time'

There are also irregular patterns:

tanetonêmowa 'is speaking': **tahitanêmowa** 'is talking away'
ihêwa 'goes to {somewhere}': **ayahayêwa** 'always goes to {somewhere}'

The dictionary lists words in the reduplicated form when this is the only one attested and in some other cases as examples, especially where the formation or the meaning might be unpredictable.

Diminutives. Diminutive forms are made for nouns, intransitive and transitive verbs, and some types of particles and pronouns, though not from demonstrative or emphatic pronouns. In addition to small size or amount, the diminutive may indicate other kinds of diminution and attenuation or an attitude of endearment or pity on the part of the speaker. In a diminutive verb the diminutive effect may apply to the verbal notion or to the subject or object, or both. With verbs denoting qualities that have a scalar value the diminutive provides a comparative:

mâtesêhi 'little knife' (compare **mâtesi** knife)
anâkâhi 'little bowl' (**anâkani** 'bowl')
âhkwamatamôhiwa 'the small or pitiful one is sick' (**âhkwamatamwa** 'he or she is sick')
anâkwîhiwi 'it is early evening' (**anâkwiwi** 'it is evening')
makekinôhiwa 'is big (diminutive), quite big, bigger' (**makekinwa** 'he or she is big')
kenwêshîmêhi 'for quite a long time' (**kenwêshi** 'for a long time')
nômakêhe 'for a short time' (**nômake** 'for a short time'; little difference in meaning)

The dictionary provides only a sample of diminutives, indicated as "(dimin.)." These include some words that have been found only in the diminutive form, some irregular or unpredictable forms, and some that happened to be found in the writings that have been most completely analyzed.

Reciprocal verbs. Reciprocal forms are freely formed from TA stems by adding **-etî** (or **-tî**), sometimes with adjustments in shape:

asemihetîwaki 'they help each other' (from **asemihêwa** 'helps s.o.')
neshkitîwaki 'they admonish each other' (from **neshkimêwa** 'admonishes s.o.')
wîtamâtîwaki 'they tell each other' (from **wîtamawêwa** 'tells s.o.')

These are inflected as AI verbs, and as they are most naturally found with a plural subject they are given as plurals in the dictionary. Singular subjects are, however, occasionally found. The meaning is typically that the action is performed reciprocally by the subjects on each other, but often the meaning is that one of a pair or some of a group act on the other or others. Only a small sample of reciprocal forms is included in the dictionary; for some of these the underlying TA was not found. Some verbs with stems ending in **-tî** do not have a reciprocal meaning, although it can be assumed that they were reciprocals in origin (for example **mîkâtîwa** 'fights, engages in mortal combat').

Participles. Meskwaki verbs very freely form participles, which can be used like nouns ('the one who, which, or that is or does (whatever it is)') or like relative clauses dependent on a noun ('who, which, or that is or does (whatever it is)'). The dictionary includes a number of participles that are conventional designations; these are labeled as participles because they inflect differently from nouns:

nêhâkapita 'son-in-law living with his in-laws' (animate singular)
êkwîchika 'hippopotamus' (animate singular)
sîkenaka 'tavern-keeper, bootlegger' (animate singular)
wênekwanichiki 'the man's parents-in-law' (animate plural)
âhkwahki 'weaponry' (inanimate singular)
mêyôwisekini 'wailing songs' (inanimate plural)

An important class of participles are those that center on the oblique complement of a relative root:

êyâyâni 'where I am going or went' (goal)
êh=nasawâki 'where it forks or they fork' (location)

wêchi-kechikâki 'where it flows out from' (source)
êhpîhchîchi 'with all one's possible speed or strength' (speed, intensity).
Interrogative participles are used when the identity is unknown; they convey they notion of 'whoever' or 'whatever'. The dictionary gives some that are used as idiomatic expressions:
êwiyêhikwêna, **wêwiyêhikwêna** 'someone or other, some unidentified creature'

William Jones. The texts and grammar of William Jones contain a good many words that have not been found in the writings of other speakers or confirmed by fieldwork. Some of these are undoubtedly genuine archaisms and are a valuable record of older usage. Other words unique to Jones look like idiosyncratic formations or outright errors, presumably reflecting his attempts to recall a language in which he was never fully fluent and that he remembered imperfectly. The words and translations labeled "(Jones)" are included on Jones's sole authority as part of the documentation of the language even though some of them appear on other evidence to be dubious.

Song words. Meskwaki writings sometimes include texts of songs that are either sung by characters in stories or are to be sung in ceremonies. These songs often include words that are not otherwise used, and even ordinary words may be sung with conventional distortion or in a form unique to songs. Some words from songs that Jones recorded appear to be so distorted as to be uninterpretable. The notation "(song word)" indicates a word from a song that is not used elsewhere.

Using the dictionary. Although many words can be found simply by looking them up, the radically different word and sentence structures of Meskwaki and English mean that it will often be useful to explore both halves of the dictionary creatively in order to find words of interest. For example, looking up 'red' in the English-Meskwaki section will find **meshkwi** 'red' and other words that begin with **meshkw-** or **meshko-** and include 'red' in their meanings. Looking then in the Meskwaki-English section under **meshkw-** and **meshko-** will reveal many additional words, such as **meshkwâhkonowa** 'paints oneself red' and **meshkonâtêwi** 'it is painted red'. Going back to the English-Meskwaki section and looking up, for example, 'paint' will lead to other words that include the idea of 'paint' as well as similarly formed words referring to other colors. These can then be searched in turn in the Meskwaki-English section. And so on, indefinitely. Also, when **meshkwi** 'red' is checked in the Meskwaki-English section, the identical word **meshkwi** 'blood' will be found, and next to the words with **meshko-** 'red' will be seen words with **meshkow-** 'bloody'. In fact, these similarities point to an ancient derivation of the initial **meshkw-** 'red' from the noun **meshkwi** 'blood'.

When multiple Meskwaki words are given under a single English keyword they are grouped in logical sets and the more common, basic words are generally given before the less common and more specialized words.

The Meskwaki-English section sometimes has inflected and related forms for a word that are not in the English-Meskwaki section.

Selected Bibliography

Bloomfield, Leonard. 1925-1927. Notes on the Fox Language [Part 1]. *International Journal of American Linguistics* 3:219-232 (1925). [Part 2]. *International Journal of American Linguistics* 4:181-219 (1927).

Dahlstrom, Amy. 2003. Warrior Powers from an Underwater Spirit: Cultural and Linguistic Aspects of an Illustrated Meskwaki Text. *Anthropological Linguistics*, 2003, 45(1):1-56.

Goddard, Ives. 1991. Observations Regarding Fox (Mesquakie) Phonology. *Papers of the Twenty-Second Algonquian Conference*, ed. William Cowan, pp. 157-181. Ottawa: Carleton University.

_____. 1994. *Leonard Bloomfield's Fox Lexicon: Critical Edition*. Algonquian and Iroquoian Linguistics Memoir 12. Winnipeg: University of Manitoba.

_____. 2002. The Linguistic Writings of Alfred Kiyana on Fox (Meskwaki). *Anthropology, History, and American Indians: Essays in Honor of William Curtis Sturtevant*, ed. William Merrill and Ives Goddard, pp. 285-293. Smithsonian Contributions to Anthropology 44. Washington: Smithsonian Institution Press.

_____. 2006. *The Autobiography of a Meskwaki Woman: A New Edition and Translation*. Algonquian and Iroquoian Linguistics Memoir 18. Winnipeg.

_____. 2007. *The Owl Sacred Pack: A New Edition and Translation of the Meskwaki Manuscript of Alfred Kiyana*. Algonquian and Iroquoian Linguistics Memoir 19. Winnipeg.

Jones, William. 1907. *Fox Texts*. American Ethnological Society Publications, no. 1. Leiden: E.J. Brill for the American Ethnological Society.

_____. 1911. Algonquian (Fox). *Handbook of American Indian Languages*, Part 1, ed. Franz Boas, pp. 735-873. Bureau of American Ethnology Bulletin 40. Washington: G.P.O.

_____. 1939. *Ethnography of the Fox Indians*, ed. by Margaret Welpley Fisher. Smithsonian Institution, Bureau of American Ethnology Bulletin 125. Washington: G.P.O.

Michelson, Truman. 1921. *The Owl Sacred Pack of the Fox Indians*. Smithsonian Institution, Bureau of American Ethnology Bulletin 72. Washington: G.P.O.

_____. 1925. Accompanying Papers. *Smithsonian Institution, Bureau of American Ethnology Annual Report* 40, pp. 21-658. Washington: G.P.O.

Smith, Huron H. 1928. Ethnobotany of the Meskwaki Indians. *Bulletin of the Public Museum of the City of Milwaukee* 4(2):175-326.

Thomason, Lucy G. 2003. The Proximate and Obviative Contrast in Meskwaki. Ph.D. dissertation, University of Texas, Austin. (Contains analyzed text excerpts.)

Voorhis, Paul. 1971. New Notes on the Mesquakie (Fox) Language. *International Journal of American Linguistics* 37:63-75.

Whittaker, Gordon. 2005. *A Concise Dictionary of the Sauk Language*. Stroud, Oklahoma: The Sac and Fox National Public Library.

Additional Meskwaki texts with translations are on the Smithsonian webpage "Meskwaki texts from the Truman Michelson collection" at http://si-pddr.si.edu/handle/10088/17270.

MESKWAKI-ENGLISH

a

achâhmeko	then, only then, for the first time, for the first time in a long time (also **châhmeko**)
achichîkwêsêwa	falls and hits one's face on the ground
achihkwihêwa	he makes her pregnant
achihkwimêwa	she is pregnant with s.o.
achihkwiwa	she is pregnant
achikêwi	it drips, leaks (**êh=achikâki** that it drips, leaks)
achikoshkêwa	gulps, gasps, hiccups
achikwânêwa, achikwâtamwa	sews s.o., it
achikwâsowa	sews, is sewing
achikwitêhêshkêwa	sighs from the heart
achipwêwa (archaic **ochipwêwa**)	Ojibwe, Chippewa
achisowa, achihtêwi	(animate, inanimate) shrivels, shrinks from heat
achitamôha	redsquirrel
achitawanahkisêwa	falls headfirst
achitawânakwakôchinwa	hangs upside-down
achitawânakwekêwa	he (slain warrior in the Land of the Dead) dances upside-down
achitawânowakôchinwa	hangs upside-down
achitawânowâshkêwa	falls headfirst, upside-down
achitawenamwa	tips it up (as, to drink from it)
ahchikâtisowa	raises (it) for oneself from seed
ahchikêwa	plants, plants (it)
ahchîhi	lacrosse-stick
ahkamawêwa	lies in wait for s.o.
ahkanâhkwa	bracelet (**otôhkanâhkomani** her bracelet)
ahkanêhi	small bone (dimin.)
ahkani (1)	bone (**otôhkanemi** his or her bone)
ahkani (2)	for the duration of (also **nahkani, nehkani**)
ahkanikomêsamwa	hardens its tip in the fire
ahkanîhiwa	is emaciated
ahkanyâwi	it is hard, rocklike
ahkapîhtamwa	stakes it out; lies in wait
ahkasamawêwa	burns (it) up for s.o.
ahkasowa, ahkatêwi	(animate, inanimate) burns up
ahkaswêwa, ahkasamwa	burns s.o., it up
ahkawâpakêmowa	guards people, protects people
ahkawâpamâsowa	is watched over
ahkawâpamêwa, ahkawâpatamwa	watches over s.o., it, guards s.o., it
ahkawâpamêweniwiwa	is watched over
ahkawâpatahêwa	has s.o. watch over (it)
ahkawâpatahiwêwa	has people watch over (it)
ahkawâpatâtêwi	it is watched over
ahkawâpihêwa, ahkawâpihtôwa	makes s.o., it watch, places s.o., it as a guard
ahkawâpiwa	watches, guards, oversees
ahkawihêwa	is on s.o.'s tracks, comes upon s.o.'s tracks
ahkânehkwâni	dandruff

ahki	land, ground, earth (**ahkîki** on the ground; **otahkimi, otahkîmi, otôhkimi, otôhkîmi** his or her land or earth; **netahki** my garden; **ketahkinânani, ketahkînânani** our gardens)
ahkihkêwa	plants things, works a garden
ahkiki	down below, below
ahkiwiwi	it is earth, earthy
ahkohkwa	kettle; drum (**netahkohkwa** my kettle, drum)
ahkohtâkosiwa, ahkohtâkwatwi	(animate, inanimate) is heard from {so far} away
ahkomîwa	is {so far} in the water
ahkopyêwi	the water comes {so far}
ahkoshamawêwa	cuts (it) {so long} for s.o.
ahkoshkamwa	wears it out
ahkoshkânawêwa	wears out one's clothes
ahkowechîha	the youngest brother or sister
ahkowi	after, afterwards, behind, as the last one
ahkônwêwa	his penis is {so long}, extends {so far}
ahkôtamwa	carries it on one's back {so far}
ahkôtawêhtôwa	lengthens it (a house) {so far}
ahkôtêwi	it (house) is {so long} (**êhkôtêki** the length of the lodge)
ahkôwêwa	comes next after s.o., follows next after s.o.
ahkwa	louse (**netehkomaki** my lice)
ahkwahkamikatwi	the world ends
ahkwahkamikesiwa	it is the end of the world for one
ahkwahtêwa	one's arrow goes {so far}
ahkwamowa	runs out of food
ahkwanahkesiwa, ahkwanahkatwi	(animate, inanimate) is {so} tall
ahkwanahkikâpâwa	stands with one's top {so} high
ahkwanahkisenwi	it begins, has its source; it ends
ahkwanâmowa (1)	cannot breathe anymore, draws one's last breath
ahkwanâmowa (2)	swims {so far} under water
ahkwashkotêwiwi	the meadow goes {so far}
ahkwâchimekosiwa:	**îni êhkwâchimekosichi** that is the end of the story about him, her
ahkwâchimêwa, ahkwâtotamwa	tell of s.o., it {so far}
ahkwâchimohêwa	stops telling s.o.
ahkwâchimowa	narrates {so far}
ahkwâhkonamawêwa	sets it {so long, so far} for s.o.
ahkwâhkonâtêwi	it is set {so long, so far}
ahkwâhtêwi	its heat extends {so far}
ahkwânaketonêmowa	ends one's talk or speech
ahkwânowêwa	has a tail that is {so} long
ahkwâpiwa	sees {so far}
ahkwâpyêhtôwa	extends it {so far}
ahkwâpyêsetâkêwa	extends it {so far} for s.o.
ahkwâpyêwi	it (a river) extends {so far}
ahkwâpyêyâwi	it (life) extends {so far}
ahkwâshkêwa	falls {so far}
ahkwâwahokowa	floats filling (the body of water)
ahkwâwanetîwaki (plural)	they go {so far} in a large group
ahkwâwi (1)	full, filling, to fullness (particle, preverb)
ahkwâwi (2)	it is {so long}
ahkwâwinechâtamwa	has one's hands or claws full of it
ahkwâwishimêwa, ahkwâwisetôwa	fill s.o. (kettle), it; fill container with s.o., it (contents)
ahkwâwishinwa, ahkwâwisenwi	(container) is full, (contents) fill the container
ahkwetonêmowa	is done talking, comes to the end of one's talking

ahkwênemêwa	thinks of s.o. {so far}, (deity) blesses s.o. {so far}
ahkwêyâmihkiwi	tract of wooded bottomland
ahkwi	{so far}, to {such a} point (preverb); until (particle)
ahkwichi	on top (particle, preparticle)
ahkwichitasane	on top of the platform
ahkwichitepe	on top of the head
ahkwihkanawêwa	reaches the end of one's road (euphemism for dying)
ahkwihkawêwa	one's tracks go {so far}, one's tracks end
ahkwikenwi	it grows {so long}
ahkwi-mâchîwa	gives out in running, becomes exhausted
ahkwisetawêwa	sets it {so far, so long} for s.o.
ahkwisêwa, ahkwisêwi	ends, runs out; it runs out, it is the end of it
ahkwishinwa, ahkwisenwi	(animate, inanimate) goes {so far}
ahkwitahâkani	shelf, storage rack
ahkwitahkamiki	on top of the earth (particle)
ahkwitanasite	on the top of the foot (particle)
ahkwitapahkwe	on top of the roof (particle)
ahkwitapiwa	sits on top
ahkwitâhkiwi	the top of a hill, bank, ridge (**ahkwitâhkîki** on top of a hill, bank, ridge)
ahkwitâkone, ahkwitakône	on top of the snow (particle)
ahkwitânaki	at the top of the hole, grave (particle)
ahkwitâsîwenêwa	takes s.o. up on top
ahkwitâsîyôtêwa	climbs crawling up on top
ahkwitepyêhokowa	floats on top of the water
ahkwitepyêki	on top of the water (particle)
ahkwitêhêwa	one's thought goes {so far}
ahkwiwa, ahkonwi	(animate, inanimate) is {so} long, tall (**îni êhkwichi** that is as far as one's story goes)
ahkwiwenêwa, ahkwiwetôwa	helps, guides s.o., it {so far}
ahkwiyâchi, ahkwiyâhi	especially, more so, more and more (particle)
ahkwîchisahowa	jumps up on top, mounts one's horse, mounts (s.o., a horse)
ahkwîtemyâwi	it (water) is {so} deep
ahkwîwa	goes {so far}, ends
ahpahamêwa	sings about (s.o., it) (**kîh=ahpahama** you will —)
ahpahamwa	patches it
ahpahikani	patch
ahpahikanimotêhi	sewing bag
ahpahôni, tahpahôni	woman's hair binder (wrapped around a bun or club at the back of the head)
ahpanasitêkâpâwa	stands with one's feet on (it)
ahpanasitêwosêwa	treads on (it) as one walks
ahpanehkîwa	steps
-ahpanehkîwene	(at) a distance of (so many) paces (in particle compounds)
ahpapiwa	sits on (it)
ahpapîni	chair, seat
ahpashkinanihêwa	butchers s.o. (animal) on leaves
ahpashkinanishikêwa	butchers on leaves
ahpatamôni	cuff
ahpâpowanâsowa	(corn) is cooked with something added
ahpâpowâni (ahpâpowâhi dimin.)	something added to the cooking; seasoning; wild ginger
ahpâpowêwa	adds (it) to the cooking
ahpeme	moreover, at the same time
ahpemeki (ahpemêheki dimin.)	up, aloft (particle)
ahpenêchi	always, every time (particle)

ahpenêwenehkêhêwa	causes s.o. to have a disease
ahpenêwenehkêwa	has a disease (**âkwi ahpenêwenehkâchini** does not have a disease)
ahpenêweni	disease
ahpenya, ahpenîha	potato, tuber
ahpesowa	burns along with (it)
ahpênemônotawêwa, **ahpênemônotamwa**	relies on s.o., it; depends on s.o., it
ahpênemowa	relies on (it), places trust in (it)
ahpênemowitêhêwa	places one's faith in (it)
ahpi	along with it all (preverb)
ahpihkanêwa	leaves s.o. behind with (it)
ahpihkyêhokowa	was pinned to the ground
ahpihokônêwa	lets (it) fall on top of s.o.
ahpihwêwa	piles (it) on top of s.o.
ahpikâhiwa	has one's feet on (it)
ahpishkawêwa, ahpishkamwa	steps on s.o., it
ahpishkamawêwa	steps on (it) for s.o.
ahpitiyêpîni	afterbirth
ahpîhchawiwa	acts {so}
ahpîhchâwi	it is {so} great, {so} intense, {so} powerful
ahpîhchi (1)	{to such extent, so intense, so fast} (preverb, particle)
ahpîhchi (2)	as one goes along, in the meantime, repeatedly, constantly, gradually (preverb, particle)
ahpîhchikenwi	it is {so} effective, powerful
ahpîhchikiwa (**ahpîhchikîhiwa** dimin.)	is {so} effective, powerful, old
ahpîhchinâkêwa	sings {so long}
ahpîhchinehki	for {so long} (particle)
ahpîhchitêhêwa	feels {so} deeply
ahpîhchiwanakesiwa, ahpîhchiwanakatwi	(animate, inanimate) weighs {so much}
ahpîhchîhkawêwa	occupies oneself {so long} with s.o.
ahpîhchîhkâtisowa	takes {so long} to do the task for oneself
ahpîhchîwa	goes {so far}, does {so much} (**êhpîhchîchi** with all one's possible speed or strength)
ahpîhtamatamwa	has {so much} pain, is in {so much} pain
ahpîhtapenêhtôwa:	**ahpîhtapenêhtôwa owîyawi** makes oneself starve {so long}
ahpîhtâshkêwa	goes {so} fast
ahpîhtâpatâniwi	it looks {so} intense
ahpîhtekahowa	dances {so much}
ahpîhtesêhkwêwa	one's cooking progresses {so far}
ahpîhtesiweni	age
ahpîhtesiwa	takes {so long}, is {so} old
ahpîhtetêwi	it is cooked {so far}
ahpîhtetonêmowa	talks {so long}
ahpîhtêhkamiki	of {such} age (**nashawaye ahpîhtêhkamiki** of ancient age)
ahpîhtênetâkwatwi	it is considered {so much}
ahpîhtênemêwa, ahpîhtênetamwa	thinks {so much} of s.o., it
ahpîhtêtwa	is gone {so long}
ahpîhtosêwa	walks {so far}
ahpîhtwêwêsenwi	it sounds {so loud}
ahpwâkana	tobacco pipe (**netôhpwâkana** my pipe) (older **ohpwâkana**)
ahpwâkanimotêha	tobacco pouch (**netôhpwâkanimotêha** my tobacco pouch) (older **ohpwâkanimotêh[a]**)
ahpwâkanimôha	tobacco pouch
ahtawâni	chief's staff of office

ahtawêwa (1)	has, places (it) {somewhere} for s.o.
ahtawêwa (2)	puts medicine on s.o.
ahtâtîwaki (plural)	they place (it) for each other
ahtenêwa	blames s.o.
ahtesowa, ahtehtêwi	(animate, inanimate) is ripe, ripening
ahtêhiminehkêwa	picks strawberries
ahtêhimini	strawberry
ahtêhimishi	strawberry vine
ahtêwi	it exists, there exists, is ({somewhere}); it is placed {somewhere}; there is a time (when), there are times (when)
ahtômepyâni	yoke for carrying two buckets of sap
ahtômyâkani	saddle
ahtôwa	(see **asêwa**)
ahtwâkani	poultice
ahtwêwa	applies (it as) a poultice (**wîh=ahtwâyâni** what I will use as a poultice)
akahkwi	blunt arrow (all wood) (**netakahkôni** my blunt arrows)
akashkwâha	bloodsucker
akayâshkwa	gull or tern (generic)
akâkwa	porcupine
akâmâhkiwe	over on another hill (particle)
akâmetêki	at the other side of the lodge (inside); on the other side of the fire (particle)
akâmêheki	on the other shore, on the other side of the stream or lake (particle)
akâmi	across (preparticle) (**akâmi-kehchikamîwe** on the other side of the lake, across the lake)
akâwânêwa, akâwâtamwa	desires s.o., it
akâwâtamâtisowa	desires (it) for oneself
akâwi	barely, for just a short time (preverb, particle)
akihêwa, akihtôwa	loses s.o., it
akikwâha	phlegm (**netakikwâha** my phlegm)
akimêwa, akitamwa	counts them
akitâsowa	counts, is counting
akiwa, akenwi	(animate, inanimate) disappears
akonamwa	applies it as a poultice
akosêhkwêwa	has one's cooking stick
akoswêwa	makes s.o. adhere by heat
akotêwi	it adheres because of heat, it sticks from being heated
akoshêwe	barely, minimally, as if not seriously (particle)
akôchikani	hanger, pothook
akôchinwa, akôtêwi	(animate, inanimate) hangs, is resting aloft
akôna	snow
akônêwa, akôtôwa	hangs s.o., it, places s.o., it aloft; buries s.o. on a scaffold
akôsîhtawêwa	climbs up after s.o.
akôsînehkawêwa	chases s.o. climbing
akôsîpahômikatwi	it runs climbing
akôsîsêwa	climbs fast
akôsîwa	climbs
akôsîyâpi	ladder
akôsîyôtêwa	crawls climbing
akôtêwâkanaki (plural)	earrings that hang
akwamowa, akwamowi	(animate, inanimate) sticks, sticks on, sticks shut
akwanahowa	covers oneself (as, with a blanket)
akwanahwêwa	covers s.o. (as, with a blanket)
akwanakôtêwi	it overhangs

akwanwîwi	the snow is sticking to the trees
akwapinêwa	bandages s.o.
akwapisowa	is bandaged
akwâchisahowa	jumps out of the water
akwâhesowa	ladles some food from the pot for oneself
akwâhkonamawêwa	holds (it) against s.o., against part of s.o.'s body
akwâhkwapinêwa, akwâhkwapitôwa	ties s.o., it to, against
akwâhkwapisowa, akwâhkwapitêwi	(animate, inanimate) is tied to, against
akwâhkwâpamêwa	sees s.o. against some ground
akwâhwêwa, akwâhamwa	fishes s.o., it out of water, fire (as, with a stick)
akwâpyêhamwa	fishes it out of the water with something, dips it out of the kettle
akwâpyêhesowa	ladles some food from the pot for oneself
akwâpyêhônêwa	drags s.o. out of the water
akwâpyêhtamwa	pulls it out of the water with one's mouth
akwâpyêkîwa	comes ashore, comes out of the water
akwâpyênêwa, akwâpyênamwa	lifts s.o., it out of the water
akwâpyêsêwa	runs out of the water
akwâsenwi	it lies out of the water, on the shore
akwâsêwa, akwâsêwi	jumps ashore; (canoe) runs ashore
akwâyâshowîwa	wades out of the water
akwâyôtêwa	crawls out of the water
akwihêwa	puts (it, a blanket or robe) on s.o. to wear
akwishkahkiwiwi	it is muddy land
akwishkehpowi	it is snowing wet snow
akwiwa	wears, puts on, or wraps oneself in (it, a blanket or robe)
akwîchimêwa, akwîtôwa	soaks s.o., it, has s.o., it in water (also **akwînêwa**)
akwîchinwa, akwîtêwi	(animate, inanimate) is in water, soaking, floating
akwîkwâtamwa	puts it on one's face
akwînêwa	soaks s.o., has s.o. in water (archaic) (see **akwîchimêwa,**)
akwîtawêwa	soaks (it) for s.o.
amehkwa	beaver
amehkwaya	beaver skin
amehkwânowi	beaver tail
amehkwikani	beaver bone
amênâkosiwa	shows a reaction
amênotawêwa, amênotamwa	reacts to s.o., it, is responsive to s.o., it
amêwa	acts, reacts promptly, takes action, goes into action, is roused to action
amotamawêwa	eats (it) of s.o.
amwêwa	eats s.o. (compare **mîchiwa**)
amwêweniwiwa:	**menwi-amwêweniwiwa** is good enough to eat (as, ripe corn or beans)
ana-shashâpwi	all alone (particle compound)
anahokowa	chokes on a fishbone
anahônêwa	fills s.o. (water drum), tightens the drumhead on s.o. (skin drum)
anahôtawêwa	fills (it) for s.o.
anahôtâsowa	(drum) has its drumhead tightened
anahpinêwa	dresses her up as a bride
anahpisowa	she is dressed in bridal finery, as a bride
anahtakîwa	braids string
anakêhkwa	sheet of bark (on house or for house covering)
anakêhkwi	bark, piece of tree bark
anakêhkwikâni (anakêhkwikâhi dimin.)	bark house
anakêweni	bark canoe (**otônakêweni** his bark canoe)
ana-kîshâkochi	extremely much (particle compound)
anakwêwa	rainbow

anakwêwiwi	there is a rainbow
anakwiwa	is fat
anakwîmikatwi	it is fat
ananeshiwi	terrific; awful (particle) (also **naneshiwi, aneneshiwi, neneshiwi**)
anapishkwêha	mink (archaic)
anasâki	exceptionally, exceedingly (particle)
anashawaye (anashawe =)	long ago (particle) (also **nashawaye, ashawaye**)
anashkenachikêwa	fills (something, esp. a pipe) (also **aneshkenachikêwa**)
anashkenanêwa, anashkenatôwa	fills s.o. (a person [metaphorically], a pipe), it, loads it (a firearm) (also **aneshkenanêwa, aneshkenatôwa**)
anawêwa, anamwa	resembles, imitates s.o., it
anawinêwa, anawitamwa	sneaks up on s.o., it
anawiwa	goes on a distant hunt
anâhamwa	stirs it
anâhkahamawêwa	spreads (it) for s.o., spreads mats or blankets for s.o.
anâhkahamwa	spreads it down for sitting, lying
anâhkahêwa	spreads something, (it) down for s.o. to sit or lie on
anâhkahikêwa	spreads mats or carpeting
anâhkahowa	spreads something, (it) down to sit or lie on
anâhkani	mat (to cover a surface)
anâhkêwa	uses something, (it) as a mat to sit on or lie on
anâhkohanwi	there is a downdraft blowing back through the smoke hole
anâhkwâtamawêwa	puts (it) on sticks for s.o.
anâhkwênêwa	strings s.o. (a bow)
anâhkwêsahêwa	quickly strings s.o. (a bow)
anâhpawânêwa, anâhpawâtamwa	he recites his dream of s.o., it to invoke the power of his blessing
anâhpawêwa	he recites his dream to invoke the power of his blessing (**êh=anâhpawâchi** he recited his dream)
anâkani (archaic **onâkani**)	bowl (**netônâkani** my bowl)
anâkâhi	little bowl (**netônâkâhi** my little bowl)
anâkowe	yesterday
anâkwa (**anâkôha** dimin.)	star
anâkwashiwa	has or gets a share of game (to keep or distribute)
anâkweshihamwa	goes on an evening hunt
anâkwiwi (**anâkwîhiwi** dimin.)	it is evening
anâpôhkawêwa	boils (it) for s.o.
anâpôhkêwa	boils (it, liquid)
anâpôsamwa	boils it
anâpôsikêwa	boils medicine
anâsowa	wrestles, horses around, tussles amorously
anâshkahamwa	spreads it as matting or undercloth (to sit on or to put something over)
anechîmini	pea, peas (also, **anechîminani** peas)
anehka	Canada goose
anehkawêwa, anehkamwa	is or gets used to s.o., it, is or gets acquainted with s.o.
anehkâchihêwa	associates with s.o., is an acquaintance of s.o.
anehkâtîwaki (plural)	they get acquainted with each other
anehkîhi	a little, a small amount (particle)
anehkîhiwa, anehkîhenwi	is few; there is not much of it
anemahokowa	(fish, bird) swims away, off, on
anemahowa	paddles away, off, on
anemapiwa	sits riding away
anematahwêwa	strikes, hits s.o. as one goes along
anemâmowa	flees away, on
anemâpatâniwi	there is a view, one can see some distance

anemâpyêwi	it (stringlike) extends away
anemâsîwa	climbs along
anemâshkêwa, anemâshkêwi	flies along, rushes along
anemâyêniwa	goes off laughing
anemehkawêwa	greets s.o. (archaic)
anemehkêwa	goes away, walks on
anemehkohamwa	uses something to turn it over
anemehkonamwa	turns it over
anemehkwisenwi	it lies upside down
anemehkwisetôwa	sets it upside down
anemeshihamwa	goes off hunting
anemi	away, continuing, along, on down the line, in time (preverb)
anemihêmikatwi	it goes {some way}
anemihêmikihtawêwa	makes (it) go {some way} for s.o.
anemihêwa	goes {some way}
anemikawiwaki (plural)	they go on as a group
anemikâshinwa	one's footprints can be seen continuing on
anemikiwa	lives on (**ênemikichiki, wîh=anemikichiki** the people to come)

anemi-mehtosêneniwa,
    anemi-mehtosêneniwaki
	the people to come, the human race (as referred to in the
	       myth age)

aneminâkêwa	goes singing
anemipahowa	runs off, on, away
anemipokôtêwi	it drifts, floats off
anemisenwi	it lies extending away
anemiwenêwa, anemiwetôwa	takes s.o., it away, leads s.o. off
anemiwetawêwa	takes (it) away for s.o.
anemona	ocher (**netônemonema** my ocher)
anemotêwa	moves camp, continues moving on
anemôha	dog
anemôhêha	puppy
anemôhiwa	is a dog
anemômêwa, anemôtamwa	carries s.o., it along on one's back
anemômowa	goes along weeping (song word)
anemôtêwa	crawls along, away
anemwêkesiwa, anemwêwêkesiwa	goes off, along shouting or wailing
anemwêwêshkâtîwaki (plural)	they collide with noise
anemwêwêshkêwi	it goes off with a noise
anemwêwêshinwa, anemwêwêsenwi	one's steps go sounding off, it goes off with noise
anemwêwêpahowa	runs with noise
anemwêwêsikêwa	goes on firing, shooting a firearm
anemyâka	downstream, down the (railroad) line, east (particle)
aneneshiwi	terrific; awful (particle) (also **ananeshiwi, naneshiwi, neneshiwi**)
anenêwi	smokehole (locative **anenêki**)
anenôtêwa	Indian (archaic; see **nenôtêwa**)
anenôtêwi	Indian, native (prenoun) (archaic; see **nenôtêwi**)
anenôtêwiwa	is an Indian (archaic; see **nenôtêwiwa**)
anenôtêwîha	Indian tobacco (archaic; see **nenôtêwîha**)
anenwa, anetwi	(animate, inanimate) rots, is rotten
anenwîwa	bathes, swims
anepyêhâsowa, anepyêhâtêwi	(animate, inanimate) is drawn, painted, diagrammed, written
anepyêhikawêwa	writes to s.o.
anepyêhikêwa	writes
anepyêhotîwaki (plural)	they write each other down, enroll each other
anepyêhwêwa, anepyêhamwa	draws a picture of s.o.; writes it

anesâchi	sober, being sober (particle)
aneshamawêwa	cuts (it) out for s.o., cuts (it) to shape for s.o.
aneshamwa	cuts it out, cuts it to shape
aneshâsowa, aneshâtêwi	an image of (animate, inanimate) is carved
aneshinenîhaki (plural)	common people
aneshkenachikawêwa	fills (something, esp. a pipe) for s.o.
aneshkenachikêwa	fills (something, esp. a pipe) (also **anashkenachikêwa**)
-aneshkenachikêwene	pipeful (in a particle compound) (**nekoti-aneshkenachikêwene** one pipeful)
aneshkenanêwa, aneshkenatôwa	fills s.o. (a person [metaphorically], a pipe), it, loads it (a firearm) (also **anashkenanêwa, anashkenatôwa**)
aneshkêwa, aneshkêwi	(animate, inanimate) takes shape, forms up
anetehkwa	goat
anihaniwânakîkwêwa	has wide-open, bright, piercing eyes
anihêwa, anihtôwa	defeats s.o., wins it; wins
anihiwêwa	wins
anika	further away (particle)
anikashi	besides, otherwise, beyond (particle)
anikânâhi	yonder, there (further away, further on) (particle)
anikânâka	that (further away; animate) (plural **anikânêke**)
anikâne	that (further away; inanimate) (plural **anikânêne**)
anikâtepi	way off (in distance or time), way beyond (particle)
anikêmêhi	a little further, beyond (particle)
anikêmêhiwa	is worse (than the other), is moreso, overdoes it
anikônêwa, anikôtôwa	offers s.o., it as a prize
anikwa	squirrel (generic)
anisêwa	flies up, flies away
aniwashiwa	carries a heavy burden
aniwatawâpiwa	looks about too much
aniwâchimowa	says too much, blabs, tells tales, is a tattle-tale
aniwânakîkwêwa	has strong, sharp eyesight
aniwânematwi	it blows hard, there is a wind storm
aniwâpehkesowa, aniwâpehketêwi	(animate, inanimate) shines brightly (stone, metal, or the like)
aniwâshkêwa, aniwâshkêwi	(animate, inanimate) goes, flies, falls fast, speeds along
aniwâshohwêwa	is a good shot with a bow or gun
aniwekêwa	dances very well
aniweshawêwa	has a big fire going
aniweshêwi	it burns big, blazes big
aniweshkamwa	walks much on it
aniwetonêmowa	talks a lot, speaks well; is a big talker, is a good speaker
aniwêmêwa	angrily rebuffs s.o., retorts to s.o. spitefully or meanly
aniwênemêwa	thinks much of s.o.
aniwêwêyâkêposowa, aniwêwêyâkêpotêwi	(animate, inanimate) whizzes loudly through the air
aniwêwi, aniwêwe	contrariwise, oddly, in contrast, then (in contrast) (particle)
aniwihtanwi	it flows swiftly, the current is fast
aniwikenwi	it grows fast
aniwinâsamwa	boils it vigorously
aniwipotêwi	it (as, an arrow) flies fast and hard
aniwisahowa	jumps or moves quickly
aniwisêwa	runs fast
aniwishimowa	uses a loud voice
aniwiyâmêwa, aniwiyâtamwa	can smell s.o., it at a distance
aniwîhkawêwa, aniwîhkamwa	concerns oneself much with s.o., it

anîhwêwa	competes against s.o., tries to beat or outdo s.o.
anîpi	American elm (plural **anîpyêni**)
anîpiwiwa	is an American elm
anohkâhkyêwa	employs people
anohkânêwa	sets s.o. to work, gives s.o. an errand, asks s.o. to help
anoshkâhaki (plural)	Drum Society
anôhwêwa	points at s.o. (archaic)
anôkahkiwiwi	the ground is muddy
anôkîwa	gets stuck in the mud
anwâchi	(with negative): not as much as before, seldom (preverb)
anwâchinawêmêwa	makes s.o. willing by speech
anwâchînohkatâtîwaki (plural)	they are willing towards each other
anwâchîwa	consents, is willing
anwâhtôwa	sings beautifully
anwâtênemêwa, anwâtênetamwa	consents to s.o., it, is willing with regard to s.o., it
anwêwêhâsowa	is drummed on
anwêwêhchikêwa	blows on something to play it or make it whistle
anwêwêhikêwa	drums
anwêwêhtamwa	blows it (wind instrument)
anwêwêhwêwa	makes s.o. (drum) sound by beating, twangs s.o. (bow)
anwêwêkatwi	it makes noise; a sound is heard
anwêwêkihêwa, anwêwêkihtôwa	makes s.o., it shout, cry out, resonate
anwêwênamwa	rattles it
anwêwênawîwa	stirs noisily
anwêwêpahkwênikêwa	raps on the side of the lodge
anwêwêsahtôwa	rattles it
anwêwêsenwi	it falls noisily
anwêwêsikêwa	fires a shot, shoots
anwêwêshkêwi	it moves with noise
anwêwêtepêhwêwa	thumps s.o. on the head
anwêwêyâpôshinwa	lands in the water with an audible splash
anwi	bullet; arrow (archaic)
apahapanênemêwa	laughs at s.o.
apahapanêniwa	laughs
apahkôhaya	small cattail-reed mat
apahkwaya	cattail reed; cattail-reed mat (for covering a lodge)
apahkwayikâni	cattail-reed lodge
apahkwâhkêwa	makes cattail-reed mats
apahkwâki êshikeki	blue flag
apahkwêwa	makes a roof or lodge-covering (of it)
apahkwêweni	roofing material, lodge-covering
apanênemêwa	smiles at s.o.
apanênetîwaki (plural)	they smile at each other
apanêniwa	smiles
apanôtêwi	it (as, a house) is warm
apashi (**apashîhi** dimin.)	lodgepole, side post, door post (plural **apashêni**; **otôpashîwâwani** their lodgepoles)
apatêhkîki	on the side of the hill (particle)
apâhkwisetawêwa	places (it) as a padding for s.o.
apâhkwîwa	has something to go by, to base oneself on
apâsesowa	suns oneself (also **apâsiwasowa**)
apâsetêhkêwa	basks in the sun
apâsetêwi	there is sunshine, the sun shines
apâsiwasowa	suns oneself (also **apâsesowa**)

apehkwêhiwa	places one's head on (it)
apehkwêshimôna	pillow (**netôpehkwêshimôna** my pillow)
apehkwêshimôni	thing used to lay the head on
apehkwêshinwa	lies with one's head on (it)
apenôha	child
apenôhâpachihêwa	dresses s.o. like a child
apenôhêha	baby
apenôhêhiwa	is a baby
apenôhêhaya	baby skin
apenôhiwa	is a child
apesokowêhiwa	warms one's back (also **apesôwêhiwa, apisikiwêhiwa**)
apesokowêpiwa	sits warming one's back
apesokowêshinwa	lies warming one's back
apesowa, apetêwi	(animate, inanimate) is warm, gets warm
apesôwêhiwa	warms one's back (also **apesokowêhiwa, apisikiwêhiwa**)
apeswêwa, apesamwa	warms s.o., it, heats s.o., it up
apihkâni	pack strap, tumpline
apikâsowa	warms one's feet
apimotêsowa	warms one's belly
apina	in fact, to this extent, even (particle)
apisikiwêhiwa	warms one's back (also **apesokowêhiwa, apesôwêhiwa**)
apiwa	sits, exists, is ({somewhere}); is laid out; (dried meat) keeps
apîhtawêwa, apîhtamwa	sits (as, in a ceremony) for s.o., it ({somewhere}), stays in it
apônêwa	roasts (it) for s.o.
apôsowa	roasts (it) for oneself
apwâchikani	grill, rack for roasting and drying meat
apwâchikêwa	roasts meat over the fire
apwâkana	frying pan
apwânêwa, apwâtamwa	roasts s.o., it
apwîhêwa, apwîhtôwa	waits for s.o., it
apwîhi	paddle
asamonamwa	grabs a handful of it (as, cloth, hair, skin, or flesh), pinches it up
asamwisahêwa	grabs a handful of s.o.'s skin
asamwitepênêwa	seizes s.o. by the hair
asanâmishi (archaic **asenâmishi**)	sugar maple
asapâpi	string, thread, cord (plural **asapâpyêni**; **netôsapâpîmi** my string)
asapâpîhi	string, thread, cord (dimin.)
asapi-pîminihkwâni	Indian hemp cordage
asapihkêwa	gathers Indian hemp
asapiwêkenwimôhi (also **asapimôhi**)	burlap bag ("gunny sack")
asapya	Indian hemp (*Apocynum*) (**otôsapîmahi** her Indian hemp strips)
asaya	skin (of a small or medium-sized animal), buckskin
asayi	skin (of a larger animal)
asayîhi	buckskin thing
asâkînâki	in the Sauk country (locative noun)
asâkîwa	Sauk
asâmehkâchi	too much (preverb)
asâmehkonowa	overeats
asâmekwamâsowa	over-fasts
asâmekwamêwa	over-fasts (**êh=asâmekwamâchi** he or she over-fasted)
asâmekwâmwa	oversleeps
asâmesiwa	is excessive, goes too far
asâmesowa	is cooked too much
asâmi	too much (preverb, particle); certainly! (particle)

asâmihêwa	is too cruel or mean to s.o., goes too far mistreating s.o.
asâminâkwatwi	it is beautiful
asâmîhkawêwa, asâmîhkamwa	occupies oneself too much with s.o., it; spends too much time with s.o., it
asâmîhkânowa	overdoes it, does something out of line
asâwanamona, asâwanemona	yellow ocher
asâwanamoniwiwi, asâwanemoniwiwi	it is rusty
asâwanikwa	fox squirrel
asâwâhkatêwi	it (as, meat) is cured
asâwâkatwi	brass
asâwâkatwi-nâpihchîha	brass armband
asâwâkeshêwa	wears brass earrings
asâwesiwa, asâwâwi	(animate, inanimate) is yellow
asâwêkisowa	(rawhide) is smoke-cured, tanned
asâwêkiswêwa	smoke-cures s.o. (rawhide) into yellow leather
asâwi	yellow; brown (archaic) (prenoun)
asâwi-mahkwa	member of the Brown Bear lineage of the Bear Clan
asâwinameshkêwa	has brown skin (**êsâwinameshkâta** Indian) (archaic)
asâwi-shôniyâhi	gold
asâwitepêwa	has blond or brown hair; has a yellow head (**êsâwitepâta** the blonde one, the yellow-headed one)
asemihetîwaki (plural)	they help each other
asemihêwa, asemihtôwa	helps s.o., it; helps it on, favors it
asemihiwêwa	helps people, helps out
asenâmishiwa	is a sugar maple (archaic; see **asanâmishi**)
asenâpêneniwa, asanâpêneniwa	"stone man," "grandfather rock" (large, isolated boulder revered as a spirit)
aseneshkêwa	gets hard as a rock
aseni (1)	stone, rock (plural **asenyêni; netôsenîmi** my rock)
aseni (2)	(of) stone, (of) rock (prenoun)
asenihkihkîki	on the rocks, in a rocky place (locative noun)
asenikâni	stone house
asenipi	lead
asenipihkêwa	mines lead
asenipikâni	lead mine
aseniwiwa, aseniwiwi	(animate, inanimate) is or becomes stone
asenya	stone used in sweatbath; rocky precipice
-asenye	stone, rock (in particle compounds) (**ahkwichi-asenye** on top of the stone; **nâmi-asenye** under the rock or rocks)
asetîwaki (plural)	they place each other {somewhere}
asêha	piece of buckskin
asêhkêwa	tans, prepares hides; tans (s.o., as a deerskin)
asêhkêhtôwa	tans it (as, a bearskin)
asêmâwa	tobacco (**netasêmâwa** my tobacco [rare]) (also **nesêmâwa**)
asêwa, ahtôwa	has s.o., it; places, puts s.o., it {somewhere}
asipapitôwa	ties them (inanimate) in a bunch
asipechênamwa	carries it bunched up in the hand, carries a bunch of them
asipehkwêkêwaki (plural)	they dance with heads together
asipehkwêkâpâwaki (plural)	they stand with heads together
asipi	all together (preverb)
asipîwaki (plural)	they go in a group
asipôhkwêpinêwa	ties their necks together
asipôhpowaki (plural)	they eat in a group
asipôshinôki (plural)	they lie in a group, they all sleep together

asitâpi	moccasin-string, shoestring (plural **asitâpyêni; netôsitâpi** my moccasin-string)
asîmini	pawpaw
asôtepêpisowa	has something tied around one's head, one's head is bandaged
aswâpamêwaki (plural)	they all had their eyes on s.o.
aswênemêwaki (plural)	their thoughts center on s.o.
aswi	all together (preverb)
aswisêwaki (plural)	they quickly gather, all crowd around
ashahashawêhkwênwa	moves one's head from side to side
ashahashawêkikanwi	it (tree or wood) is uneven
ashakêmowa	serves (someone) a meal
ashametîwaki (Jones)	they feed each other
ashamêwa	feeds s.o., gives s.o. food
ashamôchîhi	bait
ashamôtawêwa	baits s.o. with (it)
ashashkôha	small muskrat
ashashkwa (1)	muskrat
ashashkwa (2)	kneecap (**netashashkoma** my kneecap)
ashatîwaki (plural)	they feed each other
ashatwa	gives a return feast (after ceremonial adoption)
ashawaye (**ashawe=**)	long ago (also **anashawaye, nashawaye**)
ashawêhkamiki	long ago, long before, in ancient days (particle) (also **nashawêhkamiki**)
ashawêshkêwi	it tips to one side
ashâha	a Sioux person
ashâhâtowêwa	speaks the Sioux language
ashâhihkwêwa	Sioux woman
ashâhikâni	a Sioux lodge
ashâhinâwi	the Sioux country (**ashâhinâki** in the Sioux country)
ashâhkîwa	crayfish
ashâsha	an Osage (older **washâsha**)
ashâshesiwa, ashâshâwi	(animate, inanimate) is slippery, slick
ashâshinehkêwa	one's hands are very slippery
ashâshikôha	slippery elm ("red elm")
ashâtîhânowêwa	has a tail that ends in a spear point
ashâtîhi	headed arrow (with stone or metal arrowhead)
ashe	just, merely, just naturally or spontaneously, just to be doing it (particle) (also **ishe**)
ashe inowêwa (or **ishe inowêwa**)	says something false, is just kidding
ashe ishimêwa (or **ishe ishimêwa**)	tells s.o. something false, is just kidding s.o.
ashenowa, ashenowi	(animate, inanimate) is gone, absent, has a part or parts missing
ashenowâpamêwa	sees s.o. missing, does not see s.o. present
ashenowihêwa, ashenowihtôwa	is without s.o., it
ashewêna (and **ashewê=**)	but, still (also **ishewêna, shewêna**)
ashênawîwa	slides back, moves back
ashêshkêwi	it draws back, is drawn back, becomes shorter
ashêwosêwa	walks backwards
ashêyâmowa	flees back
ashichi	near, nearly (particle)
ashichikâpawînotâtîwaki (plural)	they stand next to each other
ashichikênotâtîwaki (plural)	they live near each other
ashihchikêwêwa	makes something, things, (it) with (it), out of (it)
ashihêwa, ashihtôwa	makes s.o., it; installs s.o.

ashihkanwi	tallow; wax (also **oshihkanwi**)
ashihkawêwa	flushes s.o. (bird, animal) up, scares s.o. (bird, animal) up
ashihpanêwa	has tuberculosis, has consumption
ashihpowa	eats using (it as) a dip or sauce
ashihtawêwa	makes (it) for s.o.
ashihtâtêwi	it is made
ashihtâtisowa	makes (it) for oneself
ashihwêwa	chases s.o. away, shoos s.o. away
ashikahamwa	cuts it to shape by chopping
ashikana	bass; member of the Fish Clan
ashikani (1)	on one side (of two), on the other side (particle)
ashikani (2)	of the Fish Clan (prenoun)
ashikaninehke	in, using, or affecting one hand (as opposed to the other) (particle)
ashikasowa	puts a liner in one's moccasins; puts on or wears socks or stockings
ashikasôni	stocking
ashikawêwa	builds a house for s.o.
ashikêwa	builds a house
ashinawêwa	is happy at someone's arrival
ashishkiwâhkonowa	puts mud on oneself
ashishkiwi	mud (also **ashkishkiwi**)
ashitahi	(with negative): not for a long time (particle)
ashitâhkwakôchinwa	hangs close to a solid
ashitâhkwapisowa	is tied to something (as, a tree or post)
ashiwanehkêwa	makes (it) into a bundle for a back-load
ashkachi (1) (**ashkachîmêhi** dimin.)	after a while, later, taking a long time (particle)
ashkachi (2)	be impatient to (preverb)
ashkachihkamêwa	is impatient for a smoke (**ashkachihkamâwâte** if they are —)
ashkachipwîhêwa	impatiently awaits s.o.
ashkachitepehki	late at night
ashkachitepehkîwi	it is late at night
ashkachîhiwiwi	it is some time later
ashkachîmekîhi	after a little while
ashkanamîkwêha	young man (endearing; archaic)
ashkanâmowa	is out of breath, is smothering
ashkanwîwi	the first snow (of the season) is on the ground
ashkapiwa	is tired of sitting
ashkâchimowa	first talks, gives one's first talk
ashkâhtamwa	sucks it (water) all up
ashkâhtêwi	it (lake, river) dries up
ashkâpêwa (1)	the younger of two brothers
ashkâpêwa (2)	ceremonial runner
ashkâpowi	fresh soup
ashkâsêwi	it dries up (also **ashkisêwi**)
ashkenwa, ashkenwi	(animate, inanimate) is raw
ashkepyanêwa, ashkepyatôwa	drowns s.o., it
ashkepyêwa	drowns
ashkesikêwa	makes maple syrup
ashkesowa, ashketêwi	(kettle) boils dry; it dries up from the heat
ashkênemêwa	worries about s.o.
ashki	first, for the first time (particle, preverb); new (prenoun)
ashkichâhi	at first, in the first place (particle)
ashkihkwêwiwa	she has her first menstruation
ashkihkwêwiweni	menarche, girl's first menstruation
ashkikiwa, ashkikenwi	is young, new, fresh; it is new, fresh

ashkimâhaki (plural)	hog peanuts ("Indian peanuts") (*Amphicarpa monoica*)
ashki-mesâhkwa	ear of green corn
ashki-mesîkwaki (plural)	green corn
ashkinawêhêwa	makes s.o. feel uneasy
ashkipakanenwa, ashkipakanetwi	(animate, inanimate) is green with rot
ashkipakâmehkisenwi	it lies green as the earth (also **ashkipakâmehkwisenwi**)
ashkipakâmehkwisetôwa	makes it green as the earth
ashkipakâmehkwisenwi	it lies green as the earth (also **ashkipakâmehkisenwi**)
ashkipakânahkwakôtêwi	it hangs as blue ("green") sky
ashkipakânahkwakôtôwa	hangs it as blue ("green") sky
ashkipakânahkwisetôwa	makes it blue ("green") sky
ashkipakânehkwêsetôwa	makes its (the earth's) hair green (ritual)
ashkipakâpatâniwi	it looks green
ashkipakâpehkatwi	it is a green stone
ashkipakepyêhâtêwi	it is painted green
ashkipakesiwa, ashkipakyâwi	(animate, inanimate) is green (Note: in older usage this included blue.)
ashkipakipiwêwa	has green feathers
ashkipakipyêwa	has green leaves or boughs (**êshkipakipyâta** evergreen)
ashkipwâha	"sweet potato"
ashkisêwi	it ebbs, recedes, dries up
ashkishehkîtamwa	wears new clothes
ashkishkiwi	mud (more commonly **ashishkiwi**)
ashkitêhêwa	worries
ashkiwêpi	at the start
ashkiwêpîhiwa	first starts (doing something never done previously)
ashkohkêwa	stays back (when others go on)
ashkonamâtisowa	saves (it) for oneself
ashkonêwa, ashkonamwa	saves s.o., it; has s.o., it left; has s.o. stay behind with one
ashkosowa, ashkotêwi (1)	(animate, inanimate) is left unburnt or uncooked
ashkoshâkanaki (plural)	bone beads (as a necklace)
ashkotêhkâni	match; firesteel (for making fire with a flint) (archaic)
ashkotêhkêwa	makes fire
ashkotênêsiwa	the Spirit of Fire
ashkotêwâpowi	whiskey
ashkotêwâshkêwi	there is a flash of fire
ashkotêwi (2)	fire (**netôshkotêmi** my fire)
ashkwatamawêwa	saves (it, food) for s.o.
ashkwatamwa	has it left over from eating or drinking, leaves it unconsumed
ashkwânêhketêwi	firebrand, firestick (**otôshkwânêhketêmwâwi** their fire stick)
ashkwâtêmi	door (**netashkwâtêmi** my door)
ashkwâtêmiwiwi	it has a door
ashkwênasichi	little toe
ashkwênechi	little finger, endclaw (**netashkwênechi, neteshkwênechi** my little finger)
ashkwêyawi	at the very end (particle)
ashkwêyawikâpâwa	stands at the end
ashkwi	saving, leaving, missing the chance (preverb)
ashkwihêwa	leaves, spares s.o.
ashkwinêwa (**ashkwinêhiwa** dimin.)	is left alive
ashkwisêwa	has food left; is left over (see **êshkwisâchiki**)
ashkwiwetawêwa	leaves (it) to s.o.
ashkwîwa (**ashkwîhiwa** dimin.)	stays behind (when others leave)
ashwahtêwa	takes aim to shoot a bow
ashwinôhwêwa	aims (it) at s.o.
atamâkanâhkwi	pipe stem

atamêhetîwaki (plural) — they give each other a smoke
atamêhêwa, atamêhtôwa — gives s.o., it a smoke; offers s.o., it a smoke
atamêwa — smokes a pipe (**atamâno** smoke!), smokes (it, tobacco or pipe)
atamêwapiwa — sits smoking
atasani — platform (for sitting, sleeping, working)
atâhanahka — over this way (particle)
    atâhanahka-'shi this way, towards here; since then
    atâhanahk-ochîmêhi a little later
atâhi (**atâhîmêhi** dimin.) — over here; come here! (archaic) (particle)
    atâhi-'shi on this side; since then, after that
    atâh-ochîmêhi a little nearer; a little later, a little more recently
atâhkwêpisowa — has cramps
atâhpahwêwa, atâhpahamwa — draws s.o., it in (as, with a stick)
atâhpâpyêsahtôwa — yanks it on a string
atâhpehkwêhtawêwa — motions with one's head for s.o. to come
atâhpehkwênêwa — takes s.o.'s head in one's hands
atâhpenamawêwa — takes hold of (it) for s.o.
atâhpenamâhkwîwa — pulls on (it) for support
atâhpenêwa, atâhpenamwa — takes (hold of) s.o., it, picks s.o., it up
atâhpinehkênêwa — takes s.o. by the hand, takes s.o.'s hand
atâhpisahêwa, atâhpisahtôwa — jerks s.o., it away
atâhpisêwa — is jerked away
atâmêwa — sells (it) to s.o.
atâmina — corn plant, corn (generic), maize
atâminêha — kernel of corn (maize)
atânahka — over this way; come over this way (particle)
    atânahka='shi this way, towards here; since then; come over here
atâpyâna — wagon
atâwêneniwa — trader; merchant
atâwêwa — sells (it)
atechâhkwa — crane (probably generic but especially sandhill crane)
atehchi (**atehchîmêhi** dimin.) — away someplace, a distance off
atehchihkanawe — away from the road
atekôwa — large wave
atekôwâshkêwi (also **atakôwâshkêwi**) — there are large waves, it has large waves
atemêhkôha — my dear grandchild
atenâwênemêwa — thinks less of s.o.
atenâwi (**atenâwîmêhi** dimin.) — less (particle)
ateshêwêhikani (or **ahteshêwêhikani**) — poker (for rearranging the fire) (archaic; shape uncertain)
ateshkâha, atashkâha — kingfisher
ateshkawi — all sorts of demands or excuses (particle)
atosowa — burns oneself
atôhposôni — feast blanket (used when placing a meal on the ground); tablecloth
atôhpowa — eats from (it, a dish or bowl)
atôwa — blood clot
atôwâha — wad of bark thrown in the air as a target
atôwâhiwaki (plural) — they have a contest shooting at wads of bark thrown in the air
atôwiwi — it is bloodshot
awachipahônêwa, awachipahôtôwa — runs off, over with s.o., it
awachipahôtâkêwa — runs off with (it) of others
awahîna, awahîma — what's-his-name; the one called (so-and-so)
awahîni, awahîmi — what-you-may-call-it; the thing called (so-and-so)
awahkyêwa — takes someone away, escorts someone to one's home
awanêwa, awatôwa — takes s.o., it away, home

awanwi (1)	there is thick fog
awanwi (2)	thick fog
awasowa	warms oneself
awatahônêwa	drags or hauls s.o. over (to somewhere)
awatawêwa	takes (it) away for s.o., takes (it) to s.o.
awatâhêwa	makes s.o. take (it), sends (it) by s.o.
awatâhiwêwa	sends (it) along
awatâhkawêwa	throws (it) over to s.o.
awatâkêwa	takes it over
awatâpowanêwa	takes food over to s.o.
awatâsetawêwa	sends it to s.o. on the wind
awatâsowa (Jones)	sails on the wind
awatâshimêwa	sends s.o. wafting
awatechênamwa	carries off an armload of it (as, firewood)
awatehkwêwêwa	he takes home a wife
awatenamawêwa	hands (it) over to s.o.
awatenamâkêwa	hands (it) over, yields (it)
awatenêwa, awatenamwa	hands s.o., it over
awatômêwa, awatôtamwa	carries s.o., it off on one's back
awatôtahêwa	makes s.o. carry (it) off on their back
awatôtamawêwa	carries (it) off on one's back for s.o.
awâsowa	is used, is put to work
awêwa, ayôwa	uses s.o., it; puts s.o. to work; wears it (clothing), sings it (song)
awihêwa	lends (it) to s.o.; borrows (it) from s.o.
awihiwêwa	lends (it); borrows (it)
awita	not (with potential verb) (particle)
awiwa (1)	is, stays {somewhere}
awiwa (2)	is intending to, is on the verge of
awiwêwa (1), **awiwa** (3)	gets, buys, has, keeps s.o., it
awiwêwa (2)	buys (it) for s.o.
awiyâtoke	still the same, still the case (particle)
awîmikatwi	it is {somewhere}
awotamawêwa	mentions (it) to s.o.
awotamwa	mentions it, one's words refer to it
ayahayêhêwa	always makes or lets s.o. go {somewhere} (see **ihêhêwa**)
ayahayêwa	always goes {somewhere} (see **ihêwa**)
ayâpami	back (returning) (particle, preverb)
ayâpamîwa	goes back
ayâpamotêwa	moves camp back
ayâpêwa	male deer, buck, stag; buffalo bull
ayâw-ahpîhchi	the extent to which respectively (particle compound)
ayâwi	respectively, correspondingly (preverb)
ayâwihchîhiwa	shoots with the bow, contests at archery
ayâwi-'nenikêwa	makes signs, gestures
ayâwi-ishimêwa, ayâwi-'shimêwa	dictates what to do to s.o.
aye	early, earlier, already (particle)
ayênahkatêwi	it is still anchored in place, still stuck in the ground
ayêshi, ayîshi, ayêhi	keep on, still, yet, remaining, continue to (preverb, particle)
ayêshishinwa, ayêshisenwi	(animate, inanimate) is still lying there, remains behind
ayîhkwapiwa	is tired of sitting
ayîhkwihêwa	tires s.o.
ayîhkwinehkêhokowa	one's arms get tired from one's load
ayîhkwiwa	is tired, weary
ayîkwâmâchimêwa	gives a great reputation to s.o.

ayîkwâmesiwa, awîkwâmesiwa	is alert, quick to act, pays sharp attention
ayîkwâmi	with best effort, trying one's best (preverb)
ayîkwâmimêwa	exhorts s.o., urges s.o. strongly, tells s.o. to do their best
ayîkwâmitîwaki (plural)	they exhort each other
ayîkwâmîwa	does one's utmost, tries one's best
ayînâpiwa	remains with a fixed stare on one's face
ayînêhka	persisting aimlessly or inappropriately (particle)
ayîshi: see **ayêshi**	
ayôchiwêpi	from now on
ayôhetîwaki (plural)	they make each other use or wear (it)
ayôhi	here
ayôninâhi	now, at this time; here, in this place (particle)
ayôtenêwa	uses (it) on s.o.
ayôtêwi, ayôtâtêwi	it is used
ayôtîwaki (plural)	they use (it) on each other
ayôwenehki	it takes a while, it took a while
ayôweni	tool

â

âchêwîwa	tries again, starts over
âchi	again, in addition, over again (preverb)
âchihkâhkênêwa	puts one's hands on s.o.'s chest to stop them or push them back
âchihtôwa	remakes it, makes it anew
âchikashîwa	beetle
âchikêwa	rebuilds one's house
âchimekosiwa	is told about
âchimekôha	the famous one, the one talked about, the hero of the tale
âchimekôhi	the famous thing
âchimetisowa	tells about oneself
âchimêwa, âtotamwa	tells of s.o., it
âchimôni	story, historical or traditional account
âchimohêwa	informs, instructs s.o.
âchimohetîwaki (plural)	they inform each other
âchimowa (**âchimôhiwa** dimin.)	narrates, reports, tells one's story, speaks
âchimwihtawêwa	tells (it) for s.o., speaks for s.o.
âchimwihtôwa	tells about it, talks about it
âchinehkawêwa	chases s.o. away, sends s.o. away
âchinehkamawêwa	chases (s.o.) away for s.o.
âchinehkamâtisowa	chases (s.o.) away for oneself
âchipanakichi	all different kinds, all different ways
âchipîshi	different each time, a succession of different ones (particle)
âhâmêha	nuthatch
âhchîhkatôwa	stands it leaning against (something)
âhchîpiwa	sits leaning
âhchîshinwa	leans; leans on (it)
âhkonêwa	Indian tobacco (also **wâhkonêwa**)
âhkohtamwa	has a keen sense of hearing for it
âhkowi	every time (preverb)
âhkôtêwesiwa	he goes armed, always has a deadly weapon with him
âhkwahki (participle)	weaponry (**otâhkwatomi** his weapon or weapons) (see **âhkwatwi** (2))
âhkwamachihêwa	makes s.o. sick

âhkwamatamwa	is sick, indisposed, injured (**âhkwamatamôhiwa** dimin.)
âhkwamatamôweni	sickness, disease
âhkwamatamôhkânowa	pretends to be sick
âhkwamatamôhkêwa	has sickness in one's family
âhkwamênotawêwa, âhkwamênotamwa	is on the lookout for s.o., it
âhkwamêwa	is on the lookout, on one's guard
âhkwatwi (1)	it is dangerous, it is painful
âhkwatwi (2) (only possessed):	**otâhkwatomi** his weapon or weapons (see **âhkwahki**)
âhkwâpitêwa	has a sharp bite
âhkwâshkêwi	it is painful, causes pain
âhkwâtêmeki	at the far end of the lodge (particle) (also **êhkwâtêmeki**)
âhkwêhêwa	makes s.o. angry
âhkwêhtawêwa	is angry at s.o., it
âhkwêmikatwi	it is angry
âhkwênechikana (only possessed):	**otâhkwênechikanani** his beloved
âhkwênemêwa, âhkwênetamwa	thinks a great deal of s.o., it
âhkwêwa	is angry; is in a rage
âhkwêwi	angrily, in anger (preverb)
âhkwêwinâkosiwa	seems angry
âhkwi	sharply, dangerously, (of perception) plainly (preverb)
âhkwihpokwatwi	it tastes sour, strong (**âhkwihpokwatôhiwi** dimin.)
âhkwikomêwa	has a sharp beak, (thorn) has a sharp point
âhkwimêwa	speaks to s.o. firmly, strictly forbids s.o.
âhkwitêhêwa	is sullen
âhkwiyâmêwa	has a keen sense of smell for s.o. (as, tobacco)
âhpawêwa	dreams (**netâhpawa** I dream)
âhpechi	all the time, permanently, for good (particle, preverb)
âhpechimêwa	tells s.o. all the time
âhpechinanêwa	kills s.o. for good, kills s.o. outright
âhpechîwa	goes for good
âhpene	both or all alike, regularly the same (particle)
âhpenêhêwa	prevails against s.o. one-sidedly, does not give s.o. a chance in the fight
âhpenêwe, âhpenêwi	nothing but, only onesidedly (not the reverse) (particle, preverb)
âhpenêyâwi	there is nothing but it
âhpesehkêwa	keeps on (uncontrollably)
âhpetânakîkwêwa	keeps one's eyes staring open, one's eyes stay open staring
âhpetâpiwa	freezes staring, has a frozen expression of astonishment
âhpetâpyêsenwi	it lies endless
âhpetosêwa	walks all the time
âhtawânêwa	puts s.o. on their back
âhtawâsêwa	falls over backwards
âhtawâshimêwa	lays s.o. on their back
âhtawâshinwa, âhtawâsenwi	lies on one's back, it lies on its back
âhtêsenwi	its fire dies down or goes out, it (fire) goes out
âhtêsetôwa	lets its fire go out
âhtêwa, âhtêwi	(sweatlodge stone) cools off; it (fire) goes out
âkema	snowshoe
âkowiyêhiwa	does not exist, is gone, is not there
âkôhôni	dividing pole (on the floor of the lodge)
âkôhôswêwaki (plural)	they hunt buffalo by running after them (and driving them)
âkwapiwa	sits to rest; takes a break
âkwasowa, âkwatêwi	(animate, inanimate) is piled up, forms a pile (**âyâkwatêwi** it lies in piles)
âkwêchênamwa	carries a bundle or bunch of them

âkwêhanohkiwi, âkwêhanohkihkiwi	driftpile, pile of river debris (plural **âkwêhanohkyêni, âkwêhanohkihkiwani**)
âkwi	not; no; it is not the case that (particle)
âkwi-kanâkwa	it is, was impossible; one cannot do it; there is no other possibility; it cannot be helped (particle phrase)
âkwikanâkwâhiwa	fails, is a failure
âkwikêkôhenwi	it does not exist, is gone, is no more
âkwi-kêkôhi	it does not exist (plural **âkwi-kêkôhani**) (particle phrase)
âmanêha	sexually promiscuous woman, whore
âmanohkatawêwa	engages in sexual activity with s.o.
âmanôneniwa	man with a great sexual appetite
âmanôwâchimowa	talks about sex
âmanôwitêhêwa	lusts
âmanwa	has sexual inclinations, has sex, (deer) is rutting
âmehkwâhi	(see **êmehkwâhi**)
âmi	would, should, could (preverb)
âmihtahi	would (after **îni, ôni** then)
âmiwenêwa	moves s.o. away
âmîhetêwi	camp is broken, everyone moves
âmîhetîwaki (plural)	they move camp together
âmîwa	moves camp, moves to winter camp
âmôwa	bee, wasp
âmôwi (1)	honey
âmôwi (2)	of bees (prenoun) (**âmôwi-ashihkanwi** beeswax)
ânawapwîhêwa	gives up waiting for s.o.
ânawâpamêwa	looks for s.o. and doesn't see them
ânawesiwa	fails
ânawênemêwa	thinks s.o. is inadequate, assumes s.o. is not up to it, gives up on s.o., does not have faith in s.o., purposely leaves s.o. out
ânawênetamwa	thinks it is not enough, gives up on it; gives up hope
ânawihêwa, ânawihtôwa	fails to get s.o., it
ânawihowa	is unsuccessful
ânehkênohtawêwa	interprets for s.o.
ânehkênoshêwa	interprets, is an interpreter (also **ênehkênoshêwa**)
ânehkêwi	next in sequence, in turn (particle, preverb)
	ânehkêwi nôshisemaki my great-grandchildren
ânehkôchi	next in order (prenoun)
	ketânehkôchi-kôshisemêha your great-grandchild
ânehkôchikenwi	it grows joined together, (bone) sets
ânehkôkanêyâwi	it is a joint
ânehkôtamwa	puts an addition on it
ânehkwikiwa	adds the next generation
ânemachiwa	is extremely cold, is dangerously cold
ânemapenêwa	is starving
ânemâpiwa	looks with alarm
ânemesiwa	is in a plight, in dire straits
ânemesowa	it is almost unbearably hot for one
ânemeshkêwa, ânemeshkêwi	vomits and retches uncontrollably, trembles uncontrollably, darts around at random; it moves or rolls about rapidly and confusedly
ânemênemêwa	is worried about s.o., thinks s.o. is in danger
ânemihêwa	puts s.o. in dire straits
ânemimêwa	nervously insists or demurs to s.o., implores s.o.
ânemitêhêwa	is ill at ease
ânemwêwa	nervously insists or demurs

âneta	some (of it, of them); partly (particle)
ânochimêwa	refuses s.o.'s request, tells s.o. one disagrees with their decision
ânohamwa	fails to deal with it by tool
ânohtawêwa	fails to hear s.o., denies s.o.'s request
ânohtâkêwa	mishears people, disobeys people
ânomêwa	fails to persuade s.o.
ânonêwa, ânonamwa	is unable to lift s.o., it
ânosiwa	is unable to finish the food one is served
ânotîwaki (plural)	they refuse each other's requests
ânotwêwa	refuses, refuses a request
ânowêwa	fails to persuade people
ânôhpenanêwa	is unable to kill s.o., fails to get s.o.
ânônamêwa	is unable to get around (**êh=ânônamâchi** he or she was unable to get around)
ânômêwa, ânôtamwa	is unable to carry s.o., it on one's back
ânwâkonîwa	is barely able to get through the deep snow
ânwêhtawêwa, ânwêhtamwa	disbelieves, refuses s.o., it
ânwênemêwa	thinks ill of s.o., disapproves of s.o., dislikes what s.o. does
ânwênetâkosiwa	is thought ill of, disapproved of
ânwi	fail to, is unable to (preverb)
ânwikanêwa	is too exhausted or weak to move
ânwishkiwêhamwa	is unable to stir it as a thick mass
ânwîhkawêwa	fails to deal with s.o.
âpatahowa	walks with a cane
âpatahôni	cane
âpaweshkêwa	thaws out
âpechi	come on! hurry up! (particle)
=âpehe	always, generally, usually
âpehtawâhkiwe	halfway down the hill (particle)
âpehtawâhkwe	half the height of a tree (particle)
âpehtawapahkwe	halfway up to the roof (particle)
âpehtawawahîne	half a year (particle)
âpehtaweche	up to the waist (particle)
âpehtawesîha	halfbreed
âpehtawi	half (of it), halfway (particle, preparticle)
âpehtawi-kîshekwe	halfway to the sky (particle)
âpehtawipwâme	halfway up the thigh (or thighs) (particle)
âpehtawi-wâsêyâwe	a half day (particle)
âpehtôneniwiwa	is middle-aged
âpenôyâwi	it is sheltered from the wind
âpesîhêwa	brings s.o. back to life
âpesîwa	comes back to life
âpesîwanêhpwêwa	restores s.o. to life by breathing
âpi	have gone and, have been (preverb)
âpi-chîpêwa	comes back from the dead (ritual)
âpihamawêwa	unties it for s.o.
âpihêwa	went {somewhere} and returned, has been {somewhere}
âpihiwanehkêwa	unties a pack
âpihwêwa, âpihamwa	unties s.o., it
âpinahwêwa, âpinahamwa	unties s.o., it, unties a bag containing s.o., it
âpipahtôwa	goes alone to spy on the enemy as a scout
âpishkonêwa, âpishkonamwa	unties s.o., it
âpishkwâkwatawêwa	unties and lays (it) out for s.o.
âpishkwisahtôwa	rapidly unties it

âpôchi	contrarywise, on the contrary, in reverse (preverb)
âpôchîwa	goes backwards, the wrong way
âpôshkechênamwa	turns it over
âpôshkechêsahêwa	flips s.o. over
âpôshkenamwa	turns it inside out
âpôtahamwa	turns it inside out using something
âpôtakôtôwa	hangs it the wrong way around
âsamahanoki	north (ritual) (locative noun)
âsami	upstream, up the (railroad) line, west (particle)
âsiyahkâha	gnat
âsiyâni	breechcloth
âsônêwa	supports s.o., helps s.o. stand or walk
âsôwânakwêpisôni	suspenders
âsôyâhkwishimêwa	lays s.o. propped up at an angle
âshakachi	contrariwise, the other way around instead, with roles reversed (particle)
âshakachîhkawêwa	opposes or objects to s.o. forcibly; forces s.o. against their will
âshakachîhkâsowa	objects, uses force
âshakachîhkâtîwaki (plural)	one forces the other
âshihêwa	gets s.o. to be or act like one by example, gets s.o. into the habit
âshihiwêwa	gets people into doing something by example
âshimetîwaki (plural)	they coax each other
âshimêwa, âshotamwa	coaxes, urges, tempts s.o., eggs s.o., it on; urges (it) on s.o.; urges it, advises it
âshishimôhkêwa	has a still-born child
âshita, âshitami	in turn, in return (particle)
âshitawâhêwa	retaliates the same way against s.o., gets even with s.o.
âshitônikêwa	trades
âshitônikawêwa	trades with s.o.
âshkâchi	contrary, in a contrary way (preverb)
âshkâchimêwa	speaks against s.o., opposes s.o.
âshkâchitêhêwa	is obstinate, bull-headed, stubbornly opposed
âshkâtahkasowa	braces oneself in resistance
âshkâtesiwa	is opposed, resists
âshkâtênemêwa	is opposed to s.o.
âshkâtowêwa	speaks in opposition
âshowakâme	on the other side of the stream (particle)
âshowanâmowa	swims across underwater
âshowanehkîwa	steps over
âshowâhkiwe	over the hill, on the other side of the hill (particle)
âshowânakohamwa	wears it as a cross-belt (also **âshowânekohamwa**)
âshowânekwahâtêhi	cross-belt
âshowânekoshkamwa	has it slung over one shoulder and under the other arm (like a cross-belt)
âshowâsîwa	climbs across
âshowâshkêwa	flies across
âshowi	over, on the other side, beyond an obstruction or expanse (particle, preparticle)
âshowichimêwa	swims across
âshowi-menôta (âshowi-menôtane)	over in the enemy village, on the enemy side (ritual) (particle compound) (see **menôtani**)
âshowîwa	wades, wades across
âshôhkamwa	crosses it
âshôhowa	paddles across

âtahwêwa	drives s.o. back
âtametonêmowa	chatters away
âtamênetisowa	thinks more of oneself than of anything else
âtami	persistently, persist in (preverb)
âtamitêhêwa	is (rashly) insistent
âtamosêwa	walks briskly
âtapiwa	moves to a new location
âtawahâtêwi	it is sung over again
âtawinâkêwa	sings over again
âtawinâkwihtôwa:	âyâtawinâkwihtôwa owîyâwi (the Earth) repeatedly renews the appearance of her body (ritual)
âtâkahâtêwi	it is propped up, held up by a support
âtenêwa	pushes s.o. back
âtesapitêwi	it is tied separately
âtesehkawêwa	heads s.o. off, cuts s.o. off
âtesehkwêshinwa	is stranded on the wrong side of the river or lake
âteseshkêwaki (plural)	they divide into two groups
âtesôhkawêwa	tells a sacred story to s.o.
âtesôhkâkana (âtesôhkâkâha dimin.)	sacred story ("winter story")
âtesôhkâkani	written text of a sacred story
âtesôhkânêwa	tells a sacred story of s.o.
âtesôhkâsowa	sacred stories are told of one
âtesôhkêwa	tells a sacred story
âteshi (âteshîmêhi dimin.)	separately (particle, preverb)
âteshikêwa	builds a separate house
âteshisetôwa	places it (them) separately, by itself (by themselves)
âtotamawêwa	tells of (it) to s.o.
âtotamâtîwaki (plural)	they tell of (it) to each other
âtotamwa	(see âchimêwa)
âtotâtêwi	it is told of
âwahkîkwêsahêwa	scratches s.o.'s face
âwahkyêhtamwa	gobbles it up in one bite
âwahkyênamwa	takes a handful of it, them
âwasâchimowa	exaggerates
âwasi	more; (with subjunctive) it would be best (if) (particle)
âwasinawe	on the other side (of it), over (it) (particle)
âwasi-wâpake	the day after tomorrow (subjunctive compound verb)
âwasîmêhi	more (particle)
âwâchi	even (particle)
âwêkenwi	it is similar (to it); (with negative): there is no sign if it
âwênemêwa	thinks it is s.o., thinks s.o. is it
âwêwi	somewhat like (it) (particle)
âwinôhikanechi	forefinger, index finger (otâwinôhikanechîki on his or her forefinger)
âwinôhikawêwa	points things out to s.o.
âwinôhikêwa	points
âwinôhwêwa	points at s.o.
âwîtênemêwa	favors s.o., thinks more of s.o.
âwîtêni	as the first priority, as the first choice (particle) (also âyîtêni)
âyachîchi	earnestly, insistently (particle, preverb) (also âyâchîchi)
âyachîchimêwa (also âyâchîchimêwa)	gives s.o. strict instructions, insists that s.o. comply strictly
âyachîtapinêwa, âyachîtapitôwa	ties s.o., it securely
âyachîtapisowa, âyachîtapitêwi	(animate, inanimate) is tied securely
âyachîtwêwa (also âyâchîtwêwa)	gives strict instructions, insists on strict compliance

âyahkôhkwêwa	one's hair is {so long}
âyahkwi	{so} long each, {so} far each (particle)
âyahkwinîsîpinechêwa	one's fingers are {so} long
âyahkwiwinêwa	one's horns are {so} long
âyahpîhchinâhi	once in a while, every once in a while, often (particle)
âyakâmâhkiwe	from hill to hill (particle)
âyakâmetêwe	on opposite sides of the lodge from each other (particle)
âyakwamenwi	each time (particle, preparticle)
âyakwami	each time; (with negative): not all the time (particle, preparticle)
âyakwami-kehkatwe	year by year (particle compound)
âyakwami-wâpanwe	day by day (particle compound)
âyakwîchi	more and more, over and over, to excess (particle, preverb)
âyakwîchihêwa	makes things still worse for s.o.
âyamâsowa	yawns
âyashikaninehke	in or using one hand each
âyashkachi	at long intervals, not too often (particle)
âyatehchi	away from each other, each by oneself, separately (particle)
âyâhchîhtanâhiwa	is skipping (along)
âyâhkoshawêwa	gets, has a blazing hot fire going
âyâhkwâchimêwa	tells on s.o.
âyâhkwâchimowa	goes and tells everything
âyâhpene	each the same, each kind separate (particle)
âyâkwachi	in piles (particle)
âyâkwachipokôtêwani (plural)	piles of them (inanimate) drift ashore
âyâkwêshkâtîwaki (plural)	they are all bumping into each other
âyâkwêyâwi	there is a bunch or mob
âyânehki	for {so} long a time each (particle)
âyânehkîhi	a little each (particle)
âyânehkôtîmikatwi	it is in mutual succession
âyânehkami, âyânehkêwi	one after the other (particle)
âyânehpesiwaki (plural)	they (animate) are {so} high (also **inehpesiwaki**)
âyânekihkwâhkosiwaki, âyânekihkwâhkwatôni (plurals)	they (animate, inanimate) are {so} big around
âyânekinôki, âyânekihkwâwani (plurals)	they (animate, inanimate) are {so} big (**âyânekinôhiwaki, âyânekihkwâhenôni** dimin.)
âyânesênemêwa, âyânesênetamwa	avoids thinking about s.o., it
âyânesowêwa	drops the subject
âyânîhotîwaki (plural)	they have a contest
âyânikêmêhi	each (time) a little further on
âyâninâhi	at {such} distances (particle)
	mesh-âyâninâhi separated by a moderate distance or distances
	menw-âyâninâhi a good distance from each other
âyâpôchîkwêshkamwa	wears them (footwear) on the wrong feet
âyâpôtânakeshêwa	one's ears are on backwards (said of a disobedient child)
âyâpyêchi	on top of everything else, going so fas as to (particle)
âyâshôhka	by turns, alternately (particle)
âyâshôkâsêwa	staggers
âyâshowi-wâpanwe	every other day (particle compound)
âyâtaswi	{so many} each, {so much} each (particle, preverb)
âyâtasenwi	there is {so much} of it each (plural **âyâtasenôni**)
âyâtashiwaki (plural)	there are {so many} of them (animate) each
âyâtenamâtîwaki (plural)	they keep passing (it, them) on to each other
âyâteshi	separately from each other (particle)
âyâwasanehkîwa	goes with bounding strides

âyâwasi	here and there (particle)
âyêniwe	steadily, in one place, staying the same (particle) (also **êyêniwe**)
âyênîha, êyênîha	possum
âyîtêni	as the first priority, as the first choice (particle) (also **âwîtêni**)
âyohowêwa, âyahowêwa	Iowa Indian

ch

chachawîhi	sometimes (particle)
chachâhkwi	short (plural) (prenoun)
chachâkeshîhiwaki (plural)	they (animate) are small
chachâki	small (plural) (prenoun)
chachâtapi (also **chachâtepi**)	discretely, each separately, each dealing with one's own (particle)
chachâtapinawe, chachâtapinowe	each separately (particle) (also **chachâtepinowi**)
chachâtapowêwaki (plural)	each of them says words
chachâtepinowi	each separately (particle) (also **chachâtapinawe**)
chahkwâhkonamawêwa	shortens (it) for s.o.
chahkwâpyêwi	it (stringlike) is short
chahkwi	short (prenoun)
chahkwipâhi	pistol
chahkwiwinêwa (Jones)	is short-horned
chahkwîhiwa, chahkonôhiwi	(animate, inanimate) is short
chahkwîtemyâhiwi	it is shallow
chakâhenôhiwi	it is small
chakâhenwi (found with a negative)	it is small
chakâhkosîhiwa	is slim-waisted
chakânaketonwa	has a small mouth
chakâpêwesiwa	is small in bodily build
chakeshîhiwa (chakeshîhêhiwa dimin.)	is small
chakênetamôhiwa	thinks it to be small (dimin.)
chakênetisôhiwa	thinks oneself to be small (dimin.)
chaki	small (prenoun or preverb)
chaki-mônahâkâhi	little hoe (see **mônahâkani**)
chakinâkâhi	small bowl
chaki-nemêsîha	little fish
chakinehpîhiwi	it is low
chakinehpyâhiwi	it is low
chapôkâhkwisenwi	it lies extending into the water
chapôkâmowa	flees into the water
chapôkâsenwi	it blows into the water
chapôkâshowîwa	wades into the water
chapôkenêwa, chapôkenamwa	dips s.o., it in water
chapôkisêwa, chapôkisêwi	(animate, inanimate) falls into the water
chapôkisahêwa, chapôkisahtôwa	throws s.o., it into the water
chapôkisahowa	jumps into the water
chapôkôtêpahowa	crawls rapidly into the water
châhchâmowa	sneezes
=châhi	so, for, well (idiomatic)
châhmeko	then, only then, for the first time, for the first time in a long time (particle) (older **achâhmeko**)
châkahôtêwi	it is worn out by being dragged
châkahwêwa (1)	beats s.o. out of everything, wins everything from s.o.

châkahwêwa (2)	uses up the supply of (it)
châkamêwa, châkatamwa	eats s.o., it up
châkashkitepêwa	all the hair is gone from one's head
châkatahwêwa	clubs them all
châkatamawêwa	eats it up for s.o.
châkâwanetîwaki (plural)	they all go off in a large group
châkâwanêwa, châkâwatôwa	takes all of them (animate, inanimate)
châkâpiwa	sees everywhere
châkechêhtêwi	it is blown up
châkechênawêwa, châkechênamwa	hits all of s.o., it with a shot
châkenamwa (1)	takes all of them (inanimate)
châkenamwa (2)	tears it all up
châkenawêwa	wins everything from s.o., wipes s.o. out (gambling)
châkenwi	every time; every way (particle)
châkesiwa	is cut all over
châkesowa, châketêwi	(animate, inanimate) is burned up
châkeswêwa, châkesamwa	burns s.o., it up
châkeshitôwa	makes the whole round
châkeshkamwa	wears it out, kicks it to pieces, tears it up by action of the body
châkeshkânawêwa	wears out one's clothing
châkeshkâtêwi	it is trampled up
châkeshkêwi	it (hair) falls out, it (tooth) decays
châki	all, everywhere (particle, preverb)
châkihêwa	kills all of them, kills both of them
châkihtawêwa	kills all of (them) for s.o.
châkinêwaki (plural)	they both died, they all died
châkisahtôwa	tears it to pieces; vomits it all up
châkisêwi	it is all gone, spent
châkisenyêwa	eats all
châkiwetawêwa	takes all of (it) away from s.o.
châkîkwêhâsowa	is badly beaten about the face
châkîwaki (plural)	they all go
châkochi (particle):	(in idioms) how bad, how stupid (**châkochi=nîhka keteshiwêpesi.** How stupid can you get!)
châkônêwaki (plural)	they all carry s.o.
châkôhkawêwaki (plural)	they all assail s.o.
châkôhkâtîwaki (plural)	they assail each other in full force
châkyâwi	it is all torn, all in tatters
chemôka	old woman (see also **mechemôka**)
chêchêkechênêwa	carries or hugs s.o. making them scream
chêchêkesowa	cries out from being burned, heated, or scalded
chêchêkihêwa	makes s.o. scream
chêchêkipahowa	runs crying
chêchêkwa	screams, cries out
chêchêwi	alike, the same as each other (preverb)
chêchêwinâhi	both or all at the same time; at equal distances apart
chêpahkwâni	area of sleeping platform against the lodge-wall
chêwi	equally, the same (preverb, preparticle)
chêwinâhi	at the same time (particle)
chêwinehki	in between, halfway (particle)
chêwinehkîhiwa	is around the place
chêwîshenwi	both times, both ways, double (particle)
chêwîshwi	both (particle)
chêyêneswi	all three (particle)

chêyênyêwi	all four (particle)
chihihwî!	Gosh!
chî!	Halloo! Say!
chîhchê!	Oh my! Look at that! How cute! How odd! (also **shîhchê!**)
chîhchîkenamwa	keeps holding it out
chîhchîkoma	wart (**nechîhchîkoma** my wart)
chîhchîkoswêwa	burns all of s.o.'s flesh off
chîhchîkahkwahâha	robin
chîhchîkwapisowa	she hikes up her skirt
chîhchîkwatamwa	eats everything off of it (as, all meat off bone)
chîhchîkwânakapisowa	he hikes up his breechcloth
chîhchîkwânakitiyêpisowa	hikes up one's breechcloth or skirt
chîhchîpinîkwêwa	is blinking (see also **chîpinîkwêwa**)
=chîhi	it was (suddenly, surprisingly) seen, discovered, found, or learned
chîkahkatêwi	it is anchored in place sticking out
chîkakohamwa	sweeps it
chîkakohikêwa	sweeps
chîkakonamwa	pulls or pushes it (as, a skirt) up
chîkakôtênêwa	raises s.o.'s skirt
chîkashkôhi	clitoris
chîkashkote	by the fire (particle)
chîkawahîme, chîkawahîne	nearby (particle)
chîkâhkiwe	next to a hill or cliff (particle)
chîkâhkwe	next to a tree (particle)
chîkânakwe	next to a hole (particle)
chîkânowêwa	holds up one's tail
chîkâpyêshwêwa, chîkâpyêshamwa	cuts a thin strip or slice off s.o. (as, hide or fat), it
chîkâshkahwêwa	shoots one's urine out
čîkenamawêwa	holds (it) out to s.o.
chîkepyêki	close to the water
chîkeshkwênwa	holds up one's head, sticks one's neck out
chîketôhi	tea-kettle
chîkêshkote	by the prairie (particle)
chîki	close to, near (preparticle)
chîkihtâhpêwa	the nape of one's neck sticks out
chîkikâpâwa	stands sticking out (as, of the water)
chîkikomêsenwi	its end, point projects
chîkishkwâte	by the door (particle)
chîkitepêsîhi	single-bladed axe
chîkitepêwa	has a long head
chîkitiyêkâpâha	bluebird
chîkitiyêkâpâwa	stands with rump out
chîkitiyêshinwa	is on one's hands and knees, gets down on one's hands and knees
chîkitiyêwi (preverb):	**chîkitiyêwi-pasekwîwa** gets up on all fours
chîkonwâwa	living skeleton
chîkômyêhokowa	goes with (it as) a load sticking up on one's back
chîkôtêwene	at or along the edge of the village
chîkwêsota (participle)	member of the Thunder Clan
chîkwêwa	thunderer, thunder being
chîmâni	canoe
chînawêmêwa, chînawêtamwa	is related to s.o.; is related to it, has relatives
chînishkatamôha	katydid
chînishkesowa, chînishketêwi	exudes matter liquefied by heat, it oozes out liquefied by heat
chînishkikomênowa	blows one's nose with one's hands

chînishkinenyênêwa	milks her (as, a cow)
chîpachisenwi	it is stiff
chîpahwêwa	prods him
chîpatâkesiwa	(a bow) is stiff
chîpatesiwa	is stiff
chîpaya	corpse; ghost
chîpayi-owîshi	skull
chîpânâki	in the Land of the Dead (locative noun)
chîpechênêwa	nudges s.o.
chîpechêsahêwa	pokes s.o.
chîpenêwa, chîpenamwa	touches s.o., it with something pointed; nudges, pokes s.o., it
chîpêhkohkwêweni	"Ghost Feast," memorial feast
chîpêhkohkwêwa	gives a "Ghost Feast," a memorial feast
chîpênâwesiwa	sees or is visited by a ghost
chîpêtehkwa	ghost
chîpinîkwêwa	blinks (once)
chîpisahowa	jumps with a start
chîpîkwêhtawêwa	winks at s.o.
chîpîkwêwa	winks
chîshkâkani	intestinal gas
chîshkâtamwa	breaks wind on it
chîshkêwa	breaks wind
chîtapenêwa	sits s.o. up, sits s.o. down
chîtapihêwa	makes s.o. sit upright
chîtapisêwa	ducks down, drops down
chîtapisahowa	jumps into sitting position
chîtapiwa (chîtapîhiwa dimin.)	sits, sits down, sits upright

e

ehehe!	Hey! (look sharp! wake up!)
ehehê!, ehehyê!	Oh dear!; Uh-oh!; Hard luck!
ehêhe (ê is optionally nasalized)	yes (answering a question)

ê

êh=	(aorist; marks aorist modes and locative participles) (proclitic preverb or prefix)
êhêpikwa	tarantula; water spider (**nepîki tashi-êhêpikwa**)
êhêwa	swan
êhêwekêwa	dances the Swan Dance
êhêwisowa (Jones)	is a member of the Swan Clan
êhkanyâhi	maple sugar cake
êhkawâpîha	guard, sentry
êhkawâpîhi	thing that watches
êhki	lo and behold (particle) (also **êshki**)
êhkwâtêmeki	at the far end of the lodge (particle) (also **âhkwâtêmeki**)
êhtameko	Oh how well, much, etc. (archaic) (particle) (also **tameko**)
êhtesikêha	locust (insect)
êhyê!	Uh-oh! Tough it out! Darn it! Phooey!

êkwikwâtêhi	ribbonwork appliqué
êkwikwâtêhi-manetôwêkenwi	broadcloth blanket with ribbonwork appliqué
êkwîchika (participle)	hippopotamus
êmehkwâhi (archaic êmehkwâni)	spoon (also **âmehkwâhi**)
êmehkwânahikêwa	uses a spoon
êmehtekôshîha	(see **mêmehtekôshîha**)
ênawîha	hunter
ênâpatamwa	fails to see it
ênehkênohtawêwa	interprets for s.o.
ênehkênoshêwa	interprets, is an interpreter (also **ânehkênoshêwa**)
ênêkiwa, ênêkenwi	(animate, inanimate) is left over, not paired off, an uneven number
ênikâwi, ênikâwe	in opposite directions, on opposite sides (particle)
ênikehtawêwa	laughs when hearing s.o.
ênikênemêwa	laughs at s.o.
ênikimêwa	says something funny to s.o., gives s.o. a funny answer
ênikitêhêwa	feels amused, thinks it's funny
ênikîkwêhtawêwa	smiles at s.o.
ênikîkwêkâpâwa	stands with smiling face
ênikîkwêwosêwa	walks with smiling face
ênikonôsa	ant
ênikonôsiwiwi	it is full of ants, has ants on it
ênikowêwa	says funny things to people
êniwakitêhi	expensive item
êniwânemahki	wind storm (see **aniwânematwi**)
ênîhka	in opposite directions (particle)
ênowênemâchihi,	(the warparty leader's) hand-picked men
ênawênemâchihi (participles)	
ênowêni	pretty, handsome (prenoun) (archaic) (see **nawêni**)
ênowênihkwêhêha	pretty young woman (archaic)
ênowênihkwêhêhiwa	she is a pretty young woman (archaic)
ênwêwêhâsôha	drum
êsapîhkêha	spider (Jones: spiderweb)
êsapîhkêhêyâpi	spiderweb
êsâwâhkasota kôhkôsha	bacon
êsepana, êsepâha	raccoon
êsepanaya, êsepâhaya	raccoon skin
-êsepane	quarter-dollar (in particle compounds) (**nesw-êsepane** seventy-five cents)
êsepâhêha	small raccoon
êsikâkwa	tick (plural êsikâkwaki)
êsîha	shellfish, mussel; bivalve shell
êshikanisota (participle)	member of the Fish Clan (literally, Bass Clan)
êshkamesiwa	gets sicker and sicker
êshkami	gradually, more and more (particle)
êshkamîwa	goes straight (to {somewhere})
êshki	(see **êhki**)
êshkikîha	young person
êshkipakipyâta (participle)	evergreen (see **ashkipakipyêwa**)
êshkotêwîhi	steam boat; railroad train
êshkotêwîhi-myêwi	railroad, railroad tracks
êshkwisâchiki (plural)	change (from a purchase)
êwiyêhikwêna (interrogative participle)	someone or other, some unidentified creature (also **wêwiyêhikwêna**) (see **owiyêhiwa**)
êyêhkwêwa	berdache (man dressing and living as a woman)
êyêhkwêwênemêwa	considers s.o. to be a berdache

êyêniwe	steadily, in one place, staying the same (particle) (also **âyêniwe**)
êyêshi-pwâwi-, êyêh-pwâwi-	before (preverbs with changed conjunct)
êyîki	and, also, too, as well, likewise (particle)

h

hâhâw ([âʔâwᵘ], [haʔhaʔhâʔᵘ])	(the town crier's call)
hao, hawo ([haôʔ])	hello; all right, yes (agreeing to a suggestion or request)
hwâ!	Oh no! Oh dear! Too bad (for him, etc.)! (also **wâ!**)

i

ihêhêwa	makes or lets s.o. go {somewhere} (future **wîh=êhêwa**)
ihêmikatwi	it goes {somewhere} (future **wîh=êmikatwi**)
ihênotawêwa	goes {somewhere} to s.o. (future **wîh=ênotawêwa**)
ihêwa (**ihêhiwa** dimin.)	goes {somewhere} (**neta** I go {somewhere}; **êyâyâni** where I am going, where I went; future **wîh=êwa**)
=ihi (**='hi=, ='h=, ='=**)	not (highly idiomatic; often with sarcastic intonation)
ihihwî!	Oh my!
ihihyâ!	Oh my! Oh boy!
ihketowa	speaks {so}
ihketômikatwi	it speaks {so}
ihkwêha	female
ihkwêhêha	young woman
ihkwêwa	woman
ihkwêwanohkyâni	women's products; women's equipment and supplies
ihkwêwawahîma	female (animal or bird)
ihkwêwimini	seed
ihkwêwiwa	she is a woman (**wêchi-ihkwêwichi** what makes her a woman, her private parts)
ihkwêwiweni	womanhood
ihkyêwa	says {so}, says {so} to someone
ihpahowa	runs to {somewhere} (**îtepi êh=ihpahowâchi** they ran there)
ihpahôtêwi	it (as, a train) runs to {somewhere}
ihpinêwa, ihpitôwa	ties s.o., it {so} (also **inapinêwa, inapitôwa**)
ihpisowa, ihpitêwi	is tied {so}, it is tied {so} (**êhpisochi** the way [anim.] was tied)
ihpokosiwa, ihpokwatwi	(animate, inanimate) tastes {so}
=ih=wêna	what about? why not?; obviously not!; or rather (meaning partly depends on intonation)
inachimêwa	cools, freezes s.o. {so}
inahamwa	sings the songs {so}; strikes it {so}
inahkamikesiwa	gets along {so}, has things go for one {so} (**ênahkamikesichi** how one is getting along)
inahkamikihtôwa	makes out {so}
inahkiwiwi	there is {such} going on (**ênahkiwiki** what went on)
inahowa	paddles to {somewhere} (**îtepi êh=inahowâchi** they paddled there)
inahômowa	gives {such} a cry
inahônêwa	drags s.o. to {somewhere}
inakimowa, inakitêwi	it is priced {so}
inakitamawêwa	pays s.o. {so much} for (it)

inakôtêwi	it hangs {so}
inakôtôwa	hangs it {so}
inamatamwa	has {such} a feeling or pain
inamowa	eats {so}
inanawiwa	goes on a hunting trip to {somewhere}
inanohkyêwa	does things {so}
inapenêhtôwa:	**inapenêhtôwa owîyawi** starves oneself {so}
inapinêwa, inapitôwa	ties s.o., it {so} (also **ihpinêwa, ihpitôwa**)
inapiwa	sits {so}
inashkôsowa	has {such} a feeling, understanding, or condition after eating (also **ineshkôsowa**)
inashkwi	{such} herbal medicine (**châki-'nashkwi** all kinds of herbal medicine)
inatahwêwa	strikes him {so} with tool
inatamwa	eats it {so} (**wîh=inatamowâchi** how they must eat it)
inawêmêwa	is related to s.o. {so} (**ênawêmâchi** the way he or she is related to s.o.)
inâchimêwa, inâtotamwa	speaks {so} of s.o., it
inâchimêweniwiwa	is told of {so}
inâchimekosiwa, inâchimekwatwi	is told of {so}, it is told of {so}
inâchimowa	narrates {so}
inâchimôhiwa	narrates {so} (dimin.)
inâchimohêwa	tells, informs s.o. {so}
inâchimohetîwaki (plural)	they inform each other {so}
inâhkêwa	throws (it) to {somewhere}
inâhkiwiwi	(elevated land) extends or slopes {so}
inâhkonamawêwa	makes {such} a law or rule for s.o.
inâhkonâsowa	is subject to {such} a rule or law
inâhkonikêwa	makes {such} a rule or law
inâhkowiwa, inâhkowiwi	(animate, inanimate) is {such} a tree
inâhkwichinwa	is {so} snagged
inâhpatesiwa	has {such} ability or skill
inâhpawêwa	dreams {so} (**ênâhpawâchi** his or her dream)
inâhpenanêwa, inâhpenatôwa	treats, deals with, manages to get s.o. {so}; uses it for {such} purpose
inâhpenêwa	is ill, afflicted {so}
inâkêwa	has {such} wings (**châk-ênâkâchiki** all the kinds of birds, [literally] those of every wing)
inâkômêwa, inâkôtamwa	is related to s.o. {so}, has relatives {so} (**châki ênâkômakiki** all my different relatives)
inâkôpehkêwa	uses {such} term of relationship for (s.o.)
inâkôtîwaki (plural)	they are related to each other {so}
inâkwapiwa	sits assembled {so}
inâkwasowa, inâkwatêwi	lies about {so}, it lies about {so}
inâkwâtwi	it is {so} far off (**tâni ênâkwâhki** how far away is it?)
inâmohtâtîwaki (plural)	they drive it {so} to each other
inâmowa	flees to {somewhere}
inânahkwatwi	the clouds are {so}, the sky is {so}
inânaketonêmowa	says {so} in talk or speech
inânaketonêsetôwa	lays it (as, a flute or whistle) with its "mouth" (i.e., the far end) {some way}
inânakîkwêshkêwa	one's eyes become {so}
inânematwi	the wind blows {so}, to {somewhere}
inâpamêwa, inâpatamwa	looks at s.o., it {so}, sees s.o., it {so}
inâpatâniwa	appears {so}
inâpihêwa	makes s.o. look to {somewhere}
inâpiwa	looks to {somewhere}

inâsamapiwa	sits facing {some way}
inâsamekêwa	dances facing {some way}
inâsamikâpâwa	stands facing {some way}
inâsowa (1)	is told (to do) {so} (see **itâtêwi**)
inâsowa (2), **inâtêwi**	(animate, inanimate) is colored {so}
inâshinwa, inâsenwi	(animate, inanimate) is blown {some way} by the wind
inâshkêwa, inâshkêwi	falls, rushes, flies {so}
inâtowêwa	speaks {such} language (**kotaki ênâtowâta** one that speaks another language, another tribe)
inâwakîwi	it has {such} earth, soil
inehkwêkôtôwa	hangs it with the head end oriented {some way}
inehkwêmêwa	attracts s.o.'s attention {some way} by speech
inehkwêmowa	pleads to {somewhere} for help
inehkwênamwa	makes its head end point {some way} (song word)
inehkwêshinwa	lies with head oriented {some way}
inehkwêshitîwaki (plural)	they lay each other with heads oriented {some way}
inehpapiwa	sits {so} high
inehpashkatwi	the grass is {so} high
inehpâkwanêwa, inehpâkwatôwa	makes a pile of s.o., it {so} high
inehpâkwasowa, inehpâkwatêwi	there is a pile {so} high of (animate, inanimate)
inehpowi	it snows {so}
inehpesiwa, inehpyâwi	(animate, inanimate) is {so} high
inehtawêwa	hears s.o. {so}, hearing s.o. thinks they are {so}
inehtâkêwa	hears it said {so}
inehtâkosiwa	sounds {so}, is heard {so}
inekihkoshkamwa	belongs to it in {such} numbers (**ênekihkoshkamowâchi** as many of them as belong to it)
inekihkwatêkiwi	it (as, a river) is {so} wide
inekihkwâhiwi, inekihkwâhenwi, inekihkwâhenôhiwi	it is {so} big (dimin.) (**ênekihkwâhenôhiki** its small size)
inekihkwâhkosiwa, inekihkwâhkwatwi	(animate, inanimate) is {so} big around
inekihkwâpêwesiwa	is {so} big in bodily build
inekihkwâwi	(see **inekinwa**)
inekihkwênemêwa	thinks of {such} a number of them
inekihkwi	{so} big, to {such} extent, {so many} (particle, preverb)
inekihkwihtôwa	makes it {so} big
inekihkwimêwa	speaks to {such} a number of them
inekihkwinechêwa:	**ênekihkwinechêchi** as much as one's hand holds
inekihkwishimowa	one's voice is {so} big, {so} low
inekihkwishinwa	lies {so} big
inekihkwishkwêkanwa	one's neck is {so} big around
inekinôhiwa; inekihkwâhenwi, inekihkwâhenôhiwi, inekihkwâhiwi	(animate, inanimate) is {so} big (dimin.)
inekinwa, inekihkwâwi	(animate, inanimate) is {so} big (**ênekineki** his or her size, his or her whole body; **ênekihkwâki** its size, its extent)
inenamâkêwa	hands (it) out {so}
inenehkwêwânetîwaki (plural)	they go as a couple to {somewhere}
inenehkwêwâsowa	she is taken as a bride to {somewhere}
inenekowa	carries on {so}
inenetîwa	fights {so}, to {somewhere}
inenêhamwa	fans it to {somewhere}
inenêwa, inenamwa	holds, handles s.o., it {so}, hands s.o., it on to {somewhere}
inenêwi	it burns to {somewhere}, {so}
inenikawêwa	makes signs to s.o. {so}

inenikêwa	makes signs {so}
ineniwiwa	he is a man (**êneniwiyane** you men!) (also **neniwiwa**)
inenoswa	buffalo (archaic; see **nenoswa**)
ineswêwa, inesamwa	heats, burns, cooks s.o., it {so}
ineshêwa	hears {so}
ineshêwi	it (fire) burns, blazes {so}
ineshihamwa	goes to {somewhere} to hunt
ineshkawêwa:	**ineshkâkwiwa** it (food) has a good affect on s.o.
ineshkêwa, ineshkêwi	moves (involuntarily), is moved, is taken {so, to somewhere}, retches {so}
ineshkôsowa	(see **inashkôsowa**)
inetonêmowa	talks {so}
inênechikani	thought, blessing
inênekêmowa	has {such} thoughts or feelings towards people
inênemêwa, inênetamwa	thinks {so} of s.o., it
inênemêweniwiwa	is the subject of {such} thought
inênetamawêwa	thinks of (it) for s.o. {so}
inênetâkaniwiwa	is the subject of {such} thought
inênetâkosiwa, inênetâkwatwi	is thought of {so}, it is thought of {so}
inênetisowa	thinks of oneself {so}
inênetîwaki (plural)	they think of each other {so}
inêtwa	is away {so long} (**nehki wîh=inêtowâchi** how long they will be gone for)
inêwa, itamwa	says {so} to s.o., it; tells s.o. {so}; calls s.o., it {so}
inêweniwiwa	is called {so}
inosêwa	walks {so}, to {somewhere}
inotâtêwi	it is told {so}, it is mentioned {so}, it is planned {so}
inotêwa	moves camp to {somewhere}
inowâkani	saying, word
inowânêwa	addresses s.o. {so} (**pêmi-'nowâshiki** the sequence in which I was addressed)
inowêhiwa	declares {so} (dimin.)
inowêwa	speaks to people {so}, talks, declares, states, answers {so}
inômekowa	rides on horseback to {somewhere}
inômêwa, inôtamwa	carries s.o., it on the back {so}, to {somewhere}
inôtêwa	crawls to {somewhere}
inwâsowa	pretends {so}
inwêwa, inwêwi	(animate, inanimate) sounds {so}
inwêwêkihêwa	makes s.o. shout, cry out {so}
inwêwêkesiwa, inwêwêkatwi	wails {so}, there is {such} sound
inwêwêtepêhwêwa	hits s.o. on the head with {such} noise
=ipi (=ipihi)	they say, it is said, supposedly, you're supposed to, let's say
ishawiwa	does {so}, fares {so}; {such} happens to one
ishawiweni	({such a}) kind of ceremony, activity, doing, experience, performance, way of life
ishawiwêwa	teases s.o. {so}
ishe	just, merely, just naturally or spontaneously, just to be doing it (particle) (also **ashe**)
ishenemêsîha, shenemêsîha, nemêsîha	minnow
ishewêna (and **ishewê=**)	but, still (particle) (also **ashewêna, shewêna**)
ishêwîwa	does things {so}
ishêwîweni	custom
ishêwîweniwiwi	the custom is {so}
ishi-wîsowa	is of {such} clan (**îni êshi-wîsochiki** ones of that clan)

ishi	{some} way, {so}, {thus}, to {somewhere} (particle, preverb, prenoun)
ishihchikâsowa, ishihchikâtêwi	(animate, inanimate) is fixed up or decorated {so}
ishihchikêwa	does things {so}
ishihchikêweniwiwi	it is {so} performed
ishihêwa, ishihtôwa	makes s.o., it {so}
ishihtanwi	it flows {so}
ishihtawêwa	makes (it) {so} for s.o.
ishikanêhiwa (dimin.; idiom):	**êshikanêhichi** nothing but (skin and) bones
ishikawiwaki (plural)	they go to {somewhere} as a group
ishikâhiwa	one's feet are {so} (**êshikâhichi** (to) where his or her feet are)
ishikâpawihêwa	makes s.o. stand {so}
ishikâpâwa	sets foot {somewhere}
ishikâsêwa	moves one's feet {so} (song word)
ishikihetîwaki (plural)	they make each other {so}
ishikihêwa	makes s.o. be {so}
ishikiwa, ishikenwi	(animate, inanimate) is {so}, is of {such} kind, nature, or purpose
ishikwamwa	sews it {so}
ishimâkaniwiwa	is addressed {so}
ishimêwa	speaks {so} to s.o.
ishimini	{such} kind of fruit (**châki ishimini** fruit of every kind)
ishinameshkêwa	has {such} skin, is of {such} race
ishinawêhêwa	makes s.o. feel {so}
ishinawîwa	slides or moves {so; to somewhere}
ishinâkêwa	sings {so}
ishinâkosiwa, ishinâkwatwi	looks {so}, it looks {so}
ishinâkwihêwa	makes s.o. look {so}
ishinehkâkêwa	chases people to {somewhere}
ishinehkêwa	moves one's hand to {somewhere}
ishinohtawêwa	says s.o. says {so}
ishisahetîwaki (plural)	they push each other to {somewhere}; they kill each other {so}
ishishinwa, ishisenwi	lies or is laid {so}, it lies or is set {so}, it is a rule {so}
ishisetawêwa	lays (it) {so} for s.o.
ishisêwa	speeds, flies to {somewhere}
ishisêwiwa	is {such} a bird (**châki êshisêwita** every kind of bird)
ishisowa	one's name is {so}, one's clan is {so}
ishisômikatwi	its name is {so}
ishiswihêwa	names s.o. {so}
ishishehkîhowa	dresses {so}
ishishehkîtamwa	wears {such} clothing, is dressed {so}
ishishimêwa, ishisetôwa	lays s.o., it {so}
ishishimowa	speaks with {such} voice
ishishkwêkihtôwa	leaves a trail of blood to {somewhere}
ishitanekowa	acts {so}, does {so}
ishitehkânetîwaki (plural)	they name each other {so}
ishitehkânêwa, ishitehkâtamwa	names s.o., it {so}
ishitehkâsowa, ishitehkâtêwi	is named {so}, it is named {so}
ishitêhatamwa, ishitêhâtamwa	thinks of it {so}
ishitêhâkani	thought
ishitêhêkêwa	thinks {so} as one dances, dances with {such} thought
ishitêhênawêsiwa	it comes into one's heart to think {so}
ishitêhêpiwa	thinks {so} as one sits
ishitêhêwa (1)	thinks {so}
ishitêhêwa (2)	has a heart of {some} sort, has a heart like {something}

ishitêhêweni	thought, desire
ishitêhêpiwa	sits thinking {so}
ishitêhêwosêwa	walks with {such} thought
ishitîwaki (plural)	they speak to each other {so}
ishitîweni:	**ashe ishitîweni** untruth
ishiwanakesiwa	weighs {so much}
ishiwehkyêwa	takes someone to {somewhere}
ishiwenêwa, ishiwetôwa	takes s.o., it to {somewhere}
ishiwêpawiwa	how one is or does has {such} a reason, significance
ishiwêpehtawêwa	understands s.o. to be saying {so}, to mean {so}
ishiwêpesiwa	how one is has {such} significance (**êshiwêpesikwêni** what might be the matter with him, why he was so; for whatever reason; **êshiwêpesiwânêni** I wonder what is or was the matter with me)
ishiwêpi	for, standing for, signifying {so} (particle, preverb)
ishiwêpikenwi	it is, signifies {so} (**êshiwêpikeki** what it is all about, what it represents or corresponds to, what the matter with it is)
ishiwêpitêhêwa	imagines {so}
ishiwêpiyôhkawêwa	tricks s.o. into doing {so}
ishiwêpîhkânowa	pretends {so}
ishiwêpowêwa	means {so}, means to imply {so}
ishiwêwa	says {so} to people
ishiyâkosiwa, ishiyâkwatwi	(animate, inanimate) smells {so}
ishiyâsikêwa	makes {such} an odor by burning, cooking, or smoking something
ishîhkawêwa, ishîhkamwa	occupies oneself with s.o., it {so}, deals with s.o., it {so}, keeps trying to get s.o. to do {so}
ishîhkânowa	pretends to be or do {so}; puts on {such} a ceremony or performance
ishîhtêwa (1)	dresses {so} (**êshîhtâchi** the way he or she was dressed)
ishîhtêwa (2)	works {so}, does {so} (**wîh=ishîhtâyâni** what I will do)
ishîkwêhtawêwa	signals s.o. {so} by the expression on one's face
ishîkwêkâpâwa	stands facing {so}
ishîkwêshkêwa	moves one's face {so}
ishîkwêshimêwa	places s.o. facing {so}
ishîkwêshinwa	lies facing {so} (**êshîkwêshiki** the way he or she faces, in front of his or her face)
=ishkwe	(woman's mild expletive)
ishkwêsêha	girl
ishkwêsêhêha	little girl (**neteshkwêsêhemêhenâna** our (exc.) little girl)
ishkwêsêhiwa	she is a girl
itamawêwa	says {so} of (it) to s.o., means {so} in saying (it) to s.o.
itâtêwi	{such} is said of it, it is called {so} (see **inâsowa** (1))
itesowa	calls oneself {so}
itîwaki (plural)	they say {so} to each other, one says to the other or others
itîwenahkiwiwi	people are saying {so} to each other
itômikatwi	it fares {so} (**êtômikahki** how it fared, what happened)
itwa	fares {so} (**kashi=châh=ketete** what's the matter with you?; **mani=mana wîh=twa** this is what shall happen to this person; **tâni êteyani** what has happened to you?; **wîh=teyâni** what will happen to me; **êtowânêni, êtôhiwânêni** whatever may happen to me)
iwa	says {so} (**nesi** I say {so}, **êh=iyowâchi** they said {so})
=iyo	for, (I say this) because; excuse me for asking or contradicting
=iyo=kêhi	now, remember; now, bear in mind
iyoweni	thing said, what is said

iyômikatwi   it says {so}
=iyôwe   former, formerly (rarely **iyôwe**)

î

îchina   Indian
-îkese (Jones)   acre, acres (in particle compounds) (**nekoti-îkese** one acre)
îna   that, that one (animate gender) (plural **îniki;** obviative singular **înini,** obviative plural **înihi**)
înahi (1)   there
înahi (=**înahi**) (2)   and there was also (particle) (**kwîyesêhâ='nah=nekoti.** And there was a boy, as well.)
=înahi (3)   after that, with that (happening), and; now, now you can; (idiomatic)
înâhiwa   is the one: **înâhikwêni** if it is him or her, if that is the one
înâka   that (yonder, invisible; animate) (plural **înâmâhaki, înêke**)
înâmani   that (yonder, invisible; inanimate) (plural **înâmâhani**)
înâmâhi   way over there, at that distant place or time
îni (1)   it, that, that one (inanimate gender) (plural **înini**)
îni (2)   then, now
=îni (3)   in that case
îni ishi   that way, like that; only (with numbers); immediately, right away
îni=meko   immediately, right then; the same (inanimate)
îninâhi   at that time; by now (particle)
îninâhiwiwi   it is that time
îni-nehki   for that long a time
îniya   that (past, absent, previous; animate) (plural **îniyêka, îniyêke**)
îniye   that (past, absent, previous, going away; inanimate) (plural **îniyêna, îniyêne**)
înoki   today, now, this time (particle)
îtepi   (to) there (a goal), thither (particle) (**îtepi êh=âyâni** I went there)
îyâhi   (to) there (an ending point) (particle) (**îyâhi êh=pyâyâni** I got there)
îyâka   this other one (visible; animate) (plural **îyâmâhaki**)
îyâmani   this other one (visible; inanimate) (plural **înâmâhani**)
îyâmâhi   over there, at that other place or future time
îye   once upon a time, in the past (particle)
îyêmêhi   a little while back (particle)

k

kahkamîwa   goes by a short cut
kahkâhkachîha   salamander
kahkenamwa   strips it (fiber), separates it (inner bark) from the outer bark
kahkenikopyêwa   strips basswood bark
kahkeshêwi   charcoal (also **kehkeshêwi**)
kahkikâpisowa   wears garters, wears (them) as garters
kahkikâpîha   garter (**okahkikâpîhahi** his garters)
kahkinêwa, kahkitôwa   hides s.o., it
kahkinôhi   we shall see! (particle)
kahkisowa   hides oneself, keeps what one does a secret
kahkisôhtawêwa   hides oneself from s.o.

kahkitawêwa	hides (it) from s.o.
kahkîwishinwa	is lying well wrapped up
kaho!	accordingly, well (conjunction) (particle)
kahôni, kôni	and then, so then (particle)
kakamachitêhêwa	is bitterly angry, is seething with bitter grief
kakanônetîwa	converses (with s.o.)
kakanônetîhêwa	converses with s.o.
kakapâchishinwa	lies in a gigantic heap
kakatâni	even though, even in that case, the reverse of what would be expected; it will be good (particle)
	kakatâni='h=wêna (it will be) very good!
	kakatâni='hi='yo (it will be) very good!
kakâchi	jokingly (preverb); "teasing" (of certain relatives) (prenoun)
kakâchichi	paying no heed, even so, anyway (particle)
kakâchihêwa	plays a joke or trick on s.o., teases s.o.
kakâchimêwa	jokes with s.o.
kakânoshêwa	has long ears
kakânôhkwêwa	has long hair
kakânôsiwaki (plural)	they (animate) are long, tall (see **kenôsiwa**)
kakânwâpitêwa	has long teeth
kakânwêshi	for a long time each time (particle) (see **kenwêshi**)
kakânwi	long (plural) (prenoun, preverb) (see **kenwi**)
kakânwikahkwanwa	has long legs
kakânwikashêwa	has long claws, nails
kakânwinîsîpinechêwa	has long fingers
kakânwiwinêwa	has long horns
kakâtâkômêwa	has s.o. as a "teasing" relative
kakâtônêwa	urges s.o.
kakâtwêwa	jokes, teases
kakishashîpye	reluctantly, without wanting to, dragging one's feet (particle) (also **kekishashîpita, kekishashîpye**)
kamayâchi	nevertheless (particle)
kamishinêha	commissioner
kanakanawiwa	gives a speech, says some (formal) words
kanakanawîni	speech, formal speaking, homilies and prayers
kanamâhi	even more so (particle) (also **kanomâhi**)
kanawiwa	speaks
kanawiweni	speech, speaking, form of speech
kanawîni	speech, word
kanâhi	at least (particle)
kanâkwa	it is impossible, it was impossible (particle) (short for **âkwi-kanâkwa**)
kanomâhi	even more so (particle) (also **kanamâhi**)
kanôhkyêwa, kanôhkyêmowa	speaks
kanônâsowa	is addressed
kanônetîwaki (plural)	they speak to each other
kanônetisowa	speaks to oneself
kanônêwesiwa	is addressed by a spirit or spirits
kanônêwa, kanôtamwa	speaks to s.o., it
kanôtamawêwa	speaks to (s.o.) for s.o.
kapôtwe	at some point, some time later, soon, in time, as time went by
kashi (1)	what? (as an oblique complement) (particle) (**kashi keteshawi** what's the matter with you? what happened to you? what did you do?)

kashi! (2)	Why! (exclamation); Well now!
kashinâkwa, kashinâhi, kashinâ!	Gosh! Why! Well! Well now! Well? (also **shinâkwa, shinâ!**)
kashi=wê=towi	yes, of course, to be sure (as an answer) (also **'shi=wê=towi**)
kashkâchimohêwa	is able to tell s.o., manages to tell s.o.
kashkâhkasowa, kashkâhkatêwi	(animate, inanimate) dries up, dries hard
kashkahwêwa, kashkahamwa	manages to deal with s.o., it by tool
kashkatamwa	(with negative): is not able to eat it (as it is too hard)
kashkatesiwa	is unwilling, holds back
kashkenawêwa, kashkenamwa (1)	is able to shoot s.o., it
kashkenêwa, kashkenamwa (2)	is able to lift or carry s.o., it
kashkeshihwêwa	is able to drive s.o. off
kashketiwa	is constipated
kashki	be able to, can; manage to, have the nerve to; possibly; be persuaded to, be successfully made to (preverb)
kashkihêwa, kashkihtôwa	manages, can do or succeed with, gets, buys s.o., it
kashkihkesowa, kashkihketêwi	(animate, inanimate) is naturally dried, seasoned (as, wood)
kashkihowa	succeeds (for oneself), is able; succeeds in getting (s.o., it)
kashkihtâtêwi	it is bought
kashki-mâchîwa, kashki-mâchîmikatwi	(animate, inanimate) is able to move
kashkimêwa	persuades s.o.
kashkipokowa (Jones)	is able to float
kashkishkapisowa, kashkishkapitêwi	(animate, inanimate) is curtained off, separated by hanging blankets
kashkishki (**kashkishkîmêhi** dimin.)	across the path, to or at a place in (someone's) path (particle)
kashkitenwi	it is stuck (in a tight place)
kashkitêhamêwa, kashkitêhatamwa	succeeds with s.o., it, succeeds against s.o., is able to persuade s.o.
kashkîhkawêwa	manages to deal with s.o., succeeds with s.o.
kashkîpâhkwi	tree that squeaks in the wind
kashkîpeshkâtîmikatôni (plural)	they (as, trees) squeak from rubbing against each other
kashkîpwêwêshkêwi	it makes a squeaking noise (as, by rubbing)
kashkowêwa	gets what one asks for, gets (it) as something asked for
kashkôhpenanêwa, kashkôhpenatôwa	prevails over s.o., it, is able to get or kill s.o.
katawi	nearly, almost; (with future) soon (preverb, preparticle, particle)
katawinêwa	almost dies
katôshkashâha	horse (also **nêkatôkashêha, nêkatôshkashâha, nêkatôshkashêha**)
kawapenêwa	collapses from hunger
kawekwashiwa	falls asleep
kawenawêwa	knocks s.o. down by shooting
kawenêwa, kawenamwa	lays, pushes s.o., it down
kawiponêwa, kawipotôwa	cuts s.o. (as, a tree), it down with a saw
kawisêwa, kawisêwi	(animate, inanimate) falls over (as, a standing feather, a tree)
kawishêwi	deadfall, a tangle of fallen timber and brush
kawîshâni	beforehand (particle)
kayêchîhi, kayêchîhe	recently, a short while ago; soon, soon after (particle) (also **keyêchîhi, keyêchîhe**)
kâchimêwa	persuades s.o.
kâchinawêhêwa	tempts or induces s.o. to act
kâchinawêmêwa	persuades s.o. to act
kâchinehkawêwa	urges s.o., drives s.o. on
kâchipitôwa	leads it (a song)
kâchisahêwa, kâchisahtôwa	pushes s.o., it
kâchitâsetôwa	rams it in
kâhkami	directly, from the very beginning, right from the start (particle)
kâhkâchisahêwa	keeps shoving s.o.

kâhkâhkenowa	scratches oneself hard
kâhkâhkesowa, kâhkâhketêwi	(animate, inanimate) is or gets extremely hot (as, from a fire)
kâhkâhki	deeply (of pain, yearning) (particle)
kâhkâhkitêhêwa	is anxious, one's heart aches
kâhkâtenêwa	keeps pushing s.o.
kâhkâwahowêha	fuzzy caterpillar, woollybear
kâhkâwamêwa, kâhkâwatamwa	crunches s.o., it up with one's teeth
kâhkâwêhani (plural)	hackberries
kâhkesowa, kâhketêwi	dries up, gets scorched; it dries up, dries out, gets scorched
kâhkeswêwa, kâhkesamwa	dries s.o., it (by heat)
kâhkeshkawêwa:	**kîwi-kâhkeshkawêwa** is always close by s.o.'s side
kâhki	barehanded, without anything (particle)
kâhkihkenawêwa	scratches s.o. with a shot
kâhkihkenêwa	scratches s.o. deeply (with the hand or hands)
kâhkihkichinwa	gets scratched on something
kâhkihkinameshkênawêwa	scratches s.o.'s skin with a shot
kâhkimotêhi	a bag of (basswood) bark fiber
kâhpîhi	coffee
kâhtosiwa	feels grieved, sorry, disappointed at a loss
kâhtwênemêwa	feels grieved about s.o.
kâhtwênetamawêwa	feels grieved about (s.o.) for s.o.
kâhtwihêwa	causes s.o. grief, loss, dashed hopes
kâkâkiwa	crow
kâkâkiwekêwa	dances the Crow Dance
kâkânwakôchîhaki (plural)	long hanging earrings
kâkânwikashêwa	grizzly bear (also **kêkânwikashêwa, kêkânwikashêha**)
kâkânwichitîha	pintail
kâkâsapi	each alone in turn, a little at a time (particle)
kâkikapôtwe	all at once (particle)
kâkikêneniwiwa	is an immortal, is one who lives forever
kâkikêwi	forever, eternal (prenoun, preverb)
kâkikêwineniwiwa (Jones)	is an immortal, one who lives forever
kânikanîhâhkôni (plural)	rasps (notched sticks used as musical instruments)
kânôhi	quilt; diamond card
kâpâchichi	just barely able (particle)
kâsîhamwa	erases it, rubs it out
kâsîkâshinwa	wipes one's foot
kâsîkwêhôni	handkerchief
kâsîkwêhowa	wipes one's face
kâsîmitiyêhowa	wipes one's bottom
kâsînamwa	wipes it off with one's hand
kâsînechêhowa	wipes one's hands, wipes one's hands on (it)
kâsîshkêwa, kâsîshkêwi	is rubbed clean, it rubs off
kâsîtepêhowa	wipes one's head
kâsîtonêhowa	wipes one's mouth, wipes one's mouth with (it)
kâshamatamwa	feels a stinging or burning sensation
kâshanasitêshinwa	has sore feet
kâshenamwa	makes it sting or burn by touching it
kâshkahowa	gets a shave, shaves
kâshkanachîhtawêwa	whispers to s.o.
kâshkanasowa	whispers
kâshkanâmowa	can be heard breathing
kâshkatahamawêwa	scrapes (it) for s.o.

kâshkâchâwi	there is not too much of it
kâshkâchi	not (too) much, not (too) many (particle)
kâshkâshkahwêwa, kâshkâshkahamwa	scrapes s.o., it clean
kâshkehtâkosiwa	one's voice is heard (speaking, singing, or weeping)
kâshkehtawêwa, kâshkehtamwa	hears s.o., it
kâshkesiwa	is aware of something, feels or hears something
kâshkihêwa, kâshkihtôwa	becomes aware of s.o., it, of s.o.'s, its presence or imminence
kâshkikôhiwa	snores
kâshôha	domestic cat
kâta	don't; not (with a prohibition) (particle)
kâtahamwa	starts singing it
kâtanahamîwa	leaps forward, up (as, to run or fly), shoves off with the feet, bolts
kâtehkwêhwêwa	strikes s.o. on the head, pushes or knocks s.o.'s head
kâtenêwa, kâtenamwa	pushes s.o., it
kâtenikanani (plural)	dried pumpkin slices
kâtetonêhwêwa	strikes or pushes s.o. on the mouth
kâwesiwa, kâwâwi	(animate, inanimate) is rough
kâwimina	gooseberry
kâwipôhi, kâwipochikani	file
kâwisehkawêwa	intercepts s.o. and gets ahead
kechichêpihkâsenwi	it is uprooted by the wind
kechihkâhkêpiwa	sits with one's chest out
kechihtanwi	it flows out, it flows forth, runs out (as liquid)
kechikêwi	it flows out (**wêchi-kechikâki** what flows out from {somewhere}, where it flows out from)
kechinakeshênêwa	eviscerates s.o., takes s.o.'s intestines out
kechinechênêwa	takes (it) out of s.o.'s hands
kechinehkawêwa	chases s.o. out
kechinehkêwa	pulls one's hand out
kechipahowa	runs out, runs out in to open or into view
kechisahêwa, kechisahtôwa	quickly takes or gets s.o. out; takes it (as, clothing) off quickly
kechisêwa	runs out, runs into view
kechîmikihêwa, kechîmikihtôwa	makes s.o. (non-sentient), it come out
kechîwa	emerges, goes out into the open or into view; (sun) rises
kechîmikatwi	it comes out
kehchawahîma	great one
kehchawahîminâkosiwa	looks like one is great, acts important
kehchi	great, larger (than others) (prenoun); as great, greatly, much, more (than others) (preverb); great, greatly, a great way (preparticle); (with numbers) full, whole, a good
kehchihkwêwiwa	she is a grown woman
kehchikamîwi	sea
kehchikânânâha, kehchikânâha	chickadee
kehchikâpâwa	stands still
kehchikiwa, kehchikenwi	(animate, inanimate) is old
kehchi-kwêhtâni	very greatly, frightfully (particle compound)
kehchi-manetôwa	Great Spirit
kehchi-menwâhi	quite enough, quite soon, rather; (with negative): not too bad, not too much (particle phrase)
kehchine (kehchinêhe dimin.)	close by, near; for the near term (particle)
kehchinechi	thumb
kehchinêwe, kehchinêwi	in person, oneself (particle)
kehchipenowa	runs at top speed
kehchishinwa	lies flat

kehchitâwesiwa	is adult
kehchitâwi	when adult (particle)
kehchitâwinâkosiwa, kehchitâwinâkwatwi	looks like a grown-up, it looks like a grown-up's
kehchitâwitêhêwa	thinks like a grown-up, is grown up in one's thinking
kehchîhkawêwa	sticks to s.o., sticks with s.o.
kehchîhkâsowa	is stubborn, stubbornly remains {somewhere}
kehchîkiyâpi	big house
kehchîpîhi	belt (**kehchîpîheki** at the belt or belt-line)
kehchîpîha	woven belt
kehchîpisôni	belt (prenoun) (**kehchîpisôni-neniwaki** belt men [of the Drum Society])
kehekwiwa	one's prisoner or intended victim gets away (**kehekwipi nîyawi** I escaped)
kehekwîhtawêwa	lets (it) get away from s.o., makes s.o. lose or miss out on (s.o., it)
kehkahamawêwa	points (it) out to s.o., makes (it) known to s.o.
kehkahamâkêwa	gives specific instructions (about how to do something)
kehkahamâtîwaki (plural)	they name, designate (it) for each other
kehkahâtêwi	it is named, designated
kehkahikawêwa	names, designates for s.o.
kehkahikêwa	names, designates
kehkahwêwa, kehkahamwa	names, designates s.o., it
kehkanasitêkâpâwa	there are marks from s.o.'s feet where they stood
kehkatwi	year
kehkâhkwîhi	marker, tally stick
kehkechêshinwa	a mark is left where one lay
kehkeshêwi	charcoal (also **kahkeshêwi**)
kehkênemêwa, kehkênetamwa	knows s.o., it, knows or learns about s.o., it; has carnal knowledge of s.o.; has one's senses, has understanding
kehkênetâkosiwa, kehkênetâkwatwi	(animate, inanimate) is known
kehkênetamawêwa	knows (it) from, of s.o.
kehkênetamâtisowa	knows (it) of oneself
kehkênetamôwênemêwa	thinks s.o. knows (it), thinks s.o. has their senses
kehkênetamôwitêhêwa	thinks one knows (it)
kehkênetamwihêwa	makes s.o. know (it), lets s.o. know (it)
kehkênetisowa	knows about oneself
kehkichikenamwa	wraps one's arms or hands around it to hold on to it (as, a limb)
kehkichikenêpinêwa	ties (it) around s.o.'s forehead
kehkichitepêpinêwa	ties (it) around s.o.'s head
kehkichitepêpisôni	headband
kehkihtawêwa	starts (it) for s.o. (to show how)
kehkihtôwa	starts it (to show how)
kehkikenwi	there is a sign or trace of it
kehkinawâchawiwa	acts recognizably, characteristically
kehkinawâchi	indicatively, distinctively, significantly, as a sign, as an indication, you can tell (particle)
kehkinawâchihtôwa	marks it
kehkinawâpamêwa, kehkinawâpatamwa	watches s.o., it to learn
kehkinawâpihêwa	makes s.o. learn by looking
kehkinawâpiwa	learns by looking
kehkinechêpiwa	there are marks from s.o.'s hands where they sat
kehkinôhamawêwa	teaches s.o., demonstrates (it) to s.o., points (it) out to s.o., shows s.o. how
kehkinôsowa	observes (it) and learns, memorizes (it), is knowledgeable about (it)

kehkinôwenêwa	shows s.o. how, shows s.o. the way
kehkisenwi	there is a mark, a trace, or signs where it was
kehkishinwa	there is a mark, a trace, or signs where one lay
kehkitâhkwêpinêwa	puts a belt on s.o.
kehkitâhkwêpisowa	puts a belt on oneself
kehkitechênêwa	takes hold of s.o. around the body, takes s.o. in one's arms
kehkitehkwênêwa	hugs s.o. around the neck
kehkiwesa	the older or eldest brother (also **machîhkiwesa**)
kehkiwêhôni	flag, battle standard
kehkyêwa	is old, gets old (**kehkyâyane** when you get old)
kehkyêwahkyêsenwi	the earth is in its old age
kehkyêweni	old age
kehkyêweniwiwa	is aged
kehpakesiwa (Jones)	is thick of skin
kehpaketonwa	has thick lips
kehpaki	thickly, solidly (intensifier) (preverb)
kehpakyâwi	it is thick
kehpetawâpitêwa	has a full set of teeth
kehpetawi	whole, complete, in full number (particle)
kehtahkyênêwa	holds s.o. down, in place
kehtanasichi	big toe
kehtâchimowa	tells everything
kehtâpamêwa, kehtâpatamwa	looks fixedly at s.o., it
kehtenamâhkwîwa	holds on tight (for support)
kehtenêwa	holds s.o. fast
kehtesiwa (1)	is big, old, older
kehtesiwa (2) (only possessed):	**kekehtesîmenânaki** our old people, ancestors, elders
kehtesîhiwa	is old (dimin.), is older
kehtênemêwa	has one's mind on s.o., has s.o. on one's mind
kehtikâni	farm, field
kehtwêwesiwa	has a knack at getting game, is an excellent hunter
kekakôtêwi	it is hanging ready (in the kettle)
kekapenôhe	including the children (particle) (also **keki-apenôhe**)
kekapihêwa	makes s.o. sit having (it)
kekapiwa	sits having (it)
kek-ashki	(while still) raw, uncooked (particle)
kekawêwaya, kekawêwayi	a skin with the hair on
kekekêwa	dances having (it)
kekenahowa	paddles fast
kekenekowa	has (it) with oneself in one's activities
kekenesamwa	cooks it fast
kekenesiwa	acts quickly, works quickly, is fast (doing something)
kekeneshihikêwa	hurries one's horse
kekeni	quickly (particle, preverb)
kekeninêwa	dies fast
kekenîhiwa	goes quickly, walks fast
kekenîmikatwi	it goes quickly
kekenyêkiwa, kekenyêkenwi	(animate, inanimate) grows fast
kekesiwa	has (it), possesses (it), has (it) in one
kekeshkawêwa, kekeshkamwa	has s.o., it in one, on one, with one
keki	having, provided with (preverb, prenoun, preparticle, particle)
keki-chîmâne	including the canoe (particle compound)
kekihkwêwe	including the women (particle)
kekikane	bones and all (particle)

kekikepwitîhêpiwa	sits wearing pants
keki-mahkesene	with one's moccasins on (particle compound)
kekimesi	everyone, each one (particle)
kekinâkanêshinwa, kekinâkanêsenwi	there is a bowl of it (animate, inanimate)
kekinechêkâpâwa	stands with (it) in hand
kekinechêwosahêwa	makes s.o. walk with (it) in hand
kekinenwêshinwa, kekinenwêsenwi	(animate, inanimate) has the fat on
keki-nepôpe	along with the broth, broth and all (particle)
keki-nêse	(while still) alive (particle)
keki-oneshiwe	including the testicles (particle)
kekisenwi	it is in (it as) a container
kekisetôwa	puts it in a container, has it in a container
kekishashîpye (Jones: **kekishashîpita**)	reluctantly, without wanting to, dragging one's feet (particle)
	(also **kakishashîpye**)
kekisheyêpa	in the morning (particle)
kekishinwa	lies having (it), is buried with (it)
keki-shîkâwe	(while still) in unreleased widowhood or widower-hood (particle)
kekishôshîhêpiwa	sits with shoes on
keki-tahkye	(while still) cold (particle)
keki-tepehkwe	that same night (particle)
kekîwa	goes having (it)
kekômyêkêwa	dances with (it) on one's back
kekômyêpahowa	runs with (it) on one's back
kekômyêpiwa	sits with (it) on one's back
kekônakapiwa	sits in a canoe
kekôpyêshinwa	lies in the water
kekôshânêpiwa	she sits holding a child
kekyêchinîkwêshkêwa	one's eyes bulge out
kekyêhchi	big, great (plural) (prenoun)
kekyêhkahamawêwa	names, designates (them) to s.o.
kekyêhkimêwa	teaches s.o.
kekyêhkinawâchi	as a repeated sign (particle) (see **kehkinawâchi**)
kekyêhtâhi	hazelnut
kekyêhtenâmehtawêwa	takes what s.o. says seriously
kekyêhtenâmênemêwa, kekyêhtenâmênetamwa	takes s.o. seriously, thinks seriously about it
kekyêhtenâmi	seriously (preverb) (see **kêhtenâmi**)
kekyêhtenâmimêwa	means what one says to s.o.
kekyêhtenâminâkosiwa	has a serious expression on one's face
kekyêhtenâmitêhêwa	is serious-minded
kekyênapinêwa	ties s.o. fast
kekyênenamâhkwîwa	holds on (to it) (for support)
kekyênenêwa, kekyênenamwa	holds s.o., it firmly, holds on to s.o., it
kekyênichîkwanênêwa	holds s.o.'s knees
kekyêninehkênêwa	holds s.o. by the hand
kekyêpâtesiwa	is stupid
kekyêpeshêwa	is deaf
kekyêpîkwêmowa	has one's eyes closed as one sings
kekyêpîkwêsowa	is blinded by the light
kekyêpîkwêwa	is blind
kekyêshkachihêwa	begrudges s.o. unrightfully, holds things back from s.o.
kekyêshkatawênemêwa	resents, begrudges s.o.
kekyêtâmehkisêwaki (plural)	they shoot forth from the ground
kekyêtâshkêwaki (plural)	they are jolted from their places

kekyêteshkinechênêwa	pulls s.o.'s hands away breaking their grip
kemiyânâpowi	rain water
kemiyâneshiwa	gets caught in the rain
kemiyânwihtôwa	makes it rain
kemiyâwi	it rains
kemôtemêwa	steals (it) from s.o.
kemôtwa	steals; steals (it)
=kena	(emphatic; archaic) (usually **=kena=wîna**)
kenahamawêwa	forbids, dissuades s.o.
kenahôchikani, kenahôchikanêyâpi	prisoner-tie (braided strap for securing war captives)
=kena=wîna	very much (archaic)
kenâchi	slowly, carefully (particle)
kenâchihtôwa	is careful with it, goes easy on it
kenekenâsowa	is mixed in
keneki	mixed, mixed in, mixed with (particle, preverb)
kenekisetôwa	mixes it in
kenêpikwamêkwa	eel
kenîkamêwa	nibbles at s.o.
kenîkesiwa	is ticklish
kenîkihpanêshkawêwa	tickles s.o.'s throat
kenoshkêwi	it gets longer
kenôsiwa, kenwâwi	(animate, inanimate) is long, tall (**kênôsita** the tall one)
kenôshêwa	pike (fish)
kenôtawêhtôwa	builds it as a longhouse
kenôtêwi	it is a longhouse
kenwâchimowa	talks long, gives a long talk
kenwânakatwi	it is a deep hole
kenwânowêwa	has a long tail
kenwâpyêyâwi	it is long
kenwêshi (kenwêshîmêhi dimin.)	for a long time (particle)
kenwi	long (prenoun, preverb)
kenwishkwêkanwa	has a long neck
kenwîtemyâwi	it (water) is deep
kepachihikani	stopper, cork (for bottle)
kepachihwêwa, kepachihamwa	plugs s.o. up (as, in a hole or bottle), plugs it
kepanâmoshkawêwa	smothers s.o. by pressing
kepanohwêwa, kepanohamwa	encloses s.o. in a container, closes it (as, a container) with a lid
kepanohikani	lid
kepanonamwa	closes it (as, a container) with one's hand
kepanoshkêwi	its opening closes
kepashkenamwa	blocks it (as, a hole with mud)
kepashkahowa	blocks oneself in
kepatenwi	it freezes over, is frozen over
kepâhkohwêwa, kepâhkohamwa	locks s.o., it up; closes it up securely
kepâhkonamwa	closes it (as, with a lid)
kepâhkoshkamawêwa	blocks (it) for s.o.
kepâhkwikâpâwa	hides behind (it) standing
kepâhkwimêwa	blocks or hems in s.o. by warning or argument
kepâhkwishinwa	hides behind (it) lying
kepânakwêshkawêwa	gets s.o. trapped in a hole, has s.o. trapped in a hole
kepenamwa	blocks it (by hand), puts one's hand against it
kepenikani	dam (**amehkwi-kepenikani** beaver dam)
kepenowa	she covers herself with her hand
kepetonênêwa	covers s.o.'s mouth with one's hand, holds s.o.'s mouth closed

kepetonênowa	covers one's mouth with one's hand
kepetonêpinêwa	ties s.o.'s mouth closed
kepikomêwa	has a stuffed up nose
kepinêwêhpwêwa	chokes s.o. by biting
kepinêwênêwa	chokes s.o. with the hands, strangles s.o.
kepishimêwa	lays s.o. to block
kepishinwa, kepisenwi	(animate, inanimate) lies blocking, is an obstacle
kepishkawêwa, kepishkamwa	blocks s.o.'s way, prevents s.o., blocks it (as, a door)
kepishkwâtawêhôni	door-flap
kepishkwâte	in the doorway (particle)
kepishkwênotwa, kepishkwênatwa	chokes on something (and cannot breathe)
kepiwi	twig, small piece of brushwood (Jones also "osier stem")
kepîhi	little twig
kepîhikani	fence
kepîhikêwa	encloses things, fences
kepîhwêwa	fences s.o. in
keponêwa, keponamwa	closes up a hole in s.o., closes it up (as, with hand or lid)
keposhkawêwa	surrounds, besieges s.o.
keposhkêwi	it closes up, it goes shut
kepôkwâtamwa	sews it shut
kepwikiwa	heals up, one's wound heals
kepwapitôwa	ties it closed
kepwipahôtêwi	it (as, a grass fire) spreads rapidly to surround completely
kepwisahtôwa	quickly closes it up
kepwitîhi	pants, a pair of pants
kesâpiwa	peeks in, peeks out
kesehkêwi	it comes out, comes into view; (eye) bulges out
kesîkwênêwa	washes s.o.'s face
kesîkwêwa	washes one's face (kesîkwâno wash your face)
kesînechêwa	washes one's hands (kesînechâno wash your hands)
kesîyâwi	it is very cold weather (wêchi-kesîyâki north)
keshâchi	gently, kindly (particle, preverb, prenoun)
keshâchi-metemôhiwa	she is a kind old woman
keshâchihêwa	is kind to s.o.
keshâchihetîwaki (plural)	they are kind to each other
keshâchihkwêwiwa	she is a kind woman
keshâchinâkosiwa	looks gentle
keshâchîneniwa	a kind man
keshâchîneniwiwa	he is a kind man
keshâchinohkatawêwa	is kind or friendly to s.o., (animal or bird) is tame towards s.o.
keshâchinotawêwa	is kind or friendly to s.o., (animal or bird) is tame towards s.o.
keshâtesiwa	is kind
keshâtesiweni	kindness
keshâtênemêwa	thinks kindly of s.o.
keshâtênetîwaki (plural)	they think kindly of each other
keshâwêwa	envies s.o., is jealous of s.o. (if not a sexual rival)
keshê-manetôwa	the Gentle Spirit
keshêmowa	pets and speaks soothingly to (s.o., it)
keshihkahwêwa	stabs s.o.
keshihkâpyêhikani	fork (meat-spear)
keshihkihkawêwa	one's tracks are deep, clear
keshihkisenwi	it is stuck in (as, a knife)
keshikîwa	travels rapidly, goes without delay
keshîpenêwa	scratches s.o.

keshîpenowa	scratches (an itch)
keshîpesiwa	itches
keshîpitepênowa	scratches one's head
keshôpyêhtêwi (1)	water is heated, getting warm (**kêshôpyêhtêki** warm water)
keshôpyêhtêwi (2)	warm water
keshôpyêsamwa	warms it (as, water)
keshôpyêyâwi	it (as, a river) has warm water
ketahashkwêwa	digs herbs
ketahôtêwi	it is dragged out, it drags out, flows out solidly
ketahwêwa (1), **ketahamwa**	digs s.o., it up, out
ketahwêwa (2)	digs Indian potatoes (**nîh=ketahwa** I'm going to dig Indian potatoes)
ketakânowêwa	has a striped tail
ketakesiwa, ketakyâwi	(animate, inanimate) is striped, spotted
ketakikanwi	it (stick, arrow, tail) is striped
ketakihkâhkêwa	(bird) has a spotted breast
ketakinêwâkani	choker (neckpiece)
ketasâni	parched corn (ground fine); parched-corn mush
ketatahokowa	emerges carrying (it as) a load on one's back
ketatêwa	otter
ketâkana	one of the large central posts holding up the roof of a traditional Meskwaki house
ketâpihkâtêwi	a marching line emerges into view
ketâsînehkawêwa	chases s.o. up
ketâsîpahowa	runs climbing
ketâsîwa	climbs up (a hill)
ketâsîyôtêwa	crawls up, crawls uphill
ketâshkêwi	it falls out, rushes out, gushes out
kete=kêhi	with consequences that cannot be ignored (particle + enclitic)
ketemahêwa	abuses s.o.
ketemâkesiwa, ketemâkyâwi	(animate, inanimate) is miserable, poor
ketemâkesiweni	misery
ketemâkênemêwa, ketemâkênetamwa	has compassion for s.o., it; thinks s.o., it is wretched
ketemâkênetisowa	feels oneself wretched
ketemâki	wretchedly (preverb)
ketemâkihêwa, ketemâkihtôwa	ill-treats s.o., it, makes s.o., it wretched, brings ruin, ill fate upon s.o., it
ketemâkihkanêwa	leaves s.o. wretched, in misery
ketemâkimêwa	makes s.o. miserable by speech, causes grief by mentioning s.o.
ketemâkinawêhêwa	makes s.o. feel sad
ketemâkinâkêwa	sings wretchedly
ketemâkishehkîhowa	dresses poorly
ketemâkishehkîtamwa	dresses poorly
ketemâkitêhâkani	a feeling of wretchedness
ketemâkitêhêwa	is sad, feels sorry, disappointed, one's feelings or thoughts are miserable; is humble-hearted
ketemâkitêhêwênemêwa	thinks s.o. feels wretched
ketemâkîhtêwa	dresses miserably
keteminamawêwa	blesses (s.o.) for s.o.
keteminawesiwa	is blessed
keteminawesiweni	blessing; religion (in the Drum Society)
keteminawesiweniwiwi	there is blessing
keteminawêwa	pities, blesses s.o.
keteminâhkwêwa	bestows a blessing or blessings
keteminâkêwa	bestows a blessing or blessings

keteminohtawêwa	hears and blesses s.o.
ketenamawêwa	takes (it) out for s.o.
ketenêwa, ketenamwa	takes s.o., it out, off
ketepe	surely, it's a sure thing (particle)
ketesakenêwa	gets s.o. out of it (as, danger)
ketesamawêwa	extracts (it) from s.o. by medicine
ketesowa	comes forth in the heat
keteshkanonêwa	takes (it) out of s.o.'s mouth
keteshkanwisahêwa	yanks s.o. off breaking their bite
keteshkenêwa, keteshkenamwa	releases s.o., it
keteshkesiwa	is helpful, bustles about helpfully
keteshkinechênêwa	takes (it) out of s.o.'s hands
keteshkîhêwa	escapes from s.o.
keteshkîwa	gets free, escapes
keteshkwênotawêwa	sticks one's head out to see s.o., peeks out at s.o.
keteshkwênwa	sticks one's head out (or in)
ketê='nahi	with second thoughts, with changed attitude, with fortunes reversed; too bad! (particle + enclitic)
ketiwa	eagle; golden eagle
ketiwikona	golden eagle tail-feather
ketowa	hoots, quacks, makes the characteristic sound of the species
ketômyênêwa	takes (it) from s.o.'s back
ketôtêwa	crawls out
keyêchîhi, keyêchîhe	recently, a short while ago; soon, soon after (particle) (also **kayêchîhi, kayêchîhe**)
keyêhapa	in fact, as it turns out (particle)
kêchichikwêha	mole
kêhchikamîwisota (participle)	member of the Water Clan (literally, Sea or Ocean)
=kêhi	moreover, to be precise, including, or perhaps (often idiomatic)
kêhkêhkwa	duck hawk, peregrine falcon
kêhkyâha	old person (**nekehkyâmaki** or **nekêhkyâmaki** my elders, my ancestors)
kêhta	old, former (prenoun); formerly, previously, originally (preverb, particle)
kêhtena	truly, sure enough (as stated or predicted); it is true; Go ahead! You should do that! (particle)
kêhtenâmi	seriously (preverb) (see **kekyêhtenâmi**)
kêhtenâhiwi	it is true
kêhtenâhênetamwa	thinks it true
kêhtêkiwa, kêhtêkenwi	(animate, inanimate) is or gets old (as, growing things); it (tree) is dead
kêhtêwi	old (of things) (prenoun) (**kêhtêwi-âchimôni** old stories)
kêkânôhkwêsîhi	long-fringed shawl
kêkânwikashêwa, kêkânwikashêha	grizzly bear (also **kâkânwikashêwa**)
kêkeyâhi, kêkayâhi	finally, eventually, in time, before long (particle)
kêkêwâchi	the last one (or ones) (particle)
kêkineshîha	bull
kêkisaki	right away, immediately, as soon as possible (particle)
kêkôhehtawêwa	(with negative): pays no heed to what s.o. says
kêkôhênemêwa	(with negative): thinks nothing of s.o., thinks s.o. worth nothing
kêkôhênetâkosiwa	(with negative): is considered nothing, is not respected
kêkôhi (1) (**kêkôhêhi** dimin.)	something, anything; (with negative): not anything, nothing, nothing bad, no problem (see **âkwi-kêkôhi**)
kêkôhi (2)	thing (**okêkôhemi** one's things; **châki-kêkôhi** everything)
kêkôhi-'shi	in some or any way; (with negative): not at all, not under any circumstances

kêkôhiwa, kêkôhenwi:	(with negative): (animate, inanimate) is nothing, nothing serious, not helpful, not important; **kêkôhenokwêni** some unidentified thing (obviative **kêkôhenikwêni**), **kêkôhenôtoke** there seems to be something, something or other (obviative **kêkôhenîtoke**)
kêkyâta	nearly (particle)
kêkyêpêha	mentally retarded person
kênakîha	snow goose or blue goose (**wâpi-kênakîha** snow goose)
kênemâpi, kehkênemâpi	I don't know (particle)
kênemâpi='h=wêna	I wonder whether, it might be that (particle + enclitics)
kênôtêhi	longhouse
kênwâpihkâtêhi	freight train
kênwâsowêwa	mountain lion
kênwâsowêwikihônowa	transforms oneself into a mountain lion
kênwâsowêwîhkâsowa	pretends to be a mountain lion
kêpyâhi	thimble
kêsehkawêwa	catches s.o. in the act, catches s.o. still doing something
kêsehkwi	just in time (to not be caught doing something)
kêsenwi	how many times? (particle)
kêsipi	only (myself, him, her, them) (particle)
kêsokoneshkamwa	how many days does he or she go?
kêsokonêtwa	how many days is he or she away?
kêsokoni	how many days? (particle)
kêsôchênawêwa	how many of s.o. does he or she hit with a shot?
kêswi	how many? (particle)
kêshawahamwa	loosens it by tool
kêshawahokowa	is made loose by weight or mass
kêshawenamwa	holds it loosely, loosens it
kêtakenêha	fawn
kêtakishehkîtâha	clown
kêtemâha	poor person
kêwaki	as yet; still; yet a while; wait a bit (particle)
kêwapenêwa	one's hunger begins to slack off
kêwapisowa	one's bonds are loosened a bit
kêwâshkêwa, kêwâshkêwi	(animate, inanimate) starts to slow down, slacks off
kêyêhchine	pretty soon, shortly, in a short time (particle)
kî	about, in places (preverb) (see **kîwi**)
kîh	have done, have completed or finished (preverb) (see **kîshi**)
kîhka	all around (particle)
kîhkapiwa	sits closer
kîhkâmêwa	calls s.o. out, berates s.o.
kîhkâpahônekwiwa	circles around on horseback at a gallop
kîhkâwosêwa	circles around, walks in a circle or on a circular route
kîhkenêwa, kîhkenamwa	moves s.o., it (on), extends it (as, a life, a house)
kîhkeshkêwa, kîhkeshkêwi	moves further involuntarily, it extends further, is lengthened
kîhki	further (preverb) (**kîhki-mehtosêneniwêhiwa** lives a little longer)
kîhkihêwa	prolongs s.o.'s life
kîhkikawêwa	sets up a new dwelling at some remove for s.o.
kîhkikêwa	sets up a new dwelling at some remove
kîhkiwenêwa	leads s.o. further, moves s.o. on
kîhkiwetawêwa	leads (it) further for s.o.
kîhkîchi	tenderly, solicitously, indulgently; sensitive, requiring solicitude (preverb)
kîhkîchinawêwa	is hurting ({somewhere})
kîhkîhkesiwa	is contrary

kîhkîhki	in defiance, insisting, all the same, undeterred (particle)
kîhkîhkihêwa	forces s.o. against their will
kîhkîhkikenwi	it grows on and on
kîhkîhkimêwa	bids or persuades s.o. against their will
kîhkîhkinawêhêwa	vexes s.o. by acting contrary to their wishes
kîhkîhkinawêhtôwa	vexes it by acting contrary to its wishes
kîhkîhkinotawêwa, kîhkîhkinotamwa	acts in spite of s.o., it, defies s.o., it, keeps on despite s.o., it
kîhkîhkitîwaki (plural)	they argue with each other, quarrel
kîhkîhkiwenêwa (1)	moves s.o. on again and again
kîhkîhkiwenêwa (2)	takes s.o. against their will
kîhkîhkowêwa	insists, persists in asking or claiming, expresses doubts
kîhkîtesiwa	something is hurting one, is sore, aches
kîhkîtwêha	crybaby
kîhkîtwêwa	is a cry-baby
kîhkîwa	moves further on or away, lives longer
kîhpene	in the event that, (if) ever, once (that happens), as soon as (particle)
kîhpochanêwa, kîhpochatôwa	fills s.o.'s stomach, satisfies s.o.'s, its hunger
kîhpochânêwa, kîhpochâtamwa	fills up on s.o., it, gets full on s.o., it
kîhpochêwa	one's stomach is full
kîhpochêshkawêwa	(what is eaten) satisfies s.o.
kîkesiwa	has a strong constitution, endurance, stamina
kîkesîmikatwi	it is strong
kîkênâwa	captive, prisoner of war
kîkênâwiwa	is a captive
kîkênemêwa	thinks s.o. is better, recovered
kîkênowa	gives, has a clan feast (Michelson: "gens-festival"); gives a clan feast with (it) as food
kîkênoweni	the clan feast (generic), the celebration of the clan feast, food offered in the clan feast
kîkênowapiwa	sits at the clan feast
kîkênowi	of a clan feast (prenoun), in a clan feast (preverb)
kîkênôhiwa	gives, has a clan feast (dimin.); gives a small clan feast
kîkênôni	clan feast, food offered in the clan feast
kîkênwihêwa	holds a clan feast over s.o.
kîkihêwa	makes s.o. feel better
kîkikanêsamwa	makes it strong by heat (e.g. by medicine)
kîkikanêwa	regains one's strength
kîkinawêmêwa	makes s.o. feel better by what one says
kîmâhêwa, kîmâhtôwa	sees, approaches s.o., it unobserved
kîmâshkawêwa	steals up on s.o.
kîmenêwa	feels s.o. intimately
kîminîchêwa	she is having, has an illegitimate baby (**kîminîchête** if she has an illegitimate baby)
kîmisenyêwa	eats secretly
kîmîhkâtîwa	has illicit sex, cheats on one's spouse
kîmîwa	sneaks away
kîmôchâwi	it is secret
kîmôchi	stealthily, secretly (particle, preverb)
kîmôchikenwi	it is sneaky, underhanded
kîmôchîhtawêwa	puts something over on s.o., acts stealthily undetected by s.o.
kîmôsehtawêwa	hears s.o. say things they do not know are being heard
kîmôtanohkyêwa	does things in secret
kîmôtâyêniwa	laughs secretly
kîmôtesiwa	is stealthy, secretive

61

kîmôtosêwa	walks stealthily
kîna	you (singular) (emphatic or contrastive); (by) yourself
=kîna	there you go; (you) see!
kînâkwi	freely, confidently, without worry (particle)
kînâna	we (inclusive, including "you") (emphatic or contrastive); (by) ourselves
kînesiwa, kînyâwi	(animate, inanimate) is sharp
kînihêwa, kînihtôwa	sharpens s.o., it
kînwâwa	you (plural) (emphatic or contrastive); (by) yourselves
kîpehkwêsêwa	one's head nods down
kîpenamwa	pushes it down
kîpeshkamwa	tips it over by foot
kîpisêwa	falls over
kî-pyêmashkatwi	the grass is pushed down in places
kîsâchi	in a bind, having second thoughts, as a difficult task or obligation, as a firm commitment; nothing can be done about it (particle, preverb)
kîsâchihêwa	puts s.o. in a terrible fix
kîsâchimêwa	imposes a bothersome obligation on s.o. by speech
kîsâchisahtôwa	rams it in and gets it stuck, wedged in
kîsâtenêwa	holds s.o. in an inescapable hold
kîsâtesiwa, kîsâchâwi	has a difficult time overcoming or getting over something; it is hard to overcome or get over
kîsâtesowa	is badly wounded by gunshot
kîsâtênemêwa, kîsâtênetamwa	feels reluctantly obliged about s.o., it, feels in a bind or of two minds about s.o., it, feels worried and helpless about s.o., it
kîsâtênemowa	considers the requirement burdensome, has second thoughts
kîsâtosêwa	has the bother of walking
kîshahamwa	has cut it (e.g. wood)
kîshanohikêwa	owes money
kîshapinêwa, kîshapitôwa	finishes tying s.o., it
kîshatahwêwa	finishes s.o. off with a club
kîshâchimowa	finishes one's story
kîshâhkasowa, kîshâhkatêwi	(animate, inanimate) has dried out
kîshâhkonamawêwa	has laid down the rule for (it) for s.o.
kîshâkochi	extremely, as much as possible, more than ever (particle, preverb)
kîshâkochihtôwa	does terrible things to it
kîshâkochikanêhiwa	is extremely emaciated (dimin.)
kîshâkochikanêwa	is extremely emaciated
kîshâkochikâmowa	is extremely fat
kîshâkochinawêhêwa	makes s.o. feel terrible
kîshâkochinâkosiwa	looks splendid
kîshâkochishinwa	has a bad fall, lands hard
kîshâkochitêhâkani	great grief
kîshâkochitêhêwa	feels bad, feels terrible
kîshâkotamatamwa	feels terrible pain
kîshâkotapenêwa	is terribly hungry
kîshâkotapisowa, kîshâkotapitêwi	(animate, inanimate) is very tightly bound
kîshâkotâpatâniwa	looks splendid; runs extremely fast
kîshâkotekwâmwa	sleeps soundly
kîshâkotesiwa	is in a terrible state (of grief, fear), is excited, is desperate; it is hard on one
kîshâkotênemêwa	feels bad about s.o.
kîshâkotwêwêkesiwa	wails terribly, screams as loudly as possible

kîshâkotwêwêyâkêposowa	goes whizzing through the air with tremendous noise
kîshâkwanêwa, kîshâkwatôwa	finishes setting s.o., it out, finishes laying s.o., it in place
kîshâkwapiwa	has already sat as a group
kîshânehkêwa	finishes digging
kîshâpôhkêwa	finishes boiling (it, liquid)
kîshâpôsamwa	finishes boiling it, has boiled it
kîshâpyêsetawêwa	has it strung out for s.o.
-kîshekatwi	it is a day (of such weather) (in compound verbs):
	menwi-kîshekatwi it is a nice day
	ishi-kîshekatwi it is a day of {such} weather
kîshekwi	sky, day
kîshekwi-wâpatâha	least bittern
kîshenêwa, kîshenamwa	already holds s.o., it
kîshenâtêwi	it is already in hand (**shêshki kîshenâtêwi** it is partly finished)
kîshenikawêwa	finishes fixing the place for s.o. to sleep, has made s.o.'s bed
kîshepyêhwêwa, kîshepyêhamwa	finishes drawing s.o., it
kîshesamawêwa	cooks (it) done for s.o.
kîsheswêwa, kîshesamwa	cooks s.o., it done
kîshesêhkwêwa	finishes cooking
kîshesikêwa	finishes cooking things
kîshesowa, kîshetêwi	(animate, inanimate) is cooked done
kîshesowiwi	it is sunny, the sun is up; it gets the sun
kîsheswa	sun; moon, month
kîsheswiwa	is the sun
kîsheshkawêwa, kîsheshkamwa	has acted bodily on s.o., it; has put it on
kîshetêwi	cooked food (**nekîshetêmenâni** our (offering of) cooked food)
kîshetonêmowa	finishes speaking
kîshênemêwa	has formed a plan about s.o., has made up one's mind about s.o.
kîshêwîwa	finishes
kîshi	have done, have completed or finished, do and be done (preverb) (also **kîh**)
kîshihâsowa, kîshihtâtêwi	(animate, inanimate) is made, already made, finished
kîshihêwa, kîshihtôwa	finishes making, completes s.o., it; institutes it
kîshihowa	makes oneself (be some way or do something)
kîshihtawêwa	finishes making, completes (it) for s.o.
kîshikawêwa	finishes building a house for s.o.
kîshikâmowa	fattens up; becomes (politically) powerful
kîshikâmônêwa	fattens s.o. up
kîshikâpawihêwa	has made s.o. stand
kîshikâpâwa	has taken one's position standing
kîshikenamâtisowa	raises (s.o., it, as a crop) for oneself
kîshikenêwa	brings s.o. up, raises s.o. (as, a child or animal)
kîshikêwa	finishes building a house
kîshikihtôwa	raises it (as, a crop)
kîshikiwa (kîshikîhiwa dimin.), kîshikenwi	is grown, is grown up, has matured; it is grown
kîshikiwênemêwa	thinks s.o. grown up
kîshi-kîkênowênemêwa	thinks s.o. done with the clan-feast
kîshikwâtêwi	it (as, a blanket) has ribbonwork sewn on it
kîshimêwa	settles on a plan for s.o., promises s.o.
kîshinâkanwi	it has been put into dishes, it is already in dishes
kîshinâkêwa	finishes singing
kîshinotamwa	obtains it, procures it by effort
kîshipyêyâwi	it has leafed out
kîshisenyêhêwa	has made s.o. eat

kîshisetawêwa	lays (it) away for s.o.
kîshisetânawêwa	has everything prepared, has it all set (as, for a ceremony)
kîshishimêwa	has laid s.o. away, out, in place; buries s.o.
kîshishinwa, kîshisenwi	has lain down; it is finished, decided, set, ready, already there
kîshitêhêwa	has formed a plan, has made up one's mind
kîshitîwaki (plural)	they settle on a plan
kîshîchawiwêwa	has been married to s.o. (also **kîshi-wîchawiwêwa**)
kîshîhkawêwa, kîshîhkamwa	finishes with, succeeds with, completes preparing s.o., it
kîshîhkâtêwi	it is finished with
kîshîhkâtisowa	finishes doing the task for oneself
kîshîhtêhêwa	finishes dressing s.o.
kîshîseniwa	has eaten (also **kîshi-wîseniwa**)
kîshkahamwa	cuts or chops it (off), gets it by cutting or chopping
kîshkahtêyâwi, kîshkahtêkenwi	it (coat) narrows at the waist
kîshkapehkotêyâwi	it is dark (in a place)
kîshkapehkotêwi	it is dark
kîshkatahikêwa	whips one's horse
kîshkatahwêwa	whips s.o.
kîshkatamwa	bites it off
kîshkatâtêwi	it is gnawed through
kîshkâhkiwiwi	it is a steep hill or mountain
kîshkâkwatêwi:	**pemi-kîshkâkwatêwani** they (inanimate) lie in a row
kîshkânowêshwêwa	cuts off s.o.'s tail
kîshkâpachîkwêwi (preverb):	**kîshkâpachîkwêwi-mahkatêwesiwa** has black stripes on one's face
kîshkâpehkatenwi (1), **kîshkâpehkatwi** (1)	it is a steep cliff
kîshkâpehkatenwi (2), **kîshkâpehkatwi** (2)	a steep cliff
kîshkenamwa	tears it
kîshkeshâtêwi	it is cut off
kîshkeshêshwêwa	cuts off s.o.'s ear
kîshkeshêwa (Jones)	has no ears (see **kîshkîshkeshêwa**)
kîshkeshwêwa, kîshkeshamwa	cuts s.o., it off
kîshki	steep (preverb) (**kîshki-penekwâhkiwiwi** it is a steep overhanging cliff)
kîshkikomêhpwêwa	bites off s.o.'s nose
kîshkikomêshwêwa	cuts off s.o.'s nose
kîshkikwêhokowa	has one's head cut off (in an accident)
kîshkikwêhwêwa	chops off s.o.'s head
kîshkikwêpinêwa	hangs s.o. (by the neck, as punishment)
kîshkikwêpisowa	is hanged (as punishment)
kîshkikwêshkêwa	one's head falls off
kîshkikwêshwêwa	cuts off s.o.'s head
kîshkinehkêshwêwa	cuts off s.o.'s hand
kîshkiponêwa, kîshkipotôwa	he saws s.o. (board), it off
kîshkitepêhikani	stump, tree-stump
kîshkitiyêshwêwa	cuts off s.o.'s tail
kîshkitiyêwa	one's tail is cut off
-kîshkîshkâpehkatenwe	cliffs (in particle compounds) (**nâwi-kîshkîshkâpehkatenwe** among the cliffs)
kîshkîshkâpehkatenwi	there are steep cliffs
kîshkîshkâpehkatenôni (plural)	steep cliffs
kîshkîshkeshêshwêwa	cuts off both s.o.'s ears
kîshkîshkeshêwa	has both ears cut off
kîshkîshkeshkêwi	it gets torn to shreds
kîshkîshkinehkêshwêwa	cuts off both s.o.'s hands

Meskwaki–English

kîshkîshkinekwêyâhi	sleeveless jacket, vest
kîshkôha	Kishko, member of the Kishko division
kîshkôhihkwêwa	Kishko woman
kîshkôhiwa	is a Kishko
kîshkôhkwêha	Kishko (archaic)
kîshkôhkwêhiwa	is a Kishko (archaic)
kîshkônwêshwêwa	cuts off s.o.'s penis
kîshkyâwi	there is a cliff
kîshowâhkwa	sycamore
kîshowâhkowiwa	is a sycamore
kîshowânêwa	declares a decision, plan, or promise for s.o.
kîshoweshkawêwa	keeps s.o. warm
kîshowêwa	declares a decision, plan, or promise
kîshowihowa	puts on or wears warm clothing
kîshowishinwa, kîshowisenwi	(animate, inanimate) lies warm
kîshowîhtêwa	dresses warmly (**kîshowîhtâno** dress warmly!)
kîwahokowa	floats about in a boat; (fish, bird) swims about
kîwahowa	paddles about
kîwakamôha	member of the Singing-Around Rite
kîwakamôhiwa	is a member of the Singing-Around Rite, performs the Singing-Around Rite
kîwakamôhiweni	the Singing-Around Rite
kîwapenêwa	goes about hungry
kîwashkwêpyêwa	is drunk
kîwatokêmowa	goes about inviting
kîwatomêwa	goes about inviting s.o.
kîwawiwêwa, kîwawiwa	has s.o., it with one, keeps s.o., it
-kîwâchâwe	lonely area (in a particle compound) (**nâwi-kîwâchâwe** in the middle of nowhere)
kîwâchâwi (kîwâchâhiwi dimin.)	it is lonely, sad (see **kîwâtesiwa**)
kîwâchihêwa	makes s.o. lonely
kîwâchimowa	goes around telling, reporting
kîwâchinawêhêwa	makes s.o. feel lonesome
kîwâchinawêmêwa	makes s.o. feel lonely or sad by what one says
kîwâchinâkosiwa	looks lonely
kîwâchitêhêwa	feels lonely
kîwâkwasowa, kîwâkwatêwi	lies about (dead), it lies about (destroyed)
kîwâkwatôwa	leaves it lying about (abandoned)
kîwâmohêwa	makes s.o. flee about
kîwâmowa	flees about
kîwânîsêwa	loses one's way
kîwânîwa	is lost (not knowing where one is), makes a mistake (as, in conducting a ceremony)
kîwânîwenêwa	leads s.o. astray
kîwânîwi	mistakenly, foolishly (preverb)
kîwâpamêwa, kîwâpatamwa	goes about seeing s.o., it
kîwâpyêhi	crawling vine (Huron Smith: climbing bittersweet)
kîwâshkêwa	flies about, rushes about
kîwâtesiwa (kîwâtesîhiwa dimin.)	is lonely, is lonesome (see **kîwâchâwi**)
kîwekêwa	dances around
kîwesiwa (dim. kîwesîhiwa)	is an orphan
kîweshawêwa	goes about lighting (song word)
kîweshkawêwa, kîweshkamwa	wears s.o. (clothing), it around, has s.o. (clothing), it on (archaic)
kîweshkêwa	travels, goes on a journey

kîweshkêwîhi	passenger train
kîwêpahowa	runs back
kîwêtamwa	goes about wailing (song word)
kîwêwa	turns back
kîwêwenêwa	leads s.o. back, pulls s.o. back
kîwi	around, about, in places, for a while (preverb)
kîwikâpâwa	stands around
kîwikîwikahêwa	repeatedly provides dwellings for them in different places (song word)
kîwikwânêwa, kîwikwâtamwa	bores around in s.o., it
kîwinehkâtîwaki (plural)	they chase each other about
kîwinêwa	is in one's death-throes, thrashes about as one dies
kîwipahowa	runs about
kîwisêwa	flies about
kîwishinwa	lies about (song word)
kîwitêmikatwi	it stays around
kîwitênotamwa	stays on it, has it (territory) as home
kîwitêwa	stays, stays around ({somewhere}) (**nekîwita** I —)
kîwiwenêwa	leads s.o. about
kîwîhkawêwa	goes about dealing with s.o., tags around after s.o.
kîwîtêmêwa	goes about with s.o. (also **kîwi-wîtêmêwa**)
kîyamowêwa, kîyamoshtîha	cannibal giant (in stories)
kîyosênotamwa	walks about on it
kîyosêwa	walks about
kîyômêwa, kîyôtamwa	carries s.o., it about on one's back
kîyômekowa	rides about on horseback
kîyôtêneniwa	snake
kîyôtêwa	crawls about
kochawiwa	tries
kochi (1)	try to, try and (preverb)
=kochi (2)	you know, as you know, of course, don't you remember, all I can say is
kochihêwa, kochihtôwa	tries to make, tries, tests s.o., it
kochikêhkwi	for of course, but of course
kochikwamwa	tries to sew it
kochimâchîwa	tries to see how fast one can run
kochimêwa	asks s.o., makes a request of s.o.
kochipanîwa	tries to weave
kochisahowa	tries to jump; ventures to ask (to court or marry)
kochiyâmêwa, kochiyâtamwa	sniffs at s.o., it, tries the smell of s.o., it
kochiyâtahêwa	makes s.o. try the smell of (it)
kochîhi	although, granted, concededly (particle)
kochîhkawêwa	tries to consort with s.o., tries to persuade s.o., tries to help s.o.
=kohi	certainly, definitely
kohkahamwa (1)	turns it over by tool
kohkahamwa (2)	crosses it (as, a bridge)
kohkahikanehkawêwa	makes a bridge for s.o.
kohkahikani	bridge
kohkahikêwa	turns something over by tool
kohkapiwa	turns around in one's seat
kohkâpatâniwa, kohkâpatâniwi	s.o.'s, its appearance changes
kohkenamwa	turns it over, switches or changes it; exchanges them
kohkeshkêwa, kohkeshkêwi	changes, changes places, turns around; it changes, turns around
kohkikâpâwa	turns around standing
kohkikihônowa	transforms oneself
kohkikiwa	is transformed, changes one's bodily form

kohkinawîwa	turns around
kohkinâkosiwa, kohkinâkwatwi	(animate, inanimate) changes in appearance
kohkinâkwihowa	transforms oneself
kohkinâkwihtôwa	changes how it looks
kohkisêwa	quickly reverses direction
kohkishimêwa, kohkisetôwa	changes s.o.'s, its position
kohkishinwa	rolls over, turns over or changes position as one lies
kohkitêhêwa	changes one's mind
kohkîhtêwa	changes one's clothes (**nekohkîhta** I —)
kohkîwa	turns around
kohkoseni	granite rock (plural **kohkosenyêni**)
kohkoseniwiwa	is a granite rock
kohpichi	on the prairie (particle); of the prairie (prenoun)
kohpichi-nenoswa	buffalo
kohpichîha	buffalo
kohtamwa	(see **kosêwa**)
kohtâchiwa	is afraid
kohtâmekosiwa, kohtâmekwatwi	(animate, inanimate) is the object of fear (archaic)
kokonamwa	handles it with a quick motion, jerks it
kokowêha	whippoorwill
kokowêhi-mahkesêhi	pink lady's-slipper, moccasin-flower
kokowêwa	lets out a sudden, loud scream
kokwâshkêwa, kokwâshkêwi	is suddenly jerked, tossed; it is suddenly jerked, swung
kokwêchimêwa	asks s.o.
kokwêchikwâsikawêwa	tries to sew for s.o.
kokwêchikwâsowa	tries to sew
kokwêchi	try to, practice (preverb)
kokwêchisêwa	tries to fly
kokwêhkâmehkwisetôwa	keeps changing it as earth
kokwêhkânehkwêsetôwa	keeps changing its (earth's) hair
kokwêhkâpiweni	change of seasons
kokwêhkâpatamwa	sees it keep changing
kokwêhkâpatânihtôwa	keeps changing its appearance
kokwêhkâpatâniwi	its appearance repeatedly changes (see **kohkâpatâniwi**)
kokwêhkinâkwatwi	it keeps changing in appearance (see **kohkinâkwatwi**)
kokwêhkinâkwihtôwa	makes it keep changing in appearance
kokwêhkishinwa	keeps turning over as one lies (see **kohkishinwa**)
kokwêhtâni	(with negative): not terribly, not frightfully (particle, preverb) (see **kwêhtâni**)
kokwênakoshêwa	has pierced ears
kokwênepâpamêwa	looks at s.o. all around
kokwênepechêhamwa	turns it around and around or over and over with something
kokwênepitepêsahêwa	wags s.o.'s head from side to side
kokwêtahtêwa	practices shooting with a bow
kokwêtawîwaki	(see **kotawîwa**)
kokwêtâshohwêwa	practices shooting with a bow or gun
kokwêtenêwa, kokwêtenamwa	tries to feel s.o., it
kokwêtowêwa	tries to decide on a plan; practices speaking
kokwi	suddenly, abruptly (preverb)
kokwimêwa	speaks sharply to s.o.
kokwisahtôwa	gives it a sharp jerk
komêwa, kotamwa	swallows s.o., it
konakwi	getting through the danger or difficulty (preverb)
konakwiwenêwa	leads s.o. through danger

konakwîwa	passes through, gets through danger
konashkosiwa, konashkwâwi	(animate, inanimate) has a dent or groove
konepâshkêwi	it wheels around
konepâchi	wicked, naughty (preverb)
konepechênamwa	rolls it over
konwâshkêha	frog
kosâkaniwiwa	is feared
kosâpyêshkawêwa	sinks s.o. by one's weight
kosâpyêwi	it sinks
kosehkyêwa	fears people, gets frightened
kosekwanwa, kosekwanwi	(animate, inanimate) is heavy
kosekwênetamwa	thinks it heavy
kosetawêwa, kosetamwa	avoids s.o., it out of reserve or respect, respects or defers to s.o., shies away from s.o.
kosetâkaniwiwa	is treated with reserve or respect
kosetâtîwaki (plural)	they avoid each other out of reserve or respect
kosêwa, kohtamwa	fears s.o., it, stays away from s.o.
kosikanaki (plural)	dice (of the bowl-and-dice game)
kosikêwa	plays bowl-and-dice
koshimâchikâwosêwa	steps gingerly
koshimâchishinwa	lies motionless
koshimâtapiwa	sits gingerly
koshkoshkwâtotamwa	reports it to be potentially dangerous
koshkoshkwâwi	it is risky, potentially dangerous
koshkwâtatawâpiwa	looks around eagerly, impatiently
kotaka, kotaki	other, another (animate, inanimate)
kotakapenêhêwa	makes s.o. suffer with hunger
kotakapenêhtôwa:	**kotakapenêhtôwa owîyawi** makes oneself suffer with hunger
kotakesowa	suffers from heat
kotakêhiwa	is some one else, is another person
kotakênemêwa, kotakênetamwa	knows s.o. to suffer; suffers
kotakênetamwihêwa	causes s.o. to suffer, is the cause of s.o.'s suffering
kotakihêwa, kotakihtôwa	makes s.o., it suffer; suffers, has a hard time
kotamêwa, kotatamwa	tastes s.o., it, tries the taste of s.o., it
kotapiwa	tries to sit
kotawâmehkîwa	sinks into the ground
kotawepyêhwêwa	pushes s.o. under the water with something
kotawiwenêwa	drags s.o. under the water
kotawîwa	goes under the water (plural **kokwêtawîwaki**)
kotawîhtawêwa	dives in after s.o.
kotâhkohikêwa	practices shooting
kotenamawêwa	feels of (it) for or of s.o.
kotenêwa, kotenamwa	feels of s.o., it
kotowêwa	tries to make a sound; asks permission
kotwâshikânameki	sixth, the sixth time (also **nekotwâshikânameki**)
kotwâshika	six (also **nekotwâshika**)
kotwâshikanesiwe, kotwâshikanîsiwe	sixteen
kotwâshika tashiwaki, kotwâshika tasenôni (plurals)	they (animate, inanimate) are six, there are six of them
kotwâshikenwi	six times
kotwêwêhamwa	tries its sound by hitting
kôhkâhanwi	it tipped over (in the water), was overset
kôhkâsahêwa	tips s.o. over
kôhkâwêwa	tips over in canoe

kôhkôhkâyâwi	it rocks
kôhkôhkohôwâ, kôhkôhkohôwâ!	(hoot of an owl)
kôhkôsha (**kôhkôshêha** dimin.)	pig, hog; pork
kôhkôtenîha	alligator
kôkawisahtôwa	rinses it
kôkâhkonowa	washes oneself all over
kôkechênêwa	washes s.o.'s belly
kôkenamawêwa	washes (it) for s.o.
kôkenêwa, kôkenamwa	washes s.o., it, cleans s.o., it
kôkenikêwa	washes, does washing
kôketonênêwa	washes s.o.'s mouth
kôkikenênowa	washes one's forehead
kôkinameshkênowa	washes one's skin
kôkinechêwa	washes one's hands (**êh=kôkinechâwâchi** they washed their hands)
kôkinechênêwa	washes s.o.'s hands
kôkinekwênêwa	washes s.o.'s armpits
kôkitepênowa	washes one's head
kôkîwa	mires, wallows
kônachîhi	kinnikinnick, inner bark of "red willow" (red-osier dogwood) used for smoking
kônachîhiyâhtêwi	there is the smell of kinnikinnick being smoked
kônanôhaki (plural)	double ball used in shinny
kônanôhiwa	plays the double-ball game, plays shinny
kôti	coat
kwahkwîtenêwa	lifts s.o. to their feet, helps s.o. up
kwakwinôha	chipmunk
kwananachîha	tree frog
kwananâhaki (plural)	tubular beads
kwayahkowêwa	promises, declares a decision
kwayahkwênetamwa	thinks it proper, prudent
kwayahkwi	taking the prudent course, deciding to go ahead (and be done with it), making the best of it, might as well; one had better (particle)
kwayahkwimêwa	promises s.o., tells s.o. it is definite, decides about s.o.
kwayânanohkyêwa	commits murder
kwayânâhkêwa	throws (it) too far
kwayânâshkêwa	keeps running (or metaphorically, reaching) beyond where one knows where one is
kwayâshi	already, already and it is too late, irreversibly (particle, preverb)
kwayêshi	that way, if that is done (particle)
kwâhkwâtêha	grasshopper
kwâhkwâpâhkêwa	throws (it, them) in different directions
kwâhkwâpiwiwa, kwâhkwâpiwiwi	(animate, inanimate) is decorated with porcupine-quills
kwâkohômêwa, kwâkohôtamwa	shouts to s.o., shouts
kwâpahamawêwa	dips (it) up for s.o.
kwâpahamwa	dips it up, out
kwâpahikani	dipper, ladle
kwâpâkwasowa	lies scattered
kwâpâshkêwa, kwâpâshkêwi	(animate, inanimate) flies or falls scattering
kwâpenêwa, kwâpenamwa	scatters s.o. (as, tobacco), it
kwâpinehkâtîwaki (plural)	they chase each other making them scatter
kwâpisêwaki (plural)	they fly in all directions
kwâpôhikani, akwâpôhikani	net, seine, screen for washing hominy
kwâshkopyêhamwa	splashes it, makes it splash
kwâshkopyêkîwa	(fish) makes a splash in the water

kwâshkwachikêwa	drops food from one's mouth
kwâshkwamêwa, kwâshkwatamwa	drops s.o., it in eating
kwâshkwatamâkêwa	drops (it) of others in eating
kwâshkwinâsowa, kwâshkwinâtêwi	(animate, inanimate) boils
kwâshkwisahowa	jumps off, dismounts, disembarks
kwêhchipa	repeatedly (particle)
kwêhkwêwi	going too far (particle, preverb)
kwêhkwêwîwa	goes past, passes by, goes too far
kwêhtânamachihêwa	hurts s.o. severely
kwêhtânamachihtôwa	is hurt severely
kwêhtânamêwa	bites s.o. severely
kwêhtâni	very, frightfully, so very much; it is terrible (that) (particle, preverb)
kwêhtânihêwa	gives s.o. a terrible beating, inflicts a terrible death on s.o.
kwêhtânimêwa	hits s.o. hard by what one says
kwêhtânisahowa	jumps or flinches noticeably (being startled or jolted)
kwêshêha	girl (as a pet name)
'kwi	(see âkwi)
kwichi (Jones)	ten ("in counting hurriedly")
kwîchi	at just the wrong time (preverb); just had to be (ironic) (particle)
kwîkocha	white grub; woodcock (plural kwîkochyêki) (also wîkocha)
kwînatawesiwa	is at a loss
kwînatawi	at a loss, destitute (preverb)
kwînatonêhwêwa, kwînatonêhamwa	fails to find s.o., it
kwînomêwa, kwînotamwa	longs for s.o., it
kwîtike	confound it! I'll get even! (particle)
kwîyena	exactly, just happen to; right (particle)
kwîyenâhiwa	acts right
kwîyesêha	boy
kwîyesêhêha	small boy
kwîyesêhiwa	is a boy
kyâchikenwi	it is concealed (êh=kyâchikeki in a concealed place)
kyâkomêwa	she is jealous of her (a sexual rival) (archaic)
kyâkotîwaki (plural)	they (two women) are jealous of each other (archaic)
kyâkowitêhêwa	she feels jealous (archaic)
kyâkwiwa	she is jealous (archaic)
kyâsowa	keeps (it) a secret
kyâtamawêwa	keeps (it) a secret from s.o.
kyâtamâtîwaki (plural)	they keep (it) a secret from each other
kyâtamwa	keeps it a secret
kyâwamêwa	is jealous of s.o. (a sexual rival)
kyâwatîwaki (plural)	they are jealous of each other (in older usage, only of two men)
kyâwêwa	is jealous (in older usage, only of a man)

m

machawahîna, machawahîma	rascal, good-for-nothing
machâhîni	drygoods
machi	bad (prenoun, preverb)
machi-manetôha	evil spirit; Devil
machinawêwa, machinamwa	dares with regard to s.o., it, challenges s.o.
machinâhkwêwa	challenges (mêchinâhkwâta the challenger)
machinâkêwa	challenges (mêchinâkâta the challenger)

machinâkosiwa	is ugly, is not good-looking
machitêhêwa	feels bad, has bad thoughts
machîhkiwesa	the older or eldest brother (also **kehkiwesa**)
machowiyêhiwa	is ill-tempered, cross, mean
mahkahkôhi	little box; pail
-mahkahkwe	thousand (in particle compounds) (**neswi-mahkahkwe** three thousand)
mahkahkwi	box, trunk
mahkatamwa	bites it off
mahkatêmina	highbush blackberry
mahkatêwâhkonêwa	paints s.o. black
mahkatêwâhkonowa	paints oneself black, has one's body painted black
mahkatêwânahkwatwi	there are dark clouds
mahkatêwânehkwêwa	has black hair
mahkatêwâpatâniwi	it looks black
mahkatêwâpehkatwi	it is black stone
mahkatêwesiwa, mahkatêwâwi	(animate, inanimate) is black
mahkatêwi	gunpowder
mahkatêwikanwi	it is black (as, a tree or stick)
mahkatêwinîkwênêwa	blackens s.o. across the eyes
mahkatêwishehkîtamwa	wears black clothing
mahkatêwitepêwa	has black hair
mahkatêwînêwa	makes s.o. fast, paints s.o.'s face black to fast
mahkatêwîwa	fasts (typically by not eating until a certain time of day)
mahkatêwîweni	fasting
mahkenamwa	breaks it off, pulls it off, picks it (as, a flower)
-mahkesene	moccasins (in particle compounds) (**keki-mahkesene** with one's moccasins on)
mahkesenehkêwa	makes moccasins
mahkesêhi	moccasin (**nemahkesêhani** my moccasins)
mahkeshamwa	cuts it off (as, something attached)
mahkeshkêwi	it breaks off
mahkikwêhpwêwa	bites s.o.'s head off
mahkikwêhwêwa	chops s.o.'s head off
mahkisahtôwa	snatches it off, jerks it off, breaks it off
mahkohpenya	groundnut ("bear potato")
mahkohtawakâha	sunfish
mahkomishi	sumac
mahkôha	cub
mahkôsesêha	fawn (archaic)
mahkwa	bear
mahkwayi	bearskin
mahkwâchi	quiet, quietly, gently, calmly (particle, preverb, prenoun); be quiet! (particle)
mahkwâchishinwa	lies still
mahkwâchîhiweni	quietness
mahkwâhkêha	mud turtle
mahkwâmôwa	bumblebee
mahkwânakwi	bear den
mahkwâtâpôsenwi	the water is calm, quiet
mahkwâtesiwa	is quiet, is of a quiet nature
mahkwâtesiweni	quietness
mahkwâtênetâkosiwa	is thought quiet
mahkweshihamwa	goes on a bear hunt

71

mahkwi-pakâni	black walnut (literally, bear nut)
mahkwisowa	is member of the Bear Clan
mahwêmowa	calls like a wolf
mahwêwa	wolf
mahwêwisowa	is a member of the Wolf Clan
mahwêwiwa	is a wolf
makahtakatwi	it is wide (as, a belt)
makanêhtamwa	takes or has a big mouthful of it
makapitêwi	it is tied in a large bundle (plural **makapitêwani** or **mamâkapitêwani**)
makatêkiwi (**makatêkîhiwi** dimin.)	it is a wide stream
makâhkwatwi	it is a big tree, stick (plural **mamâkâhkwatôni**)
makâkwasowa, makâkwatêwi	there is a large pile or mass of it (animate, inanimate)
makânakatwi	it is a big hole, it is a big cave
makânaketonwa	has a large mouth
makânakitiyêshkêwa	is working to widen the opening of one's anus
makekinôhiwa	is big (dimin.), quite big, bigger (plural **mamâkekinôhiwaki**)
makekinwa	is big, large (**êh=makekineki** he or she was big) (plural **mamâkekinôki**)
maki	big, much (particle, preverb)
makikamîyâwi	it is a wide stream
makikâpâwaki (plural)	they stand in a large group
makimini	"large berry" (probably chestnut)
makinehpashiwa	has a load piled high on one's back
makinehpâhkiwiwi, makinehpâhkîwi	it is high ground
makinehpâkwasowa, makinehpâkwatêwi	(animate, inanimate) is piled high
makinehpâkwêkiwa, makinehpâkwêkenwi	(ice) is thick, it has thick walls
makinehpi	high (preverb)
makinehpîwa, makinehpîwi	(animate, inanimate; as, a plant) is high
makinehpyâwi	it is high
makishimowa	talks with a deep voice
makohkwayi	hat (**nemakohkwayi** my hat)
makochêshkêwi	it swells up
makwahki, makwahkiwi	large hill (**makwahkîki** on a large hill)
makwahkiwiwi	it is a large hill
makwanowêwa	has a swollen cheek
makwêwêkatwi	there is a big noise
makwikenêwa	has a bump on the forehead
makwîtamwa	has a swelling, has a boil
mamahkânahkwatwi	there are clouds scattered here and there
mamahkâpyêwa	has smallpox (**êh=mamahkâpyâwâchi** as they have smallpox)
mamahkenêwa, mamahkenamwa	picks them (as, berries, flowers) (see **mahkenamwa**)
mamahkeshêshwêwa	cuts s.o.'s ears off
mamahkêha	toad
mamahkyâwi	it is bumpy
mamakoshkêwa	develops bumps
mamakwahkiwiwi	there are hills (see **makwahkiwiwi**)
mamakwipehkwanwa	has bumps on one's back
mamakwîwa	makes bumps in the outside surface (as, of a bag or stomach) by moving around inside
mamamamâwakâsenwi	chunks of earth are torn off by the wind (see **mamâwakâsenwi**)
mamâchisahêwa	shakes s.o.
mamâchîhêwa	makes s.o. move, gives s.o. life

mamâchîwa	moves, stirs
mamâkanowêwa	has big cheeks
mamâkapitêwani (plural)	they are tied in a large bundles
mamâkâhkwatôni (plural)	they are big trees, sticks (see **makâhkwatwi**)
mamâkâpitêwa	has big teeth
mamâkekinôhiwaki (plural)	they are big (dimin.), bigger (see **makekinôhiwa**)
mamâkekinôki (plural)	they are big, large (see **makekinwa**)
mamâkeshêwa	has big ears
mamâki	big (plural), in large numbers (preverb) (**mamâki-nêmowa** takes deep breaths)
mamâkinahakêwa	has large scales
mamâkinowêtiyêwa	has big buttocks
mamâkipwâmêwa	has big thighs
mamâkitenyêwa	is big-shouldered
mamâkôchi	somehow, by some chance (particle)
mamâkôchimêwa	talks about s.o. inappropriately or going too far (as, implying one is dead)
mamâkôtahômowa	makes inappropriate outcries (as, exaggerating the pain) (also **makomakôtahômowa**)
mamâne	many each (or each time), a lot each (or each time) (particle)
mamânêhêwaki, mamânêhtôwaki (plurals)	they each have or get a lot of (animate, inanimate)
mamânokoni	for many days each or each time (particle)
mamânôtamôki (plural)	they each carried many of them (inanimate) on their backs
mamânôwanakihtôwaki (plural)	they each had many bags of it
mamânwipepônwêwaki (plural)	they are each many years old (**mâmânwipepônwâchiki** those of advanced age)
mamâsehkêwa, mamâsehkêwi	(animate, inanimate) moves, is moving about
mamâtâpôsêwi	it (water) moves, has ripples
mamâtâpôshkêwi	it flows
mamâtâwi	marvelously; how marvelous! (particle, preverb) (archaic)
mamâtomêwa, mamâtotamwa	prays to s.o., it; requests medical aid from s.o.
mamâtomohêwa	makes s.o. worship
mamâtomowa	prays, worships
mamâtomowapiwa	sits in prayer
mamâtomoweni	worship, religion
mamâtomowitêhêwa	is prayerful
mamâtomôni	worship, religion
mamâtwêwa	moans, is moaning
mamâwakâsenwi	a chunk of earth is torn off by the wind
mamâwakeshkêwi	a chunk of earth tears away
mamenamwa	takes off some of it, takes off a bit of it
mameshamwa	cuts it off
mameshkamwa	catches the blame (for it)
mamêwa	picks the crop (of corn, tobacco) (**êh=wêpi-mamâwâchi** they began picking)
mamîkwâchi	severely, rigorously (preverb)
mamîkwâhtawêwa	makes great efforts with s.o., bears down hard on s.o., gets tough with s.o.
mamîkwânêwa	makes great efforts with s.o., bears down hard on s.o., comes down hard on s.o.
mamîkwâsowa	tries very hard or harder, makes great efforts, tries one's best
mamînâwâchimowa	gives a complete and detailed account, explanation, or answer
mamînâwâchimohêwa	gives s.o. a complete and detailed account, explanation, or answer
mamînâwâpamêwa, mamînâwâpatamwa	looks at s.o., it closely (also **mînâwâpamêwa**)

73

mamînâwesiwa	inquires closely, examines things in detail (also **mînâwesiwa**)
mamînâwi	in all parts or details, attentively, closely (particle, preverb) (also **mînâwi**)
mamînâwihêwa, mamînâwihtôwa	examines s.o., it closely (also **mînâwihêwa**)
mamînâwinawêmêwa	makes s.o. consider carefully by speech
mamîshamâkêwa	acts as attendant for people
mamîshamawêwa	acts as attendant for s.o.
mamîshipwâmêwa	has hairy thighs
mamîshîha	ceremonial attendant; chief's attendant (**nemamîshîhema** my attendant)
mamîshîhiwa	is a ceremonial attendant; is a chief's attendant
mana	this (animate) (plural **mâhaki**)
manahka	a distance off (particle)
manâchi	rich, in a rich way (preverb)
manâtesiwa	is rich
manesenôhi	war
manesenôkimâwa	member of the War Chief Clan (the highest lineage of the Fox Clan)
manesenôkimâwisowa	is a member of the War Chief Clan
manesenôwehkwêsetôwa	sets war on it (the earth)
manesenôwinêwa	dies in war
manesawêwa	gathers firewood for s.o.
manesêwa	gathers firewood
manetîwaki (plural)	they copulate
manetôhêha	little snake
manetôhkâsowa	conjures, calls up one's spiritual power
manetôhkwêwa	manitou woman
manetôhkwêwiwa	she is a manitou woman
manetômîmîwa	mourning dove
manetônâki	in the land of the spirits (locative noun)
manetôsêha	insect, worm
manetôwa	manitou, spirit, god, snake, monster
manetôwâchimowa	talks like a manitou, speaks with spiritual power
manetôwâhtekwi	manitou tree
manetôwâtakesiwa	has spiritual power
manetôwaya	manitou-skin, snakeskin
manetôwêkenwi	fine broadcloth blanket (deep indigo)
manetôwênemêwa, manetôwênetamwa	thinks s.o., it supernatural
manetôwênetâkaniwiwa	is thought a supernatural being
manetôwi (1)	powerful thing, thing having spiritual power
manetôwi (2)	(of) manitou, (of) snake (prenoun, preverb)
manetôwisenyêwa	eats spiritually
manetôwitehkâsowa	is called a manitou
manetôwiwa, manetôwiwi	(animate, inanimate) has spirit power
manetôwîmikatwi	it has spirit power
manêwa, matamwa	he copulates with her, it (Note: this word is used in winter stories but is generally avoided.)
mani (1)	this (inanimate) (plural **mâhani**); consider this (as follows); (with preverb **tashi**) meanwhile, all the while; **mani ênâpiyâni** just as I looked
=**mani** (2)	now, as it is now
manihetîwaki (plural)	they rob each other (of it)
manihêwa	robs s.o. (of it)
manimotêwa	she collects clothing off a returning warrior (in celebration) (**êh=manimanimotâwâchi** they were [doing this])
manômini	rice; wild rice

74

manôminînâki	in Menominee country (locative noun)
manôminîwa	Menominee Indian
masahkamikohkwêwa	the Earth (Grandmother Earth) (archaic **mesahkamikohkwêwa**)
masahkwêha	hairy or downy woodpecker
masakahkwa	badger
masakomiwâpôkatwi	the water is dirty
masakomiwiwa, masakomiwiwi	(animate, inanimate) is dirty
masakôchitêhêwa	is suspicious
masasâhkwa	horsefly
masatôwa	punk (spongy rotten wood that sometimes glows in the dark)
masâchi	barely, with difficulty (particle)
masâna	nettle (Huron Smith: wood nettle)
masânikâpiwa	one's leg goes to sleep as one sits
mashahkwânâsowa	is scalped
mashahkwânêwa	scalps s.o. (also **meshahkwânêwa**)
mashahkwâshwêwa	scalps s.o. (also **meshahkwâshwêwa**)
mashishki	blade of grass (plural **mashishkyêni**) (also **mashkishki**)
mashishkiwi (archaic)	blade of grass, reed, herb, medicine plant (plural **mashishkiwani**) (also **mashkishkiwi**)
mashishkihkiwiwi	it is grass-grown (also **mashkishkihkiwiwi**)
mashishkiwâpowi	tea
mashishkîhani (plural)	grass, grasses (also **mashkishkîhani**)
mashkihkyêni (plural)	grass
mashkimotêhi (**mashkimotêhêhi** dimin.)	bag, sack
mashkimotêhkêwa	she makes a woven bag
mashkishki	blade of grass (plural **mashkishkyêni**) (more commonly **mashishki**)
mashkishkiwihtôwa	makes it of grass
mashkochîsa	bean; beans (collectively)
mashkochîsêha	a bean
mashkotêhkwanwi	blade of grass
mashkotêwêtowêha	curlew
mashkotêwi	prairie
mashkotêwiwi	it is prairie
mashkotêwîtekôwa	burrowing owl
=mata	alternatively, instead, rather, but
matahkyêwa	catches up, overtakes people
matakohokowa	is covered over by something
matakohowa	covers oneself (also **mâtak-**)
matakohwêwa, matakohamwa	covers s.o., it with something (also **mâtak-**; also **matakwahwêwa, matakwahamwa**)
matakôhkwêhowa	covers one's head (also **mâtak-**)
matakôhkwêshinwa	lies with covered head (also **mâtak-**)
matakôhkwêpiwa	sits with covered head (also **mâtak-**)
matakwahwêwa, matakwahamwa	covers s.o., it with something (also **mâtak-**; also **matakohwêwa, matakohamwa**)
mâtakwapitôwa	ties it covering (also **mâtakw-**)
matakwâkonêwa	is covered with snow
matakwâmehkahwêwa	covers s.o. with earth (also **mâtakw-**)
matakwâmehkwatôwa	covers it with earth; fills it in (as, a hole) (also **mâtakw-**)
matakwinenêwêhamwa	covers the smokehole of it
matakwishinwa	lies covered up (also **mâtakw-**)
matanêwa	overtakes s.o., catches up with s.o.
matâkwâchimowa	tells an enjoyable, entertaining, or interesting tale

matâkwâhpawêwa	has an enjoyable dream
matâkwâpamêwa, matâkwâpatamwa	enjoys watching s.o., it; looks at s.o., it with pleasure
matâkwênemêwa, matâkwênetamwa	enjoys s.o., it, thinks s.o., it is interesting, fascinating, curious
matâkwi	enjoyable, interesting, curious; with enjoyment, interest, curiosity (prenoun, preverb)
matâkwikiwa, matâkwikenwi	(animate, inanimate) is new and interesting
matâkwîhkawêwa, matâkwîhkamwa	enjoys s.o.'s company; likes to frequent it (a place)
matâkwîneniwiwa	is jovial, amusing, fun to be with
matepwi	bare lodge-frame (plural **matepôni**)
matetêhi	leggin (**nematetêhani** my leggins)
matonwâwi	for fun (particle)
matôteshawanêwa	gives s.o. a sweat-bath, treats s.o. with a sweat-bath
matôteshêwa	takes a sweat-bath (**nematôtesha** I take a sweat-bath)
matôteshêwikâni	sweat-lodge
mawâpamêwa, mawâpatamwa	goes to see s.o., it
mawi	go to, go and (preverb)
mawimêwa, mawitamwa	weeps for s.o., it, mourns s.o.
mawinachihêwa	goes to help s.o.
mawinachikêwa	goes and grabs things
mawinahkyêwa	runs over, rushes over, attacks
mawinanetîwaki (plural)	they attack each other
mawinanêwa	runs up to s.o., rushes up to s.o., attacks s.o.
mawinêhikêwa	goes or attempts to recoup one's losses; stakes (it) to try to win back one's losses
mawinêhwêwa	goes after s.o., goes in pursuit of s.o.
mawitisowa	weeps for oneself
mawîhkawêwa	goes to deal with s.o.
mawîhtawêwa, mawîhtamwa	makes a grab for s.o., it
mayakahômowa	gives a strange cry
mayakechênêwa	finds s.o. strange to the touch
mayakihtôwa	does, makes it in a strange way
mayakikiwa, mayakikenwi	(animate, inanimate) is strange, odd
mayakimêwa	says strange things to s.o.
mayakinehkêwa	has a peculiar hand
mayakiyâkwatwi	it smells strange
mayakowêwa	says something strange, asks a strange question
mayâshkawêwa, mayâshkamwa	comes directly to s.o., it, encounters s.o., it
mayâshkôsowa	encounters (it)
mayâwâpamêwa	looks straight at s.o.
mayâwi	mainly, exactly; right in, on, or at (particle, preverb, preparticle)
mayâwihkeshe	in the center of the forehead (particle)
mayâwi-makwahkiwe	on top of the hill (particle compound)
mayâwimêwa	speaks mainly to s.o.
mayâwi-sîkêyâwe	right at the bend (particle compound)
mayâwîwa:	**wêchi-mayâwîchi** on one's right
mayâwosêwa	leads a warparty (**mêyâwosâta** leader of a warparty)
mayôhêwa	makes s.o. weep
mayôhiwêwi	that makes people weep (prenoun)
mayôhkatamwa	weeps over it, bewails it
mayôhtâkêwa	makes (s.o.) weep for people
mayôhkânowa	pretends to weep
mayômêwa	makes s.o. weep by speaking, singing, weeping
mayômowa	weeps as one speaks
mayôshinwa	lies weeping

mayôtanekowa	weeps as one works
mayôwa	weeps
mayôwi	it weeps (song word)
mayôwisenwi	it is for wailing (in **mêyôwisekini** wailing songs)
mâchihêwa	gets s.o. started
mâchikamîwi	it is moving water, the spring was swollen with water
mâchikanwêwa	he has an erection
mâchikâpâwa	moves one's feet while standing
mâchinawîhtawêwa	moves about for s.o.
mâchinehkêwa	moves one's arm
mâchiwenêwa	shows s.o. the way
mâchîhkawêwa	is after s.o. (as, criticizing or forcing s.o.)
mâchîwa	moves (see **ahkwi-mâchîwa, kashki-mâchîwa, mamâchîwa**)
mâhaki	these (animate)
mâhani	these (inanimate)
mâhi (1)	over there, over here (particle)
=**mâhi** (2)	of course, you see, as you know, to be sure, I mean, obviously
mâhiya	that (animate; recently present, recently mentioned, going away)
mâhiye	that (inanimate; recently present, going away)
mâhkwiwa	he copulates
mâkinîha	young male deer
mâkoshkêwaki (plural)	they rush as a group, all rush together, all rush forward
mâkwa	loon
mâkwayi	furband headdress, fur cap
mâkwihêwa	attacks s.o. massively, focused on a single target
mâkwinawîwa	struggles hard, puts up a strong resistance
mâmahkatêwanowêpiwa	sits with blackened cheeks
mâmahkatêwanowêwa	has blackened cheeks
mâmahkatêwimâmâwêwa	has black eyebrows
mâmahkâchi	necessarily, it is necessary (particle); (with negative intonation): it is not necessary, should not have, why did (they)?
mâmahkechêyâhi, mâmahkechêsîhi	cucumber
mâmahkesêhiwa	plays the moccasin game
mâmahkoshi	patiently at length or repeatedly; expecting in vain; it still has not happened (that) (particle)
mâmanîninâhi	every little while, at short intervals of time (particle)
mâmatâkwâchimohêwa	tells s.o. enjoyable or interesting things
mâmatâkwâhpawêwa	has enjoyable dreams
mâmatâkwâpiwa	enjoys looking, enjoys the sights
mâmatâkwi	how delightful, what a pleasure; as a pleasant surprise (particle, preverb)
mâmatânihetîwaki (plural)	they entertain each other
mâmatânahkiwihtôwaki (plural)	they have lively doings, a good time, a celebration
mâmatânahkiwiwi	there are lively doings, there is a celebration
mâmaya	soon, in the near future; early (particle)
mâmâhkatamwa	picks at them and eats them (as, scattered bits of food)
mâmâhki	(removing) every little bit
mâmâkeshêha	mule
mâmânami (also **mâmânomi**)	barging in, not allowing others the opportunity (particle)
mâmânetîhiwaki (plural)	they have a contest
mâmânwikâtêha	centipede
mâmâtwêha	catbird (also **mêmâtwêha**)
mâmîhkôhiwaki (plural)	they play tag
mâmôshkihtanwi	it flows bubbling

mânahwêwa	beats s.o. out of much
mânamêwa	see **mânomêwa**
mâne	much, many (particle)
mânenwi	many times (particle)
mânêhêwa, mânêhtôwa	has much, many of s.o., it
mânêwa, mânêtwi	(animate, inanimate) is much, many, numerous
mânêshêha	mud puppy
mânokonakatwi	it is many days
mânokoni	for many days (particle)
mânokonîwa	fasts for many days
mânomêwa	beats s.o. (as, by doing something better or faster) (also **mânamêwa**)
mânomihêwa	beats s.o. to it
mânôchênêwa	holds many of s.o.
mânôhkawêwaki (plural)	many (of them) go at s.o.
mânôhkwêwêwa	he has many wives
mânôhpowaki (plural)	many (of them) eat together
mânwawahîme	many years (particle)
mânwawahîmêhe	many years (dimin.) (particle)
mânwawahîne (mânwawahînêhe dimin.)	many years (particle)
mânwawahîmakatwi	it is many years
mânwayaki	many sets or groups (particle)
mânwikamikesiwaki (plural)	there are many houses of them
mânwipepônakatwi	it is many winters
mânwipepônwêwa	is many years old
mâshkôha	Creek Indian
mâtak(w)-	cover (see **matak(w)-**)
mâtakôchinwa, mâtakôtêwi	moves from the place where one (as, a star) hangs, it moves from the place where it (as, a cloud) hangs
mâtapiwa	moves one's seat, moves from one's place
mâtânakîkwêshkêwa	moves one's eyes
mâtâshkamwa	comes to it (a larger path or road)
mâtâyâwi	it (a river or stream) joins another river or stream
mâtenêwa, mâtenamwa	moves s.o., it
mâtesi (mâtesêhi dimin.)	knife
mâwachi	gathering; among all, only one of all, most (etc.) of all (superlative) (preverb, preparticle)
mâwachikawihtôwa	gathers it as it drips
mâwachimêwa	calls them together
mâwachipahowaki (plural)	they all run together, they gather together by running
mâwachishimêwa, mâwachisetôwa	brings, sets, keeps them (animate, inanimate) all together
mâwachiwenêwa, mâwachiwetôwa	gathers them (animate, inanimate) together
mâwachîwaki (plural)	they gather, assemble, meet together
mâwatâkwapiwaki (plural)	they sit assembled
mâwatenâtêwi	it is gathered
mâwatenêwa, mâwatenamwa	gathers s.o., it
mâwâkâni	village
mâwâkêwaki (plural)	they are in camp together
mâwâsenwi	there is a village, a group of lodges ({somewhere})
mâwâsetôwaki (plural)	they have a village, they have their houses all together
mâwâshimôwikâni	hotel
mâwâshkêwaki (plural)	they gather together, assemble
mechemôka	old woman (**mechemôke** wife! [term of address]) (also **chemôka, metemôha, metemôka, metenêka**)

mechi	rather, quite (particle); (with negative intonation) surely not! obviously not!
mechichimêwa	gives s.o. a message to deliver, sends a message by s.o.
mechi='hi	(with negative intonation) quite obviously not!
mechimatahwêwa	beats s.o. badly
mechimâpamêwa, mechimâpatamwa	looks closely, fixedly at s.o., it; stares at s.o., it
mechimâpiwa	stares fixedly
mechimênemowa	hesitates, holds back
mechimihêwa	is always after s.o., is always beating s.o. up; kills many of s.o.
mechiminahkyêwa	commits murder
mechiminanêwa	murders s.o.
mechiminehkênâtêwi	it is scratched by claws, has scratch marks
mechimiwetâkêwa	leads men to their death
mechimîwa	(always) gets beaten up; loses a man
mechitwêwa	sends a message
mehchawiwa	acts openly; gives away the secret by how one acts, shows it
mehchâwi:	**êh=mehchâki** in the open, in plain sight; **êhkwi-mehchâki** at the edge of an open space
mehchi (1)	openly, plainly, ostensibly; out in the open (particle, preverb)
mehchi (2)	by hand (like **mehtâhkwi**) (particle)
mehchi (3)	down, to the ground (like **mehchîki**) (particle) **mehchi pakinêwa** throws s.o. to the ground; he rapes her
mehchihêwa, mehchihtôwa	has an clear view of s.o., it; sees s.o. exposed
mehchihkatwi	the ground is bare of snow
mehchihkawêwa	leaves or has left a plain trail
mehchikahkwanwa	is bare-legged
mehchikâtêwa	is barefoot
mehchikiwa	is naked
mehchinameshkêpiwa	sits naked
mehchinameshkêwa	is naked, is minimally dressed
mehchinawe	naked, dressed only in a breechcloth (particle)
mehchinawênêwa	undresses s.o.
mehchinawênowa	undresses
mehchinawêwa	is undressed
mehchinowêtiyênêwa	uncovers s.o.'s buttocks
mehchitiyênêwa	uncovers s.o.'s bottom
mehchîki	down, to the ground, down on the ground (particle)
mehkawêwa, mehkamwa	finds s.o., it
mehkawishinwa	stumbles
mehkochêhtamwa	finds it with one's mouth, takes it into one's mouth
mehkochêmêwa	asks, names, or calls s.o. who is just the right one
mehkochênamawêwa	finds (it) for s.o. by touch
mehkochênamwa	finds it by touch
mehkokwawêwa	finds s.o. in a dream
mehkonêweni	blanket, robe (**nehkonêhi** my blanket)
mehkoshkawêwa, mehkoshkamwa	comes upon s.o., it by accident; he finds s.o., it with one's foot
mehkwachiwa	gets frostbite
mehkwami	the ice surface (**mehkwamîki** on the ice)
mehkwatomêwa	finds s.o. by inquiry
mehkwênemâsowa	is remembered
mehkwênemêwa, mehkwênetamwa	thinks of, remembers s.o., it
mehkwênetamawêwa	thinks of, remembers (it) for s.o.
mehkwênetîwaki (plural)	they remember each other

mehkwi	happen to (preverb)
mehkwinawêhêwa	reminds s.o.
mehkwinawêmêwa	reminds s.o. by speech
mehkwitêhêwa	remembers, calls to mind
mehkwiyâtamwa	finds the scent of it
mehpowi	it snows
mehpôshêwa	she infects her unborn child by violating a pregnancy taboo
mehtahokowa	is hit (by a falling or thrown object)
mehtahwêwa	hits s.o. with a thrown object
mehtami	first (particle) (also **menehta, menehtami, nenehtâmi**)
mehtanasite	barefoot (particle)
mehtanasitêkêwa	dances barefoot
mehtanasitêwa	is barefoot
mehtapihetîwaki (plural)	they bury each other out in the open in a sitting position
mehtapishkwe	stark naked (particle)
mehtapishkwêwa	is stark naked
mehtawakêwa	wears earrings (also **ohtawakêwa**)
mehtawakêwenaki (plural)	earrings
mehtawakêwâhaki (plural)	earrings (dimin.)
mehtâchimowa	tells plainly, tells the real truth
mehtâhkwi (Jones: **mehtâhkwe**)	without anything, without a proper weapon, using one's hands, without doing anything, without what might be usual or expected (particle, preverb)
mehtâhkwinameshke	naked (particle)
mehtâhkwinameshkêwa	is naked
mehtâhtêwi	it is out in the heat of the sun
mehtâkwasowa, mehtâkwatêwi	is piled in plain sight, is sprawled naked; it is piled in plain sight
mehtâpitêwa	bares one's teeth, one's teeth are exposed
mehtâsenwi	it is exposed to the wind
mehtâwaki	on the ground, on dry land (particle)
mehtekomishi	oak, black oak (plural **mehtekomishyêni, mehtekomishêni**)
mehtekomishiwa	is an oak
mehtekôhi	small tree, bough, little stick
mehtekôshîha	(see **mêmehtekôshîha**)
mehtekwahkihkiwi	woods, wooded area
mehtekwahkihkiwiwi	there is a wooded area
mehtekwanwi	arrow (modern term, as if "wooden bullet")
mehtekwapenôha	walkingstick
mehtekwâpi	bowstring (plural **mehtekwâpyêni**)
mehtekwi	tree, stick, wood
mehtekwihkîki, mehtekwahkîki	in the woods (locative nouns)
mehtekwinâkani	wooden bowl
mehtekwinâkâhi	wooden bowl (dimin.)
mehtenêwa, mehtenamwa	unwraps s.o., it, exposing them, it to view
mehtenôhi	only, except, unless; especially, moreso (particle)
mehtêha	bow (**nemehtêha** my bow)
mehtênemêwa	knows full well about s.o.
mehtênetâkwi	naturally, there is no doubt, for sure (particle)
mehtosêneniwa	person, human being
mehtosêneniwahkiwiwi	it is a peopled earth, the earth has people on it
mehtosêneniwahkyâwi (Jones?)	it is a peopled earth (ritual)
mehtosêneniwahkyâwiwi (Jones)	it is a peopled earth (ritual)
mehtosêneniwahkyâniwiwi	it is a peopled earth, the earth has people on it
mehtosêneniwâpamêwa	sees s.o. as a person

mehtosêneniwêhiwa	lives (dimin.)
mehtosêneniwihêwa	makes s.o. live; turns s.o. into a human being
mehtosêneniwikihônowa	transforms oneself into a human being
mehtosêneniwitehkânetîwaki (plural)	they call each other human beings
mehtosêneniwitehkâsowa	is called a human being
mehtosêneniwiwa	is a human being, lives
	(**wîh=anemi-mehtosêneniwita,**
	wîh=anemi-mehtosêneniwichiki
	the people to come, the future human race)
mehtosêneniwiweni	life
mehtosênenîha	human being (song word)
-mehtosênenîkêwa	(see **wîchi-mehtosênenîkêwa**)
-mehtosênenîmêwa	(see **wîchi-mehtosênenîmêwa**)
mehtôchi	like, as if, as it were, as though (particle)
mehtôchinawîhtawêwa	reveals oneself to s.o.
mehtôsâpatâniwi	it is visible
mekesiwa	bald eagle
mekesiwaki (plural)	Eagle Clan members
mekesiwisowa	is a member of the Eagle Clan
mekinêwa, mekitamwa	barks at s.o., it
mekiwa	barks
=meko, =mekoho	indeed, precisely (a weak emphatic)
mekochi	plainly visible or audible (particle)
mekosi	awl
mekôtêweni	a dress (**nekôtêhi** my dress)
memekohkwêsêwa	shakes one's head
memekwahikêwa (and **memekohikêwa**)	parches corn on the coals
memekwinîkwênowa	rubs one's eyes
memekwisahêwa	shakes s.o. hard
memênawâwi	there is room
memênawênemêwa	spares s.o. out of fondness or high regard
memênawi	enough room, space, time (particle, preverb)
memênawichinwa	has enough room to fit
memênawishinwa	has time
memêsachitêhêwa	has lascivious thoughts, has a randy feeling
memêsatesiwa	is lustful, randy, oversexed
memêshâhiwani (plural)	they (inanimate) are large (dimin.), larger
memêshâwani (plural)	they (inanimate) are large
memyênôwinâkêwa	sings a non-religious song
memyênwa (archaic)	sings a non-religious song
memyêshi	big (plural) (prenoun)
memyêshkanahamîwa	has difficult footing
memyêshkâkwapiwaki (plural)	they sit in scattered, disordered groups
memyêshkânehkwêshinwa	lies with one's hair mussed up
memyêshkâpitêwa	has irregular teeth
memyêshkênemêwa	plans trouble for s.o., makes things rough for s.o.
memyêshki	carelessly, not thoroughly, messily, crossly (particle, preverb)
memyêshkihêwa	makes trouble for s.o.
memyêshkîhkamwa	ruins it
memyêshkikâwosêwa	walks with irregular steps
memyêshkimêwa	says something out of line to s.o.
memyêshkyâwi	it is wrong, bad, wicked, ruinous
menahêwa	gives s.o. drink, gives s.o. (it) to drink
menahkwatwi	cloud

menâkosiwa, menâkwatwi	(animate, inanimate) smells bad, stinks
menâkwitepêwa	one's head stinks
menâmêwa, menâtamwa	smells s.o., it
menânawiwa	has a strange experience
menânâhpawêwa	has a strange dream (**nemenânâhpawa** I had a strange dream)
menâni	strangely, in a weird, unexpected, or inexplicable way (particle, preverb)
menâshkonowa	eats fresh meat
menâshkonôni	fresh meat
menechîha	glove
menehta	first (particle) (also **mehtami, menehtami, menehtâmi**)
menehtami, menehtâmi	first (particle, preverb)
menehtâmisenwi	it is the first one that lies or is set
menesêwa, menehtôwa	stretches s.o. (as, a hide), it (as, a scalp)
menehtêwîmêhi	a little before
menesi (dim. **menesêhi**)	island (**kemenesemenâni** our island, our continent)
menêshishi (dim. **menêshishîhi**)	maple syrup
menêwihêwa	makes s.o. resentful of being left out or not treated the same
menêwimêwa	complains that s.o. left one out or did not treat one the same
meni	pus
menihki	milk
menipowaki (plural)	they gang-rape (her) (**menipopi** she was gang-raped)
menipyâkahkiwiwi	there is a shout from the crowd (also **menwipyâkahkiwiwi**)
menipyâkimêwaki (plural)	they raise a shout at s.o. (also **menwipyâkimêwaki**)
menishkîkwêkwâmwa	sleeps with mattery eyes
meniwiwa, meniwiwi	has pus, has a pussy sore, is pussy; it is pussy
menohtawêwa, menohtamwa	hears s.o., it with pleasure
menohtâkosiwa	is heard with pleasure, one's voice sounds nice
menohtâtisowa	likes hearing oneself
menonamawêwa	straighten it up nicely for s.o.
menonêwa, menonamwa	gets or has a good grip on s.o., it
menosikêwa	cooks well
menoshêwa	hears with pleasure, likes what one hears
menoshkawêwa, menoshkamwa	has a good fit or mount of s.o., it; **menoshkâkwiwa** it (food) has a good affect on s.o.
menosowa, menotêwi	(animate, inanimate) is cooked nicely
menowa	drinks; drinks (it)
menowêwa	says something good, right, correct, pleasing
menôhkamîwi (**menôhkamîhiwi** dimin.)	it is springtime
menôtani	enemy village (**menôtaneki** in the enemy village; **ashâhi-menôtani** Sioux village) (also in **âshowi-menôta, âshowi-menôtane**)
menwahkiwiwi	it is good land
menwamatamwa	feels good, has a nice feeling
menwamêwa	makes a good meal of s.o., satisfies one's hunger eating s.o.; bites s.o. just right, has a good hold on s.o. with one's mouth
menwamowa	has a fine meal
menwamônêwa	feeds s.o. well
menwapiwa	sits well, has a comfortable seat, has a nice place to sit
menwashkatwi	there is nice grass covering the ground
menwashkôsowa	feels good after eating
menwatahwêwa	strikes s.o. just right, in just the right spot
menwawiwa	acts well, does well, does good
menwâchimowa	speaks well
menwâchimêwa, menwâtotamwa	speaks well of s.o., it

-menwâhi (only in a particle phrase):	(see **kehchi-menwâhi**)
menwâhkonikêwa	has a good rule, law
menwâkômêwa, menwâkôtamwa	likes s.o.'s ways, is pleased with it
menwâpamêwa	likes to see s.o.
menwâpatâniwa, menwâpatâniwi	(animate, inanimate) looks nice
menwâpatîwaki (plural)	they like to see each other
menwâpiwa	sees well, has good eyesight
menwâshkêwi	it works, fits, suits
menwâtotamawêwa	speaks well of (it) to s.o.
menwâtotamâtîwaki (plural)	they speak well of (it) to each other
menwâyêniwa	has a pretty laugh
menwênechikêwa	likes someone or something, has likes
menwênemêwa, menwênetamwa	likes s.o., it
menwênetamawêwa	likes (s.o.) for s.o.
menwi	good, well, pleasantly, nicely, in good order, safely (preverb, preparticle)
menwihchikêwa	does things well, does right
menwihkwêwiwa	she has a nice womanly shape
menwihtanwi	it flows nicely
menwikiwa, menwikenwi	is good, is well formed, grows the right way; it is good
menwi-kîshekatwi, menwikîshekatwi	it is a fine day
menwi-mehtosêneniwiweni	healthy life
menwimêwa	speaks nicely to s.o.; gives s.o. good advice; says something nice about s.o.
menwinawêhêwa, menwinawêhtôwa	gives s.o., it joy
menwinawêmêwa	pleases s.o. with words
menwinawêshkawêwa	goes through s.o. doing them good
menwinâhi (1)	some distance away, not far away; soon (particle)
menwinâhi (2)	(it is) the right time, a good time (particle)
menwinehki (**menwinehkîmêhi** dimin.)	for a good while, for some time, for not very long (particle)
menwi-pemâtesiwa	feels good, feels better, is in good health
menwi-pemâtesiweni	good health
menwipyâkahkiwiwi	there is a shout from the crowd (also **menipyâkahkiwiwi**)
menwipyâkimêwaki (plural)	they raise a shout at s.o. (also **menipyâkimêwaki**)
menwipyâkôki (plural)	they all shout in unison
menwisenyêwa	eats well
menwishimêwa, menwisetôwa	places s.o., it nicely
menwishimowa	has a nice-sounding voice, has a sweet or pretty voice
menwishinwa, menwisenwi	lies well, comfortably; it lies well
menwi-taswi	not (too) many, not (too) much, (only) a few, (only) a little (particle compound)
menwitêhâkani	good thoughts
menwitêhêwa	is glad; is good-hearted, has good thoughts
menwiwetôwa	conducts it well
menwiyâkosiwa, menwiyâkwatwi	(animate, inanimate) smells nice
menwiyâkotonwa	one's mouth smells nice
menwiyâmêwa, menwiyâtamwa	likes the smell of s.o., it
menwiyâsikêwa	makes or has nice smells of cooking or burning
menwiyâsowa, menwiyâhtêwi	(animate, inanimate) smells good in cooking, burning
menwîhkâtêwi	it is well taken care of, well tended
menwîhkawêwa, menwîhkamwa	takes good care of s.o., it
menwîhtêwa (1)	does right (**kemenwîhta** you do right)
menwîhtêwa (2)	dresses well
mepwâmi êsâwâhkatêki	ham (see **nepwâmi, asâwâhkatêwi**)

mesachiwa, mesatenwi	(animate, inanimate) is frozen solid
mesahkamikohkwêwa (archaic)	the Earth (Grandmother Earth) (see **masahkamikohkwêwa**)
mesatonêhwêwaki (plural)	they all looked for s.o.
mesawinawêwa, mesawinamwa	is tempted by hunger or desire for s.o., it
mesawinâkosiwa	looks tempting, is coveted as a meal
mesawinoshêwa	likes what one hears
mesâhkwa	ear of corn
mesâpêwa	giant (human giant)
mesechêwa	has a big belly
mesehkwêwa (Jones)	has long hair
mesenahikani, mesanahikani	paper, something written
mesepyêhtawêwa	sends a flood upon s.o.
mesepyêyâwi	there is a flood all over
mesêhi (**mesêhêhi** dimin.)	piece of firewood (**nemesemani** my firewood)
mesênemêwa, mesênetamwa	benefits from s.o., it; s.o. is of use to one
mesênetamâkêwa	benefits, gets good from (it) for people
mesi	all, whole (particle, preverb)
mesihâwa	headless body, corporeal body
mesihkwa	ice, piece of ice
mesihkwâpowi	ice water
mesihkwiwi	it is hailing
mesikiwa, mesikenwi	(animate, inanimate) is whole, survives in one piece
mesimesiwêshkêwa	flops about limply
mesisahêwa, mesisahtôwa	swallows s.o., it whole
mesiwêhkatêwani (plural)	they (inanimate, as trees) stand all over
mesiwêkâpâwani (plural)	they (inanimate) stand all over
mesiwêmêwaki (plural)	they all ask s.o. (as, in prayer)
mesiwêshinôki (plural)	they (animate) are all over
mesiwêwi, mesiwêwe	all, in general, entirely, all over (preverb, particle)
mesiwêwosêwa	walks all over
mesiwêyâhkohwêwa	roasts s.o. whole on a stick by the fire
mesiwêyâkwatêwani (plural)	they (inanimate) are all over the ground
mesiwêyâkwatôwa	litters the ground with them (inanimate)
mesîkwa	dried, shelled corn (generic); usually plural: **mesîkwaki** (**mesîkôhaki** dimin.)
mesômêwa	carries s.o. whole on one's back
mesônwêwa	he has a big penis
mesôtêwi, mesôtêwe	all, universally, all over, wholly (preverb, particle)
mesôtêwimêwa	speaks to all of s.o., includes all of s.o. in what one says
mesôtêwôtêwaki (plural)	they crawl all over
meshahkwânêwa	scalps s.o. (also **mashahkwânêwa**)
meshahkwâshwêwa, meshahkwâshamwa	scalps s.o., it (also **mashahkwâshwêwa**)
meshahkwatwi	it is clear sky
meshâhiwi	it is large (dimin.), larger
meshâpamêwa	sees s.o.'s private parts
meshâwi	it is large
mesh-âyâninâhi	separated by a moderate distance or distances (particle compound)
meshe	let it be, freely; or; in some way, moderately; it's up to you, if that's what you want (particle)
meshe=kêhi	(or) perhaps, (or) for example
meshe=meko	freely, peacefully, contentedly, as one pleases; let it be
meshe=mekô='nahi	any, anyone, anytime, any place
meshenahkyêwa	takes captives, arrests people
meshenamawêwa	catches (it) for s.o.

meshe-nâhinâhi, meshe=meko nâhinâhi	a little ways off (particle compound, particle phrase)
meshenâhinâhiwiwi	it is not a long time
meshenêwa, meshenamwa	catches s.o., it; arrests s.o., captures s.o.
meshesiwa	is infected
meshe=wêna	well after all
meshê='nahi, meshê='nah=meko	perhaps, may, can, could, at will, if one likes; about, roughly speaking, as much as, some or other, whatever it was; going so far as to; in the course of time; one lets it happen; let it go, forget it
meshêwêmonêha	flicker
meshêwêwa	elk
meshi	big (prenoun)
meshi-nemêsa (archaic **meshi-namêsa**)	big fish
meshihêwa	infects s.o.
meshihkatwi	war
meshihkenâhkwa	snapping-turtle (archaic)
meshihkêha	snapping-turtle; Turtle (character in stories)
meshihtâwihêwa	gets s.o. in trouble, causes trouble for s.o.
meshihtâwimêwa	gets s.o. in trouble by what one says'
meshikenêpikwa	underwater bear (a bearlike water monster)
meshiketenêwa, meshihketenêwa	she has a large vagina
meshimowêwa	eats a lot, is a glutton
meshinâkosiwa	looks big
meshinepisôni	sweet flag, calamus
meshinowêwa	osprey
meshipahtêhani (plural)	grapes
meshisêwa	prairie chicken
meshishipa	mallard
meshiwâhkwa	dead fallen tree
meshîmina	apple
meshînamêkwa, meshînamêwa	whale
meshkâkwasowa, meshkâkwatêwi	is sprawled out exposed, it is spread out exposed
meshkehtêhi	mayapple
meshkekwâmwa	is sleeping indecently exposed
meshkenamwa	opens it; turns it (as, a card) face up
meshketonênêwa	opens s.o.'s mouth
meshketonêshinwa	lies with one's mouth open
meshketonwa	opens one's mouth, has one's mouth open
meshkikoma, oshkikoma	snot (**neshkikoma** my snot)
meshkikwêwa	his foreskin is retracted
meshkinechêhtawêwa	holds one's hand open to s.o.
meshkinechêwa	opens one's hand, holds one's hand open
meshkisetawêwa	spreads (it) out for s.o.
meshkisetôwa	spreads it out
meshkishinwa, meshkisenwi	lies sprawled indecently exposed, it lies open
meshkohkamwa	reddens it by going there
meshkohpwâkana	catlinite pipe, redstone pipe
meshkohpwâkâha	catlinite pipe, redstone pipe (dimin.)
meshkonâtêwi	it is painted red
meshkonêwa, meshkonamwa	makes, paints s.o., it red
meshkopyêhâtêwi	it is painted red
meshkosiwa, meshkwâwi	(animate, inanimate) is red
meshkoshawêwa	(sun) is giving a red glow
meshkowâhkosiwa, meshkowâhkwatwi	(animate, inanimate) is all bloody, it is covered with blood
meshkowâpôkatwi	it is a bloody liquid

meshkoweshkamwa	bloodies it by walking, tracks blood in it
meshkoweshkamawêwa	bloodies (it) by walking for s.o., tracks blood in (it) for s.o.
meshkoweshkêwa	bleeds
meshkowiwa, meshkowiwi	is bloody, has blood in one; it is bloody
meshkwahkîha	Meskwaki
meshkwahkîhâtowêwa	speaks Meskwaki
meshkwahkîhi	Meskwaki (prenoun)
meshkwahkîhi-mehtosêneniwiwa	is a Meskwaki
meshkwahkîhinâki	in Meskwaki country (locative noun)
meshkwahkîh-okimâwiwa	is a Meskwaki chief
meshkwahkîhiwa, meshkwahkîhiwiwa	is a Meskwaki, becomes a Meskwaki
meshkwahtakawêwa	(animal) is red, has a red coat
meshkwanamona, meshkwanemona	red ocher
meshkwanôsamwa	heats it red-hot
meshkwanôsowa, meshkwanôtêwi	s.o. (as, a sweatlodge stone), it is heated red-hot
meshkwanwîwa	has no teeth, has only bare gums
meshkwâha	anus (**nemeshkwâha** my anus)
meshkwâhkonêwa, meshkwâhkonamwa	paints s.o., it red
meshkwâhkonikani	scalp-stick (for a warrior's niece to carry in the Scalp Dance with an attached scalp)
meshkwâhkonowa	paints oneself red
meshkwânahkwatwi	it is red sky
meshkwâpîmishi	"red willow" (red-osier dogwood)
meshkwâpôkatwi	it is red liquid
meshkwâswâhkêwa	she makes a "yarn belt" (finger-woven sash)
meshkwâswâwa	"yarn belt" (finger-woven sash)
meshkwâwâhkwa	cedar, red cedar
meshkwêhpîha	throwing stick (thrown on the ground or snow in a distance contest)
meshkwêhpîhiwa	plays the game with the throwing-stick
meshkwêkenwi	red woolen broadcloth blanket (red with white stripe)
meshkwi (1)	blood (**nemeshkomi** my blood)
meshkwi (2)	red (prenoun)
meshkwichitôwa	great-crested flycatcher
meshkwikenâtêwi	it (stick or sticklike) is painted red
meshkwinekwêwa:	**êh=meshkwinekwêchi** in one's armpit
meshkwipakatwi	its leaves are red
meshkwipiwêwa	has red feathers
meshkwitiyêshkêwa	one's anus keeps working, alternately showing red
meshkwîkitêwa	is exasperated, loses patience
meshkwîkitêwowêwa	talks annoyingly
meshoshkêwa	is smitten, is in love, is courting; is smitten with (s.o.), is courting (her)
meshotîwa	is smitten (with s.o.) (**meshotîwaki** they fall in love with each other)
meshwêha	rabbit
meshwêhikani	rabbit bone
meshwêwa, meshotamwa	shoots s.o., it, hits s.o., it with a shot (**meshwâpi** is shot; is smitten with love)
metamwa	groans, gives a groan (archaic)
metawamêwa	envies s.o., is jealous or resentful of s.o.'s success or better treatment
metawêwa	sulks, is resentful
metawêwitêhêwa	feels resentful
metâchâhiwa	enjoys oneself (also **mêmetâchâhiwa**)
metâchinehkawêwa	pleasantly chases s.o.
metâsenwi	ten times (particle)
metâsenwi nyânanenwi	fifteen times (particle phrase)

metâsokonakatwi	it is ten days
metâsokoni	ten days (particle)
metâsokonîwa	fasts for ten days
metâsônameki	tenth, the tenth time (particle)
metâsôshkene	ten bags (of something), ten bagfuls (particle)
metâsôwane	ten backloads; ten bundles or sacks (of something) (particle)
metâswawahîme, metâswawahîne	ten years (particle)
metâswâhkwe	ten hundred, a thousand (particle)
metâswi	ten (particle)
metâswi-kotwâshika	sixteen (particle compound) (also **kotwâshikanesiwe, kotwâshikanîsiwe**)
metâswi-nekoti	eleven (particle compound)
metâswi-nekotinîsiwe	eleven (particle compound) (also **nekotinesiwe** and variants)
metâswi-neswi	thirteen (particle compound)
metâswi-neswinesiwe	thirteen (particle compound) (also **neswinesiwe**)
metâswi-neswinîsiwe	thirteen (particle compound) (also **neswinîsiwe**)
metâswi-nîshwi	twelve (particle compound) (also **nîshwinîsiwe**)
metâswi-nyânanwi	fifteen (particle compound) (also **nyânanwinesiwe** and variants)
metâswi-nyêwi	fourteen (particle compound) (also **nyêwinîsiwe**)
metâswipepônwêwa	is ten years old
metâswi-shwâshika	eighteen (particle compound) (also **shwâshikanesiwe, shwâshikanîsiwi**)
metâshiwaki (plural)	they (animate) are ten, there are ten of them
metâtehtawêwa	likes to hear s.o.
metâtênetamwa	thinks it pleasant
metemôha (**metemôhêha** dimin.)	old woman (**metemo** wife! [term of address]) (also **mechemôka, metemôka, metenêka**)
metemôhêhiwa	she is an old woman, a little old lady
metemôhiwa	she is an old woman
metemôka	old woman (**metemôke** wife! [term of address])
metêwa	member of the Midewiwin
metêwesêhkwêwa	cooks for the Midewiwin
metêwiweni	Midewiwin (Mystic Rite, Grand Medicine Rite)
metopwâwi:	(equivalent to **metwi-pwâwi**)
metwêyawi	(with negative): not very often, seldom (particle)
metwi	(with negative idioms): it's about time that ...! (etc.) (particle)
mêchimôkwâtêwi	it is sewed together permanently
mêchimônêwa	has an unbreakable grip on s.o.
mêchimôshinôki (plural)	are or become stuck or fused together
mêchimôwi	committed to continuing, irreversibly (preverb)
mêhi	yet (preverb); before (preverb with prioritive modes)
mêhkatêwesita mahkwa	member of the Black Bear lineage of the Bear Clan
mêhkohpeniwisota (participle)	member of the Bear Potato Clan
mêhkwisota (participle)	member of the Bear Clan
mêhkwisôha	member of the Bear Clan
mêhwêwisota (participle)	member of the Wolf Clan
mêhwêwisôha	member of the Wolf Clan
mêkechîwa	belches
mêkesiwisota (participle)	member of the Eagle Clan
mêkwâchi	be well into, keep on the same, have become and continue with equal intensity (particle)
mêkwêhe	I believe, I think, probably, likely (particle)
mêkwênâhi	quite a ways, a considerable distance (particle)
mêkwêtanekowa	is advanced in one's work or activity

mêkwêwâpatâniwa	presents a confident sight
mêkwêwowêwa	he is well into his speech, has talked for some time
mêkwisikîha	camel
mêmâtwêha	catbird (also **mâmâtwêha**)
mêmechinêhi	for the last time (particle)
mêmechinêhiweni	last thing, conclusion
mêmechishkêhi	finally (particle)
mêmehchi	ostensibly, openly (particle) (see **mehchi**)
mêmehchichîkwanêyâshinwa	her knees are exposed by the wind (as, in running)
mêmehtânesha	sheep
mêmehtekôshîha	Frenchman (archaic **wêmehtekôshîha**; also **êmehtekôshîha, mehtekôshîha**)
mêmekenahwêwa, mêmekenahamwa	gathers them (animate, inanimate) up
mêmenachâkani	vomit
mêmenachâtamwa	vomits it up
mêmenatamwa	vomits
mêmenatêhowa	induces vomiting, takes (it as) an emetic
mêmenatêhwêwa	administers an emetic to s.o.
mêmenatêsowa	is made to vomit (by it)
mêmenwikâwosêwa	steps gracefully
mêmenwinâhi	every so often, often, regularly, not frequently; every little way, not great distances apart (particle)
mêmenwi-wîchênotamâkêwa	always plays nicely with (them) of others
mêmesôsi	extraordinary, out of the ordinary, beyond the norm, going too far
mêmeshe	any in each case (particle)
mêmeshe-nânâhinâhi	a little ways from each other (particle compound)
mêmeshihka	perhaps, probably, for example (particle)
mêmeshkomêhaki (plural)	young buffaloes, young horses
mêmeshkowinechêwa	one's hands are bleeding
mêmeshkwatayêha	earthworm
mêmeshkwatowinîkwêwa	has bloodshot eyes
mêmeshkwikashêwa	has red hoofs
mêmeshkwimatetêha	Red-Leggins (man in story)
mêmeshkwinîkwêwa	has red eyes
mêmeshkwiwinêwa	has red horns
mêmetâchâhi	fun, a good time
mêmetâchâhiwa	has a good time (also **metâchâhiwa**)
mêmetâchâhiwi	it is fun, one has a good time
mêmêchikâchimohêwa	gives s.o. definite instructions
mêmêchikesiwa	makes certain
mêmêchikênemêwa, mêmêchikênetamwa	is sure about s.o., it
mêmêchiki	I'm sure, one is sure, being sure, positively (particle)
mêmêchikihêwa, mêmêchikihtôwa	makes sure about s.o., it, gets the facts from s.o.
mêmêkêha	butterfly
mêmêkwêshawi, mêmêkwêshawe	out of turn as the first, butting in before anyone else, already prematurely (particle)
mêmênesowêwa	speaks unbelievably, unconvincingly
mêmêswêwe, mêmêswêwi	excessively, in excessive amounts, greedily
mêmêshâhi	large bead
mêmêwa	pileated woodpecker
mêmyêhchi	necessarily, unavoidably; it must be (that) (particle)
mênawânêwa	loves s.o., admires s.o.
mênawâtâkana (only possessed):	**kemênawâtâkana** the object of your affection
mênâkochêha	daddy longlegs

mênâkwashkîhi	purple giant hyssop
mênânesiwa	is missing one's opportunity
mênesenôkimâwisota (participle)	member of the War Chief lineage of the Fox Clan
mêneshâwi	it is shameful
mêneshi	so as to cause shame (preverb)
mêneshihêwa	disgraces s.o., makes s.o. feel ashamed, embarrassed, bashful
mêneshikêmowa	shames people by what one says
mêneshimêwa, mêneshotamwa	shames, embarrasses s.o., it by speech
mêneshitêhâkani	shame
mêneshitêhêwa	is ashamed, embarrassed
mêneshîhkânowa	does something that brings shame and ridicule
mêneshîhtawêwa, mêneshîhtamwa	is ashamed before s.o.; is ashamed to do it, is ashamed of it
mêneshîkwêkâpâwa	stands shamefaced
mênetîha	fornicator; harlot; screw-up
mêsi	too soon (preverb)
mêsiwêyâhi	maple sugar cake
mêshânehkwênowa	touches one's hair
mêshehkawêwa, mêshehkamwa	touches s.o., it by foot or body, infects s.o., it
mêshenêwa, mêshenamwa	touches s.o., it
mêsheshkawêwa	touches s.o. by foot or body
mêshêwêwisota (participle)	member of the Elk Clan
mêshinawâtîwaki (plural)	they come into contact with each other, their bodies touch
mêshinehkênêwa	touches s.o.'s hand
mêshisîpôwi, mêsisîpôwi	Mississippi River
mêshîsêwi	it touches the ground
mêshkowêhi	bloodroot
-mêshkwâpehkîhe	cent, cents (in particle compounds) (**nekoti-mêshkwâpehkîhe** one cent)
mêshkwâshakwêha, mêshkwâshekwêha	red sucker
mêshkwihkenôha	bedbug
mêshkwitepâta (**masahkwêha**)	red-headed woodpecker
mêtâsôpita (participle)	the President, the United States Government
mêtenôshki	easy, easily; huge (particle, preverb)
mêyâwosêha (only possessed):	**omêyâwosêhemwâwani** the leader of their warparty
mêyôwisekini (plural participle)	wailing songs
mîchikwâmwa	soils one's bed
mîchinêwa, mîchitamwa	defecates on s.o., it
mîchipêha	game animal or game bird
mîchipêhi	game (animals, collective)
mîchipêhiwa	is a game animal
mîchiwa (**mîchîhiwa** dimin.)	eats it (compare **amwêwa**)
mîchiweni (**mîchiwâhi** dimin.)	food
mîhkawihetîwaki (plural)	they meet and become friends, strike up a friendship
mîhkechêwîha	worker, hired hand, employee
mîhkechêwîwa	works
mîhkechêwîweni	work
mîhkechihâwa	patient (of a doctor)
mîhkechihêwa	doctors s.o.
mîhkechihiwêwa	doctors people
mîhkechihtâkêwa	doctors (s.o.) for people
mîhkemâsowa	she is courted
mîhkemehkwêwêwa	he courts a woman
mîhkemehkwêwêwitêhêwa	he thinks of courting women
mîhkemetîwa	courts or is courted, makes out (also **mîhketîwa**)

mîhkemêwa, mîhketamwa	works at s.o., it; courts s.o.; picks it; mines it
mîhkemêwitêhêwa	thinks of courting (s.o.)
mîhketamawêwa	he courts (her) of s.o.
mîhketîwaki (plural)	they court (for marriage)
mîhketîweni	courtship
mîhketîwênemêwa	he thinks of her for courtship
mîhketîwi	in a courting way (preverb), of courting (prenoun)
mîhketîwitêhêwa	he thinks of courting
mîhkônamwa	happens to get it
mîhkôshkawêwa	catches s.o. eating, arrives while s.o. is eating
mîhkôwêwa	says the appropriate thing, says just the right thing
mîhkwênemêwa (1) (Jones)	dotes on s.o.
mîhkwênemêwa (2), **mîhkwênetamwa**	(with negative): has no particular care for s.o., it
mîhkwênetâha:	(see **pwâwi-mîhkwênetâha**)
mîhkwi	happen to (by chance)
mîhkwihêwa, mîhkwihtôwa	happens to get, make, pick out the particular one of s.o., it
mîhkwinawêhêwa	reminds s.o., makes s.o. remember, put s.o. in mind of someone
mîhkwinawêhtâkêwa	makes (s.o.) mindful for people
mîhtamênemêwa	vexes s.o. by thought, is vexed thinking about s.o. (archaic)
mîhtamimêwa	vexes s.o. greatly with words (archaic)
mîka	mink
mîkânêwa (Jones, one example)	fights s.o. (probably not a genuine Meskwaki word)
mîkâtîhêwa, mîkâtîhtôwa	fights s.o., it
mîkâtîhetîwaki (plural)	they fight each other
mîkâtîwa	fights, engages in mortal combat; fights (s.o.)
mîkâtîweni	fighting, mortal combat
mîkâtîwi	of war (prenoun, preverb)
mîkesa	wampum bead (Jones: "cowrie shell")
mîkesâtepêwa	has wampum in one's hair
mîkesêtepêwa	has wampum in one's hair
mîkesiwiwi	it is decorated with wampum
mîkona (**mîkonêha** dimin.)	feather (especially, long feather from wing or tail)
mîkoni-mâkwayi	feather headdress; warbonnet
mîkoniwihtôwa	puts feathers on it
mîkoniwiwa, mîkoniwiwi	(animate, inanimate) is feathered
mîkwanôha	baby whose mother is about to have another baby (and is fussy)
mînâsowa	is given (it)
mînâwâpamêwa, mînâwâpatamwa	examines s.o., it visually; notices s.o., it (also **mamînâwâpamêwa**)
mînâwâpiwa	looks closely, takes a hard look
mînâwênemêwa, mînâwênetamwa	thinks seriously of s.o., it; realizes about s.o., it
mînâwênetâkwatwi	it is thought of seriously, given close consideration
mînâwesiwa	inquires closely, examines things in detail, is attentive to detail (also **mamînâwesiwa**)
mînâwi	attentively, closely, in detail (particle, preverb) (also **mamînâwi**)
mînâwihêwa, mînâwihtôwa	examines s.o., it closely (also **mamînâwihêwa**)
mînâwinawêhêwa	makes s.o. pay close attention
mînâwitêhêwa	thinks intently, realizes
mînetîwaki (plural)	they give (it) to each other
mînêwa	gives (it) to s.o.
mîsâhkoni	moss, pond scum
mîsâhkoniwipehkwanêyâwi	its roof is covered with moss
mîsechêha	peach
mîsechêwa	has a hairy body
mîsechêyâhi	muskmelon

mîsenamwa	makes it fuzzy by handling
mîsetonâkani	mustache, beard (**atâmini-mîsetonâkanani** corn tassels)
mîsetonwa	has a mustache, beard
mîsimîsîha	Jerusalem artichoke
mîsîwa	defecates
mîsîwamatamwa	feels as if one is going to defecate
mîsôni	name; clan (Michelson: "gens") (**nîsôni** my name, **owîsôni** his or her name)
mîshâchi	for fun, to show off
mîshâchihchikêwêwa	decorates things with (it)
mîshâchihêwa, mîshâchihtôwa	dresses s.o. up; decorates it
mîshâchinâkêwa	sings for fun
mîshâchinâkwatwi	it is magnificent, gorgeous
mîshâchinâkwihowa	makes oneself look dressed up
mîshâchiyâkwatwi	it has a nice fragrance
mîshâchiyâkwihowa	makes oneself smell nice
mîshâchîhtawêwa	shows off to s.o., gets all dressed up for s.o.
mîshâmêhi	small sacred bundle, minor sacred bundle
mîshâmi	sacred bundle, sacred pack, medicine bundle, "misham"
mîshâmiwi or **mîshâmiwiwi**	it is a sacred bundle
mîshâmiyâkwatwi	it smells of urine
mîshâtenowa	puts on one's best clothes, shows oneself off
mîshâtesiwa	dresses up
mîshâtesiweni (**mîshâtesiwâhi** dimin.)	finery, fancy clothes
mîshâtênemowa	is proud, glad
mîshâtênemômikatwi	it is proud, glad
mîshâtênemwihêwa, mîshâtênemwihtôwa	makes s.o., it glad
mîshehkwayi, owîshehkwayi	a scalp (**nîshehkwayi** my scalp; **owîshehkwayi, omîshehkwayi** his scalp; **nenoswi-owîshehkwayi** buffalo head [buffalo skull used in ceremony])
mîshêhiwa	puts on one's fancy clothes (archaic)
mîshikwâkani	a pubic hair (**omîshikwâkanani** his or her pubic hair)
mîshimishi	white oak, bur oak
mîshimotêhi, mîshimôhi, omîshimôhi	paunch (of ruminant's stomach), rumen
mîshinehkêwa:	**mâmîshinehkêwa** has hairy arms
mîshishehkîtamwa	wears fur clothing
mîshiwêwa	gives (it) away
mîshîkwêwa	is hairy-faced, has a beard
mîshkawesiwa, mîshkawâwi	is strong, has great power or ability; it is strong
mîshkawi	powerfully, forcefully, strongly (preverb)
mîshkawinâkwatwi	it looks strong
mîshkota	on top of that, what's more, what's worse (particle)
mîtwîwa	cottonwood; quaking aspen
mîtwîwiwa	is a cottonwood
mîwahônêwa	drags s.o. away
mîwahwêwa	pushes s.o. aside with something
mîwashiweni	pack, bundle carried on the back (also **wîwashiweni**)
mîwawisetôwa	washes it away
mîwâsetôwa	blows it away, fans it away
mîwâshinwa	he is blown away
mîwenamawêwa	removes (it) for s.o.
mîwenêwa, mîwenamwa	removes s.o., excludes s.o., discharges s.o.; removes it
mîweshihwêwa	drives s.o. off, away

mîweshkamawêwa	kicks (it) out of s.o.
mîwênetamawêwa	drives (it) away for s.o. by thought
mîwihêwa	crowds s.o. out (as, a romantic rival)
mîwikâpâwa	stands aside
mîwinawîwa	slides away, moves off
mîwinehkênêwa	moves s.o.'s arm away
mîwisahêwa	casts s.o. away
mîwisahowa	jumps aside
mîwîhtamawêwa	stands aside from (it) for s.o., gives s.o. a chance
mîwîwa	walks away, moves away, moves out of the way
môhchi	even; but, anyway, in any case, at any rate (particle)
môhkahanwi	it is sunrise (**wêchi-môhkahaki** east)
môhkahwêwa, môhkahamwa	digs s.o., it up
môhkâshkêwa	shoots out of the water
môhkâyêniwa	bursts out laughing
môhkenêwa, môhkenamwa	brings or takes s.o., it out, takes s.o., it from a place of concealment or burial
môhkeshkêwa, môhkeshkêwi	(animate, inanimate) emerges, appears, becomes evident
môhkisêhowa	paddles out (of a stream)
môhkisêsenwi	it (as a path or trail) comes out
môhkisêwa	runs into view
môhkîhtawêwa	rushes out to attack s.o.
môhkîhtâkêwa	rushes out to attack people
môhkîwa	emerges, comes up to the surface
môhkomâna	(white) American; (loosely) white man
môhkomâni	American, Euro-American, of the white man (prenoun)
môhkomânihkwêwa	white (American) woman
môhkomânikâni	white man's house
môhkomâni-peshishkesa	domestic goose
môhkomâniwa, môhkomâniwiwa	is or becomes an American, a white person
mônahâkani	hoe (**chaki-mônahâkâhi** little hoe)
mônashkahikêwa	digs weeds
mônashkenamwa	pulls it (a plant) up by the roots
mônashkitepênêwa	pulls out s.o.'s hair
mônashkwêwa	pulls up grass, weeds
mônânêha	woodchuck (groundhog)
mônepyâni	waterhole in the ice
mônenamwa	weeds it
mônênemêwa	suspects s.o., thinks s.o. likely, thinks one knows about s.o.
mônêwa	plucks s.o. (a bird)
mônihkeshêhôni	fire poker
mônisêwêwa	plucks a bird or birds
môsêhkêwa	has a toothache (**nemôsêhka** I have a toothache)
môsênikwa	groundsquirrel
môsêwa	wood worm, borer
môswa	moose
môswênemêwa	is suspicious of s.o., suspects something bad of s.o.
môshaki	only, exclusively, no one else but, nothing else but (particle)
môshakihkwêwiwa	she lives without a man in the house
môshakîha	bachelor
môshihêwa, môshihtôwa	has a vision of s.o., it
môshitêhêwa	is suspicious, suspects something
môshîkwêhêwa	finds s.o. out by their expression
môshkahanwi	there is a flood, it is flooded

môshkahokowa	is threatened by high water, is flooded out
môshkakwisêwa, môshkakwisêwi	comes to the surface, (sun) comes out from behind a cloud; it comes to the surface
môshkâpowêwa	adds (it as) water to the cooking
môshkisikiwêshkêwa	bows one's spine
môshowa	gets a haircut
môshowâkani	pair of scissors
môshôni	scalp-lock
môshwêhi	shawl
môshwêwa	cuts s.o.'s hair
môtayi	bottle (**omôtayi** his or her bottle, **omôtâhêhi** dimin.)
môwechi	dung, excrement, piece of dung (plural **môwechêni**)
môwechiwâhkosiwa, môwechiwâhkwatwi	(animate, inanimate) is covered with excrement
môwechiwiwi	it is dungy
môwechiwiyâkosiwa, môwechiwiyâkwatwi	(animate, inanimate) smells of dung
môwechîhkêha	dung beetle
môwesiwa, môwâwi	(animate, inanimate) is soiled
myâhkenawêwa	cripples s.o. by shot
myâhkesiwa	is crippled
myâhkesowa	is crippled by gunshot
myâhkeshkawêwa	cripples s.o. by foot or body
myâhkihêwa	wounds s.o., injures s.o.
myâhkosêwa	limps
myâhpamêwa, myâhpetamwa	dislikes the taste of s.o., it
myâhpechikêwa	dislikes the taste of what one is eating
myâhpokosiwa, myâhpokwatwi	(animate, inanimate) tastes bad
myânanahamîwa	one's step falters
myânahîwa	catfish (also **myânamêkwa**)
myânahokowa	is made to feel bad (by something said)
myânahônêwa	obtains mercy from s.o., persuades s.o. to take pity on one
myânamêkwa	catfish (also **myânahîwa**)
myânaw-	(see also **myânow-**)
myânawamatamwa	is overcome by pain (in it)
myânawitêhêmêwa	gets the best of s.o. by talking
myânâchimohêwa	gives s.o. bad news, a bad report
myânâhpawêwa	has a bad dream
myânâhpenanêwa	ill-treats s.o.
myânâhpenêwa	is ill, has a disease or affliction
myânâkômêwa, myânâkôtamwa	dislikes s.o., it; is not comfortable with s.o., it
myânâshkêwi	it does not go well
myânâshohwêwa	is a bad shot with a bow or gun
myânehkêwa	craves meat (**nemyânehka** I crave meat)
myânehtawêwa	does not like what one hears s.o. say
myânekêwa	dances poorly
myânenawêwa	injures s.o. by shot
myânesiwa, myânetwi	is bad, ugly; it is bad, wrong
myâneshkawêwa:	**myâneshkâkwiwa** it gives one indigestion, does not agree with one
myânênemêwa, myânênetamwa	dislikes s.o., it, does not like s.o., it; feels or becomes angry (over it), is dissatisfied (over it)
myânowâpamêwa, myânawâpamêwa	stares s.o. down, overpowers s.o. by staring
myânowehtawêwa	feels sorry for s.o., hearing them
myânowesiwa	is overcome, cannot cope
myânowêwa	speaks crossly

myânowihêwa, myânawihêwa	overcomes s.o.
myânowihtôwa, myânawihtôwa	prevails, overcomes ones opponent
myânôtêwa	she menstruates, she is in her period
myânôtêkâni	menstrual lodge
myâshawiwa	is bad, mean; acts badly, does wrong
myâshêwîwa	does the wrong thing, does the work poorly
myâshi	ill, badly; sort of (preverb)
myâshihêwa	eats up s.o.'s food
myâshihtôwa	makes it bad, makes it badly
myâshikahesêwa	does not chop the firewood right
myâshikiwa, myâshikenwi	(animate, inanimate) is bad, ill-formed, not right, bodes ill
myâshimêwa	speaks crossly to s.o.
myâshinawêhêwa	makes s.o. feel bad
myâshinawêmêwa	makes s.o. feel bad by speech
myâshinâkosiwa	looks ugly
myâshi-pemâtesiwa	feels bad, is in bad health
myâshipenanêwa, myâshipenatôwa	treats s.o. badly, does not treat s.o. right, does harm to s.o., it
myâshisêwi	it is, becomes dull
myâshishehkîtamwa	wears shabby clothing
myâshishinwa, myâshisenwi	lies uncomfortably, it (as, a song) is bad; (animate, inanimate) spoils, goes bad
myâshitanêwa	mistreats s.o.
myâshitêhêwa	feels bad (about something), feels sad
myâshiyâmêwa, myâshiyâtamwa	smells s.o., it as bad
myâshiyâkosiwa, myâshiyâkwatwi	(animate, inanimate) smells bad
myâshîkwêwa	has bad eyesight, cannot see well
myêhkawêwa	makes a road for s.o.
myêwi	road, path (**myêki** on the road; **nemyêmi** my road)
myêwiwi	it is a road

n

nahanâmowa	is able to breathe
nahatamwa	likes to eat it, likes it
nahâkanihkwêwa	daughter-in-law living with her in-laws
nahâkanihkwêwiwa	she lives with her in-laws
nahâkapiwa	he lives with his in-laws
nahânaketonêmowa	is an accomplished speaker
nahâtesiwa	recovers, gets well, feels better, acts normal
nahâwinwi	it is warm weather, a warm day
nahehkwêpiwa	is able to sit up
nahesêhkwêwa (nahesêhkwêhiwa dimin.)	knows how to cook
nahetonêmowa (nahetonêmôhiwa dimin.)	knows how to talk
nahêka	in a low tone, quietly, slowly (particle)
nahêkashe	quietly, slowly (particle)
nahênemêwa, nahênetamwa	thinks s.o., it fit
nahênetamawêwa	thinks (s.o., it) fit for, of s.o.
nahêwîwa	is a good hand at the job, works skillfully
nahi (1)	know how to, used to, subject to, given to, keep, frequently (preverb)
nahi (2)	(with negative): never (preverb)
nahi! (3)	Well, Hey, Listen (to get attention or give an order)

='nahi	(see =**înahi**)
nahichimêwa	knows how to swim
nahihêwa, nahihtôwa	knows how to make s.o., it
nahikenwi	it is proper
nahikwamwa	knows how to sew it
nahikwâsowa (**nahikwâsôhiwa** dimin.)	knows how to sew
nahinawêmêwa	makes s.o. feel good by speech
nahinâkêwa	knows how to sing
nahipahowa	is able to run
nahipanîwa	knows how to weave
nahisenyêwa	knows how to eat
nahisetwêwa	puts (it) away (as, a store of food) (**êh**=**nahisetwâchi** he or she put (it) away)
nahishimêwa, nahisetôwa	puts s.o., it away
nahitêhêwa	recovers one's composure, feels good again
nahîhkânowa	knows how to work, knows how to make things
nahîhtêwa	knows how to do work
nahîwesiwa	knows how, knows how to do things, does it right, is clever
nahkani	for the duration of (preparticle or stem component) (also **nehkani, ahkani**)
nahkochênamwa	gets one's hand on it
nahkohamawêwa (1)	hits (it) back to s.o.
nahkohamawêwa (2)	assists s.o. in singing
nahkohwêwa	stops s.o. with a blow
nahkokêwa, nahkowêwa	she "hums" along (singing a ceremonial song with closed mouth)
nahkomêwa, nahkotamwa	agrees with s.o., it; answers s.o., it affirmatively
nahkonamawêwa	takes (it) in one's hand, accepts (it), catches (it) for s.o.
nahkonâtêwi	it is accepted
nahkonêwa, nahkonamwa	takes s.o., it in one's hand; accepts s.o., it; catches s.o., it
nahkotîwaki (plural)	they answer each other
nahkowêwa	(see **nahkokêwa**)
nahkwamêwa	takes s.o. in one's mouth, accepts s.o. (as, a pipe)
nahkwamôchikani	fishhook, fishing tackle
nahkwamônêwa	catches s.o. (fish) with a hook and line
nahkwamôtawêwa	fishes for s.o. (fish)
nahkwamôtôwa	fishes, goes fishing
nahkwâhpetamawêwa	eats (it, ceremonial offering) for s.o. (spirit) receiving a blessing
nahkwâhpetamâkêwa	eats (it) for the spirits receiving a blessing
nahkwâhpetamwa	eats it and receives a blessing
nahkwâpamêwa	sees s.o. right off
nahkwâpatâniwa	is easily noticed, is readily seen
nahkwi	as one gets there, each as they come (as, in serving guests), catching on to each (song) as it is sung (preverb)
nahkwinechênêwa	grabs s.o.'s hand
nahkwinehkênêwa	grabs s.o.'s arm
nahkwitêhamêwa, nahkwitêhêmêwa	readily accepts s.o.'s opinion, wish, or blessing
nahmeko	right then and there (particle)
nahosêwa	is able to walk
nahowêwa	is able to talk, is clever at speaking or talking, says a clever thing
nahômekowa, nahômekwiwa	knows how to ride a horse
nahpamêwa, nahpatamwa	eats s.o., it in one's food (disregarding or unaware)
nahpamônêwa	poisons s.o.'s food
nahpawisenwi	it soaked through, is soaking wet
nahpawishimêwa	gets s.o. soaking wet

nahpenâsowa, nehpenâsowa	is a stepchild
nahpenêwa	has s.o. as a stepchild (**nêhpenita** my step-parent)
nah=penani!	Wait up! Hang on!
nahpi	at the same time (preverb)
nah=wêna!	Go ahead then, Alright then
nakachi	get used to (preverb)
nakachihêwa	trains s.o. (an animal) to follow commands
nakahkawikiwa	is ugly, is a weird creature
nakahkawinâkosiwa	is bizarrely deformed
nakamowa	sings
nakamôni	song, ceremonial song
nakamôniwiwi	it is a song
nakamwihêwa, nakamwihtôwa	sings over s.o., it
nakamwihtawêwa	sings for s.o.
nakanêwa, nakatamwa	leaves s.o., it
nakapehkwêsahowa	ducks one's head down
nakapehkwêsêwa	lowers one's head
nakapeshkêwa	bends one's body over forward
nakashkipahowa	runs bent forward
nakatamawêwa	leaves (it) for s.o.
nakâmowa	stops in flight
nakenêwa, nakenamwa	stops s.o. (as, to talk to a woman), it
nakeshkêwa	stops walking, stops changing
nakikâpâwa	stops and stands
nakimêwa	stops s.o. by speaking
nakinotawêwa	stops for or because of s.o.
nakipahowa	stops in one's run
nakisêwa, nakisêwi	stops running; (animate, inanimate) halts suddenly
nakishinwa	stops, halts
nakishkawêwa	meets s.o., goes to meet s.o.
nakishkâtîwaki (plural)	they meet each other
nakîmikatwi	it stops
nakîwa	stops
nakwâhtakwi	missing one's sharing of food (ritual)
nakyâwi	(with negative): **âkwi nakyâkini** there was no pause, hesitation, holding back
namâne	it is strange, unparalleled, unprecedented (particle)
namânike	it is strange, unprecedented (that) (particle)
namêsiwa, namêsiwiwa (archaic)	is a fish (also **nemêsiwa**, **nemêsiwiwa**)
namêwa	sturgeon (also **nemêwa**)
nanaîhta, nanaîhtâwi	it just so happens that, unexpectedly
nanakâchimowa	(with negative): does not hesitate to tell
nanakesiwa	(with negative): hesitates at nothing, does not hesitate to do anything, will do just anything
nanakîwa	keeps stopping (while walking)
nanakotêki	in the center of the lodge (particle)
nanakowêwa	(with negative): does not hesitate to say anything, will say just anything
nanakwi	in between (particle, preparticle)
nanakwishinwa:	**êh=nanakwishinowâchi** between them as they lay
nanakwitenyêwa:	**êh=nanakwitenyêchi** between his or her shoulders
nanakwiwine	between the horns (particle)
nanakwi-wahkwiye	in mid-sky (particle compound) (song word; shape uncertain)
nanakwîkwêwa:	**êh=nanakwîkwêchi** in the middle of one's face, right in one's face

nanamahkwêwi	it roars, there is a roar
nanawahkwi	in the middle of the sky (particle) (song word)
nanawapenêhtôwa:	**nanawapenêhtôwa owîyawi** makes oneself hungry in vain
nanawashkote	in the middle of the prairie (particle)
nanawâtâyêniwa	snickers, chuckles, laughs to oneself
nanawâtesiwa	he is useless as a hunter, never kills anything
nanawêhkami, nanawêhkamiki	in or to a remote area (particle)
nanawênemêwa	wastes one's thoughts on s.o.
nanawêyâhkopyêyâwi	the water extends way out into the forest
nanawi	off in some isolated place; in vain, uselessly, for nothing (particle)
nanawitanekowa	one's work or effort is for naught
nanayêna	in various places, in various directions (particle)
nanâhahkanêwa, nanâhahkatôwa	sets, fixes s.o., it (as, into the ground) to stand; hangs s.o. (kettle), it (water) over the fire
nanâhahtôwa	puts it in place
nanâhakônêwa, nanâhakôtôwa	hangs s.o. (as, a kettle), it in place
nanâhapinêwa, nanâhapitôwa	ties s.o., it up
nanâhapisowa	girds oneself; puts on one's skirt
nanâhapitawêwa	ties (it) for s.o.
nanâhapiwa	seats oneself
nanâhapîhtawêwa	takes a seat by s.o.
nanâhawiwa	makes ready, gets (oneself) ready (as, to travel), prepares
nanâhâhkonamwa	arranges it
nanâhâhkwisetôwa	set it (as, a log) in position
nanâhâkwanêwa, nanâhâkwatôwa	lays s.o., it in position
nanâhâkwapiwaki (plural)	they seat themselves in a group or in groups
nanâhâmehkisetawêwa	arranges (it) as earth for s.o.
nanâhâpyênamwa	gets it ready to tie it, loops it
nanâhenêwa, nanâhenamwa	attends to s.o., it; grabs hold of s.o., it; releases (deceased relative) by holding a ceremonial adoption
nanâhenikawêwa	fixes the bedding for s.o.
nanâhenikêwa	fixes the bedding
nanâhenowa	fixes oneself up
nanâheswêwa, nanâhesamwa	attends to s.o.'s, its cooking, prepares s.o., it (by cooking)
nanâhesêhkwêwa	attends to one's cooking
nanâhesikêwa	attends to the cooking
nanâheshkahêwa	dresses s.o.
nanâheshkamwa	dons it
nanâheshkawêwa	he positions himself on her (for intercourse)
nanâhênemêwa, nanâhênetamwa	tends, controls, takes charge of s.o., it; does as one sees fit with s.o., settles things for s.o.; is in control
nanâhêwîwa	attends to things, prepares
nanâhi (1)	get set or ready to, get set or ready by, try to, start to (preverb)
nanâhi (2)	(idiom; for example, with first person subject): I should not have; I regret; why did I? (preverb)
nanâhikâpâwa	takes one's position (in line, etc.), sets one's feet in position
nanâhimêwa	tells s.o. what to do, advises s.o., gives s.o. instructions; discusses, considers, judges s.o. (see **nanâhotamwa**)
nanâhinawîwa	gets ready
nanâhinâkosiwa	is looking better
nanâhinechâmêwa, nanâhinechâtamwa	takes care of s.o., it
nanâhisahowa	drops down, flops down, jumps into bed
nanâhishimêwa, nanâhisetôwa	lays s.o., it in place

nanâhishinwa	lies down, goes to bed
nanâhishitîwaki (plural)	they lay each other to rest
nanâhitêhênêwa	directs s.o.'s thoughts
nanâhiwanehkawêwa	arranges s.o.'s back-load for them
nanâhiwenêwa	guides s.o.
nanâhîhkamawêwa	attends to (it) for s.o., arranges things for s.o.
nanâhîhkamâkêwa	attends to (it) for people
nanâhîhkawêwa, nanâhîhkamwa	attends to s.o., it; holds an adoption feast for s.o. (deceased)
nanâhîhkâsowa	is attended to; an adoption feast is held for one (deceased)
nanâhîhkâtisowa	attends to oneself, takes care of oneself
nanâhîhtêwa	gets dressed (**nanâhîhtâno** get dressed!)
nanâhîhtêhêwa	gets s.o. dressed
nanâhîkwênowa	fixes oneself up, attends to one's face
nanâhkawâchimowa	says something negative or hostile, says something in rebuttal
nanâhkawesiweni	witchcraft
nanâhkawi	wickedly, meanly (preverb)
nanâhkawitêhêwa	has bad feelings, a bad feeling; has evil thoughts or intent
nanâhkomêwa	talks back to s.o.
nanâhkonêwa	fights back against s.o., defends oneself against s.o.
nanâhkwîwa	fights back, defends oneself
nanâhotamwa	talks it over, decides it by deliberation; directs it, manages it (as, a ceremony or activity); is in charge, gives the orders (see **nanâhimêwa**)
nanâhotâtêwi	it is arranged or decided by discussion
nanâhowêwa	gives instructions, directs others; discusses the question
nanâhônakapiwa	sits down inside (as, a canoe)
nanâhônakisetâsowa	loads a canoe (or the like)
nanâhônakishimêwa	puts s.o. in a box or canoe
nanâhpamêwa	keeps eating them (animate) in one's food (disregarding them)
nanâhpi	along with that, also at the same time (particle, preverb)
nanâhpinohtawêwa	repeats what s.o. says, mocks s.o. by imitating
nanânehtawêwa	follows and understands what s.o. says
nanânikâpyêshwêwa	cuts s.o. (as, fat, meat) into small strips
nanânishkwihpikêshkêwa	one's ribs slip out of joint
nanânishkwinehkêwa	pulls one's hands loose
nanânishkwisêwani (plural)	they (inanimate) slip out of their attachment
nanâsitâpihkanênêwa	pulls s.o.'s jaws apart
nanâshenêwa	strokes s.o. (repeatedly) on the head, shoulder
nanâshi	(with negative): never (particle)
nanâtahkwênemêwa	holds a grudge against s.o., harbors ill feelings toward s.o.
nanâtochêhwêwa, nanâtochêhamwa	feels around for s.o., it (as, with a stick), strikes blindly at s.o., it
nanâtochênêwa	feels around for s.o.
nanâtochêshkamâtisowa	tries to get hold of (it) for oneself by foot
nanâtohkwihêwa, nanâtahkwihêwa	picks on s.o., picks a fight with s.o.
nanâtohtawêwa	asks s.o. (a question)
nanâtohtâtîwaki (plural)	they ask each other
nanâtomêwa	asks after s.o., asks questions about s.o.
nanâtoshêwa	asks
nanâtwêwêmêwa, nanâtwêwêtamwa	wails for s.o., it; tries to make s.o. come by calling or wailing
nanâtwiyêwa	sniffs at an odor, takes a whiff
naneshiwi	terrific; awful (particle) (also **ananeshiwi, aneneshiwi, neneshiwi**)
nanôchi (1)	persisting to the end, not quit until (preverb)
nanôchi (2)	up to this time, finally, eventually (particle)
nanôchimêwa	says something bad about s.o. that is false

nanônemi	on the quiet, without saying anything (particle)
nanôpehka	a great deal, many, considerable, very (particle)
nanôpehkâchi	extensively (particle)
nanôpehkâchinâhi	a great distance, a long period of time (particle)
nanôshkwe	at random, without knowing if it would be correct or effective, without knowing what it is (particle)
nanôshkwêhiwa	acts at random
nanôshkwipokôtêwi (Jones)	it drifts about at random
nanôtênemêwa	has the wrong idea about s.o.
napahki	the very idea of it! the idea (that)! (particle)
nasahtêwa	releases the bow, pulls the trigger
nasahtêwi	it (as, a house) is deserted, there are no people about
nasahtêwinâkwatwi	it (as, a house) looks deserted
nasatâwi	crossly, grumpily, standoffishly (particle, preverb)
nasatâwikenwi	it is fierce, wild, cruel
nasatâwinohkatawêwa	acts crossly toward him
nasatâwîneniwiwa	is ill-natured
nasawanahkesiwa:	**êhkwinasawanahkesiyani** as far as your crotch
nasawapêpiwa	sits with thighs astraddle
nasawapiwa	sits astride
nasawâwi	it (as, a river) forks (**êh=nasawâki** where it forks or they fork)
nasawikiwa, nasawikenwi	is forked (**wêchi-nasawikichi, êh=nasawikichi** in one's crotch); it (as, a tree) is forked (**êh=nasawikeniki** in the fork of a tree)
nasawisenwi	it (as, a road) forks, has a fork
nasâhkohikani	roasting stick (set in the ground)
nasâhkohikêwa	roasts on a roasting stick
nasâhkohwêwa, nasâhkohamwa	roasts s.o., it on a roasting stick set in the ground
nasenamwa	breaks through it (as, poking through cloth, breaking up a small dam to let water flow out); pulls its trigger
nasikani	roasting stick; roasting stick of meat (archaic)
nashawaye (nashawe=)	long ago (**nashawêmêhi** dimin.) (particle) (also **anashawaye, ashawaye**)
nashawêhkamiki	long ago (particle) (also **ashawêhkamiki**)
natawâchi	might as well, resolving accordingly; without further ado (particle)
natawâhtôwa	reconnoiters it; reconnoiters, scouts (**nêtawâhtôta** a scout)
natawâpamêwa, natawâpatamwa	looks for s.o., it
natawâpiwa	tries to see
natawâpiweni	vision, eyesight
natawênemêwa, natawênetamwa	wants s.o., it; seeks to know about, remember, find, get s.o., it; expects s.o. to come
natawênetamawêwa	wants (it) for s.o.
natawênetamâtisowa	wants (it) for oneself
natawênetâkosiwa	is sought
natawi	seek to, try to, expect to, plan to; it is time to (preverb)
natawihêwa	tries to get s.o. (to), sounds s.o. out (for something)
natawimêwa	tries to persuade s.o. (to)
natâhamwa	stirs it up
natâshêwêhamwa	stirs the coals of the fire
natâshkêwaki (plural)	they (all) mill around
natâwosêwaki (plural)	they (all) walk around switching places
natâyâpôhamwa	stirs it (as, medicine) together
natâyâwi	there is a milling around
natochêhwêwa, natochêhamwa	pokes around searching for s.o., it, pokes around in it
natochênikêwa	tries to find or get hold of something by hand, rummages around

natochêshkamwa	seeks to come to it
natokwawêwa	seeks to dream of s.o., seeks s.o. in a dream
natomâsowa	is asked to come
natomêwa, natotamwa	asks for s.o., it; asks for s.o. to come, calls, summons, invites s.o.
natomêweniwiwa	is invited
natonamawêwa	looks for lice on s.o.
natonehkwêwêwa	he seeks a woman
natonêhamawêwa	seeks (it) for s.o.
natonêhwêwa, natonêhamwa	seeks s.o., it
natopanihkatawêwa	goes on the war-path against s.o.
natopaniwa	goes on the war-path
natopaniwenahkiwiwi	a warparty is organized to go out
natotamawêwa	asks for (it) from s.o.
natotâsêwa	prays to s.o., begs from s.o.; prays to s.o. for (it), begs for (it) from s.o. (**natotâshiyane** if you pray to me for it)
natotâsetîwaki (plural)	they beg each other
natotâsikawêwa	begs of s.o.
natotâsowa	begs, prays
natotîwaki (plural)	they invite each other
natwihkawêhêwa	looks for s.o.'s tracks
natwipahwânêwa	runs to look for s.o.
natwipekwêhamwa	pokes through the ashes searching for it
nawachi	first, before going on, having a brief opportunity (particle, preverb); wait a moment! (particle)
nawachisahêwa (Jones)	grabs s.o. on the way
nawachisêwa	grabs (it) on the run
nawahpowa	takes food for the journey
nawahpwâhêwa	sends food with s.o.
nawasehkawêwa	comes by and asks s.o. along
nawasohkyêwa	outruns people, wins the race
nawaswêwa	outruns s.o.
nawatenêwa, nawatenamwa	picks s.o., it up on the way by
nawêni	pretty, handsome (prenoun) (archaic **ênowêni**)
nawênihkwêhêha	pretty young woman
nawênihkwêhêhiwa	she is a pretty young woman
nawêni-kwîyesêhêhiwa	he is a handsome boy
nawêni-nenîhêha	a handsome man
nawêni-nenîhêhiwa	he is a handsome man
nawihetîwaki (plural)	they visit each other
nawihêwa	visits s.o.
nawôtêwêwa	visits and gets a meal
nayênenwi	one's own (particle)
nâchinehkawêwa	chases, drives, or herds s.o. back, home
nâchinêhwêwa, nâchinêhamwa	buys s.o., it; ransoms s.o.
nâchinêhikêwa	buys (it)
nâchinêhotisowa	buys one's own life, buys one's own release
nâchipahônêwa, nâchipahôtôwa	runs after s.o., it; runs to get s.o., it
nâchiyâmêwa, nâchiyâtamwa	seek out s.o., it by smell, follows the odor of s.o., it
nâchiyêwa	follows an odor, is attracted by an odor
nâchîhiwêwa	goes to seek refuge
nâhinâhi	(at) the time, distance; (it is) the first time (particle)
nâhka (also **nâhkachi**)	also, and, again; in turn, as well (as another instance), this time
nâhka=kêhi	one after another, different (ones, places, ways) successively

nâhkatahônêwa	strands s.o., leaves s.o. behind when departing by boat
nâhkateshimêwa, nâhkateshitamwa	abandons s.o., it in flight (also **âhkateshitamwa**)
nâhtasenwi	several times, a few times (particle)
nâhtasokonakatwi	it is several days
nâhtasokonakatôhiwi	it is a few days (dimin.)
nâhtasokonêtwa	is away for a few days
nâhtasokoni	several days (particle)
nâhtaswawahîme, nâhtaswawahîmêhe	several years (particle)
nâhtaswi	several, a few (particle)
nâhtaswikamiki	several households (particle)
nâhtashiwaki (plural)	there's several of them, a small number of them
nâkanêwa, nâkatamwa	follows s.o., it, trails s.o., follows s.o.'s tracks
nâkasawâpamêwa, nâkasawâpatamwa	keeps one's eye on s.o., it; keeps one's eye on where s.o., it goes
nâkatawênemêwa, nâkatawênetamwa	keeps s.o., it in mind, keeps track of s.o., it, watches s.o., it, pays close attention to it
nâkatawênetisowa	watches oneself, watches out for oneself
nâkatawênechikêwa	watches over things, keeps track of things
nâkatawênekêmowa	watches over, keeps track
nâkatôhowa	paddles along (it)
nâkatônehkawêwa	chases s.o. along (it)
nâkatôsêwa	runs following (s.o., it)
nâkatôwâmowa, nâkatôyâmowa	flees following along (it)
nâkosiwa	shows up, appears or is seen in public
nâkwêwa	leaves, goes away, goes on, goes back, sets out, heads out (**nenâkwa** I —)
nâmahkamiki	underground, under the earth, in the underworld (particle)
nâmahkîki (**nâmahkîmêhi** dimin.)	underground, under the earth, down in the ground (particle)
nâmanasite	on the sole of the foot or feet (particle)
nâmatâsîha	fetus
nâmâkone, nâmakône	under the snow (particle)
nâmânaki	inside the hole, cave (particle)
nâmeche	in the belly (stomach or womb) (particle)
nâmeki	inside, underneath (particle)
nâmepyêki (also **nâmâpyêki**)	under the water (**nâmepyêkîmêhi** dimin.) (particle)
nâmêyâhkwe	in the forest, through the forest (particle)
nâmêyâhkwisâha	large forest-dwelling hawk (probably goshawk)
nâmi	under (preparticle)
nâminawâkani	innards, insides (**onâminawâkani** his or her insides)
nâminawe	within the body (particle)
nâminekwe	under the arm (particle)
nâmi-peshiwa	Great Lynx, Underwater Panther (also **peshipeshiwa**)
nâmitasane	under the platform (particle)
nâmi-tâhtapakwe	under a leaf (particle) (see **tâhtapakwi**)
nâmitêhe	in the heart, in one's heart (particle)
nâmôchi	down in one's heart, secretly (particle)
nânawasotîwaki (plural)	they race (each other)
nânawasotîhêwa	races s.o. (a horse), makes s.o. race
nânâkachi	exactly (particle)
nânânikâhiwa	is hopping (on one foot)
nânâpi	the same repeatedly or successively (particle)
nânekoti	one apiece, one by one (particle) (also **nênekoti**)
nânekotôhpwêwa	eats them (animate) one by one
nâneshkwêpochîhi	dart

nânêwa, nâtwa	goes after s.o., it; goes to get s.o., it
nânishkonamwa	slips it out, off, loose
nânishkwihkanêwa	outdistances s.o., leaves s.o. behind
nânîkihtôha	lazy person
nânîkihtôhitêhêwa	feels lazy, does not feel like doing anything
nânîkihtôhiwa	is lazy, never wants to do anything
nânîkinawêtîwaki:	**wîh=nânîkinawêtîkini** in a discouraging way, as if to discourage someone
nânîmêsahowa	jumps up and down; hops
nânîsikâpôhaki (plural)	split feathers (worn on head)
nânôchîha	tramp, bum, hobo
nânôhkatahwêwa	finishes s.o. off (as, with a club)
nânôhkatamwa	eats what was left uneaten on it (as, discarded bones)
nânôhkenawêwa	finishes s.o. off with a shot
nânôkechêha	water moccasin
nânômahamwa	makes it rock back and forth by hitting it
nânômasakîha	wren
nânômâsenwi (also **nanômâsenwi**)	it sways in the wind
nânômehkwêsêwa	shakes one's head
nânômeshkêwi	it sways, it rocks back and forth
nânômipahowa	jogs, runs along at an easy pace
nânôta	repeatedly too soon (particle)
nâpahkohkwawêwa	(deity) refills the kettle for s.o. (grants the killing of enemies in exchange for the ritual meal)
nâpanohwêwa	sticks (it) into s.o.'s mouth
nâpâchimowa	repeats what has been said by another; (spiritual intercessor) repeats people's prayers (to convey them to the deities)
nâpâshkahwâtamwa	lets it (an arrow) fly on the same trajectory (see next)
nâpâshkahwâtôwa	lets it (an arrow) fly on the same trajectory (see previous)
nâpehkwâni	ship, sailing vessel
nâpehkwênêwa	catches s.o. by the neck
nâpehkwêhwêwa	lassoes s.o. by the neck
nâpenêwa	is a replacement spouse for s.o. (after the death of their spouse)
nâpênemowa	regards (s.o.) as a replacement
nâpêshitêhêwa	has a gnawing suspicion
nâpi	better, instead, at least; the good thing is (that) (particle)
nâpihchîhaki (plural)	armbands
nâpikêwa	rebuilds in the same spot
nâpinêwa, nâpitôwa	has s.o., it tied around one's neck, wears s.o., it around one's neck
nâpisetawêwa	replaces (it) for s.o.
nâpishâmêwa	urinates on the same spot as s.o.
nâpishimêwa	makes s.o. a replacement
nâpishinwa	is a substitute or replacement (for s.o.), takes the place of (s.o.)
nâpishkamawêwa	takes s.o.'s place, stands in for s.o.
nâpitâhêwa	puts (it) around s.o.'s neck
nâpitâtêhi	necklace
nâpitâwêwa	wears a necklace, necklaces
nâpitâwâkani	necklace
nâpiwêna	why don't you, I, we; I think I'd better
nâpyêwêsêwa	gets one's strength back
nâsâpatamwa	keeps one's eye on it as one approaches it
nâsâwi	not enough to be satisfying (preverb)
nâsâwishimowa	one's voice is weak
nâsehkawêwa, nâsehkamwa	goes up to s.o., it

nâsehtawêwa	approaches s.o.'s sound
nâshâshkêwa	flies down, flies downward
nâshêkihikani	wooden hide-scraper (for softening a stretched hide)
nâshêkihikêwa	softens a hide with a wooden hide-scraper
nâshitepênêwa	strokes s.o.'s head (once)
nâshîkwênêwa	strokes s.o.'s face (once)
nâshîwa	goes down; becomes reduced in size
nâtahâpyêwa	he checks his traps
nâtawêwa	goes after (it) for s.o.
nâtawihowa	doctors oneself
nâtawinônahwêwa	uses medicine on s.o. (to cast a spell)
nâtawinôni	medicine
nâtâhkwêshinwa	seeks help, goes after help
nâtâtisowa	goes after (it) for oneself
nâteswêwa	tries to make s.o. come by using medicine or burning tobacco
nâtômêwa, nâtôtamwa	goes to carry s.o., it on one's back
nâtwa	(see **nânêwa**)
nâtwêwêkahwêwa	makes s.o. come by drumming
nâwahkwêwi	it is noon (**wêchi-nâwahkwêki** south)
nâwakâme	in the middle of the stream or lake (particle)
nâwanonehkwêwêwa	pursues a woman or women
nâwanonêhwêwa	pursues s.o., goes following after s.o.
nâwanwâpamêwa	follows s.o. keeping them in sight
nâwashkote	in the fire (particle)
nâwênemêwa, nâwênetamwa	thinks s.o., it is inadequate; doesn't think much of s.o., it
nâwi	in the middle of (preparticle)
nâwi-nenoswahkiwe	in the middle of a herd of buffalo (particle compound)
nâwi-pekeshe	in the smoke (particle compound)
nâwi-pîkwashki	in the middle of thick weeds (particle compound)
nâwi-pîkwâwe	in the middle of a thicket (particle compound)
nâwi-sasakanwe	in the middle of a thicket (particle compound)
nâwisêwa	loses weight
nâwitepehkîwi	it is midnight
nâwîkwêhôni	cradle-board bow
nechêmôhi	my part (in hair)
nechîkwani	my knee (**ochîkwani** his or her knee; **mechîkwani** a knee)
nehchiwa	my upper arm
nehkani	for the duration of (preparticle or stem component) (also **ahkani, nahkani**)
nehkanipenâwe, nahkanipenâwe	all summer long (particle)
nehkanipepônwe, nahkanipepônwe	all winter long (particle)
nehkanitepehkwe, nahkanitepehkwe	all night long (particle)
nehkâchi	my foot (**nehkâtani** my feet; **ohkâchi, mehkâchi** a foot)
nehkâhki	my chest (**ohkâhkeki** on his or her chest)
nehkâpamêwa, nehkâpatamwa	watches s.o., it disappear from view
nehkâpatâniwa	disappears from view
nehkâshkêwa	falls out of sight
nehkenamawêwa	pushes (it) into s.o.
nehkenamwa	slips it out of sight
nehkepyêhtêwi	it soaks into what is cooking
nehkeshawêwa	goes out of sight shining
nehkeshkêwa	goes out of sight
nehketonwa	one's mouth goes out of sight
nehki	for {so} long a time, as long as {such time} (particle)

nehkiwani	my nose (**ohkiwani** his or her nose, beak; **mehkiwani** a nose)
nehkîwa	goes out of sight, (sun) sets
nehkonêhi	my blanket, robe (**mehkonêweni** blanket, robe)
nehkwêkani	my neck
nehkwêtamwa	one's voice grows faint as one moves away
nehkwêwêyâkêposowa	goes whizzing out of sight
nehtamawêwa	kills (s.o.) for, of s.o.
nehtamâkêwa	kills (s.o.) for, of people
nehtawakayi	my ear
nehtâhpi	my nape, the back of my neck (**ohtâhpeki** at his or her nape)
nehtâkyâwi	it is completely calm and quiet
nehtâwêwa	kills, makes a kill
nehtâwêmikatwi	it kills
nehtômapiwa	sits pensively, sits alone with one's thoughts
nekahkwani	my shin, my lower leg, my leg (**okahkwani** his or her shin; a shin)
nekakâchi-nesekwisa	my "teasing" aunt (my mother's brother's wife)
nekakâchi-nemeshôha	my "teasing" grandfather (my mother's mother's brother and the son of anyone I call this)
nekesowa, neketêwi	(snow, ice) melts; it (as, lard) melts
nekeshkêwa	(snow, ice) melts
nekîha	my maternal aunt, my mother's sister; my father's brother's wife; my mother's father's sister; my step-mother
nekohwêwa, nekohamwa	roasts s.o., it in ashes (also **nekwahwêwa, nekwahamwa**)
nekoshkamwa	covers it over by foot, kicks it over (as, tracks)
nekotahi	somewhere, anywhere; somewhere else; to some degree, about; (with negative): not in any way, not one of them (particle)
nekotawahîme, nekotawahîne	one year (particle)
nekotawahînakatwi	it is one year
nekotayakatwi (**nekotayakatôhiwi** dimin.)	it is one kind; it's the only one (of its kind), there is only one kind of it
nekotayaki	one group, set, pair, couple, kind (particle)
nekotenwi	once (particle)
nekotetone	one mouthful (of words) (particle)
nekoti (1)	one (particle, preparticle)
nekoti (2)	once and for good, once and for all, over and done with (preverb)
nekotihêwa, nekotihtôwa	has one of s.o., it
nekotikamiki	one household, one family (particle)
nekotinâkane	one bowlful (particle)
nekotinesiwe, nekotinîsiwe, nekotinîsiwi, nekotinesiwi (Jones)	eleven (particle) (also **metâswi-nekotinîsiwe** eleven)
nekotipenâwe	for one summer (particle)
nekotisetôwa	places one of it
nekoti-tepehkwe, nekotitepehkwe	for one night (particle compound or particle)
nekoti-wâsêyâwe	for one day, in one day (particle)
nekotîchishe	one inch (particle)
nekotîhiwa, nekotenôhiwi (diminutives)	(animate, inanimate) is one, there is (only) one
nekotokoni	one day (particle)
nekotôhkohkwe	one kettleful (particle)
nekotôhpôhiwa	eats alone (dimin.)
nekotôhpwâkane (**nekotôhpwâkâhe** dimin.)	one pipeful (particle)
nekotôkêwa	lives alone, lives by oneself
nekotôkôtêwi	it hangs singly
nekotwayaki (Jones)	one group (particle) (see **nekotayaki**)
nekotwâhkwe	one hundred (particle)

nekotwânahkwatwi	the sky is uniform; the sky is uniformly cloudless or overcast
nekotwâpyêki	one portion (particle)
nekotwâpyêkatwi	it is one portion
nekotwâshika	six (particle) (also **kotwâshika**)
nekotwâshikânameki	sixth, the sixth time (particle) (also **kotwâshikânameki**)
nekotwâshikâpitaki	sixty (particle)
nekotwêyawi	one of the two (particle)
nekôtêhi (**mekôtêweni** a dress)	my dress
nekwachihikêwa	hills, does hilling in the garden
nekwahwêwa, nekwahamwa	roasts s.o., it in ashes (also **nekohwêwa, nekohamwa**)
nekwâmehkahwêwa	buries s.o. in soil
nekwânahkwatwi	it is cloudy
nekwâpichikani	snare
nekwâpichikêwa	catches something in a trap, snare, spiderweb
nekwâpinêwa	snares s.o.
nekwâpisowa	is snared
nekwipekwêhamwa	puts it under ashes
nekwisa (**nekwisêha** dimin.)	my son (**okwisani** his or her son); (of a man) the son of my brother or anyone else I call "brother"; (of a woman) the son of my sister or anyone else I call "sister," or of my father's sister
nekya	my mother (**okyêni** his or her mother; **okiki** at his or her mother's, like his or her mother; **anêhe** Mother!)
nemachîninâki	left (side) (locative noun): **nemachîninâk=ochi** from the left (see **nenemachîneki**)
nemachîwa, nêmachîhiwa	is left-handed
nemahwêwa, nemahamwa	swings at s.o., it with something as if to strike
nemanêwa, nematôwa	sets s.o., it up
nemasohotîwaki (plural)	they have sex standing up
nemasowa, nematêwi	(animate, inanimate) stands
nemaswi	standing (preverb)
nemaswisenyêwa	eats standing up
nemaswisêwa	lands on one's feet
nematapiwa	sits upright
nemayâwîneki	on my right (locative noun)
nemenêwa, nemenamwa	motions towards s.o., it (with it) without striking; motions with it without striking
nemenamawêwa	motions towards s.o. with (it) without striking
nemesôtânaki (plural)	my parents (only plural)
nemeshôma	my father-in-law (**omeshômani** his or her father-in-law)
nemeshômesa, nemeshôha	my grandfather; my grandparent's brother
nemêhkwâni	wax; glue
nemêsa (archaic **namêsa**)	fish
nemêsiwa, nemêsiwiwa	is a fish
nemêsîha	minnow
nemêsiyâkwatwi	it smells like fish
nemêshâhema	my brother-in-law (of a man) (**omêshâhemani** his brother-in-law; **mêsha** brother-in-law!)
nemêwa	sturgeon (also **namêwa**)
nemisêha	my elder sister (**omisêhani** his or her elder sister); also applied to a father's brother's daughter and a mother's sister's daughter
nemisêwa	lunges, makes a quick, incomplete movement
nenakahkwi	the back of my mouth (**onakahkoki** in the back of one's mouth)
nenawêwa, nenamwa	recognizes s.o., it
nenâna	the calf of my leg (**onânani** his or her calf; **menâna** a calf)

nenâpêma	my husband
nenâtîwaki (plural)	they recognize each other
nenehkênemêwa, nenehkênetamwa	thinks of s.o., it, thinks about s.o., it
nenehkênetamawêwa	thinks about (it) for s.o.
nenehkênetamâtisowa	thinks about (it) for oneself
nenehkênetâkosiwa	is thought about
nenehkênetisowa	thinks about oneself
nenehkênetîwaki (plural)	they think about each other
nenehki	my hand (**menehki** a hand)
nenehkimêwa, nenehkotamwa	mentions s.o., it
nenehkinawêhêwa	makes s.o. mindful
nenehkinawêmêwa	makes s.o. mindful by speech; stirs up memories or feelings in s.o. by speech
nenehkitêhêwa	thinks
nenekapenôha	screech owl
nenekapisowa	trembles, is shaking
nenekashkahamwa	one's voice trembles
nenekâpihkanêshkêwa	one's jaw is quivering
nenekâpôshkêwi	its water trembles
nenekâpyêwa	has chills, shakes with fever (**nenenekâpya** I have chills)
nenekepyêyâwi	its water trembles
nenekesiwa	is trembling
nenekeshkêwi	it trembles, quakes
nenekikanêwa	shakes from weakness, becomes weak and shaky
nenekisêwi	it shakes, it (as, the earth) quakes
nenekishimowa	speaks with a quivering voice (as if about to cry)
nenekitêhêshkêwa	one's heart trembles
nenekwana	my son-in-law (**onekwanani** his or her son-in-law)
nenekwâha (older **nenekwanesa**)	my cross-nephew: (of a man) the son of my sister or anyone else I call "sister," or of my father's sister; (of a woman) the son of my brother or anyone else I call "brother"
nenekwêwêhikêwa	drums rapidly
nenekwîkani	my arm, my wing
nenekyêwêshkêwa	is trembling all over
nenemachîneki	on my left (**onemachîneki** on his or her left) (locative noun) (see **nemachîninâki**)
nenemehkiwa	thunderer, thunder being
nenemehkiwi-ashkotêwi	bolt of lightning
neneshiwi	terrific; awful (particle) (also **ananeshiwi, naneshiwi, aneneshiwi**)
neneshkenêwa, neneshkenamwa	spreads s.o. (as, a buckskin), it out
neneshkisahtôwa	throws it (as, a blanket) over a surface, spreads it with a flick of the wrists
neneshkisenwi	it lies spread out
neneshkishimêwa, neneshkisetôwa	spreads s.o., it out
neneshkoki	on my groin (locative noun only)
nenikosiwa, nenikwâwi	(animate, inanimate) is limber
neniwa (archaic **ineniwa**)	man; male human, guy, fellow
neniwawahîma	male (animal or bird)
neniwihêwa	makes him a man
neniwiwa	he is a man; he is a made warrior (**wêchi-neniwichi** what makes him a man, his penis) (also **ineniwiwa**)
nenîchânesa	my child; (of a man) the child of my brother or anyone else I call "brother"; (of a woman) the child of my sister or anyone else I call "sister," or of my father's sister (**nenîchânesêha** dimin.; **onîchânesani** his or her child, his brother's child, her sister's child)

nenochêhtamwa	perceives its taste
nenohpamêwa, nenohpetamwa	recognizes, makes out the taste of s.o., it
nenohtawêwa, nenohtamwa	understands s.o., it, believes s.o., it, hears s.o., it
nenohtâkosiwa, nenohtâkwatwi	(animate, inanimate) is heard
nenosohkêwa	hunts buffalo
nenosowiwa (also **nenoswiwa**)	is a buffalo
nenosôhêha	calf, buffalo calf
nenosômowa	bellows like a buffalo (also **nenoswimowa**)
nenoswa	buffalo (ceremonial, older usage); cow, ox, steer (archaic **inenoswa** and **anenoswa**)
-nenoswahkiwe	herd of buffalo (in a particle compound) (**nâwi-nenoswahkiwe** in the middle of a herd of buffalo)
nenoswahkiwi	herd of buffalo
nenoswayêyâpi	buffalo-hide rope
nenoswayi	buffalo-robe
nenoswekêwa	dances the Buffalo Dance
nenoswimowa	bellows like a buffalo (also **nenosômowa**)
nenoswiwa	is a buffalo (also **nenosowiwa**)
nenoshêwa	heeds, listens, obeys
nenowayi	my cheek (**onowayi** his or her cheek)
nenôkani	my hip
nenôtêwa	Indian (archaic **anenôtêwa**); person; Meskwaki
nenôtêwâtowêwa	speaks Meskwaki (literally, speaks Indian)
nenôtêwi	Indian, native, wild (prenoun, preverb) (archaic **anenôtêwi**)
nenôtêwi-ahpenya, nenôtêwi-ahpenîha	"Indian potato"
nenôtêwi-asêmâwa	Indian tobacco
nenôtêwi-meshîminêhi	crab apple
nenôtêwi-pehkiwêhi	wild cherry
nenôtêwiwa	is an Indian (archaic **anenôtêwiwa**)
nenôtêwîha	Indian tobacco (archaic **anenôtêwîha**)
nenwamatamwa	feels pain, feels it
nenwapenêwa	feels hunger
nenwâpatâniwa, nenwâpatâniwi	(with negative): is invisible, there is no visibility
nenwâpiwa	has eyesight, can see
nenwinâkosiwa, nenwinâkwatwi	the look on one's face says everything; how it is can be told by looking at it
nenwishinwa	(with negative): does not feel the pain
nenwiyâkosiwa, nenwiyâkwatwi	the odor of (animate, inanimate) is recognizable
nenwiyâmêwa, nenwiyâtamwa	recognizes the smell of s.o., it
nenwiyêwa	has a sense of smell, can smell
nenyêhpachiwa	is numb and weak from the cold
nenyêhpapiwa	is weak and has trouble moving from sitting too long
nenyêhpesiwa	is weak, has trouble moving or doing anything; is crippled
nenyêhpihêwa	makes s.o.'s limbs go weak
nenyêhpinehkêwachiwa	one's fingers are numb from the cold
nenyêhpishinwa	is weak and has trouble moving from lying too long
nenyêmasowa, nenyêmatêwi	stands there, is standing; it is standing there (see **nemasowa**)
nenyêmatôkanêpiwa	sits with one's knees up
nenyêmatôkanêshinwa	lies with one's knees up
nenyêshkwâsenwi	it blows in various directions
nenyêshkwâhkêwa	throws (it) in various directions
nenyêshkwi	in different or various directions (particle)
nepachikâwachiwa	has cold feet
nepachiwa	is cold

nepahetîwa	sleeps with someone (secretly)
nepahêwa	puts s.o. to bed, gives s.o. a place to sleep, puts s.o. up for the night
nepâkani	bed
nepâtâhkosiwa	is beaten to a pulp
nepâtwêwêkesiwa	screams bloody murder
nepehkwani	my back (**opehkwani** s.o.'s back; a back)
nepêhêwa	puts s.o. to sleep, lets s.o. sleep
nepêhkânowa	pretends to sleep
nepêwa	sleeps; sleeps {somewhere} (**nenepa** I sleep)
nepêwêwa	sleeps at s.o.'s house
nepêwêwêkahwêwa	puts s.o. to sleep by drumming
nepêwotîwaki (plural)	they sleep at each other's houses
nepêwowêwa	sleeps at someone else's house, spends the night
nepi	water (**nepîki** in the water)
nepinâtôhkanawi	water path (to stream where water is obtained)
nepinâtwa	goes after water (**nenepinâte** I went after water)
nepisêhi	pond, small lake
nepisi	lake
nepisiwiwi	it is a lake
nepisowa, nepihtêwi	(animate, inanimate) is cooked well done
nepiswêwa, nepisamwa	cooks s.o., it well done
nepiwashkatwi	the grass is wet
nepiwâhkosiwa	is wet (all over)
nepiwikâtêwa	one's feet get wet, are wet
nepiwinameshkênêwa	wets s.o.'s skin
nepiwiwi	it is wet, has some water on it
nepôhiwa	dies
nepôhkânowa	plays dead
nepôhkêwa	has a death in the family
nepômikatwi	it dies
nepôpi (**nepôpêhi** dimin.)	soup
nepôpihkâsowa	makes soup for oneself
nepôtêwâwi:	**nêpôtêwâki** sex, sexual matters
nepôtêwesiwa	has strong sexual desires
nepôtêwi	sexual, sexually; extremely (preverb, particle)
nepôtêwimêwa	speaks to s.o. about sex or with off-color remarks
nepôweni	death
nepôwênemêwa	thinks s.o. is dead
nepwa	dies (archaic) (**kenepe** you're dead! [as a threat])
nepwâhkânotawêwa, **nepwâhkânotamwa**	is knowledgeable about s.o., it
nepwâhkâwa (also **nepwâhkêwa**)	is wise, smart, clever, bright
nepwâhkâweni (also **nepwâhkêweni**)	wisdom, intelligence, (piece of) knowledge, cleverness
nepwâhkâhêwa (also **nepwâhkêhêwa**)	makes s.o. wise
nepwâmi	my thigh (**opwâmani** his or her thighs; **mepwâmi** a thigh)
-nepwêwa (only with a preverb):	**otehchi-nepwêwa** catches on
	tahpi-nepwêwa begins to realize things, gets smarter (**êh=tahpi-nepwâchi** has (now) gotten smarter)
nesapiwa (**nesapîhiwa** dimin.)	stays home (when others leave)
nesapiwi	(used for) staying at home (prenoun)
-nesapîmêwa	(see **wîchi-nesapîmêwa**)
nesâsowa	is put to death
nesekwisa	my paternal aunt, my father's sister; also, my mother's brother's wife (in full **nekakâchi-nesekwisa** 'my "teasing" aunt')

nesemya	my daughter-in-law (**osemyêni** his or her daughter-in-law)
nesenwi	three times (particle)
nesesêha	my older brother (**osesêhani** his or her older brother); also applied to a father's brother's son and a mother's sister's son
neseyâhiwi	it is dusk (dimin.)
nesêmâwa	tobacco (**nenesêmâwa** my tobacco) (also **asêmâwa**)
nesêwa, nehtôwa	kills s.o., it; beats s.o. up
nesiwaki, nesenôni (plurals)	they (animate, inanimate) are three, there are three of them
nesîma (nesîmêha)	my younger brother or sister (**osîmani, osîmêhani** his or her younger brother or sister); also applied to a father's brother's son or daughter, or a mother's sister's son or daughter
nesîsepetonâkani	my saliva, my drool
nesîsepinîkwâkanani (plural)	my tears
nesokonakatwi	it is three days
nesokonakesiwa	is three days old
nesokoni	three days (particle)
nesôhokowaki (plural)	they (as, fish) swim three together
nesôpiwaki (plural)	they sit three together
nesôshinôki (plural)	they lie three together
neswawahîme, neswawahîne	three years (particle)
neswayaki	three kinds, ways, sets, pairs (particle)
neswâhkwe	three hundred (particle)
neswâpitaki	thirty (particle)
neswâpyêki	three portions (particle)
neswâpyêkatwi	it is three portions
neswi (1)	three (particle, preparticle)
neswi (2)	all three together (preverb)
neswihêwa, neswihtôwa	has, gets three of them (animate, inanimate)
neswinesiwe, neswinîsiwe	thirteen (particle)
neswipepônwêwa	is three years old
neswipite (Jones)	three bits (37½ cents) (particle)
neshawiwa	is alone, is by oneself (**neshawiwaki** they are by themselves, they are alone together)
neshehki	my side (**meshehki** side (of someone's body))
neshemisa, neshemîha	my cross-niece: (of a man) the daughter of my sister or anyone else I call "sister," or of my father's sister; (of a woman) the daughter of my brother or anyone else I call "brother"
neshi	alone, on one's own, only (particle, preverb, preparticle)
neshihka	alone (particle)
neshihkêwênemêwa	thinks only of s.o.
neshihkêwênemowa	thinks only of oneself, thinks it is only oneself
neshihkêwi	alone (preverb)
neshikêwa	has a home of one's own
neshisêha	my maternal uncle, my mother's brother; the son of any man I call "mother's brother" (**oshisêhani** his or her mother's brother, archaic **oshisani**)
neshi-shâpwêshi	off alone by oneself (particle compound)
neshiwanâchâwi	it is destroyed, ruined, destructive
neshiwanâchihêwa, neshiwanâchihtôwa	ruins s.o., it; makes s.o. miserable
neshiwanâchikiwa, neshiwanâchikenwi	is hideous, deformed; it is evil, it is destroyed
neshiwanâchimêwa	speaks evilly against s.o.
neshiwanâchinâkosiwa, neshiwanâchinâkwatwi	(animate, inanimate) is ugly, looks awful, looks a mess

neshiwanâchitanekowa	does something wrong, destructive
neshiwanâchitêhêmêwa	tempts to do wrong
neshiwanâchitêhêwa	is demoralized
neshiwanâchîhkâsowa	does something terrible, wicked, destructive
neshiwanâtahkamikatwi	the world is destroyed
neshiwanâtahkiwiwi	the world is destroyed
neshiwanâtahwêwa, neshiwanâtahamwa	ruins s.o. (as, a drum), it by striking
neshiwanâtehkawêwa	ruins s.o. (as, by getting s.o. drunk), ruins s.o.'s reputation
neshiwanâtehtawêwa, neshiwanâtehtamwa	dislikes hearing s.o., it
neshiwanâtenêwa, neshiwanâtenamwa	ruins s.o. (as, a watch), it by handling
neshiwanâtesiwa	is destroyed; takes it hard; is good-for-nothing
neshiwanâtesiweni	destruction
neshiwanâteswêwa, neshiwanâtesamwa	ruins s.o. (as, corn, beans, potatoes), it by heating
neshiwanâteshkawêwa, neshiwanâteshkamwa	ruins s.o. (as, corn or beans), it by trampling
neshiwanâteshwêwa, neshiwanâteshamwa	ruins s.o. (as, s.o.'s hair), it by cutting
neshiwanâtênetâkosiwa	is considered worthless, good-for-nothing
neshiwanâtowêwa	says something inappropriate, offensive
neshiwâkwasowa, neshiwâkwatêwi	there is a huge pile, mass, or cluster of (animate, inanimate)
neshiwâpamêwa	sees s.o. as something terrible
neshiwâpatâniwa	looks terrific; looks dreadful; is going fast
neshiwâwi, neshiwatwi	it is dangerous
neshiwesiwa	is dangerous, fierce, mighty, powerful
neshiwêwêkatwi	there is a terrific, terrible, awful noise
neshiwi (also **neshîwi**)	terribly, to an extreme degree (particle, preverb)
neshiwihêwa	overpowers s.o., gets the best of s.o.
neshiwihtanwi	it flows dangerously
neshiwimêwa	overcomes s.o. with words, has commanding power over s.o.
neshiwinâkosiwa, neshiwinâkwatwi	(animate, inanimate) looks terrible, awful, fierce
neshiwiyâkosiwa, neshiwiyâkwatwi	(animate, inanimate) stinks, smells awful
neshiwîhkânowa	is doing a dangerous thing
neshîhkâtîwa	does the task alone
neshîkani	the small of my back, my lower back, my hindquarters (**oshîkani** his or her lower back; a creature's hindquarters)
neshîkwi-nenekwana	my late daughter's husband
neshkasha	my nail, my claw (plural **neshkashêki; meshkasha** a nail, claw, hoof)
neshkênemêwa	bears ill will towards s.o., harbors bad feelings towards s.o.
neshkênetîwaki (plural)	they have hatred for each other
neshki	angrily (preverb)
neshkikêmowa	forbids
neshkimâkaniwiwa	is prohibited
neshkimâwasowa	gives a direct warning not to do something
neshkimêwa	scolds, forbids, admonishes s.o.
neshkinamawêwa	hates (it) for s.o.
neshkinawêhêwa	makes s.o. angry
neshkinawêwa, neshkinamwa	hates s.o., it, dislikes s.o., it, does not like s.o., it
neshkinâkaniwiwa	is hateful
neshkitêhêwa	feels angry, offended, upset, disheartened
neshkitîwaki (plural)	they admonish each other
neshkîshekwi	my eye (**neshkîshekôni** my eyes; **meshkîshekôni** eyes)
neshwâshika	eight (particle) (see **shwâshika**)
neshwâshikânameki	eighth, the eighth time (particle) (see **shwâshikânameki**)
neshwâshikâpitaki	eighty (particle) (see **shwâshikâpitaki**)
netahtakâkwani	my backbone, spine (**otahtakâkwani** his or her spine; a backbone)

netapenôhema	my own child
netawêmâwa	my brother (of a woman) (**otawêmâwani** her brother)
netawêpemaki (plural)	my people, my men (**otawêpemahi** his people, his men)
netaya (**netayîha** dimin.)	my pet, my dog, my horse (plural **netayêki**)
netâhînemi, netâhwînemi, netâhîhemi, netâhwîhemi	my thing, my possession
netâkwa	my sister-in-law (of a woman) (**otâkwani** her sister-in-law)
netâmihkani	my jaw (**metâmihkani** a jaw)
netânesa (**netâneseha** dimin.)	my daughter (**otânesani** his or her daughter); (of a man) the daughter of my brother or anyone else I call "brother"; (of a woman) the daughter of my sister or anyone else I call "sister," or of my father's sister
netehkwêma	my sister (of a man) (**otehkwêmani** his sister)
netehkwêyôma, netôhkwêyôma	my woman, female member of my group
netêhi	my heart (**otêhi** his, her, or its heart; **metêhi** a heart)
netôni	my mouth (**otôni** his or her mouth; **metôni** a mouth)
netôshkwani	my elbow (**metôshkwani** an elbow)
netôtani	my heel
netôtêma	my brother or sister; my clan totem (animal or spirit; also used reciprocally)
nêhâpita, nêhâpîha	seer, clairvoyant
nêhâkapita (participle)	son-in-law living with his in-laws (see **nahâkapiwa**)
nêhi, =nêhi	too; (also in idioms: **âpechi=wê=nêhi!** Alright, let's do it!)
nêhishimêwa, nêhisetôwa	puts s.o., it away
nêhtawâkwapiwaki (plural)	they sit together in a separate group (of one kind)
nêhtawi	in a separate group (of one kind) (particle, preverb)
nêhtawihetîwaki (plural)	they get together by themselves
nêhtôpiwaki (plural)	they sit together in a separate group (of one kind)
nêhtôsetôwa	places them (inanimate) separately by themselves
nêkamêhkwâni	maple-sap spile (collecting spout)
nêkatôkashêha	horse, pony (also **katôshkashâha** and the following)
nêkatôshkashâha	horse, pony
nêkatôshkashêha	horse, pony
nêkatôkashêhikâni	stable, horse barn
nêkawahkiwi	sand-bar, sandy place
nêkawi	sand (**nêkawîki** in or on the sand)
nêkâhikêwa	makes maple syrup into sugar (by heating it and working it with a paddle)
nêkonamawêwa	slides (it) into s.o.
nêkwamowa	is choking, has a tickle in the throat
nêkwâhkwisetôwa	slips it in, slips it into a space between
nêkwânahkwahki	cloud (see **nekwânahkwatwi**)
nêkwâpamêwa	peers up at s.o. (out of the tops of one's eyes), glares up at s.o.
nêkwichishkiwêsêwa	sinks into mud or quicksand
nêkwisetôwa	slips it in, on, under
nêkwîwa	slips away, withdraws
nêmatêhi	upright pole (in a summer house)
nêmêsisota (participle)	member of the Fish Clan (Jones: Sturgeon Clan)
nêmowa	breathes
nêmoweni	breath
nênawênemêwa	has mercy on s.o.
nênawihtôwa	camp policeman
nênâhotâha	director of a ceremony, manager, one in charge
nênehkowêwa	the sound of one's voice dies away

nênekakôtêhani (plural)	extralong earrings with shimmery danglers
nênekoti	one apiece, one by one (particle) (also **nânekoti**)
nênekotwânehkwêhiwa	has thin hair, one's head is sparsely covered with hair
nênekotwêyâhkwâwi	grove of scattered trees (**nênekotwêyâhkwâki** in a grove of scattered trees)
nênekotwêyâhkwâwiwi	it is sparsely wooded, a grove of scattered trees
nênekîwiwa	runs with a rolling gait
nênekwêhi	"flute," the end-blown Woodland flute or flageolet
nênêhtawi	in separate groups (each of one kind) (particle)
nênêhtôsetôwa	sorts them (inanimate) out
nênêkwâpiwa	is peering up (out of the tops of one's eyes), glaring up
nênêsowa	is panting, is puffing
nênosohkêha	buffalo hunter
nênôchîha	wild animal, wild horse
nênôchîhi (**nênôchîhêhi** dimin.)	wild plants
nêpehe	or rather; or I should have said; oh I forgot (particle)
nêpiwisota (participle)	member of the Water Clan
nêpôha	dead one, dead person or animal
nêpôtêha	man with a great sexual appetite
nêsawâhi	forked support post of a platform
nêsemênâkwatwi	it looks dangerous, potentially a mortal danger
nêsemêwênetâkosiwa	is considered a potential mortal threat
nêsêhêwa	cures s.o.
nêsêhetîwaki (plural)	they cure each other
nêsêhtawêwa	cures (s.o.) for s.o.
nêsêmikihtawêwa	cures (it) for s.o.
nêsêwa	gets well, survives, lives after a brush with death, is alive
nêsêwênemêwa	thinks s.o. alive
nêsêweni	cure, recovery
nêsêwitêhêwa	thinks oneself cured, safe
nêsônameki	third, the third time (particle)
nêtamawêwa	sees (it) of s.o.
nêtamâtisowa	sees (it) for oneself
nêtonamâshîha	monkey
nêtopâha	man on the war-path
nêwa	hog-nosed snake, "puff adder"
nêwêwa, nêtamwa	sees s.o., it
nêwotisowa	sees oneself
nêwotîwaki (plural)	they see each other, they meet, they are together
nêwowêwa	sees people, sees
nêyâpapitôwa	ties it back up again
nêyâpi	back (to its former state), the same as before (particle, preverb)
nêyâpimêwa	says the same thing to s.o. as was said before
nêyâpisenwi	it is the same as it was, it is back to the same place or amount as before
='ni	(see **îni, =îni**)
nîchâpa	doll (**nenîchâpa** my doll)
nîchi- (prenoun with prefix)	my fellow (+ noun) (**owîchi-** his or her fellow —)
nîchi-manetôwaki (plural)	my fellow manitous, the other manitous besides me (**owîchi-manetôwâwani** their fellow manitou)
nîchi-mehtosêneniwa	my fellow human being (**owîchi-mehtosênenîwâwahi** their own people)
nîchi-pashitôha	my fellow old man (**owîchi-pashitôhani** his fellow old man)
nîchîshkwêha	my enemy (**owîchîshkwêhwâwahi** their enemies)
=nîhka	(man's mild expletive)
nîhkasehkêwa	(drum) has its drumhead burst

nîhkâna	my friend (generic); my close male friend (of a man or boy) (**owîhkânani** his or her friend)
nîhkwi	my chin (**owîhkwi** his or her chin; **kîhkwîki** on your chin)
nîhtâwa	my brother-in-law (of a man) (**owîhtâwani** his brother-in-law)
nîkahamâtîwaki (plural)	they divide (it) up for each other
nîkahamwa	divides it up
nîkatahwêwa	chops s.o. (as, a block of ice) to pieces
nîkateshwêwa	cuts s.o. into pieces
nîkânekêwa	leads in the dance
nîkânesiwa	is, becomes the leader, the leading one
nîkâni	in the lead, on ahead; in future, ahead of time (particle, prenoun, preverb)
nîkânîhêwa	makes s.o. the leader
nîkânîhtawêwa	is the leader of s.o.
nîkânîmikatwi	it leads
nîkânîmikihtawêwa	makes (it) be the leading thing for s.o.
nîkânîwa (1)	leads, is the leader (for example, of a dance)
nîkânîwa (2) (only possessed):	**onîkânîmwâwani** their leader
nîkâni-kechitâha	headman of a drum in the Drum Society
nîkâninehkâkani	front hoof, paw
nîkâninâkêwa	leads in singing
nîkânishinwa	is in the lead
nîkenamwa	distributes it, divides it up and passes it out
nîki (1)	my house (**owîki** his or her house)
nîki (2)	in small pieces (preverb)
nîkikiwa	multiplies, has numerous descendants
nîkiwa	is born
nîmahâha	Missouri River Sauk
nîmahâhinâki	in Nebraska (locative noun)
nîmahikani	pole (or pair of poles) for carrying or holding aloft (as, a scalp pole); **chîpayi-nîmahikani** litter for carrying a body
nîmahwêwa, nîmahamwa	sets or carries s.o., it on a stick, pole (or poles), or the like
nîmamêwa, nîmatamwa	holds s.o., it in one's mouth or using one's mouth
nîmashkahôtenêwa	fastens something (especially a feather) in s.o.'s hair
nîmashkahwêwa, nîmashkahamwa	fastens s.o. (as, a feather), it in one's hair, has s.o., it fastened in one's hair
nîmatahêwa	makes s.o. hold (it) in their mouth
nîmênêwa, nîmênamwa	lifts s.o., it up (in the air), holds s.o., it up
nîmêsahowa	jumps up in the air
nîmêshkêwa, nîmêshkêwi	(animate, inanimate) rises up in the air
nîmêwenêwa	carries s.o. up
nîmêyâhkêwa	throws (it) aloft
nîmêyâshkêwa, nîmêyâshkêwi	jumps up in the air, it flies up in the air
nîmihchikêwa	gives a dance
nîmihchîha	whip top (spun with a small whip)
nîmihetêwi	there is a dance
nîmihetîwaki (plural)	they have a dance together
nîmihetîwi	of dancing (prenoun)
nîmihetînenîhaki (plural)	Drum Society (Michelson: Religion Dance)
nîmihêwa	makes s.o. dance, has s.o. dance
nîmihiwêwa	makes people dance, has people dance, gives a dance for people
nîmihkamêkêwa	dances smoking
nîmihkamêpiwa	sits smoking
nîmihkawêwa, nîmihkamwa	dances for, over s.o., it

nîmiwa	dances
nîmiwi	of dancing (prenoun)
nîmiwahamawêwa	sings for s.o. to dance
nîmiwahamwa	sings for dancing
nîmiwahikani	dancing song
nîmiwisekini (plural participle)	dancing songs
nîmîhtamwa	dances on it
nîna	I (emphatic or contrastive); (by) myself
nînakayi	my penis (**owînakayi** his penis; **mînakayi** a penis)
nînaniwi	my tongue (**owînaniwi** his or her tongue; a tongue)
nînawesiwa, nînawâwi	(animate, inanimate) is weak
nînawi	weakly (preverb)
nînawihêwa, nînawihtôwa	weakens s.o., it
nînâna	we (exclusive, excluding "you") (emphatic or contrastive); (by) ourselves
nînemwa	my brother-in-law (of a woman), my sister-in-law (of a man) (**owînemôni** her brother-in-law, his sister-in-law)
nînesani (plural)	my hair, the hair on my head (**owînesani** his or her hair)
nînesi	a hair of my head (**owînesi** one of his or her head hairs; **mînesi** one head hair)
nînêtepi	my brain (**nînêtepîki** in my brain; **owînêtepi** his or her brain)
nîpâshimêwa	holds or attends a wake for s.o.
nîpenêhamwa	sings them (inanimate) in order
nîpenêsenôni (plural)	they (inanimate) are in order, in a particular sequence
nîpenêwi	in order, in a particular sequence (preverb)
nîpeni-wîseniweni, nîpenîseniweni	ripe garden crops (as food)
nîpenwi	it is the time when the garden crops are ripe, it is the middle of summer
nîpetesiwa	garden crop
nîpêwenêwa	hunts all night with dogs
nîpi	my arrow (plural **nîpani; owîpi** his or her arrow)
nîpikoshkawêwa	wears s.o. (as, an animal skin) over one's head
nîpikwahamwa	threads it, strings it
nîpikwakôtêwi	it is hung up over the end of something (as, a moccasin over the end of a branch)
nîpikwêhaki (plural)	the ring-and-pin game (nested cup-shaped bones, attached to a stick by a buckskin string, which are thrown up and caught on the end)
nîpikwêhiwaki (plural)	they play the ring-and-pin game
nîpikwitôshkwanâmêwa, nîpikwitôshkwanâtamwa	carries s.o., it on one's arm, in the crook of one's elbow
nîpinêwa, nîpitôwa	weaves s.o. (as, a yarn belt), it
nîpitawêwa	weaves (it) for s.o.
nîsamôhi	deadfall trap (also **mehtekwi-nîsamôhi**)
nîsatamwa	bites it to fall down
nîsâhkêwa	throws (it) down
nîsâsîwa	climbs down
nîsehkwêsahowa	pulls one's head down quickly
nîsehkwêsêwa	bows one's head
nîsehkwêwi	there is a roar from the crowd (as it speaks in chorus), a rumble of assent
nîsenâkwâwêwa	takes down the meat supply
nîsenêwa, nîsenamwa	lowers s.o., it, sets s.o., it down, takes s.o., it down
nîsênetamwa	imagines it descending
nîsinawîwa	slides down
nîsisahowa	jumps down

nîsiwenêwa, nîsiwetôwa	takes, brings, or carries s.o., it down
nîsiwetawêwa	leads (it) down for s.o.
nîsîkishehkîtamwa	is dressed in ragged clothes
nîsîkyâwi	it is all torn, shredded
nîsîpanasitâkani	toe (**kenîsîpanasitâkanani** your toes)
nîsîpinechâkani	finger (**nenîsîpinechâkanani** my fingers)
nîsîwa	descends, comes or goes down, gets down
nîshenwi	twice (particle)
nîshi	my head (**nîsheki, newîshemeki** on my head; **owîshi** his or her head; a head) (**owîshani** heads)
nîshiwaki, nîshenôni (plurals)	they (animate, inanimate) are two, there are two of them; they join up together
nîshîhiwaki, nîshenôhiwani (plurals)	they (animate, inanimate) are two, there are two of them (dimin.)
nîshkahtakawêshkêwa	(animal's) hair stands up on end
nîshkâmêwa	growls at s.o.
nîshkâmowa	growls
nîshkâpatâniwa	is all decked out; is burdened, is burdened as one runs
nîshkâpitêshkêwa	bares one's teeth
nîshkehkawêwa	crowds s.o., is in s.o.'s way
nîshkesiwa	has a big load on one's back; (woman) has many children
nîshkeshkawêwa	gets in s.o.'s way; messes things up for s.o.
nîshkênemêwa, nîshkênetamwa	thinks s.o., it a bother, in the way
nîshki	overly, messily, heavily, awkwardly, almost too (much) (preverb)
nîshkihêwa	is a burden to s.o. (to care for)
nîshkikomêshkêwa	wrinkles up one's nose
nîshkinâkwatwi	it looks messy, it looks a mess
nîshkishêwa	urinates in a large stream
nîshkitepêwa	one's hair is mussed up
nîshkiwetôwa	has the bother or inconvenience of carrying it
nîshokonakatwi	it is two days
nîshokoni	two days (particle)
nîshôchêhpwêwa	holds or carries two of them together in one's mouth
nîshôchênêwa	holds, carries, or catches two of them (animate) together
nîshôhkatêwani (plural)	the two of them (inanimate) stand set in the ground together
nîshôhkatôwa	sets them (inanimate) in the ground as a pair
nîshôhkawêwaki, nîshôhkamôki (plurals)	the two of them (animate) deal with s.o., it, set upon s.o.
nîshôhkwêwânêwa	he has them as his two wives
nîshôhkwêwâsowaki (plural)	they are the two wives of one man
nîshôhkwêwêwa	he has two wives
nîshôhokowaki (plural)	they (as, fish) swim two together
nîshôhpowaki (plural)	they eat together as a pair
nîshôkânêwa	grabs or holds s.o. by both feet
nîshôkâpâwaki (plural)	the two of them (anim.) stand together
nîshôkâpawihêwa	makes them (anim.) stand together
nîshôkâtahwêwa	shoves s.o. with both feet
nîshôkenôni (plural)	they (inanimate) grow together, as a pair
nîshôkêhiwaki (plural)	just the two of them dwell together (dimin.)
nîshôkêwa (1)	dances together, dances with (s.o.) as a couple (**êh=nîshôkâwâchi** they danced together)
nîshôkêwaki (2)	they dwell together as a pair (**êh=nîshôkêwâchi** they dwelt together)
nîshônameki	second, the second time (particle)
nîshônêwaki, nîshônamôki (plurals)	the two of them together picked s.o., it up, carried s.o., it
nîshôpahônekowaki	they rode double at a gallop

nîshôpinêwa, nîshôpitôwa	ties the two of them (animate, inanimate) together
nîshôpiwa	sits in a pair, sits in a pair with (s.o.)
nîshôsetôwa	places two of them (inanimate) together, jointly places it
nîshôtâkani	double-barreled shotgun
nîshôtâkani-chahkwipâhi	sawed-off shotgun
nîshôtêhaki (plural)	twins
nîshôtêhehkêwa	she has, gives birth to twins
nîshôtêhiwa	is a twin
nîshwawahîmakatwi	it is two years
nîshwawahîme, nîshwawahîne	two years (particle)
nîshwayaki	two kinds, ways, groups, sets, pairs (particle)
nîshwayakihtôwa	has two sets of it
nîshwâchimowa	tells (of being) as (one of) a pair
nîshwâhkwe	two hundred (particle)
nîshwâpitakenwi	twenty times (particle)
nîshwâpitaki	twenty (particle)
nîshwâpitakesiwa	is twenty years old
nîshwâpyêki	two portions (particle)
nîshwâpyêkatwi	it is two portions
nîshwêwêmêwa	scolds them both together
nîshwi (1)	two (particle, preparticle)
nîshwi (2)	as a pair, both together (preverb)
nîshwihêwa, nîshwihtôwa	has, gets two of them (anim., inan.)
nîshwimêwa	includes them both in what one says
nîshwinîsiwa	is twelve years old
nîshwinîsiwe, nîshwinîsiwi	twelve (particle)
nîshwipepônwe	two years (particle)
nîshwipeshkwahte	two charges of gunpowder (particle)
nîshwitepehkwe	for two nights (particle)
nîshwi-wâsêyâwe	for two days (particle compound)
nîtôsha	my (man's) rival; my (woman's) co-wife (**owîtôshani, owîtôshêni** his rival, her co-wife)
nîwa	my wife (**owîwani** his wife; **owîweki** at or to his wife's)
nîyawi	my body; myself, me (object of verb) (**owîyawi** his or her body; himself, herself [object of verb])
nowahôni, nônôhôni	fan
nowâhkêwa	throws (it) out
nowâmowa	flees out
nowâshkêwa, nowâshkêwi	(animate, inanimate) falls out, rushes out
nowâwanetêwi	a large group (as, of people) goes out
nowâwanetîwaki (plural)	they go out in a large group
nowâwanêwa, nowâwatôwa	takes, carries s.o., it outside
nowenamawêwa	hands (it) out to s.o.
nowenêwa, nowenamwa	hands, puts s.o., it out, lets s.o. out
nowikawihêwa	makes (a group of) them go out
nowikawiwaki (plural)	they go out as a group
nowikâhiwa	one's feet are sticking out
nowinâkêwa	goes out singing
nowinehkawêwa	chases s.o. out
nowipahowa	runs out, goes out on the run
nowipahônêwa	runs out carrying s.o.
nowipokowa	floats out
nowisahowa	jumps out
nowisetôwa	sets it outside

nowisêwa	runs out, flies out
nowiwenêwa, nowiwetôwa	leads or conveys s.o., it out
nowîhêwa	sends or brings s.o. out, gets s.o. to come out, has s.o. come out
nowîhtawêwa, nowîhtamwa	goes out at s.o., it
nowîhtâkêwa	goes out against people
nowîmikatwi	it goes out
nowîwa	goes out
nôchi (1)	since (as, with 'long ago', 'that time') (preverb)
nôchi (2)	(prayer vocable, the equivalent of 'hear my prayer')
nôchi (3):	(see **=wê=nôchi** (2))
nôhika	seven (particle)
nôhika tashiwaki, nôhika tasenôni (plurals)	they (animate, inanimate) are seven, there are seven of them
nôhikanesiwa	is seventeen (years old)
nôhikanesiwe, nôhikanîsiwe	seventeen (particle)
nôhikanîsiwe taswipepônwêwa	is seventeen years old (or with **nôhikanesiwe**)
nôhikânameki	seventh, the seventh time (particle)
nôhikâpitaki	seventy (particle)
nôhkahâni	pemmican
nôhkawahîmakatwi, nôhkawahînakatwi	it is a new year
nôhkawiwi	there is a new year, a new growing season
nôhkâmehkonikêwa	digs to make soft earth
nôhkâmehkisenwi	it lies as soft earth
nôhkâmehkisetawêwa	loosens its earth for s.o.
nôhkâmehkisetôwa	loosens the earth in it (house)
nôhketêwi (**nôhketêhiwi** dimin.)	it is cooked soft, tender
nôhkihêwa, nôhkihtôwa (1)	easily kills s.o., it; easily gets s.o.
nôhkihtôwa (2)	creates it anew
nôhkinêwa	dies easily
nôhkinokêhiwa	has a weak constitution (dimin.)
nôhkipiwâkanaki (plural)	fine down feathers
nôhkoma	my mother-in-law (**ôhkomani** his or her mother-in-law)
nôhkomesa	my grandmother (**ôhkomesani** his or her grandmother) (**nôhkomesêha** dimin.)
nôhkyâhenôhiwi	it is weak, it is not strong (dimin.)
nôkênawa, menôkênawa	soul (**onôkênawani** his or her soul, **kenôkênawâwaki** your [plural] souls)
nômake (**nômakêhe** dimin.)	for a short time, for a little while (particle)
nômakêpihêwa	makes s.o. sit for a short while
nômakêwe	for a short time, for a little while (particle)
nômakêwi	for a short time (preverb)
nômakêwosêwa (only in "when" clause):	**nômakêwosêchi** when he had walked for a little while (changed conjunct)
nômamêwa, nômatamwa	eats part of s.o., it, eats some more of s.o., it
nômekowa, nômekwiwa	rides on horseback
nômenamwa	takes part of it
nômêwa, nôtamwa (1)	carries s.o., it on one's back
nôminêwaki (plural)	part of them die off, some more of them die off
nômisenyêwa	eats part of the food, some more of the food
nônahkatawêwa	sucks at her breast
nônâkani	breast, nipple
nônâwasowa, nôtâwasowa	she is nursing a baby
nônenamwa	picks it up and has nowhere to put it
nôneshkamâtîwaki (plural)	they are overcrowded
nôneshkamwa	does not fit it (it does not fit him or her)

117

nôneshkawêwa	crowds s.o. out (taking up their space)
nôneshkâtîwaki (plural)	they crowd in taking up all the room
nônichinwa	does not fit in or through the space
nônitepêchinwa	cannot get one's head in
nônôhkâha	hummingbird
nônôhowa	fans oneself
nônôshkatamwa	sucks it
nônwa	(infant) nurses, sucks at the breast (**nôneche** let (the baby) nurse)
nôsa	my father, my father's brother, my stepfather (**ôsani** his or her father, father's brother, stepfather; **anôse** Father!)
nôsamawêwa	fumigates (it) with smoke for s.o. (ceremonially)
nôsikêwa	fumigates things ceremonially, "smokes" things
nôsowa	"smokes" oneself (ceremonially)
nôswêwa, nôsamwa	"smokes" s.o., it (ceremonially), wafts smoke on s.o., it
nôshânêwa, nôshâtamwa	she gives birth to s.o., it
nôshêhchikêwa	she acts as a midwife
nôshêhêwa	has her give birth
nôshêmikahki (participle)	interest (on a bank account)
nôshêwa	she gives birth (to s.o.) (**êh=nôshêchi** she gave birth)
nôshisema	my grandchild (**ôshisemani** his or her grandchild)
nôshisemêhkôha	my dear grandchild
nôshkânematôhiwi	there is a soft breeze (dimin.)
nôshkânêwa, nôshkânamwa	winnows s.o. (as, corn), sifts it (as, flour)
nôshkâsêwa, nôshkâsêwi	(animate, inanimate) is sifted, winnowed
nôshkinameshkinâkosîhiwa	has delicate-looking skin (dimin.)
nôshkinâkosîhiwa	has a delicate appearance (dimin.)
nôshkwâhpwêwa, nôshkwâhtamwa	licks s.o., it
nôshkwâhtamawêwa	licks (it) for s.o.
nôta (**nôtêwîmêhi** dimin.)	too soon, before the time, before completion (particle)
nôtamawêwa	hears it of s.o.
nôtawêwa, nôtamwa (2)	hears s.o., it; hears what s.o. says
nôtâkêwa	hears (a report)
nôtâkosiwa, nôtâkwatwi	(animate, inanimate) is heard; it sounds
nôtâwasowa	(see **nônâwasowa**)
nôtehkwêwêwa	he sneaks in with a girl at night for courtship
nôtenosêwa	walks in the wind (song word)
nôtenwi (1)	the wind blows (**nôteki** wind)
nôtenwi (2)	wind
nôtêchimêwa	gives out in swimming
nôtêhkanawe	before reaching the end (of the road, journey, life) (particle)
nôtêhkohtawêwa	is unable to hear s.o. because of distance
nôtêhkwâchimowa	leaves something out in the telling
nôtêhkwâhpawêwa	one's dream is incomplete
nôtêhkwâpiwa	is unable to see a particular distance
nôtêhkwikomêsenwi	the end of it (as, a pole) falls short, it does not reach
nôtêhkwimêwa	leaves something out in telling s.o.
nôtêhkwinehkêwa	is unable to reach with the hand
nôtêhtêwi	it is underdone
nôtêkiwa, nôtêkenwi	is not full grown; it falls short
nôtênamwa	falls short of reaching it with one's hand
nôtêsetwêwa	does not get enough to eat (**êh=nôtêsetwâchi** he or she did not get enough to eat)
nôtêsêwa, nôtêsêwi	runs out of food, gets no food when it runs out; it runs out, time runs out
nôtêshinwa	falls short of the goal, does not finish

nôtêtepehkwe	before the night is (was) out (particle)
nôtêwa	she nurses s.o. (infant), breastfeeds s.o.
nôtêwi	falling short, not (yet) complete (preverb)
nyânanenwi	five times (particle)
nyânaniwaki, nyânanenôni (plurals)	they (animate, inanimate) are five, there are five of them
nyânanokonakatwi	it is five days
nyânanokoni	five days (particle)
nyânanônameki	fifth, the fifth time (particle)
nyânanônetîwaki (plural)	all five of them hold hands together
nyânanônôki	fivefold (particle)
nyânanwawahîmakatwi	it is five years
nyânanwawahîme	five years (particle)
nyânanwâpitaki (Jones)	fifty (particle) (see **shekihkanawe**)
nyânanwâhkwe	five hundred (particle)
nyânanwi	five (particle)
nyânanwinesiwe, nyânanwinîsiwe, **nyânanwinîsiwi**	fifteen (particle) (also **metâswi-nyânanwi** fifteen; also **nîshwâpitaki nyânanwinesiwe** twenty-five)
nyânanwinîsiwa	is fifteen years old
nyêwawahîme, nyêwawahîne	four years (particle)
nyêwawahîmakatwi	it is four years
nyêwayaki	four sets, pairs (particle)
nyêwâhkwe	four hundred
nyêwâpitaki	forty (particle)
nyêwâpyêki	four portions (particle)
nyêwâpyêkatwi	it is four portions
nyêwenwi	four times (particle)
nyêwi	four (particle)
nyêwihêwa, nyêwihtôwa	has, gets, uses four of them (animate, inanimate)
nyêwikîsheswakatwi	it is four months
nyêwikîsheswakesiwa	is four months old
nyêwikîsheswe (also **nyêwi-kîsheswe**)	for four months (particle and particle compound)
nyêwi-mahkahkwe	four thousand (particle)
nyêwinâkanakatwi	there are four dishes or bowls of it
nyêwinesiwe, nyêwinîsiwe	fourteen (particle)
nyêwipeshkwahte	four charges of gunpowder (particle)
nyêwiwak, nyêwenôni (plural)	they (animate, inanimate) are four, there are four of them
nyêwokonakatwi	it is four days
nyêwokonêtwa	is away for four days
nyêwokoni	four days (particle)
nyêwokonîwa	fasts for four days
nyêwôhkohkwe	four kettles (of food) (particle)
nyêwôhkwêwêwa	he has four wives
nyêwôkâpâwaki (plural)	the four of them stand together
nyêwôkôtêwani (plural)	the four of them (inan.) hang together
nyêwônameki	fourth, the fourth time (particle)
nyêwôpitêwani (plural)	the four of them (inan.) are tied together
nyêwôpinêwa	ties the four of them (anim.) together
nyêwôpiwaki (plural)	they sit four together

o

o=	or (particle) (see **o=meshe=kêhi, o=tânâhka=kêhi**)
ochawiwa	gets through or across {some way, by some route}
ochêhchi (**ochêhtêhi** dimin.)	sinew, tendon (plural **ochêhtani**)
ochêka	fisher
ochêkaya	fisher skin
ochêkishkêwa, ochêkishkêwi	(animate, inanimate) shrinks
ochêmôhiwa	has a part in one's hair (**netochêmôhi** I have a part)
ochêpihki	root
ochêpihkiwiwi	it is a root
ochêpihkyêwâkanani (plural)	tendons
ochi	from {somewhere}, because of {some reason}, in {such} direction (particle, preverb) (**îtepi ochi** in that direction); away, from there (preverb)
ochihamwa	gets or takes water from {somewhere} (see **wâwochihamwa**)
ochihêwa	kills s.o. for {some reason}
ochihkamêhiwa	smokes from {somewhere} (dimin.)
ochihkanêwa, ochihkatamwa	leaves s.o., it behind {somewhere}
ochihkanetîwaki (plural)	they leave each other behind {somewhere}
ochikâpâwa	stands on {such} side
ochikâsahowa	jerks one's foot (or feet) back
ochikâte	(at) the foot on {such} side (particle)
ochikêmowa	objects (about it)
ochikiwa, ochikenwi	(animate, inanimate) grows from {somewhere}
ochimêwa	tells s.o. because of {something}; defends s.o., takes the side of s.o.; denies s.o. (it), refuses s.o. (it), opposes s.o. doing (it)
ochinawe	on {such} side (particle)
ochinehkawêwa (idiom):	**wêchinehkawochi** was immediately pursued
ochinehkâkêwa (idiom):	**wêchinehkâkêchi** went immediately in pursuit
ochinehke	(by, in, with) the hand on {such} side (particle)
ochinêwa	is ill from {something}
ochinîkwe	(at) the eye on {such} side (particle) (**âshowi ochinîkwe** the other eye)
ochipyêchi	ever since (particle)
ochisahowa	jumps from {somewhere}
ochishimêwa	lays s.o. in {such} direction
ochishinwa	lies on {such} side, in {such} direction
ochishkwâtawêwa	has one's door in {such} direction
ochishkwâte	at, by the door in {such} direction (particle)
ochiti	tail-feather (**ochityêni** tail-feathers)
ochiwenêwa, ochiwetôwa	takes s.o., it from {somewhere}, from there
ochiwêpi	from {such time}, from then on (particle)
ochîhkawêwa	goes after s.o. for something, cheats s.o. out of what is theirs
ochîhtawêwa	goes at s.o. from {somewhere}
ochîketonâkani	lips
ochîkwanapihêwa	makes s.o. kneel
ochîkwanapiwa	kneels
ochîkwêsahowa	draws one's face back, ducks one's head
ochîmêhi	a little ways {some way} (particle) (**ahkiki ochîmêhi** a little below; **anika ochîmêhi** a little further; **petek-ochîmêhi** a little while back)
ochîmikatwi	it comes from {somewhere}
ochîwa	comes from {somewhere}
ohkâtaki (plural)	animal feet (as food) (**peshekesiwi-ohkâtaki** deer feet)

ohkechi	bird's tail, set of tail-feathers
ohkenâhkwaya, ohkenâhkwa	turtle-shell
ohkeshi	forehead, his or her forehead (**nehkeshîki** on my forehead)
ohketenani	her vulva, vagina (**mehketena** a vulva, vagina)
ohkiwani	beak (of bird); his or her nose or beak (**nehkiwani** my nose)
ohkonêhêwa	puts a blanket over s.o.
ohkonêkâpâwa	stands wearing a blanket, robe
ohkonêmowa	cries while wearing a blanket (song word)
ohkonêshkwa	cornhusk
ohkoni	liver
ohkonîkwêwa	has a black eye
ohohô!	Oh I see! Oh come on! The idea!
ohohwâ!	Oh my! Oh no! Mercy me! (also **ôhwâ!**)
ohohyâ!	Oh my! Oh no! Mercy me! (also **ôhyâ!**)
ohpikayâhkôni (plural)	logs that hold down the roof of a summer house
ohpikayi	one's rib; a rib
ohpwâkana (Jones)	tobacco pipe (archaic; see **ahpwâkana**)
ohpwâkanimotêhi (Jones)	tobacco bag (probably should be **ohpwâkanimotêha**) (archaic; see **ahpwâkanimotêha**)
ohtawakêwa	has ears, has (s.o.) as one's ears; wears (them as) earrings (**ohtawakâpi** (they) are worn as earrings) (see also **mehtawakêwa**)
okahkikâpîhiwa, okehkikâpîhiwa	has garters, has (them) as garters
okâwa, akâwa	walleye
okehchîpîhiwa:	**êh=okehchîpîhichi** at one's belt line, at one's waist
okepishkwâtawêhôniwa	has a door-flap
okepwitîhiwa	wears pants
okimâwa	chief (**netôkimâma** my chief)
okimâwihêwa	makes s.o. chief
okimâwinohkatawêwa	is chief over them
okimâwiwa	is chief
okimâwîhkâsowa	acts as chief, pretends to be chief
okimêwa	has her as mother
okiwa	has a mother; has (her) as mother (**wêkita** the son or daughter of the woman)
okîha (only possessed):	**otôkîhwâwani** their chief
okîhiwa	has an aunt (mother's sister); has (her) as an aunt (mother's sister)
okîshekomiwa	has (it) as sky (**êh=okîshekomiyani** in your heaven)
okohkahikaniwa	has a bridge
okotâkani	his or her throat; throat (**kekotâkaneki** in or at your throat)
okôtêhêhi	her little dress, her little skirt
okôtêhi	her dress, her skirt
okôtêhihêwa	makes a dress or skirt (of it) for her
okôtêhiwa (**okôtêhêhiwa** dimin.)	she has on a dress or skirt
okôtêpisowa	she puts on a skirt, wears (it as) a skirt
okwisemâwa	the son
okwisemêwa	has him as a son
okwisetîhaki (plural)	the father and son
okwisiwa	has a son; has (him) as a son
omachîkwêwa	looks surprised
omahkesêhiwa	wears moccasins, wears (them) as moccasins
omamîshîhemiwa	has (him as) a ceremonial attendant
omatekwashiwa	gets up while still sleeping, sleepwalks
omatetêhihêwa	makes leggins for s.o.
omatetêhiwa	wears leggins, wears (them) as leggins

omâha	Omaha (Indian)
omâkwêhêwa	puts a fur-band headdress on him
omâkwêkêwa	he dances with a fur-band headdress on
omâmâwaki (plural)	eyebrows (**omâmâwahi** his or her eyebrows)
omâtesiwa	has a knife, has (it) as a knife
omâwashihêwa	he gives his kill to s.o. (another hunter)
omehtekwâpiwa	has a bowstring, has (it) as a bowstring
omehtêhemêwa	has s.o. (a bow) as one's bow
omehtêhiwa	has a bow, has (it) as a bow
omekihkwêkanwa	has sores on one's neck
omekikâtêwa	has sores on one's feet
omekisikiwêwa	has sores on one's back
omekishîkanwa	has a sore on the small of one's back
omekîkwêwa	has sores on one's face
omekîwa (probably also **omekiwa**)	has a sore or sores
omesôtâniwa	has parents, has (them) as parents
omesôtâniwitêhêwa	feels as if (they) were one's own parents
o=meshe=kêhi, meshe=kêhi	or maybe
omeshkwâhiwa	has an anus
omeshôhemêwa	has him as a grandfather, is his grandchild
omeshôhiwa, omeshômesiwa	has a grandfather, has (him) as a grandfather
omeshômesemêwa, omeshômesetamwa	has him, it as a grandfather
omeshômesâkômêwa, omeshômesiwâkômêwa	addresses him and treats him as if he were one's grandfather
omeshômiwa	has a father-in-law, has (him) as a father-in-law
ometemosemêhani	his wife (**kemetemosemêhwâwaki** your wives)
omîmîwa, pêhk-omîmîwa	passenger pigeon
omînaki (plural)	berries
omîshâmehkâsowa	claims (it) as one's sacred bundle, pretends (it) is one's sacred bundle
omîshâmemêwa	has s.o. as a sacred bundle, has s.o. in a sacred bundle
omîshâmetamwa, omîshâmemetamwa	has it as a sacred bundle
omîshâmiwa	has a sacred bundle
omîshâtesiweniwa, omîshâtesiweniwiwa	has fancy clothes; uses (it) to dress up with
omônahâkaniwa	has a hoe
omôshôniwa	he has a scalp-lock
omyêmiwa	has a road
onahakayani (plural)	scales (as, of a fish)
onahakayi	shell of nut, rind of melon
onakamôniwa	has a song
onakeshi	his or her intestines; an intestine (also as plural **onakeshêni**)
onameshkaya, onamashkaya	skin (**onameshkayani, onamashkayani** his or her skin)
onameshkayiwiwa, onamashkayiwiwa	has skin
onâkani (Jones)	bowl (archaic; see **anâkani**)
onâpêmemêwa	she marries him, is married to him, has him as her husband
onâpêmiwa (**onâpêmêhiwa** dimin.)	she has a husband, she marries (him), is married to (him)
onâpêmiweni	marriage, the state of a woman being married
onâtawinôniwa	has medicine
onâtawinônemêwa	has s.o. as medicine
onâyina	African lion
onechi	a paw; s.o.'s (animal's) paw (plural **onechyêni**)
onehkinawi	one's hand
onekwanemêwa	has him as a son-in-law
onekwaniwa	has a son-in-law, has (him) as a son-in-law (**wênekwanita** the man's father-in-law or mother-in-law)

onekwâhemêwa	has him as a nephew
onekwâhetîhaki (plural)	the uncle and nephew (a man and his sister's son)
onekwâhiwa	has a cross-nephew (man's sister's son or woman's brother's son)
onekwîkani	s.o.'s (e.g. a bird's) wing; a wing (see **nenekwîkani**)
onekwîkaniwa	has wings
onepâkayi	his or her forearm
onesêmâwiwa	has tobacco
oneshiwahi (plural)	his testicles (**meneshiwaki** testicles)
onêmowihêwa	gives s.o. breath
onîchânesemâwaki (plural)	the children (of the family), other people's children
onîchânesemêwa	has s.o. as a child
onîchânesetîhaki (plural)	the parent and child or children
onîchânesiwa (**onîchânesêhiwa** dimin.)	has a child, has (s.o.) as a child
onîchâpiwa	has a doll
onowêti:	**onowêtîki** on his or her buttocks
onôkênawiwa	has a soul, reflection, or shadow
opâshinwa	(snow) is blowing up
opâshkêwi	it flies up
opetonêmowa	talks happily
opi	for fun, jolly (preverb)
opinawêhêwa	makes s.o. happy
opinawêmêwa	makes s.o. happy by speech
opisahêwa, opisahtôwa	kicks up s.o. (as, snow), it (as, dirt)
opisêtepênêwa	musses up s.o.'s hair
opisêtepênowa	musses up one's hair
opisêtepêwa (Jones: **opisêwitepêwa**)	one's head (hair or feathers) is mussed, bushy
opishkwayi	bladder; gizzard
opishkwêchêwa	has a big belly
opishkwêshkêwa	swells up
opitêhâkaniwiwi	there is happy feeling
opitêhêwa	is glad, happy
opîneniwa	jolly fellow
opîneniwiwa	he is a jolly fellow
opîsehkâhihêwa	makes a shirt for s.o.
opîsehkâhiwa	wears a shirt
opîshâkanîhiwa	wears a buckskin or leather coat
opîtanwâniwa	has a quiver, has (it) as a quiver
opîwanashkenôki, opîwayashkenôki (plurals)	reeds (smaller than cattails and not used for mats)
opîwaya	body feather, coarse down feather; Feather (man in story)
opîwayiwechênêwa	puts small feathers on s.o.'s body
opîwayiwenêwa	puts small feathers on s.o.
opwehopwêhetîwaki (plural)	they make merry together
opyâwi	it is fun, there are merry doings
opyênekêwa	dances slowly
opyênesiwa	is slow
opyêneshkêwi	it goes slowly, is slow, is a slow process
opyêni	slowly, taking one's time
osâpamêwa, osâpatamwa	sees s.o., it from {somewhere}
osehkawêwa, osehkamwa	approaches s.o., it from {somewhere}
osehkêwa, osehkêwi	(animate, inanimate) comes from {somewhere}
osekwisiwa	has a father's sister; has (her) as a father's sister
osemiwa	has a daughter-in-law; has (her) as a daughter-in-law (**wêsemita** the woman's father-in-law or mother-in-law)

osesêhiwa	has an older brother, has (him) as an older brother
ositayaki (plural)	animal feet (as food) (**mahkwi-ositayaki** bear feet)
osîkashayêshinwa	has wrinkled skin
osîkawishinwa	is wrinkled from being in water
osîkinameshkêwawishinwa	has wrinkled skin from being in water
osîkîkwêwa (**osîkîkwêhiwa** dimin.)	has a wrinkled face
osîmemâwa, osîmêhemâwa	the younger brother or sister
osîmetîhaki (plural)	the brothers
osîmetîwaki (plural)	they are brothers, they are siblings
osîmêhiwa	has a younger brother or sister, has (him) as a younger brother, has (her) as a younger sister
osîmêhemêwa	has him as a younger brother, has her as a younger sister
osowânakwi (archaic **osowânokwi**)	a tail; his or her tail (**nesowânakwi** my tail)
osowânowi	a tail; his or her tail (**nesowânowi** my tail; **mesowânowi** a tail)
oshehkîhêwa, ashehkîhêwa	clothes s.o., adopts s.o. (for a deceased relative)
oshehkîhetîwaki (plural)	they clothe each other, adopt each other (ceremonially)
oshehkîtâkani	garment, clothing
oshehkîmêwa, oshehkîtamwa	wears s.o. (as, a hide), it
oshemîhiwa	has a niece, has (her) as a niece
oshêhkwâniwa	has a mane
oshêshkesîhemiwa	has an unmarried daughter
oshihkanwi	tallow; wax (more commonly **ashihkanwi**)
oshihoshi	slowly, as a slow process (particle)
oshimôkemiwa	has a cigarette, some cigarettes
oshinekêwa	the son-in-law
oshinetamwa	he is the son-in-law (**wêshinetaka** the son-in-law)
oshisêhemâkômêwa	addresses him and treats him as if he were one's mother's brother (**wêshisêhemâkômaka** my mother's brother's son [for example])
oshisêhemêwa	has him as a mother's brother, maternal uncle
oshisêhiwa	has a mother's brother, has (him) as a maternal uncle
oshiwa	she marries of her own accord
oshkasha	Tohkan (archaic; also Sauk dialect) (plural **oshkashaki**)
oshkashiwiwa	is a Tohkan (archaic; also Sauk dialect)
oshkinawêha	young man, unmarried young man; bachelor (**ketôshkinawêmenânaki** our young men)
oshkinawêhiwa, oshkinawêhiwiwa	he is a young man, he becomes a young man
oshkîshekwaki (plural)	yellow lotus seeds
oshôniyâhemiwa	has money, silver
oshôshiwa	wears shoes
otahamêwa	stands up for (s.o.), defends (s.o.), protects (s.o.) (**netotahama** I defend (s.o.))
otakâme	on {such} side of the lodge or river (particle)
otakisowa	gets lost from {somewhere}
otamesiwa	is busy
otamêwa, otatamwa (1)	bites s.o., it {somewhere}
otatamwa (2)	(infant) draws the milk
otatôhposôniwetamwa	has it as one's feast blanket or tablecloth
otami	taking time, spending time, being busy, occupied, preoccupied (preverb)
otamihêwa	bothers, inconveniences, hinders s.o., is a bother to s.o.
otamihiwêwa	bothers people, is a nuisance
otapenêhtôwa:	**otapenêhtôwa owîyawi** makes oneself hungry because of {something}

otapinêwa:	**wêtapinâchi** in one's regular place in the lodge, in one's spot
otapiwa	sits in {such} direction, on {such} side
otashâtîhemetamwa	has it for one's headed arrow
otatasaniwa	has a platform
otawahkyânemêwa	has s.o. as a slave, makes s.o. one's slave
otawêmâwitêhêwa	she thinks of (him) as her real brother
otawêmâwiwa	she has a brother, has (him) as a brother
otayimâkana (otayimâkâha dimin.)	pet, domestic animal
otayimêwa	has s.o. for a pet or domestic animal
otayiwa	has a pet, has (s.o.) as a pet
otayôweniwa	has (it) as something to use (song word)
otâchimôniwa	has a story
otâhînemiwa, otâhwînemiwa,	has (it) as a possession, has (it) as one's own
otâhîhemiwa, otâhwîhemiwa	
otâhînemetamawêwa	has (it) as a possession from s.o.
otâhînemetamwa	has it as a possession
otâhkwatomiwa	has (it) as a weapon
otâhkwe	in {such} direction, on {such} side (particle)
otâhpenanêwa	deals with, kills s.o. because of {something}
otâhpenêwa	dies because of {something}
otâkwapiwaki (plural)	they sit as a group on {such} side
otâkwiwa	she has a sister-in-law, has (her) as a sister-in-law
otâkwatîhaki (plural)	the sisters-in-law
otâmowa (idiom):	**wêtâmochi** took flight immediately
otânakatwi	a hole goes in {such} direction (**wêtânakateniki** into the hole [obviative])
otânakwêwa	has one's hole, burrow in {such} direction
o=tânâhka=kêhi, tânâhka=kêhi	or perhaps, or what about if it was this way (full form)
o=tânâh=kêhi, tânâh=kêhi	or perhaps, or what about if it was this way (shortened form)
otânematwi	it blows from {somewhere} (**wêtânemahki** the direction the wind is from)
otânesemâwa	the daughter
otânesemêwa	has her as a daughter
otânesetîhaki (plural)	the mother and daughter
otânesiwa	has a daughter; has (her) as a daughter
otâpanwi	dawn comes from {somewhere} (**wêtâpaki** east)
otâpihkâtawêwa	puts a strap on s.o. from {somewhere}
otâsiyâniwa	is wearing a breechcloth, wears (it) as a breechcloth
otâsiyânenamwa	uses it as a breechcloth
otâshkêwa	falls off; falls from {somewhere}, falls into {somewhere}
otehchi	getting it, accomplishing it (preverb)
otehchîwi (idiom):	**mêh-otehchîkwe** in no time at all (prioritive verb)
otehkesowa	is bruised by a gunshot
otehkêwa	travels for {some} reason
otehkiwa (or **otehkîwa**)	has a bruise
otehkoni	branch
otehkwêmâkômêwa	he addresses her and treats her as if she were his sister
otehkwêmemêwa	he has her as his sister
otehkwêmetîhaki (plural)	the brother and sister
otehkwêmetîwaki (plural)	they are brother and sister
otehkwêmiwa	he has a sister, he has (her) as his sister
otehtahkiwiwi (idiom):	**mêh-otehtahkiwikwe** in no time at all (prioritive verb)
otehtâpamêwa, otehtâpatamwa	(with negative): cannot make s.o., it out, does not get a good look at s.o., it

otehtâpatâniwa, otehtâpatâniwi   (with negative): cannot be made out; it cannot be made out, things cannot be made out

otehtenetîwaki (plural)   they get each other

otehtenêwa, otehtenamwa   gets s.o., it, obtains s.o., it

otehtênemêwa, otehtênetamwa   worries about s.o., it; is concerned about s.o., it

otehtênetamawêwa   does not want s.o. to have (it)

otekêwa   dances on {such} side

otenawêwa   shoots s.o. {somewhere (on the body)}

otenâtêwi   it is gotten from {somewhere}

otenetîwa   fights because of {something}

otenêwa, otenamwa   gets s.o., it from {somewhere}

otenowa   gets something for oneself from (s.o.)

otenwi   the wind blows from {somewhere}

otenya   shoulder (**netenyêki** my shoulders; **netenîki** on my shoulder or shoulders)

otesiwa   is intent on (it), devoted to (it), intends to gain from (it)

otesowa   is shot {somewhere} (with a gun)

oteshitêhâkaniwa   has a thought

oteshkîha   spleen

oteshkwêsêhemiwa   has a girl (as a daughter)

otêhiwa   has a heart

otêhtêkwayi   temple (of the head) (**netêhtêkwâki** on my temple)

otênemêwa   resents s.o. or holds something against s.o. for {some} reason; thinks s.o. is from {somewhere}

otênetâkosiwa   is thought to come from {somewhere}, belongs {somewhere}

otowêwa   stands up for (s.o.), defends (s.o.) verbally

otôhkanâhkomiwa   has on a bracelet or bracelets

otôhkimiwa   has land, has (it) as land

otôhpwâkanimotêhiwa   has a tobacco pouch, has (it) as a tobacco pouch

otôkimâmemêwa   has s.o. as chief

otôkimâmiwa   has a chief, has (s.o.) as a chief

otônenôhaki (plural)   kidneys

otônâpi   handle (as, of pail or kettle), bail

otôniwa   has a mouth; has (s.o.) speak for one

otôshkoshâkanemiwa   has on a bone-bead necklace (see **ashkoshâkanaki**)

otôtepîmi   his or her brain (archaic)

otôtêmâkômêwa   addresses s.o. and treats them as if they were one's sibling

otôtêmekôni, otôtêmekôhani   its (dog's or horse's) master

otôtêmetîwaki   they are siblings

otôtêmetîhaki (plural)   the siblings

otôtêmiwa   has a sibling, has (s.o.) as a sibling or clan totem

otôtêweniwa   has a town

owanahkwa   corn-tassel

owânakomiwa   has a hole

owâsîsani   nest

owâsîsaniwa   has a nest, makes a nest {somewhere}

owâwani   egg (**owâwanani** eggs; **owâwanwâwani, otôwâwanwâwani** their eggs)

owênêhâhkowiwa: **ketowênêhâhkowi** what kind of tree are you? (archaic; see **wênêhâhkowiwa**)

owênêhiwa: **ketowênêhi** who are you? (plural **ketowênêhipwa**) (archaic; see **wênêhiwa**)

owiyêha   someone, anyone; animal, creature; someone else, anyone else (**âkwi owiyêha** no one; [as a predicate] there is no one, is not {somewhere})

owiyêhâpamêwa	sees s.o. as another being
owiyêhetôwa	some or any spirit
owiyêhêha	(small) animal
owiyêhêhaya	small-animal skin, fur
owiyêhêhayi	furs (collective)
owiyêhi	some kind of (prenoun)
owiyêhiwa	is someone, is some (other) kind of animal (see also **êwiyêhikwêna**)
owîchi- (1) (prenoun with prefix)	one's fellow (see **nîchi-**)
owîchi- (2) (preverb)	fellow (in verbs of possession)
owîchi-manetômêwa	has s.o. as a fellow manitou (**wêwîchi-manetômenakôwe** you whom I have as fellow manitous)
owîchi-manetôwiwa	has (s.o.) as a fellow manitou (**wêwîchi-manetôwichiki** the fellow manitous of s.o.)
owîchîshkwêhetîwaki (plural)	they are enemies
owîchîshkwêhiwa	has an enemy, has (s.o.) as an enemy
owîhkânemêwa	has s.o. as a friend
owîhkânetîhaki (plural)	the friends, (especially) the two male friends
owîhkânetîwaki (plural)	they are friends
owîhkâniwa	has a friend, has (s.o.) as a friend
owîhtâtîhaki, owîhtâwetîhaki (plural)	the brothers-in-law
owîhtâtîwaki (plural)	they are brothers-in-law
owîhtâwemêwa	he has him as a brother-in-law
owîhtâwiwa	he has a brother-in-law, has him as a brother-in-law
owîkihêwa	makes or has s.o. have a dwelling {somewhere}, makes a dwelling for s.o. {somewhere}
owîkiwa (**owîkêhiwa** dimin.)	has a dwelling, dwells {somewhere}
owînakêwa	has a penis (**wêwînakâkini** as if having a penis)
owînemotîwaki (plural)	they are brother-in-law and sister-in-law
owînemwiwa	has a sibling-in-law of the opposite sex, he has (her) as his sister-in-law, she has (him) as her brother-in-law
owînenwa	a piece of fat, bear fat
owînenwi	fat (generic)
owînenwi-mîchîha	meadowlark
owînesiwa (**owînesêhiwa** dimin.)	has hair (on one's head)
owînwi	his or her navel (**owînwîki** on his or her navel)
owînwîshi	his or her navel (**kînwîshîki** at your navel)
owîpashkwa	corncob
owîpashkwi	of corncob (prenoun) (**owîpashkwi-nîchâpa** corncob doll)
owîpichi	his or her tooth; a tooth (**kîpitani** your teeth)
owîpichiwa	has teeth
owîpikani	marrow
owîpiwa	has an arrow, has (it) as an arrow
owîsayani (plural)	fur, hair (of an animal or of the human body)
owîsayiwêhiwi	it is a fur (dimin.)
owîsayiwitepêwa	has hair on one's head
owîsi	caul
owîsônihêwa	gives s.o. (it as) a name
owîshehkwayi:	(see **mîshehkwayi**)
owîtâkapîhani	his fellow son-in-law in their in-laws' house
owîtôshetîhaki (plural)	the co-wives
owîtôshetîwaki (plural)	they are co-wives
owîtôshiwa	she has a co-wife, has (her) as a co-wife
owîwashiwa	carries a pack, a back-load

owîwehkâsowa	he pretends to have (her) as his wife
owîwemêwa	he marries her, he has her as his wife
owîwetîwaki (plural)	they are married (to each other)
owîwetîweni	marriage, married life
owîwetîhaki (plural)	married couple, husband and wife
owîwihêwa	gets him to marry (her), has him marry (her)
owîwitêhêwa	he thinks of (her) as his wife
owîwiwa (**owîwêhiwa** dimin.)	he has a wife; he marries (her), is married to (her) (**wêwîwita** the husband)
owîwîna	horn (**nîwîneki** on my horn; **owîwînahi** his or her horns; **mîwînaki** horns)
owîwîniwa	has a horn or horns
owîyawiwa	has a body, has the body of (s.o.)
owîyâsi (**owîyâsêhi** dimin.)	flesh, meat
owîyâsiwiwa, owîyâsiwiwi	has flesh on one, has raw flesh; it is flesh, meat

ô

ô!	Oh!
ôchêwa	fly, housefly
ôchêwiwi	it has flies on it
ôhkomesemêwa	has her as a grandmother, is her grandchild
ôhkomesiwa	has a grandmother, has (her) as a grandmother, is (her) grandchild (**wêyôhkomesita** her grandchild, the grandchild of the woman)
ôhkwêwa	maggot
ôhkwêwiwa, ôhkwêwiwi	(animate, inanimate) is maggoty, has maggots
ôhô! (optionally nasalized)	Oh yes! So that's it!
ôhwâ!	Oh my! Oh no! Mercy me! (also **ohohwâ!**)
ôhyâ!	Oh my! Oh no! Mercy me! (also **ohohyâ!**)
ôni	and, then, and then (particle)
ôsâkômêwa	addresses him and treats him as if he were one's father (**wêyôsâkômaka** my father's brother)
ôsemêwa	has him as father, is his son or daughter
ôsiwa	has a father; has (him) as a father (**wêyôsiyâna** my father; **wêyôsita** the son or daughter of the man)
ôshisememêwa	has s.o. as a grandchild
ôshisemetîhaki (plural)	the grandparent and grandchild
ôshisemiwa	has a grandchild, has (s.o.) as a grandchild
ôtenawêwa	fasts without eating throughout the day
ôtêwenikâni	summer house (large rectangular bark-house of summer villages; now, a ceremonial house)
ôtêwenikêwa	lives in a summer house
ôtêweni	town
ôwatesiwiwi	there is a fog that comes up at night

p

pahkahwêwa, pahkahamwa	chops through the rope holding s.o.; chops it through
pahkahâtêwi	it (stringlike) is severed by tool, chopped through
pahkatêwa	is hungry (considered a Sauk word)
pahkenamawêwa	plucks (it) off for s.o.
pahkenêwa, pahkenamwa	breaks s.o., it (stringlike) apart; pulls s.o., it off, plucks s.o., it off; picks s.o. (as, fruit), it
pahkeshamawêwa	cuts (it, something stringlike) for s.o.
pahkeshamwa	cuts it (something stringlike), cuts it loose, cuts the cord holding it
pahkeshkêwa	is cut loose; is set free
pahkeshkêwi	it (stringlike) breaks
pahkêkiwa	branches, has a limb or limbs, deviates from the norm
pahkêsenwi	it (as, a road) branches off
pahkêwa	branches off, goes off in a different direction from the others, turns aside, gets off the road
pahkêyânakatwi	the hole or cave branches off
pahkêyâwi	it branches off
pahkihêwa	distributes food to s.o.
pahkihtêhpwêwa	knocks out or kills s.o. by biting
pahkihtêhwêwa	knocks out or kills s.o. by striking with something
pahkihtêkêwa	dances oneself to exhaustion or death
pahkihtêmowa	passes out from crying
pahkihtênawêwa	knocks s.o. unconscious with a shot
pahkihtênehkawêwa	chases s.o. until they pass out
pahkihtêpahowa	passes out from running
pahkihtêpenêwa	starves to death
pahkihtêpinêwa	chokes s.o. unconscious
pahkihtêsowa	passes out from the heat
pahkihtêshinwa	falls unconscious
pahkihtêshkêwa	vomits and retches to death; trembles to death
pahkihtêwachimêwa	freezes s.o. to death
pahkikêmowa	assigns dishes of food to people in a ceremony
pahkimêwa	permits, assigns s.o.; invites s.o. to eat in a ceremony, assigns (ceremonial food) to s.o.
pahkinesêmâwêwa	plucks tobacco leaves
pahkinwiyêwa	one's umbilical cord separates off
pahkisahêwa	pulls s.o. off
pahkitêhêwa	makes up one's mind
pahkitîwi	selectively, as the ceremonial assignment to selected ones (preverb)
pahkiwa	ruffed grouse, partridge ("pheasant")
pahkiwisowa	is a member of the "Pheasant" Clan (**pêhkiwisota** member of the "Pheasant" Clan)
pahkîkwahtêwi	it is so smoky it bothers the eyes
pahkîkwasowa	one's eyes are bothered by smoke
pahkohikêwa	extracts a disease object (by traditional doctoring)
pahkonamawêwa	pulls (it) out for s.o.
pahkonêwa, pahkonamwa	pulls s.o., it out; plucks s.o. (feather); takes s.o. (kettle) off the fire; removes it (lodge-covering)
pahkoshkêwi	it fell out (as, a tooth) (plural **papahkoshkêwani**)
pahkowêwa	declares one's decision
pahkwachiwênêwa, pahkwachiwênamwa	pulls s.o. (as, a cornstalk), it up by the roots (see **papahkw-**)
pahkwachiwêsahtôwa	tears it up by the roots

pahkwachiwêshkêwi	becomes uprooted
pahkwanâshinwa	is blown off
pahkwaneshamwa	cuts it off (as, a scalp or braid)
pahkwanîwi	its bark is loose (of a tree in the spring)
pahkwâpowênikêwa	takes the kettle of soup off the fire
pahkwêhamwa	chops a piece off it
pahkwêhpwêwa, pahkwêhtamwa	bites a piece out of s.o., it
pahkwêkahesâni	wood-chip
pahkwêshamawêwa	cuts a slice of (it) from s.o.
pahkwêshikani	bread; wheat flour
pahkwêshikêwa	cuts off a slice of (it)
pahkwêshkêwi	it tears off, chips off; it is torn off, chipped off
pahkwêshwêwa, pahkwêshamwa	cuts a slice from s.o., it
pahkwihkamênowa	removes one's pipe from one's mouth
pahkwitenyêsahêwa	pulls s.o.'s shoulder out of joint
pahkwiwinêwa	sheds one's horns
pahpawihkeshêwêhwêwa	knocks the ashes out of s.o. (a pipe)
pahpawinawîwa	(bird) flaps itself
pahpawisahêwa	shakes s.o. violently (see **pawisahêwa**)
pahtêhchikawêwa	lights the pipe for s.o.
pahtêhpwêwa	lights s.o. (tobacco, pipe), puffs to get s.o. (pipe) lit
pahtêhtamawêwa	lights (it, a pipe) for s.o.
pakamahkiwiwi	there is an arrival
pakameshkawêwa	comes upon s.o., comes to s.o.
pakamênemêwa	thinks s.o. has arrived
pakamêwa, pakatamwa (1)	hits s.o., it; throws (it) at s.o., it; hurls (it) (as, insults) at s.o.
pakami	arriving (preverb)
pakamikâpawîhtawêwa	arrives and stands before s.o.
pakamikâpawînotawêwa	arrives and stands before s.o.
pakamikâpawinohkatawêwa	arrives and stands before s.o.
pakamikâpâwa	stands arrived
pakamipahowa	arrives running
pakamîtêmêwa	arrives in company with s.o. (for **pakami-wîtêmêwa**)
pakamwêwêshinwa	arrives with noise
pakanâmowa	(with negative): utters no sound
pakapahkwêhamwa	knocks on the side of it with something
pakapahkwêhikêwa	knocks on the side of the lodge with something
pakatamwa (2)	strikes the post (gives a ritual account of the killing of an enemy)
pakatisowa	hits oneself
pakâhokowa, pakâhanwi	(animate, inanimate) is reached by the rising flood
pakâhôtôwa	drags it under the water
pakânâhkwi	walnut tree
pakânâhkowiwa	is a walnut tree
pakâni	nut (generic); hickory nut (also **peshkipêhi-pakâni**); black walnut (also **mahkwi-pakâni**)
pakâshimêwa, pakâhtôwa	puts s.o., it in the kettle to boil, boils s.o., it
pakâyâshowîwa	wades into the water
pakenêshêwi	it (fire) sends out a spark
pakesowa, paketêwi	(animate, inanimate) explodes (from heat or otherwise)
pakeshkêwa:	(with negative): does not show up, is not seen around
pakikawihtôwa	pours it by drops
pakikêwi	it drips (**êh=pakikâki** it dripped)
pakinetîwaki (plural)	they release each other, hold an adoption for each other

pakinêwa (1), **pakitamwa** (1)	sets s.o., it down; throws s.o., it down or away; divorces s.o.
pakinêwa (2)	releases s.o. (deceased relative) by ceremonially adopting someone of the same sex and the same approximate age
pakisahwêwa, pakisahamwa	throws s.o., it out, headlong; serves it out
pakisapinêwa	sets s.o. loose from their bonds
pakisatahwêwa	strikes s.o. down, clubs s.o. down
pakisatamwa	drops it from one's mouth
pakisâhkwimêwa	declares s.o. free, turns s.o. loose
pakisâpamêwa	takes one's eyes off s.o., quits looking at s.o.
pakisâsetawêwa	sets (it) on the wind to fall for s.o.
pakisâshimêwa	sets s.o. on the wind to fall
pakisâshinwa	blows in on the wind and lands
pakisehkawêwa, pakisehkamwa	kicks s.o., it to land somewhere; he kicks s.o., it over; runs into s.o. and knocks them down
pakisenamawêwa	sets (it) down for s.o.; lets (it) go for s.o.
pakisenêwa, pakisenamwa	sets s.o., it down; lets s.o., it go, releases s.o.
pakisênemêwa, pakisênetamwa	puts s.o., it out of one's thoughts (also **pakitênemêwa**)
pakisowa	ducks, turns aside quickly, looks away quickly
pakishêwêshkêwa	relaxes, one's muscles relax
pakishimowi	it is sunset (**êh=pakishimoki, wêchi-pakishimoki** west)
pakishinwa, pakisenwi	lands, alights ({somewhere}); it lands ({somewhere})
pakishiwenêwa, pakishiwetôwa	takes s.o., it {somewhere}; takes s.o. {somewhere} and leaves them, it, lets them go
pakitamawêwa	throws (it) down for s.o.
pakitamôweni	ceremonial adoption (releasing deceased relative)
pakitamwa (2)	holds a ceremonial adoption (releasing deceased relative)
pakitênemêwa	puts s.o. out of one's thoughts (rare; see **pakisênemêwa**)
pakiwayâhi	piece of cloth (also **papakiwayâhi**)
pakôsosêwa	walks on ahead (archaic) (see **pakôshosêwa**)
pakôshêwîwa	does work in advance, does something ahead of time
pakôshi	beforehand, to be ready ahead of time (preverb)
pakôshosêwa	walks on ahead (also **pakôsosêwa**)
pakwachi	wild (prenoun)
pakwanawesiwa	does the wrong thing feigning ignorance
panahwêwa, panahamwa	misses hitting s.o., it by tool or thrown object
panakahamwa	chops or scrapes the bark or rind off of it
panakinameshkêshkêwa	one's skin is peeling off
panakîhaki (plural)	hominy, lye hominy
panakeswêwa, panakesamwa	scorches s.o., it; parches s.o., it
panakesikêwa	parches corn
panamêwa, panatamwa	snaps at s.o. and misses, drops it in eating
panapinêwa	fails to lasso s.o.
panashâha	young (of animal or bird)
panashâhi	interest (on a bank account)
panâchâwi	it is ruined
panâchi	at the point of suffering one's fate or succumbing (preverb) (**panâchi-nêmowa** is struggling to breathe)
panâchihêwa, panâchihtôwa	ruins s.o., it; bewitches or puts a spell on s.o., it; causes s.o.'s death
panâchimowa	gives an incorrect or incomplete account or telling
panâchishimowa	loses one's voice
panâchitêhêwa	thinks one is done for, one's heart sinks
panâpamêwa, panâpatamwa	loses sight of s.o., it
panâpatamâtisowa	loses sight of (it) for oneself

panâtesiwa	loses consciousness, loses one's strength; succumbs, perishes, meets one's fate; (wagon) collapses
panâtesîmikatwi	it (as, a life or the name of one who dies) is lost
panehtawêwa	loses s.o. from hearing
panenêwa, panenamwa	loses hold of s.o., it; drops s.o., it; skips, omits s.o.
panesihêwa	he beats s.o. in winning war honors (by killing an enemy first)
panesihtôwa	he wins top war honors
panesiwênemowa	gives up
paneshkawêwa, paneshkamwa	misses stepping on s.o., it, steps clear of s.o., it
panênetamwa	completely forgets it; loses consciousness
pani	mistakenly (preverb)
panihkamêwa	misses out on smoking
panitepêhwêwa	strikes at s.o.'s head with something and misses
panîsa	police officer
panôkâhkohamwa	scrapes the bark off of it
panôkeshamwa	peels it with a knife
panôkikeshwêwa	cuts the bark off of s.o. (a tree)
papahkenêwa, papahkenamwa	breaks s.o., it apart (with multiple breaks); picks them (animate, inanimate)
papahkeshwêwa, papahkeshamwa	cuts s.o.'s bonds, severs them (with multiple cuts)
papahkimini	nannyberry
papahkîha	soft-shell turtle
papahkonêwa, papahkonamwa	pulls them out (animate, as feathers; inanimate)
papahkoshkêwani (plural)	(see **pahkoshkêwi**)
papahkwachiwêyâsenôni (plural)	they (inanimate) are blown up by the roots
papahkwachiwênamwa	pulls them (inanimate) up by the roots (see **pahkw-**)
papahkwachiwêpokôtêwani (plural)	they are uprooted by the flood
papahkwâkênêwa	plucks s.o.'s wing-feathers
papahkwâpitêhwêwa	knocks s.o.'s teeth out
papahkwâpitênêwa	pulls s.o.'s teeth out
papahkwêshwêwa, papahkwêshamwa	cut slices or chunks off s.o., it (see **pahkwêshwêwa**)
papakanikwa	flying squirrel
papakanikwânowi	flying-squirrel tail
papakâpînamwa	braids it
papakâshkatêsêwa	falls flat on one's stomach
papakâshkatêshinwa	lies flat on one's stomach
papakâshkechêhokônêwa	flattens s.o. by letting something fall on them
papakâshkipehkwanêyâwi	it has a flat roof
papakâshkitepêshkêwa	flattens one's head (as, a snake)
papakâshkyâwi	it is flat
papakâtakwa	cedar leaves
papakehkôhi	flat ceremonial war club, gunstock war club
papakenâwa	corncake
papakesa	grasshopper (variety)
papakêhimotêshinwa	one's belly has thin skin as one lies
papakêhimotêwa	one's belly has thin skin
papakêhinechêwa	one's hands have thin skin
papakêhiwa, papakêhenôhiwi (Jones: **papakêhenwi**)	is thin (as, buckskin), it is thin
papakiwayâhi (**papakiwayâhêhi** dimin.)	cloth, piece of cloth (also **pakiwayâhi**)
papakiwayânimotêhi	cloth bag
papakiwayânikâni (also **pakiwayânikâni**)	tent
papakonamwa	loosens it (to hang loosely)
papakotonêshinwa	one's lips are loose

papakwâsiyêwa	his breechcloth hangs loosely
papakwâwi	it hangs loosely, it (as, a tent) is loose
papakwinameshkêwa	one's skin is loose
papakwîkwêwa	one's face is loose
papakyêhi (**papakyêhêhi** dimin.)	axe, hatchet
papakyêhiwiwa	(the pipe) has an axe-blade on it, is a pipe-tomahawk
papasanasitêpahowa	runs with one's feet barely touching the ground
papasipahowa	runs skipping or bouncing along
papasisêwa (also: **pasipasisêwa**)	goes bouncing along
papâmehkêwa	goes about, travels around
papâmeshkêwaki (plural)	they (animate) run or fly around; they (as, horns) fall off
papâmi	about (preverb)
papâmihêwa	goes about {some way}
papâmisêwa	flies about
papâmitâhkwikâni	log cabin
papâmitekêwa	dances facing to one side and then the other
papâmwêtamwa	goes around crying out the news or announcement
papâmwêwêsenwi	it resounds about
papâsikahwêwa, papâsikahamwa	chops s.o., it into pieces (see **pâsikahwêwa**)
papâsikâsenôni (plural)	they (inanimate) are blown down and split apart
papâsiki (particle)	half and half, in two equal parts
papîsanâkamîwa, papîsanâkamîwi	one's bubbles come up in the water, there are bubbles coming up in the water
papîsikashêwi	(of) tiny hoof (prenoun) (**wâpi-papîsikashêwi-mîshâmi** white tiny hoof sacred pack)
papîwâhenôni, papîwâhenôhiwani (plurals)	they (inanimate) are small, tiny
papîweshîhiwaki, papîweshîhêhiwaki (plurals)	they (animate) are small, tiny
papîwi	small (plural) (prenoun)
papîwikenôhiwani (plural)	they (inanimate) are small (**pêpîwikenôhiki** any little thing)
papîwi-manetôhêhiwaki (plural)	they are small spirits
pasakwachihikêwa	glues, applies (it as) glue
pasakwachihwêwa, pasakwachihamwa	sticks s.o., it on, makes s.o., it stick on, glues s.o., it on
pasakwâwi	it is sticky
pasakwishinwa	sticks to {somewhere}, is or gets up against {somewhere} (as, a wall)
pasanosiwa, pasanwâwi	has a chip out of it
pasanotonwa, pasanotonêyâwi	(kettle) has a chip out of the rim, (dish) has a chip out of the edge
pasâhkosowa	has a fever
pasâpehkesamwa	heats it as metal
pasâpehkwa	coal; lump of coal (also **pasâpehkwaki** coal)
pasâpôhtêwi	it (liquid) is piping hot
pasâpôsamwa	heats it as liquid
pasâwaketêwi	the ground or earth is or gets hot
pasechêhwêwa	gives s.o. a slap on the stomach
pasehkîki	at or to the foot of the hill (particle) (also **pasihkîki**)
pasekwîchisahêwa	jerks s.o. to their feet
pasekwîchisêwa	jumps to one's feet
pasekwîtenêwa	stands s.o. up, lifts s.o. to their feet
pasekwîwa	stands up, rises, gets to one's feet
pasesowa, pasetêwi	(animate, inanimate) is hot
paseshênawêwa	grazes s.o.'s ear with a shot
pasetonêhwêwa	slaps s.o. on the mouth
pasi (preverb):	**pasi-wâpamêwa** shoots s.o. a quick glance
pasihketêwi	it is heated all the way through

pasihkîki (**pasihkîheki** dimin.)	at or to the foot of the hill (particle) (also **pasehkîki**)
pasikâhkwa	finished board (**pasikâhkwaki** lumber)
pasikâhkwi	board
pasikomêhwêwa	grazes s.o.'s nose
pasisahêwa	skims s.o., swishes s.o. on the surface of the water
pasitiyêhikani	quirt (riding whip), switch
pasinowêtiyêhwêwa	spanks s.o.
pasitiyêhwêwa	spanks s.o.
pasîkwêchinwa	hits one's face on a branch
pasîkwêhwêwa	slaps s.o. in the face
paswêwi	it echoes
pashi	almost; (with negative): not at all (preverb)
pashichôka	poor old man
pashinanêwa, pashinatôwa	almost kills s.o., it
pashitowâkani	lies (**opashitowâkani** his or her lies)
pashitowêwa	tells a lie
pashitowêwênemêwa	thinks s.o. a liar
pashitôha (**pashitôhêha** dimin.)	old man (also **pashitôka**)
pashitôhikihtôwa	makes it be like an old man
pashitôhiwa	he is an old man (also **pashitôkiwa**)
pashitôhîhkâsowa	pretends to be an old man
pashitôka	old man (more commonly **pashitôha**)
pashitôkiwa	he is an old man (more commonly **pashitôhiwa**)
pashîshkenêwa	pulls the skin off s.o. (as, a rabbit) (also **pashôshkenêwa**)
pashîshkinameshkênêwa	pulls s.o.'s skin off
pashkichikâshkêwa	throws one's leg over
pashkichimotêhi	saddlebag
pashkichipahowa	runs over the top
pashkichisahêwa	throws s.o. (as, a hide) to hang over something
pashkichisahowa	jumps across, jumps over
pashkichishinwa, pashkichisenwi	(animate, inanimate) lies across, hangs over, crosses
pashkichiwetôwa	carries it over (as, a hill)
pashkitâsîwa	climbs over the top
pashkitôtêwa	crawls over the top
pashkohkêwi	it falls out (as, hair)
pashkonamâhkwîwa	loses one's hold, loses the grip that is supporting one's weight
pashkonamwa	drops it, fails to catch it
pashkwahikani	beaming tool, scraper for removing hair from hide
pashkwahwêwa (also **pashkohwêwa**)	scrapes the hair off s.o. (a hide)
pashkwânehkwênikêwa	does the plucking of the hair
pashkwâkômêwa	omits s.o. from one's kin
pashkwâtotamawêwa	leaves (it) out in telling s.o.
pashkwi	(with **âkwi nekotahi**): there is no place not affected (in the specified way) (preverb)
pashôshkâhkohwêwa	chops the bark of s.o. (a tree)
pashôshkenêwa, pashôshkenamwa	pulls the skin off of s.o. (as, a rabbit), husks s.o. (corn); peels it (also **pashîshkenêwa**)
pashôshkenikêwa	is husking corn
patahkahikani, patahkâpyêhikani	"fork" (wooden spear for turning meat)
patahkahwêwa, patahkahamwa	pierces (the surface of) s.o., it, sticks something sharp into s.o., it
patahkechêhwêwa	spears s.o.
patahkechêshkawêwa	spurs s.o.
patahkichinwa	is stuck by something sharp
patahkisetôwa	sets it piercing, sticks it in

patahkwêwa	singes (an animal for cooking) in the fire
patashkapitêwi	it is tied on, it is tied to the outside
patapatakwânakîkwêwa	has dreamy eyes
patashkepyêhokowa	is splashed by a mass of water
patashkikwamwa	sews it on
patashkisahtôwa	throws or slaps it against something to stick
patashkisetôwa	makes it stick on something
patashkisêwa, patashkisêwi	(animate, inanimate) falls and sticks
patashkishinwa	is plastered against something (plural **pepyêtashkishinôki**)
pawenamwa	shakes it out, shakes it clean
pawenikêwa	dusts the place
pawihkeshêwêsahêwa	shakes the ashes out of s.o. (pipe)
pawinehkêsahowa	shakes one's hand off
pawisahêwa, pawisahtôwa	shakes s.o. (as, a pipe), it out
payâhkichi	in another way or direction, in the wrong way or direction (particle)
payâhkichinâkosiwa	has an unseemly expression on one's face
payâhkitâchimowa	gets on the wrong track in what one says, says something out of the way
pâhkakonêwa	takes the covers off s.o.
pâhkakoshênowa	throws off the covers
pâhkanonêwa, pâhkanonamwa	opens what s.o. is in, opens it (as, bag or bottle)
pâhkanoshkêwi	its opening opens up
pâhkatenamwa	rips it at the seam, opens the cover on it (as, a box)
pâhkâhkohwêwa	sets s.o. free
pâhkâhkoshkêwa	becomes free, is liberated
pâhkânakeshênêwa	opens s.o.'s ears
pâhkânaketêwi (Jones)	a hole opens from heat or gunshot
pâhkenamawêwa	uncovers, opens (it) for s.o.; opens the door for s.o.
pâhkenêwa, pâhkenamwa	uncovers, opens s.o., it
pâhkeshkêwi	it opens, it opens up, falls open, comes open
pâhketonwa	opens one's mouth (see **pâhpâhketonôki**)
pâhkisenwi	it lies open, it is opened, it is allowed
pâhkisetawêwa	leaves (it) open for s.o. (a door or an opportunity)
pâhkisetôwa	leaves it open
pâhkishkwâtawênamawêwa	opens the door for s.o.
pâhkîkwênêwa	uncovers s.o.'s face
pâhkîkwênwa	opens one's eyes, uncovers one's eyes, face
pâhkîkwêshimêwa	uncovers s.o.'s face
pâhkîwa	emerges from taboo or concealment
pâhpakikêwi	it is dripping (**êh=pâhpakikâki** it dripped)
pâhpakinîkwêkâpâwa	stands shedding tears
pâhpâhketonôki nenemehkiwaki	there is (thunder and) lightning ("the thunderers are opening their mouths") (see **pâhketonwa**)
pâhpâkahwêwa	pats s.o.
pâhpâkepyêhamwa	pats it (water) repeatedly
pâhpâshânani (plural)	thin slices of dried meat
pâhpâshkahikêwa	cracks nuts
pâhpâshkâwakîwi	the earth is dried and cracked
pâhpâshkâwaketêwi	it (earth) is dried and cracked
pâhpâshkinechêwa	has chapped hands
pâhpâshkitepêhčikêwa	cracks some heads
pâhpâshkitepêshimêwa	smashes s.o.'s head against something
pâhpâshkitôtanwa	has chapped heels
pâhpiwa	performs tricks
pâhpiweni	trick

pâhpiwênêwa, pâhpiwênamwa	crumbles and sprinkles s.o. (as, tobacco), it
pâhpîha	performer (of tricks) (plural **pâhpîhaki** the circus)
pâhtâchinwa	is caught or snagged on something and injured
pâhtâhêwa	beats s.o. severely
pâhtâmêwa	says hurtful things to s.o.
pâhtâsowa	is seriously wounded by gunshot
pâkahamawêwa	knocks at (it, the door) for s.o.
pâkahatowêwa	plays lacrosse; plays baseball
pâkahâhkwâha	domestic fowl; chicken, rooster
pâkahâhkwâhehkêha	chickenhawk
pâkahâtîha (**pâkahâtîhêha** dimin.)	chicken
pâkâhkotonêshinwa	bumps oneself on the mouth
pâkâhkwishinwa, pâkâhkwisenwi	bumps against a tree or other unyielding object, cannot get in (the house); it bumps against an unyielding object
pâkechêshimêwa, pâkechêsetôwa	slaps s.o., it down or against something
pâkechêshinwa	falls on one's belly
pâkikomêshinwa	bumps one's nose
pâkitenyêhwêwa	slaps s.o. on the shoulder
pâkohwêwa	drives s.o. away by what one says, scares s.o. off
pâkosôha	whole-grain hominy (dried corn, roasted then boiled)
pâkwahikani	drumstick
pâkwîwa	goes fast (archaic)
pânachiwêpahowa	runs downhill
pânachiwêsêwa	runs downhill
pânachîwa	goes downhill, goes downslope
pânekwashiwa	emerges fully from sleep, becomes wide awake
pânêshkapihamwa	straddles it
pânêshkapiwa	sits astraddle
pânîhêwa	frees s.o. (widow or widower) from strict mourning restrictions
pânîwa	is a widow or widower no longer under strict mourning restrictions
pânôhi	not until then (particle)
pâpahkêwaki (plural)	they part company
pâpahkyênêwa	scratches s.o. up, tears s.o. up
pâpahkyêsahêwa	clawed s.o. to pieces
pâpakachikani	hammer
pâpakachikêwa	slays s.o., clubs s.o. to death
pâpakamêwa	clubs, beats s.o. to death
pâpakatamawêwa	clubs (s.o.) to death for s.o.
pâpakesôhaki (plural)	popcorn
pâpakisapenêhtôwa:	**kîwi-pâpakisapenêhtôwa owîyawi** makes oneself go around collapsing from hunger
pâpakonamwa	takes it (a covering) off; takes the covering off of it (as, a winter lodge)
pâpakonapahkwêwa	takes the covering off a winter lodge
pâpakwakoshêshkawêwa	strips the covers off s.o. by bodily movement
pâpakwisahêwa, pâpakwisahtôwa	whips the covering off s.o., it
pâpakisehkâtîwaki (plural)	they keep running into each other
pâpekwa	immediately, right away, at the first opportunity; I see you've wasted no time! you didn't hesitate! (as a criticism) (particle)
pâsa	boss
pâsanâmowa	feels bloated, has gastric bloating
pâsanenwa	is bloated from rotting
pâseshkêwa, pâseshkêwi	(animate, inanimate) swells up
pâsikahwêwa, pâsikahamwa	chops s.o., it in two
pâsikâkachiwa	(bow) snaps in two from the cold

136

pâsikenêwa, pâsikenamwa (1)	divides s.o., it in two, tears s.o., it in two
pâsikenamwa (2)	splits it in two with a shot
pâsiki	half (particle, prenoun)
pâsitawênemêwa, pâsitawênetamwa	is thinking about s.o., it all the time
pâsitawi	all the time, always (particle)
pâsiwiwa	is the boss
pâshi	until, continuing until (particle)
pâshisêwa	(the sun) goes past noon
pâshkahwêwa, pâshkahamwa	cracks s.o., it open
pâshkatamôha	parrot (originally, Carolina parakeet)
pâshkâpihêwa	lets s.o. crack open their eyes
pâshkâwesiwa	(a fish) spawns
pâshkâwêshkâtêwi	it (egg) is hatched
pâshkâwêwa	(bird) hatches
pâshkehkêwi	it burst open (as, a bag, an acorn)
pâshkechêhtamwa	bursts it open by biting it
pâshkechêshwêwa, pâshkechêshamwa	cuts s.o., it open
pâshkenamwa	breaks it, cracks it open (as, an egg in one's hand)
pâshkesikani	gun, explosive
pâshkesikêwa	shoots a firearm
pâshkeswêwa	shoots s.o. with a firearm, strikes s.o. with lightning
pâshkinêhwêwa	flicks s.o. with one's finger (especially on the forehead)
pâshkinîpîwi	it (tree) is budding out
pâshkinîkwêwa	has a broken eye
pâshkyâwi	it is cracked, burst open, has a crack
pâshkyêwakeshkêwi	its surface cracks apart
pâtôhka, pâtôhkâha	Comanche
pâtôhkenetîwa	he fights the Comanches
pâwâhiwa	holds a powwow
pâwi	not (preverb) (younger form of **pwâwi**)
pâyôhkatwi	there is a heavy dew
pe=	(see **pena!**)
pechihêwa	hinders s.o. (**nepechihekwi** it hinders me)
pechihtôwa	makes a cache (of supplies, equipment) for future use; caches (it, animate or inanimate)
pechikâchinwa	trips on something
pechikâshimôhkânowa	pretends to stumble
pechikâshinwa	stumbles, trips and falls
pechimêwa	forbids s.o.
pechinôshkawêwa	sees s.o. off, sees s.o. on their way
pehchamêhêwa	deceives s.o., fools s.o.; makes s.o. think the wrong thing
pehchamêmêwa	deceives s.o., fools s.o.; has s.o. thinking the wrong thing by what one says
pehchawiwa	makes a mistake
pehchi	by mistake (preverb)
pehchihtôwa	makes a mistake in making it
pehki	differently (preverb)
pehkiwa, pehkenwi	is different, is someone else, is an outsider; it is different
pehkiwêhehkêwa	picks cherries
pehkiwêhi	cherry
pehkiwêhimishi	cherry tree
pehkînawêwa, pehkînamwa	thinks s.o., it looks different, strange; (the other, it) does not look the same to one
pehkînawiwa	acts different

pehkînâchimowa	gives a different report or message
pehkînâkôtisowa	notices something different about oneself
pehkînâpamêwa, pehkînâpatamwa	sees something different about s.o., it (also **pehkînwâpamêwa, pehkînwâpatamwa**)
pehkînâpatâniwa	looks different
pehkînâtowêwa	speaks a different language
pehkînenîha	Potawatomi
pehkîni	different, differently (particle, preverb, prenoun)
pehkînikiwa, pehkînikenwi	(animate, inanimate) is different, changed, of a different nature
pehkîninâkêwa	sings differently
pehkîninâkosiwa, pehkîninâkwatwi	looks different from before, looks strange
pehkînisetôwa	places it differently
pehkînisowa	is of another clan
pehkînowêwa	speaks differently
pehkînwâpamêwa, pehkînwâpatamwa	sees something different about s.o., it (also **pehkînâpamêwa, pehkînâpatamwa**)
pehkînwênemêwa, pehkînwênetamwa	thinks there is something different about s.o., it, notices a change in s.o., it
pehkochâni	ball of twine
pehkochêpiwa	sits hunched up, sits on one's haunches
pehkonamwa	forms it into a ball
pehkopyêsenwi	it is a pool or puddle
pehkotênemiwa	is overtaken by nightfall
pehkotêsenwi	it is dark inside
pehkotêsêwi	it suddenly gets dark
pehkotêwi	it is night
pehkwahikani	hill (where crops are planted)
pehkwahokowaki (plural)	they drift in a bunch, they (as, fish) swim in a bunch
pehkwapichikani (**pehkwapichikâhi** dimin.)	bundle
pehkwapinêwa, pehkwapitôwa	ties s.o., it in a bundle; has s.o., it tied in a bundle
pehkwapitawêwa	ties (it) into a bundle for s.o.
pehkwapisowa, pehkwapitêwi	(animate, inanimate) is tied in a bundle
pehkwashkisenwi	there is a clump of grass, reeds
pehkwâhki	ball (**nepehkwâhki** my ball)
pehkwâhkwâwi	grove of trees
pehkwâhkwâwiwi	it is a grove of trees
pehkwâkwanêwa, pehkwâkwatôwa	lays s.o. in a heap; piles it up, leaves a pile of it
pehkwâkwasowa, pehkwâkwatêwi	(animate, inanimate) lies in a pile
pehkwâsenwi	it is blown in a lump
pehkwekêwaki	they dance in a bunch
pehkwehpowi	it snows in clumps
pehkwi	in a clump, dense (preverb)
pehkwikanâkani	ankle
pehkwikanêwa	has lumps on one's bones
pehkwikâpâwaki (plural)	they stand close together
pehkwikenôhi	knot (in wood)
pehkwikîhi	knobbed war club, ball-headed war club
pehkwitepêwa	is lump-headed
pehtatahokowa	gets accidentally hit by a thrown object
pehtatahwêwa	accidentally strikes s.o. (as, with a club)
pehtawanêwa	makes a fire for s.o.
pehtawasowa	makes a fire for oneself
pehtawatôwa	gets it (fire, log) burning, keeps it going
pehtawâni (only possessed):	**opehtawâni** his (namely, the chief's) fire (i.e., village) (archaic)

pehtawêwa	makes a fire; makes a fire with (it), burns (it) in the fire
pehtenawêwa	accidentally shoots s.o.
pehteshowa	accidentally cuts oneself
pekâchênamwa	crumbles it
pekechênêwa, pekechênamwa (1)	crumbles s.o. (as, tobacco), it
pekechênamwa (2)	shoots it to pieces
pekechêshkawêwa, pekechêshkamwa	kicks s.o., it to pieces
pekechêyâsenwi	it is blown to bits (by wind)
pekenêwa	shells s.o. (corn) (i.e., removes dried kernels from cob)
pekeshawanêwa, pekeshawatôwa	"smokes" s.o., it, fumigates s.o., it ceremonially; smokes it up (as, a house)
pekeshawêwa	makes a cloud of smoke (as, a smoker); has a fire going
-pekeshe	smoke (in a particle compound) (**nâwi-pekeshe** in the smoke)
pekeshêwi	it smokes, it is smoky, it is foggy
pekihkahwêwa, pekihkahamwa	smashes s.o., it to pieces
pekihkenêwa, pekihkenamwa	crumbles s.o. (as, tobacco), it to pieces
pekihkeshkêwi	it goes to pieces
pekihkeshwêwa, pekihkeshamwa	cuts s.o., it to bits
pekihketêwi	it is blown to bits (by gunshot or explosion)
pekihkishinwa	falls in pieces
pekihtanwa	has a nosebleed (**pekihtasa** would have a nosebleed)
pekimishâhkwa	Kentucky coffee tree
pekishkamatamwa	suffers with pain
pekishkênetamwa	thinks it troublesome, too much trouble
pekishkihêwa	pesters s.o., torments s.o.
pekishkimêwa	pesters s.o., troubles s.o. by speech
pekishkinawêhêwa	causes s.o.'s feelings to be hurt, disappoints s.o.
pekishkitêhêwa	is troubled
pekishkîhkâtîwaki (plural)	they quarrel, make trouble for each other
pekishkîyâwi	there is a stretch of bad weather
pekishkyâwi	it is troublesome, tiresome
pekiwa	pitch, gum
pekohkwêwa	gathers bark sheets (for lodge-coverings)
pekohwêwa, pekohamwa	pecks or chips s.o. (as, a tree), it; chips s.o., it out with a tool
pekonêyâwakîwi	the ground is dusty
pekoshkamwa	wears it out (as, a moccasin)
pekowâhkwihtôwa	makes it dusty
pekowechêkôtêwi	it (as, a sacred bundle) hangs with dust (of ashes) on it
pekoweshkâtêwi	it is (made) dusty from being traveled on
pekowiwa, pekowiwi	(animate, inanimate) is dusty
pekowîkwêshinwa	lies with dusty face
pekwahôkêwa	paws the earth (as, an angry bull) (**êh=pekwahôkâchi** pawed the earth)
pekwi	dust, ashes
pemahowa	paddles by in a canoe
pemahônêwa, pemahôtôwa	drags s.o., it along
pemahwêwa	is mindful or respectful of s.o.
pemanâmowa	swims along or by underwater
pematahokowa	goes by carrying (it as) a load on one's back
pematahwêwa	hits s.o. in passing
pematonêhwêwa	goes by looking for s.o.
pemâhkiwiwi	it is a hill
pemâhkwâwiwi	a grove of trees extends along
pemâhkwisenwi	it lies along as a solid
pemâhtôwa (only in an idiom):	**neshi-pemâhtôwa** manages by oneself

pemâkwapiwaki (plural)	they sit together in a row (or rows) or in a bunch
pemâkwasowaki, pemâkwatêwani (plurals)	they (animate, inanimate) are sitting or lying in one place ({somewhere})
pemâkwatôwa	puts them (inanimate) in one place ({somewhere})
pemâmehkishinwa, pemâmehkisenwi	(animate, inanimate) lies along as ground
pemâmoshkêwa	proceeds to run away
pemâmowa	flees, runs away
pemânahkwakôtêwi	it hangs along as sky
pemâpyêwi	it strings by or along, it flows by or along
pemâsenwi	it is blown by
pemâsikêwa	goes shining (**pêmâsikâta** the sun [ritual])
pemâshkêwa, pemâshkêwi	shoots through (e.g., a door), it shoots through
pemâtesiwa	lives
pemâtesiweni	life
pemâtesînotamwa	lives by it
pemâwanetîwaki (plural)	they go past in a large group
pemehkânêwa	passes s.o., gets past s.o., overtakes and passes s.o.
pemehkêwa	walks, walks along, walks on, walks by, goes by
pemehtawêwa	heeds s.o.
pemekêwa	dances past
pemenamawêwa	takes care of (it) for s.o.
pemenâkaniwiwa	is taken care of
pemenetisowa	takes care of oneself
pemenetîwaki (plural)	they take care of each other
pemenêwa, pemenamwa	takes care of s.o., it, keeps it
pemenêweniwêhiwa	is taken care of (dimin.)
pemenêweniwiwa	is taken care of
pemeniwêwa	takes care of people
pemenôshêwa	takes care of a baby, is minding a baby
pemeshihwêwa	follows along after s.o.
pemeshitôwa	makes the round, passes from one (of them) to the next
pemeshkawêwa	goes to them in sequence
pemetêwi	it continues to burn (through time)
pemetonêmonohkatawêwa	speaks for s.o.
pemetonêmowa	talks going by
pemênemêwa, pemênetamwa	continues to pay attention to s.o., it, has plans for s.o.
pemi (1)	past, by, in the course, along, in sequence; go ahead and, start to, set about, directly, right (preverb)
pemi (2)	oil, grease (**pemîki** in the grease)
pemichikapitêwi	it (as, a stick) is tied crosswise
pemichikapitôwa	ties it (as, a stick) crosswise or to one side
pemichimêwa	swims by
pemichinawe (**pemichinawêmêhi** dimin.)	off to one side (particle)
pemichitehkonêyâwi	**êh=pemichitehkonêyâki** on the branch of a tree
pemihêwa	goes by {some way} (**pêmihâchi** the way he or she went by)
pemihkawêwa	has left tracks, footprints
pemihtanwi	it (water or stream) flows, there is a current
pemikâpâwaki (plural)	they stand in a row
peminawêwa	is after s.o.
peminâkêwa	goes by singing
peminechâmêwa	takes care of s.o. on the way
peminehkawêwa	chases s.o.
peminehkâkêwa	chases people
pemipahowa, pemipahôtêwi	runs by, along; it (as, a train) runs by, along

pemipanîwa	weaves
pemipenowa	speeds off, starts running
pemipokowa, pemipokôtêwi	drifts, floats along, by
pemisahêwa	swishes s.o. (as, a skin) in or on the water
pemisêwa	flies past
pemitasakatwi	log
pemitâhkwîhi	collarbone
pemitechêshinwa	lies crossways
pemitenikana	shield
pemi-tepikîshkahokowaki (plural)	they (fish, birds) swim abreast in an even line
pemitêwi	oil, lard (**nepemitêmi** my oil)
pemitôpahkwe	through the side of the house (particle)
pemiwanêsetôwa	has one bundle or bag of it after another
pemiwenêwa, pemiwetôwa	leads s.o. along, carries it along
pemiwetonwa (or **pemiwânaketonwa**)	has a greasy mouth
pemi-wêpihkanêwa	goes off and leaves s.o.
pemiwinechêwa	has greasy fingers, hands
pemîhkawêwa, pemîhkamwa	is occupied with s.o., it through time
pemosahêwa	makes s.o. walk
pemosêhkanawi	footpath
pemosêwa	walks along
pemotamawêwa	shoots (it) for s.o.
pemotîwaki (plural)	they shoot at each other
pemowêwa	shoots people
pemômêwa, pemôtamwa	carries s.o., it along on one's back
pemôtêwa	crawls by
pemwêkesiwa	goes along wailing
pemwêwa, pemotamwa	shoots s.o., it; shoots at s.o., it
pemwêwêshinwa, pemwêwêsenwi	goes by with noise, is heard walking by; it goes by with noise
pemyêkiwa	is growing, grows for a particular length of time
pena! (**pe**= before enclitic [archaic])	O.K. now, please, why don't you, could you, you'd better; why don't I, may I, I'd better (particle, interjection)
penahâhkwawêwa	combs s.o.'s hair
penahâhkwêwa	combs one's hair (**penahâhkwâno** comb you hair!)
penahâkani	comb
penani	later; wait an instant! (particle)
pena=tâtaki	can't resist, can't help (particles)
penâneshiwa	goes on a summer hunt
penâni	summer, of summer (prenoun) (also **penâwi**)
penâsîwa	climbs down
penâte	last summer (song word) (particle)
penâwi	summer, of summer (prenoun) (also **penâni**)
penâwiwi	it is summer, it is the warm season of the year
penekwâhkiwiwi	it is an overhanging cliff
peneshkânehkwênowa	undoes one's hair
peneshkehkêwi	it comes unfastened
peneshkenamawêwa	takes it (hair) down, undoes (it) for s.o.
peneshkenamwa	takes it (hair) down, undoes it
penêhkawêwa	hunts turkeys for s.o.
penêhkêwa	hunts turkeys
penêhtôwa	cuckoo ("rain crow")
penêmowa	imitates the call of a turkey
penêsiwaya (**penêsiwâha** dimin.)	raptor skin (in a sacred bundle)
penêwa	turkey

penêwi	turkey, of turkey (prenoun)
penenowa	takes one's clothes off
peninawîwa	takes one's clothes off
penîhtêhêwa	undresses s.o., has s.o. undress
peniwêshîwa	takes off one's moccasins
penîhtêwa	gets undressed
penowa	goes away, goes home, departs
penôchâwi	it is far
penôchi	far away, a long time; easily (particle)
penôchîmêhi	quite a ways off, further; quite a long time, a longer time (particle)
penôhêwa, penohêwa	sends s.o. back, sends s.o. home
penômikatwi	it goes away
pepehchi	away from the others (particle)
pepehchîmêhi	a little ways away from the others (particle)
pepehkêhêhiwa, pepehkêhenôhiwi	(animate, inanimate) is light (of weight)
pepeshkwâwakatwi, pepeshkwâwakîwi	the ground is bare
pepeshkwikeshamwa	peels it (as, a stick) with a knife, cuts the bark off it
pepeshkwitepêwa	has a bald or shaved head
pepeshkochêshkêwa	is shedding
pepikowiwa	has fleas
pepikwa	flea
pepikwêshkowiwi	it is a whistle
pepikwêshkwi	whistle (held in the mouth by a dancer)
pepikwêyâwi	it is hollow
pepônatesiwa	Spirit of Winter
pepôneshiwa	goes on a winter hunt
pepôni	winter, in winter (prenoun, preverb) (see also **pepôwi**)
pepônoki	last winter (particle)
pepôwi (1)	it is winter
pepôwi (2)	winter (preverb) (usually **pepôni**)
pepyêhkwâkwapiwaki (plural)	they sit in groups
pepyêhkwâkwatôwa	puts them (inanimate) in piles (see **pehkwâkwanêwa**)
pepyêhkwikâpâwaki (plural)	they (animate) stand in groups
pepyêhkwishinwa	lies there curled up, doubled up
pepyêhtehtawêwa	keeps misunderstanding s.o., them
pepyêkwinechêshinwa	one's hands are chafed
pepyênowihêwa	keeps just failing to get s.o.
pepyêsakonamwa	works it into patties
pepyêsehkamwa	wears moccasins (also **pesehkamwa**)
pepyêshkonawêwa	keeps missing s.o., them with shots (see **peshkonawêwa**)
pepyêtashkishinwa, pepyêtashkisenwi	(animate, inanimate) is plastered on, adheres
pepyêtekwapinêwa	hogties s.o., ties s.o.'s ankles and wrists together
pepyêtekwâhkwapitôwa	folds it together and ties it as a bundle
pepyêtekwikwayawênêwa	bends s.o.'s neck down
pepyêtekwishinwa	lies curled up
pepyêwi	(with negative): not even close, not the least bit (preverb)
pesehkamwa	puts it on (clothing, especially moccasins); puts on or wears moccasins (compare **pepyêsehkamwa**)
peshepâhkoshkâtîmikatôni (plural)	they (as, trees) rub against each other
peshepâpitênamwa	rubs the blade of it (as, a hatchet)
peshepîhkawêwa	rubs s.o. down
peseshêwa	listens
pesetawêwa, pesetamwa	listens to s.o., it
pesetwa	has something in one's eye, has (it) in one's eye

peswêwa	smokes s.o. out (as, bees or bears)
pesipemyêsowa, pesipemyêhtêwi	(animate, inanimate) fries
peshekesiwa, peshekisiwa	deer
peshekesiwi, peshekisiwi	of deer (prenoun)
peshekesiwiwa, peshekisiwiwa	is or becomes a deer
peshekênemêwa, peshekênetamwa	thinks s.o., it cute (also **peshikênetamwa**)
peshekwâha	divorced person
peshekwâhiwa	gets divorced, is divorced
peshekwâhiweni	divorce
peshikâchinâkosiwa (Jones)	looks cute ("cunning")
peshikênetamwa	thinks it cute (also **peshekênetamwa**)
peshikwapiwa	sits straight
peshikwâchimohêwa	instructs s.o. forthrightly
peshikwâchimowa	tells the truth, tells it straight
peshikwâchimwihtawêwa	reports accurately on s.o.'s behalf
peshikwâhkwatwi	it is a straight stick
pêshikwâpyêwi	it is straight (as, a road or path)
peshikwênemêwa	thinks s.o. straight, upright, honest
peshikwi	uprightly, honestly, straight (particle, preverb)
peshikwihchikêwa	does the right thing
peshikwisetawêwa	sets (it) straight for s.o.
peshikwiwenêwa, peshikwiwetôwa	conducts s.o., it straight
peshikwiwetawêwa	conducts it straight for s.o.
peshikwîwa	acts uprightly
peshipeshiwa	Great Lynx, Underwater Panther (also **nâmi-peshiwa**)
peshishkesa	brant (**môhkomâni-peshishkesa, peshishkesa** domestic goose)
peshiwa	wildcat (lynx or bobcat) (**kehchi-peshiwa** lynx)
peshînâwa (**peshînâhêha** dimin.)	animal or bird skin (in a sacred bundle)
peshînêwa	skins s.o.
peshînikêwa	does the skinning, skins a deer
peshkâshêwi	it lights up, it flashes
peshkikwâtamwa	takes a tuck in it
peshkipanwi	it is sour, puckery to the taste
peshkipêhi	hickory tree, stick
peshkipêhi-pakâni	hickory nut
peshkipêhiwa	is a hickory tree
peshkochâhi	(see **peshkwichâhi**)
peshkonawêwa, peshkonamwa	misses s.o., it with a shot
peshkonênawachikêwa	gets the fire started with (it), uses (it) as kindling wood
peshkonêwi	it (fire) is blazing, flares up, blazes up
peshkonêwiwi	it (plant, tree) has a flower, has flowers, is a flower
-peshkwahte	charge of gunpowder (in particle compounds) (**nîshwi-peshkwahte** two charges of powder)
peshkwahtêpisowa	is caught by the springing of a snare
peshkwahtêyâkesiwa	(bow) is springy, easy to pull
peshkwâsîwa	falls in climbing
peshkwichâhi, peshkochâhi	Why then ..? So, how do you explain ..? (particle)
petasakawiwa	meets misfortune
petasakesiwa	is impeded, faces an obstacle
petasaki	as an obstacle, impediment (preverb) (also **petesaki**)
petasakikenwi	there is, it has an obstacle (also **petesakikenwi**)
petekawiwa	backs out, goes back on one's word, changes one's mind
petekênemêwa	takes back one's thought, plan, or blessing for s.o.
petekênetamawêwa	takes (it) back for s.o.

peteki (**petekîmêhi** dimin.)	in back, back (in space or time), backwards (particle)
petekwâwi	it is bent over, bent down
petekyêshihêwa	takes (it) back from s.o.
petesaki	as an obstacle, impediment (preverb) (also **petasaki**)
petesakikenwi	there is, it has an obstacle (also **petasakikenwi**)
petênemêwa	is against s.o., is opposed to s.o.'s plans or desires
pêhkênemêwa	thinks s.o. is an ordinary person
pêhki	really, fully, successfully, easily, earnestly; real, correct, natural, regular, ordinary (particle, prenoun)
pêhkiwisota (participle)	member of the Pheasant Clan
pêhpêshôni	straight razor
pêhpêshwêwa	scarifies s.o., makes small cuts in s.o.'s skin
pêhpêwinekwêwa	flaps one's wings
pêkeshêki (**pêkeshêhiki** dimin.)	smoke, its smoke; fog (see **pekeshêwi**)
pêkosiwa, pêkwâwi	(animate, inanimate) is dry
pêkosowa, pêkotêwi	(animate, inanimate) dries (after being wet) (as, from fire or sun)
pêkoshkêwi	it dries, becomes dry
pêkotêhi	bread cooked in ashes (or an oven) ("cowboy bread")
pêkôneki	at St. Louis (from the early French name "Paincourt")
pêkwâpanôhiwi	it is fully daybreak (dimin.)
pêkwâwakîwi	the earth is dry
pêkwi (preverb):	**pêkwi-menôhkamîki** when spring was fully underway
pêkwitêhêwa	is thirsty
pêmâsikâta (participle)	the Sun (see **pemâsikêwa**)
pênâneshîhaki (plural)	summer hunting party
pêpehkînâtowêwaki (plural)	they speak different languages
pêpehkînikenôni (plural)	they (inanimate) are of different kinds, do not match
pêpôhkoshkâha	click beetle
pêpyêchi	coming repeatedly to (preverb)
pêpyêhchi	have to, necessarily (particle)
pêsheshwêwa	gashes s.o.
pêshichinwa	gets a deep scratch, a gash
pêshiwisota (participle)	member of the Lynx Clan (Jones: Big Lynx)
pêshkiti (**pêshkitîhi** dimin.)	basket (plural **pêshkityêni**)
pêshkonêwahkamikatwi	the land is abloom
pêshkonêwîhi	flower
pêshkwêha	nighthawk
pêwênemowa	gives up
='pi	(see **=ipi**)
pîchi	in, entering, inside (preverb, preparticle)
pîchihkawêwa	one's tracks go in
pîchikomêwa	sniffs (it) into one's nose (as, medicine or snuff) (**pîchikomâte** if one sniffs (it) up)
pîchikwâni	knife-case; hood (on a garment)
pîchinehkawêwa	chases s.o. inside
pîchinehkêwa	puts one's hand in
pîchinihkisêwa	falls into a space
pîchisahowa	jumps inside
pîchisêwa, pîchisêwi	runs in, flies in; it flies in
pîchiwenêwa, pîchiwetôwa	takes s.o., it in
pîhpîsowa	gets blistered by the heat
pîhpîshkanehkîwa	steps very softly
pîhpîshkapiwa	sits on something soft, cushiony
pîhpîshkesiwa, pîhpîshkyâwi	(animate, inanimate) is soft, cushiony

pîhpîshkîhi (or **opîhpîshkîhi**)	lung
pîhtawâhkiwi:	**pîhtawâhkîki** in a narrow valley between high hills
pîhtawi	moreover, else, besides (particle, preverb)
pîhtawiwetôwa	carries it as an extra supply
pîhtawoshêwa	puts on an extra blanket
pîhtôkenwi	it is in tiers, layers
pîhtôpisôni	underskirt
pîhtôsenwi	it is double
pîhtôshketôha	gopher (pocket gopher)
pîkêkêwa	becomes exhausted from dancing
pîkênanêwa	completely wears s.o. out, wears s.o. down to nothing
pîkênêwa	holds s.o. until they die
pîkêpahowa	runs oneself to death
pîkêpenêwa	starves to death
pîkêshkêwa	vomits and retches to death; trembles to death
pîkêtêhêwa	worries too much, worries or grieves to death
pîkêwi	to death (preverb)
pîkêwi-ashawaye	an extremely long time ago (particle compound)
pîkihtanwi	Missouri River
pîkîhiwa	plays cards
pîkwashkatwi	the grass and weeds have grown up tall
-pîkwashki	thick weeds (in a particle compound) (**nâwi-pîkwashki** in the middle of thick weeds)
pîkwâhkwâwiwi	it is a dense grove of trees
-pîkwâwe	thicket (in a particle compound) (**nâwi-pîkwâwe** in the middle of a thicket)
pîkwâwi	there is a thicket
pîkwetonêmowaki (plural)	there is the sound of a crowd of them talking
pîkwikâpâwaki (plural)	they stand all crowded together
pîminihkwâni	cordage, string, yarn (collectively)
pînahwêwa, pînahamwa	puts s.o., it in a bag; uses love medicine on s.o. (putting a hair in a bundle)
pînâpitêwa	has a good set of teeth
pînâpiwa	sees fresh things
pînenamwa	cleans it up (as, an area)
pînesâtesiwa	is alive
pînesênetisowa	thinks of oneself spontaneously
pînesiwa, pînyâwi	(animate, inanimate) is clean
pîneshi	spontaneously, of one's own accord, acting on one's own, unprovoked (particle, preverb)
pîneshihêwa	attacks s.o. unprovoked, approaches s.o. spontaneously
pînênemêwa, pînênetamwa	thinks s.o., it clean
pînênetisowa	feels clean
pînêshkesiwa, pînêshkyâwi	is or has plenty; there is plenty (of it)
pînêshki	plentifully, in abundance, in numbers (preverb)
pînêshkisetawêwa	places (it) in abundance for s.o.
pîni	in a clean way (preverb)
pînihêwa, pînihtôwa	gets s.o., it clean; keeps s.o. in clean clothing, keeps it clean
pînihowa	makes oneself clean
pîninameshkêwa	has clean skin
pînôsowiwa	is unharmed, has no ill effects
pînôshi	innovating, doing or being something new and different (particle)
pîsâkosiwa	(food animal) has a lot of meat on it
pîsâkwi (preverb):	**pîsâkwi-ishawiwa** has plenty, is wealthy
pîsâpitêhiwa	has little teeth

pîsehkamwa	dons it, puts it on (e.g., a shirt, a dress)
pîsehkâhi	garment, shirt, blouse ("waist")
pîsehkêwa, pîsehkêwi	(animate, inanimate) comes in (with no visible effort)
pîsenamwa	makes it into small pieces
pîsêyâwi	it is loose and fine
pîsi	small (prenoun, preverb)
pîsichêpihkakatôhiwi	it has small roots (dimin.)
pîsikâwosêhiwa	walks taking short steps
pîsimîkaki (plural)	wampum beads
pîsimîki	of wampum beads (prenoun)
pîsimîkiwinêwa	has braids decorated with wampum
pîsimîkiwiwa, pîsimîkiwiwi	is decked with wampum; it is decorated with wampum
pîsîkwêha	small kernels separated out of dried corn
pîshihtâtêwi	it is made anew, made over, renewed
pîshihtôwa	makes it anew, renews it
pîshâkani (1)	rawhide, buckskin, leather
pîshâkani (2)	of rawhide, buckskin, leather (prenoun)
pîshâkanimotêhi	rawhide or leather bag; parfleche
pîshâkanîhi	buckskin or leather coat (**nepîshâkanîhi** my buckskin coat)
pîshâkaninekwêha	bat
pîshâkâhi	buckskin thong
pîshi	as the first (preverb)
pîshihtâtêwi	it is renewed
pîshihtôwa	renews it
pîshkatamwa	is or gets tired of eating or drinking it
pîshkênemêwa, pîshkênetamwa	is or gets tired of it
pîshkinâniwa, pîshkinânîha	dragonfly
pîshkyâwi	it is weak (metaphorically, as from disuse or neglect)
pîshkyêwêwa	one's muscles become tired, cramped
pîtahâsowa	is buried
pîtahotîwaki (plural)	they bury each other
pîtahônêwa	drags s.o. inside
pîtahwêwa, pîtahamwa	buries s.o., it
pîtanwâna	quiver (**nepîtanwâna** my quiver)
pîtâkwatôwa	lays them (inanimate) on the ground going inside
pîtâmowa	flees in
pîtâshinwa, pîtâsenwi	(animate, inanimate) blows in
pîtâshkêhtôwa	lets it enter
pîtâshkêwa, pîtâshkêwi	flies in, rushes in; it flies in, goes in
pîtâwanetîwaki (plural)	they enter in a large group
pîtâwanêwa, pîtâwatôwa	takes, puts, stuffs (a large amount of) s.o., it in
pîtehkwênwa	sticks one's head in
pîtenamwa	puts it in, inside
pîtênemêwa	thinks s.o. enters
pîtêyâhkwîwa	enters a forest or wooded area, enters (it) as a forest
pîtikanêwa, pîtikatôwa	brings s.o., it in
pîtikatawêwa	brings (it) in for s.o., brings (s.o.) into the dwelling of s.o.
pîtikatâtisowa	brings (it) in for oneself
pîtikawêwa	enters to where s.o. is, enters s.o.'s house to visit them, visits s.o.
pîtikâtîwaki (plural)	they visit each other
pîtike	inside (particle)
pîtikêhkamiki	"inside of the earth (meaning on earth or in wickiups)" (particle) (translation from Horace Poweshiek)
pîtikêwa	enters, comes or goes inside

pîtôchâmowa	takes (it) inside of oneself, conceals (it) in one's body
pîtôchâmêwa	takes s.o. inside of oneself
pîtônaki	down inside (as, a canoe, a nest)
pîtôtêwa	crawls in
pîwâhi	bead, small bead
pîwâhihchikâtêwi	it is decorated with beads
pîwâhikwâsowa	sews beadwork
pîwâhikwâtêhiwi	it is sewn with small beads (dimin.)
pîwâhimahkesenêwa	wears beaded moccasins
pîwâhimatetêwa	wears beaded leggins
pîwâhipahônêwa	she wears a beaded hair binder
pîwâpehkwi (1)	iron rod, iron object (also **pîyâpehkwi**)
pîwâpehkwi (2)	made of iron (prenoun) (also **pîyâpehkwi**)
pîwâpehkwîhi	metal trap (also **pîyâpehkwîhi**)
pîwêhkenesêwa	picks up small sticks (for firewood)
pîyâpehkwi (1)	iron, iron object (also **pîwâpehkwi**)
pîyâpehkwi (2)	made of iron (prenoun) (also **pîwâpehkwi**)
pîyâpehkwîhi	metal trap (also **pîwâpehkwîhi**)
pîyohkwi, pîyahkwi	punk (crumbly rotten wood)
pôchêhâni	storage corner (near the door of a traditional house)
pôchisahtawêwa	drops (it) in for s.o.
pôchisahêwa, pôchisahtôwa	throws s.o., it in (as, into a container or vertical hole)
pôchisahowa	jumps down in
pôchisetôwa	puts it in a hole and leaves it ({somewhere})
pôchisêwa, pôchisêwi	(animate, inanimate) falls in
pôchîkwêhwêwa	pierces s.o. in the eye
pôhkahamwa	pokes a hole in it, pierces it
pôhkamâha	plum
pôhkânakikomâkani	nostril
pôhkânehkêwa	digs a hole through
pôhkânehkâtôwa	digs it (as, a tunnel or burrow)
pôhkechêhwêwa	pokes a hole in s.o.'s belly
pôhkechêshkawêwa	kicks a hole in s.o.'s belly
pôhkechêshwêwa	cuts a hole in s.o.'s belly
pôhkenamwa	makes a hole in it (as, with the finger)
pôhkepyêkîwa	breaks through the caul
pôhkesowa	one's boil is opened up by the application of medicine; has a hole shot in one by a firearm
pôhkeshwêwa, pôhkeshamwa	cuts a hole in s.o., it, makes a cut in s.o.
pôhkimini	cranberry
pôhkinihkahamwa	chops a hole through into the intervening space in it
pôhkiponêwa	drills a hole in s.o. (as, a pipe)
pôhkitepêhowêha	Head-Piercer (spirit in the afterworld)
pôhkitepêhwêwa	pokes a hole in s.o.'s head
pôhkitepêwa	has a hole in one's head, has a fontanelle
pôhkîkwêwa	is missing one eye, has one eye out (plural **pôhkipôhkîkwêwaki**)
pôhkonêwa, pôhkonamwa	breaks s.o. (as, a bow), it, snaps s.o., it in two
pôhkosowa, pôhkotêwi	has a bone broken by gunshot, it is broken by gunshot
pôhkoshkamawêwa	breaks (it) in two by foot for s.o.
pôhkoshkawêwa	breaks s.o. (as, a bow) in two by foot
pôhkote	one half of the (inside space of the) house (particle)
pôhkwi	in part, half (particle)
pôhkwihpikêshinwa	falls and breaks one's rib
pôhkwikahkwanêhwêwa	hits s.o. and breaks their leg

pôhkwikanêsowa	has a bone broken by gunshot
pôhkwinehkêhwêwa	breaks s.o.'s arm
pôhkwiwinêshinwa	falls and breaks one's horn
pôhkwîha	quail
pôhkyâwi	it has a hole in it, it is a hole
pôhpôhkeshamwa	cuts holes in it
pôhpôhkyâwi	it has holes in it
pônamatamwa	ceases to feel pain
pônashiwa	drops a load of game from one's back
pônâchimowa	stops talking, stops one's telling or account
pônânematwi	the wind stops
pônâshkêwa	stops falling, stops rushing
pônekêwa	stops dancing
pônenamwa	quits handling or playing with it
pônenetîhkiwiwi	the fighting stops
pônenetîwa	stops fighting
pônepyêwa	quits drinking; no longer drinks
pônesiwa	stops misbehaving
pôneshkêwa	stops (as, vomiting or crying)
pônetonêmowa	stops talking
pônênemêwa, pônênetamwa	stops thinking of s.o., it
pôni	stop, cease, no longer (preverb)
pônihêwa	stops going {somewhere}, no longer goes {somewhere}
pônihtôwa	ceases from it
pônikahesêwa	stops chopping wood
pônikâpâwa	quits standing
pônikêwa	pays one's gambling debt
pônimêwa	stops talking to s.o., stops questioning or urging s.o.
pôninâkêwa	stops singing
pôninechâmêwa	stops taking care of s.o.
pônisenyêwa	stops eating
pônishêwa	stops urinating (**pônishâchi** when he or she stopped urinating)
pônitêhêwa	stops worrying, stops being concerned or mentally agitated
pônîhetêwi	camp is made, everyone camps
pônîhetîwa	makes a camp ({somewhere}) (**pônîhetîwaki** they camp together)
pônîhkawêwa, pônîhkamwa	leaves s.o., it alone, stops being occupied with s.o., it
pônîhkâtîwaki (plural)	they stop dealing with each other, stop with each other
pônînotawêwa, pônînotamwa	camps in with s.o., it
pônîwa	camps, camps {somewhere}
pônopônôha	saw-whet owl
pônowêwa	stops talking, stops discussing
pônômêwa, pônôtamwa	puts s.o., it down from one's back
pônwêwêhikêwa	stops drumming
pônwêwêkatwa	the noise ceases, the sound of it ceases
pônwêwêkesiwa, pônwêkesiwa	stops weeping
pôsawiwa	is worse, gets worse
pôsânahkwatwi	the clouds hang heavy
pôsâpôsamwa	boils it harder, longer
pôsâwanetîwaki (plural)	they get into a boat in a large group
pôsenekôha	worst one, one that does the worst
pôsi	very, much, more so (particle, preverb, preparticle)
pôsihtawêwa	sends (it) to s.o.
pôsihêwa, pôsihtôwa	puts s.o., it into a boat, a vehicle, or a vessel or container open at the top (as, a cauldron or mortar); gives s.o. a ride; sends s.o., it

pôsitêhêwa	feels very bad
pôsiwa	gets into a boat or vehicle
pôsôtêwi	extremely (particle, preverb)
pôswêkesiwa	cries hard, cries louder
pôtahâkana	corn mortar ("grinding mill"); coffee-mill
pôtahâtêwi	it is pounded, ground up
pôtahesowa	pounds (as, in a mortar), does one's pounding
pôtahikêwa	grinds corn
pôtahishkwâti	pestle (for grinding)
pôtahwêwa, pôtahamwa	grinds s.o. (as, corn), it fine by pounding
pôtâhkwêwa	puts (it) in the pot to boil
pôtâhkwawêwa	puts (it) in the pot to boil for s.o.
pôtânêwa, pôtâtamwa	blows on s.o., it
pôtâwatâsowa	loads up (as, a canoe)
pôtenamwa	puts it in (as, into water)
pôtetonêhpwêwa, pôtetonêhtamwa	kisses s.o., it
pwâwi	not (preverb) (also **pâwi**)
pwâwi-menwi-pemâtesiweni	bad life
pwâwi-mîhkwênetâha kêkôhi	one who does not care about anything, has no regard for anything
pyâkimini	persimmon
pyêchi	coming to, come and, coming or facing this way; have been (up to now); next in past succession (preverb)
pyêchihêwa	comes {some way}, comes back {some way}
pyêchikawiwaki (plural)	they come this way as a group
pyêchikawihêwa	comes at the head of the group of them
pyêchimêwa	makes s.o. come by singing, talking, or crying
pyêchinehkawêwa	drives s.o. this way
pyêchineniwêwa	(member of a warparty) returns victorious (with prisoners or scalps)
pyêchineniwêwisekini (plural)	victory songs
pyêchipenowa	is coming, starts on the way, starts back
pyêchipehkwanêpiwa	sits with one's back this way
pyêchisahowa	jumps this way
pyêchisêwa, pyêchisêwi	flies this way; the time comes
pyêchishkwâtawêsenwi	(house) lies with its door this way
pyêchitiyêkâpâwa	stands with rear end this way
pyêchiyâhtêwi	the smell of cooking wafts this way
pyêchîkwêshinwa	is facing this way, is face-to-face
pyêchîhiwêwa	arrives reaching refuge
pyêhêwa	waits to accost s.o.
pyêhkyêwa	brings a person (especially as wife)
pyêhpahêwa	sees evidence that enemies are near (**nepyêhpaha** I —)
pyêhpahowa	runs this way
pyêhpahônekwiwa	arrives on one's horse at a gallop
pyêhpahônêwa	brings s.o. on the run, runs s.o. in
pyêmachinowa	she has (it, as a blanket or shawl) folded up and tied around her waist
pyêmakâme	half way to the other side
pyêmashkatwi	the grass is pushed down
pyêmawiwa	deviates (as, from what is expected)
pyêmâhkohwêwa	wraps oneself around s.o.
pyêmenamawêwa	twists (it) sideways for s.o.
pyêmeshkêwi	the time goes past midnight
pyêmikatwi	it comes
pyêmikihtawêwa	sends (it) to s.o. through the mail
pyêmikihtôwa	causes it to come

pyêmikopyêhamwa	twists and tightens it (as, a rope) with a stick
pyêminawe	off at an angle; halfway between (particle)
pyêmihkanêwa	goes on a distance ahead of s.o.
pyêmishkwânakîkwêwa	is cross-eyed
pyêmishkwashayêhowa	twists one's skin
pyêmishkwâshkêwa	runs twisting and turning
pyêmishkwikanwi	it is twisted (as, a vine)
pyêmishkwinêha	snail
pyêmishkwinêhekêwa	dances the Snail Dance
pyêmishkwisêwa	runs twisting and turning
pyêmishkwitôtanêsêwa	sprains one's ankle (literally, twists one's heel)
pyêmitepehkîwi	the night is well gone, it is past midnight
pyêmîkwêwa	one's face is twisted
pyênehkawêwa	chases, drives, sends s.o. (this way, back) to {somewhere}
pyênetisowa	brings oneself
pyênetîwekêwa	dances the Victory Dance (scalps or captives having been brought home)
pyênetîwinâkêwa	sings victory songs (scalps or captives having been brought home)
pyênêwa, pyêtôwa	brings s.o., it
pyênotawêwa, pyênotamwa	comes to s.o., it
pyêpyêtatawihetîwaki (plural)	they have (it) brought to each other (ritual)
pyêsâpamêwa	sees s.o. coming
pyêsehkêwi	it comes, the time (for it) comes
pyêshiwêwa	(warrior) brings home a prisoner or scalp
pyêsho	give here! (particle)
pyêtahokowa	(fish, bird) swims this way
pyêtahowa	paddles this way
pyêtanahkeshkamwa	comes out the top end of it
pyêtanahkikâpâwi	it (tree) stands with its top inclined this way
pyêtashiwa	comes with a load of game on one's back
pyêtatahokowa	comes carrying (it as) a load on one's back
pyêtatawihtawêwa	brings, takes it to (s.o.) for s.o. (ritual)
pyêtatawihêwa	has (it) brought to s.o. (ritual)
pyêtawêwa	brings (it) to s.o.
pyêtâchimohêwa	comes and tells s.o.
pyêtâchimowa	brings a report
pyêtâhkawêwa	throws (it) to s.o.
pyêtâkêwa	brings (it) to people
pyêtâmowa	flees this way
pyêtânahkwatwi	the clouds come
pyêtânematwi	the wind blows this way
pyêtâpanwi	dawn comes
pyêtâpatâniwa	is coming fast
pyêtâpowanêwa	brings s.o. food
pyêtâpowêwa	brings (it as) food
pyêtâpyêsenwi	it lies extending this way
pyêtâsamapiwa	sits facing
pyêtâsameshkawêwa	is against s.o., turns against s.o.
pyêtâsamikâpâwa	stands facing
pyêtâsîpahowa	comes climbing at a run
pyêtâsîwa	comes climbing
pyêtâshinwa, pyêtâsenwi	blows this way, it blows this way
pyêtâshkêwa, pyêtâshkêwi	comes rushing, falls or speeds this way; it falls, flies, or speeds this way
pyêtâwanetîwaki (plural)	they arrive in numbers
pyêtâwanêwa, pyêtâwatôwa	brings a load of s.o., it

pyêtâyêniwa	arrives laughing
pyêtehkwêmowa	comes seeking help or advice
pyêtehkwêwêwa	brings a woman
pyêtenamawêwa	hands it to s.o.
pyêteshitêwi	it comes in its turn
pyêtêwênemêwa, pyêtêwênetamwa	thinks s.o., it comes, comes back, arrives ({somewhere})
pyêtosêwa	comes walking
pyêtôhêwa	make s.o. bring (it)
pyêtômâwasowa	comes carrying a baby on one's back
pyêtômêwa, pyêtôtamwa	brings s.o., it on one's back
pyêtôtashiwa	comes carrying a load on one's back
pyêtwêwêhikêwa	comes drumming
pyêtwêwêkahwêwa	makes s.o. come by sounding a drum
pyêtwêwêkatwi nenemehkiwaki	there is thunder ("the sound of the thunderers is coming")
pyêtwêwêkesiwa	comes crying
pyêtwêwêmêwa	comes scolding behind s.o.
pyêtwêwêpahowa	comes running with noise, is heard approaching on the run
pyêtwêwêshinwa, pyêtwêwêsenwi	(animate, inanimate) comes with noise
pyêtwêwêyâkêposowa	comes whizzing through the air
pyêtwêwêyâkêpotêwi, pyêtwêyâkêpotêwi	it comes whizzing through the air
pyêtwêwêyâkonîwa	comes crunching through the snow
pyêtwêyâpitêsêwa	the snapping of one's teeth can be heard approaching
pyêwa	comes, comes back, arrives or gets {somewhere} (**nepya** I come)

s

sahkahamawêwa	offers tobacco to s.o.
sahkahamôtenêwa	makes or has s.o. offer tobacco
sahkahwêhtôwa	offers tobacco to it
sahkahwêwa, sahkahamwa	sets fire to s.o., it
sahkasowa, sahkahtêwi	catches fire, burns; one's house burns down; it catches fire, burns
sahkenamwa	puts the tip up to it; touches the tip to it, puts pen to paper
sahkenikêwa	signs up
sahkikenwi	it grows attached to {somewhere}
sahkitêhêwa	fixes one's thoughts on {somewhere}
sahkowêwa	one's words rcach
sahkyêwa, sahkyêwi	(animate, inanimate) is attached or rooted {somewhere}, the base of (animate, inanimate) is {somewhere}
sakahôna	brooch (round pin with a tab, traditionally of German silver)
sakahwêwa	stings s.o.
sakakwâpiwa	looks at an angle, looks out of the corner of the eye
sakakwi	at a sharp angle, at a steep angle, diagonally (particle)
sakanahkenikêwa	touches the tip of the pen, signs one's name
sakapichikêwa	ties up one's horse
sakapinêwa, sakapitôwa	ties s.o., it fast
sakapisowa, sakapitêwi	(animate, inanimate) is tied securely, is tied up
sakâhkohwêwa, sakâhkohamwa	clamps s.o. in fetters; nails it up, buttons it, pins it
sakâhkohikani (sakâhkohikâhi dimin.)	nail (for nailing)
sakâhkohôna	button; badge
sakâhkohôni	fastener (generic)
sakâki	just barely, with difficulty (particle)

sakânehkwêchinwa	gets one's hair caught
sakânehkwênêwa	seizes s.o. by the hair
sakânowênêwa	seizes s.o. by the tail
sakânowêsahêwa	grabs s.o. by the tail
sakâpyênêwa	leads s.o. holding on (with a rope or by hand)
sakâpyênikani	leading-rope, halter, bridle
sakâpyênikêwa	leads a horse
sakenehkwêwêwa	he detains a girl or woman to court her
sakenêwa, sakenamwa	he detains her to court her; holds it in one's fingers, pinches it up (as, cloth)
sakenâhkwa	blackbird (generic)
sakeshênêwa	holds s.o. by the ear
saketonêpichikani	bridle, bit
sakihtâhpênêwa	seizes s.o. by the back of the neck
sakikânêwa	seizes or holds s.o. by the leg
sakikâpinêwa, sakikâpitôwa	ties s.o., it by the leg
sakikomêhpwêwa	bites s.o. on the nose
sakikwênêwa	takes or holds s.o. by the neck
sakikwêpinêwa	ties s.o. by the neck
sakikwêpisowa	is tied by or around the neck; ties oneself by the neck
sakikwêsahêwa	grabs s.o. by the neck
sakimêwa	mosquito
sakinechênetîwaki (plural)	they shake hands
sakinechênêwa	shakes s.o.'s hand
sakinehkênetîwaki (plural)	they take, hold, or lead each other by the hand
sakinehkênêwa	takes s.o. by the hand, holds s.o.'s hand
sakinehkêpahônêwa	runs holding s.o. by the hand
sakinekwêhpwêwa	bites s.o. on the wing
sakinekwênêwa	takes s.o. by the arm
sakinowêtiyêhpwêwa	bites s.o. on the buttocks
sakipwêwa, sakipotamwa	bites s.o., it
sakiwa	great blue heron
sakiwinênêwa	takes or holds s.o. by the horn or horns
sakwâkwasowaki (plural)	they lie packed closely together
sakwisenôni (plural)	they (as, houses) lie packed closely together
sanakâhkonamawêwa	sets difficult rules for s.o.
sanakâhkonikêwa	sets difficult rules
sanakâhpenêwa	has a serious disease or affliction
sanakesiwa, sanakatwi	is difficult to get; it is difficult to get or do
sanakênemâsowa	is thought hard to get
sanakênemêwa, sanakênetamwa	thinks s.o., it difficult, hard to get; gives s.o. a difficult blessing
sanaki	in a difficult way (preverb)
sanakihêwa, sanakihtôwa	makes it hard for s.o.; works hard at it, has trouble with it; has a hard time
sanakimêwa	asks s.o. to do a difficult thing
sanakinâkwatwi	it looks difficult, it looks impossible
sanakishinwa	is or gets stuck (as, when unable to proceed or go back while climbing), is in a tight place
sanakôpinaye	between the seats (archaic) (particle)
sanakwâwi	there is an open space (as, between houses)
sanakwi	in between (particle, preparticle)
-sasakanwe	thicket (in a particle compound) (**nâwi-sasakanwe** in the middle of a thicket)
sasakanwi	it is a thicket, thick underbrush (**sêsakaki** a thicket)

sasakânehkwêwa	has curly, kinky, or tangled hair
sasakyâwani (plural)	they are tangled (as, the hair [plural])
sasapihkâha	willow
sasapihkâhimishihkiwiwi	there are willows
sasâhkwêwa	is restricted by a taboo, strictly observant; it is taboo for one
sasâhkwêweniwiwa, sasâhkwêweniwiwi	(animate, inanimate) is subject to taboo, forbidden
sasâkihêwa, sasâkihtôwa	is careful with s.o., it; keeps s.o., it ritually clean
sasâkihêweniwiwa	is treated carefully
sasâkihowa	is careful with oneself, keeps oneself ritually clean
sasâkihtâtêwi	it is kept ritually clean
sayasayâwanasitêwa	feels a tingling in the soles of one's feet
sayâwamatamwa	feels a tingling sensation, has chills up one's spine
sayâwi	so as to ruffle or upset (preverb)
sayâwihêwa	makes s.o. tingle, shudder, or be ruffled
sayâwinawêhêwa	makes s.o. tingle (as, with fear or pleasure)
sayâwinawêshkêwa	a tingling sensation comes over one
sayâwinechêshkêwa	gets a tingling sensation in one's hand or hands
sâkahokowa, sâkahanwi	(animate, inanimate) is exposed out of the water
sâkâchimowa	tells just a little
sâkânowêkâpâwa	stands with one's tail in sight
sâkânwîwaki, sâkânwîwani (plurals)	they (animate, as corn plants, beans; inanimate, as pumpkins) are just sprouting, coming up (out of the ground)
sâkâtotamwa	talks about it just a little
sâkehtâkosiwa	is heard wailing
sâkenamwa	shows part of it
sâkepyêsowa	breaks out into a sweat
sâkeshkêwa, sâkeshkêwi	(animate, inanimate) emerges, becomes exposed
sâketonêhokowa	floats with one's mouth out of the water
sâki	exposed, partly visible, sticking out (preverb, prenoun)
sâkichi	outside (particle, prenoun)
sâkichîmêhi	a little outside (dimin.) (particle)
sâkichîwa	goes out; goes to the toilet
sâkikâshinwa	lies with a foot sticking out
sâkikomêsetôwa	sets it with the tip sticking out
sâkikomêshkêwa	sticks one's nose out
sâkikomêwa	one's nose is exposed to view
sâkinaniwêhtawêwa	sticks out one's tongue at s.o.
sâkinaniwêsêwa	sticks out one's tongue
sâkinehkêshkêwa	sticks one's arm out into view
sâkipyêyâwi	it (tree) buds; the trees bud, the leaves are out on the trees
sâkishinwa, sâkisenwi	(animate, inanimate) is sticking out, showing
sâkishkwêkatwi	it is bleeding
sâkitepêhokowa	floats with one's head out of the water
sâkitepêkâpâwa	stands with one's head exposed
sâkitepêshinwa	lies with one's head exposed
sâkitepêshkêwa	sticks one's head into view
sâkitiyêhokowa	floats with one's rear end out of the water (as, a duck feeding)
sâkiwa, sâkenwi	(animate, inanimate) grows up (as, a plant), sprouts
sâpîkwêwa	peeps (through half-open eyes)
sâsakâki	just barely each time (particle)
sâsanakwi	in between, between-times (particle)
sâsâkehtâkosiwa	is heard speaking, singing, or weeping
sâsâkeshêkâpâwa	stands with the ears exposed (as, a horse or mule)
sâsâkikashêshkêwa	one's nails or claws appear

sâsâkikâshinwa	lies with (or has) one's feet sticking out
sâsâkisâhi	underskirt
sâsâkiwinêkâpâwa	stands with one's horns partly visible
sâsâkiwinêshinwa	has one's horns partly visible
sâsîkâhkêwa	pours out sloshes of (it)
sehkwânêwa, sehkwâtamwa	spits on s.o., it
sehkwiwa	spits
sehkwiweni	spittle
sekihkatami	constantly, all the time; (with negative): seldom (particle)
sekihkênetamwa	is faithful to it, has faith in it
sekihki	assiduously, regularly (particle, preverb)
sekihkinawîwaki (plural)	they move closer together, pack themselves in
sekihkîhkawêwa, sekihkîhkamwa	is faithfully attentive to s.o., it
sesekeshêwi	it sparks, sparks come out of it
sesêsapenêwa	is so hungry one is impatient to eat
sesêsênemêwa, sesêsênetamwa	is impatient about s.o., it, in a hurry about s.o., it'
sesêsi	hurriedly, hurry to (particle, preverb)
sesêsikâwosêwa	walks with hurried steps
sesêsimêwa	hurries s.o. along with words, tells s.o. to hurry
sesêsitêhêwa	is impatient, is in a hurry
sesêsîwa	hurries, is in a hurry
sesotamwa	coughs
seswahowa	perfumes oneself
seswahôni	perfume
seswamêwa, seswatamwa	sprays (it, medicine) on s.o., it with the mouth
seswamowa	sprays (it) on oneself with the mouth
seswêhamwa	splatters it with a blow
seswêhokowa, seswêhanwi	(animate, inanimate) is splattered by the impact
seswêhtêwi	it explodes and scatters in pieces from the heat
seswêsêwa, seswêsêwi	(animate, inanimate) scatters, splatters
seswêyâhkêwa	scatters (it)
seswêyâmowaki (plural)	they scatter in flight
sêkahkiwiwi, sêkahkîwi	there is fear, people are scared
sêkahkamikatwi	there is fear, people are scared
sêkâchimowa	tells a terrifying tale
sêkâchimowenakatwi	it is a terrifying tale
sêkesiwa	is frightened
sêkihêwa, sêkihtôwa	frightens s.o., it
sêkimêwa	frightens s.o. by speech
sêkinotawêwa	is frightened over s.o.
sêkipani	it will be a bad thing (if); it won't be good (if) (particle)
sêkipanwâna	woman's hair ornament (attached to the hair at the back of the head)
sêkitêhêwa	is apprehensive
sêkitîwaki (plural)	they frighten each other by what they say
sêkîkwêshkêwa	a frightened look comes over one's face
sênawêhi	bell (also **shênawêhi**)
sênipâhi	ribbon (**osênipâhemi** her ribbon)
sênipâhikwâsôni	ribbonwork
sênipâhikwâsowa	sews ribbon-appliqué
sêsahikani	dried meat, piece of dried meat
sêsahikêwa	stores meat away
sêsahwêwa, sêsahamwa	leaves s.o., it someplace safe (to be retrieved later)
sêsahâsowa	is put away safely, in an inaccessible place
sêsenamwa	rests it temporarily on something

sêsakaki	a thicket (see **sasakanwi**)
sêsikâhiwa	rests one's leg or legs on {somewhere}
sêsikâtêkâpâwa	stands with one's foot resting {somewhere}
sêsisechikêwa	lays down a layer (of it) on top
sêsisetôwa	rests it on {somewhere}
sêsishinwa, sêsisenwi	(animate, inanimate) lies or leans on top
sêsitiyêpiwa	sits perched on {somewhere}
siche, shiche (Jones)	Hiss! Psst!
sî! (Jones)	Too bad! Oh, say!
sîhpwêhêwa	makes s.o. suffer, makes it bad for s.o.
sîhpwênetamwa	suffers, endures suffering, is in misery
sîhpwêwa	suffers (**êh=sîhpwêchi** he or she suffered)
sîkachimêwa, sîkachitôwa	freezes s.o., it
sîkachiwa, sîkatenwi	(animate, inanimate) freezes
sîkahamawêwa	serves, pours (it) for s.o.
sîkahamâtisowa	serves oneself, dishes out food to oneself
sîkahamâtîwaki (plural)	they serve (it) for each other
sîkahanwi	it spills (from being overfilled or pushed over)
sîkahikawêwa	serves food for s.o., dishes out food to s.o.
sîkahikêwa	serves food, dishes out food; serves (it) as food
sîkahwêwa (1), sîkahamwa	pours s.o., it out; serves s.o., it up
sîkahwêwa (2)	dumps (it) all out (**êh=sîkahwêchi** he or she dumped (it) all out)
sîkanwishinwa	lets something spill out of one's mouth; spills the beans
sîkâhkêwa	pours out a slosh of (it)
sîkâhpwêwa	smokes s.o. (a pipe) completely out
sîkâhtamwa	eats it all up
sîkehkwêtenwi	it is a hill that narrows down to a point
sîkenahamawêwa	pours water on (it) for s.o.
sîkenahwêwa, sîkenahamwa	pours water on s.o., it, pours (it) on s.o., it
sîkenaka (participle)	tavern-keeper, bootlegger (obviative **sîkenaminichini**)
sîkenêwa, sîkenamwa	pours or dumps s.o., it out
sîkenitepêhwêwa	sprinkles (it, liquid) on s.o.'s head
sîkenîkwêhwêwa	throws (it, liquid) in s.o.'s face
sîkeshkamwa	knocks it over, kicks it over
sîkeshkânêwa, sîkeshkânamwa	pours, spills, dumps s.o., it out
sîketiwa	has a watery bowel movement
sîkêyâwi	there is a corner or bend
sîkêyâhkwâwi	corner of a forest, where a wooded area comes to a point
sîkihkamêsêwa	jumps spilling one's pipe
sîkikêwi	it pours out
sîkiminêwa	"chickenhawk" (*Buteo* species)
sîkinâsamwa	lets it boil over
sîkinâsikêwa	lets things boil over
sîkinâtêwi	it boils over
sîkisahtôwa	empties it out, pours it out, spills it out, dumps it out
sîkisêwa, sîkisêwi	spills; it spills, flows out
sîkishinwa	falls spilling (it)
sîkîkwâtamwa	has tears pour from one's eyes
sîkomêhikani	three-pronged fish spear, leister
sîkomêhikanisahowa	dives in headfirst (with one's arms over one's head)
sînahtakîwa	makes a leather cord by rolling together strips of hide
sînâhkwapinêwa	ties s.o. clamped in
sînâhkwisahêwa	wedges s.o. in a tight space
sînepyênamwa	squeezes it out, wrings it out

155

sînepyênikêwa	wrings out the washed clothes
sînepyêkêwa	drips from the effects of dancing
sîpachikani	cupping horn (used by a sucking doctor for blood-letting)
sîpôhêhi	brook, creek
sîpôwi	river
sîpwâkana	cornstalk
sîpwâtamwa	sucks on it (a sucking horn for blood-letting)
sîpwêwa	bleeds s.o. (with a sucking horn)
sîpyêhikani	soap
sîsahkyêwa	performs as a sucking doctor (**êh=nahi-sîsahkyêči** he was a sucking doctor)
sîsamachihêwa	makes s.o. feel a sharp pain
sîsamatamwa	feels a sharp pain
sîsamêwa	nips s.o. (**nesîsamekwa** (dog, insect) nipped me)
sîsenawêwa	grazes s.o. with a shot
sîsenêwa, sîsenamwa	pinches s.o., it (with the fingers)
sîsepâhkohkêwa	makes maple sugar
sîsepâhkwi	maple sugar; sugar (**nenôtêwi-sîsepâhkwi** maple sugar)
sîsepetonêkwâmwa	drools in one's sleep
sîsepetonwa	drools, is drooling
sîsepinîkwêkâpâwa	stands with tears in one's eyes
sîsepinîkwêwa	one's eyes are watering, has tears in one's eyes
sîsitôtanênêwa	pinches s.o.'s heel
sîsîkimêwa	whimpers at s.o., before s.o.
sîsîkwa	whimpers
sîsîsi	stingingly, tinglingly; by sips (preverb)
sîswêwa, sîsamwa	fries s.o., it
sîtâwi	it is drizzling
sîwanohkêwa	picks frost grapes
sîwanwi	frost grape (plural **sîwanôni**)
sôkenamawêwa	holds (it) in one's hand for s.o.
sôkenatahêwa	makes s.o. hold (it) in their hand
sôkenêwa, sôkenamwa	holds, carries s.o., it in one's hand
sôkihchikani	cordage, string, rope
sôkihchikêwa	ties things
sôkihêwa, sôkihtôwa	ties, binds s.o., it
sôkihtawêwa	ties (it) for s.o.
sôkisowa, sôkihtêwi	(animate, inanimate) is tied
sôpihkesowa	savors one's smoking, enjoys a smoke
sôsôpamêwa, sôsôpatamwa	is sucking at s.o., it, on s.o., it

sh

shahkamowa	puts a bite of food in one's mouth
shahkamônêwa	puts food in s.o.'s mouth, hand-feeds s.o.
shahkanwi	there is a thaw
shahkapiwa	sits in a soft place, it is soft where one sits
shahkâtowêwa	is soft-spoken
shahkesiwa, shahkyâwi	is gentle; it is soft
shahki	pleasant, good-natured, gently (particle, preverb)
shahki-mehtosêneniwiwa	is good-natured
shahki-wîkanwi	it is pleasant-tasting

shahkokwâmwa	is drowsy or weak from sleep
shahkosiwa	is drowsy, listless, weak, down-hearted
shahkwikanêwa	is weak in one's limbs
shahkwîkwêpiwa	sits with a down-hearted look on one's face
shakashkwa	cocklebur
shamahtîha	soldier
shamakwaya	large, animal-rib mat needle
shamâkanesha	soldier
shamâkani	spear
shanahkîha	Cherokee
shashahkechêhiwa	(horse, dog) rolls in something
shashawenêwa	rubs s.o. down, loosens s.o. (person, hide) by rubbing
shashawesiwa, shashawâwi	is limber; it is pliant, yielding
shashawêkinêwa	loosens s.o. (a hide) up by working (the hide) with the hands
shashawikahkwanêwosêwa	walks to limber up one's legs
shashawikâwosêwa	walks to limber up one's legs
shashawosêwa	walks to limber up
shashâpwi:	(see **ana-shashâpwi**)
shashômipyêyâwi	it has bending boughs
shashôshkikâsahowa	kicks one's legs out straight
shashôshkoshêshkêwa	(dog) lays the ears back flat
shashôshkwanahamîwa	keeps slipping as one tries to get traction
shashôshkwâhkosiwa	(tree) is slippery
shashôshkwâwi	it is slippery
shashôshkwikanwi	it (as, a tree or pole) is slippery
shatôha (only in forms of address):	friend (**shato** friend!; **shatôhetike** friends!; **neshatôhetike, neshatôhemetike** my friends!)
shawesiwa	is hungry
shayôshkwêwesiwa	the warparty he leads comes through unscathed, loses no men
shâka	nine (particle)
shâka tashiwaki, shâka tasenôni (plural)	they (animate, inanimate) are nine, there are nine of them
shâkanesiwe	nineteen (particle)
shâkânameki	ninth (particle)
shâkâpitaki	ninety (particle)
shâkohkâni	piece of flint
shâkonamwa	breaks, crushes it (as, an eggshell, glass)
shâkowihêwa	overpowers s.o., gets the best of s.o.
shâkwênemowa	is unwilling;
shâkwênemowinâkwatwi	it does not look promising, it looks discouraging
shâkwênemêwa	is unwilling for s.o. to, does not want s.o. to, gets tired of s.o.
shâkwisetôwa	smashes it by hitting it against something
shâpatênawêwa, shâshâpatênawêwa	pierces s.o.'s body with a shot (song word; uncertain)
shâponikani	needle
shâposikani (**shâposikâhi** dimin.)	laxative
shâposwêwa	administers a laxative or purgative to s.o.
shâpôsiwa	has diarrhea
shâpwêshi	as the only one, by oneself (particle) (see also **neshi-shâpwêshi**)
shâshakesiwa, shâshakyâwi	(animate, inanimate) is sway-backed, curved (back)
shâshâkêha	garter-snake
shâshâkwamêwa, shâshâkwatamwa	chews s.o., it
shâshâkwêwa	chews (song word)
shâshâkwikiwa	has a trim body
shâshâkwitepêshinwa	lies with one's head smashed
shâshâkwitepêwa	one's head is smashed, one's skull is fractured

shâshâshakinekwêpinêwa	ties s.o.'s arms together behind them
shâshîpahtêpahowa	runs bounding along
shâshîpahtêsêwa	gallops
shâshôkimêwa	whistles at s.o., for s.o.
shâshôkinâkêwa	whistles a tune
shâshôkwa	whistles
shâshôpesiwa, shâshôpyâwi	(animate, inanimate) is slender
shâshôpikiwa	is slender, slim
shâwanoki	in the south (ritual) (particle)
shâwanôwa	Shawnee
shâwanôwekêwa	dances the Shawnee Dance
shâwanôwiwa	dances the Shawnee Dance
shehehyê!	Uh-oh! *Oh* boy! (also **shêhyê!**)
shekahôha	pied-billed grebe ("hell-diver")
shekâkôha	onion
shekâkwa (shekâkôhêha dimin.)	skunk
shekehkwêmêwa	makes s.o. bow their head by what one says to them
shekehkwêshinwa	has one's head down
shekenêwa, shekenamwa	spreads s.o. (as, corn), it out to dry
shekenikêwa	spreads food items out to dry
shekihkanawe	fifty (particle)
shekikwâmwa	wets one's bed
shekinêwa, shekitamwa	urinates on s.o., it
shekisahowa	throws oneself down
shekishinwa (shekishinôhiwa dimin.)	lies, lies down, is lying down ({somewhere})
shekiwa	urinates
shekiweni	urine
shekochêhokônêwa	lets or has s.o. be crushed to a pulp by (it)
shekohwêwa, shekohamwa	pounds s.o., it to pieces
shekonêwa, shekonamwa	pushes s.o. down; crushes it, squashes it, flattens it
shekopyênêwa, shekopyênamwa	squishes s.o. (as, an insect), it by hand, mashes s.o., it up
shekosa	weasel
shekoshkamwa	crushes it by one's weight
shekwakwîchinwa, shekwakwîtêwi	(animate, inanimate) falls to pieces lying in water
shekwanenwa, shekwanetwi	(animate, inanimate) rots to pieces
shekwatahwêwa, shekwatahamwa	smashes s.o., it to pieces; beats s.o. down, subdues s.o.
shekwatamwa	crushes it up in one's mouth
shekwâhkwa	pine tree
shekwi	bent down, bent over (preverb)
shekwiponêwa	crushes s.o. (as, green corn) to pieces
shenemêsîha, ishenemêsîha	minnow
shepawîhta	fortunately, luckily (particle)
-shepwâhkiwe:	**nâwi-shepwâhkiwe** in the middle of a low area surrounded by higher ground (particle compound)
sheshekâchi, sheshekâhi	frivolously, lightly, toyingly, jokingly, as make-believe (particle)
sheshekonêwa, sheshekonamwa	tears s.o., it to pieces
sheshekotêwi	it is shattered by gunshot
sheshekwatamwa	chews it to pieces
sheshekwinanêwa	crushes s.o. to pieces
sheshekwishinwa	is smashed to pieces on impact
sheshêhkami	freely, unrestrained, readily (particle)
sheshôhwêwa, sheshôhamwa	paints s.o., it, daubs or smears s.o., it (with anything)
sheshônêwa	smears s.o. (with it) using the hand
sheshôwâhkonêwa	paints s.o., paints s.o.'s body

sheshôwâhkonowa	paints oneself, paints one's body
sheshôwîkwênowa	paints one's face
shewêna (and **shewê=**)	but, still, even so (particle) (also **ashewêna, ishewêna**)
shêhyê!	Uh-oh! *Oh* boy! (also **shehehyê!**)
shêkâtêha	moorhen, common gallinule
shênawêhi	bell (also **sênawêhi**)
shêpâye	this morning (early today) (particle)
shêpyêyâwi	there is unfrozen water
shêshêhkosiwa	is generous
shêshêhkwênetisowa	she is free with herself
shêshêhkwi	generously, liberally (particle)
shêshêwiketonwa	chews the cud
shêshkesîha	teenage girl, unmarried young woman, virgin
shêshkesîhêha	young teenage girl
shêshkesîhiwa, shêshkesîhiwiwa	is an unmarried teenage girl, is a virgin
shêshketôha (**shêshketôhêha** dimin.)	kettle, cauldron (copper kettle not fitted with a lid)
shêshki	only, alone, except; unmarried, empty-handed; the only thing is (particle)
shêshkinâkâkâhani (plural)	songs unaccompanied by a drum
shêshkinâkêwa	sings unaccompanied
shêshkishinwa, shêshkisenwi	(animate, inanimate) is empty
shêshkîkwêhêwa	lets s.o. go with face unblackened (i.e., not fasting)
shêshkîkwêwa	goes with face unblackened (i.e., is not fasting)
shêtêwa	pelican
shêy!	hey there!
'shi	(see **ishi, kashi**)
shihihwî!	Oh my! Gosh! Golly! (also **shîhwî!**)
shihihyê!	Oh my!
shinâkwa, shinâhi, shinâ!	Gosh! Why! Well! Well now! Well then! (also **kashinâkwa, kashinâhi**)
'shi=wê=towi	(see **kashi=wê=towi**)
shî!	Gee! Say!
shîhchê!	Oh my! Look at that! How cute! How odd! (also **chîhchê!**)
shîhkawisetawêwa	moistens (it) for s.o.
shîhkawishimêwa, shîhkawisetôwa	moistens or dampens s.o. (as, a drum), it
shîhkyâwi	it is damp
shîhwî!	Oh my! (also **shihihwî!**)
shîkahamawêwa	disparages (it) to s.o., warns s.o. sternly against (it)
shîkâwa	widow or widower (in strict mourning)
shîkâwiwa	is a widow or widower (in strict mourning)
shîkâwiweni	widowhood, widower-hood
shîkâwîhi	purple coneflower
shîkênemêwa, shîkênetamwa	dislikes s.o., it, objects to s.o., it
shîkênetâkaniwiwa	is generally disliked
shîkona	whetstone, grindstone; cliff, rocky precipice
shîkonêwa, shîkonamwa	empties s.o., it
shîkoshkamwa	discards it after wearing it out (as, clothing)
shîkotêwi	it is left after burning
shîkônahwêwa, shîkônahamwa	chooses s.o., it, picks s.o., it out
shîkônêwa, shîkônamwa	sorts s.o., it out, separates s.o., it
shîkôsetôwa	puts it by itself, places it separately
shîkôwi	separately; only those particular ones (preverb)
shîkwanêhtaki (participle)	what (the Fire Spirit) leaves unconsumed (ritual expression for charcoal)
shîkwashkwîhi	something abandoned as unwanted

shîkwatahwêwa	he abandons her after having enough of copulating with her
shîkwatamwa	leaves it from eating
shîkwatâtêwi	it is left over from eating
shîkwênetamwa	rejects it for something better
shîkwênetâkaniwiwa	is generally rejected
shîkwêwêshinwa	falls with a dull thud
shîkwêwi	there is a hollow sound, there is a dull thud (**shîkweshîkwêwi** dull thuds are heard)
shîkwi	formerly (preverb); former (of an in-law after the death of one's relative) (prenoun)
shîkwihkatamwa	abandons it (as, a house), flees leaving it empty
shîkwihkeshêwêshinwa	(Fire Spirit) lies in the spent coals (as charcoal) (ritual)
shîkwîwa	sheds one's clothes, skin, horns
shîkwîwena	bodily form (**oshîkwîwenani** "the outside shell of his bodily frame" [Jones])
shîpachiwa	endures cold
shîpachîkwêshkêwa	one's face becomes taut
shîpapenêwa	endures hunger
shîpatenêwa, shîpatenamwa	stretches s.o., it
shîpâhikani	hole-and-slot heddle for making beadwork ("bead loom")
shîpâyôtêwa	crawls through and out the other side
shîpeshkihêwa	makes s.o. suffer a long time
shîpêyâwi	the woods are open (without thick undergrowth)
shîpi	continuing a long time (preverb)
shîpinawîwa	stretches, stretches out
shîpinêwa	takes a long time to die
shîpinokêwa	has a hardy constitution
shîpishinwa, shîpisenwi	(animate, inanimate) keeps, remains unspoiled
shîpitêhêwa	is forbearing, puts up with a lot
shîshahikani (Jones)	buffalo shoulderblade used to scrape and prepare basswood-bark fibers
shîshahwêwa	pokes s.o. with a burning stick
shîshênotamawêwa	hunts game for s.o.
shîshêwa	hunts (**neshîsha** I hunt)
shîshêwashkwi	hunting medicine
shîshêwosêwa	hunts as one walks
shî! shî! (Jones)	hush!
shîshîhkanahamîwa	walks on tiptoes
shîshîhkanehkîwa	steps softly
shîshîhkenêwa	rubs s.o., gives s.o. a rub
shîshîhkyêwakenêwa	rubs s.o. down, rubs s.o.'s muscles
shîshîkimêha	soft maple
shîshîkwani	rattle, gourd
shîshîkwêhwêwa	pokes s.o. in the face with a burning stick
shîshîkwêwa	rattlesnake
shîshîpa	duck (generic)
shîshîpikani	duck bone
shîshîshanohwêwa	gives s.o. pokes in an orifice with a burning stick
='shkwe	(see =**ishkwe**)
shohohô!	Say, look at this! Say isn't that something!
showanakeshi	grapevine (plural **showanakeshêni**)
showekwâmwa	sleeps sprawled out
showêkinamwa	holds it (as, a blanket) spread out
showihkechêshkêwa	spreads one's tail-feathers
showikâtêwa	has one's feet apart

showinekwêkwâmwa	sleeps with one's arms flung out
showinekwêsêwa	falls with wings spread
showinekwêshkêwa	spreads one's arms or wings
showinekwêwa	has one's wings spread
showishinwa	lies sprawled out
shômenamwa	bends it in or down unevenly by pushing
shômeshkawêwa	dents, bends s.o. (as, cattail-reed mats) in by body
shôniyâha	coin
shôniyâhahtakawêwa	(animal) has a silver coat
shôniyâhaki (plural)	coins; money
shôniyâhi	silver, money
shôniyâhâpehkwi	silver
shôniyâhânowâkani	silver tail
shôpyêsikêwa	blanches ears of green corn (to set the milk)
shôpyêswêwa	blanches s.o. (green corn) to set the milk
shôshîhani (plural)	shoes (**neshôshani** my shoes)
shôshkâhkwapiwa	sits up straight
shôshkâhkwikâpâwa	stands up straight
shôshkâhkwikiwa	grows straight
shôshkâhkosêwa	walks erect
shôshkâkêwa	glides on outstretched wings
shôshkâmowa	flees on a straight line
shôshkâpyêshinwa	lies at full length
shôshkâpyêwi	it (stringlike) is straight
shôshkehkêwa	stretches out
shôshkenêwa, shôshkenamwa	straightens s.o., it
shôshki	instantly, directly, at once, with ease (particle, preverb)
shôshkikâpiwa	sits with one's legs stretched out
shôshkikâsahowa	kicks one's legs out straight
shôshkikâtêwa	straightens one's leg or legs
shôshkikiwa, shôshkikenwi	is straight, grows straight; it is straight
shôshkinawîwa	straightens out
shôshkîwa	goes straight
shôshkohâhkwêwa, shôshkwahâhkwêwa	combs one's hair straight
shôshkonêwa, shôshkonamwa	has s.o., it slip from one's grasp; smooths s.o., it by hand
shôshkwanahamîwa	slips as one tries to get one's footing
shôshkwânehkwêyâshinwa	one's hair is blown back smooth
shôshkwâwakeshkâtêwi	the dirt on it (a road) was trodden smooth
shôshkwâwi	it is smooth
shôshkwêkîhi	fine broadcloth
shôshkwêkenwi	smooth cloth
shôshkwishinwa, shôshkwisenwi	slips, slips and falls; it slides and falls
shôshkyâwi	it is straight; it is easy, straightforward
shwâshika	eight (particle) (older **neshwâshika**)
shwâshikanesiwe, shwâshikanîsiwi	eighteen (particle)
shwâshika tasokoni	eight days (particle phrase)
shwâshika tashiwaki,	they (animate, inanimate) are eight, there are eight of them
shwâshika tasenôni (plurals)	
shwâshikânameki	eighth, the eighth time (particle) (older **neshwâshikânameki**)
shwâshikâpitaki	eighty (particle) (older **neshwâshikâpitaki**)
shwâshikenwi	eight times (particle)

t

tahitanachiwa	is cold all the while ({somewhere})
tahitanawasowa	stays warming oneself by the fire
tahitanâhkohwêwa	keeps s.o. imprisoned {somewhere}
tahitanânakîkwêshinwa	is lying there with one's eyes open
tahitanâyênekêmowa	is laughing away at people
tahitanâyênemêwa	is laughing away at s.o.
tahitanâyêniwa	is laughing away, laughs and laughs
tahitanehkomêwa	is whittling
tahitanenekowa	is engaged in activity, performing a task, fooling around
tahitanekahtôwa owîyawi	joins in the dance ({somewhere})
tahitanekêwa	continues to dance
tahitanekwâmwa	is sleeping away ({somewhere})
tahitanetonêmowa	is speaking at length
tahkahwêwa, tahkahamwa	cools s.o., it off (by fanning)
tahkamâhkwishinwa, tahkamâhkwisenwi	(animate, inanimate) lies stretching across a gap
tahkamipahowa	runs across an open space
tahkamisêwa	flies over an open space
tahkamîwa	crosses an open space
tahkamosêwa	walks across an open space
tahkamôtêwa	crawls across an open space
tahkawishinwa	cools off (by getting wet)
tahkâhkohikani (older tahkâhkwahikani)	arbor ("shade")
tahkâhkoshkamwa, tahkâhkoshkamômikatwi	(animate, inanimate) casts a shadow
tahkâhkwâwi	it is shady (êh=tahkâhkwâki in the shade)
tahkâshinwa	cools off in the breeze
tahkepi (tahkepîhi dimin.)	spring (of cool water); well (tahkepîki in the spring, well)
tahkepyêyâwi	its water is cold
tahkikâwawishinwa	cools one's feet in water
tahkinawêshkawêwa	(something ingested) gives s.o. a chill
tahkisenwi	it is cool, is left to cool, cools off
tahkonamwa	catches it and intercepts it
tahkoshkawêwa, tahkoshkamwa	meets, encounters s.o., it, accidentally runs into it
tahkoshkâtîwaki (plural)	they ran into each other (colliding or encountering)
tahkwe, tahkwê!	alas!
tahkyâwi (tahkyâhiwi dimin.)	it is cold
tahowêha	turkey vulture ("buzzard") (archaic)
tahpahôni	(see ahpahôni)
tahpâpatâniwi	it can be seen through; (with negative): there is no visibility (as, in a snowstorm)
tahpâpiwa	sees through
tahpehkwamye	through the (unbroken) ice
tahpehtawêwa	finally understands s.o.
tahpenêwa	dies {somewhere} (êh=tahpenêwâneni wherever I may die)
tahpênetamwa	catches on to it; finally realizes
tahpi	through (preverb) (see -nepwêwa, -wâsêyâpôkatwi)
tahpinawapahkwe	through the wall of the lodge
tahpishimowa:	masâchi (or sakâki) tahpishimôhiwa one's voice can barely be heard
tahtakwapinêwa, tahtakwapitôwa	ties them (animate, inanimate) together
tahtakoshkêwaki (plural)	they (animate) flock together
tahtakoshkêwi	it is added together

tahtakôhpowaki (plural)	they all eat together
tahtakwi	all together, collectively (particle, preverb); collective (prenoun)
tahtakwihtôwaki (plural)	they make it together
tahtakwikwamwa	sews them (inanimate) together, sews (it) to it
tahtakwikwâtêwani (plural)	they (inanimate) are sewn together
tahtakwisahêwa	shoves them (animate) together
tahtakwisenyêwaki (plural)	they all eat together
tahtakwisetôwa	places it, them (inanimate) together
tahtakwîwaki (plural)	they (animate) go together
takâwi	a little (particle)
takeshkawêwa, takeshkamwa	kicks s.o., it, stomps on s.o., it
takonêwa, takonamwa	includes s.o., it, reattaches it
takonâtêwi	it is included, it counts
takosowa	is cooked with (it)
takoswêwa, takosamwa	cooks s.o., it along with (it)
takoshkawêwa, takoshkamwa (1)	covers s.o.'s bet, bets it to cover the bet
takoshkamwa (2)	wears it over another one
takowa, takowi	(animate, inanimate) exists or is found in numbers ({somewhere}) (**êtakochiki** ones that exist {somewhere})
takwahwêwa, takwahamwa	grinds s.o., it up; grinds them together
takwahâni	corn mush (ground dried corn boiled)
takwahâhi	corn mush (dimin.)
takwahôchîhi	trap
takwahônêwa	traps s.o., catches s.o. in a deadfall, runs s.o. over
takwahôsowa	is caught in a trap or deadfall; is run over, crushed
takwahôtawêwa	is trapping for s.o. (animals)
takwahôtôwa	is trapping
takwanwi	there is a frost
takwapitôwa	ties it together with (it)
takwatamwa	chews it together with (it)
takwâkeshiwa	goes on a fall hunt
takwâkêhiwi (dimin.)	it is early autumn, fall
takwâkiwi	it is autumn, fall
takwêwêkesiwa	sounds together with (it)
takwi	both or all together, at the same time, along with (it, etc.) (particle, preverb)
takwihetîwa	makes peace (**takwihetîwaki** they make peace; they get together)
takwikenwi	it grows with (it), it is reattached
takwikihtawêwa	makes (it) grow together for s.o.
takwimêwa	includes s.o. in what one says; says s.o. is romantically involved with (someone)
takwisenwi	it lies, is placed with (it)
takwisetâtîwaki (plural)	they place (it) in addition for each other
takwishimêwa, takwisetôwa	places s.o., it in addition, together with (it)
takwîwa	joins, joins the others
tamâkishaki	too bad about him!
tameko	Oh how well, much, etc. (also **êhtameko**)
tanahâkapiwa	he lives {somewhere} with his in-laws
tanahkamawêwa	lies in wait for s.o. {somewhere}
tanahkiwihtôwaki (plural)	they are having a get-together
tanahkîwi	it goes on {somewhere}
tanahkyêhêwa	grazes s.o. (animal)
tanahkyêhtawêwa	grazes (it) for s.o.

tanahkyêshinwa	is keeping to one's bed with a serious illness
tanahwêwesiwa	spends one's time {somewhere}
tanahkyêwa	(animal) grazes
tanakihtôwa	loses it {somewhere}
tanamatamwa	has pain {somewhere}
tanamêwa	eats s.o. {somewhere}
tananohkyêwa	is doing things, performing one's tasks
tanapenêwa	continues hungry
tanapwîhêwa, tanapwîhtôwa	is waiting for s.o., it ({somewhere})
tanatahwêwa	clubs s.o. {somewhere}
tanâchimohêwa	informs, instructs s.o. {somewhere}
tanâchimêwa, tanâtotamwa	tells of s.o., it being {somewhere}; instructs {somewhere}; is talking about s.o., it
tanâchimowa	talks, reports, tells one's story {somewhere} or about what happened {somewhere}; is telling one's story
tanâhkasamwa	dries it {somewhere}
tanâhkohwêwa	imprisons s.o. {somewhere}
tanânaketonêmowa	engages in talk, is talking
tanâpamêwa	sees s.o. (as being) {somewhere}
tanâpatâniwa	keeps right on doing what one is doing
tanâpiwa	looks {somewhere}; is watchful {somewhere}
tanâsîwa	climbs {somewhere}, is climbing
tanâtotamawêwa	tells s.o. of (it) {somewhere}
tanâyêniwa	is laughing {somewhere}
tanehkwêhiwa	has one's head {somewhere}
tanehkwêshimêwa	lays s.o. with head {somewhere}
tanehkwêshinwa	lies with one's head {somewhere}
tanehtawêwa	hears s.o. {somewhere}
tanekahetîwaki (plural)	they have a dance together {somewhere}
tanekêwa	dances {somewhere}
tanekwâmwa	is sleeping {somewhere}; is (still) sleeping
tanenekowa	thrashes around, fools around, is occupied doing something ({somewhere})
tanenetîwa	fights {somewhere}; is engaged in fighting, continues fighting
tanenêwa, tanenamwa	holds s.o., it {somewhere}; keeps handling it
tanesiwa	is {somewhere}, is at {some place}
tanesowa, tanetêwi	(animate, inanimate) is burning or cooking, is burned, burned up, or cooked {somewhere}
taneswêwa, tanesamwa	cooks s.o., it {somewhere}
taneshamwa	is occupied in cutting it
taneshawêwa	has a fire going ({somewhere})
taneshêwêshinwa	(Fire Spirit) lies blazing
taneshêwi	it (fire) burns, blazes {somewhere}
taneshihamwa	is hunting, continues hunting
taneshitôwa	makes the rounds, makes the complete circuit {somewhere}
taneshkêwa	is acting (involuntarily); acts {somewhere}
tanetîneniwiwa	is a gambler
tanetîwaki (plural)	they gamble, make a bet with each other
tanetîwashkwi	gambling medicine
tanetonêmowa	engages in talk; is talking ({somewhere})
tanetonwa	moves one's mouth ({somewhere}) (song word)
tanênemêwa, tanênetamwa	expects s.o., it; thinks s.o., it is {somewhere}
tanîhka	Oh no! What have I gotten myself into! (exclamation of regret and self-reproach)

tanosêwa	walks {somewhere, in some position or location}
tanotamwa	talks about it ({somewhere}); says (bad) things about it
tanotâtêwi	it is discussed {there}
tanowêwa	discusses {somewhere}
tanôhkyanêwa, tanôhkyatôwa	keeps s.o. {somewhere}, lets or has s.o., it stay {somewhere}
tanôshêwa	she gives birth {somewhere}; (bird) nests {somewhere}
tanôtêwa	crawls {somewhere, in some location}
tanwêkesiwa	cries {somewhere}; is crying
tanwêtamwa	is wailing, shouting, making one's voice sound ({somewhere})
tanwêwêhchikêwa	is audibly chewing or gnawing
tanwêwêhikêwa	is heard drumming, pounding, or chopping ({somewhere})
tanwêwêhtôwa (Jones)	"bangs away on it"
tanwêwêhwêwa, tanwêwêhamwa	is audibly drumming, banging, or pounding on s.o. (as, a drum), it
tanwêwêkatwi	there is loud noise ({somewhere})
tanwêwêkesiwa	is making loud noise (as, wailing, [drum] being drummed on, [bird] calling) ({somewhere})
tanwêwêkihêwa, tanwêwêkihtôwa	makes s.o., it cry out, yelp, squeal ({somewhere})
tanwêwêmêwa	quarrels with s.o.
tanwêwêpochikêwa	continues noisily filing something
tanwêwêtepêhwêwa	is cracking s.o.'s skull with noise
tanwêwêtîwa	quarrels with (s.o.)
tanwêwêtîwaki (plural)	they quarrel with each other
tanwêwêyâpônikêwa	is noisily splashing water on things
tanyêkiwa, tanyêkenwi	(animate, inanimate) is growing
tanyêwîwa	is doing something, is accomplishing something
tasenwi (1)	it is {so much, so many}
tasenwi (2)	{so many} times (particle, preverb)
tasokonakatwi	it is {so many} days
tasokonêtwa	is away {so many} days
tasokoni	{so many} days (particle)
tasokonîwa	fasts for {so many} days
tasotone	{so much} speech (particle)
tasôchêhtamwa	bites of {so much} of it at once
tasôchênamwa	grabs {so many} of them at once
tasôchênawêwa	shoots {so many} of them (animate) with one shot
tasôhpowaki (plural)	{so many} of them eat together (**âyâtasôhpowâchi** as many of them as eat together each time)
tasôkâpâwaki (plural)	{so many} of them stand together
tasôkâtêwa	has {so many} feet
tasôkêwaki (plural)	{so many} of them dwell together
tasônameki	number {so many} (ordinal number) (particle) (e.g. **nîshwâpitaki tasônameki** number twenty, twentieth, the twentieth time)
tasôsetôwa	places {so much, so many} of it, them
tasôshinôki, tasôsenôni (plurals)	{so many} of them (animate, inanimate) lie together
tasôshkenêwa	fills (e.g., a lodge, village, continent) {in such numbers}
taswawahîmakatwi	it is {so many} years
taswawahîme, taswawahîne	{so many} years (particle)
taswayaki	{so many} kinds, groups, sets, pairs (particle)
taswâhkwe	{so many} hundred (particle)
taswâkwapiwaki (plural)	they sit as a group of {so many} ({somewhere})
taswâpyêshka	{so many} strands (as, of strung beads) (particle)
taswâpyêshwêwa	cuts s.o. into {so many} pieces
taswi (**taswîhi** dimin.)	{so much}, {so many} (particle)
taswihêwa, taswihtôwa	has, makes, kills {so many} of s.o., it

taswikamikesiwaki (plural)	there are {so many} houses of them
taswinekwêwa, taswinekwêyâwi	has {so many} wings, star points; it has {so many} petals
taswipepônwe	{so many} years (particle)
taswipepônwêwa	is {so many} years old
tashi (1)	{somewhere}, at or in {some place} (particle, preverb, prenoun)
tashi (2)	engaged in (preverb)
tashichimêwa	is swimming ({somewhere})
tashihêwa	makes s.o. {somewhere}, is making s.o.; kills s.o. {somewhere}
tashikahesêwa	is chopping wood
tashikâhiwa	has one's feet {somewhere}
tashikâshinwa	lies with one's feet {somewhere}
tashikiwa	lives {somewhere}, grows {somewhere}
tashikomêsetôwa	dips its tip (as, of an arrow) {somewhere}
tashimêwa	talks about s.o., gossips about s.o.
tashinâkêwa	sings {somewhere}
tashinechâmêwa	is taking care of s.o.
tashisenyêhêwa	makes or has s.o. eat {somewhere}
tashisenyêwa	eats {somewhere}
tashisêwa	flies {somewhere, in some place}
tashitashi	(with negative): it does not take long (particle)
tashitêhêwa	expects, is expecting; is thinking; one's thoughts are {somewhere}; one's thoughts are on (s.o.)
tashitiyêpiwa	is sitting, perching on (the edge of) {somewhere}; is squatting {somewhere} (Jones)
tashitiyêshimêwa	places s.o. with rump {somewhere}
tashiwaki (plural)	are {so many} (**shwâshika tashiwaki** there are eight of them; **êtashiwâchi** as many as there are of them, all of them)
tashîhkamawêwa	deals with (it) for s.o.
tashîhkawêwa, tashîhkamwa	is dealing with s.o., it, working on s.o., it; busy with s.o., it; tries to persuade s.o.
tashîhkânowa	plays, is playing (**têshîhkânôhikini** as if merely playing)
tashîhkânoweni	toy
tashîhkâtîwa	tries to persuade; courts or is courted by (s.o.), has an affair (with s.o.) (**têshîhkâtîkini** as if one is being courted)
tashîseniwa	eats {somewhere} (for **tashi-wîseniwa**)
tatakohamwa	weeds it
tatakwanwi	yard, area around the summer house kept free of grass and litter
tatakwisetôwa	cleans it up (as, a yard, a house)
tatayâchi	in quick succession (archaic) (particle)
tatâtonêwa, tatâtonamwa	tears s.o. (as, skin), it up, shreds it
tatike (or **ta=tike**)	confound (that one, them)! (particle)
tatôkikâpiwa	sits with one's legs spread apart
tatôkikomêwa	one's nostrils spread open
tatôpanahwêwa	ties s.o. up in a bag
tawashkotêyâwi	there is a clearing
tawâkonêshkânawêwa	clears a space in the snow with one's feet
tawânahi, tayânahi	would that! (particle) (archaic equivalents of **tânî='nahi**)
tawâwi (**tawâhiwi** dimin.)	there is a space, a gap
tawenamwa	clears it
tawenikêwa	clears things away
tawihtôwa	leaves a space
tawipekwêhikêwa	clears away the ashes (in the fireplace)
tayânahi	(see **tawânahi**)
tâhtapakwi (archaic **tâhtopakwi**)	leaf

tâhtâpôhkasowaki, **tâhtâpôhkatêwani** (plurals)	they (animate, inanimate) are stuck in the ground side by side
tâhtâpôkâpâwaki (plural)	they (animate) stand side by side
tâhtâpôkêwaki (plural)	they (animate) dance side by side
tâhtâpôpahowaki (plural)	they (animate) run side by side
tâhtâpôpiwaki (plural)	they (animate) sit side by side
tâhtâpôshimêwa, tâhtâpôsetôwa	places them (animate, inanimate) side by side
tâhtâpôshinôki (plural)	they (animate) lie side by side
tâhtâpôwâshkêwani (plural)	they (inanimate) fall side by side
tâhtâpôwosêwaki (plural)	they (animate) walk side by side
tâkahwêwa	touches s.o., taps s.o.
tâkamêwa, tâkatamwa	tastes s.o., it, gets a taste of s.o., it, gets to eat s.o., it
tâkamônêwa	allows s.o. a taste of (it)
tâkâhkwêhamwa	taps it (as, a tree or post) with a stick
tâkenêwa, tâkenamwa	touches s.o., it
tâkeshkawêwa, tâkeshkamwa	touches s.o., it with one's foot (feet) or body
tâkichinwa	is touched or brushed by something (as one passes)
tâkitepênêwa	touches s.o. on the head
tâkyênihikêwa	taps the drum
tâkyênihwêwa	taps s.o. (as, a drum)
tâna, tâni (1)	where is? which one is? (animate, inanimate)
tânâhka=kêhi (short form **tânâh=kêhi**)	or perhaps, or what about if it was this way (also with **o**= or)
tânahi	where? (particle)
tâni (2)	how? what? (particle)
=tâni (3)	O.K.? why don't I, if you agree, if you will, please
tâninapâchi	what else can be done (but)? all one can do (is) (particle)
tâninâhi	when? at what distance? (particle)
tâniya, tâniye	where is he or she, it?
tânî='nahi	I wish (with subjunctive verb)
tâpônamwa	puts it or them together double (as, folding a blanket)
tâpôpinêwa	wraps the two of them (animate, as hides) together
tâpôwi	on opposite sides, on both sides (preverb)
-tâshine	dozen (in particle compounds) (**nîshwi-tâshine** two dozen)
tâtakeshkawêwa	stomps s.o., kicks s.o. around
tâtaki	sort of, as it were, in a way, making like; in order to (particle)
tâtashi	{somewhere} (repeatedly) (preverb)
tâtashîhkânowa	(always) plays ({somewhere})
tâtepi	where to? where from? (particle)
tâtonêwa, tâtonamwa	tears s.o., it
tâtoshwêwa	cuts s.o. open
tâtwâhkiwi	ravine
tâtwâwi	it is torn
tâtwikashâtamwa	tears it with one's nail or claw
tâtwineshiwêshinwa	he falls and tears his testicles
tâtwisahtôwa	tears it quickly
tehkichikêwa	she puts her baby on a cradle-board
tehkinâkani (**tehkinâkâhi** dimin.)	cradle-board
tehkinêwa	puts s.o. on a cradle-board
tehkisowa	is on a cradle-board
tehtômêwa	sings a lullaby to s.o.
tepahâsowa, tepahâtêwi	(animate, inanimate) is paid
tepahwêwa, tepahamwa	pays s.o., it, pays s.o. (it)
tepasishimôhiwa	speaks in a low voice
tepatawi	in full number, amount, or extent (preverb)

tepatohachikêwa	follows (s.o.'s) advice and example
tepatohachikaniwiwa	is emulated and relied on
tepâhkiwiwi, tepâhkîwi	it is level land; it (water) is flat calm
tepâhkonikani	law
tepâhkonikênenîha	judge, lawyer
tepâhkoshkamwa	weighs it, balances them
tepânâsowa	is loved, is dearly loved
tepânekosiwa	is dearly loved
tepânetîwaki (plural)	they love each other
tepânetîweni	love
tepânêwa, tepâtamwa	loves, cherishes, is fond of, is proud of s.o., it; holds it back, keeps it for oneself
tepâpamêwa	looks s.o. over, looks into s.o.'s situation
tepâshiwêwa	loves people
tepâtesiwa	is up to it
tepehki (1)	at night (particle)
tepehki (2)	night (noun) (**îni tepehki** that night)
tepehki (3)	of night (prenoun)
tepehki-kîsheswa	moon
tepehkîwi	it is night
tepehkoki	last night (particle)
tepehkwi (1)	night (noun)
tepehkwi (2)	of night (prenoun)
tepênemêwa, tepênetamwa	owns, controls s.o., it
tepênetamôwitêhêwa	thinks one owns (s.o., it)
tepênetâkosiwa, tepênetâkwatwi	(animate, inanimate) is owned, belongs
tepênetâtêwi	it is owned, controlled
tepi	the full number or amount, being all set (preverb, preparticle, particle)
tepichîkwanêshkâtîwaki (plural)	they are in a row sitting knee-to-knee
tepihkamêwa	has a complete smoke, the full amount of smoking
tepihkesowa	has a complete smoke, the full amount of smoking
tepikiwaki (plural), **tepikenwi**	they are the right number; it is the right amount, correct
tepikîshkâkwapiwaki (plural)	they sit in a row
tepikîshkâkwasowaki (plural)	they lie on the ground in a row
tepikîshkâkwatêwi:	**pemi-tepikîshkâkwatêwani** they (inanimate) lie end-on in an even line
tepikîshki	simultaneously (particle)
tepikîshkikâpâwaki (plural)	they stand side-by-side in a row
tepikîshkishinôki (plural)	they lie side-by-side in a row
tepikîshkosêwaki (plural)	they walk in an even line abreast
tepimêwa, tepotamwa	discusses s.o., it in council
tepinâhi	in a straight line; directly opposite, above, or below; exactly (where) (particle)
tepinâhiwi, tepinâhiwiwi:	**êh=tepinâhiki** exactly where it is
tepinehki (**tepinehkîhi** dimin.)	for the right length of time, for quite a while
tepinowe, tepinawe	of one's own, of one's own family or lineage, directly related (particle)
tepinowêwe	(by) oneself
tepishkawêwa	takes s.o.'s place
tepitepi	in equal numbers or amounts (particle)
tepitêhêwa	is deciding, trying to figure out, considering what to do
tepitîhêwa	tries s.o. (in court)
tepitîwa	stands trial
tepowânêwa, tepowâtamwa	debates over, decides about s.o., it in council
tepowênenîha	councilman
tepowêwaki (plural)	they hold council

tepowêwi	of the council (prenoun)
tepowêwi-ashkotêwi	council fire
tepowêwikâni	council-house
tesôchîhi	trap (archaic)
tesôtawêwa	sets a trap for s.o. (archaic)
tesôsowa	is caught in a trap (archaic)
tetepahtakîhi	cord
tetepashkwêwa	is dizzy
tetepâhkwisetawêwa	wraps (it) around for s.o.
tetepâhkwisêwa, tetepâhkwisêwi	(animate, inanimate) wraps around
tetepâhkwishinwa	lies or is placed to wrap around
tetepâkwapiwaki (plural)	they sit around (it) in a circle
tetepâkwatôwa	places them in a circle
tetepechêsahtôwa	sets it rolling
tetepechêsêwa	falls rolling
tetepechêshkêwi	it goes rolling
tetepekêwa	dances in a circle, circles (it) dancing
tetepi	in a circle (particle, preverb)
tetepinâkêwa	circles singing, circles (it) singing
tetepinehkawêwa	chases s.o. in a circle
tetepipahowa	runs in a circle, circles (it) running
tetepipokôtêwi	it floats circling (Jones: whirling)
tetepisahêwa	swings s.o. around
tetepisêwa	flies in a circle (Jones: whirls around)
tetepishkenamwa	twists it, makes a twist of it
tetepiwenêwa	leads s.o. in a circle, leads s.o. in a circle around (it)
tetepîhi	ring
teteposahêwa	makes s.o. walk in a circle, makes s.o. circle (it) walking
teteposêwa	walks in a circle, walks in a circle around (it)
têhkinâsôha	baby on a cradle-board ("cradle baby")
têhtêpahanwi	it floats
têhtêpanwi	there is rhythmic movement, undulation
têhtêpechânâmowa	one's stomach rises and falls as one breathes
têhtêpipiwêsêwi	the pile on it (as, a bearskin) undulates
têhtêwahamwa	taps or thumps repeatedly on it
têhtêwahikêwa	gives several taps or thumps (with it)
têhtêwahkyêshkamwa	is shaking the earth with one's stomping
têhtêwâhkohamwa	taps or thumps repeatedly on it
têhtêweshkamwa	stomps repeatedly (causing vibration)
têkwâkeshîhaki (plural)	fall hunters
têpahkoshkamwa	attains it, reaches the end of it
têpahkwi	reaching, reaching the point or end of, going so far as to, living long enough to, succeeding in, all the way (preverb, particle)
têpapiwa	has enough room to sit, fits in one's seat
têpashkenêwa, têpeshkenêwa	fills, takes all the room (êhkwi-têpeshkenêwâchi as many of them as could fit in)
têpâpamêwa, têpâpatamwa	is able to see s.o., it (in the distance or clairvoyantly)
têpâpatamâkêwa	is able to see (it) in the distance for people
têpâpatâniwi	it can be seen in the distance
têpâpiwa	sees enough; is able to see (from distance or clairvoyantly)
têpehtawêwa	catches s.o.'s sound
têpenêwa, têpenamwa	reaches s.o., it, reaches out and touches s.o., it
têpesiwa (têpesîhiwa dimin.)	is glad, pleased, delighted, joyful
têpesînotawêwa, têpesînotamwa	is pleased with s.o., it

169

têpesowa	enough of (animate) is cooked (**êhkwi-têpesochi** as much of (animate) as can be cooked)
têpênemêwa	is content about (what happened to) s.o. (as, thinking it was deserved), does not feel sorry for s.o.
têpênemowa	is satisfied, has had enough
têpi	sufficiently, as long as; achieve, succeed in (particle, preverb)
	têpi=kêh=wîna (and this is) despite the fact that; although
	têpi='h=wê=kêhî='ni it is surely not too much (to ask)
têpihetîwaki (plural)	they please each other
têpihêwa (1)	goes as far as {somewhere}
têpihêwa (2), **têpihtôwa**	pleases s.o., it; does a good thing for s.o., it; has a good effect on s.o., it; does s.o., it good
têpihiwêwa	pleases people
têpihkamêwa	gets enough smoking, is satisfied smoking
têpihkesowa	gets enough smoking, is satisfied smoking
têpihtawêwa	pleases (it) for s.o.
têpikenwi	it reaches, is possible
têpimêwa	says what is true about s.o.
têpinehki	for long enough (particle)
têpi-nâhinâhi	for long enough, far enough (particle compound)
têpisenyêwa	has enough to eat
têpisêwa, **têpisêwi**	there is enough of s.o., it to go around (**êhkwi-têpisâchi, êhkwi-têpisâki** as far as s.o., it goes when distributed)
têpiwetôwa	is able to take it all the way
têpîhiwêwa	succeeds in reaching safety or refuge
têpîhkânowa	does a pleasing deed
têpîmêhi	greatly, to a great number or extent (particle)
têpôtamwa	is able to carry it on one's back
têpwêhêwa	believes s.o.; makes s.o.'s prayer come true
têpwêhtawêwa, **têpwêhtamwa**	believes s.o., it; grants s.o.'s request
têpwêhtâkaniwiwa	is believed, is heeded
têpwêmikatwi	it is true
têpwêshêwa	believes what one hears, what one is told
têpwêwa	speaks the truth; one's prayer or request is granted
têpwêwêkomêwa	can be heard (from a distance) snoring
têpwêwi	believing, granting (preverb)
têpiyâkosiwa, **têpiyâkwatwi**	the smell of (animate, inanimate) reaches
têtepechêhâtêhi	barrel, keg
têtepechêhiwa	rolls downhill
têtepisâha	wheel
têtepishkâsôha	bicycle
têwanasitêkâpâwa	stands with aching feet
têwehkwêwa	has a headache
têwêhikana	drum
têwishinwa	falls and hurts oneself
têwitepêhokowa	is bumped on the head by a falling object
têwitepêshinwa	falls and bumps one's head
têyêhtakwi	all together, in general (particle)
têyêpesiwa	leads a completely successful warparty (with scalps or prisoners taken but no casualties)
têyêpênemêwa	one's intentions against s.o. are completely fulfilled
têyêpimêwa, **têyêpotamwa**	one's words about s.o., it are completely fulfilled
têyêpîkwêshinwa:	**anenêki têyêpîkwêshika** He Who Has His Face Completely Filling the Smokehole (the Sky as an intermediary of prayer)

têyêpowêwa	foretells something completely accurately
=tike	(man's mild expletive)
tîkwêwêpahowa	the patter of one's feet can be heard as one runs
tîkwêwêshkamwa	the patter of one's feet can be heard
tîkwêwi	it patters, there is a pattering sound
tîpani (**tîpanêhi** dimin.)	table
tîtîwa	bluejay
tohitôtawêwa (also **itohitôtawêwa**)	acts {so} upon s.o. repeatedly, treats s.o. {so} repeatedly
tohkâna	Tohkan, member of the Tohkan division
tohkânihkwêwa	Tohkan woman
tohkâniwiwa, tohkâniwa	is a Tohkan
towi (**tôhiwi** dimin.) (also **tômikatwi**)	it happens {so} (in idioms):

    kashi=wîh=towi I don't care; what difference will it make? (literally: what will happen?)

    kashi wîh=tôhiwi it will be alright (if)

    kashi=wê=wîh=towi what does it matter? (literally: after all, what will happen?)

    kashi=wê=towi, 'shi=wê=towi yes, of course, to be sure (as an answer)

    kashi=châhi êh=teki. Why? How come? What for?

tôhkapenêwa	wakes up hungry
tôhkenêwa	wakes s.o. up by touching
tôhkeshkawêwa	wakes s.o. up by bodily contact
tôhki	wake up (doing whatever) (preverb)
tôhkihêwa	wakes s.o. up
tôhkikêmowa	wakes people up by calling out
tôhkikomasowa	is awakened by heat in one's nose
tôhkimêwa	wakes s.o. up by voice
tôhkinehkawêwa	rousts s.o., rouses s.o. from sleep
tôhkisahêwa	wakes s.o. up
tôhkisêwa	wakes up abruptly
tôhkîwa	wakes up
tôhkwêwêhpwêwa	wakes s.o. up by blowing (as, on a whistle)
tôhkwêwêhwêwa	wakes s.o. up by knocking, pounding, or drumming
tôhkwêwêshkawêwa	wakes s.o. up by stomping (as, by dancing)
tôkanoshkêwi	its opening spreads open
tôkapiwa	sits with one's legs spread apart
tôke (particle):	**tôke=wîna:** the idea of it! imagine that!
tôkishêsetawêwa	has it (as, a bag) open for s.o.
tôkitiyêwosêwa	walks with legs spread apart
tôpahiyâha	top (spun as a toy)
tôpâkâha	bark hoop rolled as a target
tôpâkâhiwaki (plural)	they have a contest shooting at hoops
tôshkânakîkwêshkêwa	one's eyes peep open
tôshkîkwêmowa	peeps through one's eyes while singing
tôshkîkwênwa	peeps through one's eyes
tôshkîkwêshkêwa	opens one's eyes a crack
tôshkîkwêwa	peeps, one's eyes peep open
tôtawêwa, tôtamwa (also **itôtawêwa**)	acts {so} upon s.o., it; treats s.o., it {so}

    wîh=tôtawaki!? What would I care about s.o.? Of what possible use is s.o. to me?

    kêkôhi tôtawêwa does something to s.o.; he has sex with her

tôtâtîwaki (plural)	they act {so} upon each other
tôtôsiwa	cricket

tôtôwa	bullfrog
tôtôwâwi	it is large and strong, massive, sturdy

W

wachâhêwa	cooks (it) for s.o.
wachâhetisowa	cooks for oneself
wachâhetîwaki (plural)	they cook for each other
wachâhetîweni	cooking, preparation of feasts for each other
wachâhowa	cooks (it)
wachâhôhkânowa	pretends to cook, plays at cooking
wachânotêwa	cooks for people (**nîh**=**wachânota** I'll cook for everyone)
wahkêwi	easily, readily (preverb)
wahkêwikitâsowa	gets angry easily
wahkwi (also sung as **wahkwiye**)	sky (song word)
wahônwa	howls (as, a wolf or dog) (**êh**=**wahôneki** howled)
wahpâhêwa	disrupts s.o.'s sleep
wahpâsiwa	is an early riser
wahpâtêhêwa	is kept awake by one's thoughts
wahpâwîhkâtîwaki (plural)	they are busy keeping each other awake
wanahkamiki	all over, all over the map, in all directions, on all sides (particle)
wanawosêwa (Jones)	walks to relieve one's mind of care
wanâkenêwa	raises s.o. by hand
wanâkîwa	arises from bed, gets up
wanâpêwinohkatamwa:	**wênâpêwinohkataka îni kehkeshêwi** the one who is brave towards the charcoal (i.e., who has the courage to fast)
wanâpêwiwa:	**wênâpêwita** the one who is brave
wanâtesiwa	does not know what's what, is clueless
wanihchikani	medicine for losing someone
wanenamwa	puts it somewhere and loses it
wani	as a diversion, to forget one's troubles (preverb)
wanihêwa, wanihtôwa	loses, forgets about s.o., it; misses s.o. (not knowing where they are)
wanikêmowa	fools people, makes deceptive claims or statements
wanimêwa, wanotamwa	deceives s.o., it, fools s.o.
wanimôchi	perchance, if it should happen to be that (particle)
wanimôshkwe	(with negative): not freely or randomly, only if appropriate (particle)
waninawe	in all directions, on all sides (particle)
waninêhwêwa	cheats s.o.
wanisowa	is lost (one's whereabouts are unknown), is in another world (mentally), is confused (as, about what day it is)
wanîhkamêwa	passes the time (with a diversion, pastime, rainy-day activity)
wanîhkanawesiwa	is getting forgetful, loses track
wanîhkânêwa, wanîhkâtamwa	forgets s.o., it
wanîhkâsowa	forgets
wanîhkêwa	forgets (it)
wanîkwêhêwa	deceives s.o.; tries to take (it) away from s.o. secretly
wanîkwênêwa	cheats s.o. (out if it)
wanîpahêwa	avoids being found by s.o., gets away from s.o. by concealment
wanyêwîwa	makes a mistake
wapasatamwa	eats it disrespectfully (also **wâpasatamwa**)
wapasehtawêwa	listens to s.o. disrespectfully (also **wâpasehtawêwa**)

wapasênemêwa, wapasênetamwa	is disrespectful of s.o., it, thinks s.o., it foolish, has a flippant or mocking attitude (towards it) (also **wâpasênemêwa**)
wapasotamwa	makes fun of it by speech (also **wapashotamwa**)
wapasowêwa	makes fun of people (also **wâpasowêwa**)
wapashi	disrespectfully, mockingly (preverb, particle) (also **wâpashi**)
wapashihêwa, wapashihtôwa	makes fun of, disgraces, ruins, wastes s.o., it (also **wâpashihêwa**)
wapashihtawêwa	makes fun of, disgraces, ruins, wastes (it) for s.o. (also **wâpashihtawêwa**)
wapashimêwa, wapashotamwa	makes fun of s.o., it by speech (also **wâpashimêwa; wapasotamwa**)
washâsha	an Osage (also **ashâsha**)
washâshinâki	in the Osage country (locative noun)
wawâsanosowa	(see **wâsanosowa**)
wawâsanotêwi	it sparkles
wawâsanôtêwi	(see **wâsanôtêwi**)
wawâsehkêwi	it is shiny, glistens, sparkles (also **wâsewâsehkêwi**)
wawâsesowa, wawâsetêwi	(animate, inanimate) sparkles, shines (by reflected light)
wawâsetonwa	flashes at the mouth (**wawâsetonôki nenemehkiwaki** there is lightning, "the thunderers' mouths are flashing")
wawîhkwanapiwa	sits on one's knees (with feet together on one side)
wawîhkwanisahowa	drops to one's knees (to sit)
wawîhkwanisêwa	collapses to one's knees
wawîkihêwa	consoles s.o., placates s.o., cheers s.o. up
wawîkimêwa	soothes or calms s.o. with words
wawînwâsowa	brags, boasts
wawînwânêwa, wawînwâtamwa	compliments s.o., praises s.o.; brags about it
wayachi	already (preverb)
wayachîwa	has already gone
wayatahkiwiwi	everything is already over
wayêchi	easily, with no effort or ado (particle)
wayêshi	ready (particle, preverb)
wayîhkwa (also **wayîhkwe**)	forever, since long ago, from now on (particle)
wayîhkwâwi	forever (preverb)
wâ!	Oh no! Oh dear! Too bad (for him, etc.)! (also **hwâ!**)
wâh (older **wâyi**)	what? what did you say?
wâhkamahwêwa, wâhkamahamwa	wipes s.o., it clean, polishes s.o., it
wâhkamenêwa, wâhkamenamwa	cleans s.o., it
wâhkami	clean, neat; completely (particle, preverb)
wâhkanakikesiwa, wâhkanakikanwi	(animate tree, inanimate tree) has the bark gone
wâhkanakikeshamwa	cuts the bark from it
wâhkanakitepêshwêwa	cuts the scalp from s.o.'s head
wâhkâhikani	stockade
wâhkâshamwa	cuts it around in a circle or ring
wâhkâshikêwa	cuts squash or pumpkin rings (see **kâtenikanani**)
wâhkonêwa	Indian tobacco (also **âhkonêwa**)
wâhtenamwa	offers it, sacrifices it; bets it
wâhtenikêwa	sacrifices (it), makes a sacrifice of (it)
wâkâkenamwa	bends it (something stiff), bends it over
wâkechêkâpâwa	stands bent over
wâkechêsahowa	doubles up quickly
wâkechêshinwa	lies curled up
wâkechêwosêwa	walks bent over
wâkechêyâpyêhi	bend in a stream
wâkenêwa, wâkenamwa	bends s.o. (as, a bow), it

wâkichêhtêwa:	**êh=wâkichêhtêchi** one's hamstring, the sinew behind the (animal's) hind-leg joint
wâkihpeni	yellow lotus, yellow lotus roots
wâkihpenihkêwa	gathers yellow lotus roots
wâkihpeni-oshkîshekwaki (plural)	yellow-lotus seeds
wâkihpenipakwi	yellow-lotus leaf
wâkikiwa, wâkikenwi	is bent (as, with age), it is crooked
wâkikomêwa	has a hooked nose or beak
wâkikwayawêshkêwa	arches one's neck
wâkisikiwêwa	has a crooked spine
wâkîwa	turns off, turns in, veers off (does not keep going straight)
wâkoshêha	fox
wâkôha	member of the Fox Clan
wâkôhisowa	is a member of the Fox Clan
wâkôhisota (participle)	member of the Fox Clan
wâkômowa (also **wâkôtamwa**)	gives thanks
wânahkye	peaceably, undisturbed (particle)
wânahkyêhêwa	puts them at ease, makes them feel secure
wânahkyêwa	is undisturbed, at ease, without worries, paying no attention
wânakowiwi	it has a hole in it, is hollow
wânakwi	hole, cave; open grave
wânapiwa	is peaceable, at peace, unconcerned
wânatâkani	mound of earth with concave top (ceremonial)
wânatohka	unconcerned, as if nothing were wrong or unusual (particle)
wânehkâtamwa	digs a hole in it
wânehkêwa	digs, digs a hole or grave
wânehkonamwa	hollows it out by hand, scoops it out
wânehkwâwi	it is hollow, there is a depression (in the ground)
wânehkwâwashkohkamwa	tromps down the tall grass to make a concealed space
wânihêwa	leaves s.o. in peace
wânimêwa, wânotamwa	holds one's tongue in speaking to or about s.o., it; does not say anything critical to or about s.o.
wânisetôwa	leaves it undisturbed, unused
wânotâha:	**pwâwi- kêkôhi -wânotâha** one who is quick to criticize anything
wâpachihkawêhchikêwa	looks for tracks
wâpachihkawêhêwa	looks for s.o.'s tracks, follows s.o.'s tracks
wâpachikêwa	looks, looks at something
wâpahtakawêwa	(animal) has a white coat
wâpake	tomorrow (subjunctive verb) (see **wâpanwi**)
wâpakêwa	looks on
wâpaki	the next day (in the past) (changed conjunct verb) (see **wâpanwi**)
wâpamâsowa	is looked at
wâpamêwa, wâpatamwa	looks at s.o., it
wâpamowa	looks at one's reflection
wâpamôni	mirror
wâpananâkwa	the morning star
wâpanâchihêwa	(departing soul) looks back and destroys s.o. (ritual)
wâpanâpamêwa	(departing soul) looks back at s.o. (ritual)
wâpanâtapiwa	sits as one pleases (ritual)
wâpanemiwa	is overtaken by daylight, lives till dawn
wâpanênemêwa	(departing soul) thinks back about s.o. (ritual)
wâpanohkêwa	makes the morning; morning comes for one
wâpanôwiweni	Wabano Rite

wâpanwi (wâpanôhiwi dimin.)	it dawns, is morning, is day (see also wâpake, wâpaki)
wâpanwitêhêshinwa	lies thinking until dawn
wâpasatamwa	eats it disrespectfully (also wapasatamwa)
wâpasehtawêwa	listens to s.o. disrespectfully (also wapasehtawêwa)
wâpasênemêwa, wâpasênetamwa	is disrespectful of s.o., it, thinks s.o., it foolish, has a flippant or mocking attitude (towards it) (also wapasênemêwa)
wâpasowêwa	makes fun of people (also wapasowêwa)
wâpashi	disrespectfully, mockingly (preverb) (also wapashi)
wâpashihêwa, wâpashihtôwa	makes fun of, disgraces, ruins, wastes s.o., it (also wapashihêwa)
wâpashihtawêwa	makes fun of, disgraces, ruins, wastes (it) for s.o. (also wapashihtawêwa)
wâpashimêwa, wâpashotamwa	makes fun of s.o., it by speech (also wapashimêwa)
wâpatahêwa	shows (it) to s.o., lets s.o. see it
wâpatamawêwa	looks at (it) for s.o.
wâpatisowa	looks at oneself, examines oneself
wâpatîwaki (plural)	they look at each other
wâpatôhkyêwa	shows (it), shows (it) to people
wâpatônêwa	shows (it) to s.o.
wâpawâpamêwa, wâpawâpatamwa	keeps looking at s.o., it, gazes at s.o., it
wâpesiwisowa	is a member of the Swan Clan
wâpesîhpenyêki (plural)	broad-leaved arrowheads, arrowhead roots
wâpeswêwa	leaves s.o. (corn) to dry on the stalks
wâpeshkâhkonêwa	paints s.o. white
wâpeshkâhkonowa	paints oneself white, has one's body painted white
wâpeshkesiwa, wâpeshkyâwi	is white
wâpeshkinameshkêwa	is white-skinned (wâpeshkinameshkâta white person)
wâpeshkipehkwanwa	has a white back
wâpeshkitepêwa	has a white head
wâpeshkîkwêwa	has a white face; (ear of corn) has white kernels
wâpeshkyêkiwa	(buckskin) is white
wâpetôhi	black broadcloth with light-colored edge
wâpi	pale; white (archaic) (prenoun, preverb)
wâpikaya	wolverine
wâpi-kohpichi-nenoswa	White Buffalo
wâpi-kohpichi-nenoswayi	White Buffalo skin
wâpikoni	squash, pumpkin
wâpikonôha	mouse
wâpimina	white corn
wâpinîkwêwa	is white-eyed
wâpinôha	white person (song word); a species of bird ("snow-bird")
wâpinôhi	white thing (song word)
wâpi-sîpôwi	the White River (in the sky); the Milky Way
wâpisôha	nit, louse egg
wâpisôhânehkwêwa	has nits in one's hair
wâpitenâhkwa	whooping crane
wâpitepêwa	has a gray head
wâpitepêwâtesiwa	is gray-haired
wâpitîha	antelope
wâpîwena	white clay (used for body paint)
wâpôsôha	snowshoe hare
wâsahkamikôha	person of a distant land (archaic)
wâsanosowa (or wawâsanosowa)	has something shining or sparkling on one
wâsanôtêwi (or wawâsanôtêwi)	it glows, it shines with a bright light

wâsapahkwêsenwi	its roof stands out clearly against the darker background (in the distance)
wâsâhkotawêwa	the light of one's fire can be seen glowing in the distance
wâsâhkotêwi	the light of (its) fire can be seen glowing in the distance
wâsâpanwi	it is bright dawn
wâsehkosowa, wâsehkotêwi	shines; it shines, glows, is lit up
wâsehkwi	shiny (prenoun)
wâsenamwa	flashes it (as, a mirror)
wâsesikêwa	lights things up
wâsesîha	bullhead
wâsewâsehkêwi	it glistens, sparkles (also **wawâsehkêwi**)
wâsêshawêwa	has or makes light (as, from a fire)
wâsêshêwa	(star) gives off light
wâsêshêwi	there is light from a fire; it (house) has light in it from a fire
wâsêshkamwa	lights it by walking, going, jumping
wâsêyânakatwi	it is a lighted hole
-wâsêyâwe	day (in particle compounds) (see **âpehtawi-wâsêyâwe, nekoti-wâsêyâwe, nîshwi-wâsêyâwe**)
wâsêyâwi (1)	there is light, daylight; it is day
wâsêyâwi (2)	daylight, day
wâsêyâwi (3)	in the daytime (preverb)
wâsêyâpiwa	sees as if in daytime
-wâsêyâpôkatwi:	**tahpi-wâsêyâpôkatwi** the water is clear
wâsikînahtêhi	sharp-pointed wooden arrow
wâsikînihketêwi	it is burned to a point
wâsikînikomêyâwi	it is sharp at the point
wâsikînikomêhamwa	sharpens it to a point by chopping
wâsikînikomêshamwa	sharpens it to a point by cutting
wâsikînipehkwanêyâwi	it has a sharply peaked roof
wâshkêtepêwa	has a bald spot or spots where hair has been pulled out
wâshkêtepêshinwa	lies with one's head scalped
wâsôkêwa	the northern lights
wâsôkêwiwi	the northern lights can be seen
wâsôni	brightness (?; song word)
wâshâwakahamwa	makes a hole in it (the earth) by striking it
wâshesiwa, wâshâwi	has a hole; it has a hole in it
wâshinihkatwi	it (a tree) is hollow
wâshipaka	one (of them) and not the other is the one (particle) (see **wâwâshipaka**)
wâwananâmosowa	is smothered by the heat
wâwananâmowa	is out of breath
wâwananâmwishimêwa	lays s.o. out with the wind knocked out of them
wâwanatamwa	cannot eat it
wâwanawiwa	is ignorant, does not know how, does not know what to do
wâwanâchi	confusedly, with confused excitement, all over the place, at a loss for what to do (particle, preverb)
wâwanâchitêhêwa	does not know what to think
wâwanâhpenanêwa, wâwanâhpenatôwa	is unable to deal with or get at s.o., it; has no chance with s.o.
wâwanâkômêwa, wâwanâkôtamwa	is uncomfortable with s.o., it, is not used to s.o.'s ways
wâwanâsîwa	is not good at climbing
wâwanâtâmanwa	engages in sex with wild abandon
wâwanâtesiwa	is excited, fidgety, rattled, beside oneself, at a loss for what to do
wâwanâtesowa	is foolish from heat
wâwanâtetonêmowa	is talking incoherently

wâwanâtowêhtawêwa	misinterprets to s.o.
wâwanehtawêwa	fails to hear s.o., fails to understand s.o.
wâwanekêwa	does not know how to dance
wâwaneshkâha	naughty, bad, wicked, or evil person, bad actor
wâwaneshkâhanohkyêwa	does something wicked
wâwaneshkâhawiwa	is wicked
wâwaneshkâhekêwa	dances wickedly
wâwaneshkâhênemêwa	thinks s.o. wicked
wâwaneshkâhênetâkaniwiwa	is thought wicked
wâwaneshkâhi	evilly, wickedly (preverb); evil, wicked (prenoun)
wâwaneshkâhikenwi	it is mischievous
wâwaneshkâhitêhâkani	wicked thought
wâwaneshkâhitêhêwa	is wicked at heart
wâwaneshkâhiwa, wâwaneshkâhiwi	is bad, naughty, immoral; it is bad, evil
wâwaneshkâhiwiwa	is bad, naughty, immoral
wâwaneshkâhîhkânowa	does an evil thing, an evil deed
wâwaneshkâhîhtêwa	does something wicked, acts wickedly
wâwaneshkâhowêwa	speaks evil, wickedly
wâwanênemêwa, wâwanênetamwa	fails to know s.o., it, forgets s.o., it; loses one's mind, cannot think straight, is at one's wit's end
wâwanênetamôhkânowa	pretends not to know
wâwani	be unable to, be poor at (preverb)
	wâwani-inekinôhiwa is not grown up enough
	wâwani-ishawiwa is unable to do it right, is at a loss
wâwanihchikêwa	makes a mistake, does not do it the right way
wâwanikenwi	it does not work right, turns out bad (**êh=wâwanikenôhiniki** in a somewhat unhandy or out-of-the-way place [obv.])
wâwanikihtôwa	is at a loss what to do about it
wâwaninâhi	(still) some distance away
wâwaninâkêwa	does not know how to sing correctly
wâwanîwesiwa	cannot get used to it
wâwasâhi	(see **wâwosâhi**)
wâwâchi	reciprocally, mutually; jointly (particle, preverb)
wâwâchikâshinôki (plural)	they (two) lie with their feet toe to toe
wâwâchipehkwanêkâpâwaki (plural)	they (two) stand back to back
wâwâchitiyêshinôki (plural)	they (two) lie buttocks to buttocks
wâwâchîkwêshinôki (plural)	they (two) lie facing each other
wâwâkahamwa	whoops
wâwâkapayêwa	is bow-legged (literally, has bent thigh-bones)
wâwâpachikêwa	chooses, makes one's selection
wâwâpamêwa, wâwâpatamwa	selects s.o., it; looks at, gazes at s.o., it
wâwâpatahêwa	lets s.o. select, decide
wâwâpimatetêwa	is wearing white leggins
wâwâsêsîha, wêwâsêsîha	firefly
wâwâshinîkwêwa	is hollow-eyed
wâwâshipaka	the other way around (with roles reversed), contrary to the norm (particle) (see **wâshipaka**)
wâwâtâsamapiwaki (plural)	they sit facing each other
wâwâtâsamikâpâwaki (plural)	they stand facing each other
wâwâtehkwêhiwa	lies head-to-head with (s.o.) (**wâwâtehkwêhiwaki** they lie head-to-head)
wâwâtehkwêpiwaki (plural)	they sit with their heads together
wâwiyâkahamwa	grinds it all up together
wâwiyâkesamwa	cooks it mixed together
wâwiyâki	of all kinds, mixed together (particle, preverb)

wâwiyâkisetôwa	mixes it together
wâwiyâtepâpyêshinwa	(snake) lies coiled up
wâwiyêpenwâneki êshikeki	seneca snakeroot
wâwiyêpenwâni	roach (man's headdress)
wâwiyêsiwa, wâwiyêyâwi	is round, (moon) is full; it is round
wâwiyêshâtêhi	round shield
wâwiyêwâkenamwa	bends it in a circle
wâwiyêwi	in a circle (particle, preverb)
wâwînishkîkwêwa	one's eyes are dirty with hardened tears
wâwîpekwâkêha	teal
wâwîsakichinwa	gets repeatedly caught and injured (on it)
wâwîsakwêwaki (plural)	they (thunderers) boom loudly (see also **wîsakowêwa**)
wâwîsakwêwêkatwi	there are loud crashes (as, of thunder)
wâwîsikêwa	does the singeing (of the animals for the feast)
wâwîsitepasowa	the hair of one's head gets singed
wâwîswêwa	singes the hair off s.o. (animal)
wâwîshasowa	sweats profusely
wâwîtawakâme	on opposite sides (particle)
wâwîtawâhkwâpamêwa	looks at s.o. from both sides (ritual)
wâwîtawâhkwe	on opposite sides (as, of the tree) (particle)
wâwîtawetone	(from) both sides of the mouth (particle)
wâwîtawi	on both sides, on either side (particle)
wâwîtawishkwâte	(through) the doors on both ends of the lodge (particle)
wâwîtâkosiwa	one's name is mentioned
wâwîtekwatwi	it is named
wâwîtetîwaki (plural)	they name each other
wâwîtêwa, wâwîtamwa	calls s.o. by name; speaks about it
wâwîtônehke	with both hands (particle)
wâwîyashkimêwa	says all kinds of bad things about s.o.
wâwochi	repeatedly from {somewhere}, because of {some reason}, in {such} direction (preverb)
wâwochihamwa	regularly gets water from {somewhere} (see **ochihamwa**)
wâwosâhi, wâwasâhi	expectably, unsurprisingly; even, going so far as to; at least, perhaps as many as; (with negative): it is not to be expected, not going so far as to (particle). Also used with the negative meaning even without a negative present.
wâwosâpamêwa	is watching s.o. (at length or intently) from {somewhere}
wâwotami	taking the time to, wasting one's time (preverb) (see **otami**)
=wê=	(see **=wêna**)
wêchi-	the reason why (preverb with initial change [see **ochi**])
wêchi-kesîyâki (oblique participle)	north
wêchi-mayâwîchi (oblique participle)	on one's right
wêchi-môhkahaki (oblique participle)	east
wêchi-nâwahkwêki (oblique participle)	south
wêchi-nemachîchi (oblique participle)	on one's left
wêchinowi	easily (particle, preverb)
wêchinowatwi (wêchinowatôhiwi dimin.)	it is easy
wêchinowihêwa, wêchinowihtôwa	easily kills s.o.; finds it easy
wêchinowisetôwa	places it within easy reach
wêchinowîhtêwa	is lightly clothed
wêchi-pakishimoki (oblique participle)	west
wêchitawi	very good, splendid, excellent (particle, prenoun)
wêchitawîhiwa	is a good person, is excellent
wêchinowatwi	it is easy

wêchinowâhkonikêhêwa	makes easy rules for s.o.
wêchinowesiwa	is easy to get, kill; has an easy time
wêchinowikiwa, wêchinowikenwi	is easy (to deal with); things are easy
wêchinowinâkwatwi	it looks easy
wêchinowitêhêwa	thinks something is easy, plans something easy
wêhkâchîha	Dutch oven (a cast-iron pot with a lid and small legs that is set in the coals)
wêkonêhi (1)	what? (inanimate interrogative pronoun)
wêkonêhi (2)	what? what kind of? (prenoun)
wêkonêhi wêchi-	why? (inanimate interrogative pronoun + preverb with initial change [see **ochi**])
wêmehtekôshîha	Frenchman (archaic; see **mêmehtekôshîha**)
wêmîkôha	member of the Thunder Clan
wêmîkôhisowa	is a member of the Thunder Clan
wêmîkôhisota	member of the Thunder Clan
=wêna (=wê=)	in fact; after all; rather, or actually, but actually, or at least (see =ih=**wêna**)
wênahi	(this) is it, here now, I see now (that) (particle)
wênânîhi	ginseng
wênehpenênetamwa	thinks it is easy
wênehpenihêwa (also **wênehpeshihêwa**)	gets, kills s.o. easily
wênehpeni (also **wênehpeshi**)	easily (particle, preverb)
wênekwanichiki (plural participle)	the man's parents-in-law
wênêha	who? what creature or animal? (plural **wênêhaki** and **wênewênêhaki**)
	(idiom): **wênêhani** (the observer found that) the other person was not there
wênêhâhkowiwa:	**kewênêhâhkowi** what kind of tree are you? (also **owênêhâhkowiwa**)
wênêhetôwa	what manitou?
wênêhi (1)	what? who is? (prenoun) (**wênêhi-ihkwêwa** what woman? who is the woman?)
=wê=nêhi (2)	(see **nêhi**)
wênêhiwa:	**kewênêhi** who are you? (plural **kewênêhipwa**) (also **owênêhiwa**)
wênôchi (1)	(with or without negative): surely greatly (preverb) (**wênôch-âhkwêwa='h=wêna** he will surely be angry no end)
=wê=nôchi (2):	**nîna=wê=nôchi, '..,' neteshitêhe** I had thought rather, '...'
wênôchimêwa	(with [and presumably without] negative): goes too far in what one says about s.o.
wênôchinawêhêwa	(with [and presumably without] negative): goes too far and upsets s.o.
wênôchinawêmêwa	(with or without negative): goes too far and upsets s.o. by what one says
wênôchitêhêwa	takes it hard
wênôshkâhpenanêwa	is able to readily kill s.o.
wênôshki (preverb):	**wênôshki-nesêwa** is able to readily kill s.o.
wênôshkihêwa	is able to readily kill s.o.
wênôtâhpenanêwa	(future or potential, with or without negative): kills s.o. without restraint
wênôtesiwa	(future or potential, with or without negative): stops at nothing, goes overboard, is beside oneself
wêpahinotawêwa	starts in on s.o.
wêpahîwa	starts things (as, a fight), gets started (as, misbehaving)
wêpahkiwihtôwa	starts (a general activity)
wêpahowa	starts to paddle
wêpahtêwa	shoots (with a bow), shoots (it, an arrow)
wêpamatamwa	starts to have pain

wêpanâmowa	starts swimming underwater
wêpapisowa	has an epileptic fit
wêpatahokowa	starts to carry (it as) a load on one's back
wêpatahwêwa	starts to beat s.o.
wêpatonêhwêwa	starts to seek s.o.
wêpâchimowa	starts to narrate
wêpâhkêwa	throws (it)
wêpâhpenanêwa	starts in on s.o.
wêpâmowa	flees, runs away
wêpâpyêsenwi	it begins to lie strung, it begins
wêpâsîwa	starts to climb
wêpâshkêwa, wêpâshkêwi	falls, falls down, starts; it falls (**pemi-wêpâshkêwa** starts to fall)
wêpâshowîwa	begins to wade
wêpekêwa	starts to dance
wêpenekowa	begins to fool around
wêpenetîwa	starts to fight
wêpesiwa	is crazy
wêpesîha	insane person, crazy person; one who acts foolishly; one who has a fit
wêpesîhiwa	is crazy
wêpesîhiwiwa	is crazy
wêpesîhihêwa	makes s.o. crazy
wêpetonêmowa	starts talking
wêpetonwa	moves one's mouth (song word)
wêpi	start to, begin to, set about (preverb)
wêpihkanêwa	abandons s.o.
wêpihkawêwa	one's tracks begin
wêpihtôwa	begins making it
wêpikawiwaki (plural)	they started off in a group
wêpikâwosêwa	takes a step, starts walking
wêpikiwa, wêpikenwi	begins (to exist); it begins, starts to happen
wêpikwamwa	begins to sew it
wêpimêwa	begins to talk to s.o.
wêpinanihêwa	begins to cut s.o. up, butcher s.o.
wêpinâkêwa	starts to sing
wêpinâkwihowa	begins to change one's appearance
wêpinehkâtîwaki (plural)	they begin to chase each other
wêpinehkawêwa, wêpinehkamwa	begins to chase s.o., it
wêpinekwêsêwa	swings one's arm quickly
wêpipahowa	starts to run
wêpipokôtêwi	it starts floating off
wêpipokôtôwa	sets it adrift
wêpisenyêwa	starts to eat
wêpisêwa	starts to fly
wêpishkwêhtêhi	white bread
wêpitanekowa	begins to work
wêpiwenêwa, wêpiwetôwa	starts to convey s.o., it
wêpîhkâtîwaki (plural)	they start having to do with each other, start courting
wêpîhkamwihêwa	gets s.o. to take (it) up
wêpîhkawêwa, wêpîhkamwa	starts on s.o., it, takes it up
wêpîhkwêwêwa	he beats his (own) wife (as, from jealousy)
wêposahêwa	makes s.o. start walking
wêposêwa	starts walking
wêpotêwa	starts moving camp
wêpômekwiwa	rides (as, a horse), starts riding

wêpômêwa, wêpôtamwa	starts to carry s.o., it on one's back
wêpôtashiwa	starts carrying a load on one's back
wêpôtêpahowa	starts running in a crouch
wêpôtêwa	starts crawling
wêpôtîwaki (plural)	one of them starts carrying the other on their back
wêpwêkesiwa	starts to wail
wêpwêwêhwêwa	begins to make s.o. (a drum) sound by beating
wêpwêwêkesiwa	starts to yell loudly, scream
wêpwêwêkesiwaki nenemehkiwaki	there is thunder ("the thunderers begin to scream")
wêpyêkiwa, wêpyêkenwi	(animate, inanimate) is starting to grow
wêpyêwîwa	begins the task or activity
wêsemichiki (plural)	the woman's parents-in-law
wêshinemâchihi (plural)	his parents-in-law
wêshîhêwa, wêshîhtôwa	paints s.o., it; paints s.o.'s face
wêshîhowa	paints oneself, one's face
wêshîhôni	paint
wêshkihtâhi	watermelon
wêta	Alas! Oh my! (particle)
wêtâpaki (oblique participle)	east
wêtâsêwa	warrior (who has achieved war honors)
wêtâsêwiwa	is a warrior
wêtâsêwihêwa	makes s.o. a warrior
wêtepîwa	"crane" (Jones) (perhaps specifically sandhill crane)
wêtêwi, wêtêwe	(with negative): not the least bit, not for a while, not at all close (particle)
wêtêwihtôwa	(with negative): is far from being able to do it
wêtôtêwâha	prairie dog
wêwenahkwatwi	the clouds are beautiful
wêwenashkatwi	it is beautiful grass
wêwenâhkwâwiwi	it is a beautiful grove of trees
wêwenânakîkwêwa	has pretty eyes
(also **wêwewêwenânakîkwêwa**)	
wêwenânehkwêwa	has beautiful hair
wêwenepyêhâsowa	(animate, as a buckskin) is beautifully painted
wêwenesiwa, wêwenetwi	is pretty, handsome; it is nice, good
wêwenihchikâsowa, wêwenihchikâtêwa	(animate, inanimate) is decorated
wêwenihchikâtôwa	decorates it (as, with beads, ribbons)
wêwenihchikêwa	does a good thing, does good work
wêwenihêwa, wêwenihtôwa	makes s.o., it pretty, nice
wêwenihtawêwa	makes (it) pretty for s.o.
wêwenihtâtîwaki (plural)	they make (it) pretty for each other
wêwenipyêwa, wêwenipyêyâwi	(animate, inanimate) has pretty leaves or boughs
wêwênawi	have a chance to (preverb)
wêwênawihêwa, wêwênawihtôwa	has a chance at s.o., it
wêwênênemêwa, wêwênênetamwa	has control over s.o., it, is in charge of s.o., it; has the say
wêwênênetamwihêwa	lets s.o. have their own say, lets s.o. choose
wêwênênetisowa	has control over oneself
wêwêpânehkwêwosahêwa	makes s.o. walk with swaying mane (song word)
wêwêpakôtêwi	it hangs swinging
wêwêpeshêwa	flaps one's ears (song word)
wêwêpikâpiwa	sits with one's legs dangling
wêwêpikôha	elephant
wêwêpinehkêhtawêwa	waves one's hand at s.o.
wêwêpinêwa	swings s.o. in a swing
wêwêpisowa	swings, swings oneself

wêwêpisôni	swing; baby hammock ("baby swing")
wêwêshiwawiwa	gets or is ready (to act)
wêwêshiwenêwa, wêwêshiwenamwa	holds s.o., it ready (to use)
wêwiyêhikwêna (interrogative participle)	someone or other, some unidentified creature (also **êwiyêhikwêna**) (see **owiyêhiwa**)
wêwîshêha	Rolling Skull (in story)
wêwîshêhihkwêwa	Rolling Skull Woman (in story)
wêwîtepi (1)	quickly, at once, forthwith, losing no time (preverb)
wêwîtepi (2)	for a while (particle)
wêyôhkomesita (participle)	the grandchild (of a woman), her grandchild (see **ôhkomesiwa**)
wêyôsêha	Indian agent
wêyôsita (participle)	the son or daughter (of a man), his son or daughter (see **ôsiwa**)
wêyôshisemichiki (plural participle)	the grandparents, his or her grandparents (see **ôshisemiwa**)
wihihwî!	Oh my! Gee whiz! Oh golly! Well well! How marvelous!
wîchawiwêwa	is with s.o.; he is married to her, she is married to him (**wîchawiwaka** my husband; my wife)
wîchawîtîwaki (plural)	they are married (to each other)
wîchênokêwa	enjoys life with others, associates with others, plays with others
wîchênomêwa, wîchênotamwa	enjoys life with s.o., associates with s.o., plays with s.o.; plays with it
wîchênotamâkêwa	plays with (them) of others
wîchênotîwaki (plural)	they play together, enjoy themselves together
wîchêwêwa	goes along, accompanies people
wîchi	together with, joining with (preverb, particle)
wîchihetîwaki (plural)	they live in the same dwelling
wîchihêwa, wîchihtôwa	lives with s.o., it (in the same dwelling)
wîchihiwêwa	lives with others (in the same dwelling)
wîchikêkêwa	dwells among others, with others as neighbors
wîchikêmêwa	lives in the same camp or settlement as s.o., is s.o.'s neighbor
wîchikêtîwaki (plural)	they live in the same settlement
wîchi-mahkatêwîmêwa	fasts with s.o.
wîchi-mâwâsetôkêwa	lives in a village with others
wîchi-mâwâsetômâwâchihi	their fellow villagers
wîchi-mehtosênenîkêwa	lives as a fellow mortal
wîchi-mehtosênenîmêwa	is a fellow mortal to s.o., has s.o. as a fellow human being
wîchi-nesapîmêwa	stays home with s.o.
wîchitêhamêwa	is with s.o. in thought, helps s.o. with their plan or intention
wîchitêhêmêwa	is with s.o. in thought, helps s.o. with their plan or intention
wîchi-têpesîmêwa	is pleased together with s.o.
wîchîsôkêwa	belongs to one's clan, is a clan member
wîchîsômêwa	has s.o. as fellow clan-member (also **wîchi-wîsômêwa**)
wîchîsôtîwaki (plural)	they are of the same clan
wîh= (1) (younger variant **îh**=)	will, shall, is going to, must; (in subordinate clauses) to, so that, in order to; (with subjunctive, iterative, plain interrogative, changed interrogative, prohibitive, potential, or imperative modes) wish to, dare to, be about to, be inclined to, was going to (future proclitic preverb or prefix)
wîhi- (**wîh-**) (2)	(like **wîh**= [future] but may be preceded by **êh**= [aorist] and may be followed by an enclitic) (preverb)
wîhkomâkaniwiwa	is invited to eat
wîhkomêwa	invites s.o. to eat
wîhkomêweniwiwa	is invited to eat
wîhkonemîwa	great horned owl, "hoot owl"
wîhkotîwaki (plural)	they invite each other to eat

wîhkowêwa	invites people to eat
wîhkowêhêwa	has s.o. invite people
wîhkowêwosêwa	walks inviting people
wîhkwayâchimêwa	strongly advises s.o.
wîhkwayâtowêwa	speaks or prays insistently
wîhkwênêwa	carries s.o. in a blanket
wîhkwêpichikani	bundle
wîhkwêpitawêwa	wraps (it) (as, in a buckskin) for s.o.
wîhkwêpitêwi	it is bundled up
wîhkwêwanâni, wîhkwêwanehkâni	bundle
wîhkwêwanehkêwa	makes a bundle (to be carried)
wîhkwêwashiwa	has a bundle on one's back
wîhkwêsêwa	bumps making a bulge
wîhkwêshkêwi	it bulges out
wîhkwêyâhkiwiwi	there is an area sheltered by high ground
wîhkwêyôtamwa	carries it on one's back in a blanket
wîhpêmêwa, wîhpêtamwa	sleeps with s.o., it
wîhpêtenowa	gets into someone's bed, gets into bed with (s.o.)
wîhpêtîwaki (plural)	they sleep together
wîhpêwa	sleeps double, sleeps with someone
wîhpokêwa	eats with people, eats with others
wîhpomêwa	eats with s.o.
wîhpotîwaki (plural)	they eat with each other
wîhtêwahkiwiwi	it is burnt-over land
wîhtwiyâha, wîhtwîyâha	smith, silversmith
wîhwî!	Oh my! Goodness gracious!
wîkamêwa, wîkatamwa	likes s.o.'s, its taste
wîkamosiwa	American bittern
wîkawapiwa	fidgets, moves restlessly in one's seat
wîkawi	restlessly (preverb)
wîkawihêwa	annoys s.o.
wîkawikâpiwa	sits moving one's feet
wîkehtawêwa	(with negative): pays s.o. no heed, does not respond to s.o.
wîkenwa, wîkanwi	(animate, inanimate) is good, tastes good
wîkesêhkwêwa	cooks good-tasting food
wîkeshêwa	(with negative): pays no heed, does not listen, does not mind
wîkêchi	carefully, earnestly, completely, perfectly (preverb, particle)
wîkêchihkeshêwênikêwa	carefully stirs the fire
wîkêchihêwa, wîkêchihtôwa	makes s.o., it well, fixes it up right
wîkêchinâkêwa	sings carefully
wîkêchinâkwihtôwa	fixes it up to look neat and tidy
wîkêchinechâtamawêwa	handles (it) carefully for s.o.
wîkêchishimêwa, wîkêchisetôwa	lays s.o., it carefully
wîkêchishinwa	lies comfortably, carefully; settles into position lying
wîkêchiwetôwa	conducts it carefully
wîkêchîhkawêwa, wîkêchîhkamwa	deals with s.o., it carefully
wîkêchîhkâtêwi	it is dealt with carefully
wîkêsiwa	is careful, attends to details, is precise, meticulous
wîkêtahkyêsetôwa	sets it (as, a bowl) squarely on the ground
wîkêtakoshêhowa	fixes the covers on oneself
wîkêtakôtôwa	carefully hangs it up, carefully places it (arrow) in one's quiver
wîkêtapinêwa, wîkêtapitôwa	ties s.o., it carefully
wîkêtapiwa	sits comfortably, adopts a comfortable position in one's seat

wîkêtatamwa	eats it up carefully
wîkêtatawâpiwa	takes a careful look
wîkêtâchimohêwa	carefully informs s.o., carefully explains to s.o.
wîkêtâhkonêwa, wîkêtâhkonamwa	folds s.o. (as, a skin), it up neatly
wîkêtâsiyênowa	he straightens out his breechcloth
wîkêtehtamwa	listens to it carefully
wîkêtenêwa, wîkêtenamwa	arranges s.o. with care; tidies it up, holds it in position
wîkêtenikêwa	straightens things up, tidies up the house
wîkêtesamwa	cooks it carefully
wîkêtesêhkwêwa	cooks carefully
wîkêtetêwi	it is carefully cooked
wîki	enjoy, like (preverb)
wîkihpwêwa, wîkihpetamwa	likes s.o.'s, its taste
wîkinenwêwa	has savory fat, one's fat is good eating
wîkisenyêwa	finds one's food tasty
wîkiyâpâhkwi (wîkiyâpâhkôhi dimin.)	lodgepole
-wîkiyâpe	house, houses (in particle compounds) (**keki-wîkiyâpe** along with the house; **sanakwi-wîkiyâpe** between the houses)
wîkiyâpêhi	house (dimin.) (also: **chaki-wîkiyâpêhi** little house)
wîkiyâpi	house, lodge, Meskwaki-style wickiup (plural **wîkiyâpyêni**; **wîkiyâpeki** in the house)
wîkiyâpihkîki	in the village, among the houses (locative noun)
wîkîkwêha	wood duck
wîkocha	woodcock; white grub (also **kwîkocha**)
wîkopi	(piece or string of) basswood inner bark (plural **wîkopyêni**)
wîkopihkêwa	gathers basswood inner bark
wîkopimishi	basswood tree, stick (plural **wîkopimishêni**)
wîkowashkôsowa	is sleepy from having eaten
wîkowiwa	is sleepy
wîkwâmesiwa (Jones)	(see **ayîkwâmesiwa**)
wîkwânêwa, wîkwâtamwa	(with negative): pays no attention to s.o., it
wîna (1)	he or she (emphatic or contrastive); (by) himself or herself
=wîna (2)	but, however, though you may not think so
wînamowa	eats something dirty
wînanesiwa	cuts up meat, butchers
wînanihêwa	cuts s.o. up, butchers s.o.
wînanihtawêwa	butchers (it) for s.o.
wînasamwêwiyâkochêwa	one's body reeks with dirty-dog smell
wînasamwêwiyâkosiwa	reeks with dirty-dog smell
wînâkêwa	turkey vulture ("buzzard")
wînenamwa	gets it dirty by touching or handling
wînepinenyêhpwêwa	dirties her breasts by nursing
wînepitiyêwa	has a dirty bottom; (sun or moon) has a halo
wînepyêkôhkwêwa	Winnebago woman
wînepyêkônâki	(in) Winnebago country (locative noun)
wînepyêkôwa	Winnebago
wînesiwa, wînyâwi	(animate, inanimate) is dirty, filthy
wînênemêwa, wînênetamwa	thinks s.o., it dirty, filthy
wînihêwa, wînihtôwa	makes s.o., it dirty, befouls s.o., it
wînihpanêwa	has a phlegmy cough
wînikomêwa	has a runny nose
wîninâkosiwa, wîninâkwatwi	(animate, inanimate) looks filthy
wînisetôwa	gets it dirty
wînitepêwa	has filthy hair

wînîhkâsowa	does a filthy thing
wînwâwa	they (emphatic or contrastive); (by) themselves
wîpachi	in case; if it should happen that (particle)
wîpekosiwa, wîpekwâwi	(animate, inanimate) is blue
wîpekwi	blue (prenoun, preverb)
wîponamwa	makes it narrow, makes it closer
wîposhkawêwa	approaches s.o., gets closer to s.o.
wîpôyâwi	it is narrow
wîpwinehkawêwa	chases s.o. into a corner, a narrow place
wîpwisahowa	claps one's legs together
wîsakamachihêwa	causes s.o. pain
wîsakamatamwa	suffers pain
wîsakamêwa	hurts s.o. by biting
wîsakanêshinwa:	**kewâwîsakanêshine** "you smell so strong it hurts" (song)
wîsakâhkwa	white ash (tree)
wîsakâhpenanêwa, wîsakâhpenatôwa	hurts s.o., it; causes s.o. a painful injury
wîsakenawêwa	hurts s.o. by shooting
wîsakenêwa	hurts s.o. by touching or feeling
wîsakenwa, wîsakanwi	(animate, inanimate) is bitter
wîsakeshkawêwa	hurts s.o. by foot or body
wîsakinakahkwêwachiwa	one's throat aches from being cold
wîsakinawêhêwa	hurts s.o.'s feelings
wîsakinêhwêwa	hurts s.o., injures s.o. with a blow
wîsakisetôwa:	**wîsakisetôwa owîyawi** hurts oneself
wîsakishinwa	falls and hurts oneself, hurts oneself (on it)
wîsakitîha (wîsakitîhêha dimin.)	terrier
wîsakitôtanênêwa	painfully pinches s.o.'s heel
wîsakowêwa	(thunderer) booms loudly (see **wâwîsakwêwaki**)
wîsakowêmikatwi (Jones)	there is "a mighty roar"
wîsakwêwêkatwi	there is a loud crash (as, of thunder)
wîsenihêwa	makes s.o. eat
wîseniwa	eats, has a meal; makes a meal (of it)
wîseniweni (wîseniwâhi dimin.)	food, meal
wîseniwi	eating, of eating (prenoun)
wîseniwisekini (plural participle)	eating songs
wîsenîhtawêwa	eats for s.o.
wîsenîmikatwi	it eats
wîsenîmikihtôwa	makes it eat
wîsikiwa	has a scar
wîsiyashkwikâni (wîsiyashkwikâhi dimin.)	grass lodge
wîswihêwa, wîswihtôwa	names s.o., it; gives a name to s.o., it
wîshasokwâmwa	sweats in one's sleep
wîshasowa	feels hot, sweats
wîshatêwi	it is warm weather
wîshâchi	there is (or was) an ill-advised insistence (particle)
wîshâhêwa	keeps after s.o., presses s.o. hard
wîshâmêwa	implores s.o., pleads with s.o., is insistent with s.o., presses s.o. hard (verbally), nags s.o.
wîshâpenêwa	is hungry
wîshâpenêhêwa	starves s.o.
wîshâpenêhtôwa:	**wîshâpenêhtôwa owîyawi** starves oneself
wîshâpenêwênemêwa	thinks s.o. is hungry
wîshâsiwa	is anxious, agitated
wîshâshinwa	tries one's level best (to), is anxious (to)

wîshâshkêwa	is anxious, agitated, eager
wîshâtêhêwa	is anxious
wîshâwâpiwa	looks about anxiously
wîshâwehtawêwa	hears s.o. with anxiety
wîshâwehtâkosiwa	is heard pleading (ritual)
wîshâwênemêwa	is anxious about s.o.
wîshâwêwa	screams in anguish; pleads (for spiritual aid) against (it)
wîshâwêwêkesiwa	wails loudly
wîshâwi (1)	with great agitation (preverb)
wîshâwi (2)	maybe, perhaps, likely but not certainly (particle, preverb)
wîshâwitêhêwa	is anxious, concerned
wîshikahkatêwi	it is planted firmly
wîshikahtêwa	shoots hard (with a bow)
wîshikamêwa	bites s.o. hard
wîshikanâmowa	breathes hard, pushes hard with one's breath
wîshikapinêwa, wîshikapitôwa	ties s.o., it tight
wîshikapiwa	sits firmly, sits unbudging
wîshikatahwêwa	hits s.o. hard
wîshikatenwi	it is frozen hard
wîshikâhkêwa	throws (it) hard, shakes (it) hard
wîshikâhkohwêwa, wîshikâhkohamwa	shuts s.o. up securely, fastens it firmly
wîshikâkesiwa	(bow) is stiff, hard to pull
wîshikenamâhkwîwa	holds on tight (for support)
wîshikenêwa, wîshikenamwa	holds s.o., it tightly
wîshikesiwa, wîshikyâwi	is strong, has physical strength; it is strong
wîshikeshkamwa	makes it secure by one's step, by dwelling there
wîshikênetamwa	thinks of it strongly, earnestly
wîshiki	strongly, hard, firmly, tightly, securely (particle, preverb)
wîshikihkesiwa, wîshikihkatwi	(tree, post) is very hard and dense, it is very hard and dense
wîshikihtôwa	makes it strong
wîshikikanêwa	has strength in one's body
wîshikimêwa	urges s.o. strongly
wîshikinawêshkawêwa	(blessing, ceremonial feast) hardens or strengthens s.o.'s bodily constitution or life
wîshikinawîwa	uses one's strength, makes a powerful effort to move
wîshikinâkêwa	sings loud
wîshikishinwa	lies secure
wîshikîwa	exerts oneself
wîshikowêwa	speaks, sings, screams loud
wîshikwêwêhtamwa	blows it (wind instrument) loud
wîshkenôha (**wîshkenôhêha** dimin.)	bird
wîshkenôhehkêwa	hunts birds
wîshkîhi	whiskey
wîshkopanohikani	sweetener, sugar
wîshkopanohikêwa	sweetens food, uses sugar
wîshkopanohwêwa, wîshkopanohamwa	sweetens s.o. (as, corn), it
wîshkopanosowa	eats sweet food, has something sweet
wîshkopanôheki (Jones)	at Salt Creek (in Kansas)
wîshkopanôhiwi	it is sweet, tastes sweet (dimin.)
wîshkopâpowi	sap; wine
wîshkopenwa, wîshkopanwi	(animate, inanimate) is sweet, tastes sweet
wîshkopi	sweet (prenoun)

wîshkopimina	sweet corn
wîshkopi-pahkwêshikâhi	cake
wîshkopisenyâkani	sweet food
wîshkopishinwa	(corn) turns sour
wîshkwêshkwi	of birchbark (prenoun)
wîshkwêwêkomêwa	snores loudly
wîshkwêwêsenwi	it falls with loud noise
wîshkwêwêkatwi	there is great noise
wîshkwêwêkesiwa	screams
wîshôka	large fish species (perhaps garfish)
wîtamawêwa	tells s.o.
wîtamâtîwaki (plural)	they tell each other
wîtapîkêwa	sits with people
wîtapîmêwa	sits with s.o.
wîtawakâme	on both sides, on opposite sides (participle)
wîtawi	on both ends, on both sides (participle)
wîtawîhaki (plural)	black raspberries (**meshkwi-wîtawîhaki** red raspberries)
wîtekêmêwa	dances with s.o.
wîtekômowa	gives an owl-call
wîtekôwa	owl (generic)
wîtekôwaya	owl-skin
wîtekôwi	of owl (prenoun)
wîtekôwi-mâtesi	"owl knife" (flint knife or arrowhead)
wîtekôwi-mâtesêhi	"owl knife" (dimin.)
wîtekôwiwa	is an owl
wîtêmêwa, wîtêtamwa	accompanies s.o., it
wîtôhkawêwa, wîtôhkamwa	helps, aids, collaborates or cooperates with, favors, allows s.o.; takes part in it
wîtôhkâsowa	takes part, helps, joins in, goes along (with it or the others)
wîtôhkâtîwaki (plural)	they help each other, join together, cooperate
wîwahêwa	puts (it) (as, a blanket, a bundle) on s.o.'s back
wîwahowa	puts (it) on one's back to carry
wîwapinêwa, wîwapitôwa	wraps (and ties) s.o., it
wîwenêwa, wîwenamwa	wraps s.o., it up
wîwenowa	covers one's nakedness
wîwikâpisowa	wraps one's feet (with it)
wîwikenwi	it is covered, has a covering
wîwisenwi	it is wrapped (in it)
wîwitepêpisowa	has (it as) a covering tied on one's head
wîyaki	various, of various kinds (particle, prenoun)
wîyashkâpôkatwi	its water is muddy, it is muddy water
wîyashkâpôshkamwa	made its water muddy, made it (water) muddy
wîyashkihêwa	destroys s.o., spoils s.o.'s spiritual power
wîyashkimêwa	maligns s.o., says bad things about s.o.
wîyashkinâkwatwi	it (as, a cloud or water) looks dreadful
wîyashkitêhêwa	has an upset stomach
wîyatâhêwa	makes s.o. have a bad dream
wîyatâsiwa	has a nightmare, is disturbed in one's sleep
wîyatâwêwêkesiwa	screams in terror, screams bloody murder

y

-yâche	yard, yards (in particle compounds) (**nîshwi-yâche** two yards)
=yâpani	mind you, I expect, I warn you (older **=yêpani**)
=yâpi	alright now, here I go, here we go, get ready, here's the deal; (in a question) alright tell me
=yêhapa	in fact, as it turns out
=yêpani	mind you, I expect, I warn you (also **=yâpani**)
=yêtoke	probably, I suppose, it seems
='yo	(see **=iyo**)
yohohwâ!	Whew! (as, in satisfaction after meal or escape)
yôhwâ!	Oh dear! Oh no!
='yôwe	(see **=iyôwe**)

ENGLISH-MESKWAKI

a

abandon	wêpihkanêwa	abandons s.o.
	shîkwihkatamwa	abandons it (house), flees leaving it empty
	nâhkateshimêwa, nâhkateshitamwa	abandons s.o., it in flight
	shîkwashkwîhi	something abandoned as unwanted
ability	inâhpatesiwa	has {such} ability or skill
able	kashki	be able to, can; manage to, have the nerve to; possibly; be persuaded to, be successfully made to (preverb)
	kashkenêwa, kashkenamwa	is able to lift or carry s.o., it
	kashkimâchîwa	is able to move
	kashkimâchîmikatwi	it is able to move
	nahowêwa	is able to talk, is clever at speaking or talking, says a clever thing
	têpâpamêwa, têpâpatamwa	is able to see s.o., it (in the distance or clairvoyantly)
	têpâpatâniwi	it can be seen in the distance
	têpâpiwa	sees enough; is able to see (from distance or clairvoyantly)
	têpôtamwa	is able to carry it on one's back
	wêtêwihtôwa	(with negative:) is far from being able to do it
	kâpâchichi	just barely able
about	kîwi, kî	about, in places, for a while (preverb)
	papâmi	about (preverb)
	nekotahi	somewhere, anywhere; somewhere else; to some degree, about; (with negative:) not in any way, not one of them
	meshê='nahi, meshê='nah=meko	about, roughly speaking, as much as, some or other, whatever it was; going so far as to; in the course of time;
about time	metwi	(with negative idioms:) it's about time that ...! (preverb)
absent	inêtwa	is absent {so long}
	ashenowa, ashenowi	(animate, inanimate) is gone, absent, has a part or parts missing
	ashenowâpamêwa	sees s.o. missing, does not see s.o. present
	pakeshkêwa:	(with negative:) does not show up, is not seen around
abuse	ketemahêwa	abuses s.o.
accept	nahkonêwa, nahkonamwa	takes s.o., it in one's hand; accepts s.o., it; catches s.o., it
	nahkonâtêwi	it is accepted
	nahkwamêwa	takes s.o. in one's mouth, accepts s.o. (as, a pipe)
	nahkwitêhamêwa, nahkwitêhêmêwa	readily accepts s.o.'s opinion, wish, or blessing
accompany	wîchêwêwa	goes along, accompanies
	wîtêmêwa, wîtêtamwa	accompanies s.o., it
	kîwîtêmêwa	goes about with s.o. (for kîwi-wîtêmêwa)
	pakamîtêmêwa	arrives in company with s.o. (for pakami-wîtêmêwa)
accordingly	kaho!	accordingly, well (conjunction)
ache	têwanasitêkâpâwa	stands with aching feet

across	**kashkishki**	across the path, to or at a place in (someone's) path (particle)
	kashkishkîmêhi	across the path, to or at a place in (someone's) path (dimin.) (particle)
	tahkamâhkwishinwa, tahkamâhkwisenwi	(animate, inanimate) lies stretching across a gap
	tahkamipahowa	runs across an open space
acquainted	**anehkawêwa, anehkamwa**	is or gets used to s.o., it, is or gets acquainted with s.o.
	anehkâtîwaki	they get acquainted with each other
acre	**-îkese**	{so many} acres (in particle compounds)
act	**amêwa**	acts, reacts promptly, takes action, goes into action
	ahpîhchawiwa	acts {so}
	ishitanekowa	acts {so}, does {so}
	kîhkîhkinotamwa	acts in spite of it
	kwîyenâhiwa	acts right
	menwawiwa	acts well, does well, does good
	nanôshkwêhiwa	acts at random
	nasatâwinohkatawêwa	acts crossly toward him
	peshikwîwa	acts uprightly
	âchêwîwa	acts again
activity	**tahitanenekowa**	is engaged in activity, performing a task, fooling around
	kekenekowa	has (it) with oneself in one's activities
act upon	**tôtawêwa, tôtamwa**	acts {so} upon s.o., it
	tôtâtîwaki	they act {so} upon each other
add	**ânehkôtamwa**	puts an addition on it
	ahpâpowêwa	adds (it) to the cooking
	ahpâpowanâsowa	(corn) is cooked with something added
	ahpâpowâni	something added to the cooking; seasoning; wild ginger
	ahpâpowâhi	seasoning (dimin.)
	tahtakoshkêwi	it is added together
address	**inowânêwa**	addresses s.o. {so}
	ishimâkaniwiwa	is addressed {so}
	kanônâsowa	is addressed
	kanônêwesiwa	is addressed by spirits
adhere	**akoswêwa**	makes s.o. adhere by heat
	akotêwi	it adheres because of heat, it sticks from being heated
	pepyêtashkishinwa, pepyêtashkisenwi	(animate, inanimate) is plastered on, adheres
adoption	**pakinêwa**	he releases s.o. (deceased relative) by ceremonially adopting someone of the same sex and the same approximate age
	pakitamwa	holds a ceremonial adoption (releasing deceased relative)
	pakitamôweni	ceremonial adoption (releasing deceased relative)
	pakinetîwaki	they release each other, hold an adoption for each other
	nanâhenêwa	releases (deceased relative) by holding a ceremonial adoption
	nanâhîhkawêwa	holds an adoption feast for s.o. (deceased relative)
	nanâhîhkâsowa	an adoption feast is held for one (deceased relative)
	oshehkîhêwa, ashehkîhêwa	adopts s.o. (for deceased relative) (literally, clothes s.o.)
	oshehkîhetîwaki	they adopt each other (literally, they clothe each other)
adrift	**wêpipokôtôwa**	sets it adrift
adult	**kehchitâwesiwa**	is adult
	kehchitâwi	when adult (preverb)
	kehchitâwitêhêwa	thinks like a grown-up, is grown up in one's thinking

	kehchitâwinâkosiwa, kehchitâwinâkwatwi	looks like a grown-up, it looks like a grown-up's
advice	tepatohachikêwa	follows (s.o.'s) advice and example
advise	nanâhimêwa	tells s.o. what to do, advises s.o.
	wîhkwayâchimêwa	strongly advises s.o.
affection	kemênawâtâkana	the object of your affection
afflicted	inâhpenêwa	is ill, afflicted {so}
affliction	sanakâhpenêwa	has a serious disease or affliction
afraid	kohtâchiwa	is afraid
after	ahkowi	after, afterwards, behind, as the last one (particle)
after all	=wêna (=wê=)	after all, in fact
	meshe=wêna	well after all
afterbirth	ahpitiyêpîni	afterbirth
again	âchi	again, in addition, over again (preverb)
	nâhka, nâhkachi	also, and, again; in turn, as well (as another instance), this time (particle)
	âchêwîwa	tries again, starts over
against	pyêtâsameshkawêwa	is against s.o., turns against s.o.
age	ahpîhtesiweni	age
aged	kehkyêweniwiwa	is aged
	kehkyêwahkyêsenwi	the earth is in its old age
agent	wêyôsêha	Indian agent
agitated	pônitêhêwa	stops worrying, stops being concerned or mentally agitated
	wîshâshkêwa	is anxious, eager, agitated
	wîshâsiwa	is anxious, agitated
agitation	wîshâwi	with great agitation (preverb)
agree	kîshitîwaki	they settle on a plan
	nahkomêwa, nahkotamwa	agrees with s.o., it; answers s.o., it
ahead	nîkâni	in the lead, on ahead; in future (particle, prenoun, preverb)
alarm	ânemâpiwa	looks with alarm
alert	ayîkwâmesiwa, awîkwâmesiwa	is alert, pays sharp attention
alive	ashkwinêwa	is left alive
	ashkwinêhiwa	is left alive (dimin.)
	pînesâtesiwa	is alive
	nêsêwênemêwa	thinks s.o. alive
	keki-nêse	(while still) alive (particle compound)
all	châki	all, everywhere (particle, preverb)
	châkîwa	goes in full number, all go
	châkâwanêwa, châkâwatôwa	takes all of them (animate, inanimate)
	châkâwanetîwaki	they all go off in a large group
	châkisêwi	it is all gone, spent
	mâwachi	gathering; among all, only one of all, most (etc.) of all (superlative) (preverb, preparticle)
	mesi	all, whole (particle, preverb)
	mesiwêwi, mesiwêwe	all, in general, entirely, all over (preverb, particle)
	mesiwêyâhkohwêwa	roasts s.o. whole on a stick by the fire
	mesiwêmêwaki (plural)	they all ask s.o. (as, in prayer)
	mesôtêwi, mesôtêwe	all, wholly, universally, all over (preverb, particle)
	mesôtêwimêwa	speaks to all of s.o., includes all of s.o. in what one says
	sîkâhpwêwa	smokes s.o. (a pipe) completely out
	sîkâhtamwa	eats it all up
	tepatawi	in full number, amount, or extent (particle)
	tepi	the full number or amount, being all set (preverb, preparticle)

	kâkikapôtwe	all at once (particle)
alligator	**kôhkôtenîha**	alligator
all possible	**êhpîhchîchi**	with all one's possible speed or strength
almost	**katawi**	nearly, almost; (with future) soon (preverb, preparticle, particle)
all over	**mesôtêwi, mesôtêwe**	all over, universally, all, wholly (preverb, particle)
	mesiwêhkatêwani (plural)	they (inanimate, as trees) stand all over
	mesiwêkâpâwani (plural)	they (inanimate) stand all over
	mesiwêshinôki (plural)	they (animate) are all over
	mesiwêwosêwa	walks all over
	mesiwêyâkwatêwani (plural)	they (inanimate) are all over the ground
	mesiwêyâkwatôwa	litters the ground with them (inanimate)
	wanahkamiki	all over, all over the map, in all directions, on all sides
allow	**wîtôhkawêwa**	helps, aids, allows s.o., collaborates with s.o.
allowed	**pâhkisenwi**	it lies open, it is opened, it is allowed
all sorts	**ateshkawi**	all sorts of demands or excuses (particle)
all together	**aswâpamêwaki** (plural)	they all had their eyes on s.o.
	aswênemêwaki (plural)	their thoughts center on s.o.
	aswi	all together (preverb)
	aswisêwaki (plural)	they quickly gather, all crowd around
almost	**pashi**	almost; (with negative:) not at all (preverb)
alone	**neshi**	alone, only (particle, preverb, preparticle)
	neshawiwa	is alone, by oneself
	neshawiwaki	they are by themselves, they are alone together
	neshîhkâtîwa	does the task alone
	neshihka	alone (particle)
	neshihkêwi	alone (preverb)
	neshihkêwênemêwa	thinks only of s.o.
	neshihkêwênemowa	thinks only of oneself, thinks it is only oneself
	shêshki	only, alone, except; unmarried; empty-handed (particle)
	nekotôhpôhiwa	eats alone
	nekotôkôtêwi	it hangs alone
	môshakihkwêwiwa	she dwells as a woman alone
	neshi-shâpwêshi	off alone by oneself (particle compound)
	ana-shashâpwi	all alone, alone of all (particle compound)
along	**ahpi**	along with it all (preverb)
	anemi	away, continuing, along, on down the line, in time (preverb)
already	**wayachi**	already (preverb)
	wayatahkiwiwi	everything is already over
	kwayâshi	already, already and it is too late, irreversibly (particle, preverb)
	aye	early, earlier, already (particle)
	kîshenêwa, kîshenamwa	already holds s.o., it
	kîshenâtêwi	it is already in hand (**shêshki kîshenâtêwi** it is partly finished)
alright	**nâh=wêna!**	go ahead then, alright then
	âpechi=wê=nêhi!	alright, let's do it!
alright now	**=yâpi**	alright now, here I go, here we go, get ready, here's the deal; (in a question) alright tell me
also	**nâhka, nâhkachi**	also, and, again; in turn, as well (as another instance), this time (particle)
alternate	**âyâshôhka**	by turns, alternately (particle)
alternatively	**=mata**	alternatively, instead, rather, but
although	**kochîhi**	although, granted, concededly (particle)

	têpi=kêh=wîna	(and this is) despite the fact that; although
always	**=âpehe**	always, generally, usually
	ahpenêchi	always, every time (particle)
	pâsitawi	all the time, always (particle)
American	**môhkomâna**	(white) American; white man
amused	**ênikitêhêwa**	feels amused, thinks it's funny
anchored	**ayênahkatêwi**	it is still anchored in place, still stuck in the ground
	chîkahkatêwi	it is anchored in place sticking out
and	**=înahi**	and (with nominals)
	înahi (=înahi)	and there was also (particle)
	nâhka, nâhkachi	also, and, again; in turn, as well (as another instance), this time (particle)
	ôni	and, then (particle)
and then	**kahôni, kôni**	and then (particle)
angle	**sakakwi**	at a sharp angle, at a steep angle, diagonally (particle)
angry	**âhkwêwa**	is angry
	âhkwêwi	angrily, in anger (preverb)
	âhkwêhêwa	makes s.o. angry
	âhkwêhtawêwa	is angry at s.o., it
	âhkwêmikatwi	it is angry
	âhkwêwinâkosiwa	seems angry
	neshki	angrily (preverb)
	neshkitêhêwa	feels angry, offended, upset, disheartened
	neshkinawêhêwa	makes s.o. angry
	wahkêwikitâsowa	gets angry easily
	kakamachitêhêwa	is bitterly angry, seething with bitter grief
anguish	**wîshâwêwa**	screams in anguish; pleads (for spiritual aid) against (it)
animal	**owiyêha**	animal, creature
	owiyêhêha	(small) animal
	owiyêhêhaya	small-animal skin
	mîchipêha	game animal or bird
	mîchipêhi	game (animals, collective)
	mîchipêhiwa	is a game animal
ankle	**pehkwikanâkani**	ankle
annoy	**wîkawihêwa**	annoys s.o.
another	**kotakêhiwa**	is some one else, is another person
	owiyêhâpamêwa	sees s.o. as another being
another way	**payâhkichi**	in another way or direction, in the wrong way or direction (particle)
answer	**nahkotîwaki**	they answer each other
ant	**ênikonôsa**	ant
	ênikonôsiwiwi	it is full of ants
antelope	**wâpitîha**	antelope
anus	**meshkwâha**	anus
	omeshkwâhiwa	has an anus
	makânakitiyêshkêwa	is working to widen the opening of one's anus
	meshkwitiyêshkêwa	s.o.'s anus keeps working, alternately showing red
anxious	**wîshâshkêwa**	is anxious, eager, agitated
	wîshâtêhêwa	is anxious
	wîshâwitêhêwa	is anxious, concerned
	wîshâsiwa	is anxious, agitated
	wîshâshinwa	tries one's level best (to), is anxious (to)
	wîshâwâpiwa	looks about anxiously
	wîshâwehtawêwa	hears s.o. with anxiety

	wîshâwênemêwa	is anxious about s.o.
	kâhkâhkitêhêwa	is anxious, one's heart aches
any	**meshe=mekô='nahi**	any, anyone, anytime, any place
	mêmeshe	any, in each case (particle)
	kêkôhi-'shi	in some or any way; (with negative:) not at all, not under any circumstances
	nekotahi	somewhere, anywhere; somewhere else; to some degree, about; (with negative:) not in any way, not one of them
anyone	**owiyêha**	anyone, someone; anyone else, someone else
anything	**kêkôhi**	anything, something
	kêkôhêhi	anything, something (dimin.)
anyway	**kakâchichi**	anyway, even so, paying no heed (particle)
(aorist)	**êh=** (proclitic preverb or prefix)	(marks aorist modes and locative participles)
appear	**inâpatâniwa**	appears {so}
	nâkosiwa	shows up, appears or is seen in public
apple	**meshîmina**	apple
	nenôtêwi-meshîminêha	crab apple
apprehensive	**sêkitêhêwa**	is apprehensive
approach	**wîposhkawêwa**	approaches s.o., gets closer to s.o.
	nâsâpatamwa	keeps one's eye on it as one approaches it
	nâsehtawêwa	approaches s.o.'s sound
	osehkawêwa, osehkamwa	approaches s.o. from {somewhere}
appropriate	**mîhkôwêwa**	says the appropriate thing, says just the right thing
arch	**wâkikwayawêshkêwa**	arches one's neck
arise	**wanâkîwa**	arises from bed, gets up
	pasekwîwa	arises, stands up, gets to one's feet
arm	**nenekwîkani**	my arm, wing
	nehchiwa	my upper arm
	nâminekwe	under the arm
	mâchinehkêwa	moves one's arm
	mîshinehkêwa	is hairy-armed
	mîwinehkênêwa	moves s.o.'s arm away
	nahkwinehkênêwa	grabs s.o.'s arm
	pôhkwinehkêhwêwa	breaks s.o.'s arm
	shâshâshakinekwêpinêwa	ties s.o.'s arms together behind them
	showinekwêkwâmwa	sleeps with one's arms flung out
	showinekwêshkêwa	spreads one's arms or wings
	wêpinekwêsêwa	swings one's arm quickly
armband	**nâpihchîhaki**	armbands
armed	**âhkôtêwesiwa**	he goes armed, always has a deadly weapon with him
armload	**awatechênamwa**	carries off an armload of it (as, firewood)
armpit	**êh=meshkwinekwêchi**	in one's armpit
	kôkinekwênêwa	washes s.o.'s armpits
around	**kîwi, kî**	around, about, in places, for a while (preverb)
	kîhka	all around (particle)
	chêwinehkîhiwa	is around the place
arrange	**nanâhîhkamawêwa**	attends to (it) for s.o., arranges things for s.o.
	nanâhâhkonamwa	arranges it
	nanâhâmehkisetawêwa	arranges (it) as earth for s.o.
	nanâhotâtêwi	it is arranged by discussion
arrest	**meshenêwa, meshenamwa**	arrests s.o., captures s.o.; catches s.o., it
	meshenahkyêwa	takes captives, arrests people
arrival	**pakamahkiwiwi**	there is an arrival
arrive	**pakami**	arriving (preverb)

	pakamênemêwa	thinks s.o. arrived
	pakamîtêmêwa	arrives in company with s.o. (for **pakami-wîtêmêwa**)
	pakamikâpâwa	stands arrived
	pakamikâpawîhtawêwa	arrives and stands before s.o.
	pakamikâpawînotawêwa	arrives and stands before s.o.
	pakamikâpawinohkatawêwa	arrives and stands before s.o.
	pakamipahowa	arrives running
	pakamwêwêshinwa	arrives with noise
	pyêtêwênemêwa, pyêtêwênetamwa	thinks s.o., it comes, comes back, arrives
arrow	anwi	arrow (archaic)
	mehtekwanwi	arrow (modern term, as if "wooden bullet")
	nîpi	my arrow
	owîpiwa	has an arrow, has (it) as an arrow
	akahkwi	blunt arrow (all wood)
	ashâtîhi	headed arrow (with stone or metal arrowhead)
	otashâtîhemetamwa	has it for one's headed arrow
	wâsikînahtêhi	sharp-pointed wooden arrow
	ahkwahtêwa	one's arrow goes {so far}
arrowhead (1)	wîtekôwi-mâtesi	"owl knife" (stone arrowhead found on the ground)
	wîtekôwi-mekosi	"owl awl" (stone arrowhead found on the ground)
arrowhead (2)	wâpesîhpenyêki	broad-leaved arrowheads, arrowhead roots
artichoke	mîsimîsîha	Jerusalem artichoke
as before	nêyâpi	back (to its former state), the same as before (particle, preverb)
	nêyâpapitôwa	ties it back up again
	anwâchi	(with negative:) not as much as before, seldom (preverb)
ashes	pekwi	ashes, dust
	natwipekwêhamwa	pokes through the ashes searching for it
ashore	akwâsêwa, akwâsêwi	jumps ashore; (canoe) runs ashore
ask	nanâtohtawêwa	asks s.o. (a question)
	nanâtohtâtîwaki	they ask each other
	nanâtoshêwa	asks
	nanâtomêwa	asks after s.o., asks questions about s.o.
	kochimêwa	asks s.o., makes a request of s.o.
	kokwêchimêwa	asks s.o.
	natomêwa	asks for s.o. to come, summons s.o., invites s.o.
	natotamwa	asks for it
	natotamawêwa	asks for (it) from s.o.
	kashkowêwa	gets what one asks for
	nawasehkawêwa	comes by and asks s.o. along
ask along	nawasehkawêwa	comes by and asks s.o. along
asleep	masânikâpiwa	one's leg goes to sleep as one sits
as one pleases	wâpanâtapiwa	sits as one pleases (ritual)
assemble	inâkwapiwa	sits assembled {so}
	mâwâshkêwaki	they gather together, assemble
	mâwachîwaki	they gather, assemble, meet together
assiduously	sekihki	assiduously, regularly (particle, preverb)
assign	pahkimêwa	permits, assigns s.o.; invites s.o. to eat in a ceremony, assigns ceremonial food to s.o.
	pahkikêmowa	assigns dishes of food to people in a ceremony
associate with	wîchênomêwa	enjoys life with s.o., associates with s.o., plays with s.o.
	wîchênokêwa	enjoys life with others, associates with others, plays with others
	anehkâchihêwa	associates with s.o., is an acquaintance of s.o.

astraddle	**pânêshkapiwa**	sits astraddle
	nasawapêpiwa	sits with thighs astraddle
astride	**nasawapiwa**	sits astride
at	**tashi**	{somewhere}, at, in {some place} (particle, preverb, prenoun)
	tanesiwa	is {somewhere}, at {some place}
at ease	**wânahkyêwa**	is undisturbed, at ease, without worries, paying no attention
	wânahkyêhêwa	puts them at ease, makes them feel secure
at least	**wâwosâhi, wâwasâhi**	at least, perhaps as many as; even, going so far as to; expectably, unsurprisingly
attach	**sahkyêwa, sahkyêwi**	(animate, inanimate) is attached or rooted {somewhere}, the base of (animate, inanimate) is {somewhere}
attack	**mawinanêwa**	attacks s.o., runs up to s.o.
	mawinanetîwaki	they attack each other
	mawinahkyêwa	runs over, rushes over, attacks
	môhkîhtâkêwa	rushes out to attack people
	môhkîhtawêwa	rushes out to attack s.o.
	pîneshihêwa	attacks s.o. unprovoked
attain	**têpahkoshkamwa**	attains it, reaches the end of it
attend	**nanâhîhkawêwa, nanâhîhkamwa**	attends to s.o., it; holds an adoption feast for s.o. (the dead)
	nanâhîhkamawêwa	attends to (it) for s.o., arranges things for s.o.
	nanâhîhkamâkêwa	attends to (it) for people
	nanâhîhkâsowa	is attended to; an adoption feast is held for s.o. (the dead)
	nanâhîhkâtisowa	attends to oneself
	nanâheswêwa, nanâhesamwa	attends to s.o.'s, its cooking
	nanâhesikêwa	attends to cooking
	nanâhêwîwa	attends to things
	nanâhenêwa, nanâhenamwa	attends to s.o., it
	nanâhesêhkwêwa	attends to one's cooking
attendant	**mamîshîha**	ceremonial attendant, chief's attendant
	mamîshamawêwa	acts as attendant for s.o.
	mamîshamâkêwa	acts as attendant
	omamîshîhemiwa	has (him as) a ceremonial attendant
attention	**wîkwânêwa**	pays attention to s.o.
	pemênetamwa	continues to pay attention to it
	inehkwêmêwa	attracts one's attention {some way} by speech
attentive	**mînâwi**	attentively, closely, in detail (particle, preverb)
	mînâwinawêhêwa	makes s.o. attentive
	sekihkîhkawêwa, sekihkîhkamwa	is faithfully attentive to s.o., it
attitude	**memyêshkênemêwa**	has a trouble-making attitude towards s.o.
attract	**inehkwêmêwa**	attracts one's attention {some way} by speech
audible	**ahkohtâkwatwi**	it is audible from {so far} away
aunt	**nekîha**	my maternal aunt, my mother's sister; my father's brother's wife; my mother's father's sister; my step-mother
	nesekwisa	my paternal aunt, my father's sister
	nekakâchi-nesekwisa	my "teasing" aunt; my mother's brother's wife
autumn	**takwâkiwi**	it is autumn, fall
	takwâkêhiwi	it is early autumn, fall
avoid	**wanîpahêwa**	avoids being found by s.o., gets away from s.o. by concealment

	kosetawêwa, kosetamwa	avoids s.o., it out of reserve or respect
	kosetâtîwaki	they avoid each other out of reserve or respect
awake	**wahpâsiwa**	is an early riser
	wahpâtêhêwa	is kept awake by one's thoughts
	wahpâwîhkâtîwaki	they are busy keeping each other awake
aware	**kâshkihêwa, kâshkihtôwa**	becomes aware of s.o., it, of s.o.'s, its presence or imminence
	kâshkesiwa	is aware of something, feels or hears something
	kehkênetamwa	is aware of things, has one's senses, is conscious
	kehkênetamôwênemêwa	thinks s.o. has their senses
away	**atehchi**	away someplace, a distance off (particle)
	atehchihkanawe	away from the road (particle)
	pepehchi	away from the others (particle)
	pepehchîmêhi	a little ways away from the others (particle)
awful	**ananeshiwi, naneshiwi, aneneshiwi, neneshiwi**	terrific; awful (particle)
	neshiwanâchinâkosiwa, neshiwanâchinâkwatwi	(animate, inanimate) is ugly, looks awful, looks a mess
awl	**mekosi**	awl
axe	**papakyêhi**	axe, hatchet
	chîkitepêsîhi	single-bladed axe
	papakyêhiwiwa	(the pipe) has an axe-blade, is a pipe-tomahawk

b

baby	**apenôhêha**	baby
	apenôhêhiwa	is a baby
	têhkinâsôha	baby on a cradle-board ("cradle baby")
	mîkwanôha	baby whose mother is about to have another baby (and is fussy)
	âshishimôhkêwa	has a still-born child
back	**ayâpami**	back (returning) (particle, preverb)
	ayâpamîwa	goes back
	ayâpamotêwa	moves camp back
	peteki	in back, back (in space or time), backwards (particle)
	petekîmêhi	in back, back (in space or time), backwards (dimin.) (particle)
back (of body)	**nepehkwani**	my back
	opehkwani	his or her back; a back
	wâpeshkipehkwanwa	has a white back
	wâwâchipehkwanêkâpâwaki (pl.)	they (two) stand back to back
	neshîkani	the small of my back, my lower back, my hindquarters
	oshîkani	his or her lower back; a creature's hindquarters
	omekishîkanwa	has a sore in the small of one's back
	omekisikiwêwa	has sores on one's back
	apisikiwêhiwa	warms one's back
	apesokowêhiwa	warms one's back
	apesokowêshinwa	lies warming one's back
	apesôwêhiwa	warms one's back
	âhtawâshinwa, âhtawâsenwi	lies on one's back, it lies on its back
backbone	**netahtakâkwani**	my backbone

	otahtakâkwani	his or her backbone; a backbone
back out	petekawiwa	backs out, goes back on one's word, changes one's mind
backwards	âhtawâsêwa	falls over backwards
	ashênawîwa	slides back, moves back
bacon	êsâwâhkasota kôhkôsha	bacon
bad	machi	bad (prenoun, preverb)
	myâshi	badly; sort of (preverb)
	myânesiwa, myânetwi	is bad, ugly
	myâshikiwa, myâshikenwi	(animate, inanimate) is bad, ill-formed, not right, bodes ill
	myâshawiwa	is bad, mean; acts badly, does wrong
	myâshisenwi	it (as, a song) is bad; it spoils, goes bad
	wâwaneshkâha	naughty, bad, wicked, or evil person, bad actor
	wâwaneshkâhiwa, wâwaneshkâhiwiwa	is bad, naughty, immoral;
	wâwaneshkâhiwi	it is bad, evil
	myânâshkêwi	it does not go well
	myânahokowa	is made to feel bad (by something said)
	myâshikahesêwa	does not chop the firewood right
	machitêhêwa	feels bad, has bad thoughts
	myâshitêhêwa	feels bad (about something), feels sad
	myâshi-pemâtesiwa	feels bad, is in bad health
	myâshipenanêwa, myâshipenatôwa	treats s.o. badly, does not treat s.o. right, does harm to s.o., it
	nanâhkawi	wickedly, meanly
	nanâhkawitêhêwa	has bad feelings, a bad feeling; has evil thoughts or intent
	pôsitêhêwa	feels very bad
	wâwîyashkimêwa	says all kinds of bad things about s.o.
badger	masakahkwa	badger
bad weather	pekishkîyâwi	there is a stretch of bad weather
bag	mashkimotêhi	bag, sack
	mashkimotêhêhi	small bag, sack
	mashkimotêhkêwa	she makes a woven bag
	ahpahikanimotêhi	sewing bag
	pîshâkanimotêhi	rawhide or leather bag; parfleche
	metâsôshkene	ten bags (of something), ten bagfuls (particle)
	metâsôwane	ten backloads; ten bundles or sacks (of something)
	tatôpanahwêwa	ties s.o. up in a bag
	mamânôwanakihtôwaki (plural)	they each had many bags of it
bait	ashamôtawêwa	baits s.o.
	ashamôchîhi	bait
bald	pepeshkwitepêwa	has a bald or shaved head
	wâshkêtepêwa	has a bald spot or spots where hair has been pulled out
ball	pehkwâhki	ball
	pehkonamwa	forms it into a ball
bandage	akwapinêwa	bandages s.o.
	akwapisowa	is bandaged
bang	tanwêwêhwêwa, tanwêwêhamwa	is audibly drumming, banging, or pounding on s.o. (as, a drum), it
	tanwêwêhtôwa (Jones)	"bangs away on it"
bank	ahkwitâhkîki	on top of a hill, bank, ridge (locative noun)
bare	mehtâwaki	on the bare ground (particle)
	pepeshkwâwakatwi	the ground is bare
	pepeshkwâwakîwi	the ground is bare
barefoot	mehtanasitêwa	is barefoot

	mehtanasite	barefoot (particle)
	mehchikâtêwa	is barefoot
barehanded	**kâhki**	barehanded, without anything (particle)
barely	**sakâki**	just barely, with difficulty (particle)
	sâsakâki	just barely each time (particle)
	masâchi	barely, with difficulty (particle)
	akâwi	barely (preverb)
	akoshêwe	barely, minimally, as if not seriously (particle)
barge in	**mâmânami** (also **mâmânomi**)	barging in, not allowing others the opportunity (particle)
bark (of dog)	**mekiwa**	barks
	mekinêwa, mekitamwa	barks at s.o., it
bark (of tree)	**anakêhkwi**	bark, piece of tree bark
	anakêhkwa	sheet of bark (on house or for house covering)
	wîshkwêshkwi	of birchbark (prenoun)
	wîkopi	(piece or string of) basswood inner bark
	kônachîhi	kinnikinnick (see this)
	anakêweni	bark canoe
	kâhkimotêhi	a bag of (basswood) bark fiber
	pekohkwêwa	gathers bark sheets (for lodge-coverings)
	wâhkanakikeshamwa	cuts the bark from it
	pahkwanîwi	its bark is loose (of a tree in the spring)
barrel	**têtepechêhâtêhi**	barrel, keg
bask	**apâsetêhkêwa**	basks in the sun
basket	**pêshkiti**	basket
base	**sahkyêwa, sahkyêwi**	(animate, inanimate) is attached or rooted {somewhere}, the base of (animate, inanimate) is {somewhere}
baseball	**pâkahatowêwa**	plays baseball, plays lacrosse
bass	**ashikana**	bass
basswood	**wîkopimishi**	basswood tree, stick
	wîkopi	(piece or string of) basswood inner bark
	wîkopihkêwa	gathers basswood inner bark
bat (animal)	**pîshâkaninekwêha**	bat
bathe	**anenwîwa**	bathes, swims
be	**apiwa**	sits, exists, is ({somewhere}); is laid out
	ahtêwi	it exists, is ({somewhere})
	awiwa	is, stays {somewhere}
	awîmikatwi	it is {somewhere}
	ishikiwa, ishikenwi	is {so}
bead	**pîwâhi**	bead, small bead
	pîwâhihchikâtêwi	it is decorated with beads
	pîwâhikwâtêhiwi	it is sewn with small beads (dimin.)
	pîwâhimahkesenêwa	wears beaded moccasins
	pîwâhimatetêwa	wears beaded leggins
	pîwâhipahônêwa	she wears a beaded hair binder
	mêmêshâhi	large bead
	mîkesa	wampum bead (Jones: "cowrie shell")
	pîsimîkaki	wampum beads
	kwananâhaki	tubular beads
	ashkoshâkanaki	bone beads (as a necklace)
	otôshkoshâkanemiwa	has on bone beads
beak	**ohkiwani**	beak (of bird); nose
	âhkwikomêwa	has a sharp beak
bean	**mashkochîsa**	bean, beans
	mashkochîsêha	a bean

bear	**mahkwa**	bear
	mahkweshihamwa	goes on a bear hunt
	kâkânwikashêwa	grizzly bear
	kêkânwikashêha	grizzly bear
Bear Clan	**mahkwisowa**	is a member of the Bear Clan
	mêhkwisota	member of the Bear Clan
Bear Potato Clan	**mêhkohpeniwisota**	member of the Bear Potato Clan
beard	**mîsetonâkani**	beard, mustache
	mîshîkwêwa	is hairy-faced, has a beard
bear den	**mahkwânakwi**	bear den
bearskin	**mahkwayi**	bearskin
beat (defeat)	**châkahwêwa**	beats s.o. out of everything
	mânahwêwa	beats s.o. out of much
	mânomêwa, mânamêwa	beats s.o. (as, by doing something better or faster)
	mânomihêwa	beats s.o. to it
beat (strike)	**anwêwêhwêwa**	makes s.o. (drum) sound by beating
beat up	**nesêwa**	kills s.o., beats s.o. up
	wêpîhkwêwêwa	beats his (own) wife
	mechimatahwêwa	beats s.o. badly
	mechimihêwa	is always after s.o., is always beating s.o. up; kills many of s.o.
	mechimîwa	(always) gets beaten up; loses a man
	nepâtâhkosiwa	is beaten to a pulp
	châkîkwêhâsowa	is badly beaten about the face
beautiful	**asâminâkwatwi**	it is beautiful
	wêwenahkwatwi	the clouds are beautiful
	wêwenâhkwâwiwi	it is a beautiful grove of trees
	wêwenânehkwêwa	has beautiful hair
	wêwenepyêhâsowa	(animate, as a buckskin) is beautifully painted
beaver	**amehkwa**	beaver
	amehkwânowi	beaver tail
	amehkwaya	beaver skin
be away	**inêtwa**	is away {so long}
because of	**ochi**	from {somewhere}, because of {some reason} (particle, preverb)
	wâwochi	repeatedly from {somewhere}, because of {some reason}, in {such} direction (preverb)
	ochimêwa	tells s.o. because of {something}
	otâhpenanêwa	deals with, kills s.o. because of (something)
	otenetîwa	fights because of {something}
bed	**nepâkani**	bed
	wîhpêtenowa	gets into someone's bed, gets into bed with (s.o.)
bedbug	**mêshkwihkenôha**	bedbug
bee	**âmôwa**	bee, wasp
	mahkwâmôwa	bumblebee
beetle	**âchikashîwa**	beetle
	môwečîhkêha	dung beetle
	pêpôhkoshkâha	click beetle
before	**kawîshâni**	beforehand (particle)
	menehtêwîmêhi	a little before
	pakôshi	beforehand, to be ready ahead of time (preverb)
	pakôshêwîwa	does work in advance, does something ahead of time
	mêhi	yet (preverb); before (preverb with prioritive modes)
	êyêshi-pwâwi-, êyêh-pwâwi-	before (preverbs with changed conjunct)

beg	natotâsêwa	begs from s.o.
	natotâsetîwaki	they beg each other
	natotâsikawêwa	begs of s.o.
begin	wêpi	begin, start to, set about (preverb)
	wêpikiwa, wêpikenwi	begins (to exist); it begins, starts to happen
	wêpyêwîwa	begins the task or activity
	wêpâpyêsenwi	it begins to lie strung, begins
	ahkwanahkisenwi	it begins, has its source
	wêpwêwêhwêwa	begins to drum s.o. (a drum)
	kâhkami	directly; from the very beginning (particle)
begrudge	kekyêshkachihêwa	begrudges s.o. unrightfully, holds things back from s.o.
behind	ahkowi	after, afterwards, behind (particle)
behold	êhki	lo and behold (particle)
	êshki	lo and behold (particle)
belch	mêkechîwa	belches
believe	têpwêhêwa	believes s.o.
	têpwêhtawêwa, têpwêhtamwa	believes s.o., it; grants s.o.'s request
	têpwêhtâkaniwiwa	is believed, is heeded
	têpwêwi	believing, granting (preverb)
	têpwêshêwa	believes what one hears, what one is told
	nenohtawêwa, nenohtamwa	understands s.o., it, believes s.o., it
	ânwêhtawêwa, ânwêhtamwa	disbelieves, refuses s.o., it
	sekihkênetamwa	is faithful to it, has faith in it
	mêkwêhe	I believe, I think, probably, likely (particle)
bell	sênawêhi	bell
	shênawêhi	bell
bellow	nenosômowa	bellows like a buffalo
	nenoswimowa	bellows like a buffalo
belly	nâmeche	in the belly (stomach or womb) (particle)
	kôkechênêwa	washes s.o.'s belly
	mesechêwa	has a big belly
	opishkwêchêwa	has a big belly
	pâkechêshinwa	falls on one's belly
	papakêhimotêwa	one's belly has thin skin
	papakêhimotêshinwa	one's belly has thin skin as one lies
	pôhkechêhwêwa	pokes a hole in s.o.'s belly
	pôhkechêshwêwa	cuts a hole in s.o.'s belly
	kîhpochêwa	one's belly is full
belong	inekihkoshkamwa	belongs to it in {such} numbers
	otênetâkosiwa	is thought to come from {somewhere}, belongs {somewhere}
beloved	otâhkwênechikanani	his beloved
below	ahkiki	down below (particle)
belt	kehchîpîhi	belt
	kehchîpîheki	at the belt or belt-line
	kehchîpîha	woven belt
	kehchîpisôni	belt (prenoun)
	kehkitâhkwêpinêwa	puts a belt on s.o.
	kehkitâhkwêpisowa	puts a belt on oneself
	âshowânekwahâtêhi	cross-belt
	meshkwâswâwa	finger-woven sash, "yarn belt"
bend	wâkenamwa	bends it
	wâkâkenamwa	bends it (something stiff), bends it over
	wâkechêkâpâwa	stands bent over

	wâkechêwosêwa	walks bent over
	wâkechêyâpyêhi	bend in a stream
	pepyêtekwikwayawênêwa	bends s.o.'s neck down
	shômenamwa	bends it in or down unevenly by pushing
	shômeshkawêwa	dents, bends s.o. (as, cattail-reed mats) in by body
	shashômipyêyâwi	it has bending boughs
	wâwiyêwâkenamwa	bends it in a circle
bend down	**shekwi**	bent down (preverb)
bend over	**nakapeshkêwa**	bends one's body over forward
benefit	**mesênemêwa, mesênetamwa**	benefits from s.o., it; s.o. is of use to one
	mesênetamâkêwa	benefits, gets good from (it) for people
berate	**kîhkâmêwa**	calls s.o. out, berates s.o.
berdache	**êyêhkwêwa**	berdache, man living as a woman
	êyêhkwêwênemêwa	considers s.o. to be a berdache
berry	**makimini**	"large berry" (probably chestnut)
besides	**anikashi**	besides, otherwise, beyond (particle)
	pîhtawi	moreover, else, besides (particle)
be so	**ishikiwa, ishikenwi**	(animate, inanimate) is {so}, is of {such} kind, nature, or purpose
best (verb)	**myânawitêhêmêwa**	gets the best of s.o. by talking
better	**nâpi**	better, instead, at least; the good thing is (that) (particle)
	nâpiwêna	why don't you, I, we; I think I'd better
	kîkênemêwa	thinks s.o. is better, recovered
	kîkinawêmêwa	makes s.o. feel better by what one says
between	**chêwinehki**	in between, halfway (particle)
	nanakwi	in between (particle, preparticle)
	sanakwi	in between (particle, preparticle)
	sanakwâwi	there is an open space (as, between houses)
	sanakôpinaye	between the seats (archaic) (particle)
	sâsanakwi	in between, between-times (particle)
bewitch	**panâchihêwa**	bewitches or puts a spell on s.o., ruins s.o.
beyond	**âshowi**	over, beyond an obstruction or expanse (particle, preparticle)
	anikâtepi	way off (in distance or time), way beyond (particle)
bicycle	**têtepishkâsôha**	bicycle
big	**makekinwa**	is big
	mamâkekinôki	they (animate) are large
	mamâkekinôhiwaki	they (animate) are large (dimin.), larger
	meshâwi	it is large
	meshâhiwi	it is large (dimin.), larger
	memêshâwani	they (inanimate) are large
	memêshâhiwani	they (inanimate) are large (dimin.), larger
	inekinwa	is {so} big
	inekinôhiwa	is {so} big (dimin.)
	âyânekinôki	they (animate) are {so} big
	âyânekinôhiwaki	they (animate) are {so} big (dimin.)
	inekihkwâwi	it is {so} big
	inekihkwâhiwi, inekihkwâhenwi, inekihkwâhenôhiwi	it is {so} big (dimin.)
	âyânekihkwâwani	they (inanimate) are {so} big
	âyânekihkwâhenôni	they (inanimate) are {so} big (dimin.)
	inekihkwâhkosiwa, inekihkwâhkwatwi	(animate, inanimate) is {so} big around

202

	âyânekihkwâhkosiwaki, âyânekihkwâhkwatôni	they (animate, inanimate) are {so} big around
	inekihkwâpêwesiwa	is {so} big in bodily build
	inekihkwi	{so} big, to {such} extent, {so many} (particle, preverb)
	inekihkwihtôwa	makes it {so} big
	kehchi	much, great, more or larger (than others) (prenoun, preverb)
	kekyêhchi	big, great (plural) (prenoun)
	maki	big, much (particle, preverb)
	mamâki	big (plural), in large numbers (preverb)
	mamâki-nêmowa	takes deep breaths
	meshinâkosiwa	looks big
	meshi	big (prenoun)
	memyêshi	big (plural) (prenoun)
bind (in a bind)	**kîsâchi**	in a bind, having second thoughts, as a difficult task or obligation, as a firm commitment; nothing can be done about it (particle, preverb)
	kîsâtênemêwa, kîsâtênetamwa	feels reluctantly obliged about s.o., it, feels in a bind or of two minds about s.o., it, feels worried and helpless about s.o., it
	kîsâtênemowa	considers the requirement burdensome, has second thoughts
birchbark	**wîshkwêshkwi**	of birchbark (prenoun)
bird	**wîshkenôha**	bird
	ishisêwiwa	is {such} a bird (**châki êshisêwita** every kind of bird)
birth	**nôshêwa**	she gives birth
	nôshânêwa	she gives birth to s.o.
	nôshêhêwa	has her give birth
bit	**neswipite**	three bits (37½ cents) (particle)
bite	**sakipwêwa, sakipotamwa**	bites s.o., it
	sakikomêhpwêwa	bites s.o. on the nose
	sakinekwêhpwêwa	bites s.o. on the wing
	sakinowêtiyêhpwêwa	bites s.o. on the buttocks
	kîshkamêwa, kîshkatamwa	bites s.o., it off
	kîshkikomêhpwêwa	bites off s.o.'s nose
	mahkatamwa	bites it off
	mahkikwêhpwêwa	bites s.o.'s head off
	menwamêwa	bites s.o. just right, has a good hold on s.o. with one's mouth
	otamêwa, otatamwa	bites s.o., it {somewhere}
	tasôchêhtamwa	bites of {so much} of it at once
	wîshikamêwa	bites s.o. hard
	kepinêwêhpwêwa	chokes s.o. by biting
bits	**pekechêyâsenwi**	it is blown to bits (by wind)
	pekihketêwa	it is blown to bits (by explosion)
bitter	**wîsakenwa, wîsakanwi**	(animate, inanimate) is bitter
bittern	**kîshekwi-wâpatâha**	least bittern
	wîkamosiwa	American bittern
black	**mahkatêwesiwa, mahkatêwâwi**	(animate, inanimate) is black
	mahkatêwâhkonêwa	paints s.o. black
	mahkatêwâhkonowa	paints oneself black, has one's body painted black
	mahkatêwikanwi	it is black (as, a tree or stick)
	mahkatêwâpatâniwi	it looks black
	mahkatêwâpehkatwi	it is black stone
	mahkatêwinîkwênêwa	blackens s.o. across the eyes
	mâmahkatêwanowêwa	has blackened cheeks
	mâmahkatêwanowêpiwa	sits with blackened cheeks

blackberry	**mahkatêmina**	highbush blackberry
blackbird	**sakenâhkwa**	blackbird (generic)
black eye	**ohkonîkwêwa**	has a black eye
bladder	**opishkwayi**	bladder; gizzard
blame	**ahtenêwa**	blames s.o.
	mameshkamwa	catches the blame (for it)
blanch	**shôpyêswêwa**	blanches s.o. (green corn) to set the milk
	shôpyêsikêwa	blanches ears of green corn (to set the milk)
blanket	**mehkonêweni**	blanket, robe
	nehkonêhi	my blanket, robe
	ohkonêmowa	cries while wearing a blanket
	ohkonêhêwa	puts a blanket over s.o.
	ohkonêkâpâwa	stands wearing a blanket, robe
	manetôwêkenwi	fine broadcloth blanket (deep indigo)
	meshkwêkenwi	red woolen broadcloth blanket (red with white stripe)
	pîhtawoshêwa	puts on an extra blanket
blaze	**aniweshêwi**	it burns, blazes big
	ineshêwi	it (fire) burns, blazes {so}
	taneshêwi	it (fire) burns, blazes {somewhere}
	peshkonêwi	it (fire) is blazing, flares up, blazes up
	taneshêwêshinwa	(Fire Spirit) lies blazing
bleed	**meshkoweshkêwa**	bleeds
	mêmeshkowinechêwa	one's hands are bleeding
	sâkishkwêkatwi	it is bleeding
	pekihtanwa	has a nosebleed
	sîpwêwa	bleeds s.o. (with a cupping horn)
bless	**keteminawesiwa**	is blessed
	keteminawêwa	pities, blesses s.o.
	keteminâhkwêwa	bestows a blessing or blessings
	keteminâkêwa	bestows a blessing or blessings
	keteminamawêwa	blesses (s.o.) for s.o.
	keteminohtawêwa	hears and blesses s.o.
blessing	**keteminawesiweni**	blessing; religion (in the Drum Society)
	keteminawesiweniwiwi	there is blessing
blind	**kekyêpîkwêwa**	is blind
	kekyêpîkwêsowa	is blinded by the light
blink	**chîpinîkwêwa**	blinks
	chîhchîpinîkwêwa	is blinking
bloat	**pâsanenwa**	is bloated from rotting
	pâsanâmowa	feels bloated, has gastric bloating
block	**kepishkawêwa**	blocks s.o.
	kepishinwa, kepisenwi	lies blocking
	kepishimêwa	lays s.o. to block
	kepâhkwimêwa	blocks or hems in s.o. by warning or argument
	kepâhkoshkamawêwa	blocks (it) for s.o.
blood	**meshkwi**	blood
	ishishkwêkihtôwa	leaves a trail of blood to {somewhere}
blood clot	**atôwa**	blood clot
bloodroot	**mêshkowêhi**	bloodroot
bloodshot	**atôwiwi**	it is bloodshot
	mêmeshkwatowinîkwêwa	has bloodshot eyes
bloodsucker	**akashkwâha**	bloodsucker

bloody	**meshkowiwa, meshkowiwi**	is bloody, has blood in one; it is bloody
	meshkowâhkosiwa, **meshkowâhkwatwi**	(animate, inanimate) is all bloody, is covered with blood
	meshkowâpôkatwi	it is a bloody liquid
	meshkoweshkamawêwa	bloodies (it) for s.o.
blow	**pôtânêwa, pôtâtamwa**	blows on s.o., it
	anwêwêhtamwa	blows it (wind instrument)
	anwêwêhchikêwa	blows on something to play it or make it whistle
	wîshikwêwêhtamwa	blows it (wind instrument) loud
blow (wind)	**aniwânematwi**	it blows hard
	inâshinwa, inâsenwi	(animate, inanimate) is blown {some way} by the wind
	mîwâsetôwa	blows it away, fans it away
	mîwâshinwa	he is blown away
	otânematwi	it blows from {somewhere}
	otenwi	the wind blows from {somewhere}
	pakisâshinwa	blows in on the wind and lands
	papahkwachiwêyâsenwi	it is blown up by the roots
	pehkwâsenwi	it is blown in a lump
	pekechêyâsenwi	it is blown to bits
	pemâsenwi	it is blown by
	pîtâshinwa, pîtâsenwi	(animate, inanimate) blows in
	pyêtâsenwi	it blows this way
	shôshkwânehkwêyâshinwa	one's hair is blown back smooth
blow nose	**chînishkikomênowa**	blows one's nose with one's hands
blow up	**châkechêhtêwi**	it is blown up
	pekihketêwa	it is blown to bits
blue	**wîpekwi**	blue (prenoun)
	wîpekosiwa, wîpekwâwi	(animate, inanimate) is blue
bluebird	**chîkitiyêkâpâha**	bluebird
bluejay	**tîtîwa**	bluejay
board	**pasikâhkwa**	board
board (verb)	**pôsâwanetîwaki**	they get into a boat in a large group
boat	**chîmâni**	canoe (see: canoe)
	êshkotêwîhi	steam boat
	nâpehkwâni	ship, sailing vessel
	pôsihtôwa	loads it into a boat; sends it
body	**nîyawi**	my body; myself, me (object of verb)
	owîyawi	s.o.'s body; himself, herself, him, her (object of verb)
	uwîyawiwa	has a body
	mesihâwa	headless body, corporeal body
	chakâhkosîhiwa	is small-bodied
	chakâpêwesiwa	is small in bodily build
	inekihkwâpêwesiwa	is {so} big in bodily build
	mîsechêwa	has a hairy body
	nâminawe	within the body (particle)
	shîkwîwena	bodily form
boil	**kwâshkwinâsowa,** **kwâshkwinâtêwi**	(animate, inanimate) boils
	pakâshimêwa, pakâhtôwa	boils s.o., it
	anâpôsamwa	boils it
	kîshâpôsamwa	finishes boiling it, has boiled it
	pôsâpôsamwa	boils it harder, longer
	anâpôsikêwa	boils medicine
	anâpôhkêwa	boils (it, liquid)

	kîshâpôhkêwa	finishes boiling (it, liquid)
	anâpôhkawêwa	boils (it) for s.o.
	sîkinâtêwi	it boils over
	sîkinâsamwa	lets it boil over
	sîkinâsikêwa	lets things boil over
	aniwinâsamwa	boils it vigorously
	pôtâhkwêwa	puts (it) in the pot to boil
	pôtâhkwawêwa	puts (it) in the pot to boil for s.o.
boil (noun)	makwîtamwa	has a swelling, has a boil
	pôhkesowa	one's boil is opened up by the application of medicine
bone	ahkani	bone
	ahkanêhi	small bone
	kekikane	bones and all
	pehkwikanêwa	has lumps on one's bones
	amehkwikani	beaver bone
	meshwêhikani	rabbit bone
	shîshîpikani	duck bone
	pôhkosowa, pôhkotêwi	has a bone broken by gunshot, it is broken by gunshot
boom	wîsakowêwa	booms out
born	nîkiwa	is born
borrow	awihiwêwa	borrows (it); lends (it)
	awihêwa	borrows (it) from s.o.; lends (it) to s.o.
boss	pâsa	boss
	pâsiwiwa	is the boss
both	chêwîshwi	both (particle)
	chêwîshenwi	both times, both ways, double (particle)
	châkinêwaki	they both died, they all died
	tâpôwi	on opposite sides, on both sides (preverb)
	wâwîtawi	on both sides, on either side (particle)
	wâwîtawâhkwâpamêwa	looks at s.o. from both sides (ritual)
	wâwîtawetone	(from) both sides of the mouth (particle)
	wâwîtawishkwâte	(through) the doors on both ends of the lodge (particle)
	wâwîtônehke	with both hands (particle)
	wîtawakâme	on both sides, on opposite sides (particle)
bother	otamihêwa	bothers, inconveniences, hinders s.o., is a bother to s.o.
	otamihiwêwa	bothers people, is a nuisance
	kîsâchimêwa	imposes a bothersome obligation on s.o. by speech
	nîshkênemêwa, nîshkênetamwa	thinks s.o., it a bother, in the way
	nîshkiwetôwa	has the bother or inconvenience of carrying it
bottle	môtayi	bottle
bottom	mehchitiyênêwa	uncovers s.o.'s bottom
	wînepitiyêwa	has a dirty bottom
bottomland	ahkwêyâmihkiwi	tract of wooded bottomland
bough	shashômipyêyâwi	it has bending boughs
bounce	papasipahowa	runs skipping or bouncing along
	papasisêwa	goes bouncing along
	pasipasisêwa	goes bouncing along
bound along	shâshîpahtêpahowa	runs bounding along
bow	mehtêha	bow
	omehtêhiwa	has a bow, has (it) as a bow
	omehtêhemêwa	has s.o. (a bow) as a bow
	wîshikâkesiwa	(bow) is stiff, hard to pull
	peshkwahtêyâkesiwa	(bow) is springy, easy to pull

bow (verb)	**nîsehkwêsêwa**	bows one's head
	shekehkwêshinwa	has one's head down
	shekehkwêmêwa	makes s.o. bow their head by what one says to them
bowstring	**mehtekwâpi**	bowstring
	omehtekwâpiwa	has a bowstring, has (it) as a bowstring
bowl	**anâkani**	bowl
	onâkani	bowl (archaic)
	anâkâhi	little bowl
	chakinâkâhi	small bowl
	mehtekwinâkani	wooden bowl
	nekotinâkane	one bowlful
box	**mahkahkwi**	box
	mahkahkôhi	little box, pail
boy	**kwîyesêha**	boy
	kwîyesêhiwa	is a boy
	kwîyesêhêha	small boy
bracelet	**ahkanâhkwa**	bracelet
	otôhkanâhkomiwa	has on a bracelet or bracelets
brag	**wawînwâsowa**	brags, boasts
braid	**anahtakîwa**	braids string
	papakâpînamwa	braids it
	pîsimîkiwinêwa	has braids decorated with wampum
brain	**nînêtepi**	my brain
	otôtepîmi	his or her brain (archaic)
branch	**otehkoni**	branch
	êh=pemichitehkonêyâki	on the branch of a tree
	pahkêkiwa	branches
	pahkêyâwi	it branches off
	pahkêsenwi	it (as, a road) branches off
	pahkêyânakatwi	the hole or cave branches off
brant	**peshishkesa**	brant; domestic goose
brass	**asâwâkatwi**	brass
	asâwâkatwi-nâpihchîha	brass armband
	asâwâkeshêwa	wears brass earrings
brave	**wanâpêwiwa:**	**wênâpêwita** the one who is brave
	wênâpêwinohkataka	the one who is brave towards the charcoal
	îni kehkeshêwi	(i.e., one who has the courage to fast)
bread	**pahkwêshikani**	bread; wheat flour
	pêkotêhi	bread cooked in ashes (or oven), "cowboy bread"
	wêpishkwêhtêhi	white bread
break	**pôhkonêwa, pôhkonamwa**	breaks s.o., it, snaps s.o., it in two
	pôhkoshkawêwa	breaks s.o. in two by foot
	pôhkoshkamawêwa	breaks (it) in two by foot for s.o.
	pôhkosowa, pôhkotêwi	has a bone broken by gunshot, it is broken by gunshot
	pôhkwikahkwanêhwêwa	hits s.o. and breaks their leg
	pôhkwikanêsowa	has a bone broken by gunshot
	pôhkwinehkêhwêwa	breaks s.o.'s arm
	pôhkwihpikêshinwa	falls and breaks one's rib
	pôhkwiwinêshinwa	falls and breaks one's horn
	pahkeshkêwi	it (stringlike) breaks
	pahkenêwa, pahkenamwa	breaks s.o., it (stringlike) apart; pulls s.o., it off, plucks s.o., it off; picks s.o. (as, fruit), it
	papahkenêwa, papahkenamwa	breaks s.o., it apart (with multiple breaks); picks them
	papahkeshwêwa, papahkeshamwa	cuts s.o.'s bonds, severs them (with multiple cuts)

	mahkenamwa	breaks it off, pulls it off, picks it (as, a flower)
	mahkeshkêwi	it breaks off
	mahkisahtôwa	snatches it off, jerks it off, breaks it off
	nasenamwa	breaks through it (as, poking through cloth, breaking up a small dam to let water flow out); pulls its trigger
break grip	**kekyêteshkinechênêwa**	pulls s.o.'s hands away breaking their grip
breast	**nônâkani**	breast, nipple
breath	**nêmoweni**	breath
	onêmowihêwa	gives s.o. breath
	ashkanâmowa	is out of breath, is smothering
	wâwananâmowa	is out of breath
	wâwananâmwishimêwa	lays s.o. out with the wind knocked out of them
breathe	**nêmowa**	breathes
	mamâki-nêmowa	takes deep breaths
	panâchi-nêmowa	is struggling to breathe
	kâshkanâmowa	can be heard breathing
	nahanâmowa	is able to breathe
	têhtêpechânâmowa	one's stomach rises and falls as one breathes
	wîshikanâmowa	breathes hard, pushes hard with one's breath
breechcloth	**âsiyâni**	breechcloth
	otâsiyâniwa	is wearing a breechcloth, wears (it) as a breechcloth
	otâsiyânenamwa	uses it as a breechcloth
	papakwâsiyêwa	his breechcloth hangs loosely
bride	**inenehkwêwâsowa**	she is taken as a bride to {somewhere}
bridge	**kohkahikani**	bridge
	kohkahikêwa	makes a bridge
	okohkahikaniwa	has a bridge
bridle	**sakâpyênikani**	leading-rope, halter, bridle
	saketonêpichikani	bridle, bit
bring	**pyênêwa, pyêtôwa**	brings s.o., it
	pyênetisowa	brings oneself
	pyêhkyêwa	brings a person (especially as wife)
	pyêtawêwa	brings (it) to s.o.
	pyêtâkêwa	brings (it) to people
	pyêhpahônêwa	brings s.o. on the run, runs s.o. in
	pyêtatawihtawêwa	brings, takes it to (s.o.) for s.o. (ritual)
	pyêtatawihêwa	has (it) brought to s.o. (ritual)
	pyêpyêtatawihetîwaki	they have (it) brought to each other (ritual)
	pyêshiwêwa	(warrior) brings home a prisoner or a scalp
	nâteswêwa	tries to make s.o. come by using medicine or burning tobacco
	pîtikanêwa, pîtikatôwa	brings s.o., it in
	pîtikatawêwa	brings (it) in for s.o.
	pîtikatâtisowa	brings (it) in for oneself
	pyêtômêwa, pyêtôtamwa	brings s.o., it on one's back
bring up	**kîshikenêwa**	brings s.o. up, raises s.o. (as, a child or animal)
broadcloth	**manetôwêkenwi**	fine broadcloth blanket (deep indigo)
	meshkwêkenwi	red woolen broadcloth blanket (red with white stripe)
	shôshkwêkîhi	fine broadcloth
	wâpetôhi	black broadcloth with light-colored edge
brooch	**sakahôna**	brooch (round pin with a tab, traditionally of German silver)
brook	**sîpôhêhi**	brook

brother	**neseseha**	my older brother (**osesêhani** his or her older brother); also applied to a father's brother's son and a mother's sister's son.
	netawêmâwa	my brother (of a woman) (**otawêmâwani** her brother)
	nesîma (nesîmêha)	my younger brother or sister (**osîmani, osîmêhani** his or her younger brother or sister); also applied to a father's brother's son or a mother's sister's son.
	osîmemâwa, osîmêhemâwa	the younger brother or sister
	osîmetîwaki	they are brothers, they are siblings
	osîmetîhaki	the brothers
	netôtêma	my brother or sister; my clan totem (animal or spirit; also used reciprocally)
	ahkowechîha	the youngest brother or sister
	machîhkiwesa	the older or eldest brother
	kehkiwesa	the older or eldest brother
	ashkâpêwa	the younger of two brothers
brother-in-law	**nînemwa**	my brother-in-law (of a woman), my sister-in-law (of a man) (**owînemôni** her brother-in-law, his sister-in-law)
	owînemwiwa	has a sibling-in-law of the opposite sex, he has (her) as his sister-in-law, she has (him) as her brother-in-law
	nîhtâwa	my brother-in-law (of a man) (**owîhtâwani** his brother-in-law)
	nemêshâhema	my brother-in-law (of a man) (**omêshâhemani** his brother-in-law; **mêsha** brother-in-law!)
brown	**asâwi**	brown (archaic); yellow (prenoun)
	asâwi-mahkwa	member of the Brown Bear lineage of the Bear Clan
	asâwinameshkêwa	has brown skin (**êsâwinameshkâta** Indian) (archaic)
bruise	**otehkiwa (or otehkîwa)**	has a bruise
	otehkesowa	is bruised by a gunshot
bubble	**papîsanâkamîwa**	one's bubbles come up in the water
	papîsanâkamîwi	there are bubbles coming up in the water
	mâmôshkihtanwi	it flows bubbling
buckskin	**asaya**	skin, buckskin
	asayîhi	buckskin thing
	pîshâkani	rawhide, buckskin
	pîshâkanîhi	buckskin coat
bud	**pâshkinîpîwi**	it (tree) is budding out
	sâkipyêyâwi	it (tree) buds; the trees bud
buffalo	**kohpichi-nenoswa**	buffalo
	kohpichîha	buffalo
	nenoswa	buffalo (ceremonial, older usage); cow, ox, steer
	inenoswa and **anenoswa**	buffalo (archaic)
	nenoswayi	buffalo-robe
	nenoswiwa	is a buffalo
	nenosômowa	bellows like a buffalo
	nenosohkêwa	hunts buffalo
	nênosohkêha	buffalo hunter
	nenoswekêwa	dances the Buffalo Dance
	nenoswahkiwi	herd of buffalo
	nâwi-nenoswahkiwe	in the middle of a herd of buffalo
	ayâpêwa	buffalo bull (also: male deer)
	mêmeshkomêhaki	young buffaloes, young horses

build	**ashikêwa**	builds a house
	ashikawêwa	builds a house for s.o.
	kîshikêwa	finishes building a house
	kîshikawêwa	finishes building a house for s.o.
	nâpikêwa	builds in the same spot
bulge	**wîhkwêshkêwi**	it bulges out
	wîhkwêsêwa	bumps making a bulge
	kekyêchinîkwêshkêwa	one's eyes bulge out
bull	**kêkineshîha**	bull (of cattle)
bullfrog	**tôtôwa**	bullfrog
bullhead	**wâsesîha**	bullhead
bump (verb)	**pâkâhkwishinwa, pâkâhkwisenwi**	(animate, inanimate) bumps against an unyielding object; cannot get in (the house)
	pâkâhkotonêshinwa	bumps oneself on the mouth
	pâkikomêshinwa	bumps one's nose
	wîhkwêsêwa	bumps making a bulge
	âyâkwêshkâtîwaki	they are all bumping into each other
bump (noun)	**makwikenêwa**	has a bump on the forehead
	mamakoshkêwa	develops bumps
	mamakwipehkwanwa	has bumps on one's back
	mamakwîwa	makes bumps in the outside surface (as, of a bag or stomach) by moving around inside
bumpy	**mamahkyâwi**	it is bumpy
	mamahkânahkwatwi	there are clouds scattered here and there
bunch	**asipechênamwa**	carries it bunched up in the hand, carries a bunch of them
	âkwêchênamwa	carries a bundle or bunch of them (inanimate)
	âyâkwêyâwi	there is a bunch or mob
	pehkwahokowaki	they drift in a bunch, they (as, fish) swim in a bunch
	pehkwikâpâwaki	they stand close together
	pemâkwapiwaki (plural)	they sit together in a row (or rows) or in a bunch
	pemâkwasowaki, pemâkwatêwani	they (animate, inanimate) are sitting or lying in one place ({somewhere})
	pemâkwatôwa	puts them (inanimate) in one place ({somewhere})
bundle	**mîwashiweni**	pack, bundle carried on the back
	pehkwapichikani	bundle
	wîhkwêpichikani	bundle
	wîhkwêwanâni	bundle
	wîhkwêwanehkâni	bundle
	makapitêwi	it is tied in a large bundle
	makapitêwani	they are tied in a large bundles
	mamâkapitêwani	they are tied in a large bundles
	pehkwapitêwi	it is tied into a bundle
	wîhkwêpitêwi	it is bundled up
	wîhkwêwanehkêwa	makes a bundle (to be carried)
	wîhkwêwashiwa	has a bundle on one's back
	metâsôwane	ten backloads; ten bundles or sacks (of something)
bundle (sacred)	**mîshâmi**	sacred bundle, sacred pack, medicine bundle
	mîshâmêhi	small sacred bundle
	omîshâmiwa	has a sacred bundle
	omîshâmemêwa	has s.o. as a sacred bundle, has s.o. in a sacred bundle
	omîshâmetamwa	has it as a sacred bundle
	omîshâmemetamwa	has it as a sacred bundle
	omîshâmehkâsowa	claims (it) as one's sacred bundle, pretends (it) is one's sacred bundle

bur	**shakashkwa**	bur
burden	**nîshkihêwa**	is a burden to s.o. (to care for)
	nîshkâpatâniwa	is all decked out; is burdened, is burdened as one runs
burlap bag	**asapiwêkenwimôhi**	burlap bag ("gunny sack") (also **asapimôhi**)
burn	**ahkasowa, ahkatêwi**	burns up, it burns up
	ahkaswêwa, ahkasamwa	burns s.o., it up
	ahkasamawêwa	burns (it) up for s.o.
	ineswêwa, inesamwa	heats, burns, cooks s.o., it {so}
	pemetêwi	it continues to burn (through time)
	tanesowa, tanetêwi	(animate, inanimate) is burning or cooking, is burned, burned up, or cooked {somewhere}
	sahkasowa, sahkahtêwi	catches fire, burns; one's house burns down
	sahkahwêwa, sahkahamwa	sets fire to s.o., it
	châkeswêwa, châkesamwa	burns s.o., it up
	châkesowa, châketêwi	is burned up
	ahpesowa	burns along with (it)
	atosowa	burns oneself
	chîhchîkoswêwa	burns all of s.o.'s flesh off
	shîshîkwêhwêwa	pokes s.o. in the face with a burning stick
	pekeshawatôwa	burns incense to it
	sahkahwêhtôwa	burns tobacco for it
	wâsikînehketêwi	it is burned to a point
burn (fire)	**aniweshêwi**	it burns, blazes big
	âhtêsenwi	it (fire) dies down
	inenêwi	it burns to {somewhere}, {so}
	ineshêwi	it (fire) burns, blazes {so}
	taneshêwi	it (fire) burns, blazes {somewhere}
burnt land	**wîhtêwahkiwiwi**	it is burnt-over land
burrow	**otânakwêwa**	has one's hole, burrow in {that direction}
burst	**nîhkasehkêwa**	(drum) has its drumhead burst
	pâshkechêhtamwa	bursts it open by biting it
bury	**kekishinwa**	lies having (it), is buried with (it)
	kîshishimêwa	buries s.o.; has laid s.o. away, out, in place
	mehtapihetîwaki	they bury each other out in the open in a sitting position
	nekwâmehkahwêwa	buries s.o. in soil
	pîtahwêwa, pîtahamwa	buries s.o., it
	pîtahotîwaki	they bury each other
	pîtahâsowa	is buried
busy	**otami**	taking time, spending time, being busy, occupied, preoccupied (preverb)
	wâwotami	taking the time to, wasting one's time (preverb)
	otamesiwa	is busy
but	**shewêna (shewê=)**	but, still (particle)
	ashewêna (ashewê=)	but, still (particle)
	ishewêna	but, still (particle)
	môhchi	even; but, anyway, in any case, at any rate (particle)
	=wîna	but, however, though you may not think so
butcher	**wînanihêwa**	cuts s.o. up, butchers s.o.
	ahpashkinanihêwa	butchers s.o. (animal) on leaves
	ahpashkinanishikêwa	butchers on leaves
butt in	**mêmêkwêshawi, mêmêkwêshawe**	out of turn as the first, butting in before anyone else, already prematurely
butterfly	**mêmêkêha**	butterfly
buttocks	**onowêtîki**	on his or her buttocks

	mamâkinowêtiyêwa	has big buttocks
	mehchinowêtiyênêwa	uncovers s.o.'s buttocks
	sakinowêtiyêhpwêwa	bites s.o. on the buttocks
	wâwâchitiyêshinôki	they lie buttocks to buttocks
button	sakâhkohôna	button
	sakâhkohôni	fastener (generic)
	sakâhkohamwa	nails it up, buttons it, pins it
buy	kashkihêwa, kashkihtôwa	gets, buys s.o., it
	kashkihtâtêwi	it is bought
	nâchinêhwêwa, nâchinêhamwa	buys him, it, ransoms him
	nâchinêhikêwa	buys (it)
	nâchinêhotisowa	buys one's own life, buys one's own release
	awiwêwa	buys (it) for s.o.

buzzard: → turkey vulture

c

cache	pechihtôwa	makes a cache (of supplies, equipment) for future use; caches (it, animate or inanimate)
cake	wîshkopi-pahkwêshikâhi	cake
calf	nenosôhêha	calf
calf of leg	nenâna	the calf of my leg (**onânani** his or her calf; **menâna** a calf)
call	inêwa, itamwa	calls s.o., it {so}; says {so} to s.o., it
	itâtêwi	it is called {so}
	itesowa	calls oneself {so}
	mâwachimêwa	calls them together
	mahwêmowa	calls like a wolf
	natomêwa, natotamwa	calls, asks for s.o., it
	wâwîtêwa	calls s.o. by name
call for	nanâtwêwêmêwa,	tries to make s.o. come by calling or wailing
calm	mahkwâchi	calmly, gently, quiet, quietly (particle, preverb, prenoun)
	mahkwâtâpôsenwi	the water is calm, quiet
	nehtâkyâwi	it is completely calm and quiet
	tepâhkiwiwi, tepâhkîwi	it (water) is flat calm (also: it is level land)
camel	mêkwisikîha	camel
camp	pônîwa	camps
	pônîhetîwa	makes a camp ({somewhere})
	pônîhetîwaki	they camp together ({somewhere})
	pônîhetêwi	camp is made, everyone camps
	pônînotawêwa, pônînotamwa	camps in with s.o., it
	mâwâkêwaki	they are in camp together
	inotêwa	moves camp to {somewhere}
	wêpotêwa	starts moving camp
cane	âpatahôni	cane
	âpatahowa	walks with a cane
canoe	chîmâni	canoe
	keki-chîmâne	including the canoe (particle compound)
	anakêweni	bark canoe
	kekônakapiwa	sits in a canoe
	nanâhônakisetâsowa	loads a canoe (or the like)
	nanâhônakishimêwa	puts s.o. in a box or canoe
	kôhkâwêwa	tips over in canoe

	pemahowa	paddles by in a canoe
capacity	tasôshkenêwa	holds {so much}, has {such} a capacity
captive	kîkênâwa	captive, prisoner of war
	kîkênâwiwa	is a captive
	pyênetîwekêwa	dances the victory dance (scalps or captives having been brought home)
	pyênetîwinâkêwa	sings victory songs (scalps or captives having been brought home)
capture	meshenêwa	captures s.o., catches s.o., arrests s.o.
	meshenahkyêwa	takes captives, arrests people
card	pîkîhiwa	plays cards
care about	mîhkwênemêwa, mîhkwênetamwa	(with negative:) does not care a bit about s.o., it, thinks nothing of s.o., it
	pwâwi-mîhkwênetâha kêkôhi	one who does not care about anything, has no regard for anything
	wîh=tôtawaki!?	What would I care about s.o.? Of what possible use is s.o. to me?
careful	wîkêchi	carefully, earnestly, completely, perfectly (preverb, particle)
	wîkêsiwa	is careful, attends to details, is precise, meticulous
	wîkêchiwetôwa	conducts it carefully
	wîkêtahkyêsetôwa	sets it (as, a bowl) squarely on the ground
	wîkêtakôtôwa	carefully hangs it up, carefully places it (arrow) in one's quiver
	wîkêtatawâpiwa	takes a careful look
	wîkêtâchimohêwa	carefully informs s.o., carefully explains to s.o.
	wîkêtenêwa, wîkêtenamwa	arranges s.o. with care; tidies it up, holds it in position
	kenâchi	slowly, carefully (particle)
	kenâchihtôwa	is careful with it, goes easy on it
	sasâkihêwa, sasâkihtôwa	is careful with s.o., it, keeps s.o., it ritually clean
	sasâkihowa	is careful with oneself, keeps oneself ritually clean
	sasâkihêweniwiwa	is treated carefully
careless	memyêshki	carelessly, messily, crossly (particle, preverb)
carry	kîwawiwêwa, kîwawiwa	has s.o., it with one, keeps s.o., it
	sôkenêwa, sôkenamwa	holds, carries s.o., it
	nîmahwêwa, nîmahamwa	sets or carries s.o., it on a stick, pole (or poles), or the like
	châkônêwaki	they all carry s.o.
	aniwashiwa	carries a heavy burden
	pîhtawiwetôwa	carries it as an extra supply
	wîhkwênêwa	carries s.o. in a blanket
	âshowânekoshkamwa	has it slung over one shoulder and under the other arm
	nîpikwitôshkwanâmêwa, nîpikwitôshkwanâtamwa	carries s.o., it on one's arm, in the crook of one's elbow
carry a load	owîwashiwa	carries a pack, a backload
	pematahokowa	goes by carrying (it as) a load on one's back
	ketatahokowa	emerges carrying (it as) a load on one's back
	pyêtatahokowa	comes carrying (it as) a load on one's back
	pyêtômâwasowa	comes carrying a baby on one's back
	pyêtôtashiwa	comes carrying a load on one's back
	wêpôtashiwa	starts to carry a load on one's back
	wêpatahokowa	starts to carry (it as) a load on one's back
	makinehpashiwa	has a load piled high on one's back
	chîkômyêhokowa	goes with (it as) a load sticking up on one's back
	ashiwanehkêwa	makes (it) into a bundle for a back-load
	nanâhiwanehkawêwa	arranges s.o.'s back-load for them

carry on	**inenekowa**	carries on {so}
carry on back	**nômêwa, nôtamwa**	carries s.o., it on one's back
	pemômêwa, pemôtamwa	carries s.o., it along on one's back
	ânôtamwa	is unable to carry it on one's back
	anemômêwa, anemôtamwa	carries s.o., it along on one's back
	awatômêwa, awatôtamwa	carries s.o., it off on one's back
	awatôtahêwa	makes s.o. carry (it) off on one's back
	awatôtamawêwa	carries (it) off on one's back for s.o.
	kîyômêwa, kîyôtamwa	carries s.o.,it about on their back
	inômêwa, inôtamwa	carries s.o., it on the back {so}, to {somewhere}
	mesômêwa	carries s.o. whole on back
	nâtômêwa, nâtôtamwa	goes to carry s.o., it on one's back
	têpôtamwa	is able to carry it on one's back
	wêpômêwa, wêpôtamwa	starts to carry s.o., it on one's back
	wêpôtîwaki	one of them starts carrying the other on their back
	wîhkwêyôtamwa	carries it on one's back in a blanket
	wîwahêwa	puts it (as, a blanket, a bundle) on s.o.'s back
	wîwahowa	puts (it) on one's back to carry
cast away	**mîwisahêwa**	casts s.o. away
cat	**kâshôha**	domestic cat
catbird	**mâmâtwêha, mêmâtwêha**	catbird
catch	**meshenêwa, meshenamwa**	catches s.o., it; arrests s.o., captures s.o.
	meshenamawêwa	catches (it) for s.o.
	nahkonamwa	catches it
	nâpehkwênêwa	catches s.o. by the neck
	sakânehkwêchinwa	gets one's hair caught
	têpehtawêwa	catches one's sound
catch eating	**mîhkôshkawêwa**	catches s.o. eating, arrives while s.o. is eating
catch in the act	**kêsehkawêwa**	catches s.o. in the act, catches s.o. still doing something
catch on	**otehchi-nepwêwa**	catches on
catch up: → overtake		
caterpillar	**kâhkâwahowêha**	fuzzy caterpillar, woollybear
catfish	**myânamêkwa**	catfish
	myânahîwa	catfish
	wâsesîha	bullhead
cattail	**apahkwaya**	cattail reed; cattail-reed mat
	apahkôhaya	small cattail-reed mat
	apahkwâhkêwa	makes cattail-reed mats
	apahkwayikâni	cattail-reed lodge
caul	**owîsi**	caul
	pôhkepyêkîwa	breaks through the caul
cause death	**panâchihêwa, panâchihtôwa**	ruins s.o., it; bewitches or puts a spell on s.o., it; causes s.o.'s death
cave	**wânakwi**	hole, cave; open grave
cease: → stop		
cease thinking	**pakisênemêwa, pakisênetamwa**	puts s.o., it out of one's thoughts
	pakitênemêwa	puts s.o. out of one's thoughts (rare)
cedar	**meshkwâwâhkwa**	cedar, redcedar
	papakâtakwa	cedar leaves
celebration	**mâmatânahkiwiwi**	there are lively doings, there is a celebration
	mâmatânahkiwihtôwaki	they have lively doings, a good time, a celebration
cent	**-mêshkwâpehkîhe**	(so many) cents (in particle compounds)
	nekoti-mêshkwâpehkîhe	one cent
centipede	**mâmânwikâtêha**	centipede

214

ceremony	**ishawiweni**	({such a} kind of) ceremony, activity, doing, experience, performance, way of life
certain	**mêmêchikesiwa**	makes certain
certainly	**=kohi**	certainly
chair	**ahpapîni**	chair, seat
challenge	**machinawêwa, machinamwa**	dares with regard to s.o., it, challenges s.o.
	machinâkêwa	challenges (**mêchinâkâta** the challenger)
	machinâhkwêwa	challenges (**mêchinâhkwâta** the challenger)
chance	**wêwênawi**	have a chance to (preverb)
	wêwênawihêwa, wêwênawihtôwa	has a chance at s.o., it
change (noun)	**êshkwisâchiki**	change (from a purchase)
change (verb)	**kohkeshkêwa, kohkeshkêwi**	changes, changes places, turns around; it changes, turns around
	kohkinâkosiwa	changes in appearance
	kohkitêhêwa	changes one's mind
	kohkîhtêwa	changes one's clothes
	kohkâpatâniwi	it changes its appearance
	kohkishimêwa, kohkisetôwa	changes s.o.'s, its position
	kokwêhkâpatamwa	sees it keep changing
	kokwêhkâpatânihtôwa	keeps changing its appearance
	kokwêhkinâkwatwi	it keeps changing in appearance
	kokwêhkinâkwihtôwa	makes it keep changing in appearance
	kokwêhkâmehkwisetôwa	keeps changing it as earth
	kokwêhkânehkwêsetôwa	keeps changing its (earth's) hair
chapped	**pâhpâshkinechêwa**	has chapped hands
	pâhpâshkitôtanwa	has chapped heels
charcoal	**kehkeshêwi**	charcoal
	kahkeshêwi	charcoal (rare)
	shîkwanêhtaki	what (the Fire Spirit) leaves unconsumed (ritual)
chase	**peminehkawêwa**	chases s.o.
	peminehkâkêwa	chases
	ashihwêwa	chases s.o. away, shoos s.o. away
	akôsînehkawêwa	chases s.o. climbing
	âchinehkawêwa	chases s.o. away, sends s.o. away
	âchinehkamawêwa	chases (s.o.) away for s.o.
	âchinehkamâtisowa	chases (s.o.) away for oneself
	ishinehkâkêwa	chases people to {somewhere}
	kechinehkawêwa	chases s.o. out
	ketâsînehkawêwa	chases s.o. up
	kîwinehkâtîwaki	they chase each other about
	kwâpinehkâtîwaki	they chase each other to scatter
	metâchinehkawêwa	pleasantly chases s.o.
	nâchinehkawêwa	chases, drives, or herds s.o. back, home
	nâkatônehkawêwa	chases s.o. along s.t.
	nowinehkawêwa	chases s.o. out
	pahkihtênehkawêwa	chases s.o. until they pass out
	pîchinehkawêwa	chases s.o. inside
	pyênehkawêwa	chases, drives, sends s.o. (this way, back) to {somewhere}
	tetepinehkawêwa	chases s.o. in a circle
	wêpinehkawêwa, wêpinehkamwa	begins to chase s.o., it
	wêpinehkâtîwaki	they begin to chase each other
chatter	**âtametonêmowa**	chatters away
cheat	**wanîkwênêwa**	cheats s.o. (out if it)

	waninêhwêwa	cheats s.o.
	ochîhkawêwa	goes after s.o. for something, cheats s.o. out of what is theirs
	kîmîhkâtîwa	has illicit sex, cheats on spouse
cheek	**nenowayi**	my cheek
	makwanowêwa	has a swollen cheek
	mamâkanowêwa	has big cheeks
	mâmahkatêwanowêpiwa	sits with blackened cheeks
Cherokee	**shanahkîha**	Cherokee (archaic)
cherry	**pehkiwêhi**	cherry
	nenôtêwi-pehkiwêhi	wild cherry
	pehkiwêhehkêwa	picks cherries
	pehkiwêhimishi	cherry tree
chest	**nehkâhki**	my chest (**ohkâhkeki** on his or her chest)
	kechihkâhkêpiwa	sits with the chest out
	ketakihkâhkêwa	(bird) has a spotted breast
chew	**shâshâkwamêwa,** **shâshâkwatamwa**	chews s.o., it
	shâshâkwêwa	chews (song word)
	takwatamwa	chews it together
	sheshekwatamwa	chews it to pieces
	tanwêwêhchikêwa	is audibly chewing or gnawing
chickadee	**kehchikânânâha**	chickadee
	kehchikânâha	chickadee
chicken	**pâkahâhkwâha**	domestic fowl; chicken, rooster
	pâkahâtîha	chicken
	pâkahâtîhêha	chicken
chief	**okimâwa**	chief
	okimâwiwa	is chief
	okimâwîhkâsowa	acts as chief, pretends to be chief
	okimâwihêwa	makes s.o. chief
	okimâwinohkatawêwa	is chief over them
	otôkimâmiwa	has a chief, has (s.o.) as a chief
	otôkimâmemêwa	has s.o. as chief
	otôkîhwâwani	their chief (**okîha** not used unpossessed)
child	**apenôha**	child
	netapenôhema	my own child
	apenôhiwa	is a child
	kekapenôhe	including the children (particle)
	nenîchânesa	my child; (of a man) the child of my brother or anyone else I call "brother"; (of a woman) the child of my sister or anyone else I call "sister," or of my father's sister
	nenîchânesêha	my child (dimin.)
	onîchânesiwa	has a child
	kekôshânêpiwa	she sits holding a child
chill	**tahkinawêshkawêwa**	(something ingested) gives s.o. a chill
chills	**nenekâpyêwa**	has chills, shakes with fever (**nenenekâpya** I have chills)
chin	**nîhkwi**	my chin (**owîhkwi** his or her chin; **kîhkwîki** on your chin)
chip	**pekonamwa**	chips it with one's hand(s)
	pekohamwa	pecks it, chips it with a tool
	pasanosiwa, pasanwâwi	has a chip out of it
	pasanotonwa, pasanotonêyâwi	(kettle) has a chip out of the rim, (dish) has a chip out of the edge
	pahkwêkahesâni	wood-chip

chipmunk	kwakwinôha	chipmunk
choke	nêkwamowa	is choking, has a tickle in the throat
	anahokowa	chokes on a fishbone
	kepishkwênotwa, kepishkwênatwa	chokes on something (and cannot breathe)
	kepinêwênêwa	chokes s.o. with the hands, strangles s.o.
	kepinêwêhpwêwa	chokes s.o. by biting
	pahkihtêpinêwa	chokes s.o. unconscious
choker	ketakinêwâkani	choker (neckpiece)
choose	wâwâpamêwa, wâwâpatamwa	selects s.o., it
	wâwâpachikêwa	chooses, makes one's selection
	wâwâpatahêwa	lets s.o. select, decide
	shîkônahwêwa, shîkônahamwa	chooses s.o., it, picks s.o., it out
chop	kîshahamwa	has chopped it, has cut it (as, wood)
	pahkahwêwa, pahkahamwa	chops through the rope holding s.o.; chops it through
	tanwêwêhikêwa	is heard drumming, pounding, or chopping ({somewhere})
	tashikahesêwa	is chopping wood
	pônikahesêwa	stops chopping wood
	mahkikwêhwêwa	chops s.o.'s head off
cigarette	oshimôkemiwa	has a cigarette, some cigarettes
circle	tetepi	in a circle (particle, preverb)
	tetepâkwapiwaki	they sit in a circle
	tetepâkwatôwa	places them in a circle
	tetepekêwa	dances in a circle
	tetepinâkêwa	circles singing
	tetepinehkawêwa	chases s.o. in a circle
	tetepiwenêwa	leads s.o. in a circle
	tetepipahowa	runs in a circle
	teteposêwa	walks in a circle
	teteposêhêwa	makes s.o. walk in a circle
	kîhkâwosêwa	circles around, walks in a circle or on a circular route
	kîhkâpahônekwiwa	circles around on horseback at a gallop
	wâwiyêwi	in a circle (particle, preverb)
clairvoyant	têpâpiwa	sees enough; is able to see (from distance or clairvoyantly)
	têpâpamêwa, têpâpatamwa	is able to see s.o., it (in the distance or clairvoyantly)
clan	mîsôni	name, clan (Michelson: "gens")
	wîchîsômêwa	has s.o. as fellow clan-member
	wîchîsôtîwaki	they are of the same clan
	ishi-wîsowa	is of {such} clan (îni êshi-wîsochiki ones of that clan)
	pehkînisowa	is of another clan
clan-feast	kîkênowa	gives, has a clan feast (Michelson: "gens-festival")
	kîkênowa	gives a clan feast with (it) as food
	kîkênôhiwa	gives, has a clan feast (dimin.)
	kîkênwihêwa	holds a clan feast over s.o.
	kîkênôni	clan feast
	kîkênoweni	clan feast
	kîkênowi	of a clan feast (prenoun), in a clan feast (preverb)
	kîshi-kîkênowênemêwa	thinks s.o. done with the clan-feast
	kîkênowapiwa	sits at the clan feast
clap together	wîpwisahowa	claps one's legs together
claw	neshkasha	my nail, my claw
	meshkasha	a nail, claw, hoof
	sâsâkikashêshkêwa	one's nails, claws come out
	papîsikashêwa	has small claws or hooves
	kakânwikashêwa	has long claws, nails

217

	ahkwâwinechâtamwa	has one's hands or claws full of it
	tâtwikashâtamwa	tears it with one's nail or claw
clay	wâpîwena	white clay (used for body paint)
clean	pîni	in a clean way (preverb)
	pînesiwa, pînyâwi	(animate, inanimate) is clean
	pînihêwa, pînihtôwa	gets s.o., it clean; keeps s.o. in clean clothing, keeps it clean
	pînihowa	makes oneself clean
	pînênemêwa, pînênetamwa	thinks s.o., it clean
	pînênetisowa	feels clean
	sasâkihtôwa	is careful with it, keeps it ritually clean
	sasâkihtâtêwi	it is kept ritually clean
	tatakwisetôwa	cleans it up (as, a yard, a house)
	wâhkami	clean, neat; completely (particle, preverb)
clear	mehchihêwa, mehchihtôwa	has an clear view of s.o., it; sees s.o. exposed
	tahpi-wâsêyâpôkatwi	the water is clear
clear away	tawenikêwa	clears things away
	tawâkonêshkânawêwa	clears a space in the snow with one's feet
	tawipekwêhikêwa	clears away the ashes (in the fireplace)
clearing	tawashkotêyâwi	there is a clearing
clever	nahîwesiwa	is clever, knows how
	nahowêwa	is clever at speaking or talking, says a clever thing
cliff	kîshkâpehkatenwi, kîshkâpehkatwi	it is a steep cliff
	kîshkâpehkatenwi, kîshkâpehkatwi	steep cliff
	kîshki-penekwâhkiwiwi	it is a steep overhanging cliff
	kîshkyâwi	there is a cliff
	shîkona	cliff, rocky precipice; whetstone
climb	akôsîwa	climbs
	akôsîsêwa	climbs fast
	akôsîyôtêwa	crawls climbing
	akôsînehkawêwa	chases s.o. climbing
	ahkwitâsîyôtêwa	climbs crawling up on top
	anemâsîwa	climbs along
	âshowâsîwa	climbs across
	ketâsîwa	climbs up (a hill)
	nîsâsîwa	climbs down
	penâsîwa	climbs down
	peshkwâsîwa	falls in climbing
	pyêtâsîwa	comes climbing
	pyêtâsîpahowa	comes climbing at a run
	tanâsîwa	climbs {somewhere}, is climbing
	wâwanâsîwa	is not good at climbing
	wêpâsîwa	starts to climb
clitoris	chîkashkôhi	clitoris
close	pepyêwi	(with negative:) not even close, not the least bit (preverb)
close (verb)	kepanohamwa	closes it (as, a container) with a lid
	kepanonamwa	closes it (as, a container) with the hand
	kepâhkohwêwa, kepâhkohamwa	locks s.o., it up; closes it up securely
	kepâhkonamwa	closes it
	kepwapitôwa	ties it closed
	kepetonêpinêwa	ties s.o.'s mouth closed
close eyes	kekyêpîkwêmowa	has one's eyes closed as one sings
closely	mînâwâpiwa	looks closely

closely packed	**sakwâkwasowaki**	they lie packed closely together
	sakwisenôni	they (as, houses) lie packed closely together
cloth	**papakiwayâhi**	cloth, piece of cloth (archaic)
	papakiwayâhêhi	piece of cloth (dimin.)
	pakiwayâhi	cloth, piece of cloth
	papakiwayânimotêhi	cloth bag
	shôshkwêkîhi	fine broadcloth
	shôshkwêkenwi	smooth cloth
clothe	**oshehkîhêwa**	clothes s.o.; adopts s.o.
	oshehkîhetîwaki	they clothe each other; adopt each other
	wîwenowa	covers one's nakedness
clothing	**oshehkîtâkani**	garment, clothing
	mahkatêwishehkîtamwa	wears black clothing
	myâshishehkîtamwa	wears shabby clothing
cloud	**menahkwatwi**	cloud
	nekwânahkwatwi	it is cloudy
	nêkwânahkwahki	cloud
	inânahkwatwi	the clouds are {so}, the sky is {so}
	mamahkânahkwatwi	there are clouds scattered here and there
	mahkatêwânahkwatwi	there are dark clouds
	nekotwânahkwatwi	the sky is uniformly cloudless or overcast
	pôsânahkwatwi	the clouds hang heavy
	wêwenahkwatwi	the clouds are beautiful
clown	**kêtakishehkîtâha**	clown
club	**pâpakamêwa**	clubs, beats s.o. to death
	pâpakatamawêwa	clubs (s.o.) to death for s.o.
	châkatahwêwa	clubs them all
	tanatahwêwa	clubs s.o. {somewhere}
	pehkwikîhi	knobbed war club, ball-headed war club
	papakehkôhi	flat ceremonial war club, gunstock war club
	wanâtesiwa	does not know what's what, is clueless
clump	**pehkwi**	in a clump (preverb)
coal	**pasâpehkwa**	coal; lump of coal
	pasâpehkwaki (plural)	coal
coals	**shîkwihkeshêwêshinwa**	(Fire Spirit) lies in the spent coals (as charcoal) (ritual)
coat	**kôti**	coat
	pîshâkanîhi	buckskin or leather coat
	opîshâkanîhiwa	wears a buckskin or leather coat
	wâpahtakawêwa	(animal) has a white coat
coax	**âshimêwa, âshotamwa**	coaxes, urges, tempts s.o., eggs s.o., it on; urges (it) on s.o.; urges it, advises it
	âshimetîwaki	they coax each other
cocklebur	**shakashkwa**	cocklebur
coffee	**kâhpîhi**	coffee
coil	**wâwiyâtepâpyêshinwa**	(snake) lies coiled up
cold	**tahkyâwi**	it is cold
	keki-tahkye	(while still) cold (particle compound)
	nepachiwa	is cold
	nepachikâwachiwa	has cold feet
	ânemachiwa	is extremely, dangerously cold
	nenyêhpachiwa	is numb and weak from the cold
	nenyêhpinehkêwachiwa	one's fingers are numb from the cold
	shîpachiwa	endures cold
	tahitanachiwa	is cold all the while ({somewhere})

	wîsakinakahkwêwachiwa	one's throat aches from being cold
collaborate	wîtôhkawêwa	helps, aids, collaborates with, allows s.o.
collapse	panâtesiwa	(wagon) collapses
	wawîhkwanisêwa	collapses to one's knees
	pâpakisapenêhtôwa owîyawi	makes oneself collapse from hunger
collarbone	pemitâhkwîhi	collarbone
collide	anemwêwêshkâtîwaki	they collide with noise
colored	inâsowa, inâtêwi	(animate, inanimate) is colored {so}
comb	penahâkani	comb
	penahâhkwêwa	combs one's hair
	penahâhkwawêwa	combs s.o.'s hair
comb	shôshkohâhkwêwa	combs one's hair straight
	shôshkwahâhkwêwa	combs one's hair straight
come	pyêwa	comes, comes back
	pyêmikatwi	it comes
	pyêchipenowa	is coming, has started on the way
	pyêchi	coming to, come and, coming or facing this way; have been (up to now); next in past succession (preverb)
	pêpyêchi	coming repeatedly to (preverb)
	pyêchihêwa	comes, comes back {some way}
	pyêchimêwa	makes s.o. come by singing, talking, or crying
	nâtwêwêkahwêwa	makes s.o. come by drumming
	pyêchikawiwa	comes this way as a group
	pyêchikawihêwa	comes at the head of the group of them
	pyêtanahkeshkamwa	comes out the top end of it
	pyêchisêwa, pyêchisêwi	flies this way; the time comes
	pyêtâshkêwa, pyêtâshkêwi	comes rushing, falls or speeds this way; it falls or speeds this way
	pyênotawêwa, pyênotamwa	comes to s.o., it
	pyêsehkêwi	it comes, the time (for it) comes
	pyêtashiwa	comes with a load of game
	pyêtehkwêmowa	comes seeking help or advice
	pyêtwêwêshinwa, pyêtwêwêsenwi	comes with noise
	pyêchiyâhtêwi	the smell of cooking wafts this way
	mayâshkawêwa, mayâshkamwa	comes directly to s.o., it, encounters s.o., it
come back	âpi-chîpêwa	comes back from the dead (ritual)
come from	ochîwa	comes from {somewhere}
	ochîmikatwi	it comes from {somewhere}
	osehkêwa	comes from {somewhere}
come out	nowîwa	comes out, goes out
	kesehkêwi	it comes out, comes into view; (eye) bulges out
	akwâpyêkîwa	comes ashore, comes out of the water
come upon	pakameshkawêwa	comes upon s.o., comes to s.o.
comfortable	wîkêtapiwa	sits comfortably, adopts a comfortable position in one's seat
	wîkêchishinwa	lies comfortably, carefully; settles into position lying
command	neshiwimêwa	has commanding power over s.o., overcomes s.o. with words
commission	mechichimêwa	commissions s.o.
commissioner	kamishinêha	commissioner
compassion	ketemâkênemêwa, ketemâkênetamwa	has compassion for s.o., it; thinks s.o., it is wretched
compete	anîhwêwa	competes against s.o., tries to beat or outdo s.o.
complete	kehpetawi	whole, complete, in full number (particle)
	kehpetawâpitêwa	has a full set of teeth
	mamînâwâchimowa	gives a complete and detailed account, explanation, or answer

220

	mamînâwâchimohêwa	gives s.o. a complete and detailed account, explanation, or answer
	tepihkamêwa	has a complete smoke, the full amount of smoking
	tepihkesowa	has a complete smoke, the full amount of smoking
	wâhkami	clean, neat; completely (particle, preverb)
compliment	wawînwânêwa	compliments, praises s.o.
conceal	wanîpahêwa	avoids being found by s.o., gets away from s.o. by concealment
conceited	âtamênetisowa	thinks more of oneself than of anything else
concerned	wîshâwitêhêwa	is anxious, concerned
	otehtênemêwa, otehtênetamwa	worries about s.o., it; is concerned about s.o., it
	otehtênetamawêwa	does not want s.o. to have (it)
conclusion	mêmechinêhiweni	last thing, conclusion
conduct	peshikwiwetawêwa	conducts it straight for s.o.
	menwiwetôwa	conducts it well
	peshikwiwenêwa, peshikwiwetôwa	conducts s.o., it straight
	wîkêchiwetôwa	conducts it carefully
	pakishiwenêwa, pakishiwetôwa	conducts s.o., it to freedom; sets s.o., it down
coneflower	shîkâwîhi	purple coneflower
confident	kînâkwi	freely, confidently, without worry (particle)
	mêkwêwâpatâniwa	presents a confident sight
confused	wâwanâchi	confusedly, with confused excitement, all over the place, at a loss for what to do (particle, preverb)
	wanâtesiwa	does not know what's what, is clueless
	wâwanênemêwa, wâwanênetamwa	fails to know s.o., it, forgets s.o., it; loses one's mind, cannot think straight, is at one's wit's end
conjure	manetôhkâsowa	conjures, calls up one's spiritual power
consciousness	panênetamwa	loses consciousness
consent	anwâchîwa	consents, is willing
	anwâtênemêwa, anwâtênetamwa	consents to s.o., it, is willing with regard to s.o., it
consider	ahpîhtênetâkwatwi	it is considered {so much}
	mamînâwinawêmêwa	makes s.o. consider carefully by speech
console	wawîkihêwa	consoles s.o., placates s.o., cheers s.o. up
constantly	sekihkatami	constantly, all the time; (with negative) seldom (particle)
	ahpîhchi	as one goes along, in the meantime, repeatedly, constantly, gradually (preverb, particle)
constipated	kashketiwa	is constipated
constitution	shîpinokêwa	has a hardy constitution
	nôhkinokêhiwa	has a weak constitution
container	kekisenwi	it is in (it as) a container
	kekisetôwa	puts it in a container, has it in a container
content	têpênemêwa	is content about (what happened to) s.o. (as, thinking it was deserved), does not feel sorry for s.o.
contest	âyânîhotîwaki	they have a contest
	mâmânetîhiwaki	they have a contest
	atôwâhiwaki	they have a contest shooting at wads of bark thrown in the air
	meshkwêhpîhiwaki	they have a contest throwing the throwing-stick
	tôpâkâhiwaki	they have a contest shooting at hoops
continue	anemi	away, continuing, along, on down the line, in time (preverb)
	ayêshi, ayîshi, ayêhi	keep on, still, yet, remaining, continue to (preverb, particle)
	mêchimôwi	committed to continuing, irreversibly (preverb)
	shîpi	continuing a long time (preverb)
contrariwise	âshakachi	contrariwise, the other way around instead, with roles reversed (particle)

contrary	**âshkâchi**	contrary, in a contrary way (preverb)
	kîhkîhkesiwa	is contrary
	kîhkîhkinawêhtôwa	is contrary with s.o., it, defies the wishes of s.o., it
control	**wêwênênemêwa, wêwênênetamwa**	has control over s.o., it, is in charge of s.o., it; has the say
	wêwênênetamwihêwa	lets s.o. have their own say, lets s.o. choose
	wêwênênetisowa	has control over oneself
	tepênemêwa, tepênetamwa	owns, controls s.o., it
	tepênetâtêwi	it is owned, controlled
converse	**kakanônetîwa**	converses (with s.o.)
	kakanônetîhêwa	converses with s.o.
convey	**nowiwenêwa**	conveys s.o. out
	wêpiwenêwa, wêpiwetôwa	starts to convey s.o., it
cook	**wachâhowa**	cooks (it)
	wachâhêwa	cooks (it) for s.o.
	wachâhetisowa	cooks for oneself
	wachâhetîwaki	they cook for each other
	wachâhetîweni	cooking, preparation of feasts for each other
	wachâhôhkânowa	plays at cooking
	wachânotêwa	cooks for people
	ahpîhtetêwi	it is cooked {so far}
	asâmesowa	is cooked too much
	ineswêwa, inesamwa	heats, burns, cooks s.o., it {so}
	kekenesamwa	cooks it fast
	kîsheswêwa, kîshesamwa	cooks s.o., it done
	kîshesamawêwa	cooks it done for s.o.
	kîshesowa, kîshetêwi	(animate, inanimate) is cooked done
	menosowa, menotêwi	(animate, inanimate) is cooked nicely
	nanâheswêwa, nanâhesamwa	attends to s.o.'s, its cooking, prepares s.o., it (by cooking)
	nepiswêwa, nepisamwa	cooks s.o., it well done
	nepisowa, nepihtêwi	(animate, inanimate) is cooked well done
	nôhketêwi	it is cooked soft, tender
	nôhketêhiwi	it is cooked soft, tender (dimin.)
	takoswêwa, takosamwa	cooks s.o., it along with (it)
	takosowa	is cooked with (it)
	taneswêwa, tanesamwa	cooks s.o., it {somewhere}
	tanesowa, tanetêwi	(animate, inanimate) is burning or cooking, is burning or cooking {somewhere}
	wîkêtesamwa	cooks it carefully
	wîkêtetêwi	it is carefully cooked
	ahpîhtesêhkwêwa	one's cooking progresses {so far}
	akosêhkwêwa	has one's cooking stick
	kîshesêhkwêwa	finishes cooking
	metêwesêhkwêwa	cooks for the Midewiwin
	nahesêhkwêwa	knows how to cook
	nanâhesêhkwêwa	attends to one's cooking
	wîkesêhkwêwa	cooks good-tasting food
	kîshesikêwa	finishes cooking things
	menosikêwa	cooks well
	nanâhesikêwa	attends to the cooking
cooked food	**kîshetêwi**	cooked food
	nekîshetêmenâni	our (offering of) cooked food
cool	**tahkyâhiwi**	it is a little cool
	tahkâshinwa	cools off in the breeze
	tahkisenwi	it is cool, is left to cool, cools off

	tahkahwêwa, tahkahamwa	cools s.o., it off (by fanning)
	tahkawishinwa	cools off (by getting wet)
	tahkikâwawishinwa	cools one's feet in water
	inachimêwa	cools, freezes s.o. {so}
cooperate	**wîtôhkawêwa**	helps s.o., aids s.o., collaborates or cooperates with s.o.
	wîtôhkâtîwaki	they help each other, join together, cooperate
cord	**tetepahtakîhi**	cord
	sînahtakîwa	makes a leather cord by rolling together strips of hide
corn	**atâmina**	corn plant, corn
	atâminêha	kernel of corn
	mesîkwa	dried, shelled corn (generic)
	mesîkwaki (plural)	dried, shelled corn (usual term)
	mesîkôhaki (plural)	dried, shelled corn (dimin.)
	mesâhkwa	ear of corn
	ketasâni	parched corn (ground fine); parched-corn mush
	pâkosôha	roasted dried corn
	pîsîkwêha	small kernels separated out of dried corn
	wâpimina	white corn
	wîshkopimina	sweet corn
corncake	**papakenâwa**	corncake
corncob	**owîpashkwa**	corncob
	owîpashkwi	of corncob (prenoun) (**owîpashkwi-nîchâpa** corncob doll)
corner	**sîkêyâwi**	there is a corner or bend
	mayâwi-sîkêyâwe	right at the bend (particle compound)
	sîkêyâhkwâwi	corner of a forest, where a wooded area comes to a point
	wîpwinehkawêwa	chases s.o. into a corner, a narrow place
corn mush	**takwahâni**	corn mush (ground dried corn boiled)
cornstalk	**sîpwâkana**	cornstalk
corn-tassel	**owanahkwa**	corn-tassel
corresponding	**ayâwi**	respectively, correspondingly (preverb)
cotton	**papakiwayâhêhi**	a bit of cotton cloth
cottonwood	**mîtwîwa**	cottonwood; quaking aspen
	mîtwîwiwa	is a cottonwood
cough	**sesotamwa**	coughs
	wînihpanêwa	has a phlegmy cough
council	**tepowêwa**	holds council
	tepimêwa	discusses s.o. in council
	tepowânêwa, tepowâtamwa	debates over, decides about s.o., it in council
	tanowêwa	discusses {somewhere}
council-house	**tepowêwikâni**	council-house
councilman	**tepowênenîha**	councilman
count	**akimêwa, akitamwa**	counts them
	akitâsowa	counts, is counting
couple	**inenehkwêwânetîwaki**	they go as a couple to {somewhere}
court	**mîhkemêwa**	he courts her
	mîhketamawêwa	he courts (her) of s.o.
	mîhkemâsowa	she is courted
	mîhketîwa	courts or is courted, makes out
	mîhkemetîwa	courts or is courted, makes out (less common)
	mîhketîwaki	they court (for marriage)
	mîhketîwi	in a courting way (preverb)
	mîhketîweni	courtship
	mîhketîwitêhêwa	he thinks of courting
	mîhkemêwitêhêwa	thinks of courting (s.o.)

	mîhkemehkwêwêwa	he courts a woman
	mîhkemehkwêwêwitêhêwa	he thinks of courting women
	mîhketîwênemêwa	he thinks of her for courtship
	meshoshkêwa	is smitten, is in love, is courting; is smitten with (s.o.), is courting (her)
	nôtehkwêwêwa	he sneaks in with a girl at night for courtship
	sakenêwa	he detains her to court her
	sakenehkwêwêwa	he detains a girl or woman to court her
	tashîhkâtîwa	tries to persuade; courts (before or outside marriage)
	wêpîhkâtîwaki	they start having to do with each other, start courting
cover	**matakohwêwa, matakohamwa**	covers s.o., it with something (also **mâtak-**)
	matakohowa	covers oneself (also **mâtak-**)
	matakohokowa	is covered over by something
	matakwishinwa	lies covered up
	akwanahwêwa	covers s.o. (as, with a blanket)
	akwanahowa	covers oneself (as, with a blanket)
	matakwâmehkahwêwa, matakwâmehkwatôwa	covers s.o., it with earth (also **mâtakw-**)
	nekoshkamwa	covers it over by foot, kicks it over (as, tracks)
	akwiwa	covers oneself with (it, a blanket or robe)
	akwihêwa	covers s.o. with (it, a blanket or robe)
	anâshkahamwa	spreads it as matting or undercloth (to sit on or to put something over)
	ohkonêhêwa	puts a blanket over s.o.
	kepenowa	she covers herself with her hand
	wîwikenwi	it is covered, has a covering
cover head	**matakôhkwêhowa**	covers one's head
	mâtakôhkwêhowa	covers one's head
	matakôhkwêshinwa	lies with covered head
	wîwitepêpisowa	has (it as) a covering tied on one's head
cover mouth	**kepetonênêwa**	covers s.o.'s mouth with one's hand, holds s.o.'s mouth closed
	kepetonênowa	covers one's mouth with one's hand
covers	**pâhkakonêwa**	takes the covers off s.o.
	pâhkakoshênowa	throws off the covers
	wîkêtakoshêhowa	fixes the covers on oneself
cow	**nenoswa**	cow, ox, steer; buffalo (ceremonial, older usage)
crab apple	**nenôtêwi-meshîminêha**	crab apple
crack	**pâshkyâwi**	it is cracked, burst open, has a crack
	pâshkyêwakeshkêwi	its surface cracks apart
	pâshkenamwa	breaks it, cracks it open (as, an egg in the hand)
	pâshkahwêwa, pâshkahamwa	cracks s.o., it open
	tanwêwêtepêhwêwa	is cracking s.o.'s skull with noise
cradle-board	**tehkinêwa**	puts s.o. on a cradle-board
	tehkisowa	is on a cradle-board
	tehkichikêwa	she puts her baby on a cradle-board
	tehkinâkani	cradle-board
	têhkinâsôha	baby on a cradle-board ("cradle baby")
	nâwîkwêhôni	cradle-board bow
cramp	**atâhkwêpisowa**	has cramps
	pîshkyêwêwa	one's muscles become tired, cramped
cranberry	**pôhkimini**	cranberry
crane	**atechâhkwa**	crane (probably generic but especially sandhill crane)
	wâpitenâhkwa	whooping crane

	wêtepîwa	"crane" (Jones) (perhaps specifically sandhill crane)
crash	wîsakwêwêkatwi	there is a loud crash (as, of thunder)
	wâwîsakwêwêkatwi	there are loud crashes (as, of thunder)
crayfish	ashâhkîwa	crayfish
crawl	pemôtêwa	crawls by
	anemôtêwa	crawls along, away
	inôtêwa	crawls to {somewhere}
	ketôtêwa	crawls out
	kîyôtêwa	crawls about
	pîtôtêwa	crawls in
	tanôtêwa	crawls {somewhere}
	wêpôtêwa	starts crawling
	ahkwitâsîyôtêwa	climbs crawling up on top
	akôsîyôtêwa	crawls climbing
	akwâyôtêwa	crawls out of the water
	ketâsîyôtêwa	crawls uphill
	pashkitôtêwa	crawls over the top
	tahkamôtêwa	crawls across an open space
crazy	wêpesiwa	is crazy
	wêpesîhiwa	is crazy
	wêpesîhiwiwa	is crazy
	wêpesîhihêwa	makes s.o. crazy
Creek	mâshkôha	Creek (Indian)
cricket	tôtôsiwa	cricket
cripple	myâhkenawêwa	cripples s.o. by shot
	myâhkeshkawêwa	cripples s.o. by foot or body
crippled	myâhkesiwa	is crippled
	myâhkesowa	is crippled by gunshot
	nenyêhpesiwa	is crippled; is weak, has trouble moving or doing anything
criticize	mâchîhkawêwa	is after s.o. (as, criticizing or forcing s.o.)
crooked	wâkikenwi	it is crooked
crop	nîpetesiwa	garden crop; Harvest Spirit
	nîpeni-wîseniweni	ripe garden crops (as food)
	nîpenîseniweni	ripe garden crops (as food)
cross	tahkamîwa	crosses an open space
	âshôhkamwa	crosses it (as, a stream)
	kohkahamwa	crosses it (as, a bridge)
cross-belt	âshowânakohamwa	wears it as a cross-belt
	âshowânekohamwa	wears it as a cross-belt
crosswise	pemichikapitôwa	ties it (as, a stick) crosswise or to one side
	pemichikapitêwi	it (as, a stick) is tied crosswise
crotch	wêchi-nasawikichi	in one's crotch (oblique participle)
	êh=nasawikichi	in one's crotch (locative participle)
	êhkwinasawanahkesichi	as far as one's crotch (oblique participle)
crouch	wêpôtêpahowa	starts running in a crouch
crow	kâkâkiwa	crow
crowd	nôneshkawêwa	crowds s.o. out (taking up their space)
	nôneshkâtîwaki	they crowd in taking up all the room
	nôneshkamâtîwaki	they are overcrowded
	nîshkehkawêwa	crowds s.o., is in s.o.'s way
	pîkwikâpâwaki	they stand all crowded together
cruel	asâmihêwa	is too cruel or mean to s.o., goes too far mistreating s.o.
crumble	pekihkenêwa, pekihkenamwa	crumbles s.o., it
	pekechênamwa	crumbles it

	pekâchênamwa	crumbles it
crunch	kâhkâwamêwa, kâhkâwatamwa	crunches s.o., it up with one's teeth
crush	shekohwêwa, shekohamwa	pounds s.o., it to pieces
	shekoshkamwa	crushes it by one's weight
	shekwatamwa	crushes it up in one's mouth
	shekwiponêwa	crushes s.o. (as, green corn) to pieces
	sheshekwinanêwa	crushes s.o. to pieces
	shekopyênêwa, shekopyênamwa	squishes s.o. (as, an insect), it by hand, mashes s.o., it up
	shekochêhokônêwa	lets or has s.o. be crushed to a pulp by (it)
cry	mayôwa	weeps
	chêchêkwa	screams, cries out
	anemômowa	goes along weeping
	chêchêkipahowa	runs crying
	chêchêkesowa	cries out from being burned, heated, or scalded
	inahômowa	gives {such} a cry
	ohkonêmowa	cries while wearing a blanket (song word)
	pôswêkesiwa	cries hard, cries louder
	pyêtwêwêkesiwa	comes crying
	tanwêkesiwa	cries {somewhere}
cry out	tanwêwêkihêwa	makes s.o. cry out, yelp, squeal ({somewhere})
cry-baby	kîhkîtwêwa	is a cry-baby
cub	mahkôha	bear cub
cuckoo	penêhtôwa	cuckoo, "rain crow"
cud	shêshêwiketonwa	chews the cud
cupping horn	sîpachikani	cupping horn (used in blood-letting)
cure	nêsêhêwa	cures s.o.
	nêsêhetîwaki	they cure each other
	nêsêhtawêwa	cures (s.o.) for s.o.
	nêsêmikihtawêwa	cures (it) for s.o.
	nêsêweni	cure, recovery
	nêsêwitêhêwa	thinks oneself cured, safe
curlew	mashkotêwêtowêha	curlew
curl up	pepyêhkwishinwa	lies there curled up, doubled up
	pepyêtekwishinwa	lies curled up
	wâkechêshinwa	lies curled up
curtain	kashkishkapisowa, kashkishkapitêwi	(animate, inanimate) is curtained off, separated by hanging robes or blankets
curved back	shâshakesiwa, shâshakyâwi	(animate, inanimate) is sway-backed, curved (back)
custom	ishêwîweni	custom
	ishêwîweniwiwi	the custom is {so}
cut	kîshkeshwêwa, kîshkeshamwa	cuts s.o., it off
	kîshkeshâtêwi	it is cut off
	kîshkahamwa	cuts or chops it (off), gets it by cutting or chopping
	ahkoshamawêwa	cuts (it) {so long} for s.o.
	aneshamawêwa	cuts (it) ready for s.o.
	kîshkeshêshwêwa	cuts off s.o.'s ear
	kîshkikwêshwêwa	cuts off s.o.'s head
	kîshkinehkêshwêwa	cuts off one's hand
	mahkeshamwa	cuts it off (as, something attached)
	mameshamwa	cuts it off
	pahkeshamwa	cuts it (something stringlike), cuts it loose, cuts the cord holding it
	pahkeshamawêwa	cuts (it) for s.o.
	pahkwêshamawêwa	cuts a slice of (it) from s.o.

	pehteshowa	accidentally cuts oneself
	pôhkeshwêwa, pôhkeshamwa	cuts a hole in s.o., it
	pahkwêshwêwa	cuts a slice from s.o.
	pekihkeshwêwa, pekihkeshamwa	cuts s.o., it to bits
	taneshamwa	is occupied in cutting it
	wâhkanakikeshamwa	cuts the bark from it
	wêpinanihêwa	begins to cut s.o. up, butcher s.o.
	wînanihêwa	cuts s.o. up, butchers s.o.
	wînanesiwa	cuts up meat
cute	peshekênemêwa, peshekênetamwa	thinks s.o., it cute
	peshikênetamwa	thinks it cute
	peshikâchinâkosiwa	looks cute
cut loose	pahkeshkêwa	is cut loose; is set free
cut open	pâshkechêshwêwa, pâshkechêshamwa	cuts s.o., it open
	tâtoshwêwa	cuts s.o. open

d

daddy longlegs	mênâkochêha	daddy longlegs
dam	kepenikani	dam
dance	nîmiwa	dances
	nîmihêwa	makes s.o. dance, has s.o. dance
	nîmihetîwaki	they have a dance together
	nîmihetêwi	there is a dance
	nîmihiwêwa	makes people dance, has people dance, gives a dance for people
	nîmiwi	of dancing (prenoun)
	nîmihetîwi	of dancing (prenoun)
	nîmihiwêwa	makes people dance, gives a dance for people
	nîmihchikêwa	gives a dance
	nîmihkawêwa, nîmihkamwa	dances for s.o., it; dances over s.o., it
	nîmîhtamwa	dances on it
	nîmihkamêkêwa	dances smoking
	ahpîhtekahowa	dances {so much}
	aniwekêwa	dances very well
	asipehkwêkêwaki	they dance with heads together
	inâsamekêwa	dances facing {some way}
	ishitêhêkêwa	dances with {such} thought
	kekekêwa	dances having (it)
	kekômyêkêwa	dances with (it) on one's back
	kîwekêwa	dances around
	mehtanasitêkêwa	dances barefoot
	myânekêwa	dances poorly
	nîkânekêwa	leads in the dance
	opyênekêwa	dances slowly
	otekêwa	dances on {such} side
	pahkihtêkêwa	dances oneself to exhaustion or death
	pemekêwa	dances past
	pônekêwa	stops dancing
	sînepyêkêwa	drips from the effects of dancing
	tanekêwa	dances {somewhere}

	tahitanekêwa	continues to dance
	tahitanekahtôwa owîyawi	joins in the dance ({somewhere})
	tetepekêwa	dances in a circle
	wâwanekêwa	does not know how to dance
	wâwaneshkâhekêwa	dances wickedly
	wêpekêwa	starts to dance
	wîtekêmêwa	dances with s.o.
	nenoswekêwa	dances the Buffalo Dance
	kâkâkiwekêwa	dances the Crow Dance
	shâwanôwekêwa	dances the Shawnee Dance
	shâwanôwiwa	dances the Shawnee Dance
	êhêwekêwa	dances the Swan Dance
	pyênetîwekêwa	dances the Victory Dance (scalps or captives having been brought home)
danger	**konakwiwenêwa**	leads s.o. through danger
dangerous	**neshiwesiwa**	is dangerous, fierce, mighty, powerful
	neshiwâwi, neshiwatwi	it is dangerous
	neshiwîhkânowa	is doing a dangerous thing
	âhkwi	dangerously, sharply, (of perception) plainly (preverb)
	âhkwatwi	it is dangerous, it is painful
	koshkoshkwâtotamwa	reports it to be potentially dangerous
	nêsemênâkwatwi	it looks dangerous, potentially a mortal danger
	nêsemêwênetâkosiwa	is considered a potential mortal threat
dangle	**wêwêpikâpiwa**	sits with one's legs dangling
dark	**pehkotêsêwi**	it suddenly gets dark
	kîshkapehkotêyâwi	it is dark (in a place)
dart	**nâneshkwêpochîhi**	dart
daughter	**netânesa**	my daughter (**otânesani** his or her daughter); (of a man) the daughter of my brother or anyone else I call "brother"; (of a woman) the daughter of my sister or anyone else I call "sister," or of my father's sister
	otânesiwa	has a daughter; has (her) as a daughter
	otânesemêwa	has her as a daughter
	otânesemâwa	the daughter
	wêyôsita	the son or daughter (of a man), his son or daughter (see **ôsiwa**) daughter-in-law
	nesemya	my daughter-in-law (**osemyêni** his or her daughter-in-law)
	osemiwa	has a daughter-in-law; has (her) as a daughter-in-law
	nahâkanihkwêwa	daughter-in-law living with her in-laws
	nahâkanihkwêwiwa	she lives with her in-laws
dawn	**wâpanwi**	it dawns, is morning, is day (**wâpanôhiwi** dimin.)
	otâpanwi	dawn comes from {somewhere}
	pêkwâpanôhiwi	it is fully daybreak
	pyêtâpanwi	dawn comes
	wâsâpanwi	it is bright dawn
	wâpanemiwa	daylight overtakes one; lives till dawn
	wâpanwitêhêshinwa	lies thinking until dawn
day	**kîshekwi**	sky, day
	-kîshekatwi	it is a day (of such weather) (requires a preverb)
	menwi-kîshekatwi	it is a fine day
	menwikîshekatwi	it is a fine day
	wâsêyâwi	it is daylight
	wâsêyâwi	day, daylight
	âpehtawi-wâsêyâwe	a half day (particle compound)

	nekoti-wâsêyâwe	for one day, in one day (particle compound)
	nîshwi-wâsêyâwe	for two days (particle compound)
	âyakwami-wâpanwe	day by day (particle compound)
	âyâshowi-wâpanwe	every other day (particle compound)
	nekotokoni	one day (particle)
	nîshokoni	two days (particle)
	nîshokonakatwi	it is two days
	nesokoni	three days (particle)
	nesokonakatwi	it is three days
	nesokonakesiwa	is three days old
	nyêwokoni	four days (particle)
	nyêwokonakatwi	it is four days
	nyêwokonêtwa	is away for four days
	nyânanokoni	five days (particle)
	nyânanokonakatwi	it is five days
	metâsokoni	ten days (particle)
	metâsokonakatwi	it is ten days
	tasokoni	{so many} days (particle)
	tasokonakatwi	it is {so many} days
	tasokonêtwa	is away {so many} days
	mânokoni	many days (particle)
	mânokonakatwi	it is many days
	nâhtasokoni	several days (particle)
	nâhtasokonakatwi	it is several days
	kêsokoneshkamwa	how many days does one go?
dead	chîpaya	corpse; ghost
	âpi-chîpêwa	comes back from the dead (ritual)
	chîpânâki	in the Land of the Dead (locative noun)
	nêpôha	dead one, dead person or animal
	kîwâkwasowa, kîwâkwatêwi	lies about (dead)
	nepôhkânowa	plays dead
	nepôwênemêwa	thinks s.o. dead
deadfall	kawishêwi	deadfall, a tangle of fallen timber and brush
deadfall trap	nîsamôhi	deadfall trap
	mehtekwi-nîsamôhi	deadfall trap
deaf	kekyêpeshêwa	is deaf
deal with	tashîhkawêwa, tashîhkamwa	is dealing with s.o., it
	tashîhkamawêwa	deals with (it) for s.o.
	ânwîhkawêwa	fails to deal with s.o.
	kashkîhkawêwa	manages to deal with s.o., succeeds with s.o.
	kîwîhkawêwa	goes about dealing with s.o., tags around after s.o.
	nîshôhkawêwaki, nîshôhkamôki	the two of them (anim.) deal with s.o., it, set upon s.o.
	wîkêchîhkawêwa, wîkêchîhkamwa	deals with s.o., it carefully
	wîkêchîhkâtêwi	it is dealt with carefully
	ânohamwa	fails to deal with it by tool
	kashkahwêwa, kashkahamwa	manages to deal with s.o., it by tool
	otâhpenanêwa	deals with, kills s.o. because of (something)
death	nepôhkêwa	has a death in the family
	nepôweni	death
	pîkêpahowa	runs oneself to death
	kîwinêwa	is in one's death throes, thrashes about as one dies
	nesâsowa	is put to death
debt	pônikêwa	pays one's gambling debt
decay	châkeshkêwi	it (tooth) decays, it (hair) falls out

deceive	**wanimêwa, wanotamwa**	deceives s.o., it, fools s.o.
	wanikêmowa	fools people, makes deceptive claims or statements
	pehchamêmêwa	deceives s.o., fools s.o.; has s.o. thinking the wrong thing by what one says
	pehchamêhêwa	deceives s.o., fools s.o.; makes s.o. think the wrong thing
	wanîkwêhêwa	deceives s.o.; tries to take (it) away from s.o. secretly
	kîmôchîhtawêwa	puts something over on s.o., acts stealthily undetected by s.o.
decide	**nanâhotamwa**	talks it over, decides it by deliberation
	nanâhotâtêwi	it is arranged or decided by discussion
	kîshimêwa	settles on a plan for s.o., promises s.o.
	kîshitêhêwa	has formed a plan, has made up one's mind
	kîshênemêwa	has formed a plan about s.o., has made up one's mind about s.o.
	kîshisenwi	it is decided
	kokwêtowêwa	tries to decide on a plan
	tepitêhêwa	is deciding, trying to figure out, considering what to do
decision	**kîshowânêwa**	declares a decision, plan, or promise for s.o.
	pahkowêwa	declares one's decision
decked out	**nîshkâpatâniwa**	is all decked out
declare	**inowêwa**	declares {so}
	inowêhiwa	declares {so} (dimin.)
	kîshowêwa	declares a decision or promise
	kîshowânêwa	declares a decision or promise for s.o.
	pakisâhkwimêwa	declares s.o. free, turns s.o. loose
	pahkowêwa	declares one's decision
decorate	**mîshâchihêwa, mîshâchihtôwa**	dresses s.o. up; decorates it
	mîshâchihchikêwêwa	decorates things with (it)
	ishihchikâsowa, ishihchikâtêwi	(animate, inanimate) is fixed up or decorated {so}
	wêwenihchikâtôwa	decorates it (as, with beads, ribbons)
	wêwenihchikâsowa, wêwenihchikâtêwa	(animate, inanimate) is decorated
	kwâhkwâpiwiwa, kwâhkwâpiwiwi	(animate, inanimate) is decorated with porcupine-quills
deep	**ahkwîtemyâwi**	it (water) is {so} deep
	kenwîtemyâwi	it (water) is deep
	kenwânakatwi	it is a deep hole
	nâmahkîki	deep in the ground (particle)
deeply	**kâhkâhki**	deeply (of pain, yearning) (particle)
deer	**peshekesiwa**	deer
	peshekisiwa	deer
	peshekesiwi	of deer (prenoun)
	peshekisiwi	of deer (prenoun)
	peshekesiwiwa	is or becomes a deer
	peshekisiwiwa	is or becomes a deer
	ayâpêwa	male deer, buck, stag; buffalo bull
	mâkinîha	young male deer
defeat	**anihêwa, anihtôwa**	defeats s.o., wins it
defecate	**mîsîwa**	defecates
	mîchinêwa, mîchitamwa	defecates on s.o., it
	mîchikwâmwa	soils one's bed
	mîsîwamatamwa	feels as if one is going to defecate
defend	**ochimêwa**	defends s.o., takes the side of s.o.
	otowêwa	stands up for (s.o.), defends (s.o.) verbally
	otahamêwa	stands up for (s.o.), defends (s.o.), protects (s.o.)
defiance	**kîhkîhki**	in defiance, insisting, all the same, undeterred (particle)

definite	**mêmêchikâchimohêwa**	gives s.o. definite instructions
deformed	**neshiwanâchikiwa**	is hideous, deformed
delicate	**nôshkinâkosîhiwa**	has a delicate appearance
	nôshkinameshkinâkosîhiwa	has delicate-looking skin
delightful	**mâmatâkwi**	how delightful, what a pleasure; as a pleasant surprise (particle, preverb)
demoralized	**neshiwanâchitêhêwa**	is demoralized
demur	**ânemwêwa**	nervously insists or demurs
dent	**konashkosiwa, konashkwâwi**	(animate, inanimate) has a dent or groove
deny	**ânohtawêwa**	fails to hear s.o., denies s.o.'s request
	ochimêwa	denies s.o. (it), refuses s.o. (it), opposes s.o. doing (it)
descend	**nîsênetamwa**	imagines it descending
deserted	**nasahtêwi**	it (as, a house) is deserted, there are no people about
	nasahtêwinâkwatwi	it (as, a house) looks deserted
desire	**ishitêhêweni**	desire
	akâwânêwa, akâwâtamwa	desires s.o., it
	akâwâtamâtisowa	desires (it) for oneself
despite	**kîhkîhkinotawêwa, kîhkîhkinotamwa**	acts in spite of s.o., it, defies s.o., it, keeps on despite s.o., it
destitute	**kwînatawi**	at a loss, destitute (preverb)
destroy	**neshiwanâchâwi**	it is destroyed, destructive
	neshiwanâtesiwa	is destroyed; takes it hard; is good-for-nothing
	neshiwanâchikenwi	it is evil, it is destroyed
	neshiwanâtahkiwiwi	the world is destroyed
	neshiwanâtahkamikatwi	the world is destroyed
	wîyashkihêwa	destroys s.o., spoils s.o.'s spiritual power
	châkeshkamwa	wears it out, kicks it to pieces, tears it up by action of the body
destruction	**neshiwanâtesiweni**	destruction
destructive	**neshiwanâchitanekowa**	does something wrong, destructive
	neshiwanâchîhkâsowa	does something terrible, wicked, destructive
detail	**mînâwesiwa**	is attentive to detail
	mamînâwesiwa	inquires closely, examines things in detail
	mînâwi	attentively, closely, in detail (particle, preverb)
	mamînâwi	in all parts or details, attentively, closely (particle, preverb)
deviate	**pyêmawiwa**	deviates (as, from what is expected)
	pyêminawe	off at an angle; halfway between (particle)
dew	**pâyôhkatwi**	there is a heavy dew
	nepiwashkatwi	the grass is wet
dictate	**ayâwi-ishimêwa**	dictates what to do to s.o.
diarrhea	**shâpôsiwa**	has diarrhea
	sîketiwa	has a watery bowel movement
dice	**kosikanaki**	dice (of the bowl-and-dice game)
die	**nepôhiwa**	dies
	nepwa	dies (older form)
	nepômikatwi	it dies
	châkinêwaki	they both or all die
	katawinêwa	almost dies
	kekeninêwa	dies fast
	manesenôwinêwa	dies in war
	shîpinêwa	takes a long time to die
	tahpenêwa	dies {somewhere}
	otâhpenêwa	dies because of {something}
	âhtêsenwi	it (fire) dies down

	pahkihtêkêwa	dances oneself to exhaustion or death
	pahkihtêshkêwa	vomits and retches to death; trembles to death
	pahkihtêwachimêwa	freezes s.o. to death
	pîkêshkêwa	vomits and retches to death; trembles to death
	pîkêtêhêwa	worries too much, worries or grieves to death
die away	**nênehkowêwa**	the sound of one's voice dies away
different	**pehki**	differently (preverb)
	pehkîni	differently (particle, preverb, prenoun)
	pehkiwa, pehkenwi	is different, is a different one, is an outsider
	pehkînikiwa, pehkînikenwi	(animate, inanimate) is different, changed, of a different nature
	pêpehkînikenôni	they (inanimate) are of different kinds, do not match
	pehkînawêwa, pehkînamwa	thinks s.o., it looks different, strange; (the other, it) does not look the same to one
	pehkîninâkosiwa, pehkîninâkwatwi	(animate, inanimate) looks different from before, looks strange
	pehkînâchimowa	gives a different report or message
	pehkînâpamêwa, pehkînâpatamwa	sees something different about s.o., it
	pehkînwâpamêwa, pehkînwâpatamwa	sees something different about s.o., it
	pehkînwênemêwa, pehkînwênetamwa	thinks there is something different about s.o., it, notices a change in s.o., it
	âchipîshi	different each time, a succession of different ones (particle)
	nâhka=kêhi	one after another, different (ones, places, ways) successively
difficult	**sanaki**	in a difficult way (preverb)
	sanakesiwa, sanakatwi	is difficult to get; it is difficult to get or do
	sanakihêwa, sanakihtôwa	makes it hard for s.o.; works hard at it, has trouble with it; has a hard time
	sanakimêwa	asks s.o. to do a difficult thing
	sanakinâkwatwi	it looks difficult, it looks impossible
	kîsâchi	in a bind, as a difficult obligation (particle, preverb)
	kîsâtesiwa, kîsâchâwi	has a difficult time overcoming or getting over something; it is hard to overcome or get over
	memyêshkanahamîwa	has difficult footing
	masâchi	barely, with difficulty (particle)
	sakâki	just barely, with difficulty (particle)
dig	**wânehkêwa**	digs, digs a grave
	wânehkâtamwa	digs a hole in it
	kîshânehkêwa	finishes digging
	pôhkânehkêwa	digs a hole through
	pôhkânehkâtôwa	digs it (as, a tunnel or burrow)
	môhkahwêwa, môhkahamwa	digs s.o., it up
	ketahwêwa, ketahamwa	digs s.o., it up, out
	ketahwêwa	digs Indian potatoes (**nîh=ketahwa** I'm going to dig Indian potatoes)
	ketahashkwêwa	digs herbs
	nôhkâmehkonikêwa	digs to make soft earth
dip	**chapôkenêwa, chapôkenamwa**	dips s.o., it in water
	kwâpahamwa	dips it up, out
	kwâpahamawêwa	dips (it) up for s.o.
	tashikomêsetôwa	dips its tip (as, of an arrow) {somewhere}

dip (noun)	**ashihpowa**	eats using (it as) a dip
dipper	**kwâpahikani**	dipper, ladle
dire straits	**ânemihêwa**	puts s.o. in dire straits
	ânemesiwa	is in a plight, in dire straits
direct	**nanâhotamwa**	directs it, manages it (as, a ceremony or activity); is in charge
	nênâhotâha	director of a ceremony, manager, one in charge
direction	**ochi**	in {such} direction (particle, preverb)
	ochîmêhi	a little ways {some way} (particle)
	wâwochi	repeatedly from {somewhere}, because of {some reason}, in {such} direction (preverb)
	otâhkwe	in {some} direction, on {such} side (particle)
	ênikâwi, ênikâwe	in opposite directions, on each side (particle)
	nenyêshkwi	in different directions (particle)
	payâhkichi	in another direction, in the wrong direction (particle)
	tepinâhi	in straight direction, directly opposite, above, or below (particle)
	waninawe	in all directions, on all sides (particle)
	nenyêshkwâsenwi	it blows in various directions
	pahkêwa	branches off, goes off in a different direction from the others, turns aside, gets off the road
directly	**kâhkami**	directly; from the very beginning (particle)
dirt	**shôshkwâwakeshkâtêwi**	the dirt on it (a road) was trodden smooth
dirty	**masakomiwiwa, masakomiwiwi**	(animate, inanimate) is dirty
	masakomiwâpôkatwi	the water is dirty
	wînesiwa, wînyâwi	(animate, inanimate) is dirty, filthy
	wînihêwa, wînihtôwa	makes s.o., it dirty, befouls s.o., it
	wînisetôwa	gets it dirty
	wînênemêwa, wînênetamwa	thinks s.o., it dirty, filthy
	wînepitiyêwa	has a dirty bottom
	wâwînishkîkwêwa	one's eyes are dirty with hardened tears
	wînasamwêwiyâkosiwa	reeks with dirty-dog smell
	wînasamwêwiyâkochêwa	one's body reeks with dirty-dog smell
	wînepinenyêhpwêwa	dirties her breasts by nursing
disappear	**akiwa, akenwi**	disappears
	nehkâpamêwa, nehkâpatamwa	watches s.o., it disappear from view
	nehkâpatâniwa	disappears from view
	nehkwêwêyâkêposowa	goes whizzing out of sight
disappoint	**pekishkinawêhêwa**	causes s.o.'s feelings to be hurt, disappoints s.o.
disapprove	**ânwênemêwa**	thinks ill of s.o., disapproves of s.o., dislikes what s.o. does
	ânwênetâkosiwa	is thought ill of, is disapproved of
discouraging	**shâkwênemowinâkwatwi**	it looks discouraging, it does not look promising
discovered	**=chîhi**	it was seen, discovered, found, learned
discuss	**tanowêwa**	discusses {somewhere}
	tanotâtêwi	it is discussed {there}
	tepimêwa	discusses s.o. in council
	nanâhimêwa	discusses, considers, judges s.o.; tells s.o. what to do, advises s.o., gives s.o. instructions
	nanâhowêwa	discusses the question; gives instructions, directs others
disease	**ahpenêweni**	disease
	ahpenêwenehkêwa	has a disease
	ahpenêwenehkêhêwa	causes s.o. to have a disease
	sanakâhpenêwa	has a serious disease or affliction
	pahkohikêwa	extracts a disease object (by traditional doctoring)

disgrace	**mêneshihêwa**	disgraces s.o.
dislike	**ânwênemêwa**	thinks ill of s.o., disapproves of s.o., dislikes what s.o. does
	ânwênetâkosiwa	is thought ill of, disapproved of
	myânênemêwa, myânênetamwa	dislikes s.o., it, does not like s.o., it; feels or becomes angry (over it), is dissatisfied (over it)
	myânâkômêwa, myânâkôtamwa	dislikes s.o., it; is not comfortable with s.o., it
	myânehtawêwa	does not like what one hears s.o. say
	myâhpamêwa, myâhpetamwa	dislikes the taste of s.o., it
	myâhpechikêwa	dislikes the taste of what one is eating
	neshiwanâtehtawêwa, neshiwanâtehtamwa	dislikes hearing s.o., it
	shîkênemêwa, shîkênetamwa	dislikes s.o., it, objects to s.o., it
	shîkênetâkaniwiwa	is generally disliked
disobey	**ânohtâkêwa**	mishears people, disobeys people
disparage	**shîkahamawêwa**	disparages (it) to s.o., warns s.o. sternly against (it)
	tanotamwa	talks about it ({somewhere}); says (bad) things about it
disrespectful	**wapasênemêwa**	is disrespectful of s.o., thinks s.o. foolish
	wâpasênemêwa, wâpasênetamwa	is disrespectful of s.o., it, thinks s.o., it foolish, has a flippant or mocking attitude (towards it)
	wapasehtawêwa	listens to s.o. disrespectfully
	wâpasehtawêwa	listens to s.o. disrespectfully
	wapasatamwa	eats it disrespectfully
	wâpasatamwa	eats it disrespectfully
disrupt	**wahpâhêwa**	disrupts s.o.'s sleep
dissuade	**kenahamawêwa**	forbids, dissuades s.o.
distance	**nâhinâhi**	(at) the time, distance (particle)
	chêchêwinâhi	both or all at the same time; at equal distances apart (particle)
	menwinâhi	some distance away, not far away; soon (particle)
	mêmenwinâhi	every little way, not great distances apart (particle)
	mesh-âyâninâhi	separated by a moderate distance or distances (particle compound)
	menw-âyâninâhi	a good distance from each other (particle compound)
	mêkwênâhi	quite a ways, a considerable distance (particle)
	nanôpehkâchinâhi	a great distance, a long period of time (particle)
	têpi-nâhinâhi	for long enough, far enough (particle)
	tâninâhi	at what distance? when? (particle)
	wâwaninâhi	(still) some distance away (particle)
	manahka	a distance off (particle)
distant land	**wâsahkamikôha**	person of a distant land (archaic)
distribute	**nîkenamwa**	distributes it, divides it up and passes it out
dive	**kotawîhtawêwa**	dives in after s.o.
	sîkomêhikanisahowa	dives in head-first (with one's arms over one's head)
diversion	**wani**	as a diversion, to forget one's troubles (preverb)
	wanîhkamêwa	passes the time (with a diversion, pastime, rainy-day activity)
	wanawosêwa (Jones)	walks to relieve one's mind of care
divide	**nîkahamâtîwaki**	they divide (it) up for each other
	nîkahamwa	divides it up
divorce	**peshekwâha**	divorced person
	peshekwâhiwa	gets divorced, is divorced
	peshekwâhiweni	divorce
	pakinêwa, pakitamwa	sets s.o., it down; throws s.o., it away; divorces s.o.
dizzy	**tetepashkwêwa**	is dizzy
do	**ishawiwa**	does, fares {so}

	ishihchikêwa	does things {so}
	inanohkyêwa	does things {so}
	menwawiwa	acts well, does well
	mamîkwâsowa	does one's best
	menwihchikêwa	does things well, does right
	menwinawêshkawêwa	goes through s.o. doing s.o. good
	pakôshêwîwa	does work in advance
	peshikwihchikêwa	does the right thing
	tananohkyêwa	is doing things, performing one's tasks
	tanyêwîwa	is doing something, is accomplishing something
	wînîhkâsowa	does a filthy thing
doctor	**mîhkechihêwa**	doctors s.o.
	mîhkechihiwêwa	doctors people
	mîhkechihtâkêwa	doctors (s.o.) for people
	nâtawihowa	doctors oneself
	sîsahkyêwa	performs as a sucking doctor
dog	**anemôha**	dog
	anemôhiwa	is a dog
	anemôhêha	puppy
	netaya	my dog, my horse, my pet
doll	**nîchâpa**	doll
	onîchâpiwa	has a doll
done for	**panâchi**	at the point of suffering one's fate or succumbing (preverb)
	panâchitêhêwa	thinks one is done for, one's heart sinks
	panâtesiwa	is about to succumb, is done for
door	**ashkwâtêmi**	door
	ashkwâtêmiwiwi	it has a door
	chîkishkwâte	by the door (particle)
	kepishkwâte	in the doorway (particle)
	ochishkwâte	at, by the door in {some} direction (particle)
	ochishkwâtawêwa	has one's door in {such} direction
	pyêchishkwâtawêsenwi	(house) lies with its door this way
	pâhkishkwâtawênamawêwa	opens the door for s.o.
door-flap	**kepishkwâtawêhôni**	door-flap
	okepishkwâtawêhôniwa	has a door-flap
dote	**mîhkwênemêwa**	dotes on s.o.
double	**pîhtôsenwi**	it is double
double up	**wâkechêsahowa**	doubles up quickly
dove	**manetômîmîwa**	mourning dove
down	**mehchîki**	down, to the ground, down on the ground (particle)
	mehchi	down, to the ground (with some verbs) (particle)
	mehchi pakinêwa	throws s.o. to the ground; he rapes her
	nâshîwa	goes down; becomes reduced in size
	nâshâshkêwa	flies down, flies downward
	nîsîwa	descends, comes or goes down, gets down
	nîsenêwa, nîsenamwa	lowers, sets down s.o., it
	nîsisahowa	jumps down
	nîsiwenêwa, nîsiwetôwa	takes, brings, or carries s.o., it down
	nîsehkwêsahowa	pulls one's head down quickly
	kawenêwa, kawenamwa	lays, pushes s.o., it down
downdraft	**anâhkohanwi**	there is a downdraft blowing back through the smoke hole
down-hearted	**shahkosiwa**	is drowsy, listless, weak, down-hearted
	shahkwîkwêpiwa	sits with a down-hearted look on one's face
downhill	**pânachîwa**	goes downhill, goes downslope

235

	pânachiwêpahowa	runs downhill
	pânachiwêsêwa	runs downhill
downstream	**anemyâka**	downstream, down the (railroad) line, east (particle)
dozen	**-tâshine**	(so many) dozen (in particle compounds)
	(nîshwi-tâshine two dozen)	
drag	**pemahônêwa, pemahôtôwa**	drags s.o., it along
	awatahônêwa	drags or hauls s.o. over (to somewhere)
	inahônêwa	drags s.o. to {somewhere}
	mîwahônêwa	drags s.o. away
	pakâhôtôwa	drags it under the water
	pîtahônêwa	drags s.o. inside
	akwâpyêhônêwa	drags s.o. out of the water
	ketahôtêwi	it is dragged out, it drags out, flows out solidly
dragonfly	**pîshkinâniwa, pîshkinânîha**	dragonfly
draw	**kîshepyêhwêwa, kîshepyêhamwa**	finishes drawing s.o., it
	anepyêhâtêwi	it is drawn, painted, diagrammed
	anepyêhwêwa	draws a picture of s.o.
	atâhpahwêwa	draws s.o. in
draw milk	**otatamwa**	(infant) draws the milk
dreadful	**neshiwâpatâniwa**	looks dreadful; looks terrific; is going fast
	wîyashkinâkwatwi	it (as, a cloud or water) looks dreadful
dream	**âhpawêwa**	dreams
	inâhpawêwa	dreams {so}
	matâkwâhpawêwa	has an enjoyable dream
	myânâhpawêwa	has a bad dream
	menânâhpawêwa	has a strange dream
	wîyatâhêwa	makes s.o. have a bad dream
	anâhpawêwa	he recites his dream to invoke the power of his blessing
	natokwawêwa	seeks to dream of s.o., seeks s.o. in a dream
	mehkokwawêwa	finds s.o. in a dream
dreamy eyes	**patapatakwânakîkwêwa**	has dreamy eyes
dress (noun)	**mekôtêweni**	a dress
	nekôtêhi	my dress
dress (verb)	**ishîhtêwa**	dresses {so}
	ishishehkîhowa	dresses {so}
	anahpisowa	she is dressed in bridal finery, as a bride
	anahpinêwa	dresses her up as a bride
	apenôhâpachihêwa	dresses s.o. like a child
	ketemâkîhtêwa	dresses miserably
	ketemâkishehkîhowa	dresses poorly
	ketemâkishehkîtamwa	dresses poorly
	kîshîhtêhêwa	finishes dressing s.o.
	kîshowîhtêwa	dresses warmly
	kohkîhtêwa	changes one's clothes
	menwîhtêwa	dresses well
	nanâheshkamwa	dons it
	nanâheshkahêwa	dresses s.o.
	nanâhîhtêwa	gets dressed
	nanâhîhtêhêwa	gets s.o. dressed
	wêchinowîhtêwa	is lightly clothed
dress up	**mîshâtesiwa**	dresses up
	mîshâchihêwa, mîshâchihtôwa	dresses s.o. up; decorates it
	mîshâtenowa	puts on one's best clothes, shows oneself off
	mîshâchîhtawêwa	shows off to s.o., gets all dressed up for s.o.

	omîshâtesiweniwa	has fancy clothes; uses (it) to dress up with
	omîshâtesiweniwiwa	has fancy clothes; uses (it) to dress up with
dried	**pâhpâshkâwakîwi**	the earth is dried and cracked
	pâhpâshkâwaketêwi	it (earth) is dried and cracked from heat
drift	**pemipokowa, pemipokôtêwi**	drifts, floats along, by; it drifts, floats along, by
	anemipokôtêwi	it drifts, floats off
	nanôshkwipokôtêwi	it drifts about at random
driftpile	**âkwêhanohkiwi**	driftpile, pile of river debris
	âkwêhanohkihkiwi	driftpile, pile of river debris
drill	**pôhkiponêwa**	drills a hole in s.o. (as, a pipe)
drink	**menowa**	drinks; drinks (it)
	menahêwa	gives s.o. drink, gives s.o. (it) to drink
	pônepyêwa	quits drinking; no longer drinks
drip	**achikêwi**	it drips, leaks, flows
	pakikêwi	it drips
	pâhpakikêwi	it is dripping
drive	**âtahwêwa**	drives s.o. back, repulses s.o.
	inâmohtâtîwaki	they drive it {so} to each other
	mîwênetamawêwa	drives (it) away for s.o. by thought
	pyêchinehkawêwa	drives s.o. this way
drive away	**kashkeshihwêwa**	is able to drive s.o. off
	mîweshihwêwa	drives s.o. off, away
	pâkohwêwa	drives s.o. away by what one says, scares s.o. off
drizzle	**sîtâwi**	it drizzles
drool	**sîsepetonwa**	drools, is drooling
	sîsepetonêkwâmwa	drools in one's sleep
	nesîsepetonâkani	my saliva, my drool
drop	**panenêwa, panenamwa**	loses hold of s.o., it; drops s.o., it; skips, omits s.o.
	panatamwa	drops it in eating
	pakisatamwa	drops it from one's mouth
	pashkonamwa	drops it, fails to catch it
	kwâshkwamêwa, kwâshkwatamwa	drops s.o., it in eating
	kwâshkwatamâkêwa	drops (it) of others in eating
	kwâshkwachikêwa	drops food from one's mouth
drop down	**nanâhisahowa**	drops down, flops down, jumps into bed
	wawîhkwanisahowa	drops to one's knees (to sit)
drop in	**pôchisahtawêwa**	drops (it) in for s.o.
drop subject	**âyânesowêwa**	drops the subject
drown	**ashkepyêwa**	drowns
	ashkepyanêwa, ashkepyatôwa	drowns s.o., it
drowsy	**shahkosiwa**	is drowsy, listless, weak, down-hearted
	shahkokwâmwa	is drowsy or weak from sleep
drum (noun)	**ahkohkwa**	drum, kettle
	têwêhikana	drum
	ênwêwêhâsôha	drum
	anahônêwa	fills s.o. (water drum); tightens the drumhead on s.o. (skin drum)
	anahôtâsowa	(drum) has its drumhead tightened
	nîhkasehkêwa	(drum) has its drumhead burst
drum (verb)	**anwêwêhikêwa**	drums
	anwêwêhâsowa	is drummed on
	anwêwêhwêwa	makes s.o. (drum) sound by beating
	tanwêwêhwêwa, tanwêwêhamwa	is audibly drumming, banging, or pounding on s.o. (as, a drum), it

	wêpwêwêhwêwa	begins to make s.o. (drum) sound by beating
	nâtwêwêkahwêwa	makes s.o. come by drumming
	pyêtwêwêkahwêwa	makes s.o. come by sounding a drum
	nenekwêwêhikêwa	drums rapidly
	pyêtwêwêhikêwa	comes drumming
	tanwêwêhikêwa	is heard drumming, pounding, or chopping ({somewhere})
	tâkyênihikêwa	taps the drum
Drum Society	**nîmihetînenîhaki** (plural)	Drum Society (Michelson: Religion Dance)
	anoshkâhaki (plural)	Drum Society
	nîkâni-kechitâha	headman of a drum in the Drum Society
drunk	**kîwashkwêpyêwa**	is drunk
dry	**pêkwâwi**	it is dry
	pêkwâwakîwi	the earth is dry
	pêkotêwi	it dried (after being wet) (as, in the sun)
	pêkoshkêwi	it dries, becomes dry
	kâhkeswêwa, kâhkesamwa	dries s.o., it (by heat)
	wâpeswêwa	leaves s.o. (corn) to dry on the stalks
	kîshâhkasowa, kîshâhkatêwi	(animate, inanimate) has dried out
	kashkihkesowa, kashkihketêwi	(animate, inanimate) is naturally dried, seasoned (as, wood)
	tanâhkasamwa	dries it {somewhere}
dry up	**ashkisêwi**	it ebbs, recedes, dries up
	ashkâsêwi	it dries up
	ashkâhtêwi	it (lake, river) dries up
	kashkâhkasowa, kashkâhkatêwi	dries up, dries hard
	kâhkesowa, kâhketêwi	(animate, inanimate) dries up, dries out, gets scorched
drygoods	**machâhîni**	drygoods
duck	**shîshîpa**	duck (generic)
	meshishipa	mallard
	kâkânwichitîha	pintail
	wâwîpekwâkêha	teal
	wîkîkwêha	wood duck
	shîshîpikani	duck bone
duck (verb)	**pakisowa**	ducks, turns aside quickly, looks away quickly
	chîtapisêwa	ducks down, drops down
	ochîkwêsahowa	draws one's face back, ducks one's head
	nakapehkwêsahowa	ducks one's head down
duck hawk	**kêhkêhkwa**	duck hawk, peregrine falcon
dull	**myâshisêwi**	it is, becomes dull
dull (sound)	**shîkwêwêshinwa**	falls with a dull thud
	shîkwêwi	there is a hollow sound, there is a dull thud
	shîkweshîkwêwi	dull thuds are heard
dump out	**sîkahwêwa**	dumps (it) all out
dung	**môwechi**	dung, excrement
	môwechiwiwi	it is dungy
	môwechiwâhkosiwa, môwechiwâhkwatwi	(animate, inanimate) is covered with excrement
	môwechiwiyâkosiwa, môwechiwiyâkwatwi	(animate, inanimate) smells of dung
duration	**nehkani**	for the duration of (archaic) (preparticle or initial)
	nahkani	for the duration of (preparticle or initial)
	ahkani	for the duration of (preparticle or initial)
dusk	**neseyâhiwi**	it is dusk
dust	**pekwi**	dust, ashes
dust (verb)	**pawenikêwa**	dusts the place

dusty	**pekowiwa, pekowiwi**	(animate, inanimate) is dusty
	pekoweshkâtêwi	it is (made) dusty from being traveled on
	pekowâhkwihtôwa	makes it dusty
	pekowîkwêshinwa	lies with dusty face
	pekowechêkôtêwi	it (as, a sacred bundle) hangs with dust (of ashes) on it
	pekonêyâwakîwi	the ground is dusty
dwell	**owîkiwa**	has a dwelling, dwells {someplace}
	owîkêhiwa	has a dwelling, dwells {someplace} (dimin.)
	owîkihêwa	makes or has s.o. have a dwelling {someplace}, makes a dwelling for s.o. {someplace}
	neshikêwa (**neshikêhiwa** dimin.)	has a home of one's own
	nekotôkêwa (**nekotôkêhiwa** dimin.)	lives alone, lives by oneself
	nîshôkêhiwaki (plural)	they dwell together as just a pair
	tasôkêwaki (plural)	{so many} of them dwell together
	wîchikêmêwa	lives in the same camp or settlement as s.o., is s.o.'s neighbor
	wîchikêtîwaki	they live in the same settlement
	wîchikêkêwa	dwells among others, with others as neighbors
	môshakihkwêwiwa	she dwells as a woman alone
dwelling	**kîwikîwikahêwa**	repeatedly provides dwellings for them in different places (song word)
	kîhkikêwa	sets up a new dwelling at some remove
	kîhkikawêwa	sets up a new dwelling at some remove for s.o.

e

each	**âyânikêmêhi**	each (time) a little further on (particle)
	nahkwi	as one gets there, each as they come (as, in serving guests), catching on to each (song) as it is sung (preverb)
each time	**âyakwami**	each time; (with negative:) not all the time (particle, preparticle)
	âyakwamenwi	each time (particle, preparticle)
eager	**wîshâshkêwa**	is eager, anxious, agitated
	koshkwâtatawâpiwa	looks around eagerly, impatiently
eagle	**ketiwa**	eagle, golden eagle
	mekesiwa	bald eagle
Eagle Clan	**mekesiwaki**	Eagle Clan members
	mekesiwisowa	is a member of the Eagle Clan
	mêkesiwisota	member of the Eagle Clan
ear	**nehtawakayi**	my ear
	ohtawakêwa	has ears, has (s.o.) as one's ears; wears (them as) earrings
	kakânoshêwa	has long ears
	kîshkîshkeshêwa	has both ears cut off
	kokwênakoshêwa	has pierced ears
	mamâkeshêwa	has big ears
	wêwêpeshêwa	flaps one's ears (song word)
	âyâpôtânakeshêwa	one's ears are on backwards (said of a disobedient child)
	shashôshkoshêshkêwa	(dog) lays the ears back flat
	kîshkeshêshwêwa	cuts off s.o.'s ear
	pâhkânakeshênêwa	opens s.o.'s ears
	sakeshênêwa	holds s.o. by the ear
early	**aye**	early, earlier, already (particle)

	mâmaya	early; soon, in the near future (particle)
	peteki (petekîmêhi dimin.)	in back, back (in space or time) (particle)
	petek-ochîmêhi	a little while back (particle compound)
earnestly	âyachîchi (also âyâchîchi)	earnestly, insistently (particle, preverb)
earring	ohtawakêwa	wears (them as) earrings
	mehtawakêwa	wears (them as) earrings
	mehtawakêwenaki	earrings
	mehtawakêwâhaki	earrings (dimin.)
	akôtêwâkanaki	earrings that hang
	kâkânwakôchîhaki	long hanging earrings
	nênekakôtêhani	extralong earrings with shimmery danglers
	asâwâkeshêwa	wears brass earrings
earth	ahki	land, ground, earth
	ahkwitahkamiki	on top of the earth (particle)
	mehtosêneniwahkyâwi	it is a peopled earth (ritual)
	mehtosêneniwahkyâwiwi	it is a peopled earth (ritual)
	mehtosêneniwahkyâniwiwi	it is a peopled earth (ritual)
	ashkipakâmehkisenwi	it lies green as the earth
	ashkipakâmehkwisenwi	it lies green as the earth
	ashkipakâmehkwisetôwa	makes it green as the earth
	masahkamikohkwêwa	the Earth (Grandmother Earth)
	mesahkamikohkwêwa	the Earth (Grandmother Earth) (archaic)
	nanâhâmehkisetawêwa	arranges it as earth for s.o.
	nôhkâmehkisenwi	it lies as soft earth
	mamâwakâsenwi	a chunk of earth is torn off by the wind
	mamamamâwakâsenwi	chunks of earth are torn off by the wind
	mamâwakeshkêwi	a chunk of earth tears away
	pêkwâwakîwi	the earth is dry
	têhtêwahkyêshkamwa	is shaking the earth with one's stomping
	wâshâwakahamwa	makes a hole in it (the earth) by striking it
east	wêtâpaki	east
	wêchi-môhkahaki	east
	anemyâka	east, downstream, down the (railroad) line (particle)
easy	wêchinowi	easily (particle, preverb)
	wêchinowesiwa	is easy to get, kill; has an easy time
	wêchinowatwi	it is easy
	wêchinowikiwa, wêchinowikenwi	is easy (to deal with); things are easy
	wêchinowinâkwatwi	it looks easy
	wêchinowihêwa, wêchinowihtôwa	easily kills s.o.; finds it easy
	nôhkihêwa, nôhkihtôwa	easily kills s.o., it; easily gets s.o.
	nôhkinêwa	dies easily
	wêchinowisetôwa	places it within easy reach
	wêchinowâhkonikêhêwa	makes easy rules for s.o.
	wêchinowitêhêwa	thinks something is easy, plans something easy
	wênehpeni	easily (particle, preverb)
	wênehpeshi	easily (particle, preverb)
	wênehpenihêwa	gets, kills s.o. easily
	wênehpeshihêwa	gets, kills s.o. easily
	wênehpenênetamwa	thinks it is easy
	shôshki	instantly, directly, at once, with ease (particle)
	shôshkyâwi	it is straight; it is easy, straightforward
	wayêchi	easily, with no effort or ado (particle)
	penôchi	far away, a long time; easily (particle)
	mêtenôshki	easy, easily; huge (particle, preverb)

eat	**amwêwa**	eats s.o.
	amotamawêwa	eats (it) of s.o.
	menwi-amwêweniwiwa	is good enough to eat (as, ripe corn or beans)
	mîchîwa	eats it
	mîchîhiwa	eats it (dimin.)
	wîseniwa	eats, eats a meal, feasts
	wîseniwi	eating, of eating (prenoun)
	wîsenîmikatwi	it eats
	wîsenihêwa	makes s.o. eat
	wîsenîmikihtôwa	makes it eat
	wîsenîhtawêwa	eats for s.o.
	atôhpowa	eats from (it, a dish or bowl)
	ânosiwa	is unable to finish the food one is served
	meshimowêwa	eats a lot
	inatamwa	eats it {so}
	inamowa	eats {so}
	ashkwatamwa	leaves it from eating
	châkamêwa, châkatamwa	eats s.o., it up
	châkatamawêwa	eats it up for s.o.
	chîhchîkwatamwa	eats everything off of it (as, all meat off bone)
	kashkatamwa	(with negative:) is not able to eat it (as it is too hard)
	menwamêwa	makes a good meal of s.o., satisfies one's hunger eating s.o.
	menwamowa	has a fine meal
	nanâhpamêwa	eats s.o. in one's food (not bothering to remove s.o.)
	sîkâhtamwa	eats it all up
	tanamêwa	eats s.o. {somewhere}
	wâpasatamwa	eats it wastingly
	wâwanatamwa	cannot eat it
	wîkêtatamwa	eats it up carefully
	wînamowa	eats something dirty
	nânekotôhpwêwa	eats s.o. one by one
	tasôhpowaki	{so many} of them eat to a bowl
	nîshôhpowaki	they eat together as a pair
	asipôhpowaki	they eat in a group
	mânôhpowaki	many (of them) eat together
	châkisenyêwa	eats all
	kîmisenyêwa	eats secretly
	kîshisenyêhêwa	has made s.o. eat
	kîshîseniwa	has eaten
	kîshi-wîseniwa	has eaten
	manetôwisenyêwa	eats spiritually
	menwisenyêwa	eats well
	nahisenyêwa	knows how to eat
	nemaswisenyêwa	eats standing up
	pônisenyêwa	stops eating
	tahtakwisenyêwaki (plural)	they eat together
	takwisenyêwa	eats joining others
	tashisenyêwa	eats {somewhere}
	tashisenyêhêwa	makes s.o. eat {somewhere}
	tashîseniwa	eats {somewhere}
	tashi-wîseniwa	eats {somewhere}
	têpisenyêwa	has enough to eat
	wêpisenyêwa	starts to eat
	wîkisenyêwa	finds one's food tasty

	wîhpomêwa	eats with s.o.
	wîhpotîwaki	they eat with each other
	wîhpokêwa	eats with people, eats with others
	nahkwâhpetamwa	eats it (ceremonial offering) and receives a blessing
	nahkwâhpetamawêwa	eats (it) for s.o. (spirit) receiving a blessing
	nahkwâhpetamâkêwa	eats (it) for the spirits receiving a blessing
eat food of	myâshihêwa	eats up s.o.'s food
echo	paswêwi	it echoes
eel	kenêpikwamêkwa	eel
effect of food	inashkôsowa	has {such} a feeling, understanding, or condition after eating
	ineshkôsowa	has {such} a feeling, understanding, or condition after eating
	ineshkâkwiwa	it (thing eaten) has {such} an effect on one
	menwashkôsowa	feels good after eating
	menoshkâkwiwa	it (thing eaten) has a good effect on one
	wîshikinawêshkâkwiwa	it (thing eaten) has a strong effect on one
effort	wayêchi	easily, with no effort or ado (particle)
	mamîkwâsowa	tries very hard or harder, makes great efforts, tries one's best
	mamîkwânêwa	makes great efforts with s.o., bears down hard on s.o., comes down hard on s.o.
	mamîkwâhtawêwa	makes great efforts with s.o., bears down hard on s.o., gets tough with s.o.
egg	owâwani	egg (**owâwanani** eggs)
	wâpisôha	nit, louse egg
eight	shwâshika	eight (particle)
	neshwâshika	eight (older form) (particle)
	shwâshika tashiwaki, shwâshika tasenôni	they (animate, inanimate) are eight, there are eight of them
	shwâshikenwi	eight times
	shwâshika tasokoni	eight days
eighteen	shwâshikanesiwe, shwâshikanîsiwi	eighteen (particle)
	metâswi-shwâshika	eighteen (particle compound)
eighth	shwâshikânameki	eighth, the eighth time (particle)
	neshwâshikânameki	eighth, the eighth time (older form) (particle)
eighty	shwâshikâpitaki	eighty (particle)
	neshwâshikâpitaki	eighty (older form) (particle)
elbow	netôshkwani	my elbow (**metôshkwani** an elbow)
elephant	wêwêpikôha	elephant
eleven	nekotinesiwe	eleven (particle)
	nekotinîsiwe	eleven (particle)
	metâswi-nekoti	eleven (particle compound)
	metâswi-nekotinîsiwe	eleven (particle compound)
elk	meshêwêwa	elk
Elk Clan	mêshêwêwisota	member of the Elk Clan
elm	anîpi	American elm
	anîpiwiwa	is an American elm
	ashâshikôha	slippery elm ("red elm")
emaciated	ahkanîhiwa	is emaciated
	ishikanêhiwa (dimin.; idiom):	**êshikanêhichi** nothing but (skin and) bones
	kîshâkochikanêwa	is extremely emaciated
	kîshâkochikanêhiwa	is extremely emaciated (dimin.)
embark	pôsiwa	gets into a boat or vehicle, embarks
emerge	môhkîwa	emerges, comes up to the surface
	môhkeshkêwa, môhkeshkêwi	(animate, inanimate) emerges, appears, becomes evident
	môhkisêsenwi	it (as, a path or trail) comes out

	sâkeshkêwa	emerges
	pâhkîwa	emerges from taboo or concealment
	môshkakwisêwa, môshkakwisêwi	comes to the surface, (sun) comes out from behind a cloud; it comes to the surface
employ	**anohkâhkyêwa**	employs people
empty	**shêshkishinwa, shêshkisenwi**	(animate, inanimate) is empty
	shîkonêwa, shîkonamwa	empties s.o., it
	sîkisahtôwa	empties it out, pours it out, spills it out, dumps it out
emulate	**tepatohachikaniwiwa**	is emulated and relied on
enclose	**kepîhikêwa**	encloses things, fences
	kepwipahôtêwi	it (as, a grass fire) spreads rapidly to enclose completely
encounter	**mayâshkôsowa**	encounters (it)
	mayâshkawêwa, mayâshkamwa	comes directly to s.o., it, encounters s.o., it
end (noun)	**ashkwêyawi**	at the very end (particle)
	wîtawi	on both ends, on both sides (particle)
	pîkêwi	to the end, to weariness, to death (preverb)
	ahkwihkanawêwa	reaches the end of one's road (euphemism for dying)
	ashkwêyawikâpâwa	stands at the end
	chîkikomêsenwi	its end, point projects
end (verb)	**ahkwîwa**	goes {so far}, ends
	îni êhkwichi	that is as far as one's story goes
	ahkwahkamikatwi	the world ends
	ahkwahkamikesiwa	it is the end of the world for one
	ahkwanahkisenwi	it ends
endure	**shîpachiwa**	endures cold
	shîpapenêwa	endures hunger
enemy	**nîchîshkwêha**	my enemy
	menôtani	enemy village
	ashâhi-menôtani	Sioux village
	âshowi-menôta	over in the enemy village, on the enemy side (ritual) (particle compound)
	âshowi-menôtane	over in the enemy village, on the enemy side (ritual) (particle compound)
	pyêhpahêwa	sees evidence that enemies are near
engaged in	**tashi**	engaged in (preverb)
enjoy	**matâkwi**	enjoyable, interesting, curious; with enjoyment, interest, curiosity (prenoun, preverb)
	mâmatâkwi	how delightful, it is delightful (particle)
	matâkwênemêwa, matâkwênetamwa	enjoys s.o., it, thinks s.o., it is interesting, fascinating, curious
	matâkwîhkawêwa, matâkwîhkamwa	enjoys s.o.'s company; likes to frequent it (a place)
	mâmatâkwâchimohêwa	tells s.o. enjoyable or interesting things
	mâmatâkwâhpawêwa	has enjoyable dreams
	mâmatâkwâpiwa	enjoys looking, enjoys the sights
	metâchâhiwa	enjoys oneself
	mêmetâchâhiwa	enjoys oneself
enough	**têpi**	sufficiently, as long as; achieve, succeed in (particle, preverb)
	têpinehki	for long enough (particle)
	têpi-nâhinâhi	for long enough, far enough (particle)
	têpênemowa	is satisfied, has had enough
	têpisêwa, têpisêwi	there is enough of s.o., it to go around
	têpesowa	enough of (animate) is cooked
	têpihkamêwa	gets enough smoking, is satisfied smoking

	têpihkesowa	gets enough smoking, is satisfied smoking
	têpisenyêwa	has enough to eat
enter	pîtikêwa	enters, comes or goes inside
	pîtikawêwa	enters to where s.o. is, visits s.o. at home
	pîtikâtîwaki	they visit to each other
	pîsehkêwa, pîsehkêwi	(animate, inanimate) comes in (with no visible effort)
	pîtâwanetîwaki	they enter in a large group
	pîtâshkêhtôwa	lets it enter
	pîtênemêwa	thinks s.o. enters
entertain	mâmatânihetîwaki	they entertain each other
	mâmatânahkiwiwi	there is some entertainment going on
envy	keshâwêwa	envies s.o., is jealous of s.o. (if not a sexual rival)
	metawamêwa	envies s.o., is jealous or resentful of s.o.'s success or better treatment
equal	chêwi	equally (preverb, preparticle)
	chêchêwinâhi	both or all at the same time; at equal distances apart (particle)
	papâsiki	half and half, in two equal parts (particle)
erase	kâsîhamwa	erases it, rubs it out
erection	mâchikanwêwa	he has an erection
errand	anohkânêwa	sets s.o. to work, gives s.o. an errand
escape	kehekwiwa	one's prisoner or intended victim gets away
	kehekwipi nîyawi	I escaped
	kehekwihtawêwa	lets (it) get away for s.o.
	keteshkîhêwa	escapes from s.o.
	keteshkîwa	gets free, escapes
especially	ahkwiyâchi, ahkwiyâhi	especially, more so, more and more (particle)
	mehtenôhi	only, except, unless; especially, moreso (particle)
eternal	kâkikêwi	forever, eternal (prenoun, preverb)
	kâkikêneniwiwa	is an immortal
even	âwâchi	even (particle)
	apina	in fact, to this extent, even (particle)
	môhchi	even; but, anyway, in any case, at any rate (particle)
	wâwosâhi	even, going so far as to (particle)
	wâwasâhi	even, going so far as to (particle)
evening	anâkwiwi	it is evening
	anâkwîhiwi	it is evening (dimin.)
evergreen	êshkipakipyâta	evergreen
every	kekimesi	everyone, each one (particle)
	châkenwi	every time; every way (particle)
	âhkowi	every time (preverb)
every	mesôtêwe	everybody, universally (particle)
evil	wâwaneshkâhi	evilly, wickedly (preverb); evil, wicked (prenoun)
	neshiwanâchikenwi	it is evil, it is destroyed
	wâwaneshkâhîhkânowa	does an evil thing
	neshiwanâchimêwa	speaks evilly against s.o.
eviscerate	kechinakeshênêwa	eviscerates s.o., takes s.o.'s intestines out
exactly	kwîyena	exactly, just happen to; right (particle)
	nânâkachi	exactly (particle)
exaggerate	âwasâchimowa	exaggerates
examine	mînâwesiwa	inquires closely, examines things in detail, is attentive to detail
	mamînâwesiwa	inquires closely, examines things in detail
	mînâwihêwa, mînâwihtôwa	examines s.o., it closely
	mamînâwihêwa, mamînâwihtôwa	examines s.o., it closely
	mînâwâpiwa	looks closely, takes a hard look

	mînâwâpamêwa, mînâwâpatamwa	examines s.o., it visually; notices s.o., it
	tepâpamêwa	looks s.o. over, looks into s.o.'s situation
exasperated	**meshkwîkitêwa**	is exasperated, loses patience
exceedingly	**anasâki**	exceptionally, exceedingly (particle)
excessive	**asâmesiwa**	is excessive, goes too far
excessively	**mêmêswêwe, mêmêswêwi**	excessively, in excessive amounts, greedily (particle)
excited	**kîshâkotesiwa**	is in a terrible state (of grief, fear), is excited, is desperate; it's hard on one
	wâwanâtesiwa	is excited, fidgety, rattled, beside oneself, at a loss for what to do
excitedly	**wâwanâchi**	confusedly, with confused excitement (particle, preverb)
excuses	**ateshkawi**	with all kinds of delays and excuses (particle)
exert self	**wîshikîwa**	exerts oneself
exhausted	**ahkwimâchîwa**	gives out in running, becomes exhausted
	pahkihtêkêwa	dances oneself to exhaustion or death
	pîkêkêwa	becomes exhausted from dancing
exhibit	**môhkenamwa**	exhibits it, takes it from concealment
exhort	**ayîkwâmimêwa**	exhorts s.o., urges s.o. strongly, tells s.o. to do their best
	ayîkwâmitîwaki	they exhort each other
exist	**ahtêwi**	it exists, there exists, is ({somewhere}); it is placed {somewhere}
	takowa, takowi	(animate, inanimate) exists or is found in numbers ({somewhere})
	âkwi=kêkôhi	it does not exist (plural **âkwi=kêkôhani**)
expect	**tanênemêwa, tanênetamwa**	expects s.o., it
expectably	**wâwosâhi, wâwasâhi**	expectably, unsurprisingly; even, going so far as to; (with a negative:) it is not to be expected, not going so far as to (particle). Also used with a negative meaning even without a negative present.
expensive	**êniwakitêhi**	expensive item
explain	**wîkêtâchimohêwa**	carefully informs s.o., carefully explains to s.o.
expletive	**=ishkwe**	(woman's mild expletive)
	=nîhka	(man's mild expletive)
	=tike	(man's mild expletive)
explode	**pakesowa, paketêwi**	(animate, inanimate) explodes (from heat or otherwise)
	seswêhtêwi	it explodes and scatters in pieces from the heat
explosive	**pâshkesikani**	gun, explosive
exposed	**sâki**	exposed, partly visible, sticking out (preverb, prenoun)
	sâkahokowa, sâkahanwi	is exposed out of the water
	sâkikomêwa	one's nose is exposed to view
	sâkitepêkâpâwa	stands with the head exposed
	mehtâsenwi	it is exposed to the wind
	mehchihêwa	sees s.o. exposed; has an clear view of s.o.
	mehtâkwasowa	is sprawled naked; is piled in plain sight
	mehtâpitêwa	bares one's teeth, one's teeth are exposed
	mêmehchichîkwanêyâshinwa	her knees are exposed by the wind (as, in running)
	meshkâkwasowa, meshkâkwatêwi	is sprawled out exposed, it is spread out exposed
	meshkishinwa, meshkisenwi	lies sprawled indecently exposed, it lies open
	meshkekwâmwa	is sleeping indecently exposed
	sâkeshkêwa, sâkeshkêwi	(animate, inanimate) emerges, becomes exposed
	sâkânowêkâpâwa	stands with one's tail in sight
	sâkikomêsetôwa	sets it with the tip sticking out
	sâsâkeshêkâpâwa	stands with the ears exposed (as, a horse or mule)
	sâsâkiwinêshinwa	has one's horns partly visible

extend	**ahkwâpyêwi**	it extends {so far}
	ahkwâpyêyâwi	it extends {so far}
	ahkwâpyêhtôwa	extends it {so far}
	ahkwâpyêsetâkêwa	extends it {so far} for s.o.
	pyêtâpyêsenwi	it lies extending this way
extent	**ahpîhchi**	{to such extent, so intense, so fast} (preverb, particle)
	ayâw-ahpîhchi	the extent to which, respectively (particle compound)
extract	**ketesakenêwa**	gets s.o. out of it (as, danger)
	ketesamawêwa	extracts (it) from s.o. by medicine
extremely	**kîshâkochi**	extremely, as much as possible, more than ever (particle, preverb)
	pôsôtêwi	extremely (particle, preverb)
	nepôtêwi	extremely; (literally) sexually (preverb)
exude	**chînishkesowa, chînishketêwi**	exudes matter liquefied by heat, it oozes out liquefied by heat
eye	**neshkîshekwi**	my eye
	ochinîkwe	(at) the eye on {such} side (particle)
	âshowi ochinîkwe	the other eye
	anihaniwânakîkwêwa	has wide-open, bright, piercing eyes
	mêmeshkwinîkwêwa	has red eyes
	pâshkinîkwêwa	has a broken eye
	pyêmishkwânakîkwêwa	is cross-eyed
	tahitanânakîkwêshinwa	is lying there with one's eyes open
	wâpinîkwêwa	is white-eyed
	wâwâshinîkwêwa	is hollow-eyed
	wêwenânakîkwêwa	has pretty eyes
	wêwewêwenânakîkwêwa	has pretty eyes
	inânakîkwêshkêwa	one's eyes become {so}
	mâtânakîkwêshkêwa	moves one's eyes
	mahkatêwinîkwênêwa	blackens s.o. across the eyes
	menishkîkwêkwâmwa	sleeps with mattery eyes
	pesetwa	has something in one's eye, has (it) in one's eye
	pahkîkwasowa	one's eyes are bothered by smoke
eyebrow	**omâmâwaki**	eyebrows
	omâmâwahi	his or her eyebrows
	mâmahkatêwimâmâwêwa	has black eyebrows
eyesight	**nenwâpiwa**	has eyesight, can see
	aniwânakîkwêwa	has strong, sharp eyesight
	menwâpiwa	has good eyesight
	myâshîkwêwa	has bad eyesight, cannot see well
	natawâpiweni	vision, eyesight

f

face (noun)	**kesîkwêwa**	washes one's face
	kesîkwênêwa	washes s.o.'s face
	mîshîkwêwa	is hairy-faced, has a beard
	wâpeshkîkwêwa	has a white face
	osîkîkwêhiwa	has a wrinkled face (dimin.)
	omekîkwêwa	has sores on one's face
	papakwîkwêwa	one's face is loose
	pyêmîkwêwa	one's face is twisted
	wâpeshkîkwêwa	has a white face; (ear of corn) has white kernels

	shêshkîkwêhêwa	lets s.o. go with face unblackened (i.e., not fasting)
	akwîkwâtamwa	puts it on one's face
	ishîkwêshkêwa	moves one's face {so}
	sêkîkwêshkêwa	a frightened look comes over one's face
	shîpachîkwêshkêwa	one's face becomes taut
	pâhkîkwêshimêwa	uncovers s.o.'s face
	pâhkîkwênêwa	uncovers s.o.'s face
	sîkenîkwêhwêwa	throws (it, liquid) in s.o.'s face
	shîshîkwêhwêwa	pokes s.o. in the face with a burning stick
facing	**inâsamapiwa**	sits facing {some way}
	inâsamikâpâwa	stands facing {some way}
	ishîkwêkâpâwa	stands facing {so}
	ishîkwêshimêwa	places s.o. facing {so}
	pyêchi	coming to, come and, coming or facing this way (preverb)
	pyêchishkwâtawêsenwi	(house) lies with its door this way
	pyêchitiyêkâpâwa	stands with rear end this way
	pyêchîkwêshinwa	is facing this way, is face-to-face
	pyêtanahkikâpâwi	it (tree) stands with its top inclined this way
	pyêtâsamapiwa	sits facing
	pyêtâsamikâpâwa	stands facing
	wâwâchikâshinôki (plural)	they (two) lie with their feet toe to toe
	wâwâchipehkwanêkâpâwaki (pl.)	they (two) stand back to back
	wâwâchîkwêshinôki (plural)	they (two) lie facing each other
fact (in fact)	**=wêna (=wê=)**	in fact; after all; rather, or actually, but actually, or at least
fade	**nehkwêtamwa**	one's voice fades as one moves away
fail	**ânawesiwa**	fails
	âkwikanâkwâhiwa	fails, is a failure
	ânwi	fail to, is unable to (preverb)
	pepyênowihêwa	keeps just failing to get s.o.
fall	**wêpâshkêwa, wêpâshkêwi**	(animate, inanimate) falls
	inâshkêwa, inâshkêwi	(animate, inanimate) falls, rushes, flies {so}
	otâshkêwa	falls off; falls from {somewhere}, falls into {somewhere}
	ahkwâshkêwa	falls {so far}
	achitawanahkisêwa	falls headfirst
	achitawânowâshkêwa	falls headfirst, upside-down
	achichîkwêsêwa	falls and hits one's face on the ground
	anwêwêsenwi	it falls noisily
	âhtawâsêwa	falls over backwards
	chapôkisêwa, chapôkisêwi	(animate, inanimate) falls into the water
	kawɪsêwa, kawɪsêwi	(animate, inanimate) falls over (as, a standing feather, a tree)
	kîpisêwa	falls over
	kîshâkochishinwa	has a bad fall, lands hard
	ketâshkêwi	it falls out, rushes out
	kwâpâshkêwa	falls scattering
	nowâshkêwa, nowâshkêwi	falls out, rushes out
	pakisâshimêwa	sets s.o. on the wind to fall
	papâmeshkêwaki (plural)	they (animate) run or fly around; they (as, horns) fall off
	pakisâsetawêwa	sets (it) on the wind to fall for s.o.
	pâkechêshinwa	falls on one's belly
	peshkwâsîwa	falls in climbing
	pîchinihkisêwa	falls into a space
	pôchisêwa, pôchisêwi	(animate, inanimate) falls in
	pônâshkêwa	stops falling, stops rushing
	showinekwêsêwa	falls with wings spread

	shôshkwishinwa, shôshkwisenwi	(animate, inanimate) slips and falls
	wîsakishinwa	falls and hurts oneself
	wîshkwêwêsenwi	it falls with loud noise
fall off	kîshkikwêshkêwa	one's head falls off
fall out	châkeshkêwi	it (hair) falls out, it (tooth) decays
fall short	nôtêwi	falling short, not (yet) complete (preverb)
	nôtêkiwa, nôtêkenwi	is not full grown; it falls short
	nôtêshinwa	falls short of the goal, does not finish
	nôtêhkanawe	before reaching the end (of the road, journey, life) (particle)
	nôtêhkwikomêsenwi	the end of it (as, a pole) falls short, it does not reach
	nôtêhkwinehkêwa	is unable to reach with the hand
false	ashe inowêwa	says something false, is just kidding
	ishe inowêwa	says something false, is just kidding
	ashe ishimêwa	tells s.o. something false, is just kidding s.o.
	ishe ishimêwa	tells s.o. something false, is just kidding s.o.
famous	âchimekôha	the famous one, the one talked about, the hero of the tale
	âchimekôhi	the famous thing
fan	nowahôni, nônôhôni	fan
	nônôhowa	fans oneself
	mîwâsetôwa	blows it away, fans it away
	inenêhamwa	fans it {some way}
fancy clothes: → finery		
far	penôchi	far away, a long time; easily (particle)
	penôchîmêhi	quite a ways off, further; quite a long time, a longer time (particle)
	penôchâwi	it is far
	ahkwi	{so far} (preverb); until (particle)
	ahkomîwa	is {so far} in the water
	inâkwâtwi	it is {so} far off
	nanôpehkâchinâhi	a long period of time, a great distance (particle)
	têpi-nâhinâhi	for long enough, far enough (particle compound)
fare	itwa	fares {so}
	itômikatwi	it fares {so}
	inahkamikesiwa	gets along {so}, has things go for one {so}
farm	kehtikâni	farm, field
fast (verb)	mahkatêwîwa	fasts (typically by not eating until a certain time)
	mahkatêwînêwa	makes s.o. fast
	mahkatêwîweni	fasting
	wîchi-mahkatêwîmêwa	fasts with s.o.
	nyêwokonîwa	fasts for four days
	metâsokonîwa	fasts for ten days
	mânokonîwa	fasts for many days
	tasokonîwa	fasts for {so many} days
	asâmekwamâsowa	over-fasts
	asâmekwamêwa	over-fasts
	ôtenawêwa	fasts without eating throughout the day
	wênâpêwinohkataka îni kehkeshêwi	the one who is brave towards the charcoal (i.e., who has the courage to fast) (see: wanâpêwinohkatamwa)
fast (go fast)	aniwâshkêwa, aniwâshkêwi	(animate, inanimate) goes, flies, falls fast, speeds along
	kîshâkotâpatâniwa	looks splendid; runs extremely fast
	neshiwâpatâniwa	looks terrific; looks dreadful; is going fast
	nîshkâpatâniwa	is burdened as one runs
	pyêtâpatâniwa	is coming fast
fasten	wîshikâhkohamwa	fastens it firmly

fat	**owînenwi**	fat (generic)
	owînenwa	a piece of fat, bear fat
	wîkinenwêwa	has savory fat, one's fat is good eating
	kekinenwêshinwa,	(animate, inanimate) has the fat on
	kekinenwêsenwi	
fat (be fat)	**anakwiwa**	is fat
	anakwîmikatwi	it is fat
	kîshikâmowa	fattens up; becomes (politically) powerful
	kîshikâmônêwa	fattens s.o. up
	kîshâkochikâmowa	is extremely fat
father	**nôsa**	my father, my father's brother
	ôsiwa	has a father; has (him) as a father
	okwisetîhaki (plural)	the father and son
father-in-law	**nemeshôma**	my father-in-law
favor	**âwîtênemêwa**	favors s.o., thinks more of s.o.
	wîtôhkawêwa	helps, aids, favors, allows s.o.
fawn	**kêtakenêha**	fawn
	mahkôsesêha	fawn (archaic)
fear	**kosêwa, kohtamwa**	fears s.o., it, stays away from s.o.
	kosehkyêwa	gets frightened
	kosâkaniwiwa	is feared
	sêkahkiwiwi, sêkahkîwi	there is fear, people are scared
	sêkahkamikatwi	there is fear, people are scared
feast	**chîpêhkohkwêweni**	"Ghost Feast," memorial feast
	chîpêhkohkwêwa	gives a "Ghost Feast"
	ashatwa	gives a return feast (after ceremonial adoption)
	kîkênowa	gives a clan feast; gives a clan feast with (it) as food
feast blanket	**atôhposôni**	feast blanket (used when placing a meal on the ground); tablecloth
feather	**mîkona**	feather
	mîkoniwiwa, mîkoniwiwi	(animate, inanimate) is feathered
	mîkoniwihtôwa	puts feathers on it
	ketiwikona	golden eagle feather
	opîwaya	body feather, coarse down feather; Feather (man in story)
	opîwayiwenêwa	puts small feathers on s.o.
	opîwayiwechênêwa	puts small feathers on s.o.'s body
	ochiti	tail-feather (**ochityêni** tail-feathers)
	ohkechi	bird's tail, set of tail-feathers
	nôhkipiwâkanaki	fine down feathers
	ashkipakipiwêwa	has green feathers
	meshkwipiwêwa	has red feathers
	nânîsikâpôhaki	split feathers (worn on head)
feed	**ashamêwa**	feeds s.o., gives s.o. food
	ashatîwaki	they feed each other
	ashametîwaki (Jones)	they feed each other
	ashakêmowa	serves (someone) a meal
	menwamônêwa	feeds s.o. well
	shahkamônêwa	puts food in s.o.'s mouth, hand-feeds s.o.
	shahkamowa	puts a bite of food in one's mouth
feel	**kotenêwa**	feels of s.o.
	kotenamawêwa	feels of (it) for or of s.o.
	kokwêtenêwa, kokwêtenamwa	tries to feel s.o., it
	kîmenêwa	feels s.o. intimately
feel (bodily)	**kîkihêwa**	makes s.o. feel better

	ineshkôsowa	is made to feel {so} by eating
	inamatamwa	has {such} a feeling or pain
	menwamatamwa	feels good, has a nice feeling
	nenwamatamwa	feels pain, feels it
	nenwapenêwa	feels hunger
	pekishkamatamwa	suffers with pain
	pônamatamwa	ceases to feel pain
feel (mentally)	**ahpîhchitêhêwa**	feels {so} deeply
	kîshâkochitêhêwa	feels bad, feels terrible
	kîshâkotênemêwa	feels bad about s.o.
	ishinawêhêwa	makes s.o. feel {so}
	ashkinawêhêwa	makes feel uneasy
	myâshinawêhêwa	makes s.o. feel bad
	myâshinawêmêwa	makes s.o. feel bad by speech
	nahinawêmêwa	makes s.o. feel good by speech
	pînênetisowa	feels clean
feel for	**nanâtochêhwêwa,**	feels around for s.o., it (as, with a stick)
	nanâtochêhamwa	
	nanâtochênêwa	feels around for s.o.
feel good	**menwi-pemâtesiwa**	feels good, feels better, is in good health
feel sorry for	**myânowehtawêwa**	feels sorry for s.o., hearing them
fellow	**nîchi-** (prenoun with prefix)	my fellow (+ noun)
	owîchi- (1) (prenoun with prefix)	one's fellow (+ noun)
	nîchi-manetôwaki	my fellow manitous, the other manitous
	nîchi-pashitôha	my fellow old man
	owîchi- (2) (preverb)	fellow (in verbs of possession)
	owîchi-manetômêwa	has s.o. as a fellow manitou
	wêwîchi-manetômenakôwe	you whom I have as fellow manitou
	owîchi-manetôwiwa	has (s.o.) as a fellow manitou
	wêwîchi-manetôwichiki	the fellow manitous of one
female	**ihkwêwawahîma**	female (animal or bird)
fence	**kepîhwêwa**	fences s.o. in
	kepîhikani	fence
fetus	**nâmatâsîha**	fetus
fever	**pasâhkosowa**	has a fever
few	**anehkîhiwa, anehkîhenwi**	is few; there is not much of it
	menwi-taswi	not (too) many, not (too) much, (only) a few, (only) a little (particle compound)
	nâhtasenwi	several times, a few times (particle)
	nâhtasokonêtwa	is away for a few days
	nâhtashiwaki	there's several of them, a small number of them
fidget	**wîkawapiwa**	fidgets, moves restlessly in one's seat
fidgety	**wâwanâtesiwa**	is fidgety
fierce	**nasatâwikenwi**	it is fierce, wild, cruel
fierce	**neshiwinâkosiwa,**	(animate, inanimate) looks terrible, awful, fierce
	neshiwinâkwatwi	
fifth	**nyânanônameki**	fifth, the fifth time (particle)
fifteen	**nyânanwinesiwe**	fifteen (particle)
	nyânanwinîsiwe	fifteen (particle)
	nyânanwinîsiwi	fifteen (particle)
	metâswi-nyânanwi	fifteen (particle compound)
	nyânanwinîsiwa	is fifteen years old
fifty	**shekihkanawe**	fifty (particle)
	nyânanwâpitaki (Jones)	fifty (particle)

fight	**mîkâtîwa**	fights, engages in mortal combat; fights (s.o.)
	mîkâtîhêwa	fights s.o.
	mîkâtîhetîwaki	they fight each other
	mîkâtîwi	of war (prenoun, preverb)
	mîkâtîweni	fighting, mortal combat
	mîkânêwa (Jones, one example)	fights s.o. (probably not a genuine Meskwaki word)
	châkôhkawêwaki	they all assail s.o.
	châkôhkâtîwaki	they assail each other in full force
	inenetîwa	fights {so}, to {somewhere}
	otenetîwa	fights because of {something}
	pônenetîwa	stops fighting
	tanenetîwa	fights {somewhere}; is engaged in fighting, continues fighting
	wêpenetîwa	starts to fight
	pônenetîhkiwiwi	the fighting stops
fight back	**nanâhkonêwa**	fights back against s.o., defends oneself against s.o.
	nanâhkwîwa	fights back, defends oneself
file	**kâwipôhi, kâwipochikani**	file
	tanwêwêpochikêwa	continues noisily filing something
fill	**anahônêwa**	fills s.o. (a water drum); tightens the head on s.o. (a drum)
	anahôtawêwa	fills (it) for s.o.
	anashkenatôwa	fills, loads it
	aneshkenachikawêwa	fills things for s.o.
	têpashkenêwa	fills, takes all the room
	têpeshkenêwa	fills, takes all the room
	êhkwi-têpeshkenêwâchi	as many of them as could fit in
	kîhpochanêwa, kîhpochatôwa	fills s.o.'s stomach, satisfies s.o.'s, its hunger
	kîhpochânêwa, kîhpochâtamwa	fills up on s.o., it, gets full on s.o., it
filthy	**wînesiwa, wînyâwi**	(animate, inanimate) is dirty, filthy
	wîninâkosiwa, wîninâkwatwi	(animate, inanimate) looks filthy
	wînitepêwa	has filthy hair
	wînîhkâsowa	does a filthy thing
finally	**kêkeyâhi, kêkayâhi**	finally, eventually, in time, before long (particle)
	mêmechishkêhi	finally (particle)
	nanôchi	up to this time, finally, eventually (particle)
find	**mehkawêwa, mehkamwa**	finds s.o., it
	mehkochênamwa	finds it by touch
	mehkochênamawêwa	finds (it) for s.o. by touch
	mehkochêhtamwa	finds it with one's mouth, takes it into one's mouth
	mehkwatomêwa	finds s.o. by inquiry
find out	**môshîkwêhêwa**	finds s.o. out by their expression
finery	**mîshâtesiweni**	finery
	mîshâtesiwâhi	finery (dimin.)
	omîshâtesiweniwa, omîshâtesiweniwiwa	has fancy clothes; uses (it) to dress up with
finger	**nîsîpinechâkani**	finger
	âwinôhikanechi	forefinger
	ashkwênechi	little finger, endclaw
	âyahkwinîsîpinechêwa	one's fingers are {so} long
	kakânwinîsîpinechêwa	has long fingers
	nenyêhpinehkêwachiwa	one's fingers are numb from the cold
	pemiwinechêwa	has greasy fingers, hands
finish	**kîshihêwa, kîshihtôwa**	finishes making, completes s.o., it
	kîshihtawêwa	finishes making, completes (it) for s.o.
	kîshi, kîh	have completed, finish (preverb)

	kîshîhkâtêwi	it is finished with
	kîshânehkêwa	finishes digging
	kîshêwîwa	finishes
	kîshikêwa	finishes building a house
	kîshikawêwa	finishes building a house for s.o.
	kîshîhkamwa	finishes with it
	shêshki kîshenâtêwi	it is partly finished
finish off	nânôhkatahwêwa	finishes s.o. off (as, with a club)
fire	ashkotêwi	fire
	ashkotêhkêwa	makes fire
	ashkotênêsiwa	the Spirit of Fire
	ashkotêwâshkêwi	there is a flash of fire
	aniweshawêwa	has a big fire going
	âyâhkoshawêwa	gets, has a blazing hot fire going
	taneshawêwa	has a fire going ({somewhere})
	pehtawêwa	makes a fire; makes a fire with (it), burns (it) in the fire
	pehtawanêwa	makes a fire for s.o.
	pehtawasowa	makes a fire for oneself
	pehtawatôwa	gets it (fire, log) burning, keeps it going
	peshkonênawachikêwa	gets the fire started with (it), uses (it) as kindling wood
	chîkashkote	by the fire (particle)
	nâwashkote	in the fire (particle)
firebrand	ashkwânêhketêwi	firebrand, firestick
firefly	wâwâsêsîha, wêwâsêsîha	firefly
firewood	mesêhi	piece of firewood
	mesêhêhi	small piece of firewood
	manesêwa	gathers firewood
firm	wîshiki	firmly (particle, preverb)
firmly	âhkwimêwa	speaks to s.o. firmly, strictly forbids s.o.
first	ashkichâhi	at first, in the first place (particle)
	ashki	first, for the first time (particle, preverb, prenoun)
	ashkiwêpîhiwa	first starts (doing something never done previously)
	ashkihkwêwiwa	she has her first menstruation
	mehtami	first (particle)
	menehta	first (particle)
	menehtami, menehtâmi	first (particle, preverb)
	mêmêkwêshawi, mêmêkwêshawe	as the first, before anyone else, already (particle)
	nawachi	first, before going on, having a brief opportunity (particle, preverb); wait a moment!
	pîshi	as the first (preverb)
	âwîtêni	as the first priority, as the first choice (particle)
	âyîtêni	as the first priority, as the first choice (particle)
first time	achâhmeko	then, only then, for the first time, for the first time in a long time (particle)
	châhmeko	then, only then, for the first time, for the first time in a long time (younger form) (particle)
fish	nemêsa	fish
	namêsa	fish (archaic)
	meshi-namêsa	big fish
	chaki-nemêsîha	little fish
	namêsiwa, namêsiwiwa	is a fish
	wîshôka	large fish species (perhaps garfish)
fish (verb)	nahkwamôtôwa	fishes, goes fishing
Fish Clan	nêmêsisota	member of the Fish Clan (Jones: Sturgeon Clan)

	êshikanisota	member of the Fish Clan (literally, Bass Clan)
	ashikanaki	members of the Fish Clan (Jones: Bass)
	ashikani	of the Fish Clan (prenoun)
fisher	ochêka	fisher
	ochêkaya	fisher skin
fit (noun)	wêpapisowa	has an epileptic fit
	wêpesîha	insane person, crazy person; one who acts foolishly; one who has a fit
fit (verb)	nahênemêwa, nahênetamwa	thinks s.o., it fit
	nahênetamawêwa	thinks (it) fit for, of s.o.
	menoshkawêwa, menoshkamwa	has a good fit or mount of s.o., it
fit	menwâshkêwi	it works, fits, suits
	nôneshkamwa	does not fit it (that is, it does not fit him or her)
	nônichinwa	does not fit in or through the space
	nônitepêchinwa	cannot get one's head in
five	nyânanwi	five (particle)
	nyânaniwaki, nyânanenôni	they (animate, inanimate) are five, there are five of them
	nyânanenwi	five times (particle)
	nyânanônôki	fivefold (particle)
	nyânanônetîwaki	all five of them hold hands together
	nîshwâpitaki nyânanwinesiwe	twenty-five
fix	wîkêchihêwa, wîkêchihtôwa	makes s.o., it well; fixes it up right, completes making it
	wîkêchinâkwihtôwa	fixes it up to look better
	wîkêtakoshêhowa	fixes the covers on oneself
fix (in a fix)	kîsâchihêwa	puts s.o. in a terrible fix
fixedly	kehtâpamêwa, kehtâpatamwa	looks fixedly at s.o., it
	mechimâpamêwa, mechimâpatamwa	looks closely, fixedly at s.o., it, stares at s.o., it
fix on	sahkitêhêwa	fixes one's thoughts on {somewhere}
fix self up	nanâhenowa	fixes oneself up
	nanâhîkwênowa	fixes oneself up, attends to one's face
flag (1)	kehkiwêhôni	flag, battle standard
flag (2)	apahkwâki êshikeki	blue flag
flap	pahpawinawîwa	(bird) flaps itself
	pêhpêwinekwêwa	flaps one's wings
	wêwêpeshêwa	flaps one's ears (song word)
flare up	peshkonêwi	it flares up
flash	wâsêshêwi	it flashes
	peshkâshêwi	it lights up, it flashes
	wâsetonwa	(thunderer) flashes at the mouth
	wawâsetonwa	(thunderer) flashes at the mouth
flat	papakâshkyâwi	it is flat
	papakâshkatêsêwa	falls flat on one's stomach
	papakâshkechêhokônêwa	flattens s.o. by letting something fall on them
	papakâshkipehkwanêyâwi	it has a flat roof
	papakâshkitepêshkêwa	flattens one's head (as, a snake)
	shashôshkoshêshkêwa	(dog) lays the ears back flat
flatulence	chîshkêwa	breaks wind
	chîshkâkani	intestinal gas
flea	pepikwa	flea
	pepikowiwa	has fleas
flee	wêpâmowa	flees, runs away
	pemâmowa	flees, runs away
	anemâmowa	flees on

	ashêyâmowa	flees back
	chapôkâmowa	flees into the water
	inâmowa	flees to {somewhere}
	kîwâmowa	flees about
	kîwâmohêwa	makes s.o. flee about
	nakâmowa	stops in flight
	nâkatôwâmowa	flees following along (it)
	nâkatôyâmowa	flees following along (it)
	nowâmowa	flees out
	wêtâmochi	took flight immediately (idiom)
	pîtâmowa	flees in
	pyêtâmowa	flees this way
	seswêyâmowaki (plural)	they scattered in flight
	shôshkâmowa	flees on a straight line
flesh	**owîyâsi**	flesh, meat
	owîyâsêhi	a little flesh, meat
	owîyâsiwiwa	has flesh on one,
	owîyâsiwiwi	it is flesh, meat
flick	**pâshkinêhwêwa**	flicks s.o. with one's finger (especially on the forehead)
flicker (bird)	**meshêwêmonêha**	flicker
flint	**shâkohkâni**	piece of flint
float	**pemipokowa, pemipokôtêwi**	(animate, inanimate) drifts, floats along, floats by
	têhtêpahanwi	it floats
	ahkwitepyêhokowa	floats on top of the water
	ahkwâwahokowa	floats filling (the body of water)
	kashkipokowa	is able to float
	nowipokowa	floats out
	sâketonêhokowa	floats with one's mouth out of the water
	sâkitepêhokowa	floats with one's head out of the water
	tetepipokôtêwi	it floats whirling
	kîwahokowa	floats about in a boat; (fish, bird) swims about
flood	**pakâhokowa, pakâhanwi**	(animate, inanimate) is reached by the rising flood
	môshkahokowa	is threatened by high water, is flooded out
	môshkahanwi	there is a flood, it is flooded
	mesepyêyâwi	there is a flood all over
	mesepyêhtawêwa	sends a flood upon s.o.
	papahkwachiwêpokôtêwani	they (inanimate) are uprooted by the flood
flop about	**mesimesiwêshkêwa**	flops about limply
flour	**pahkwêshikani**	(wheat) flour
flow	**pemihtanwi**	it (water or stream) flows, there is a current
	aniwihtanwi	it flows swiftly
	ishihtanwi	it flows {so}
	kechihtanwi	it flows out, it flows forth, runs out (as liquid)
	mâmôshkihtanwi	it flows bubbling
	menwihtanwi	it flows nicely
	neshiwihtanwi	it flows dangerously
	mamâtâpôshkêwi	it flows
	kechikêwi	it flows out
	pemâpyêwi	it strings, flows by
	ketahôtêwi	it is dragged out, it drags out, flows out solidly
flower	**pêshkonêwîhi**	flower
	peshkonêwiwi	it (plant, tree) has a flower, has flowers, is a flower
flute	**nênekwêhi**	"flute" (the end-blown Woodland flute or flageolet)
fly	**anisêwa**	flies up, flies away

	ishisêwa	speeds, flies to {somewhere}
	kîwisêwa	flies about
	pemisêwa	flies past
	papâmisêwa	flies about
	papâmeshkêwaki (plural)	they (animate) run around. fly around
	pyêchisêwa	flies this way
	tahkamisêwa	flies over an open space
	tashisêwa	flies {somewhere}
	wêpisêwa	starts to fly
	anemâshkêwa, anemâshkêwi	(animate, inanimate) flies along, rushes along
	âshowâshkêwa	flies across
	inâshkêwa, inâshkêwi	(animate, inanimate) falls, flies {so}
	kîwâshkêwa	flies about, rushes about
	nâshâshkêwa	flies down, flies downward
	opâshkêwi	it flies up
	pîtâshkêwa, pîtâshkêwi	flies in, rushes in; it flies in, goes in
	aniwipotêwi	it (as, an arrow) flies fast and hard
fly (insect)	ôchêwa	fly, housefly
	ôchêwiwi	it has flies on it
flycatcher	meshkwichitôwa	great-crested flycatcher
fog	pekeshêwi	it is foggy, it is smoky
	pêkeshêki	fog; smoke
	awanwi	there is thick fog; thick fog
	ôwatesiwiwi	there is a fog that comes up at night
fold	wîkêtâhkonêwa, wîkêtâhkonamwa	folds s.o. (as, a skin), it up neatly
	pepyêtekwâhkwapitôwa	folds it together and ties it as a bundle
	tâpônamwa	puts it or them together double (as, folding a blanket)
follow	ahkôwêwa	comes next after s.o., follows next after s.o.
	nâkanêwa, nâkatamwa	follows s.o., it, trails s.o., follows s.o.'s tracks
	nâwanonêhwêwa	follows after s.o.
	kîwîhkawêwa	goes about dealing with s.o., tags around after s.o.
	pemeshihwêwa	follows along after s.o.
follow by eye	nâkasawâpamêwa, nâkasawâpatamwa	keeps one's eye on s.o., it; keeps one's eye on where s.o., it goes
food	mîchiweni	food
	wîseniweni	food, meal
	ashkwisêwa	has food left
	awatâpowanêwa	takes food over to s.o.
	pyêtâpowêwa	brings food
	pyêtâpowanêwa	brings s.o. food
	nawahpowa	takes food for the journey
	nawahpwâhêwa	sends food with s.o.
	nawôtêwêwa	visits and gets a meal
fool	wanimêwa, wanotamwa	deceives s.o., it, fools s.o.
	wanikêmowa	fools people, makes deceptive claims or statements
	pehchamêmêwa	deceives s.o., fools s.o.; says something to s.o. that is misunderstood
	pehchamêhêwa	deceives s.o., fools s.o.; makes s.o. think the wrong thing
fool around	tahitanenekowa	is engaged in activity, performing a task, fooling around
	wêpenekowa	begins to fool around
foolish	wêpesîha	insane person, crazy person; one who acts foolishly; one who has a fit
	kîwânîwi	mistakenly, foolishly (preverb)
	wâwanâtesowa	is foolish from heat

foot	**nehkâchi**	my foot
	ohkâchi	his or her foot; a foot
	mehkâchi	a foot
	ohkâtaki (plural)	animal feet (as food)
	ahkwitanasite	on the top of the foot (particle)
	nâmanasite	on the sole of the foot or feet (particle)
	ochikâte	at the {specified} foot (particle)
	omekikâtêwa	has sores on one's feet
	showikâtêwa	has one's feet apart
	tasôkâtêwa	has {so many} feet
	ahpikâhiwa	has one's feet on (it)
	ishikâsêwa	moves one's feet {so} (song word)
	masânikâpiwa	sits with foot asleep
	nowikâhiwa	one's feet are sticking out
	ochikâsahowa	jerks one's foot (or feet) back
	sêsikâhiwa	rests one's leg or legs on {somewhere}
	sêsikâtêkâpâwa	stands with one's foot resting {somewhere}
	tahkikâwawishinwa	cools one's feet in water
	tashikâhiwa	has one's feet {somewhere}
	tashikâshinwa	lies with feet {somewhere}
	têwanasitêkâpâwa	stands with aching feet
	wâwâchikâshinôki (plural)	they (two) lie with their feet toe to toe
	nanâtochêshkamâtisowa	tries to get hold of (it) for oneself by foot
	pôhkoshkawêwa	breaks s.o. (as, a bow) in two by foot
footing	**memyêshkanahamîwa**	has difficult footing
	shôshkwanahamîwa	slips as one tries to get one's footing
footprints: → tracks		
for	**ishiwêpi**	for, standing for (particle, preverb)
	=iyo	for, (I say this) because; excuse me for asking or contradicting
forbear	**shîpitêhêwa**	is forbearing, puts up with a lot
forbid	**neshkimêwa**	scolds, forbids, admonishes s.o.
	neshkitîwaki	they admonish each other
	neshkikêmowa	forbids
	kenahamawêwa	forbids, dissuades s.o.
	pechimêwa	forbids s.o.
	kîhkîhkihêwa	forces s.o. against their will
force	**mâchîhkawêwa**	is after s.o. (as, criticizing or forcing s.o.)
	âshakachîhkawêwa	opposes or objects to s.o. forcibly; forces s.o. against their will
	âshakachîhkâsowa	objects, uses force
	âshakachîhkâtîwaki	one forces the other
forearm	**onepâkayi**	his or her forearm
forefinger	**âwinôhikanechi**	forefinger, index finger
forehead	**ohkeshi**	forehead, his or her forehead
	makwikenêwa	has a bump on the forehead
	kôkikenênowa	washes one's forehead
	mayâwihkeshe	in the center of the forehead
foreskin	**meshkikwêwa**	his foreskin is retracted
forest	**nâmêyâhkwe**	in the forest, through the forest
	pîtêyâhkwîwa	enters a forest or wooded area, enters (it) as a forest
forever	**kâkikêwi**	forever, eternal (prenoun, preverb)
	wayîhkwa	forever, since long ago, from now on (particle)

	wayîhkwe	forever, since long ago, from now on (particle)
	wayîhkwâwi	forever (preverb)
forget	**wanihêwa, wanihtôwa**	loses, forgets about s.o., it
	wanîhkânêwa	forgets s.o.
	wanîhkâsowa	forgets
	wanîhkêwa	forgets (it)
	wanîhkanawesiwa	is getting forgetful, loses track
	wâwanênemêwa, wâwanênetamwa	fails to know, forgets s.o., it
	wâwanênetamôhkânowa	pretends not to know
	pakitênemêwa	cast s.o. out of one's thoughts
fork (noun)	**keshihkâpyêhikani**	fork (meat-spear)
	patahkahikani	fork (meat-spear)
	patahkâpyêhikani	fork (meat-spear)
fork (verb)	**nasawâwi**	it (as, a river) forks
	nasawikiwa, nasawikenwi	(animate, inanimate) is forked
	nasawisenwi	it (as, a road) forks, has a fork
former	**kêhta**	old, former (prenoun); formerly, previously, originally (preverb, particle)
	shîkwi	formerly (preverb); former (of in-law after death of relative) (prenoun)
	neshîkwi-nenekwana	my late daughter's husband
	=iyôwe	former, formerly
fortunately	**shepawîhta**	fortunately (particle)
forty	**nyêwâpitaki**	forty (particle)
four	**nyêwi**	four (particle)
	nyêwihêwa, nyêwihtôwa	has, gets, uses four of them (animate, inanimate)
	nyêwiwak, nyêwenôni	they (animate, inanimate) are four, there are four of them
	nyêwokonêtwa	is away for four days
	nyêwôhkohkwe	four kettles (of food) (particle)
	nyêwôhkwêwêwa	he has four wives
	nyêwôkâpâwaki	the four of them stand together
	nyêwôkôtêwani	the four of them (inanimate) hang together
	nyêwôpinêwa	ties the four of them (animate) together
	nyêwôpiwaki	they sit four together
	nyêwikîsheswe	for four months (particle)
	nyêwi-kîsheswe	for four months (particle compound)
	nyêwikîsheswakatwi	it is four months
	nyêwinâkanakatwi	there are four dishes or bowls of it
	chêyênyêwi	all four (particle)
fourteen	**nyêwinesiwe**	fourteen (particle)
	nyêwinîsiwe	fourteen (particle)
	metâswi-nyêwi	fourteen (particle compound)
fourth	**nyêwônameki**	fourth, the fourth time (particle)
fox	**wâkoshêha**	fox
Fox Clan	**wâkôha**	member of the Fox Clan
	wâkôhisowa	is a member of the Fox Clan
	wâkôhisota	member of the Fox Clan
fragrance	**mîshâchiyâkwatwi**	it has a nice fragrance
free	**keteshkîwa**	gets free, escapes
	pahkeshkêwa	is cut loose; is set free
	pâhkâhkohwêwa	sets s.o. free
	pâhkâhkoshkêwa	becomes free, is liberated
	pâhkeshkêwa	is set free

freely	**meshe**	freely, peacefully, contentedly, as one pleases; or; in some way, moderately; let it be, it's up to you, if that's what you want (particle)
	sheshêhkami	freely, unrestrained, readily (particle)
	wanimôshkwe	(with negative:) not freely or randomly, only if appropriate (particle)
freeze	**sîkachiwa, sîkatenwi**	(animate, inanimate) freezes
	sîkachimêwa, sîkachitôwa	freezes s.o., it
	mesachiwa, mesatenwi	(animate, inanimate) is frozen solid
	kepatenwi	it freezes over, is frozen over
	wîshikatenwi	it is frozen hard
	pahkihtêwachimêwa	freezes s.o. to death
Frenchman	**mêmehtekôshîha**	Frenchman
	wêmehtekôshîha	Frenchman (archaic)
friend	**nîhkâna**	my friend (generic); my close male friend (of a man or boy) (**owîhkânani** his or her friend)
	owîhkâniwa	has a friend, has (s.o.) as a friend
	owîhkânetîwaki	they are friends
	owîhkânetîhaki	the friends, (especially) two male friends
	shatôha	friend (only used in forms of address)
frighten	**sêkesiwa**	is frightened
	sêkihêwa	frightens s.o.
	sêkimêwa	frightens s.o. by speech
	sêkitîwaki	they frighten each other by what they say
	sêkinotawêwa	is frightened over s.o.
	sêkîkwêshkêwa	a frightened look comes over one's face
	sêkâchimowenakatwi	it is a terrifying tale
frightfully	**kwêhtâni**	frightfully, so very much (particle, preverb)
	kokwêhtâni	(with negative): not terribly, not frightfully (particle, preverb)
	kehchi-kwêhtâni	very greatly, frightfully (particle compound)
frivolously	**sheshekâchi**	frivolously, lightly, toyingly, jokingly, as make-believe (particle)
	sheshekâhi	frivolously, lightly, toyingly, jokingly, as make-believe (particle)
frog	**konwâshkêha**	frog
	kwananachîha	tree frog
from	**ochi**	from {somewhere}, because of {some reason}, in {such} direction (particle, preverb); away, from there (preverb)
	wâwochi	repeatedly from {somewhere}, because of {some reason}, in {such} direction (preverb) (preverb)
	ochiwêpi	from {such time}, from then on (particle)
	otênemêwa	resents s.o. or holds something against s.o. for {some} reason; thinks s.o. is from {somewhere}
	otênetâkosiwa	is thought to come from {somewhere}, belongs {somewhere}
frost	**takwanwi**	there is a frost
frostbite	**mehkwačiwa**	gets frostbite
fry	**sîswêwa, sîsamwa**	fries s.o., it
	pesipemyêsowa, pesipemyêhtêwi	(animate, inanimate) fries
frying pan	**apwâkana**	frying pan
full	**ahkwâwi**	full, filling, to fullness (particle, preverb)
	ahkwâwishinwa, ahkwâwisenwi	(container) is full, (contents) fill the container
	ahkwâwishimêwa, ahkwâwisetôwa	fill s.o. (kettle), it; fill container with s.o., it (contents)
	anashkenachikêweni	pipeful

	kîhpochêwa	one's belly is full
fully	pêhki	really, fully, successfully, easily, earnestly (particle)
	pêkwi (preverb):	
	pêkwi-menôhkamîki	when spring was fully underway
fumigate ceremonially: → smoke		
fun	mêmetâchâhi	fun, a good time
	metâchâhiwa	has a good time
	mêmetâchâhiwa	has a good time
	mêmetâchâhiwi	it is fun, one has a good time
	opi	for fun; jolly (preverb)
	opyâwi	it is fun, there are merry doings
	matonwâwi	for fun (preverb)
fur	owîsayani (plural)	fur, hair (of an animal or of a human body)
	owîsayiwêhiwi	it is a fur
	mîshishehkîtamwa	wears fur clothing
further	anika	further away (particle)
	anikêmêhi	a little further, beyond (particle)
	anika ochîmêhi	a little further
	kîhkeshkêwa, kîhkeshkêwi	moves further involuntarily, it extends further, is lengthened
fused	mêchimôshinôki	are or become stuck or fused together
future	nîkâni	in the lead, on ahead; in future, ahead of time (particle, prenoun, preverb)
future people	anemi-mehtosêneniwa, anemi-mehtosêneniwaki	the people to come, the human race (as referred to in the myth age)
	wîh=anemi-mehtosêneniwita, wîh=anemi-mehtosêneniwičiki	the people to come, the future human race
	ênemikichiki, wîh=anemikichiki	the people to come, the future human race

g

gallop	shâshîpahtêsêwa	gallops
gamble	tanetîwaki (plural)	they gamble, make a bet
	tanetîneniwiwa	is a gambler
	tanetîwashkwi	gambling medicine
	châkenawêwa	wins everything from s.o., cleans s.o. out (gambling)
game	kosikêwa	plays bowl-and-dice
	kônanôhiwa	plays the double-ball game, shinny
	mâmahkesêhiwa	plays the moccasin game
	mâmîhkôhiwaki (plural)	they play tag
	meshkwêhpîhiwa	plays with the throwing-stick
game (animal)	mîchipêha	game animal or bird
	mîchipêhi	game (animals, collective)
	mîchipêhiwa	is a game animal
	pônashiwa	drops a load of game from one's back
	pyêtashiwa	comes with a load of game on one's back
	shîshênotamawêwa	hunts game for s.o.
garment	oshehkîtâkani	garment, clothing
	pîsehkâhi	garment, shirt, blouse ("waist")
garter	kahkikâpîha	garter
	kahkikâpisowa	wears garters
	okahkikâpîhiwa	has garters, has (them) as garters
	okehkikâpîhiwa	has garters, has (them) as garters

gash	**pêsheshwêwa**	gashes s.o.
	pêshichinwa	gets a deep scratch, a gash
gasp	**achikoshkêwa**	gulps, gasps, hiccups
gather	**mâwâshkêwaki**	they gather together, assemble
	mâwachipahowaki (plural)	they gather together by running, they all run together
	mâwatenêwa, mâwatenamwa	gathers s.o., it
	mâwatenâtêwi	it is gathered
	mâwachiwenêwa, mâwachiwetôwa	gathers them together
	mâwachikawihtôwa	gathers it as it drips
	mêmekenahwêwa	gathers s.o. up
	wîkopihkêwa	gathers basswood inner bark
gathering	**mâwachi**	gathering; among all, only one of all, most (etc.) of all (superlative) (preverb, preparticle)
gaze at	**wâpawâpamêwa, wâpawâpatamwa**	gazes at s.o., it, keeps looking at s.o., it
generation	**ânehkwikiwa**	adds the next generation
generous	**shêshêhkwi**	generously, liberally (particle)
	shêshêhkosiwa	is generous
	shêshêhkwênetisowa	she is free with herself
gens: → clan		
gens-festival: → clan feast		
gentle	**keshâchinâkosiwa**	looks gentle
	mahkwâchi	quiet, quietly, gently, calmly (particle, preverb, prenoun); be quiet!
get	**awiwêwa, awiwa**	gets, buys, has, keeps s.o., it
	otehchi	getting it, accomplishing it (preverb)
	otehtenêwa, otehtenamwa	gets s.o., it
	otehtenetîwaki	they get each other
	otenêwa, otenamwa	gets s.o., it from {somewhere}
	otenâtêwi	it is gotten from {somewhere}
	otenowa	gets something for oneself from (s.o.)
	ânawihêwa, ânawihtôwa	fails to get s.o., it
get away	**kehekwîhtawêwa**	lets (it) get away from s.o., makes s.o. lose or miss out on (s.o., it)
get hold of	**nanâtochêshkamâtisowa**	tries to get hold of (it) for oneself by foot
get through	**konakwi**	getting through the danger or difficulty (preverb)
	konakwîwa	passes through, gets through danger
	ochawiwa	gets through or across {some way, by some route}
get-together	**tanahkiwihtôwaki** (plural)	they are having a get-together
get water	**ochihamwa**	gets or takes water from {somewhere}
	wâwochihamwa	regularly gets water from {somewhere}
ghost	**chîpaya**	corpse; ghost
	chîpênâwesiwa	sees or is visited by a ghost
	chîpêtehkwa	ghost
giant	**kîyamowêwa**	cannibal giant (in stories)
	kîyamoshtîha	cannibal giant (in stories)
	mesâpêwa	giant (human giant)
gigantic	**kakapâchishinwa**	lies in a gigantic heap
ginger	**ahpâpowâni** (**ahpâpowâhi** dimin.)	something added to the cooking, seasoning, wild ginger
gingerly	**koshimâtapiwa**	sits gingerly
	koshimâchikâwosêwa	steps gingerly
ginseng	**wênânîhi**	ginseng
gird	**nanâhapisowa**	girds oneself; puts on one's skirt
girl	**ishkwêsêha**	girl

	ishkwêsêhêha	little girl
	ishkwêsêhiwa	she is a girl
	oteshkwêsêhemiwa	has a girl (as a daughter)
	kwêshêha	girl (as a pet name)
give	mînêwa	gives (it) to s.o.
	mînâsowa	is given (it)
	mînetîwaki	they give (it) to each other
	mîshiwêwa	gives it
	atamêhêwa	gives s.o. a smoke
	atamêhetîwaki	they give each other a smoke
	ashamêwa	gives s.o. food, feeds s.o.
	ashatwa	gives a return feast
	omâwashihêwa	he gives his kill to s.o. (as, another hunter)
	wâkômowa, wâkôtamwa	gives thanks
give birth	tanôshêwa	she gives birth {somewhere}
give out	pahkikêmowa	gives out food to people in a ceremony
give up	pêwênemowa	gives up
	panesiwênemowa	gives up
	ânawênetamwa	thinks it is not enough, gives up on it; gives up hope
gizzard	opishkwayi	gizzard; bladder
glad	mîshâtênemowa	is proud, glad
	mîshâtênemômikatwi	it is proud, glad
	mîshâtênemwihêwa, mîshâtênemwihtôwa	makes s.o., it glad
	menwitêhêwa	is glad; is good-hearted, has good thoughts
	opitêhêwa	is glad, happy
	têpesiwa	is glad, pleased, delighted, joyful
	wîchi-têpesîmêwa	is pleased together with s.o.
glide	shôshkâkêwa	glides on outstretched wings
glove	menechîha	glove
glue	nemêhkwâni	glue; wax
gnat	âsiyahkâha	gnat
gnaw	nânôhkatamwa	eats what was left uneaten on it (as, discarded bones)
	kîshkatâtêwi	it is gnawed through
go	ihêwa	goes {somewhere}
	ihêhiwa	goes {somewhere} (dimin.)
	ihêmikatwi	it goes {somewhere}
	ihêhêwa	makes or lets s.o. go {somewhere}
	ihênotawêwa	goes {somewhere} to s.o.
	ayahayêwa	always goes {somewhere}
	ayahayêhêwa	always makes or lets s.o. go {somewhere}
	asipîwaki	they go in a group
	âhpechîwa	goes for good
	âpihêwa	went {somewhere} and returned, has been {somewhere}
	ahkwâwanetîwaki	they go {so far} in a large group
	ahpîhtâshkêwa	goes {so} fast
	anemehkêwa	goes away, walks on
	anemihêwa	goes {some way}
	anemihêmikatwi	it goes {some way}
	anemihêmikihtawêwa	makes (it) go {some way} for s.o.
	ishikawiwaki	they go to {somewhere} as a group
	anemikawiwaki	they go on as a group
	châkîwaki	all go
	kekîwa	goes having (it)

	nowîwa	goes out, comes out
	nowîmikatwi	it goes out
	nowâwanetîwaki	they go out in a large group
	nowâwanetêwi	a large group (as, of people) goes out
	nowîhtamwa	goes out at it
	nowîhtâkêwa	goes out against people
	nowinâkêwa	goes out singing
	nowikawihêwa	makes (a group of) them go out
	pemâsikêwa	goes shining
	pemâwanetîwaki	they go past in a large group
	pemihêwa	goes {some way}
	papâmihêwa	goes about {some way}
	papâmehkêwa	goes about, travels around
	pyêmihkanêwa	goes on a distance ahead of s.o.
	sâkichîwa	goes out; goes to the toilet
	têpihêwa	goes as far as {somewhere}
	wâsêshkamwa	lights it by walking, going, jumping
	wayachîwa	has already gone
go after	mawinêhwêwa	goes after s.o., goes in pursuit of s.o.
	ochîhkawêwa	goes after s.o. for something, cheats s.o. out of what is theirs (see also: go to get)
go along	wîtôhkâsowa	takes part, helps, joins in, goes along (with it or the others)
go ahead	kêhtena	Go ahead! You should do that! (particle)
go at	ochîhtawêwa	goes at s.o. from {somewhere}
	mânôhkawêwa	many of them go at s.o.
goat	anetehkwa	goat
go away	penowa	goes away, goes home, departs
	penômikatwi	it goes away
gobble up	âwahkyêhtamwa	gobbles it up in one bite
go by	apâhkwîwa	has something to go by, to base oneself on
go downhill	pânachîwa	goes down a hill
go fast	kekenîhiwa	goes quickly, walks fast
	kekenîmikatwi	it goes quickly
	pâkwîwa	goes fast (archaic)
gold	asâwi-shôniyâhi	gold
gone	ashenowa, ashenowi	(animate, inanimate) is gone, absent
good	menwi	good, well, pleasantly, nicely, in good order, safely (preverb, preparticle)
	menwikiwa, menwikenwi	is good, is well formed, grows the right way; it is good
	menwitêhêwa	is good-hearted, has good thoughts; is glad
	wîkenwa, wîkanwi	(animate, inanimate) is good, tastes good
	wîkinenwêwa	has savory fat, one's fat is good eating
	wêchitawi	very good, splendid, excellent (particle, prenoun)
	wêchitawîhiwa	is a good person, is excellent
	kakatâni='hi='yo	(it will be) very good
	kakatâni='h=wêna	(it will be) very good
	mesênetamâkêwa	benefits, gets good from (it) for people
	pînâpitêwa	has a good set of teeth
	wêwenihchikêwa	does a good thing, does good work
good-for-nothing	machawahîna	rascal, good-for-nothing
	machawahîma	rascal, good-for-nothing
go on	inahkiwiwi	there is {such} going on
	tanahkîwi	it goes on {somewhere}
goose	anehka	Canada goose

	kênakîha	snow goose or blue goose
	wâpi-kênakîha	snow goose
	peshishkesa	domestic goose; brant
	môhkomâni-peshishkesa	domestic goose
gooseberry	kâwimina	gooseberry
go out, go cold	âhtêwa, âhtêwi	(sweatlodge stone) cools off; it (fire) goes out
	âhtêsenwi	its fire dies down or goes out, it (fire) goes out
	âhtêsetôwa	lets its fire go out
go past	kwêhkwêwîwa	goes past, passes by, goes too far
gopher	pîhtôshketôha	gopher (pocket gopher)
go so far	ahkwishinwa, ahkwisenwi	goes {so far}
	ahpîhchîwa	goes {so far}, does {so much}
gosh	kashinâkwa, kashinâhi, kashinâ!	Gosh! Why! Well! Well now! Well?
	shinâkwa	Gosh! Why! Well! Well now!
	shinâ!	Gosh! Why! Well! Well now!
gossip	tashimêwa	talks about s.o., gossips about s.o.
	takwimêwa	says s.o. is romantically involved with (someone)
go to	mawi	go to, go and (preverb)
	mawâpamêwa, mawâpatamwa	goes to see s.o., it
	mawîhkawêwa	goes to deal with s.o. go to get
	nânêwa, nâtwa	goes after s.o., it; goes to get s.o., it
	nâtawêwa	goes after (it) for s.o.
	nâtâtisowa	goes after (it) for oneself
go too far	wênôchi	(with or without negative:) surely greatly (preverb)
	wênôtesiwa	(future or potential, with or without negative:) stops at nothing, goes overboard, is beside oneself
	wênôchimêwa	(with [or, presumably, without] negative:) goes too far in what one says about s.o.
	wênôchinawêhêwa	(with [or, presumably, without] negative:) goes too far and upsets s.o.
	wênôtâhpenanêwa	(future or potential, with or without negative:) kills s.o. without restraint
go up to	nâsehkawêwa, nâsehkamwa	goes up to s.o., it
gourd	shîshîkwani	rattle, gourd
government	mêtâsôpita	the President, the U.S. Government
grab	nanâhenêwa, nanâhenamwa	grabs hold of s.o., it, takes hold of s.o., it
	tasôchênamwa	grabs {so many} of them at once
	asamonamwa	grabs a handful of it (as, cloth or s.o.'s hair or flesh)
	mawinachikêwa	goes and grabs things
	mawîhtawêwa, mawîhtamwa	makes a grab for s.o., it
	nawachisahêwa (Jones)	grabs s.o. on the way
	nawachisêwa	grabs (it) on the run
	kehkitechênêwa	grabs s.o. around the body
	nahkwinechênêwa	grabs s.o.'s hand
	nahkwinehkênêwa	grabs s.o.'s arm
	sakânehkwênêwa	grabs s.o. by the hair
	sakihtâhpênêwa	seizes s.o. by the back of the neck
	sakikwênêwa	takes or holds s.o. by the neck
	sakikwêsahêwa	grabs s.o. by the neck
gradually	êshkami	gradually (particle)
grandchild	nôshisema	my grandchild (**ôshisemani** his or her grandchild)
	nôshisemêhkôha	my dear grandchild
	atemêhkôha	my dear grandchild
	ôshisememêwa	has s.o. as grandchild

	ôshisemiwa	has a grandchild, has (s.o.) as a grandchild
	wêyôhkomesita	the grandchild (of a woman), her grandchild
grandfather	**nemeshômesa**	my grandfather
	nemeshôha	my grandfather
	omeshômesiwa	has a grandfather, has (him) as a grandfather
	omeshôhiwa	has a grandfather, has (him) as a grandfather
	omeshôhemêwa	has him as a grandfather, is his grandchild
	omeshômesemêwa	has him as a grandfather
	omeshômesetamwa	has it as a grandfather
	omeshômesâkômêwa	addresses him and treats him as if he were one's grandfather
	omeshômesiwâkômêwa	addresses him and treats him as if he were one's grandfather
grandmother	**nôhkomesa**	my grandmother
	nôhkomesêha	my grandmother (dimin.)
	ôhkomesiwa	has a grandmother, has (s.o.) as a grandmother, is the grandchild of (s.o.)
grandparent	**wêyôshisemichiki**	the grandparents, his or her grandparents
	ôshisemetîhaki	the grandparent and grandchild
granite	**kohkoseni**	granite rock
	kohkoseniwiwa	is a granite rock
grapes	**meshipahtêhani**	grapes
	sîwanôni	frost grapes
grass	**mashishki**	blade of grass
	mashkishki	blade of grass (less common)
	mashishkiwi	blade of grass, reed, herb, medicine plant
	mashkishkiwi	blade of grass, reed, herb, medicine plant (less common)
	mashishkîhani (plural)	grass, grasses
	mashkishkîhani (plural)	grass, grasses
	mashkihkyêni (plural)	grass
	mashishkihkiwiwi	it is grass-grown
	mashkishkiwihtôwa	makes it of grass
	mashkotêhkwanwi	blade of grass
	pehkwashkisenwi	there is a clump of grass, reeds
	inehpashkatwi	the grass is {so} high
	menwashkatwi	there is nice grass covering the ground
	kî-pyêmashkatwi	the grass is pushed down in places
	mônashkwêwa	pulls up grass, weeds
	wânehkwâwashkohkamwa	tromps down the tall grass to make a concealed space
	wêwenashkatwi	it is beautiful grass
grasshopper	**kwâhkwâtêha**	grasshopper
	papakesa	grasshopper (variety)
grass lodge	**wîsiyashkwikâni**	grass lodge
	wîsiyashkwikâhi	grass lodge (dimin.)
grave	**wânakwi**	hole; open grave
	wânehkêwa	digs, digs a grave
gray	**wâpitepêwa**	has a gray head
	wâpitepêwâtesiwa	is gray-haired
graze (1)	**sîsenawêwa**	grazes s.o. with a shot
	paseshênawêwa	grazes s.o.'s ear with a shot
	pasikomêhwêwa	grazes s.o.'s nose
graze (2)	**tanahkyêwa**	(animal) grazes
	tanahkyêhêwa	grazes s.o. (animal)
	tanahkyêhtawêwa	grazes (it) for s.o.
greasy	**pemiwinechêwa**	has greasy fingers, hands
	pemiwetonwa	has a greasy mouth

	pemiwânaketonwa	has a greasy mouth
great	**kehchi**	great, larger (than others) (prenoun); as great, greatly, much, more (than others) (preverb); great(ly), a great way (preparticle); (with numbers) full, whole, a good
	kehchawahîma	great one
	kehchawahîminâkosiwa	looks like one is great, acts important
	kehchi-kwêhtâni	very greatly, frightfully (particle compound)
	têpîmêhi	greatly, to a great number or extent (particle)
greatly	**wênôchi**	(with or without negative:) surely greatly (preverb)
	wênôchitêhêwa	takes it hard
Great Lynx	**peshipeshiwa**	Great Lynx, Underwater Panther
grebe	**shekahôha**	pied-billed grebe, "hell-diver"
green	**ashkipakesiwa, ashkipakyâwi**	(animate, inanimate) is green
	ashkipakâpatâniwi	it looks green
	ashkipakanenwa, ashkipakanetwi	(animate, inanimate) is green with rot
	ashkipakânehkwêsetôwa	makes its hair green
	ashkipakâmehkwisetôwa	makes it green as earth
	ashkipakepyêhâtêwi	it is painted green
green corn	**ashki-mesîkwaki** (plural)	green corn
	ashki-mesâhkwa	ear of green corn
greet	**anemehkawêwa**	greets s.o.
grief	**kîshâkochitêhâkani**	great grief
grieve	**kâhtosiwa**	feels grieved, sorry, disappointed at a loss
	kâhtwênemêwa	feels grieved about s.o.
	kâhtwênetamawêwa	feels grieved about (s.o.) for s.o.
	kâhtwihêwa	causes s.o. grief, loss, dashed hopes
	kîshâkotesiwa	grieves, is in a terrible state; it's hard on one
	pîkêtêhêwa	worries too much, worries or grieves to death
grind	**takwahwêwa, takwahamwa**	grinds s.o., it up; grinds them together
	pôtahwêwa, pôtahamwa	grinds s.o. (as, corn), it fine by pounding
	pôtahikêwa	grinds corn
grip	**menonêwa, menonamwa**	gets or has a good grip on s.o., it
	pashkonamâhkwîwa	loses one's hold, loses the grip that is supporting one's weight
groin	**neneshkoki**	on my groin (locative forms only)
ground	**mehtâwaki**	on the bare ground, on dry land (particle)
	kekyêtâmehkisêwaki	they shoot forth from the ground
	pepeshkwâwakatwi	the ground is bare
	pepeshkwâwakîwi	the ground is bare
groundnut	**mahkohpenya**	groundnut, "bear potato"
group	**nêhtawi**	in a separate group (of one kind) (particle, preverb)
	nênêhtawi	in separate groups (particle)
	mâkoshkêwaki (plural)	they rush as a group, all rush together, all rush forward
	mâkwihêwa	attacks s.o. massively, focused on a single target
	ishikawiwaki (plural)	they go to {somewhere} as a group
	nowikawiwaki (plural)	they go out as a group
	pepyêhkwâkwapiwaki (plural)	they sit in groups
	pepyêhkwikâpâwaki (plural)	they (animate) stand in groups
group (set)	**taswayaki**	{so many} kinds, groups, sets, pairs (particle)
	nekotayaki	one group, set (particle)
	nekotwayaki (Jones)	one group (particle)
	mânwayaki	many groups (particle)
grouse	**pahkiwa**	ruffed grouse, partridge ("pheasant")
grove	**pehkwâhkwâwi**	grove of trees
	pehkwâhkwâwiwi	it is a grove of trees

	pemâhkwâwiwi	a grove of trees extends along
	pîkwâhkwâwiwi	it is a dense grove of trees
	wêwenâhkwâwiwi	it is a beautiful grove of trees
	nênekotwêyâhkwâwi	grove of scattered trees
	nênekotwêyâhkwâwiwi	it is sparsely wooded, a grove of scattered trees
grow	kîshikiwa, kîshikenwi	is grown, is grown up, has matured
	kîshikiwênemêwa	thinks s.o. grown up
	sâkenwi	it grows out, sprouts
	ahkwikenwi	it grows {so long}
	aniwikenwi	it grows fast
	ahpîhchikîhiwa	is {so far} grown up
	ânehkôchikenwi	it grows joined together, (bone) sets
	ânehkwikiwa	grows to the next generation
	kekenyêkiwa, kekenyêkenwi	(animate, inanimate) grows fast
	kîhkîhkikenwi	it grows on and on
	nôtêkiwa	is not full grown
	ochikiwa, ochikenwi	grows from {somewhere}
	pemyêkiwa	is growing, grows for a particular length of time
	sahkikenwi	it grows attached to {somewhere}
	shôshkâhkwikiwa	grows straight
	takwikenwi	it grows with (it), it is reattached
	takwikihtawêwa	makes (it) grow together for s.o.
	wêpyêkiwa, wêpyêkenwi	(animate, inanimate) is starting to grow
growl	nîshkâmowa	growls
	nîshkâmêwa	growls at s.o.
grub	kwîkocha	white grub; woodcock
grumpily	nasatâwi	crossly, grumpily, standoffishly (particle, preverb)
guide	ahkwiwenêwa, ahkwiwetôwa	helps, guides s.o., it {so far}
	nanâhiwenêwa	guides s.o.
gull	akayâshkwa	gull or tern (generic)
gun	pâshkesikani	gun, explosive
gunpowder	mahkatêwi	gunpowder
	nîshwipeshkwahte	two charges of gunpowder (particle)
	nyêwipeshkwahte	four charges of gunpowder (particle)

h

habituate	âshihêwa	gets s.o. to be or act like one by example, gets s.o. into the habit
	âshihiwêwa	gets people into doing something by example
hackberry	kâhkâwêhani (plural)	hackberries
hail	mesihkwiwi	it is hailing
hair	nînesani	my hair, the hair on my head
	nînesi	a hair of my head
	owînesiwa	has hair (on one's head)
	owînesêhiwa	has hair (on one's head) (dimin.)
	âyahkôhkwêwa	one's hair is {so long}
	kakânôhkwêwa	is long-haired
	mesehkwêwa	has long hair
	ashkipakânehkwêsetôwa	makes its (the earth's) hair green (ritual)
	memyêshkânehkwêshinwa	lies with one's hair mussed up
	mêshânehkwênowa	touches one's hair

	sakânehkwêchinwa	gets one's hair caught
	sasakânehkwêwa	has curly, kinky, or tangled hair
	shôshkwânehkwêyâshinwa	one's hair is blown back smooth
	nênekotwânehkwêhiwa	has thin hair, one's head is sparsely covered with hair
	wêwenânehkwêwa	has beautiful hair
	mahkatêwitepêwa	has black hair
	owîsayiwitepêwa	has hair on one's head
	wâpeshkitepêwa	has a white head
	wâpitepêwa	has a gray head
	wâpitepêwâtesiwa	is gray-haired
	wînitepêwa	has filthy hair
	châkashkitepêwa	all the hair is gone from one's head
	mônashkitepênêwa	pulls out s.o.'s hair
	nîshkahtakawêshkêwa	(animal's) hair stands up on end
	têhtêpipiwêsêwi	the pile on it (as, a bearskin) undulates
	nîmashkahwêwa, nîmashkahamwa	fastens s.o. (as, a feather), it in one's hair; has s.o., it fastened in one's hair
	nîmashkahôtenêwa	fastens something (especially a feather) in s.o.'s hair
hair binder	ahpahôni	woman's hair binder (wrapped around a bun or club at the back of the head)
	tahpahôni	woman's hair binder
	pîwâhipahônêwa	she wears a beaded hair binder
haircut	môshwêwa	cuts s.o.'s hair
	môshowa	gets a haircut
hair ornament	sêkipanwâna	woman's hair ornament (attached to the hair at the back of the head)
hairy	mîsechêwa	has a hairy body
half	âpehtawi	a half, halfway (particle, preparticle)
	âpehtawi-kîshekwe	halfway to the sky (particle compound)
	pâsiki	half (particle, prenoun)
	papâsiki	half and half, in two equal parts (particle)
	pôhkwi	in part, half (particle)
	pôhkote	one half of the (inside space of the) house (particle)
halfbreed	âpehtawesîha	halfbreed
halfway	chêwinehki	in between, halfway (particle)
	pyêmakâme	halfway to the other side (particle)
	pyêminawe	off at an angle; halfway between (particle)
halo	wînepitiyêwa	(sun or moon) has a halo (literally, has a dirty bottom)
ham	mepwâmi êsâwâhkatêki	ham
hammer	pâpakachikani	hammer
hamstring	êh=wâkichêhtêchi	one's hamstring, the sinew behind the (animal's) hind-leg joint
hand	nenehki	my hand
	onehkinawi	one's hand
	ashikaninehke	in, using, or affecting one hand (as opposed to the other) (particle)
	âyashikaninehke	in or using one hand each
	ochinehke	(by, in, with) the hand on {such} side (particle)
	wâwîtônehke	with both hands (particle)
	atâhpinehkênêwa	takes s.o. by the hand, takes s.o.'s hand
	ishinehkêwa	moves one's hand to {somewhere}
	kechinehkêwa	pulls one's hand out
	kîshkinehkêshwêwa	cuts off s.o.'s hand
	mayakinehkêwa	has a peculiar hand

267

	mêshinehkênêwa	touches s.o.'s hand
	nanânishkwinehkêwa	pulls one's hands loose
	pîchinehkêwa	puts one's hand in
	sakinehkênêwa	takes s.o. by the hand, holds s.o.'s hand
	sakinehkênetîwaki	they take, hold, or lead each other by the hand
	sakinehkêpahônêwa	runs holding s.o. by the hand
	kechinechênêwa	takes (it) out of s.o.'s hands
	kesînechêwa	washes one's hands
	keteshkinechênêwa	takes (it) out of s.o.'s hands
	kôkinechêwa	washes one's hands
	kôkinechênêwa	washes s.o.'s hands
	meshkinechêwa	opens one's hand, holds one's hand open
	meshkinechêhtawêwa	holds one's hand open to s.o.
	nahkwinechênêwa	grabs s.o.'s hand
	papakêhinechêwa	one's hands have thin skin
	nahkochênamwa	gets one's hand on it
	sôkenamawêwa	holds (it) in one's hand for s.o.
	sôkenatahêwa	makes s.o. hold (it) in the hand
hand (verb)	pyêtenamawêwa	hands it to s.o.
	awatenamwa	hands it over
	awatenamawêwa	hands (it) over to s.o.
	inenamâkêwa	hands (it) out {so}
	nowenamawêwa	hands (it) out to s.o.
handful	asamonamwa	grabs a handful of it (as, cloth, hair, skin, or flesh)
	asamwisahêwa	grabs a handful of s.o.'s skin
	âwahkyênamwa	takes a handful of it, them
	ênekihkwinechêchi	as much as one's hand holds
handkerchief	kâsîkwêhôni	handkerchief
handle (noun)	otônâpi	handle (as, of pail or kettle), bail
handle (verb)	kokonamwa	handles it jerkily, with a quick motion
	wîkêchinechâtamawêwa	handles (it) carefully for s.o.
hand-picked	ênowênemâchihi	(the warparty leader's) hand-picked men
	ênawênemâchihi	(the warparty leader's) hand-picked men
handprints	kehkinechêpiwa	there are marks from s.o.'s hands where they sat
handsome	nawêni-kwîyesêhêhiwa	he is a handsome boy
	nawêni-nenîhêhiwa	he is a handsome man
hang	akônêwa, akôtôwa	hangs s.o., it, places s.o., it aloft
	akôchinwa, akôtêwi	hangs
	akwanakôtêwi	it overhangs
	ashitâhkwakôchinwa	hangs close to a solid
	inakôtôwa	hangs it {so}
	mâtakôchinwa, mâtakôtêwi	moves from the place where one (as, a star) hangs, it moves from the place where it (as, a cloud) hangs
	nanâhakôtôwa	hangs it in place
	nanâhahkanêwa, nanâhahkatôwa	hangs s.o. (kettle), it (water) over the fire
	nekotôkôtêwi	it hangs alone
	nyêwôkôtêwi	it hangs as four
	pemânahkwakôtêwi	it hangs along as sky
	kîshkikwêpinêwa	hangs s.o. (as punishment)
	kîshkikwêpisowa	is hanged (as punishment)
hanger	akôchikani	hanger, pothook
happen	towi (tôhiwi dimin.)	it happens {so} (in idioms):
	kashi=wîh=towi	I don't care; what difference will it make? (literally: what will happen?)

	kashi=wîh=tôhiwi	it will be alright (if)
	kashi=wê=wîh=towi	what does it matter? (literally: after all, what will happen?)
	kashi=wê=towi	yes, of course, to be sure (as an answer)
	'shi=wê=towi	yes, of course, to be sure (as an answer)
	kashi=châhi êh=teki.	Why? How come? What for? (literally: So, what happened?)
	tômikatwi	it happens {so}
	mehkwi	happen to (preverb)
	mîhkwi	happen to (by chance) (preverb)
	mîhkwihêwa, mîhkwihtôwa	happens to get, make, pick out the particular one of s.o., it
	mîhkônamwa	happens to get it
	wanimôchi	perchance, if it should happen to be that (particle)
happy	opitêhêwa	is glad, happy
	opinawêhêwa	makes s.o. happy
	opinawêmêwa	makes s.o. happy by speech
	opitêhâkaniwiwi	there is happy feeling
	ashinawêwa	is happy at someone's arrival
hard	ahkanyâwi	it is hard, rocklike
	aseneshkêwa	gets hard as a rock
	wîshikihkesiwa, wîshikihkatwi	(tree, post) is very hard and dense, it is very hard and dense
	ahkanikomêsamwa	hardens its tip in the fire
hare	wâpôsôha	snowshoe hare
hat	makohkwayi	hat
hatch	pâshkâwêwa	(bird) hatches
	pâshkâwêshkâtêwi	it (egg) is hatched
hate	neshkinawêwa, neshkinamwa	hates s.o., it, does not like s.o., it
	neshkinamawêwa	hates (it) for s.o.
	neshkênemêwa	bears ill will towards s.o., harbors bad feelings towards s.o.
	neshkênetîwaki	they have hatred for each other
hateful	neshkinâkaniwiwa	is hateful
have	awiwêwa, awiwa	gets, has, keeps s.o., it
	keki	having, provided with (it) (preverb, prenoun, preparticle)
	kekesiwa	has (it)
	kekeshkawêwa, kekeshkamwa	has s.o., it in one, on one, with one
	kîsheshkamwa	already has it with one, on one
	nekotihêwa, nekotihtôwa	has one of s.o., it
	kîwawiwêwa, kîwawiwa	has s.o., it with one
	kîshi-atâhpenêwa	has picked s.o. up
have been	pyêchi	coming to, come and, coming or facing this way; have been (up to now); next in past succession (preverb)
have done	âpi	have gone and, have been (preverb)
have to	pêpyêhchi	have to, necessarily (particle)
hawk	sîkiminêwa	"chickenhawk" (*Buteo* species)
	pâkahâhkwâhehkêha	chickenhawk
	kêhkêhkwa	duck hawk, peregrine falcon
	nâmêyâhkwisâha	large forest-dwelling hawk, probably goshawk
hazelnut	kekyêhtâhi	hazelnut
he	wîna	he or she (emphatic or contrastive); (by) himself or herself
head	nîshi	my head
	owîshi	his or her head; a head

	ahkwichitepe	on top of the head (particle)
	anwêwêtepêhwêwa	thumps s.o. on the head
	chîkitepêwa	has a long head
	kôkitepênowa	washes one's head
	nônitepêchinwa	cannot get one's head in
	panitepêhwêwa	strikes at s.o.'s head with something and misses
	pâhpâshkitepêshimêwa	smashes s.o.'s head against something
	pâhpâshkitepêhčikêwa	cracks some heads
	pehkwitepêwa	is lump-headed
	pôhkitepêhwêwa	pokes a hole in s.o.'s head
	sâkitepêshkêwa	sticks one's head into view
	sîkenitepêhwêwa	sprinkles (it, liquid) on s.o.'s head
	shâshâkwitepêshinwa	lies with one's head smashed
	shâshâkwitepêwa	one's head is smashed, one's skull is fractured
	tâkitepênêwa	touches s.o. on the head
	wâpeshkitepêwa	one's head is white
	wâpitepêwa	one's head is white
	apehkwêshinwa	lies with one's head on (it)
	asôtepêpisowa	has something tied around one's head, one's head is bandaged
	atâhpehkwêhtawêwa	motions with one's head for s.o. to come
	atâhpehkwênêwa	takes s.o.'s head in one's hands
	matakôhkwêhowa	covers one's head
	matakôhkwêpiwa	sits with covered head
	nakapehkwêsêwa	lowers one's head
	nîsehkwêsahowa	pulls one's head down quickly
	nîsehkwêsêwa	bows one's head
	pîtehkwênwa	sticks one's head in
	tanehkwêhiwa	has one's head {somewhere}
	tanehkwêshinwa	lies with one's head {somewhere}
	kîshkikwêhokowa	has one's head cut off (in an accident)
	kîshkikwêhwêwa	chops off s.o.'s head
	kîshkikwêshwêwa	cuts off s.o.'s head
	mahkikwêhpwêwa	bites s.o.'s head off
	mahkikwêhwêwa	chops s.o.'s head off
	chîkeshkwênwa	holds up one's head
headache	**têwehkwêwa**	has a headache
headband	**kehkichitepêpisôni**	headband
headdress	**mâkwayi**	furband headdress, fur cap
	mîkoni-mâkwayi	feather headdress; warbonnet
	omâkwêhêwa	puts a fur-band headdress on him
	omâkwêkêwa	he dances with a fur-band headdress on
headman	**nîkâni-kechitâha**	headman in the Drum Society
head off	**âtesehkawêwa**	heads s.o. off, cuts s.o. off
Head-Piercer	**pôhkitepêhowêha**	Head-Piercer (spirit in the afterworld)
head-to-head	**wâwâtehkwêhiwa**	lies head-to-head with (s.o.)
	wâwâtehkwêhiwaki	they lie head-to-head
	wâwâtehkwêpiwaki	they sit with their heads together
health	**menwi-pemâtesiweni**	good health
hear	**kâshkehtawêwa, kâshkehtamwa**	hears s.o., it
	nenohtawêwa, nenohtamwa	understands s.o., it, believes s.o., it, hears s.o., it
	nenohtâkosiwa, nenohtâkwatwi	(animate, inanimate) is heard
	menohtawêwa, menohtamwa	hears s.o., it with pleasure
	menohtâkosiwa	is heard with pleasure, one's voice sounds nice

	menohtâtisowa	likes hearing oneself
	menoshêwa	hears with pleasure
	nôtawêwa	hears s.o., hears what s.o. says
	nôtamawêwa	hears it of s.o.
	nôtâkêwa	hears (a report)
	nôtâkosiwa, nôtâkwatwi	(animate, inanimate) is heard; it sounds
	ânohtawêwa	fails to hear s.o.; denies s.o.'s request
	âhkohtamwa	has a keen sense of hearing for it
	inehtawêwa	hears s.o. {so}
	inehtâkêwa	hears it said {so}
	ineshêwa	hears {so}
	metâtehtawêwa	likes to hear s.o.
	kâshkehtâkosiwa	one's voice is heard (speaking, singing, or weeping)
	nôtêhkohtawêwa	is unable to hear s.o. because of distance
	sâkehtâkosiwa	is heard wailing
	sâsâkehtâkosiwa	is heard speaking, singing, or weeping
	tanehtawêwa	hears s.o. {somewhere}
	wâpasehtawêwa	hears s.o. in jest
	wâwanehtawêwa	fails to hear s.o., fails to understand s.o.
heart	netêhi	my heart
	metêhi	a heart
	otêhiwa	has a heart
	nâmitêhe	in the heart, in one's heart (particle)
	nenekitêhêshkêwa	one's heart trembles
heat	pasâpehkesamwa	heats it as metal
	pasâpôsamwa	heats it as liquid
	meshkwanôtêwi	it is heated red-hot
	meshkwanôsamwa	heats it red-hot
	ahkwâhtêwi	its heat extends {so far}
	mehtâhtêwi	it is out in the heat of the sun
	akoswêwa	makes s.o. adhere by heat
	ketesowa	comes forth in the heat
heavy	kosekwanwa, kosekwanwi	(animate, inanimate) is heavy
	kosekwênetamwa	thinks it heavy
heed	nenoshêwa	heeds, listens, obeys
	pemehtawêwa	heeds s.o.
	pemênetamwa	continues to pay attention to it, heed it
	kakâchichi	paying no heed (particle)
	kêkôhehtawêwa	(with negative:) pays no heed to what s.o. says
	wikehtawêwa	(with negative:) pays s.o. no heed, does not respond to s.o.
	wîkeshêwa	(with negative:) pays no heed, does not listen, does not mind
heel	netôtani	my heel
	sîsitôtanênêwa	pinches s.o.'s heel
	wîsakitôtanênêwa	painfully pinches s.o.'s heel
help	asemihêwa, asemihtôwa	helps s.o., it; helps it on, favors it
	asemihetîwaki	they help each other
	asemihiwêwa	helps people, helps out
	wîtôhkawêwa, wîtôhkamwa	helps, aids, collaborates or cooperates with, favors, allows s.o.; takes part in it
	wîtôhkâtîwaki	they help each other, join together, cooperate
	wîtôhkâsowa	takes part, helps, joins in, goes along (with it or the others)

	mawinachihêwa	goes to help s.o.
	inehkwêmowa	pleads to {somewhere} for help
	pyêtehkwêmowa	comes seeking help or advice
	ahkwiwenêwa, ahkwiwetôwa	helps, guides s.o., it {so far}
helpful	keteshkesiwa	is helpful, bustles about helpfully
hemp	asapya	Indian hemp
	asapihkêwa	gathers Indian hemp
	asapi-pîminihkwâni	Indian hemp cordage
herb	inashkwi	{such} herbal medicine
	ketahashkwêwa	digs herbs
herd	nenoswahkiwi	herd of buffalo
	nâwi-nenoswahkiwe	in the middle of a herd of buffalo (particle compound)
here	ayôhi	here
	ayôninâhi	now, at this time; here, in this place (particle)
here	atâhanahka-'shi	this way, towards here; since then
	âyâwasi	here and there (particle)
heron	sakiwa	great blue heron
hesitate	mechimênemowa	hesitates, holds back
	nakyâwi	(with negative:) **âkwi nakyâkini** there was no pause, hesitation, holding back
	nanakesiwa	(with negative:) hesitates at nothing, does not hesitate to do anything, will do just anything
	pwâwi-nanakesita	one who hesitates at nothing
	nanakâchimowa	(with negative:) does not hesitate to tell
	nanakowêwa	(with negative:) does not hesitate to say anything, will say just anything
Hey!	ehehe!	Hey! (look sharp! wake up!)
hickory	peshkipêhi	hickory tree, stick
	peshkipêhiwa	is a hickory tree
hickory nut	peshkipêhi-pakâni	hickory nut
	pakâni	hickory nut; also nut (generic), black walnut
hide (verb)	kahkisowa	hides oneself, keeps what one does a secret
	kahkisôhtawêwa	hides oneself from s.o.
	kahkinêwa, kahkitôwa	hides s.o., it
	kahkitawêwa	hides (it) for s.o.
hide (noun)	asaya	skin (of a small or medium-sized animal), buckskin
	asêha	piece of buckskin
	asayi	skin (of larger animal)
	asêhkêwa	tans, prepares hides
	pîshâkani	rawhide, buckskin, leather
	pîshâkanimotêhi	parfleche (hide bag)
hide behind	kepâhkwikâpâwa	hides behind (it) standing
	kepâhkwishinwa	hides behind (it) lying
hide-scraper	pashkwahikani	hide-scraper (for removing hair)
high	makinehpi	high (preverb)
	makinehpîwa, makinehpîwi	(animate, inanimate; as, a plant) is high
	makinehpesiwa, makinehpyâwi	(animate, inanimate) is high
	inehpesiwa, inehpyâwi	(animate, inanimate) is {so} high
	âyânehpesiwaki (plural)	they (animate) are {so} high
	makinehpâhkiwiwi	it is high ground
	makinehpâhkîwi	it is high ground
	makinehpâkwasowa, makinehpâkwatêwi	(animate, inanimate) is piled high
	ahkwanahkikâpâwa	stands with one's top {so} high

hike up	**chîhchîkwapisowa**	she hikes up her skirt
	chîhchîkwânakapisowa	he hikes up his breechcloth
	chîhchîkwânakitiyêpisowa	hikes up one's breechcloth or skirt
hill (noun)	**makwahki, makwahkiwi**	large hill
	makwahkiwiwi	it is a large hill
	mamakwahkiwiwi	there are large hills
	kîshkâhkiwiwi	it is a steep hill
	pemâhkiwiwi	it is a hill
	ahkwitâhkiwi	the top of a hill, bank, ridge
	ahkwitâhkîki	on top of a hill, bank, ridge (locative noun)
	mayâwi-makwahkiwe	on top of the hill (particle compound)
	akâmâhkiwe	over on another hill (particle)
	apatêhkîki	on the side of the hill (particle)
	âpehtawâhkiwe	halfway down the hill (particle)
	âshowâhkiwe	over the hill, on the other side of the hill (particle)
	âyakâmâhkiwe	from hill to hill (particle)
	chîkâhkiwe	next to a hill or cliff (particle)
	pasihkîki	at or to the foot of the hill (particle)
	pasehkîki	at or to the foot of the hill (particle)
	sîkehkwêtenwi	the hill narrows down to a point
hill (in garden)	**pehkwahikani**	hill (where crops are planted)
	nekwachihikêwa	hills, does hilling in garden
hinder	**pechihêwa**	hinders s.o.
hip	**nenôkani**	my hip
hippopotamus	**êkwîchika**	hippopotamus
hit	**pakamêwa, pakatamwa**	hits s.o., it
	pakatisowa	hits oneself
	mehtahwêwa	hits s.o. with a thrown object
	mehtahokowa	is hit (by falling or thrown object)
	pehtatahokowa	gets accidentally hit by a thrown object
	anematahwêwa	strikes, hits s.o. as one goes along
	inatahwêwa	strikes him {so} with tool
	menwatahwêwa	strikes s.o. just right, in just the right spot
	pehtatahwêwa	accidentally strikes s.o. (as, with a club)
	pematahwêwa	hits s.o. in passing
	inwêwêtepêhwêwa	hits s.o. on the head with {such} noise
	kotwêwêhamwa	tries its sound by hitting
	pasîkwêchinwa	hits one's face on a branch
hobo	**nânôchîha**	hobo, tramp, bum
hoe	**mônahâkani**	hoe
	omônahâkaniwa	has a hoe
	chaki-mônahâkâhi	little hoe
hold	**sôkenêwa, sôkenamwa**	holds s.o., it in one's hand
	sôkenamawêwa	holds (it) in one's hand for s.o.
	sôkenatahêwa	makes s.o. hold (it) in their hand
	atâhpenêwa, atâhpenamwa	takes hold of s.o., it
	atâhpenamawêwa	takes hold of (it) for s.o.
	čîkenamawêwa	holds (it) out to s.o.
	chîhchîkenamwa	keeps holding it out
	tanenêwa, tanenamwa	holds s.o., it {somewhere}; keeps fiddling with it
	inenêwa, inenamwa	holds, handles s.o., it {so}, hands s.o., it on to {somewhere}
	kehkitechênêwa	takes hold of s.o. around the body, takes s.o. in one's arms
	kehtahkyênêwa	holds s.o. down, in place

	kehtenêwa	holds s.o. fast
	kekyênenêwa, kekyênenamwa	holds s.o., it firmly, holds on to s.o., it
	kekyênichîkwanênêwa	holds s.o.'s knees
	kekyêninehkênêwa	holds s.o. by the hand
	nîmamêwa, nîmatamwa	holds s.o., it in one's mouth or using one's mouth
	sakeshênêwa	holds s.o. by the ear
	sakenamwa	holds it in one's fingers, pinches it up (as, cloth)
	sakinehkênêwa	takes s.o. by the hand, holds s.o.'s hand
	sakinehkênetîwaki	they take, hold, or lead each other by the hand
	sakinehkêpahônêwa	runs holding s.o. by the hand
	sakiwinênêwa	takes or holds s.o. by the horn or horns
	tasôshkenêwa	holds, s.o.'s capacity is {such an amount}
	wîkêtenêwa, wîkêtenamwa	holds it in position
	wîshikenêwa, wîshikenamwa	holds s.o., it tightly
hold against	**otênemêwa**	resents s.o. or holds something against s.o. for {some} reason
hold on	**kehkichikenamwa**	wraps one's arms or hands around it to hold on to it (as, a limb)
	atâhpenamâhkwîwa	pulls on (it) for support
	kehtenamâhkwîwa	holds on tight (for support)
	kekyênenamâhkwîwa	holds on (to it) (for support)
	wîshikenamâhkwîwa	holds on tight (for support)
	pashkonamâhkwîwa	loses one's hold, loses the grip that is supporting one's weight
hold tongue	**wânimêwa, wânotamwa**	holds one's tongue in speaking to or about s.o., it; does not say anything critical to or about s.o.
hole	**wânakwi**	hole, cave; open grave
	wânakowiwi	it has a hole in it, is hollow
	owânakomiwa	has a hole
	wânehkêwa	digs, digs a hole or grave
	otânakwêwa	has one's hole, burrow in {such} direction
	otânakatwi	a hole goes in {such} direction
	ahkwitânaki	at the top of the hole (particle)
	nâmânaki	inside the hole, cave (particle)
	chîkânakwe	by the hole (particle)
	makânakatwi	it is a big hole, it is a big cave
	pâhkânaketêwi (Jones)	a hole opens from heat or gunshot
	wâsêyânakatwi	it is a lighted hole
	wâshesiwa, wâshâwi	has a hole, it has a hole in it
	wâshâwakahamwa	makes a hole in it (the earth) by striking it
	pôhkyâwi	it has a hole in it, it is a hole
	pôhpôhkyâwi	it has holes in it
	pôhkechêshkawêwa	kicks a hole in s.o.'s belly
	pôhkeshwêwa, pôhkeshamwa	cuts a hole in s.o., it, makes a cut in s.o.
	pôhkitepêwa	has a hole in one's head, has a fontanelle
	pôhpôhkeshamwa	cuts holes in it
	pôhkahamwa	pokes a hole in it, pierces it
hollow	**pepikwêyâwi**	it is hollow
	wânakowiwi	it has a hole in it, is hollow
	wâshinihkatwi	it (a tree) is hollow
	wâwâshinîkwêwa	is hollow-eyed
	wânehkonamwa	hollows it out by hand, scoops it out
	wânehkwâwashkohkamwa	tromps down the tall grass to make a concealed space
hominy	**panakîhaki** (plural)	hominy, lye hominy

274

	pâkosôha	whole-grain hominy (dried corn, roasted then boiled)
honey	**âmôwi**	honey
hood	**pîchikwâni**	hood (on a garment); knife-case
hoof	**meshkasha**	a nail, claw, hoof
	nîkâninehkâkani	front hoof, paw
	mêmeshkwikashêwa	has red hoofs
	papîsikashêwi	(of) tiny hoof (prenoun)
hooked	**wâkikomêwa**	has a hooked nose or beak
hoop	**tôpâkâha**	bark hoop rolled as a target
	tôpâkâhiwaki	they have a contest shooting at hoops
hoot	**ketowa**	hoots, quacks, etc.
hop	**nânânikâhiwa**	is hopping (on one foot)
	nânîmêsahowa	jumps up and down; hops
horn	**owîwîna**	horn
	owîwîniwa	has horns
	mîwînaki	horns
	nanakwiwine	between the horns (particle)
	âyahkwiwinêwa	one's horns are {so} long
	chahkwiwinêwa (Jones)	is short-horned
	kakânwiwinêwa	has long horns
	mêmeshkwiwinêwa	has red horns
	pôhkwiwinêshinwa	falls and breaks one's horn
	sakiwinênêwa	takes or holds s.o. by the horn or horns
	sâsâkiwinêkâpâwa	stands with one's horns partly visible
horse	**nêkatôkashêha**	horse, pony
	nêkatôshkashêha	horse, pony
	nêkatôshkashâha	horse, pony
	katôshkashâha	horse, pony
	mêmeshkomêhaki	young horses, young buffaloes
	sakâpyênikêwa	leads a horse
	kîshkatahikêwa	whips one's horse
hostile	**nanâhkawi**	wickedly, meanly (preverb)
	nanâhkawâchimowa	says something negative or hostile, says something in rebuttal
hot	**pasesowa, pasetêwi**	(animate, inanimate) is hot
	pasihketêwi	it is heated all the way through
	pasâpôhtêwi	it (liquid) is piping hot
	pasâwaketêwi	the ground or earth is or gets hot
	kâhkâhkesowa, kâhkâhketêwi	(animate, inanimate) is or gets extremely hot (as, from a fire)
	ânemesowa	it is almost unbearably hot for one
	wîshasowa	feels hot, sweats
	wâwîshasowa	sweats profusely
hotel	**mâwâshimôwikâni**	hotel
house	**wîkiyâpi**	house, lodge, Meskwaki-style wickiup
	wîkiyâpêhi	house (dimin.)
	-wîkiyâpe	house, houses (in particle compounds)
	nîki	my house
	kehchîkiyâpi	big house
	ôtêwenikâni	summer house (large rectangular bark-house of summer villages; now, a ceremonial house)
	ôtêwenikêwa	lives in a summer house
	môhkomânikâni	white man's house
	pôhkote	one half of the (inside space of the) house

	ashikêwa	builds a house
	ashikawêwa	builds a house for s.o.
	ahkôtawêhtôwa	lengthens it (a house) {so far}
	pemitôpahkwe	through the side of the house
household	**nekotikamiki**	one household, one family
	nâhtaswikamiki	several households
	mânwikamikesiwaki	there are many houses of them
	taswikamikesiwaki	there are {so many} houses of them
how	**tâni**	how? what?
	êshi-	how, in what way, the way that (preverb with initial change [see **ishi**])
	êhtameko, tameko	Oh how well, much, etc. (particle)
however	**=wîna**	however, but, though you may not think so
howl	**wahônwa**	howls (as, wolf or dog)
how many	**kêswi**	how many? (particle)
	kêsenwi	how many times? (particle)
	kêsokoneshkamwa	how many days does one go?
	kêsôchênawêwa	how many of s.o. does he or she hit with a shot?
	kêsokoni	how many days? (particle)
	kêsokoneshkamwa	how many days does he or she go?
	kêsokonêtwa	how many days is he or she away?
huddle	**wawîhkwanapîhiwa**	sits huddled up
hug	**kehkitehkwênêwa**	hugs s.o. around the neck
	chêchêkechênêwa	hugs s.o. till one screams
hum	**nahkokêwa**	she hums (an accompaniment), sings a religious song with closed mouth
	nahkowêwa	she hums (an accompaniment)
human being: → person		
hummingbird	**nônôhkâha**	hummingbird
hunched	**pehkochêpiwa**	sits hunched up, sits on one's haunches
hundred	**nekotwâhkwe**	one hundred (particle)
	nîshwâhkwe	two hundred (particle)
	neswâhkwe	three hundred (particle)
	nyêwâhkwe	four hundred (particle)
	nyânanwâhkwe	five hundred (particle)
	taswâhkwe	{so many} hundred (particle)
	metâswâhkwe	ten hundred, a thousand (particle)
hungry	**wîshâpenêwa**	is hungry
	wîshâpenêwênemêwa	thinks s.o. is hungry
	shawesiwa	is hungry
	kîshâkotapenêwa	is terribly hungry
	kawapenêwa	collapses from hunger
	kêwapenêwa	one's hunger begins to slack off
	kîwapenêwa	goes about hungry
	nenwapenêwa	feels hunger
	nanawapenêhtôwa owîyawi	makes oneself hungry in vain
	otapenêhtôwa owîyawi	makes oneself hungry because of {something}
	pâpakisapenêhtôwa owîyawi	makes oneself collapse from hunger
	sesêsapenêwa	is so hungry one is impatient to eat
	shîpapenêwa	endures hunger
	tanapenêwa	continues hungry
hunt	**shîshêwa**	hunts
	shîshênotamawêwa	hunts game for s.o.
	anawiwa	goes on a distant hunt

276

	anemeshihamwa	goes off hunting
	ineshihamwa	goes to {somewhere} to hunt
	taneshihamwa	is hunting, continues hunting
	penêhkêwa	hunts turkeys
	penêhkawêwa	hunts turkeys for s.o.
	nenosohkêwa	hunts buffalo
	nênosohkêha	buffalo hunter
	mahkweshihamwa	goes on a bear hunt
	pepôneshiwa	goes on a winter hunt
	penâneshiwa	goes on a summer hunt
	takwâkeshiwa	goes on a fall hunt
	kehtwêwesiwa	has a knack for getting game
	âkôhôswêwaki (plural)	they hunt buffalo by running after them (and driving them)
	nîpêwenêwa	hunts all night with dogs
	shîshêwashkwi	hunting medicine
hunter	ênawîha	hunter
hurry	sesêsi	hurriedly, hurry to (particle, preverb)
	sesêsîwa	hurries, is in a hurry
	sesêsitêhêwa	is impatient, is in a hurry
	sesêsênemêwa, sesêsênetamwa	is impatient about s.o., it, in a hurry about s.o., it'
	sesêsapenêwa	is so hungry one is impatient to eat
	sesêsikâwosêwa	walks with hurried steps
	sesêsimêwa	hurries s.o. along with words, tells s.o. to hurry
	kekeneshihikêwa	hurries one's horse
hurt	wîsakishinwa	falls and hurts oneself, hurts oneself (on it)
	wâwîsakichinwa	gets repeatedly caught and injured (on it)
	wîsakinêhwêwa	hurts s.o., injures s.o. with a blow
	wîsakisetôwa owîyawi	hurts oneself
	wîsakamêwa	hurts s.o. by biting
	wîsakâhpenanêwa, wîsakâhpenatôwa	hurts s.o., it; causes s.o. a painful injury
	wîsakenêwa	hurts s.o. by touching or feeling
	wîsakenawêwa	hurts s.o. by shooting
	wîsakeshkawêwa	hurts s.o. by foot or body
	wîsakinakahkwêwachiwa	one's throat aches from being cold
	wîsakinawêhêwa	hurts s.o.'s feelings
	wîsakitôtanênêwa	painfully pinches s.o.'s heel
	kîhkîtesiwa	something is hurting one, is sore, aches
	têwishinwa	falls and hurts oneself
	têwitepêshinwa	falls and hurts one's head
	kwêhtânamachihêwa	hurts s.o. severely
	kwêhtânamachihtôwa	is hurt severely
	pekishkinawêhêwa	causes s.o.'s feelings to be hurt, disappoints s.o.
husband	nenâpêma	my husband
	onâpêmemêwa	she has him as a husband
	onâpêmiwa	she has a husband, has or takes (him) as her husband
	opashitômêhani	her husband
husk	pashôshkenikêwa	is husking corn
hyssop	mênâkwashkîhi	purple giant hyssop

i

I	**nîna**	I (emphatic or contrastive); (by) myself
ice	**mesihkwa**	ice, piece of ice
	mesihkwâpowi	ice water
	mehkwami	the ice surface
	tahpehkwamye	through the ice surface
if ever	**kîhpene**	in the event that, (if) ever, once (that happens), as soon as (particle)
ill	**inâhpenêwa**	is ill, afflicted {so}
	myânâhpenêwa	is ill, has a disease or affliction
	ochinêwa	is ill from {something}
illegitimate	**kîminîchêwa**	she is having, has an illegitimate baby
ill-natured	**nasatâwîneniwiwa**	is ill-natured
ill-treat	**ketemâkihêwa, ketemâkihtôwa**	ill-treats s.o., it, makes s.o., it wretched, brings ruin, ill fate upon s.o., it
image	**aneshâsowa, aneshâtêwi**	an image of (animate, inanimate) is carved
imagine	**ishiwêpitêhêwa**	imagines {so}
imitate	**anawêwa, anamwa**	imitates, resembles s.o., it
	nanâhpinohtawêwa	repeats what s.o. says, mocks s.o. by imitating
immediately	**pâpekwa**	immediately, right away, at the first opportunity; I see you've wasted no time! you didn't hesitate! (as a criticism) (particle)
	îni=meko	immediately, right then
	îni ishi	immediately, right away
	kêkisaki	right away, immediately, as soon as possible (particle)
impatient	**ashkachi**	be impatient to (preverb)
	ashkachihkamêwa	is impatient for a smoke
	ashkachipwîhêwa	impatiently awaits s.o.
impede	**nîshkeshkawêwa**	gets in s.o.'s way
impeded	**petasakesiwa**	is impeded, faces an obstacle
implore	**ânemimêwa**	implores s.o.
	wîshâmêwa	implores s.o., pleads with s.o., is insistent with s.o., presses s.o. hard (verbally), nags s.o.
impossible	**âkwi-kanâkwa**	it is, was impossible; one cannot do it; there is no other possibility; it cannot be helped (particle phrase)
	kanâkwa	it is, was impossible (particle)
in	**pîchi**	in (preverb)
inadequate	**nâwênemêwa, nâwênetamwa**	thinks s.o., it is inadequate; doesn't think much of s.o., it
inappropriate	**mamâkôchimêwa**	talks about s.o. inappropriately or going too far (as, implying one is dead)
	mamâkôtahômowa	makes inappropriate outcries (as, exaggerating the pain)
	makomakôtahômowa	makes inappropriate outcries (as, exaggerating the pain)
	memyêshkimêwa	says something out of line to s.o.
	neshiwanâtowêwa	says something inappropriate, offensive
inaudible	**panehtawêwa**	loses s.o. from hearing
in case	**wîpachi**	in case; if it should happen that (particle)
incense	**pekeshawatôwa**	burns incense to it
inch	**nekotîchishe**	one inch (particle)
include	**takonêwa, takonamwa**	includes s.o., it; reattaches it
	takonâtêwi	it is included, it counts
	takwimêwa	includes s.o. in what one says
incoherent	**wâwanâtetonêmowa**	is talking incoherently

incomplete	**nôtêhkwâhpawêwa**	one's dream is incomplete
inconvenience	**otamihêwa**	bothers, inconveniences, hinders s.o.
incorrect	**panâchimowa**	gives an incorrect or incomplete account or telling
indeed	**=meko, =mekoho**	indeed, precisely (a weak emphatic)
Indian	**nenôtêwa**	Indian; person; Meskwaki
	anenôtêwa	Indian (archaic)
	îchina	Indian
	nenôtêwi	Indian, native, wild (prenoun, preverb)
	anenôtêwi	Indian, native, wild (archaic) (prenoun)
	nenôtêwiwa	is an Indian
	anenôtêwiwa	is an Indian (archaic)
	nenôtêwâtowêwa	speaks Meskwaki (literally, speaks Indian)
indicate	**kehkinawâchi**	as an indication, indicatively (particle)
	kekyêhkinawâchi	as a repeated sign (particle)
inescapable	**kîsâtenêwa**	holds s.o. in an inescapable hold
in fact	**apina**	in fact, to this extent, even (particle)
infect	**meshesiwa**	is infected
	meshihêwa	infects s.o.
	mêshehkawêwa, mêshehkamwa	infects s.o., it; touches s.o., it by foot or body
	mehpôshêwa	she infects her unborn child by violating a pregnancy taboo
inform	**âchimohêwa**	informs, instructs, tells s.o.
	tanâchimohêwa	informs s.o. {somewhere}
	wîkêtâchimohêwa	carefully informs s.o., carefully explains to s.o.
injure	**myânenawêwa**	injures s.o. by shot
	pâhtâchinwa	is caught or snagged on something and injured
	pâhtâhêwa	beats s.o. severely
	pâhtâmêwa	says hurtful things to s.o.
innocently	**pakwanawesiwa**	does the wrong thing feigning ignorance
insane	**wêpesîha**	insane person, crazy person; one who acts foolishly; one who has a fit
insect	**manetôsêha**	insect, worm (insect larva)
inside	**nâmeki**	inside, underneath (particle)
	pîtike	inside (particle)
	pîtônaki	down inside (as, a canoe, a nest)
	pîtâkwatôwa	lays them (inanimate) on the ground going inside
inside out	**âpôtahamwa**	turns it inside out
	âpôshkenamwa	turns it inside out
insides	**nâminawâkani**	innards, insides (**onâminawâkani** his or her insides)
insist	**ânemwêwa**	nervously insists or demurs
	âtamitêhêwa	is (rashly) insistent
	kîhkîhkowêwa	insists, persists in asking or claiming, expresses doubts
	âyachîchimêwa	gives s.o. strict instructions, insists that s.o. comply strictly
	âyâchîchimêwa	gives s.o. strict instructions, insists that s.o. comply strictly
	âyachîtwêwa	gives strict instructions, insists on strict compliance
	âyâchîtwêwa	gives strict instructions, insists on strict compliance
insistent	**wîshâchi**	there is (or was) an ill-advised insistence (particle)
	wîshâmêwa	implores s.o., pleads with s.o., is insistent with s.o., presses s.o. hard (verbally), nags s.o.
	wîhkwayâtowêwa	speaks or prays insistently
install	**ashihêwa**	installs s.o.
instantly	**shôshki**	instantly, directly, at once, with ease (particle, preverb)

instead	**nâpi**	better, instead, at least (particle)
instruct	**âchimohêwa**	instructs, informs, tells s.o.
	tanâchimohêwa	instructs s.o. {somewhere}
	peshikwâchimohêwa	instructs s.o. forthrightly
	kehkahamâkêwa	gives specific instructions (about how to do something)
intend	**awiwa**	is intending to, is on the verge of
intense	**ahpîhtâpatâniwi**	it looks {so} intense
intent on	**otesiwa**	is intent on (it), devoted to (it), intends to gain from (it)
interest	**panashâhi**	interest (on a bank account)
	nôshêmikahki	interest (on a bank account) (participle)
interesting	**matâkwikiwa, matâkwikenwi**	(animate, inanimate) is new and interesting
interjections	**hâhâw** ([âʔâwᵘ], [haʔhaʔhâʔᵘ])	(the town crier's call)
	âpechi	Come on! Hurry up!
	chihihwî!	Gosh!
	chî!	Halloo! Say!
	chîhchê!	Look at that! How cute! How strange!
	ehehê!	Oh dear!; Uh-oh!; Hard luck!
	ehehyê!	Oh dear!; Uh-oh!; Hard luck!
	êhyê!	Uh-oh! Tough it out!
	hao ([haôʔ])	hello; all right, yes (agreeing to a suggestion or request)
	hawo ([haôʔ])	hello; all right, yes (agreeing to a suggestion or request)
	hwâ!	too bad (for him, etc.)!
	ihihwî!	Oh my!
	ihihyâ!	Oh my! Oh boy!
	kashi!	Why! Well now!
	kashinâkwa!	Gosh! Why! Well! Well now! Well?
	kashinâhi	Gosh! Why! Well! Well now! Well?
	kashinâ!	Gosh! Why! Well! Well now! Well?
	nahi!	Well! Hey! Listen!
	ohohô!	Oh I see! Oh come on! The idea!
	ohohwâ!	Oh my! Oh no! Mercy me!
	ohohyâ!	Oh my! Oh no! Mercy me!
	ô!	Oh!
	ôhô!	Oh yes! So that's it!
	ôhwâ!	Oh my! Oh no! Mercy me!
	ôhyâ!	Oh my! Oh no! Mercy me!
	penani	Wait an instant!
	pyêsho	Give here!
	siche, shiche (Jones)	Hiss! Psst!
	sî! (Jones)	Too bad!
	shêy	Hey there!
	shihihwî!	Oh my! Gosh! Golly!
	shihihyê!	Oh my!
	shinâkwa	Gosh, Why, Well!
	shinâhi	Gosh, Why, Well!
	shinâ!	Gosh, Why, Well!
	shî!	Gee! Say!
	shî! shî! (Jones)	Hush!
	shîhchê!	Oh my! Look at that! How cute! How odd!
	shîhwî!	Oh my!
	shohohô!	Say, look at this! Say isn't that something!
	tahkwe	Alas!
	tahkwê!	Alas!
	tamâkishaki	Too bad about him!

	tanîhka	Oh no! What have I gotten myself into! (exclamation of regret and self-reproach)
	tatike	Confound him, them!
	tôke=wîna	The idea of it! Imagine that!
	wihihwî!	Oh my! Gee whiz! Oh golly! Well well! How marvelous!
	wîhwî!	Oh my! Goodness gracious!
	yohohwâ!	Whew! (as, in satisfaction after meal or escape)
	yôhwâ!	Oh dear! Oh no!
interpret	**ânehkênoshêwa**	interprets, is an interpreter
	ânehkênohtawêwa	interprets for s.o.
	ênehkênoshêwa	interprets, is an interpreter
	ênehkênohtawêwa	'interprets for s.o.
intestines	**onakeshi**	ones' intestines; an intestine
	kechinakeshênêwa	eviscerates s.o., takes s.o.'s intestines out
in vain	**nanawi**	in vain, uselessly, for nothing; off in some isolated place (particle)
	nanawitanekowa	one's work or effort is for naught
	nanawapenêhtôwa owîyawi	makes oneself hungry in vain
invisible	**nenwâpatâniwa, nenwâpatâniwi**	(with negative:) is invisible, there is no visibility
invite	**wîhkomêwa**	invites s.o. to eat
	wîhkotîwaki	they invite each other to eat
	wîhkomâkaniwiwa	is invited to eat
	wîhkomêweniwiwa	is invited to eat
	wîhkowêwa	invites people
	wîhkowêhêwa	has s.o. invite people
	wîhkowêwosêwa	walks inviting people
	kîwatomêwa	goes about inviting s.o.
	kîwatokêmowa	goes about inviting
	natomêwa	invites, calls, asks for s.o.
	natomâsowa	is asked to come
	natomêweniwiwa	is invited
	natotîwaki	they invite each other
	pahkimêwa	invites s.o. to eat in a ceremony, assigns ceremonial food to s.o.
iron	**pîyâpehkwi, pîwâpehkwi**	iron, iron object
	pîyâpehkwi, pîwâpehkwi	made of iron (prenoun)
irregular	**memyêshkikâwosêwa**	walks with irregular steps
irreversibly	**mêchimôwi**	committed to continuing, irreversibly (preverb)
	kwayâshi	already, already and it is too late, irreversibly (particle, preverb)
is after	**peminawêwa**	is after s.o.
island	**menesi**	island
isolated	**nanawi**	off in some isolated place; in vain, uselessly, for nothing (particle)
itch	**keshîpesiwa**	itches

j

jacket	**kîshkîshkinekwêyâhi**	sleeveless jacket, vest
jaw	**netâmihkani**	my jaw
	nenekâpihkanêshkêwa	one's jaw is quivering

	nanâsitâpihkanênêwa	pries s.o.'s jaws apart
jealous	**kyâwêwa**	is jealous (in older usage, only of a man)
	kyâwamêwa	is jealous of s.o.
	kyâwatîwaki	they are jealous of each other (in older usage, only of two men)
	kyâkwiwa	she is jealous (archaic)
	kyâkomêwa	she is jealous of her (a sexual rival) (archaic)
	kyâkotîwaki	they (two women) are jealous of each other (archaic)
	kyâkowitêhêwa	she feels jealous (archaic)
	metawamêwa	envies s.o., is jealous or resentful of s.o.'s success or better treatment
jerk	**atâhpisêwa**	is jerked away
	kokwâshkêwa, kokwâshkêwi	is suddenly jerked, tossed; it is suddenly jerked, swung
	kokwisahtôwa	gives it a sharp jerk
	ochikâsahowa	jerks one's foot (or feet) back
	pasekwîchisahêwa	jerks s.o. to one's feet
jog	**nânômipahowa**	jogs, runs along at an easy pace
join	**takwîwa**	joins others
	wîtôhkâsowa	takes part, helps, joins in, goes along (with it or the others)
joint	**ânehkôkanêyâwi**	it is a joint
joke	**kakâchimêwa**	jokes with s.o.
	kakâtwêwa	jokes, teases
	kakâchihêwa	plays a joke or trick on s.o., teases s.o.
	kakâchi	jokingly (preverb), teasing (prenoun)
jolly	**opi**	for fun; jolly (preverb)
	opîneniwa	jolly fellow
	opîneniwiwa	he is a jolly fellow
jolt	**kekyêtâshkêwaki** (plural)	they are jolted from their places
jovial	**matâkwîneniwiwa**	is jovial, amusing, fun to be with
joy	**menwinawêhêwa, menwinawêhtôwa**	gives s.o., it joy
jump	**nîmêsahowa**	jumps up in the air
	nânîmêsahowa	jumps up and down; hops
	akwâchisahowa	jumps out of the water
	chapôkisahowa	jumps into the water
	chîpisahowa	jumps with a start
	chîtapisahowa	jumps into sitting position
	kwâshkwisahowa	jumps off, dismounts, disembarks
	nîsisahowa	jumps down
	nowisahowa	jumps out
	ochisahowa	jumps from {somewhere}
	pasekwîchisêwa	jumps to one's feet
	pyêchisahowa	jumps this way
	pîchisahowa	jumps inside
	pôchisahowa	jumps down in
jump (flinch)	**kwêhtânisahowa**	jumps or flinches noticeably (being startled or jolted)
just	**ishe, ashe**	just, merely, just naturally or spontaneously, just to be doing it (particle)
just as	**mani** (idiom):	**mani ênâpiyâni** just as I looked
just in time	**kêsehkwi**	just in time (to not be caught doing something)

k

katydid	**chînishkatamôha**	katydid
keep	**awiwêwa, awiwa**	gets, has, keeps s.o., it
	kîwawiwêwa, kîwawiwa	has s.o., it with one, keeps s.o., it
	shîpishinwa, shîpisenwi	(animate, inanimate) keeps, remains unspoiled
	tanôhkyanêwa, tanôhkyatôwa	keeps s.o. {somewhere}, lets or has s.o., it stay {somewhere}
keep after	**wîshâhêwa**	keeps after s.o., presses s.o. hard
keep in mind	**nâkatawênemêwa,** **nâkatawênetamwa**	keeps s.o., it in mind, keeps track of s.o., it, watches s.o., it, pays close attention to it
keep on	**âhpesehkêwa**	keeps on
	tanâpatâniwa	keeps right on doing what one is doing
	kwayânâshkêwa	keeps running (or metaphorically, reaching) beyond where one knows where one is
	ayêshi, ayîshi, ayêhi	keep on, still, yet, remaining, continue to (preverb, particle)
	mêkwâchi	be well into, keep on the same, have become and continue with equal intensity (particle)
kettle	**shêshketôha**	kettle, cauldron (copper kettle not fitted with a lid)
	shêshketôhêha	kettle, cauldron (dimin.)
	ahkohkwa	kettle, drum
	chîketôhi	tea-kettle
	nekotôhkohkwe	one kettleful (particle)
	nyêwôhkohkwe	four kettles (of food) (particle)
kick	**takeshkawêwa, takeshkamwa**	kicks s.o., it, stomps on s.o., it
	tâtakeshkawêwa	stomps s.o., kicks s.o. around
	opisahêwa, opisahtôwa	kicks up s.o. (as, snow), it (as, dirt)
	pakisehkamwa	kicks it somewhere
	mîweshkamawêwa	kicks (it) out of s.o.
kid (verb)	**ashe inowêwa**	says something false, is just kidding
	ishe inowêwa	says something false, is just kidding
	ashe ishimêwa	tells s.o. something false, is just kidding s.o.
	ishe ishimêwa	tells s.o. something false, is just kidding s.o.
kidneys	**otônenôhaki**	kidneys
kill	**nesêwa, nehtôwa**	kills s.o., it; beats s.o. up
	nehtamawêwa	kills (s.o.) for s.o.
	nehtamâkêwa	kills (s.o.) for people
	nehtâwêwa	kills, makes a kill
	nehtâwêmikatwi	it kills
	âhpechinanêwa	kills s.o. for good, kills s.o. outright
	ânôhpenanêwa	is unable to kill s.o.
	châkihêwa	kills both or all of them
	châkihtawêwa	kills all of (them) for s.o.
	ishisahetîwaki	they kill each other {so}
	kîshatahwêwa	finishes s.o. off with a club
	mechimihêwa	kills many of s.o.
	ochihêwa	kills s.o. for {some reason}
	otâhpenanêwa	deals with, kills s.o. for {some reason}
	pahkihtêhpwêwa	knocks out or kills s.o. by biting
	pahkihtêhwêwa	knocks out or kills s.o. by striking with something
	pashinanêwa, pashinatôwa	almost kills s.o., it
	pâpakachikêwa	slays someone, clubs someone to death
	taswihêwa, taswihtôwa	has, makes, kills {so many} of s.o., it
	wêchinowihêwa	easily kills s.o.

kind, kindly	**keshâchi**	gently, kindly (particle, preverb, prenoun)
	keshâtesiwa	is kind
	keshâtesiweni	kindness
	keshâchîneniwa	a kind man
	keshâchîneniwiwa	he is a kind man
	keshâchihêwa	is kind to s.o.
	keshâchihetîwaki	they are kind to each other
	keshâchinohkatawêwa	is kind or friendly to s.o.
	keshâchinotawêwa	is kind or friendly to s.o.
	shahki-mehtosêneniwiwa	is good-natured
kind, type	**nekotayaki**	one group, set, pair, couple, kind (particle)
	nekotayakatwi	it's the only one (of its kind), there is only one kind of it
	nekotayakatôhiwi	it is one kind; it's the only one (of its kind), there is only one kind of it (dimin.)
	nîshwayakihtôwa	has two sets of it
	taswayaki	{so many} kinds, groups, sets, pairs (particle)
	âchipanakichi	all different kinds, all different ways (particle)
	wâwiyâki	of all kinds, mixed together (preverb)
kindling	**peshkonênawachikêwa**	gets the fire started with (it), uses (it) as kindling wood
kindly	**keshâtênemêwa**	thinks kindly of s.o.
kingfisher	**ateshkâha, atashkâha**	kingfisher
kinnikinnick	**kônachîhi**	kinnikinnick, inner bark of "red willow" (red-osier dogwood) used for smoking
	kônachîhiyâhtêwi	there is the smell of kinnikinnick being smoked
Kishko	**kîshkôha**	Kishko, member of the Kishko division
	kîshkôhiwa	is a Kishko
	kîshkôhkwêha	Kishko (archaic)
	kîshkôhkwêhiwa	is a Kishko (archaic)
	kîshkôhihkwêwa	Kishko woman
kiss	**pôtetonêhpwêwa**	kisses s.o.
knee	**nechîkwani**	my knee
	mêmehchichîkwanêyâshinwa	her knees are exposed by the wind (as, in running)
	tepichîkwanêshkâtîwaki	they are in a row sitting knee-to-knee
	wawîhkwanapiwa	sits on one's knees (with feet together on one side)
	wawîhkwanisahowa	drops to one's knees (to sit)
	wawîhkwanisêwa	collapses to one's knees
kneecap	**ashashkwa**	kneecap
	netashashkoma	my kneecap
kneel	**ochîkwanapiwa**	kneels
	ochîkwanapihêwa	makes s.o. kneel
knees up	**nenyêmatôkanêpiwa**	sits with one's knees up
	nenyêmatôkanêshinwa	lies with one's knees up
knife	**mâtesi**	knife
	mâtesêhi	knife (dimin.)
	omâtesiwa	has a knife, has (it) as a knife
	wîtekôwi-mâtesi	"owl knife" (flint knife or arrowhead)
	wîtekôwi-mâtesêhi	"owl knife" (dimin.)
knife-case	**pîchikwâni**	knife-case; hood (on a garment)
knock	**pakapahkwêhamwa**	knocks at the wall of it
	pakapahkwêhikêwa	is knocking on the wall
	anwêwêpahkwênikêwa	knocks on the side of the lodge
	pâkahamawêwa	knocks at (it, the door) for s.o.
knock out	**pahkihtêhwêwa**	knocks out or kills s.o. by striking with something
	pahkihtêhpwêwa	knocks out or kills s.o. by biting

	papahkwâpitêhwêwa	knocks s.o.'s teeth out
knock over	**sîkeshkamwa**	knocks it over, kicks it over
knot	**pehkwikenôhi**	knot (in wood)
know	**kehkênemêwa, kehkênetamwa**	knows s.o., it; has carnal knowledge of s.o.; has one's senses, is conscious, is aware of things
	kehkênetamawêwa	knows (it) from, of s.o.
	kehkênetamâtisowa	knows (it) of oneself
	kehkênetamôwênemêwa	thinks s.o. knows (it), thinks s.o. has their senses
	kehkênetamôwitêhêwa	thinks one knows (it)
	kehkênetamwihêwa	makes s.o. know (it), lets s.o. know (it)
	kehkênetisowa	knows about oneself
	kehkênetâkosiwa, kehkênetâkwatwi	(animate, inanimate) is known
	kênemâpi, kehkênemâpi	I don't know (particle)
	mehtênemêwa	knows full well about s.o.
	wâwanawiwa	is ignorant, does not know how, does not know what to do
	wâwanênemêwa, wâwanênetamwa	fails to know s.o., it, forgets s.o., it
	wâwanênetamôhkânowa	pretends not to know
	wâwanekêwa	does not know how to dance
	nahi	know how to, used to, subject to, given to, keep, frequently (preverb)
	=kochi	you know, as you know, of course, don't you remember, all I can say is
knowledgeable	**nepwâhkânotawêwa, nepwâhkânotamwa**	is knowledgeable about s.o., it

l

lack	**ashenowihêwa, ashenowihtôwa**	is without s.o., it
lacrosse	**pâkahatowêwa**	plays lacrosse; plays baseball
	ahchîhi	lacrosse-stick
ladder	**akôsîyâpi**	ladder
lady's-slipper	**kokowêhi-mahkesêhi**	lady's-slipper
ladle	**kwâpahikani**	dipper, ladle
lake	**nepisi**	lake
	nepisiwiwi	it is a lake
land	**ahki**	land
	ahkiwiwi	it is earth, earthy
	otôhkimiwa	has (it) as land
	inâhkiwiwi	it is high land {so}
	menwahkiwiwi	it is good land
	pêshkonêwahkamikatwi	the land is abloom
	tepâhkiwiwi	it is flat land
	wîhtêwahkiwiwi	it is burnt-over land
	ashkipakâmehkwisenwi	it lies as green land
land (verb)	**pakishinwa, pakisenwi**	lands, falls, strikes
large: → big		
large group	**nowâwanetêwi**	a large group (as, of people) goes out
	pôsâwanetîwaki (plural)	they get into a boat in a large group
	pyêtâwanetîwaki (plural)	they arrive in numbers

lascivious	**memêsachitêhêwa**	has lascivious thoughts, has a randy feeling
lasso	**panapinêwa**	fails to lasso s.o.
	nâpehkwêhwêwa	lassoes s.o. by the neck
last	**mêmechinêhi**	for the last time (particle)
	mêmechinêhiweni	last thing, conclusion
	ahkowi	after, afterwards, behind, as the last one (particle)
	kêkêwâchi	as the last one(s) (particle)
late	**ashkachitepehki**	late at night (particle)
	ashkachitepehkîwi	it is late at night (particle)
later	**ashkachi**	after a while, later, taking a long time (particle)
	ashkachîmekîhi, ashkachîmêhi	after a little while (particle)
	ashkachîhiwiwi	it is some time later
	atâhanahk-ochîmêhi	a little later
	atâh-ochîmêhi	a little later; a little nearer, a little more recently
laugh	**apahapanêniwa**	laughs
	apahapanênemêwa	laughs at s.o.
	ênikênemêwa	laughs at s.o.
	ênikehtawêwa	laughs when hearing s.o.
	anemâyêniwa	goes off laughing
	menwâyêniwa	has a pretty laugh
	môhkâyêniwa	bursts out laughing
	pyêtâyêniwa	arrives laughing
	tanâyêniwa	is laughing {somewhere}
	tahitanâyêniwa	is laughing away, laughs and laughs
	tahitanâyênemêwa	is laughing away at s.o.
	tahitanâyênekêmowa	is laughing away at people
laxative	**shâposwêwa**	administers a laxative or purgative to s.o.
	shâposikani	laxative
law	**inâhkonikêwa**	makes {such} laws or rules
	inâhkonamawêwa	makes {such} laws or rules for s.o.
lay	**nanâhishimêwa, nanâhisetôwa**	lays s.o., it in place
	nanâhishitîwaki (plural)	they lay each other to rest
	ishishimêwa, ishisetôwa	lays s.o., it {so}
	ishisetawêwa	lays (it) {so} for s.o.
	kîshishimêwa	has laid s.o. away, out, in place; buries s.o.
	kîshisetawêwa	lays (it) away for s.o.
	nowisetôwa	throws it outside (Jones)
	ochishimêwa	lays s.o. in {somewhere}
	wîkêchishimêwa, wîkêchisetôwa	lays s.o., it carefully
	âsôyâhkwishimêwa	lays s.o. propped up at an angle
	inehkwêshitîwaki	they lay each other with heads {some way}
	tanehkwêshimêwa	lays s.o. with head {somewhere}
	pîtâkwatôwa	lays it along toward the inside
	âpishkwâkwatawêwa	unties and lays (it) out for s.o.
	kawenêwa, kawenamwa	lays, pushes s.o., it down
layer	**pîhtôkenwi**	it is in tiers, in layers
lazy	**nânîkihtôha**	lazy person
	nânîkihtôhiwa	is lazy, never wants to do anything
lead	**nîkâni**	in the lead, on ahead; in future, ahead of time (particle, prenoun, preverb)
	nîkânîwa	leads, is the leader (for example, of a dance)
	nîkânîmikatwi	it leads
	nîkânîhêwa	makes s.o. the leader
	nîkânîhtawêwa	is the leader of s.o.

	nîkânîmikihtawêwa	makes (it) be the leading thing for s.o.
	nîkânesiwa	is, becomes the leader, the leading one
	nîkânishinwa	is in the lead
	nîkânekêwa	leads in the dance
	kîhkiwenêwa	leads s.o. further
	kîhkiwetawêwa	leads s.o., it further for s.o.
	kîhkîhkiwenêwa	leads s.o. against their will
	kîwânîwenêwa	leads s.o. astray
	kîwêwenêwa	leads, pulls s.o. back
	kîwiwenêwa	leads s.o. about
	mechimiwetâkêwa	leads men to their death
	nîsiwenêwa	leads s.o. down
	nîsiwetawêwa	leads it down for s.o.
	pemiwenêwa, pemiwetôwa	leads s.o. along, carries it along
	pîchiwenêwa	leads s.o. in
	sakâpyênêwa	leads s.o. holding on (with a rope or by hand)
	tetepiwenêwa	leads s.o. in a circle
lead (metal)	asenipi	lead
	asenipihkêwa	mines lead
	asenipikâni	lead mine
lead warparty	mayâwosêwa	leads a warparty
leaf	tâhtapakwi	leaf
	tâhtopakwi	leaf (archaic)
	nâmi-tâhtapakwe	under a leaf (particle compound)
	nâmi-tâhtopakwe	under a leaf (archaic) (particle compound)
	wâkihpenipakwi	yellow-lotus leaf
	meshkwipakatwi	its leaves are red
	ashkipakipyêwa	has green leaves or boughs
	wêwenipyêwa, wêwenipyêyâwi	(animate, inanimate) has pretty leaves or boughs
leaf out	kîshipyêyâwi	it has leafed out
leak	achikêwi	it drips, leaks
lean	âhchîshinwa	leans
	âhchîpiwa	sits leaning
leap	kâtanahamîwa	springs, bolts off, leaps up (to fly), shoves off with the feet
learn	kehkinôsowa	observes (it) and learns, memorizes (it), is knowledgeable about (it)
	kehkinawâpiwa	learns by looking
	kehkinawâpihêwa	makes s.o. learn by looking
	kehkinawâpamêwa, kehkinawâpatamwa	watches s.o., it to learn
least	kanâhi	at least (particle)
	wêtêwi, wêtêwe	(with negative:) not the least bit, not for a while, not at all close (particle)
leather	pîshâkani	rawhide, buckskin, leather
	sînahtakîwa	makes a leather cord by rolling together strips of hide
leave	ashkwatamwa	leaves it from eating
	ashkwihêwa	leaves, spares s.o.
	ashkwiwetawêwa	leaves (it) to s.o.
	kîwâkwatôwa	leaves it lying about (abandoned)
	sêsahwêwa, sêsahamwa	leaves s.o., it someplace to be retrieved later
	shîkotêwi	it is left after burning
	shîkwatamwa	leaves it from eating
	shîkwatâtêwi	it is left over from eating

leave behind	**nakanêwa, nakatamwa**	leaves s.o., it
	nakatamawêwa	leaves (it) for s.o.
	pemi-wêpihkanêwa	goes off and leaves s.o.
	ahpihkanêwa	leaves s.o. behind with (it)
	ketemâkihkanêwa	leaves s.o. wretched, in misery
	nânishkwihkanêwa	outdistances s.o., leaves s.o. behind
	ochihkanêwa, ochihkatamwa	leaves s.o., it behind {somewhere}
	ochihkanetîwaki	they leave each other behind {somewhere}
left (side)	**nemachîwa**	is left-handed
	nêmachîhiwa	is left-handed
	wêchi-nemachîchi	on one's left
	nemachîninâki	left (side)
	nenemachîneki	on my left
left over	**ashkwisêwa**	has food left; is left over (see **êshkwisâchiki**)
	ênêkiwa, ênêkenwi	(animate, inanimate) is left over, not paired off, an uneven number
leg	**kakânwikahkwanwa**	has long legs
	mehchikahkwanwa	is bare-legged
	pôhkwikahkwanêhwêwa	hits s.o. and breaks their leg
	sakikânêwa	grabs s.o. by the leg
	sakikâpinêwa, sakikâpitôwa	ties s.o., it by the leg
	shashawikahkwanêwosêwa	walks to limber up one's legs
	shashawikâwosêwa	walks to limber up one's legs
	shashôshkikâsahowa	kicks one's legs out straight
	shôshkikâtêwa	straightens one's leg or legs
	shôshkikâsahowa	kicks one's legs out straight
	tatôkikâpiwa	sits with one's legs spread apart
leg: → calf, shin, thigh		
legend: → story		
leggin	**matetêhi**	leggin
	omatetêhiwa	wears leggins, wears (them) as leggins
	omatetêhihêwa	makes leggins for s.o.
	mêmeshkwimatetêha	Red-Leggins (man in story)
	pîwâhimatetêwa	wears beaded leggins
	wâwâpimatetêwa	wears white leggins
lend	**awihêwa**	lends to s.o., lends (it) to s.o.; borrows (it) from s.o.
	awihiwêwa	lends (it), borrows (it)
length	**êhkôtêki**	the length of the lodge (see **ahkôtêwi**)
lengthen	**ahkôtawêhtôwa**	lengthens it (a house) {so far}
less	**atenâwi**	less (particle)
let fly	**nâpâshkahwâtamwa**	lets it (an arrow) fly on the same trajectory
	nâpâshkahwâtôwa	lets it (an arrow) fly on the same trajectory
let go	**pakisenêwa, pakisenamwa**	sets s.o., it down; lets s.o., it go
	pakisenamawêwa	sets (it) down for s.o.; lets (it) go for s.o.
let it go	**meshê=ʼnahi**	let it go, forget it; one lets it happen
	meshê=ʼnah=meko	let it go, forget it; one lets it happen
level	**tepâhkiwiwi, tepâhkîwi**	it is level land; it (water) is flat calm
liar	**pashitowêwênemêwa**	thinks s.o. a liar
liberated	**pâhkâhkoshkêwa**	becomes free, is liberated
lick	**nôshkwâhpwêwa, nôshkwâhtamwa**	licks s.o., it
	nôshkwâhtamawêwa	licks (it) for s.o.
lid	**kepanohikani**	lid
lie (recline)	**shekishinwa**	lies, lies down, is lying down ({somewhere})

	shekishinôhiwa	lies (dimin.)
	nanâhishinwa	lies down, goes to bed
	apehkwêshinwa	lies with one's head on (it)
	anemehkwisenwi	it lies upside down
	anemisenwi	it lies extending away
	asipôshinôki	they lie in a group, they all sleep together
	ayêshinôhiwa	still lies (dimin.)
	âhpetâpyêsenwi	it lies endless
	âhtawâshinwa, âhtawâsenwi	lies on one's back, it lies its back
	inâkwasowa, inâkwatêwi	it lies about {so}
	inekihkwishinwa	lies {so} big
	ishisenwi	it lies or is set {so}, it is a rule {so}
	ishîkwêshinwa	lies facing {so}: **êshîkwêshiki** the way he or she faces, in front of his or her face
	kehchishinwa	lies flat
	kekishinwa	lies having (it), is buried with (it)
	kîshishinwa	has lain down
	pemi-kîshkâkwatêwani	they (inanimate) lie in a row
	kîwâkwasowa, kîwâkwatêwi	(animate, inanimate) lies about (as dead or destroyed)
	kîwishinwa	lies about
	kohkishinwa	turns over as one lies
	kokwêhkishinwa	keeps turning over as one lies
	kwâpâkwasowa	lies scattered
	matakôhkwêshinwa	lies with covered head
	menehtâmisenwi	it is the first one that lies or is set
	menwishinwa, menwisenwi	lies well, comfortably; it lies well
	êh=nanakwishinowâchi	between them as they lay
	neneshkisenwi	it lies spread out
	nenyêhpishinwa	is weak and has trouble moving from lying too long
	nenyêmatôkanêshinwa	lies with one's knees up
	nîpenêsenwi	it lies in order
	ochishinwa	lies on {some} side, in {some} direction
	papakâshkatêshinwa	lies flat on one's stomach
	pemâhkwisenwi	it lies along as a solid
	pemâkwatêwi	it lies along
	pemâmehkishinwa	lies along as ground
	pemâmehkisenwi	it lies along as ground
	pemitechêshinwa	lies crossways
	sâkitepêshinwa	lies with head exposed
	shôshkâpyêshinwa	lies at full length
	tanahkyêshinwa	is keeping to one's bed with a serious illness
	takwisenwi	it lies, is placed together
	tanehkwêshinwa	lies with one's head facing {somewhere}
	tashikâshinwa	lies with feet {somewhere}
	pemi-tepikîshkâkwatêwani	they (inanimate) lie end-on in an even line
	wâwâchikâshinôki	they lie with feet together
	wâwâchitiyêshinôki	they lie buttocks to buttocks
lie (tell a lie)	pashitowêwa	tells a lie
life	pemâtesiweni	life
	mehtosêneniwiweni	life
	menwi-mehtosêneniwiweni	healthy life
	pwâwi-menwi-pemâtesiweni	bad life
	kîhkihêwa	prolongs s.o.'s life
	âpesîwa	comes back to life

	âpesîhêwa	brings s.o. back to life
	âpesîwanêhpwêwa	restores s.o. to life by breathing
lift	nîmênêwa, nîmênamwa	lifts s.o., it up, holds s.o., it up
	nîmêwenêwa	lifts s.o.
	akwâpyênêwa	lifts s.o. out of the water
	kwahkwîtenêwa	lifts s.o. to their feet, helps s.o. up
	pasekwîtenêwa	lifts s.o. to their feet
light	wâsêyâwi	there is light, daylight; it is day
	wâsêshawêwa	has or makes light (as, from a fire)
	wâsêshêwa	(star) gives off light
	wâsêshêwi	there is light from a fire; it (house) has light in it from a fire
	wâsêshkamwa	lights it by walking, going, jumping
	wâsesikêwa	lights things up
	wâsâhkotawêwa	the light of one's fire can be seen glowing in the distance
	wâsâhkotêwi	the light of (its) fire can be seen glowing in the distance
	kîweshawêwa	goes about lighting
	pahtêhpwêwa	lights s.o. (tobacco, pipe), puffs and gets s.o. (pipe) lit
	pahtêhtamawêwa	lights (it, a pipe) for s.o.
	pahtêhchikawêwa	lights the pipe for s.o.
light (weight)	pepehkêhêhiwa, pepehkêhenôhiwi	(animate, inanimate) is light (of weight)
lightly	wêchinowîhtêwa	is lightly clothed
lightning	pâhpâhketonôki nenemehkiwaki	there is thunder and lightning ("the thunderers are opening their mouths")
	wawâsetonôki nenemehkiwaki	there is lightning ("the thunderers' mouths are flashing")
	nenemehkiwi-ashkotêwi	bolt of lightning
like	wîki	enjoy, like (preverb)
	menwênemêwa, menwênetamwa	likes s.o., it
	menwênetamawêwa	likes (s.o.) for s.o.
	menwênechikêwa	likes someone or something, has likes
	menwâkômêwa	likes s.o.'s ways
	mesawinoshêwa	likes what one hears
	nahatamwa	likes to eat it, likes it
like, as	mehtôchi	like, as if, as it were, as though (particle)
limber	nenikosiwa, nenikwâwi	(animate, inanimate) is limber
	shashawesiwa, shashawâwi	is limber; it is pliant, yielding
	shashawosêwa	walks to limber up
	shashawikâwosêwa	walks to limber up one's legs
	shashawikahkwanêwosêwa	walks to limber up one's legs
limp	myâhkosêwa	limps
line	ketâpihkâtêwi	a marching line emerges into view
lion	kênwâsowêwa	mountain lion
	onâyina	African lion
lip	ochîketonâkani	lips
	kehpaketonwa	has thick lips
	papakotonêshinwa	one's lips are loose
liquid	meshkwâpôkatwi	it is red liquid
listen	peseshêwa	listens
	pesetawêwa, pesetamwa	listens to s.o., it
	ênikehtawêwa	listens laughing to s.o.
	wîkêtehtamwa	listens to it carefully
little	takâwi	a little (particle)
	anehkîhi	a little, a small amount (particle)
	âyânehkîhi	a little each (particle)

little ways	**meshe-nâhinâhi**	a little ways off (particle compound)
	mêmeshe-nânâhinâhi	a little ways from each other (particle compound)
little while	**nômakêpihêwa**	makes s.o. sit for a short while
	nômakêwe	in, for a little while (particle)
	nômake	in, for a little while (particle)
live	**pemâtesiwa**	lives
	pemâtesînotamwa	lives by it
	mehtosêneniwiwa	lives
	mehtosêneniwêhiwa	lives (dimin.)
	mehtosêneniwihêwa	makes s.o. live; turns s.o. into a human being
	nêsêwa	gets well, survives, lives after brush with death, is alive
	mamâchîhêwa	makes s.o. move, gives s.o. life
	anemikiwa	lives on (**ênemikichiki, wîh=anemikichiki** 'the people to come in the future')
	kâkikêwineniwiwa	lives forever
	tashikiwa	lives, grows {somewhere}
	wîchi-mehtosênenîkêwa	lives as a fellow mortal
live alone	**môshakihkwêwiwa**	she lives without a man in the house
live longer	**kîhki-mehtosêneniwêhiwa**	lives a little longer
	kîhkîwa	moves further on or away, lives longer
liver	**ohkoni**	liver
live with	**wîchihêwa, wîchihtôwa**	lives with s.o., it (in the same dwelling)
	wîchihetîwaki	they live in the same dwelling
	wîchihiwêwa	lives with others (in the same dwelling)
load	**pôsihêwa, pôsihtôwa**	puts s.o., it into a boat, a vehicle, or a vessel or container open at the top (as, a cauldron or mortar); sends s.o., it
lock up	**kepâhkohwêwa, kepâhkohamwa**	locks s.o., it up; closes it up securely
	tanâhkohwêwa	imprisons s.o. {somewhere}
	tahitanâhkohwêwa	keeps s.o. imprisoned {somewhere}
locust	**êhtesikêha**	locust (insect)
lodge	**akâmetêki**	at the other side of the lodge (particle)
	âhkwâtêmeki	at the far end of the lodge (particle)
	êhkwâtêmeki	at the far end of the lodge (particle)
	nanakotêki	in the center of the lodge (particle)
lodge-frame	**matepwi**	bare lodge-frame
lodge-pole	**apashi**	lodge-pole, side post, door post
	apashîhi	lodge-pole, side post, door post (dimin.)
	wîkiyâpâhkwi	lodge-pole
	wîkiyâpâhkôhi	lodge-pole (dimin.)
log	**pemitasakatwi**	log
	ohpikayâhkôni	logs that hold down the roof of a summer house
log cabin	**papâmitâhkwikâni**	log cabin
lonely	**kîwâtesiwa**	is lonely
	kîwâtesîhiwa	is lonely (dimin.)
	kîwâchâwi	it is lonely, sad
	kîwâchâhiwi	it is lonely, sad (dimin.)
	kîwâchinâkosiwa	looks lonely
	kîwâchitêhêwa	feels lonely
	kîwâchihêwa	makes s.o. lonely
	kîwâchinawêhêwa	makes s.o. feel lonesome
	kîwâchinawêmêwa	makes s.o. feel lonely or sad by what one says
	nanawêhkami	in a lonely spot
long	**kenwi**	long (prenoun, preverb)

	kenôsiwa, kenwâwi	is long, tall; it is long
	kenoshkêwi	it gets longer
	kakânwi	long (plural) (prenoun, preverb)
	kakânôsiwaki	they (animate) are long
	ahkwiwa, ahkonwi	(animate, inanimate) is {so long}
	ahkwâwi	it is {so long}
long ago	**ashawaye (ashawe=)**	long ago (particle)
	nashawaye	long ago (particle)
	anashawaye (anashawe=)	long ago (particle)
	ashawêhkamiki	long ago, long before, in ancient days (particle)
	nashawêhkamiki	long ago, long before, in ancient days (particle)
long for	**kwînomêwa, kwînotamwa**	longs for s.o., it
long time	**kenwêshi**	for a long time (particle, preverb)
	kenwêshîmêhi	for quite a long time (particle)
	kakânwêshi	for a long time each time (particle)
	meshenâhinâhiwiwi	it is not a long time
	nanôpehkâchinâhi	a long period of time; a great distance (particle)
	penôchi	far away, a long time; easily (particle)
longhouse	**kênôtêhi**	longhouse
	kenôtêwi	it is a longhouse
	kenôtawêhtôwa	builds it as a longhouse
look (appear)	**ishinâkosiwa, ishinâkwatwi**	(animate, inanimate) looks {so}
	ishinâkwihêwa	makes s.o. look {so}
	keshâchinâkosiwa	looks gentle
	kîshâkochinâkosiwa	looks splendid
	menwâpatâniwa, menwâpatâniwi	(animate, inanimate) looks nice
	meshinâkosiwa	looks big
	mîshâchinâkwihowa	makes oneself look dressed up
	nanâhinâkosiwa	is looking better
	nenwinâkosiwa	the look on one's face says everything
	neshiwinâkosiwa, neshiwinâkwatwi	(animate, inanimate) looks terrible, awful, fierce
	pehkîninâkosiwa, pehkîninâkwatwi	(animate, inanimate) looks different, strange
	sanakinâkwatwi	it looks difficult
	wîyashkinâkwatwi	it looks dreadful
look (regard)	**inâpiwa**	looks to {somewhere}
	inâpihêwa	makes s.o. look to {somewhere}
	aniwatawâpiwa	looks about too much
	mînâwâpiwa	looks closely
	sakakwâpiwa	looks at an angle, looks out of the corner of the eye
	tanâpiwa	looks {somewhere}
	wîkêtatawâpiwa	takes a careful look
	wîshâwâpiwa	looks about anxiously
look at	**wâpamêwa, wâpatamwa**	looks at s.o., it
	wâpatamawêwa	looks at (it) for s.o.
	wâpakêwa	looks on
	wâpachikêwa	looks, looks at something
	wâpamâsowa	is looked at
	wâpawâpamêwa, wâpawâpatamwa	keeps looking at s.o., it, gazes at s.o., it
	wâpatisowa	looks at oneself, examines oneself
	wâpatîwaki	they look at each other
	inâpamêwa, inâpatamwa	looks at s.o., it {so}, sees s.o., it {so}

	kehtâpamêwa, kehtâpatamwa	looks fixedly at s.o., it
	kokwênepâpamêwa	looks at s.o. all around
	mayâwâpamêwa	looks straight at s.o.
	mechimâpamêwa, mechimâpatamwa	looks closely, fixedly at s.o., it, stares at s.o., it
	pakisâpamêwa	takes one's eyes off s.o., quits looking at s.o.
Look at that!	**chîhchê!**	Oh my! Look at that! How cute! How odd! (also **shîhchê!**)
look back	**wâpanâchihêwa**	(departing soul) looks back and destroys s.o.
	wâpanâpamêwa	(departing soul) looks back at s.o.
look for: → seek		
lookout	**âhkwamêwa**	is on the lookout, on one's guard
	âhkwamênotawêwa, âhkwamênotamwa	is on the lookout for s.o., it
loon	**mâkwa**	loon
loop	**nanâhâpyênamwa**	gets it ready to tie it, loops it
loose	**papakwâwi**	it hangs loosely, it (as, a tent) is loose
	papakonamwa	loosens it (to hang loosely)
	papakotonêshinwa	one's lips are loose
	papakwâsiyêwa	his breechcloth hangs loosely
	papakwinameshkêwa	one's skin is loose
	papakwîkwêwa	one's face is loose
	pîsêyâwi	it is loose and fine
	kêshawenamwa	holds it loosely, loosens it
	kêshawahamwa	loosens it by tool
	kêshawahokowa	is made loose by weight or mass
	shâpôsiwa	is loose in the bowels, has diarrhea
loosen	**kêwapisowa**	one's bonds are loosened a bit
	nôhkâmehkisetôwa	loosens the earth in it (house)
	nôhkâmehkisetawêwa	loosens its earth for s.o.
	papakonamwa	loosens it (to hang loosely)
	shashawêkinêwa	loosens s.o. (a hide) up by working (the hide) with the hands
lose	**akihêwa, akihtôwa**	loses s.o., it
	panehtawêwa	loses s.o. from hearing
	tanakihtôwa	loses it {somewhere}
	wanihêwa, wanihtôwa	loses, forgets about s.o., it
lose mind	**wâwanênetamwa**	loses one's mind, cannot think straight, is at one's wit's end
lose sight	**panâpamêwa, panâpatamwa**	loses sight of s.o., it
	panâpatamâtisowa	loses sight of (it) for oneself
lose voice	**panâchishimowa**	loses one's voice
loss (at a loss)	**kwînatawi**	at a loss, destitute (preverb)
	kwînatawesiwa	is at a loss
	wâwanâchi	at a loss for what to do, confusedly (particle, preverb)
	wâwanâtesiwa	is at a loss for what to do, beside oneself
	wâwani-ishawiwa	is unable to do it right, is at a loss
	wâwanikihtôwa	is at a loss what to do about it
lost	**kîwânîwa**	is lost (not knowing where one is)
	kîwânîsêwa	loses one's way
	wanisowa	is lost (one's whereabouts are unknown), in another world, confused (as, about what day it is)
	otakisowa	gets lost from {somewhere}
lotus	**wâkihpeni**	yellow lotus, yellow lotus roots

	oshkîshekwaki	yellow lotus seeds
	wâkihpeni-oshkîshekwaki	yellow lotus seeds
loud	pôswêkesiwa	cries hard, cries louder
	wîshâwêwêkesiwa	wails loudly
	ahpîhtwêwêsenwi	it sounds {so loud}
louse	ahkwa	louse
	netehkomaki	my lice
	natonamawêwa	looks for lice on s.o.
love	tepânêwa, tepâtamwa	loves, is fond of, cherishes s.o., it
	tepânâsowa	is loved, is dearly loved
	tepânekosiwa	is dearly loved
	tepânetîwaki	they love each other
	tepânetîweni	love
	tepâshiwêwa	loves people
	mênawânêwa	loves s.o.
	meshotîwaki	they fall in love with each other
	meshoshkêwa	is smitten, is in love, is courting; is smitten with (s.o.), is courting (her)
low	chakinehpîhiwi	it is low
	chakinehpyâhiwi	it is low
low area	-shepwâhkiwe:	**nâwi-shepwâhkiwe** in the middle of a low area surrounded by higher ground
lower	nakapehkwêsêwa	lowers one's head
	nîsenêwa, nîsenamwa	lowers, sets down s.o., it
low voice	tepasishimôhiwa	speaks in a low voice
lullaby	tehtômêwa	sings a lullaby to s.o.
lump	pehkwâsenwi	it is blown in a lump
	pehkwikanêwa	has lumps on one's bones
lung	pîhpîshkîhi	lung
	opîhpîshkîhi	lung
lust	âmanôwitêhêwa	lusts
	memêsatesiwa	is lustful
lynx	peshiwa, kehchi-peshiwa	lynx
Lynx Clan	pêshiwisota	member of the Lynx Clan (Jones: Big Lynx)

m

maggot	ôhkwêwa	maggot
maggot	ôhkwêwiwa, ôhkwêwiwi	(animate, inanimate) is maggoty, has maggots
maiden: → teenage girl		
make	ashihêwa, ashihtôwa	makes s.o., it; installs s.o.
	ashihtawêwa	makes (it) for s.o.
	ashihtâtêwi	it is made
	ashihtâtisowa	makes (it) for oneself
	ashihchikêwêwa	makes something, things, (it) with (it), out of (it)
	kîshihêwa, kîshihtôwa	finishes making, completes s.o., it
	kîshihtawêwa	finishes making, completes (it) for s.o.
	kîshihâsowa, kîshihtâtêwi	(animate, inanimate) is made, already made, finished
	ishikihêwa	makes s.o. be {so}
	ishihêwa, ishihtôwa	makes s.o., it {so}
	ishihtawêwa	makes (it) {so} for s.o.
	ishikihetîwaki	they make each other {so}

	kîshihowa	makes oneself (be some way or do something)
	nahihtôwa	knows how to make it
	tashihêwa	makes s.o. {somewhere}, is making s.o.; kills s.o.{somewhere}
	wêpihtôwa	begins making it
make a bed	nanâhenikêwa	fixes the bedding
	nanâhenikawêwa	fixes the bedding for s.o.
	kîshenikawêwa	finishes fixing the place for s.o. to sleep, has made s.o.'s bed
	anâhkahêwa	makes a pallet for s.o.
make bad	myâshihtôwa	makes it bad, makes it badly
make fun of	wâpashihêwa, wâpashihtôwa	makes fun of, disgraces, ruins, wastes s.o., it
	wapashihêwa, wapashihtôwa	makes fun of, disgraces, ruins, wastes s.o., it
	wâpashihtawêwa	makes fun of, disgraces, ruins, wastes (it) for s.o.
	wapashihtawêwa	makes fun of, disgraces, ruins, wastes (it) for s.o.
	wâpashimêwa, wâpashotamwa	makes fun of s.o., it by speech
	wapashimêwa, wapashotamwa	makes fun of s.o., it by speech
	wapasotamwa	makes fun of it by speech
	wapasowêwa	makes fun of people
	wâpasowêwa	makes fun of people
make out (1)	inahkamikihtôwa	makes out {so}
make out (2)	otehtâpamêwa, otehtâpatamwa	(with negative:) cannot make s.o., it out, does not get a good look at s.o., it
	otehtâpatâniwa, otehtâpatâniwi	(with negative:) cannot be made out; it cannot be made out, things cannot be made out
make out (3)	mîhketîwa	courts or is courted, makes out
	anâsowa	wrestles, horses around, tussles amorously
make up	pahkitêhêwa	makes up one's mind
male	neniwawahîma	male (animal or bird)
malign	wîyashkimêwa	maligns s.o., says bad things about s.o.
man	neniwa	man
	ineniwa	man (archaic)
	neniwiwa, ineniwiwa	he is a man; he is a made warrior
	neniwihêwa	makes him a man
	keshâchîneniwiwa	he is a kind man
	oshkinawêha	young man
	pashitôha	old man
	wîchi-mehtosênenîmêwa	he is a fellow-man to s.o.
	aneshinenîhaki	common people
	môhkomâna	American; white man
manage	kashki	able to, manage to, possible (preverb)
	kashkihêwa, kashkihtôwa	manages, can do, gets, buys s.o., it
	nanâhotamwa	manages it, directs it (as, a ceremony or activity); is in charge
	neshi-pemâhtôwa	manages by oneself
	inâhpenanêwa	treats, deals with, manages to get s.o. {so}
mane	oshêhkwâniwa	has a mane
manitou	manetôwa	manitou, spirit, god, snake, monster
	manetôwi	(of) manitou, (of) snake (prenoun, preverb)
many	mâne	much, many (particle)
	mamâne	many each (or each time), a lot each (or each time)(particle)
	mânêwa, mânêtwi	(animate, inanimate) is much, many, numerous
	mânêhêwa, mânêhtôwa	has much, many of s.o., it
	mânenwi	many times (particle)
	mânokoni	for many days (particle)

	mânokonîwa	fasts for many days
	mamânokoni	for many days each or each time (particle)
	mamânôtamôki	they each carried many of them on their backs
	mânôchênêwa	holds many of s.o.
	inekihkwi	{so} big, to {such} extent, {so many} (particle, preverb)
	nanôpehka	a great deal, many (particle)
	tasenwi (1)	it is {so much, many}
	tasenwi (2)	{so many} times (particle)
maple	**asanâmishi**	sugar maple
	asenâmishi	sugar maple (archaic)
	asenâmishiwa	is a sugar maple (archaic)
	shîshîkimêha	soft maple
maple sugar	**mêsiwêyâhi**	maple-sugar cake
	êhkanyâhi	maple-sugar cake
maple syrup	**menêshishi**	maple syrup
mark	**kehkinawâchihtôwa**	marks it
	kehkishinwa	has left a mark where one lay
	kehkechêshinwa	a mark is left where one lay
	kehkisenwi	it is marked
marker	**kehkâhkwîhi**	marker, tally stick
marriage	**owîwetîweni**	marriage, married life
	onâpêmiweni	marriage, the state of a woman being married
marrow	**owîpikani**	marrow
marry	**onâpêmiwa**	she marries (him), is married to (him)
	onâpêmemêwa	she marries him, is married to him, has him as her husband
	owîwiwa	he marries (her), is married to (her)
	owîwemêwa	he marries her, is married to her, he has her as his wife
	owîwetîwaki	they are married (to each other)
	owîwetîhaki	married couple
	owîwehkâsowa	he pretends to have (her) as his wife
	owîwihêwa	gets him to marry (her), has him marry (her)
	wîchawiwêwa	is with s.o.; he is married to her, she is married to him
	wîchawîtîwaki	they are married
	kîshîchawiwêwa	has been married to s.o.
	kîshi-wîchawiwêwa	has been married to s.o.
	oshiwa	she marries of her own accord
marvelously	**mamâtâwi**	marvelously, how marvelous (particle, preverb)
master	**otôtêmekôni, otôtêmekôhani**	its (dog's or horse's) master
mat	**anâhkani**	mat (to cover a surface)
	anâhkêwa	uses something, (it) as a mat to sit on or lie on
	anâhkahamawêwa	spreads (it) for s.o., spreads mats or blankets for s.o.
	apahkwaya	cattail reed; cattail-reed mat (for covering a lodge)
match	**ashkotêhkâni**	match
matter	**ishiwêpikenwi**	it is, signifies {so}
	êshiwêpikeki	what it is all about, what it represents or corresponds to, what the matter with it is (oblique participle)
mayapple	**meshkehtêhi**	mayapple
maybe	**wîshâwi**	maybe, perhaps, likely but not certainly (particle, preverb)
meadow	**ahkwashkotêwiwi**	the meadow goes {so far}
meadowlark	**owînenwi-mîchîha**	meadowlark
mean	**machowiyêhiwa**	is ill-tempered, cross, mean
	asâmihêwa	is too cruel or mean to s.o., goes too far mistreating s.o.
mean (verb)	**ishiwêpowêwa**	means {so}, means to imply {so}
	itamawêwa	says {so} of (it) to s.o., means {so} in saying (it) to s.o.

meanwhile	**mani** (idiom):	**mani** with preverb **tashi**: meanwhile, all the while
meat	**owîyâsi**	flesh, meat
	owîyâsêhi	flesh, meat (dimin.)
	owîyâsiwiwi	it is flesh, meat
	menâshkonowa	eats fresh meat
	menâshkonôni	fresh meat
	pâhpâshânani	thin slices of dried meat (plural)
	sêsahikêwa	stores meat away
	sêsahikani	dried meat, piece of dried meat
	nîsenâkwâwêwa	takes down the meat supply
medicine	**nâtawinôni**	medicine
	onâtawinôniwa	has medicine
	onâtawinônemêwa	has s.o. as medicine
	nâtawinônahwêwa	uses medicine on s.o. (to cast a spell)
	ahtawêwa	puts medicine on s.o.
	shîshêwashkwi	hunting medicine
	tanetîwashkwi	gambling medicine
meet	**nakishkawêwa**	meets s.o., goes to meet s.o.
	nakishkâtîwaki	they meet each other
	tahkoshkawêwa, tahkoshkamwa	meets, encounters s.o., it, accidentally runs into it
	mîhkawihetîwaki	they meet and become friends, strike up a friendship
	wanihchikani	medicine for losing someone
melt	**nekesowa, neketêwi**	(snow, ice) melts; it (as, lard) melts
	nekeshkêwa	(snow, ice) melts
memorize	**kehkinôsowa**	observes (it) and learns, memorizes (it)
Menominee	**manôminîwa**	Menominee Indian
	manômininâki	in Menominee country
menstruate	**myânôtêwa**	she menstruates
	myânôtêkâni	menstrual lodge
	ashkihkwêwiweni	menarche, girl's first menstruation
mention	**nenehkimêwa, nenehkotamwa**	mentions s.o., it
	awotamwa	mentions it, one's words refer to it
	awotamawêwa	mentions (it) to s.o.
mercy	**nênawênemêwa**	has mercy on s.o.
	myânahônêwa	obtains mercy from s.o.
merry	**opyâwi**	it is fun, there are merry doings
	opwehopwêhetîwaki (plural)	they make merry together
Meskwaki	**meshkwahkîha**	Meskwaki
	meshkwahkîhâtowêwa	speaks Meskwaki
	meshkwahkîhiwa, meshkwahkîhiwiwa	is a Meskwaki, becomes a Meskwaki
	meshkwahkîhi-mehtosêneniwiwa	is a Meskwaki
	meshkwahkîh-okimâwiwa	is a Meskwaki chief
mess	**nîshki**	overly, messily, heavily, awkwardly, almost too (much) (particle)
	nîshkinâkwatwi	it looks messy, it looks a mess
	nîshkeshkawêwa	gets in s.o.'s way; messes things up for s.o.
	nîshkitepêwa	one's hair is mussed up
message	**mechichimêwa**	gives s.o. a message to deliver, sends a message by s.o.
	mechitwêwa	sends a message
messily	**memyêshki**	carelessly, not thoroughly, messily, crossly (particle, preverb)
middle	**nanawashkote**	in the middle of the prairie (particle)
	êh=nanakwîkwêchi	in the middle of one's face, right in one's face

middle-aged	**âpehtôneniwiwa**	is middle-aged
Midewiwin	**metêwiweni**	Midewiwin (Mystic Rite, Grand Medicine Rite)
	metêwa	member of the Midewiwin
midnight	**nâwitepehkîwi**	it is midnight
	pyêmeshkêwi	the time goes past midnight
midwife	**nôshêhchikêwa**	she acts as a midwife
might as well	**natawâchi**	might as well, resolving accordingly; without further ado (particle)
milk	**menihki**	milk
milk (verb)	**chînishkinenyênêwa**	milks her (as, a cow)
Milky Way	**wâpi-sîpôwi**	the White River (in the sky); the Milky Way
mill around	**natâshkêwaki** (plural)	they (all) mill around
	natâwosêwaki (plural)	they (all) walk around switching places
	natâyâwi	there is a milling around
mind	**kehtênemêwa**	has one's mind on s.o., has s.o. on one's mind
	kohkitêhêwa	changes one's mind
	pahkitêhêwa	makes up one's mind
	nâkatawênemêwa, nâkatawênetamwa	keeps s.o., it in mind, keeps track of s.o., it, watches s.o., it, pays close attention to it
mind you	**=yêpani, =yâpani**	mind you, I expect, I warn you
mindful	**pemahwêwa**	is mindful or respectful of s.o.
	nenehkinawêmêwa	makes s.o. mindful by speech
	nenehkinawêhêwa	makes s.o. mindful
	mîhkwinawêhtâkêwa	makes (s.o.) mindful for people
mine: → lead		
mink	**mîka**	mink
	anapishkwêha	mink (archaic)
minnow	**ishenemêsîha**	minnow
	shenemêsîha	minnow
	nemêsîha	minnow
mirror	**wâpamôni**	mirror
misbehave	**wâwaneshkâhiwa**	is bad, naughty, immoral
	pônesiwa	stops misbehaving
mischievous	**wâwaneshkâhikenwi**	it is mischievous
miserable	**ketemâkesiwa, ketemâkyâwi**	is miserable, poor
	ketemâkesiweni	misery
	ketemâkênetisowa	feels oneself wretched
	ketemâkimêwa	makes s.o. miserable by speech, causes grief by mentioning s.o.
	ketemâkinawêhêwa	makes s.o. feel sad
	ketemâkihkanêwa	leaves s.o. in misery
misfortune	**petasakawiwa**	meets misfortune
mishear	**ânohtâkêwa**	mishears people, disobeys people
misinterpret	**wâwanâtowêhtawêwa**	misinterprets to s.o.
miss	**panahwêwa, panahamwa**	misses hitting s.o., it by tool or thrown object
	peshkonawêwa, peshkonamwa	misses s.o., it with a shot
	pepyêshkonawêwa	keeps missing s.o., them with shots
	paneshkawêwa, paneshkamwa	misses stepping on s.o., it, steps clear of s.o., it
	panamêwa	snaps at s.o. and misses
	panitepêhwêwa	strikes at s.o.'s head with something and misses
	wanihêwa	misses s.o. (not knowing where they are); loses, forgets about s.o.
Mississippi	**mêshisîpôwi, mêsisîpôwi**	Mississippi River
Missouri	**pîkihtanwi**	Missouri River

mistake	**pehchi**	by mistake (preverb)
	pehchawiwa	makes a mistake
	pehchihtôwa	makes a mistake in making it
	kîwânîwa	is lost (not knowing where one is), makes a mistake (as, in conducting a ceremony)
	kîwânîwi	mistakenly, foolishly (preverb)
	wanyêwîwa	makes a mistake
	wâwanihchikêwa	makes a mistake, does not do it the right way
mistreat	**asâmihêwa**	is too cruel or mean to s.o., goes too far mistreating s.o.
	myâshitanêwa	mistreats s.o.
misunderstand	**pepyêhtehtawêwa**	keeps misunderstanding s.o., them
mix	**wâwiyâki**	of all kinds, mixed together (particle, preverb)
	wâwiyâkisetôwa	mixes it together
	wâwiyâkesamwa	cooks it mixed together
	kenekenâsowa	is mixed in
	keneki	mixed, mixed in, mixed with (particle, preverb)
	kenekisetôwa	mixes in
moan	**mamâtwêwa**	moans
moccasin	**mahkesêhi**	moccasin
	omahkesêhiwa	wears moccasins, wears (them) as moccasins
	mahkesenehkêwa	makes moccasins
	keki-mahkesene	with one's moccasins on (particle compound)
	pîwâhimahkesenêwa	wears beaded moccasins
	pepyêsehkamwa	wears moccasins
	ashikasowa	puts a liner in one's moccasins; puts on or wears socks or stockings
moccasin-string	**asitâpi**	moccasin-string, shoestring
mock	**wâpashi**	disrespectfully, mockingly (preverb)
	wapashi	disrespectfully, mockingly (preverb, particle)
moisten	**shîhkawisetawêwa**	moistens (it) for s.o.
mole (animal)	**kêchichikwêha**	mole
money	**shôniyâhi**	money, silver
	shôniyâhaki	coins, money
	oshôniyâhemiwa	has money, silver
monkey	**nêtonamâshîha**	monkey
month	**kîsheswa**	month; sun, moon
	nyêwikîsheswakesiwa	is four months old
	nyêwikîsheswakatwi	it is four months
	nyêwikîsheswe	for four months (particle)
	nyêwi-kîsheswe	for four months (particle)
moon	**kîsheswa**	sun, moon, month
	tepehki-kîsheswa	moon
moorhen	**shêkâtêha**	moorhen, common gallinule
moose	**môswa**	moose
more	**âwasi**	more (particle)
	âwasîmêhi	more (particle)
	âyakwîchi	more and more, over and over, to excess (particle, preverb)
	mîshkota	on top of that, what's more, what's worse (particle)
more so	**kanomâhi, kanamâhi**	even more so (particle)
	ahkwiyâchi	especially, more so (particle)
moreover	**=kêhi**	moreover, to be precise, including, or perhaps (often idiomatic)
	pîhtawi	moreover, besides (particle, preverb)
	ahpeme	moreover, at the same time (particle)

morning	**kekisheyêpa**	in the morning (particle)
	shêpâye	this morning (early today) (particle)
	wâpanwi	it dawns, is morning
	wâpanohkêwa	makes the morning; morning comes for one
morning star	**wâpananâkwa**	the morning star
mortar	**pôtahâkani**	corn mortar ("grinding mill"); coffee-mill
mosquito	**sakimêwa**	mosquito
moss	**mîsâhkoni**	moss, pond scum
	mîsâhkoniwipehkwanêyâwi	its roof is covered with moss
mother	**nekya**	my mother
	okiwa	has a mother; has (her) as mother
	okimêwa	has her as mother
mother-in-law	**nôhkoma**	my mother-in-law
motion (verb)	**atâhpehkwêhtawêwa**	motions with one's head for s.o. to come
	nemenêwa, nemenamwa	motions towards s.o., it (with it) without striking; motions with it without striking
	nemenamawêwa	motions towards s.o. with (it) without striking
mound	**wânatâkani**	mound of earth with concave top (ceremonial)
mount	**ahkwîchisahowa**	mounts one's horse, mounts (s.o., a horse)
mountain lion	**kênwâsowêwa**	mountain lion
	kênwâsowêwikihônowa	turns oneself into a mountain lion
	kênwâsowêwîhkâsowa	pretends to be a mountain lion
mouse	**wâpikonôha**	mouse
mouth	**netôni**	my mouth
	metôni	a mouth
	otôniwa	has a mouth; has (s.o.) speak for one
	chakânaketonwa	has a small mouth
	inânaketonêsetôwa	lays it (as, a flute or whistle) with its "mouth" (the end that is away from the player) {some way}
	kepetonênêwa	covers s.o.'s mouth with one's hand, holds s.o.'s mouth closed
	kepetonêpinêwa	ties s.o.'s mouth closed
	kwâshkwachikêwa	drops food from the mouth
	makânaketonwa	has a large mouth
	meshketonêshinwa	lies with one's mouth open
	meshketonênêwa	opens s.o.'s mouth
	nâpanohwêwa	sticks (it) into s.o.'s mouth
	nehketonwa	one's mouth goes out of sight
	nîmamêwa, nîmatamwa	holds s.o., it in one's mouth
	nîmatahêwa	makes s.o. hold (it) in the mouth
	pâhketonwa	opens one's mouth
	pâkâhkotonêshinwa	bumps oneself on the mouth
	pemiwetonwa	has a greasy mouth
	pemiwânaketonwa	has a greasy mouth
	tanetonwa	moves one's mouth ({somewhere})
	wawâsetonwa	flashes at the mouth (said of thunderers)
	wêpetonwa	moves one's mouth (song word)
	sîkanwishinwa	lets something spill out of one's mouth; spills the beans
mouthful	**nekotetone**	one mouthful (particle)
	makanêhtamwa	takes or has a big mouthful of it
move	**mamâchîwa**	moves, stirs
	mamâchîhêwa	makes s.o. move, gives s.o. life
	mamâsehkêwa, mamâsehkêwi	(animate, inanimate) moves, is moving about
	mâtenêwa, mâtenamwa	moves s.o., it

	âmîwa	moves camp, moves to winter camp
	âmîhetîwaki	they move camp together
	âmîhetêwi	camp is broken, everyone moves
	âmiwenêwa	moves s.o. away
	anemotêwa	moves camp
	anwêwêshkêwi	it moves with noise
	âtapiwa	moves to a new location
	ineshkêwa, ineshkêwi	moves (involuntarily), is moved, is taken {so, to somewhere}
	kîhkîwa	moves further on or away, lives longer
	kîhkîhkiwenêwa	moves s.o. on again and again
	mâchîwa	moves; runs (with preverb)
	mâchinawîhtawêwa	moves about for s.o.
	mâtapiwa	moves one's seat, moves from one's place
	mâtakôchinwa	moves from the place where one (as, a star) hangs
	mâtakôtêwi	it moves from the place where it (as, a cloud) hangs
	mîwîwa	walks away, moves away, moves out of the way
	têhtêpanwi	there is rhythmic movement, undulation
	wêpetonwa	moves one's mouth (song word)
	wîshikinawîwa	uses one's strength, makes a powerful effort to move
much	mâne	much, many (particle)
	mamâne	many each (or each time), a lot each (or each time) (particle)
	mânêwa, mânêtwi	(animate, inanimate) is much, many, numerous
	mânêhêwa, mânêhtôwa	has much, many of s.o., it
	mamânêhêwaki, mamânêhtôwaki	they each have or get a lot of (animate, inanimate)
	kehchi	much, greatly, very big (prenoun, preverb)
	maki	big, much (prenoun, preverb)
	ana=kîshâkochi	extremely much (particle compound)
	anwâchi	(with negative:) not as much as before (preverb)
mud	ashishkiwi	mud
	ashishkiwâhkonowa	puts mud on oneself
	akwishkahkiwiwi	it is muddy land
	wîyashkâpôkatwi	its water is muddy, it is muddy water
	wîyashkâpôshkamwa	made its water muddy, made it (water) muddy
	anôkahkiwiwi	the ground is muddy
mud puppy	mânêshêha	mud puppy
mule	mâmâkeshêha	mule
multiply	nîkikiwa	multiplies, has numerous descendants
murder	mechiminahkyêwa	commits murder
	kwayânanohkyêwa	commits murder
muscles	pîshkyêwêwa	one's muscles become tired, cramped
	pakishêwêshkêwa	relaxes, one's muscles relax
	shîshîhkyêwakenêwa	rubs s.o. down, rubs s.o.'s muscles
muscular	nenyêhpesiwa	loses muscular coordination
muskmelon	mîsechêyâhi	muskmelon
muskrat	ashashkwa	muskrat
	ashashkôha	small muskrat
muss up	memyêshkânehkwêshinwa	lies with one's hair mussed up
	opisêtepêwa	one's head (hair or feathers) is mussed, bushy
	opisêwitepêwa (Jones)	one's head (hair or feathers) is mussed, bushy
	opisêtepênêwa	musses up s.o.'s hair
	opisêtepênowa	musses up one's hair
mustache	mîsetonâkani	mustache, beard
	mîsetonwa	has a mustache
mutually	wâwâchi	reciprocally, mutually; jointly (particle, preverb)

n

nail (on body)	**neshkasha**	my nail, my claw (plural **neshkashêki**) (**meshkasha** a nail, claw, hoof)
	kakânwikashêwa	has long nails, claws
	sâsâkikashêshkêwa	one's nails, claws appear
nail (to nail)	**sakâhkohikani**	nail (for nailing)
	sakâhkohamwa	nails it up, buttons it, pins it
naked	**mehtâhkwinameshke**	naked (particle)
	mehchinameshkêwa	is naked, minimally dressed
	mehchinameshkêpiwa	sits naked
	mehtâhkwinameshkêwa	is naked
	mehchinawe	naked, dressed only in a breechcloth (particle)
	mehtapishkwe	stark naked (particle)
	mehtapishkwêwa	is stark naked
	meshâpamêwa	sees s.o.'s private parts
name	**ishisowa**	one's name, clan is {so}
	ishisômikatwi	its name is {so}
	mîsôni	name; clan (**nîsôni** my name, **owîsôni** his or her name)
	wîswihêwa, wîswihtôwa	names s.o., it, gives a name to s.o., it
	owîsônihêwa	gives s.o. (it as) a name
	kehkahwêwa, kehkahamwa	names, designates s.o., it
	kekyêhkahamawêwa	names, designates (them) to s.o.
	kehkahamâtîwaki	they name, designate (it) for each other
	kehkahâtêwi	it is named, designated
	kehkahikêwa	names, designates
	kehkahikawêwa	names, designates for s.o.
	ishitehkânêwa, ishitehkâtamwa	names s.o., it {so}
	ishitehkânetîwaki	they name each other {so}
	ishitehkâsowa, ishitehkâtêwi	is named {so}
	mahkwisowa	has a Bear name, is a member of the Bear Clan
	manetôwitehkâsowa	is called a manitou
	wâwîtêwa, wâwîtamwa	calls s.o. by name; speaks about it
	wâwîtetîwaki	they name each other
	wâwîtâkosiwa	s.o.'s name is mentioned
	wâwîtekwatwi	it is named
nape	**nehtâhpi**	my nape, the back of my neck
	chîkihtâhpêwa	the nape of one's neck sticks out
	sakihtâhpênêwa	seizes s.o. by the back of the neck
narrate	**inâchimowa**	narrates {so}
	inâchimôhiwa	narrates {so} (dimin.)
	wêpâchimowa	starts to narrate
narrow	**wîpôyâwi**	it is narrow
	wîponamwa	makes it narrow, makes it closer
	wîpwinehkawêwa	chases s.o. into a corner, a narrow place
	kîshkahtêyâwi	it (coat) narrows at the waist
	kîshkahtêkenwi	it (coat) narrows at the waist
	sîkehkwêtenwi	it (hill) narrows down to a point
naturally	**mehtênetâkwi**	naturally, there is no doubt, for sure (particle)
navel	**owînwi**	his or her navel
	owînwîshi	his or her navel
near	**ashichi**	near, nearly (particle)
	ashichikênotâtîwaki	they live near each other

	chîki	close to, near (preparticle)
	chîkawahîme	nearby (particle)
	chîkawahîne	nearby (particle)
	kehchine	close by, near; for the near term (particle)
	kehchinêhe	close by, near; for the near term (dimin.) (particle)
nearer	**atâh-ochîmêhi**	a little nearer; a little later, a little more recently (particle compound)
nearly	**katawi**	nearly, almost; (with future) soon (preverb, preparticle, particle)
	kêkyâta	nearly (particle)
neat	**wîkêtenikêwa**	straightens things up, neatens up the house
	wîkêchinâkwihtôwa	fixes it up to look neat and tidy
	wîkêtâhkonêwa, wîkêtâhkonamwa	folds s.o. (as, a skin), it up neatly
	menonamawêwa	straighten it up nicely for s.o.
Nebraska	**nîmahâhinâki**	in Nebraska, in Missouri River Sauk country (locative noun)
necessarily	**mâmahkâchi**	necessarily, it is necessary; (with sarcastic intonation:) it is not necessary, should not have, why did (they)? (particle)
	mêmyêhchi	necessarily, unavoidably; it must be (that) (particle)
	pêpyêhchi	necessarily, have to (particle)
neck	**nehkwêkani**	my neck
	omekihkwêkanwa	has sores on one's neck
	kenwishkwêkanwa	has a long neck
	inekihkwishkwêkanwa	one's neck is {so} big around
	pepyêtekwikwayawênêwa	bends s.o.'s neck down
	wâkikwayawêshkêwa	arches one's neck
	sakikwênêwa	takes or holds s.o. by the neck
	sakikwêsahêwa	grabs s.o. by the neck
	sakikwêpinêwa	ties s.o. by the neck
	sakikwêpisowa	is tied by or around the neck; ties oneself by the neck
	kehkitehkwênêwa	hugs s.o. around the neck
	nâpinêwa, nâpitôwa	wears s.o., it around the neck
	nâpitâhêwa	puts (it) around s.o.'s neck
necklace	**nâpitâwêwa**	wears a necklace, necklaces
	nâpitâtêhi	necklace
	nâpitâwâkani	necklace
needle	**shâponikani**	needle
	shamakwaya	large, animal-rib mat needle
nephew	**nenekwâha**	my cross-nephew: (of a man) the son of my sister or of anyone else I call "sister," or of my father's sister; (of a woman) the son of my brother or of anyone else I call "brother"
	nenekwanesa	my cross-nephew (in older usage)
	onekwâhiwa	has a cross-nephew
nephew: parallel nephew → son		
nest	**owâsîsani**	nest
	owâsîsaniwa	has a nest
net	**kwâpôhikani, akwâpôhikani**	net, seine, screen for washing hominy
nettle	**masâna**	nettle
never	**nahi**	(with negative:) never (preverb)
	nanâshi	(with negative:) never (particle)
nevertheless	**kamayâchi**	nevertheless (particle)
new	**ashkikiwa, ashkikenwi**	is young, new, fresh

	ashkishehkîtamwa	wears new clothes
	pînôshi	innovating, doing or being something new and different (particle)
	nôhkihtôwa	creates it anew
	pîshihtôwa	makes it anew, renews it
	pîshihtâtêwi	it is made anew, made over, renewed
new year	**nôhkawiwi**	there is a new year, a new growing season
	nôhkawahîmakatwi	it is a new year
	nôhkawahînakatwi	it is a new year
news	**papâmwêtamwa**	goes around crying out the news or announcement
next	**ahkôwêwa**	comes next after s.o., follows next after s.o.
	âyânehkôtîmikatwi	it is in mutual succession
	ânehkôchi	next in order (prenoun)
	âyânehkami, âyânehkêwi	one after the other (particle)
	ashichikâpawînotâtîwaki	they stand next to each other
nibble	**kenîkamêwa**	nibbles at s.o.
nice	**wêwenihêwa, wêwenihtôwa**	makes s.o., it pretty, nice
niece	**neshemisa, neshemîha**	my cross-niece: (of a man) the daughter of my sister or of anyone else I call "sister," or of my father's sister; (of a woman) the daughter of my brother or of anyone else I call "brother"

niece: parallel niece → daughter

night	**tepehkwi**	night (noun)
	tepehkwi	of night (prenoun)
	tepehki	at night (particle)
	tepehki	of night (prenoun)
	tepehkîwi	it is night
	tepehkoki	last night (particle)
	pehkotêwi	it is night
	pehkotênemiwa	is overtaken by nightfall
	keki-tepehkwe	that same night
	nehkanitepehkwe	all night long (particle)
	nahkanitepehkwe	all night long (particle)
	nekoti-tepehkwe	for one night (particle)
	nekotitepehkwe	for one night (particle)
	nîshwitepehkwe	for two nights (particle)
	pyêmitepehkîwi	the night is well gone, it is past midnight
	nôtêtepehkwe	before the night is (was) out (particle)
nighthawk	**pêshkwêha**	nighthawk
nightmare	**wîyatâsiwa**	has a nightmare, is disturbed in one's sleep
	wîyatâhêwa	makes s.o. have a bad dream
nine	**shâka**	nine (particle)
	shâka tashiwaki, shâka tasenôni	they (animate, inanimate) are nine, there are nine of them
ninety	**shâkâpitaki**	ninety (particle)
ninth	**shâkânameki**	ninth (particle)
nit	**wâpisôha**	nit
	wâpisôhânehkwêwa	has nits in the hair
no	**âkwi**	no, not (particle)
nod	**kîpehkwêsêwa**	one's head nods down
noise	**anemwêwêshkêwi**	it goes off with a noise
	anwêwêkatwi	it makes noise
	anwêwênawîwa	stirs noisily
	anemwêwêshinwa	one's steps go sounding off,
	anemwêwêsenwi	it goes off with noise

	kashkîpwêwêshkêwani (plural)	they (trees, inanimate) make noise rubbing together
	makwêwêkatwi	there is a big noise
	neshiwêwêkatwi	there is a terrific, terrible, awful noise
	pemwêwêshinwa	goes by with noise, is heard walking by
	pemwêwêsenwi	it goes by with noise
	pônwêwêkatwa	the noise ceases, the sound of it ceases
	pyêtwêwêpahowa	comes running with noise, is heard approaching on the run
	pyêtwêwêyâkonîwa	comes crunching through the snow
	tanwêwêkatwi	there is loud noise ({somewhere})
	tanwêwêyâpônikêwa	is noisily splashing water on things
	têpwêwêkomêwa	can be heard (from a distance) snoring
	wîshkwêwêkatwi	there is great noise
	kîshâkotwêwêyâkêposowa	whizzes off through the air with tremendous noise
noon	**nâwahkwêwi**	it is noon
	pâshisêwa	(the sun) goes past noon
no one	**owiyêha**	(with negative:) **âkwi owiyêha** no one; (as a predicate) there is no one, is not {somewhere}
north	**wêchi-kesîyâki**	north (oblique participle)
	âsamahanoki	north (ritual) (particle)
northern lights	**wâsôkêwa**	the northern lights
	wâsôkêwiwi	the northern lights are visible
nose	**nehkiwani**	my nose
	mehkiwani	a nose
	kîshkikomêhpwêwa	bites off s.o.'s nose
	kîshkikomêshwêwa	cuts off s.o.'s nose
	nîshkikomêshkêwa	wrinkles up one's nose
	pâkikomêshinwa	bumps one's nose
	sakikomêhpwêwa	bites s.o. on the nose
	sâkikomêshkêwa	sticks one's nose out
	tatôkikomêwa	one's nostrils spread open
	wâkikomêwa	has a hooked nose or beak
nostril	**pôhkânakikomâkani**	nostril
not	**âkwi**	not, no (particle)
	pwâwi	not (preverb)
	pâwi	not (preverb) (younger form)
	awita	not (with potential verb) (particle)
	kâta	don't; not (with a prohibition) (particle)
	=ihi (='h=)	not (highly idiomatic; often with sarcastic intonation)
	mechi	(with sarcastic intonation) surely not! obviously not! (particle)
	mechi='hi	(with sarcastic intonation) surely not! obviously not!
	pashi	(with negative:) not at all (preverb)
not enough	**nôtêhkwâpiwa**	is unable to see a particular distance
	nôtêsetwêwa	does not get enough to eat
	wâwani-inekinôhiwa	is not grown up enough
	nâsâwi	not enough to be satisfying (preverb)
not exist	**âkowiyêhiwa**	does not exist, is gone, is not there
	âkwikêkôhenwi	it does not exist, is gone, is no more
nothing	**kêkôhi**	(with negative:) not anything, nothing, nothing bad, no problem
	kêkôhêhi	(with negative:) not anything, nothing, nothing bad, no problem (dimin.)
	kêkôhiwa, kêkôhenwi	(with negative:) (animate, inanimate) is nothing, nothing serious, not helpful, not important

nothing but	**âhpenêwe**	nothing but, only onesidedly (not the reverse) (particle)
	âhpenêyâwi	there is nothing but it
notice	**pehkînâkôtisowa**	notices something different about oneself
not much	**anehkîhiwa, anehkîhenwi**	is few; there is not much of it
not too bad	**kehchi-menwâhi**	(with negative:) not too bad, not too much (particle phrase)
not too much	**kâshkâchâwi**	there is not too much of it
	kâshkâchi	not (too) much, not (too) many (particle)
	têpi='h=wê=kêhî='ni	it's surely not too much (to ask)
now	**=înahi**	after that, with that (happening), and; now, now you can
	ayôninâhi	now, at this time; here, in this place (particle)
	ayôchiwêpi	from now on
	îni	then, now
	înoki	today, now, this time (particle)
	nanôchi	up to this time, finally, eventually (particle)
	wênahi	(this) is it, here now, I see now (that) (particle)
	=mani	now, as it is now
nowhere	**nâwi-kîwâchâwe**	in the middle of nowhere (particle compound)
	nanawi	off in some isolated place; in vain (particle)
nudge	**chîpechênêwa**	nudges s.o.
	chîpenêwa	nudges s.o.
nuisance	**otamihiwêwa**	bothers people, is a nuisance
numb	**nenyêhpapiwa**	is numb from sitting
number	**inekihkwênemêwa**	thinks of {such} a number of them
numerous	**mânêwa, mânêtwi**	is much, many, numerous
nurse	**nônwa**	(infant) nurses, sucks at the breast
	nônahkatawêwa	sucks at her breast
	nôtêwa	she nurses, breastfeeds s.o.
	nôtâwasowa	she is nursing a baby
	nônâwasowa	she is nursing a baby
	wînepinenyêhpwêwa	dirties her breasts by nursing
nut	**pakâni**	nut (generic); hickory nut; black walnut
	mahkwi-pakâni	black walnut
	peshkipêhi-pakâni	hickory nut
nuthatch	**âhâmêha**	nuthatch

O

oak	**mehtekomishi**	oak, black oak
	mehtekomishiwa	is an oak
	mîshimishi	white oak, bur oak
obstacle	**petasaki**	as an obstacle, impediment (preverb)
	petesaki	as an obstacle, impediment (preverb)
	petasakikenwi	there is, it has an obstacle
	petesakikenwi	there is, it has an obstacle
	petasakesiwa	is impeded, faces an obstacle
obtain	**otehtenêwa, otehtenamwa**	gets s.o., it, obtains s.o., it
obtain mercy	**myânahônêwa**	obtains mercy from s.o., persuades s.o. to take pity on one
obvious	**nenwinâkosiwa, nenwinâkwatwi**	the look on one's face says everything; how it is can be told by looking at it
occupied with	**pemîhkawêwa, pemîhkamwa**	is occupied with s.o., it through time

	ishîhkawêwa	occupies oneself with s.o. {so}, keeps trying to get s.o. to do {so}
	ahpîhchîhkawêwa	occupies oneself {so long} with s.o.
	asâmîhkawêwa	occupies oneself too much with s.o., spends too much time with s.o.
	pônîhkawêwa, pônîhkamwa	leaves s.o., it alone, stops being occupied with s.o., it
	pônîhkâtîwaki	they stop dealing with each other, stop with each other
ocher	anemona	ocher
	meshkwanamona	red ocher
	meshkwanemona	red ocher
	asâwanamona	yellow ocher
	asâwanemona	yellow ocher
oddly	aniwêwi, aniwêwe	contrariwise, oddly, in contrast, then (in contrast) (particle)
of course	kochikêhkwi	for of course, but of course (particle)
	=mâhi	of course, you see, as you know, to be sure
	kashi=wê=towi	yes, of course, to be sure (as an answer)
	'shi=wê=towi	yes, of course, to be sure (as an answer)
off	manahka	a distance off (particle)
off to side	pemichinawe	off to one side (particle)
offer	sahkahamawêwa	offers tobacco to s.o.
	sahkahamôtenêwa	makes or has s.o. offer tobacco
	sahkahwêhtôwa	offers tobacco to it
	anikônêwa, anikôtôwa	offers s.o., it as a prize
often	âyahpîhchinâhi	once in a while, every once in a while, often (particle)
	mêmenwinâhi	every so often, often, regularly, not frequently; every little way, not great distances apart (particle)
	âyashkachi	at long intervals, not too often (particle)
Oh dear!	ehehê!, ehehyê!	Oh dear!; Uh-oh!; Hard luck!
Oh how	êhtameko	Oh how well, much, etc. (particle)
	tameko	Oh how well, much, etc. (particle)
oil	pemitêwi	oil, lard
	pemi	oil, grease
Ojibwa	achipwêwa	Ojibwa
	ochipwêwa	Ojibwa (archaic)
O.K.?	=tâni	O.K.? why don't I? if you agree, if you will, please
old	kehkyêwa	is old, gets old
	kehkyêweni	old age
	kehkyêwahkyêsenwi	the earth is in its old age
	kêhkyâha	old person
	nekehkyâmaki or nekêhkyâmaki	my elders, my ancestors
	ahpîhchikiwa, ahpîhchikenwi	is {so} powerful, old; it is {so} effective, powerful
	ahpîhtesiwa	takes {so long}, is {so} old
	kehchikiwa, kehchikenwi	(animate, inanimate) is old
	kehtesiwa	is big, old, older
	kehtesîhiwa	is old (dimin.), older
	kekehtesîmenânaki	our old people, ancestors, elders
	kêhta	old, former (prenoun)
	kêhtêwi	old (of things) (prenoun)
	kêhtêkiwa, kêhtêkenwi	(animate, inanimate) is or gets old (as, growing things); it (tree) is dead
old man	pashitôha	old man
	pashichôka	poor old man
	pashitôhiwa	he is an old man

	pashitôhîhkâsowa	pretends to be an old man
	pashitôhikihtôwa	makes it be like an old man
old woman	metemôha	old woman
	metemôhêha	old woman (dimin.)
	metemôka	old woman
	mechemôka	old woman
	chemôka	old woman
	metenêka	old woman
	metemôhiwa	she is an old woman
	metemôhêhiwa	she is an old woman (dimin.)
omit	nôtêhkwâchimowa	leaves something out in the telling
	nôtêhkwimêwa	leaves something out in telling s.o.
	pashkwâkômêwa	omits s.o. from one's kin
	pashkwâtotamawêwa	leaves (it) out in telling s.o.
on all fours	chîkitiyêshinwa	is on one's hands and knees, gets down on one's hands and knees
	chîkitiyêwi-pasekwîwa	gets up on all fours
once	nekotenwi	once, one time (particle)
	nekoti	once and for good, once and for all, over and done with (preverb)
on the way	nawatenêwa, nawatenamwa	picks s.o., it up on the way by
	nawachisêwa	grabs (it) on the run
one	nekoti	one (particle, preparticle)
	nânekoti	one apiece, one by one (particle)
	nênekoti	one apiece, one by one (particle)
	nekotayaki	one group, set, pair, couple, kind (particle)
	nekotayakatwi	it's the only one (of its kind), there is only one kind of it
	nekotayakatôhiwi	it's the only one (of its kind), there is only one kind of it (dimin.)
	nekotwêyawi	one of the two (particle)
	nekotôhkohkwe	one kettleful (particle)
	nekotisetôwa	places one of it
	îna, îni	that, that one
	înâhiwa	is the one
	wâshipaka	one (of them) and not the other is the one (particle)
one-eyed	pôhkîkwêwa	is missing one eye, has one eye out
	pôhkipôhkîkwêwaki	they are each missing one eye
oneself	tepinowêwe	(by) oneself
onion	shekâkôha	onion
only	kêsipi	only (him, her, them) (particle)
	mehtenôhi	only, except, unless; especially, moreso (particle)
	môshaki	only, exclusively, no one else but, nothing else but (particle)
	shâpwêshi	as the only one, by oneself (particle)
	îni ishi	only (with numbers)
on the back	âhtawânêwa	puts s.o. on their back
	âhtawâshinwa, âhtawâsenwi	lies on one's back, it lies on its back
on top	ahkwitâhkîki	on top of a hill, bank, ridge (locative noun)
	ahkwichitepe	on top of the head (particle)
	ahkwitahkamiki	on top of the earth (particle)
	ahkwitâsîwenêwa	takes s.o. up on top
	ahkwitepyêhokowa	floats on top of the water
	ahpihokônêwa	lets (it) fall on top of s.o.
open	pâhkenêwa, pâhkenamwa	uncovers, opens s.o., it

	pâhkenamawêwa	uncovers, opens (it) for s.o.; opens the door for s.o.
	pâhkatenamwa	rips it at the seam, opens the cover on it (a box)
	pâhkisenwi	it lies open, it is opened, it is allowed
	pâhkisetôwa	leaves it open
	pâhkisetawêwa	leaves (it) open for s.o. (a door or an opportunity)
	pâhkanonêwa, pâhkanonamwa	opens what s.o. is in, opens it (as, bag or bottle)
	pâhkanoshkêwi	its opening opens up
	pâhkeshkêwi	it opens, it opens up, falls open, comes open
	pâhkânaketêwi	it gapes open from heat
	pâhkeshkêwi	it opens up
	pâhkîkwênwa	opens one's eyes, uncovers one's eyes, face
	pâshkâpihêwa	lets s.o. crack open their eyes
	tahitanânakîkwêshinwa	is lying there with one's eyes open
	tôshkânakîkwêshkêwa	opens one's eyes again
	meshkisenwi	it lies open
	meshketonêshinwa	lies with one's mouth open
	meshkinechêhtawêwa	holds one's hand open to s.o.
openly	mehchi	openly, plainly, ostensibly; out in the open (particle, preverb)
	mehchawiwa	acts openly; gives away the secret by how one acts, shows it
	mehtâkwasowa, mehtâkwatêwi	is piled in plain sight, is sprawled naked; it is piled in plain sight
open space	êh=mehchâki	in the open, in plain sight
	êhkwi-mehchâki	at the edge of an open space
	shîpêyâwi	the woods are open (without thick undergrowth)
opportunity	mênânesiwa	is missing one's opportunity
oppose	âshkâtênemêwa	is opposed to s.o.
	âshkâtowêwa	speaks in opposition
	petênemêwa	is against s.o., is opposed to s.o.'s plans or desires
opposite	âyakâmetêwe	on opposite sides of the lodge from each other (particle)
	wîtawakâme	on both sides, on opposite sides (particle)
	wâwîtawakâme	on opposite sides (particle)
	wâwîtawâhkwe	on opposite sides (as, of the tree) (particle)
	ênîhka	in opposite directions (particle)
or	o=tânâhka=kêhi	or perhaps, or what about if it was this way
	tânâhka=kêhi	or perhaps, or what about if it was this way
	o=tânâh=kêhi	or perhaps, or what about if it was this way
	tânâh=kêhi	or perhaps, or what about if it was this way
	o=meshe=kêhi	or maybe
	meshe=kêhi	or maybe
order (in order)	nîpenêwi	in order, in a particular sequence (preverb)
	nîpenêsenôni	they (inanimate) are in order, in a particular sequence
	nîpenêhamwa	sings them (inanimate) in order
orders	nanâhotamwa	directs it, manages it (as, a ceremony or activity); is in charge, gives the orders
ordinary	pêhkênemêwa	thinks s.o. is an ordinary person
oriented	inehkwêkôtôwa	hangs it with head end oriented {some way}
	inehkwênamwa	makes its head end point {some way} (song word)
	inehkwêshinwa	lies with head oriented {some way}
	inehkwêshitîwaki	they lay each other with heads oriented {some way}
orifice	shîshîshanohwêwa	gives s.o. pokes in an orifice with a burning stick
Osage	ashâsha	an Osage
	washâsha	an Osage (archaic)
	washâshinâki	in the Osage country (locative noun)
osprey	meshinowêwa	osprey

ostensibly	**mêmehchi**	ostensibly (particle)
other	**kotaka, kotaki**	other, another (animate, inanimate)
	îyâka	this other one (visible)
other side	**âwasinawe**	on the other side (of it), over (it) (particle)
other way	**wâwâshipaka**	the other way around (with roles reversed), contrary to the norm (particle)
otherwise	**anikashi**	besides, otherwise, beyond (particle)
otter	**ketatêwa**	otter
out	**kechîwa**	emerges, goes out into the open or into view; (sun) rises
	kechîmikatwi	it comes out
	kechipahowa	runs out, runs out into the open or into view
	kechinechênêwa	takes (it) out of s.o.'s hands
	kechinehkawêwa	chases s.o. out
	kechinehkêwa	pulls one's hand out
	kechisahêwa, kechisahtôwa	quickly takes or gets s.o. out; takes it (as, clothing) off quickly
	kechîmikihêwa, kechîmikihtôwa	makes s.o. (non-sentient), it come out
	nowîwa	goes out
	nowîmikatwi	it goes out
	nowîhêwa	sends or brings s.o. out, gets s.o. to come out, has s.o. come out
	nowikawiwaki	they go out as a group
	nowipahowa	runs out, goes out on the run
	nowipahônêwa	runs out carrying s.o.
	nowisêwa	runs out, flies out
	nowenêwa, nowenamwa	hands, puts s.o., it out, lets s.o. out
	nowiwenêwa, nowiwetôwa	leads or conveys s.o., it out
	nowikâhiwa	one's feet are sticking out
out of sight	**nehkeshawêwa**	goes out of sight shining
	nehkeshkêwa	goes out of sight
	nehkâshkêwa	falls out of sight
out-of-the-way	**êh=wâwanikenôhiniki**	in a somewhat unhandy or out-of-the-way place (obv.)
out of water	**akwâsenwi**	it lies out of the water, on the shore
	akwâpyênêwa	lifts s.o. out of the water
	akwâpyêhônêwa	drags s.o. out of the water
	akwâchisahowa	jumps out of the water
	akwâyâshowîwa	wades out of the water
	akwâhwêwa, akwâhamwa	fishes s.o., it out of water, fire (with a stick)
	akwâpyêhamwa	fishes it out of the water with something, dips it out of the kettle
outrun	**nawaswêwa**	outruns s.o.
	nawasohkyêwa	outruns people, wins the race
outside	**sâkichi**	outside (particle, prenoun)
	sâkichîmêhi	a little outside (dimin.) (particle)
oven	**wêhkâchîha**	Dutch oven
over	**pashkichishinwa, pashkichisenwi**	(animate, inanimate) lies across, hangs over, crosses
	pashkichisahowa	jumps across, jumps over
	pashkitâsîwa	climbs over the top
	pashkichisahêwa	throws s.o. (as, a hide) to hang over something
	pashkichikâshkêwa	throws one's leg over
overdo	**asâmîhkânowa**	overdoes it, does something out of line
overly	**nîshki**	overly, messily, heavily, awkwardly, almost too (much) (preverb)
overpower	**neshiwihêwa**	overpowers s.o., gets the best of s.o.

over the end	**nîpikwakôtêwi**	it is hung up over the end of something (as, a moccasin over the end of a branch)
over there	**mâhi**	over there, over here (particle)
over here	**atâhi**	over here; come here! (archaic) (particle)
	atâhîmêhi	over here; come here! (dimin.) (archaic) (particle)
	atâhanahka	over this way (particle)
	atânahka	over this way; come over this way (particle)
overburdened	**nîshkesiwa**	has a big load on one's back, (woman) has many children
overcome	**myânowihêwa, myânawihêwa**	overcomes s.o.
	myânowihtôwa, myânawihtôwa	prevails, overcomes ones opponent
	myânowesiwa	is overcome, cannot cope
	nôhkihêwa	easily overcomes s.o.
	neshiwimêwa	overcomes s.o. with words, has commanding power over s.o.
overeat	**asâmehkonowa**	overeats
overpower	**neshiwihêwa**	overpowers s.o.
	shâkowihêwa	overpowers s.o.
overtake	**matanêwa**	overtakes s.o., catches up with s.o.
	matahkyêwa	overtakes people, catches up
owl	**wîtekôwa**	owl (generic)
	wîtekôwi	of owl (prenoun)
	wîtekôwiwa	is an owl
	wîtekômowa	gives an owl-call
	wîhkonemîwa	great horned owl, "hoot owl"
	nenekapenôha	screech owl
	pônopônôha	saw-whet owl
	mashkotêwîtekôwa	burrowing owl
	kôhkôhkohôwâ!	(the hoot of an owl)
own	**tepênemêwa, tepênetamwa**	owns, controls s.o., it
	tepênetâtêwi	it is owned, controlled
	tepênetamôwitêhêwa	thinks one owns (s.o., it)
	nayênenwi	one's own (particle)
	tepinowe, tepinawe	of one's own, of one's own family or lineage, directly related (particle)

p

pack: → bundle, carry bundle		
packed	**sakwâkwasowa**	lies packed closely together
pack strap	**apihkâni**	pack strap, tumpline
paddle	**pemahowa**	paddles by in a canoe
	âshôhowa	paddles across
	inahowa	paddles to {somewhere}
	kekenahowa	paddles fast
	kîwahowa	paddles about
	môhkisêhowa	paddles out (of a stream)
	nâkatôhowa	paddles along (it)
	pyêtahowa	paddles this way
	wêpahowa	starts to paddle
paddle (noun)	**apwîhi**	paddle
pain	**ahpîhtamatamwa**	has {so much} pain, is in {so much} pain
	kîshâkotamatamwa	feels terrible pain

	nenwamatamwa	feels pain, feels it
	nenwishinwa	(with negative:) does not feel the pain
	pekishkamatamwa	suffers with pain
	sîsamatamwa	feels a sharp pain
	sîsamachihêwa	makes s.o. feel a sharp pain
	tanamatamwa	has pain {somewhere}
	wêpamatamwa	starts to have pain
painful	âhkwatwi	it is dangerous, it is painful
	âhkwâpitêwa	has a sharp bite
	âhkwâshkêwi	it is painful, causes pain
paint	wêshîhôni	paint
	wêshîhêwa	paints s.o.'s face
	wêshîhowa	paints oneself, one's face
	sheshôhamwa	paints it, daubs or smears it (with paint or something else)
	sheshôwâhkonêwa	paints s.o., paints s.o.'s body
	sheshôwâhkonowa	paints oneself, paints one's body
	sheshôwîkwênowa	paints one's face
	meshkonêwa	paints s.o. red
	meshkwâhkonêwa	paints s.o. red
	meshkwâhkonowa	paints oneself red
	wâpeshkâhkonêwa	paints s.o. white
	wâpeshkâhkonowa	paints oneself white
	mahkatêwâhkonêwa	paints s.o. black
	mahkatêwâhkonowa	paints oneself black
	anepyêhâtêwi	it is drawn, painted, diagrammed
	ashkipakepyêhâtêwi	it is painted green
	meshkopyêhâtêwi	it is painted red
	wêwenepyêhâsowa	(animate, as a buckskin) is beautifully painted
pair	nîshôhkatêwani (plural)	the two of them (inanimate) stand set in the ground together
	nîshôkêhiwaki (plural)	they dwell together as just a pair (dimin.)
	nîshôpiwa	sits in a pair, sits in a pair with (s.o.)
pale	wâpi	pale; white (archaic) (prenoun, preverb)
pallet	anâhkahêwa	makes a pallet for s.o.
pant	nênêsowa	is panting, is puffing
pants	kepwitîhi	pants, a pair of pants
	okepwitîhiwa	wears pants
	kekikepwitîhêpiwa	sits wearing pants
paper	mesenahikani, mesanahikani	paper
parch corn	panakesikêwa	parches corn
	memekwahikêwa	parches corn on the coals
	memekohikêwa	parches corn on the coals
parents	nemesôtânaki	my parents
	omesôtâniwa	has parents, has (them) as parents
	omesôtâniwitêhêwa	feels as if (they) were one's own parents
parents-in-law	wêsemichiki	the woman's parent's-in-law
	wênekwanichiki	the man's parents-in-law
	wêshinemâchihi	his parents-in-law
parfleche	pîshâkanimotêhi	parfleche, rawhide bag
parrot	pâshkatamôha	parrot (originally, Carolina parakeet)
part	nômamêwa, nômatamwa	eats part of s.o., it, eats some more of s.o., it
	nômenamwa	takes part of it
	nôminêwaki	part of them die off, some more of them die off

	nômisenyêwa	eats part of the food, some more of the food
	sâkâchimowa	tells just a little
	sâkâtotamwa	talks about it just a little
part (in hair)	nechêmôhi	my part (in my hair)
	netochêmôhi	I have a part (in my hair)
part company	pâpahkêwaki (plural)	they part company
partridge	pahkiwa	partridge, ruffed grouse
Partridge Clan	pahkiwisowa	is a member of the Partridge Clan
	pêhkiwisota	member of the Partridge Clan
pass	pemehkânêwa	passes s.o.
	pemeshitôwa	makes the round, passes from one of (them) to the next
pass on	âyâtenamâtîwaki	they keep passing (it, them) on to each other
pass out	panâtesiwa	loses consciousness, loses one's strength; succumbs, perishes, meets one's fate
	pahkihtêmowa	passes out from crying
	pahkihtêshinwa	falls unconscious
	pahkihtênehkawêwa	chases s.o. until they pass out
	pahkihtêpahowa	passes out from running
	pahkihtêsowa	passes out from the heat
pass through	konakwîwa	passes through, gets through danger
past, by	pemi	past, by, in the course, along, in sequence, go ahead and, start to, set about (preverb)
pat	pâhpâkahwêwa	pats s.o.
	pâhpâkepyêhamwa	pats it (water) repeatedly
patch	ahpahamwa	patches it
	ahpahikani	patch
path	myêwi	road, path
	pemosêhkanawi	footpath
	nepinâtôhkanawi	water path (to stream where water is obtained)
	mâtâshkamwa	comes to it (a larger path or road)
patiently	mâmahkoshi	patiently at length or repeatedly; expecting in vain; it still has not happened (that) (particle)
patter	tîkwêwi	it patters, there is a pattering sound
	tîkwêwêpahowa	the patter of one's feet can be heard as one runs
	tîkwêwêshkamwa	the patter of one's feet can be heard
paunch	mîshimotêhi	paunch, rumen
	mîshimôhi	paunch, rumen
	omîshimôhi	paunch, rumen
paw	onechi	a paw; s.o.'s (animal's) paw
	nîkâninehkâkani	front hoof, front paw
paw the earth	pekwahôkêwa	paws the earth (as, an angry bull)
pawpaw	asîmini	pawpaw
pay	tepahwêwa, tepahamwa	pays s.o., it, pays s.o. (it)
	tepahâsowa, tepahâtêwi	(animate, inanimate) is paid
	inakitamawêwa	pays s.o. {so much} for (it)
	pônikêwa	pays one's gambling debt
peacefully	wânahkye	peacefully, undisturbed (particle)
	wânapiwa	is peaceable, at peace, unconcerned
	wânihêwa	leaves s.o. in peace
peach	mîsechêha	peach
peanut	ashkimâhaki	hog peanuts, "Indian peanuts"
peck	pekohamwa	pecks it, chips it with a tool
peek	kesâpiwa	peeks in, peeks out
peel	panakahamwa	chops or scrapes the bark or rind off of it

	panakinameshkêshkêwa	one's skin is peeling off
	panôkâhkohamwa	scrapes the bark off of it
	panôkeshamwa	peels it with a knife
	pashôshkâhkohwêwa	chops the bark of s.o. (a tree)
	pashôshkenêwa, pashôshkenamwa	pulls the skin off of s.o. (as, a rabbit), husks s.o. (corn); peels it
	pashîshkenêwa	pulls the skin off of s.o. (as, a rabbit), husks s.o. (corn)
	pepeshkwikeshamwa	peels it (as, a stick) with a knife, cuts the bark off it
peep	sâpîkwêwa	peeps (through half-open eyes)
	tôshkîkwêwa	peeps, one's eyes peep open
	tôshkîkwênwa	peeps through one's eyes
	tôshkîkwêshkêwa	opens one's eyes a crack
	tôshkânakîkwêshkêwa	one's eyes peep open
	tôshkîkwêmowa	peeps through one's eyes while singing
peer up	nênêkwâpiwa	is peering up (out of the tops of one's eyes), glaring up
	nêkwâpamêwa	peers up at s.o. (out of the tops of one's eyes), glares up at s.o.
pelican	shêtêwa	pelican
pemmican	nôhkahâni	pemmican
penis	nînakayi	my penis
	owînakêwa	has a penis
	mesônwêwa	he has a big penis
	ahkônwêwa	his penis is {so long}
	kîshkônwêshwêwa	cuts off his penis
peopled earth	mehtosêneniwahkiwiwi	it is a peopled earth, the earth has people on it
	mehtosêneniwahkyâniwiwi	it is a peopled earth, the earth has people on it
perch	tashitiyêpiwa	is sitting, perching on (the edge of) {somewhere}; is squatting {somewhere} (Jones)
perform	pâhpiwa	performs tricks
	pâhpîha	performer (of tricks)
	pâhpîhaki (plural)	the circus
	ishîhkânowa	puts on {such} a ceremony or performance
	ishihchikêweniwiwi	it is {so} performed
perfume	seswahowa	perfumes oneself
	seswahôni	perfume
perhaps	mêmeshihka	perhaps, for example (particle)
	meshê='nahi, meshê='nah=meko	perhaps, may, can, could, at will, if one likes; about, roughly speaking, as much as, some or other, whatever it was; going so far as to; in the course of time; one lets it happen; let it go, forget it
	meshe=kêhi	(or) perhaps, (or) for example
	wîshâwi	perhaps, maybe, likely but not certainly (particle, preverb)
perish	panâtesiwa	succumbs, perishes, meets one's fate; loses consciousness or strength
	panâtesîmikatwi	it (as, a life or the name of one who dies) is lost
permission	kotowêwa	asks permission; tries to make a sound
permit	pahkimêwa	permits, assigns s.o.; invites s.o. to eat in a ceremony, assigns (ceremonial food) to s.o.
persimmon	pyâkimini	persimmon
persist	ayînêhka	persisting aimlessly or inappropriately (particle)
	âtami	persistently, persist in (preverb)
	nanôchi	persisting to the end, not quit until (preverb)
person	mehtosêneniwa	person, human being,

	owîchi-mehtosênenîwâwahi	their own people
	mehtosênenîha	human being (song word)
	mehtosêneniwiwa	is a human being, lives
	mehtosêneniwihêwa	turns s.o. into a human being; makes s.o. live
	mehtosêneniwâpamêwa	sees s.o. as a person
	wîchi-mehtosênenîmêwa	has s.o. as a fellow human being
	mehtosêneniwitehkâsowa	is called a person, a human being
	mehtosêneniwitehkânetîwaki	they call each other human beings
	netawêpemaki	my people, my men
	kêhkyâha	old person
	kehchinêwe, kehchinêwi	in person, oneself
	wâsahkamikôha	person of a distant land
persuade	kashkimêwa	persuades s.o.
	kâchimêwa	persuades s.o.
	kâchinawêmêwa	persuades s.o. to act
	kîhkîhkimêwa	bids or persuades s.o. against one's will
	kochîhkawêwa	tries to consort with s.o., to persuade s.o.
	natawimêwa	tries to persuade s.o. (to)
	tashîhkâtîwa	tries to persuade; courts, has an affair
	ânomêwa	fails to persuade s.o.
	ânowêwa	fails to persuade
pestle	pôtahishkwâti	pestle (for grinding)
pet	netaya	my pet, my dog, my horse
	netayîha	my pet (dimin.)
	otayiwa	has a pet, has (s.o.) as a pet
	otayimêwa	has s.o. for a pet or domestic animal
	otayimâkana	pet, domestic animal
	otayimâkâha	pet, domestic animal (dimin.)
pet (verb)	keshêmowa	pets and speaks soothingly to (s.o., it)
pheasant: → grouse		
Pheasant Clan	pêhkiwisota	member of the Pheasant Clan
phlegm	akikwâha	phlegm
	wînihpanêwa	has a phlegmy cough
pick	mahkenamwa	breaks it off, pulls it off, picks it (as, a flower)
	mamahkenêwa, mamahkenamwa	picks them (as, berries, flowers)
	pahkenêwa, pahkenamwa	picks s.o. (as, fruit), it; plucks s.o., it off; pulls s.o., it off
	papahkenêwa, papahkenamwa	breaks s.o., it apart (with multiple breaks); picks them
pick at and eat	mâmâhkatamwa	picks at them and eats them (as, scattered bits of food)
pick on	nanâtohkwihêwa	picks on s.o., picks a fight with s.o.
	nanâtahkwihêwa	picks on s.o., picks a fight with s.o.
pick the crop	mamêwa	picks the crop (of corn, tobacco)
piece	pahkwêhamwa	chops a piece off it
	pahkwêhpwêwa, pahkwêhtamwa	bites a piece out of s.o., it
	pahkwêshkêwi	it tears off, chips off; it is torn off, chipped off
pieces	nîki	in small pieces (preverb)
	nîkatahwêwa	chops s.o. (as, a block of ice) to pieces
	nîkateshwêwa	cuts s.o. into pieces
	pekechênamwa	shoots it to pieces
	pekechêshkawêwa, pekechêshkamwa	kicks s.o., it to pieces
	pekihkeshkêwi	it goes to pieces
	pekihkishinwa	falls in pieces
	pekihkahwêwa, pekihkahamwa	smashes s.o., it to pieces
	pekihkenêwa, pekihkenamwa	crumbles s.o. (as, tobacco), it to pieces

	pekihketêwi	it is blown to bits (by gunshot or explosion)
	shekwakwîchinwa, shekwakwîtêwi	(animate, inanimate) falls to pieces lying in water
	shekwatahwêwa, shekwatahamwa	smashes s.o., it to pieces; beats s.o. down, subdues s.o.
	sheshekonêwa, sheshekonamwa	tears s.o., it to pieces
	sheshekwatamwa	chews it to pieces
	sheshekwishinwa	is smashed to pieces on impact
	taswâpyêshwêwa	cuts s.o. into {so many} pieces
pierce	**pôhkahamwa**	pokes a hole in it, pierces it
	patahkahwêwa, patahkahamwa	pierces (the surface of) s.o., it, sticks something sharp into s.o., it
	patahkechêhwêwa	spears s.o.
	patahkisetôwa	sets it piercing
	pôchîkwêhwêwa	pierces s.o. in the eye
pig	**kôhkôsha**	pig, hog; pork
	kôhkôshêha	pig, hog; pork (dimin.)
pigeon	**omîmîwa**	passenger pigeon
	pêhk-omîmîwa	passenger pigeon
pike	**kenôshêwa**	pike
pile	**pehkwâkwasowa, pehkwâkwatêwi**	(animate, inanimate) lies in a pile
	pehkwâkwanêwa, pehkwâkwatôwa	lays s.o. in a heap; piles it up, leaves a pile of it
	inehpâkwanêwa, inehpâkwatôwa	makes a pile of s.o., it {so} high
	inehpâkwasowa, inehpâkwatêwi	there is a pile {so} high of (animate, inanimate)
	pepyêhkwâkwatôwa	puts them (inanimate) in piles
	âkwasowa, âkwatêwi	(animate, inanimate) is piled up, forms a pile
	âyâkwatêwi	it lies in piles
	âyâkwachi	in piles
	âyâkwachipokôtêwani	piles of them (inanimate) drift ashore
	makâkwasowa, makâkwatêwi	there is a large pile or mass of (animate, inanimate)
	neshiwâkwasowa, neshiwâkwatêwi	there is a huge pile, mass, or cluster of (animate, inanimate)
	ahpihwêwa	piles (it) on top of s.o.
pillow	**apehkwêshimôna**	pillow
	apehkwêshimôni	thing used to lay the head on
pin (verb)	**sakâhkohamwa**	nails it up, buttons it, pins it
pinch	**sîsenêwa, sîsenamwa**	pinches s.o., it (with the fingers)
	sakenamwa	pinches it up (as, cloth), holds it in one's fingers
pine tree	**shekwâhkwa**	pine tree
pipe	**ahpwâkana**	tobacco pipe
	ohpwâkana	tobacco pipe (archaic [Jones])
	meshkohpwâkana	catlinite pipe, redstone pipe
	atamâkanâhkwi	pipe stem
	sîkihkamêsêwa	jumps spilling one's pipe
pipeful	**nekotôhpwâkane**	one pipeful (particle)
pitch	**pekiwa**	pitch, gum
pity	**ketemâkênemêwa, ketemâkênetamwa**	has compassion for s.o., it; thinks s.o., it is wretched
	keteminawêwa	pities, blesses s.o.
place	**kîshâkwanêwa, kîshâkwatôwa**	finishes setting s.o., it out, laying s.o., it in place
	menwishimêwa, menwisetôwa	places s.o., it nicely
	pehkînisetôwa	places it differently

316

	tashitiyêshimêwa	places s.o. with rump {somewhere}
	tasôsetôwa	places {so many} of it
place in lodge	wêtapinâchi	in one's regular place in the lodge, in one's spot (oblique participle)
place together	takwishimêwa, takwisetôwa	places s.o., it in addition, together with (it)
	takwisetâtîwaki	they place (it) in addition for each other
	tahtakwisetôwa	places them together
plain	mehchi	openly, plainly, ostensibly (particle, preverb)
	âhkwi	plainly, sharply, dangerously (preverb)
plan	inotâtêwi	it is told {so}, it is mentioned {so}, it is planned {so}
	kîshitêhêwa	has formed a plan, has made up one's mind
	kîshênemêwa	has formed a plan about s.o., has made up one's mind about s.o.
	wêchinowitêhêwa	thinks something is easy, plans something easy
plant	ahkihkêwa	plants things, works a garden
plaster (verb)	patashkishinwa	is plastered against something
platform	atasani	platform (for sitting, sleeping, working)
	otatasaniwa	has a platform
	ahkwichitasane	on top of the platform (particle)
	nâmitasane	under the platform (particle)
	chêpahkwâni	area of sleeping platform against the lodge-wall
	nêsawâhi	forked support post of a platform
play	tashîhkânowa	plays, is playing
	wîchênomêwa, wîchênotamwa	enjoys life with s.o., associates with s.o., plays with s.o.; plays with it
	wîchênokêwa	enjoys life with others, associates with others, plays with others
	wîchênotîwaki	they play together, enjoy themselves together
	mêmenwi-wîchênotamâkêwa	always plays nicely with (them) of others
	kônanôhiwa	plays the double-ball game, shinny
	kosikêwa	plays bowl-and-dice
	mâmîhkôhiwaki (plural)	they play tag
	meshkwêhpîhiwa	plays with the throwing-stick
	pîkîhiwa	plays cards
	tâtashîhkânowa	(always) plays ({somewhere})
plead	wîshâmêwa	implores s.o., pleads with s.o., urges s.o. insistently
	wîshâwêwa	pleads (for spiritual aid) against (it); screams in anguish
	wîshâwehtâkosiwa	is heard pleading (ritual)
pleasant	shahki	pleasant, good-natured (particle, preverb)
	shahki-mehtosêneniwiwa	is good-natured
	shahki-wîkanwi	it is pleasant-tasting
	metâtênetamwa	thinks it pleasant
please	têpihêwa, têpihtôwa	pleases s.o., it
	têpihetîwaki	they please each other
	têpihiwêwa	pleases people
	têpihtawêwa	pleases (it) for s.o.
	têpîhkânowa	does a pleasing deed
	menwinawêmêwa	pleases s.o. with words
	têpesînotawêwa, têpesînotamwa	is pleased with s.o., it
please!	pena!	O.K. now, please, why don't you, could you, you'd better; why don't I, may I, I'd better
	=tâni	O.K.? why don't I, if you agree, if you will, please
plenty	pîneshki	plentifully, in abundance, in numbers (preverb)

317

	pînêshkesiwa, pînêshkyâwi	is or has plenty; there is plenty (of it)
	pînêshkisetawêwa	places (it) in abundance for s.o.
	pîsâkwi-ishawiwa	has plenty, is wealthy
	pîsâkosiwa	(food animal) has a lot of meat on it
pliant	**shashawâwi**	it is pliant, yielding
plight	**ânemesiwa**	is in a plight
pluck	**pahkenêwa, pahkenamwa**	plucks s.o., it off; pulls s.o., it off, picks s.o. (as, fruit), it
	pahkenamawêwa	plucks it off for s.o.
	mônêwa	plucks s.o.
	mônisêwêwa	plucks a bird or birds
	pashkwânehkwênikêwa	does the plucking of the hair
plug	**kepachihwêwa, kepachihamwa**	plugs s.o., it up (as, in a hole or bottle)
plum	**pôhkamâha**	plum
point	**ashâtîhânowêwa**	has a tail that ends in a spear point
point at	**âwinôhwêwa**	points at s.o.
	anôhwêwa	points at s.o. (archaic)
point out	**kehkahamawêwa**	points (it) out to s.o., makes (it) known to s.o.
poke	**chîpechêsahêwa**	pokes s.o.
	pôhkahamwa	pokes a hole in it, pierces it
	pôhkitepêhwêwa	pokes a hole in one's head
	shîshahwêwa	pokes s.o. with a burning stick
	shîshîshanohwêwa	gives s.o. pokes in an orifice with a burning stick
poker	**mônihkeshêhôni**	fire poker
	ateshêwêhikani, ahteshêwêhikani	poker (for rearranging the fire) (archaic; shape uncertain)
pole	**âkôhôni**	dividing pole (on the floor of the lodge)
	nêmatêhi	upright pole (in a summer house)
policeman	**nênawihtôwa**	camp policeman
	panîsa	police officer
pond	**nepisêhi**	pond
pool	**pehkopyêsenwi**	it is a pool or puddle
poor	**kêtemâha**	poor person
popcorn	**pâpakesôhaki** (plural)	popcorn
porcupine	**akâkwa**	porcupine
portion	**nekotwâpyêki**	one portion (particle)
	nîshwâpyêki	two portions (particle)
	neswâpyêki	three portions (particle)
	nyêwâpyêki	four portions (particle)
	nekotwâpyêkatwi	it is one portion
	nîshwâpyêkatwi	it is two portions
	neswâpyêkatwi	it is three portions
	nyêwâpyêkatwi	it is four portions
position	**nanâhâkwatôwa**	lays it in position
	nanâhikâpâwa	takes one's position (in line, etc.), sets one's feet in position
possession	**netâhînemi**	my thing, my possession
	netâhwînemi	my thing, my possession
	netâhîhemi	my thing, my possession
	netâhwîhemi	my thing, my possession
	otâhînemiwa	has (it) as a possession
	otâhwînemiwa	has (it) as a possession
	otâhîhemiwa	has (it) as a possession
	otâhwîhemiwa	has (it) as a possession
	otâhînemetamwa	has it as a possession

	otâhînemetamawêwa	has (it) as a possession from s.o.
possum	âyênîha, êyênîha	possum
post	apashi	lodgepole, side post, door post
	apashîhi	lodgepole, side post, door post (dimin.)
	nêsawâhi	forked support post of a platform
	ketâkana	one of the large central posts holding up the roof of a summer house
potato	ahpenya	potato, tuber
	ahpenîha	potato, tuber
	nenôtêwi-ahpenya	"Indian potato"
	nenôtêwi-ahpenîha	"Indian potato"
	ashkipwâha	"sweet potato"
Potawatomi	pehkînenîha	Potawatomi
pothook	akôchikani	hanger, pothook
poultice	akonamwa	applies it as a poultice
	ahtwêwa	applies (it as) a poultice
	ahtwâkani	poultice
pound	pôtahesowa	pounds (as, in a mortar), does one's pounding
	tanwêwêhwêwa, tanwêwêhamwa	is audibly drumming, banging, or pounding on s.o. (as, a drum), it
	tanwêwêhikêwa	is heard drumming, pounding, or chopping ({somewhere})
pour	sîkikêwi	it pours out
	sîkâhkêwa	pours out a slosh of (it)
	sâsîkâhkêwa	pours out sloshes of (it)
	sîkahwêwa, sîkahamwa	pours s.o., it out; serves s.o., it up
	sîkisahtôwa	empties it out, pours it out, spills it out, dumps it out
	sîkenahwêwa, sîkenahamwa	pours water on s.o., it, pours (it) on s.o., it
	sîkenahamawêwa	pours water on (it) for s.o.
	sîkeshkânamwa	pours, spills, dumps it out
	pakikawihtôwa	pours it by drops
powwow	pâwâhiwa	holds a powwow
power	manetôwiwa, manetôwiwi	(animate, inanimate) has spirit power
	manetôwîmikatwi	it has spirit power
	manetôwâtakesiwa	has spiritual power
	manetôwi	powerful thing, thing having spiritual power (nemanetômi my spiritual power)
	nemanetômi	my spiritual power
	manetôwâchimowa	talks like a manitou, speaks with spiritual power
powerful	neshiwesiwa	is dangerous, fierce, mighty, powerful
	ahpîhchikiwa, ahpîhchikenwi	is {so} powerful, old; it is {so} effective, powerful
	ahpîhchâwi	it is {so} great, {so} intense, {so} powerful
practice	kokwêchi	try to, practice (preverb)
	kokwêtowêwa	practices speaking
	kotâhkohikêwa	practices shooting
prairie	mashkotêwi	prairie
	mashkotêwiwi	it is prairie
	chîkêshkote	by the prairie (particle)
	kohpichi	on the prairie (particle); of the prairie (prenoun)
prairie chicken	meshisêwa	prairie chicken
prairie dog	wêtôtêwâha	prairie dog
praise	ayîkwâmâchimêwa	gives a great reputation to s.o.
praise	wawînwânêwa, wawînwâtamwa	compliments s.o., praises s.o.; brags about it
pray	mamâtomowa	prays, worships

	mamâtomowapiwa	sits in prayer
	mamâtomowitêhêwa	is prayerful
	mamâtomêwa, mamâtotamwa	prays to s.o., it; requests medical aid from s.o.
	natotâsêwa	prays to s.o.
	natotâsowa	begs, prays
prayer word	**nôchi**	(prayer vocable, the equivalent of 'hear my prayer')
pregnant	**achihkwiwa**	she is pregnant
prepare	**kîshisetânawêwa**	has everything prepared, has it all set (as, for a ceremony)
President	**mêtâsôpita**	the President, the United States Government
press hard	**wîshâhêwa**	keeps after s.o., presses s.o. hard
	wîshâmêwa	implores s.o., pleads with s.o., is insistent with s.o., presses s.o. hard (verbally), nags s.o.
pretend	**ishîhkânowa**	pretends to be or do {so}
	ishiwêpîhkânowa	pretends {so}
	inwâsowa	pretends {so}
	mayôhkânowa	pretends to weep
	nepêhkânowa	pretends to sleep
	wachâhôhkânowa	pretends to cook, plays at cooking
	wâwanênetamôhkânowa	pretends not to know
	omîshâmehkâsowa	claims (it) as one's sacred bundle, pretends (it) is one's sacred bundle
	okimâwîhkâsowa	acts as chief, pretends to be chief
	kênwâsowêwîhkâsowa	pretends to be a mountain lion
	pashitôhîhkâsowa	pretends to be an old man
pretty	**wêwenesiwa, wêwenetwi**	is pretty, handsome; it is nice, good
	wêwenihêwa, wêwenihtôwa	makes s.o., it pretty, nice
	wêwenihtawêwa	makes it pretty for s.o.
	wêwenihtâtîwaki	they make it pretty for each other
	wêwenânakîkwêwa	has pretty eyes
	wêwewêwenânakîkwêwa	has pretty eyes
	wêwenipyêwa, wêwenipyêyâwi	(animate, inanimate) has pretty leaves or boughs
	nawêni	pretty, handsome (prenoun)
	ênowêni	pretty, handsome (prenoun) (archaic)
prevail	**kashkôhpenanêwa, kashkôhpenatôwa**	prevails over s.o., it, is able to get or kill s.o.
	âhpenêhêwa	prevails against s.o. one-sidedly, does not give s.o. a chance in the fight
price	**inakimowa, inakitêwi**	it is priced {so}
probably	**=yêtoke**	probably, I suppose, it seems
	mêkwêhe	I believe, I think, probably, likely
prod	**chîpahwêwa**	prods him
prohibit	**neshkimâkaniwiwa**	is prohibited
promise	**kwayahkwimêwa**	promises s.o., tells s.o. it is definite, decides about s.o.
	kwayahkowêwa	promises, declares a decision
proper	**kwayahkwênetamwa**	thinks it proper, prudent
	nahikenwi	it is proper
proud: → glad		
provide	**kîwikîwikahêwa**	repeatedly provides dwellings for them in different places (song word)
prudently	**kwayahkwi**	taking the prudent course, deciding to go ahead (and be done with it), making the best of it, might as well; one had better (particle)
pubic hair	**mîshikwâkani**	a pubic hair
pull	**atâhpâpyêsahtôwa**	yanks it on a string

	pahkisahêwa	pulls s.o. off
	nasenamwa	pulls its trigger
pull apart	**nanâsitâpihkanênêwa**	pulls s.o.'s jaws apart
pull hair	**mônashkitepênêwa**	pulls out s.o.'s hair
pull out	**pahkonêwa, pahkonamwa**	pulls s.o., it out; plucks s.o. (feather)
	pahkonamawêwa	pulls (it) out for s.o.
	papahkonêwa, papahkonamwa	pulls them out (animate, as feathers; inanimate)
	pahkwitenyêsahêwa	pulls s.o.'s shoulder out of joint
	papahkwâkênêwa	plucks s.o.'s wing-feathers
	papahkwâpitênêwa	pulls s.o.'s teeth out
	akwâpyêhtamwa	pulls it out of the water with one's mouth
pull up	**mônashkwêwa**	pulls up grass, weeds
	mônashkenamwa	pulls it (a plant) up by the roots
	pahkwachiwênêwa, pahkwachiwênamwa	pulls s.o. (as, a cornstalk), it up by the roots
	papahkwachiwênamwa	pulls it up by the roots
	pahkwachiwêsahtôwa	tears it up by the roots
punk	**pîyohkwi, pîyahkwi**	punk (crumbly rotten wood)
	masatôwa	punk (spongy rotten wood that sometimes glows in the dark)
pursue	**nâwanonêhwêwa**	pursues s.o., goes following after s.o.
	nâwanonehkwêwêwa	pursues a woman or women
	wêchinehkawochi	was immediately pursued (idiom)
	wêchinehkâkêchi	went immediately in pursuit (idiom)
pus	**meni**	pus
	meniwiwa, meniwiwi	has pus, a pussy sore, is pussy; it is pussy
push	**kâchisahêwa, kâchisahtôwa**	pushes s.o., it
	kâhkâtenêwa	keeps pushing s.o.
	mîwahwêwa	pushes s.o. aside
	ishisahetîwaki	they push each other to {somewhere}
	kâtehkwêhwêwa	strikes s.o. on the head, pushes or knocks s.o.'s head
	kâtetonêhwêwa	strikes or pushes s.o. on the mouth
push back	**âtenêwa**	pushes s.o. back
push in	**nehkenamawêwa**	pushes (it) into s.o.
put	**asêwa, ahtôwa**	has s.o., it; places, puts s.o., it ({somewhere})
	ahtâtîwaki	they place (it) {somewhere} for each other
	ahtawêwa	has, places (it) {somewhere} for s.o.
	akwîkwâtamwa	puts it on one's face
	pesehkamwa	puts it on (clothing, especially moccasins); puts on moccasins
	pîsehkamwa	puts it on (as, a shirt, a dress)
	apâhkwisetawêwa	places (it) as a padding for s.o.
	apehkwêhiwa	places one's head on (it)
	asetîwaki	they place each other {somewhere}
	mâwachisetôwa	puts it all together
	nanâhahtôwa	puts it in place
	nanâhônakishimêwa	puts s.o. in a box or canoe
	nekwipekwêhamwa	puts it under ashes
	pôtenamwa	puts it in (as, into water)
	pônômêwa, pônôtamwa	puts s.o., it down from one's back
	anâhkwâtamawêwa	puts (it) on sticks for s.o.
	pînahwêwa, pînahamwa	puts s.o., it in a bag; uses love medicine on s.o. (putting a hair in a bundle)
put away	**nahishimêwa, nahisetôwa**	puts s.o., it away

	nahisetwêwa	puts (it) away (as a store of food)
	nêhishimêwa, nêhisetôwa	puts s.o., it away
	sêsahwêwa, sêsahamwa	leaves s.o., it someplace safe (to be retrieved later)
	sêsahâsowa	is put away safely, in an inaccessible place

q

quail	**pôhkwîha**	quail
quarrel	**tanwêwêmêwa**	quarrels with s.o.
	kîhkîhkitîwaki (plural)	they argue with each other, quarrel
	pekishkîhkâtîwaki (plural)	they quarrel, make trouble for each other
quarter	**-êsepane**	quarter-dollar (in particle compounds)
	nesw-êsepane	seventy-five cents
quickly	**kekeni**	quickly (particle, preverb)
	kekenesiwa	acts quickly, works quickly, is fast (doing something)
	tatayâchi	in quick succession (archaic)
	wêwîtepi	quickly, at once, forthwith, losing no time (preverb)
	aniwisahowa	jumps or moves quickly
	pasi-wâpamêwa	shoots s.o. a quick glance
quiet	**mahkwâchi**	quietly, gently (particle, preverb, prenoun)
	mahkwâtesiwa	is quiet, is of a quiet nature
	mahkwâtesiweni	quietness
	mahkwâchîhiweni	quietness
	mahkwâtênetâkosiwa	is thought quiet
	nahêkashe	quietly, slowly (particle)
	nahêka	in a low tone, quietly, slowly (particle)
	nanônemi	on the quiet, without saying anything (particle)
quill	**kwâhkwâpiwiwa, kwâhkwâpiwiwi**	(animate, inanimate) is decorated with porcupine-quills
quilt	**kânôhi**	quilt; diamond card
quite	**mechi**	rather, quite; (with sarcastic intonation) surely not! obviously not! (particle)
	kehchi-menwâhi	quite enough, quite soon, rather (particle compound)
quiver (noun)	**pîtanwâna**	quiver
	opîtanwâniwa	has a quiver, has (it) as a quiver
quiver (verb)	**nenekishimowa**	speaks with a quivering voice (as if about to cry)

r

rabbit	**meshwêha**	rabbit
raccoon	**êsepana**	raccoon
	êsepâha	raccoon
	êsepâhêha	small raccoon
	êsepanaya, êsepâhaya	raccoon skin
race (verb)	**nânawasotîwaki**	they race
	nânawasotîhêwa	races s.o. (a horse), makes s.o. race
race (noun)	**ishinameshkêwa**	has {such} skin, is of {such} race
rack	**ahkwitahâkani**	shelf, storage rack
ragged	**nîsîkishehkîtamwa**	is dressed in ragged clothes
railroad	**êshkotêwîhi-myêwi**	railroad
rain	**kemiyâwi**	it rains

	kemiyâneshiwa	gets caught in the rain
	kemiyânwihtôwa	makes it rain
	kemiyânâpowi	rain water
rainbow	**anakwêwa**	rainbow
	anakwêwiwi	there is a rainbow
raise	**wanâkenêwa**	raises s.o. by hand
	chîkakonamwa	pulls or pushes it (as, a skirt) up
	chîkakôtênêwa	raises s.o.'s skirt
	kîshikenêwa	raises s.o. (as, a child or animal)
	kîshikenamâtisowa	raises (s.o., it, as a crop) for oneself
	kîshikihêwa, kîshikihtôwa	raises s.o., it (as a crop), has s.o., it mature
	ahchikâtisowa	raises (it) for oneself from seed
ram	**kâchitâsetôwa**	rams it in
random	**nanôshkwe**	at random, without knowing if it would be correct or effective, without knowing what it is (particle)
rape	**mehchi pakinêwa**	he rapes her
	menipowaki	they gang-rape (her)
rascal	**machawahîna, machawahîma**	rascal, good-for-nothing
rasp	**kânikanîhâhkwi**	rasp (notched stick used as a musical instrument)
raspberry	**wîtawîhaki** (plural)	black raspberries
	meshkwi-wîtawîhaki (plural)	red raspberries
rather	**mechi**	rather, quite (particle)
	=wêna (=wê=)	in fact, rather, after all
	=wê=nôchi (idiom):	**nîna=wê=nôchi, '...,' neteshitêhe** I had thought rather, '...'
	mata	rather, alternatively (particle)
	nêpehe	or rather; or I should have said; oh I forgot (particle)
	kehchi-menwâhi	rather, quite enough, quite soon (particle compound)
rattle	**anwêwênamwa**	rattles it
	anwêwêsahtôwa	rattles it
rattlesnake	**shîshîkwêwa**	rattlesnake
ravine	**tâtwâhkiwi**	ravine
raw	**ashkenwa, ashkenwi**	is raw
	kek-ashki	(while still) raw, uncooked (particle compound)
reach	**têpahkwi**	reaching, reaching the point or end of, going so far as to, living long enough to, succeeding in, all the way (preverb, particle)
	têpikenwi	it reaches
	têpenêwa, têpenamwa	reaches s.o., it, reaches out and touches s.o., it
	têpiyâkosiwa, têpiyâkwatwi	the smell of (animate, inanimate) reaches
	nôtênamwa	falls short of reaching it with one's hand
react	**amêwa**	act, react
	amênâkosiwa	shows a reaction
	amênotawêwa	reacts to s.o., is responsive to s.o.
readily	**wênôshkâhpenanêwa**	is able to readily kill s.o.
	wênôshkihêwa	is able to readily kill s.o.
	wênôshki-nesêwa	is able to readily kill s.o.
ready	**nanâhi**	get set or ready to, get set or ready by, try to, start to (preverb)
	nanâhawiwa	makes ready
	nanâhinawîwa	gets ready
	wêwêshiwawiwa	gets or is ready (to act)
	wêwêshiwenêwa, wêwêshiwenamwa	holds s.o., it ready (to use)
	wayêshi	ready

	kekakôtêwi	it is hanging ready (in the kettle)
realizes	**mînâwênemêwa, mînâwênetamwa**	thinks seriously of s.o., it; realizes about s.o., it
	mînâwitêhêwa	thinks intently, realizes
really	**pêhki**	really, fully, successfully, easily, earnestly (particle); real, correct, natural, regular, ordinary (prenoun)
rear end	**pyêchitiyêkâpâwa**	stands with rear end this way
reason	**ochi**	from {somewhere}, because of {some} reason (particle, preverb)
reattach	**takwikenwi**	it grows with (it), it is reattached
rebuff	**aniwêmêwa**	angrily rebuffs s.o., retorts to s.o. spitefully or meanly
rebuild	**âchikêwa**	rebuilds one's house
recede	**ashkisêwi**	it ebbs, recedes
receive	**nahkwâhpetamawêwa**	receives and eats (it) for s.o.
recently	**keyêchîhi, keyêchîhe**	recently, a short while ago; soon, soon after (particle)
	kayêchîhi, kayêchîhe	recently, a short while ago; soon, soon after (particle)
reciprocally	**wâwâchi**	reciprocally, mutually (particle)
recognize	**nenawêwa, nenamwa**	recognizes s.o., it
	nenâtîwaki	they recognize each other
	nenohpamêwa, nenohpetamwa	recognizes, makes out the taste of s.o., it
	nenwiyâmêwa, nenwiyâtamwa	recognizes the smell of s.o., it
	nenwiyâkosiwa, nenwiyâkwatwi	the odor of (animate, inanimate) is recognizable
	kehkinawâchawiwa	acts recognizably, characteristically
reconnoiter	**natawâhtôwa**	reconnoiters (it)
	âpipahtôwa	goes alone to spy on the enemy as a scout
recoup losses	**mawinêhikêwa**	goes or attempts to recoup one's losses; stakes (it) to try to win back one's losses
recover	**nahâtesiwa**	recovers, gets well, feels better, acts normal
	nahitêhêwa	recovers one's composure, feels good again
	kîkikanêwa	regains one's strength
	kîkênemêwa	thinks s.o. is better, recovered
red	**meshkwi**	red (prenoun)
	meshkosiwa, meshkwâwi	(animate, inanimate) is red
	meshkwâpôkatwi	it is red liquid
	meshkwahtakawêwa	is red (animal), has a red coat
	meshkwikenâtêwi	it (stick or sticklike) is painted red
	meshkwêkenwi	red woolen broadcloth
redden	**meshkohkamwa**	reddens it by going there
red glow	**meshkoshawêwa**	(sun) is giving a red glow
reed	**opîwanashkenôki** (plural)	reeds (smaller than cattails and not used for mats)
	opîwayashkenôki (plural)	reeds (smaller than cattails and not used for mats)
reek	**wînasamwêwiyâkosiwa**	reeks with dirty-dog smell
	wînasamwêwiyâkochêwa	one's body reeks with dirty-dog smell
refill kettle	**nâpahkohkwawêwa**	(deity) refills the kettle for s.o. (grants the killing of enemies in exchange for the ritual meal)
reflection	**onôkênawiwa**	has a soul, reflection, or shadow
refuge	**nâchîhiwêwa**	goes to seek refuge
	pyêchîhiwêwa	arrives reaching refuge
	têpîhiwêwa	succeeds in reaching safety or refuge
refuse	**ânochimêwa**	refuses s.o.'s request
	ânotwêwa	refuses, refuses a request
	ânotîwaki	they refuse each other's requests
	ânwêhtawêwa, ânwêhtamwa	disbelieves, refuses s.o., it
regular	**pêhkênemêwa**	thinks s.o. is a regular person

regularly	**sekihki**	assiduously, regularly (particle, preverb)
reject	**shîkwênetamwa**	rejects it for something better
	shîkwênetâkaniwiwa	is generally rejected
related	**chînawêmêwa, chînawêtamwa**	is related to s.o.; is related to it, has relatives
	inâkômêwa, inâkôtamwa	is related to s.o. {so}, has relatives {so}
	inâkôtîwaki	they are related to each other {so}
	inawêmêwa	is related to s.o. {so}
relationship	**inâkôpehkêwa**	uses {such} term of relationship for (s.o.)
relax	**pakishêwêshkêwa**	relaxes, one's muscles relax
release	**keteshkenêwa, keteshkenamwa**	releases s.o., it
	pakinêwa	releases s.o. (deceased relative) by the ceremonial adoption of another
	pakinetîwaki	they hold an adoption for someone (lit., they release each other)
rely on	**ahpênemônotawêwa, ahpênemônotamwa**	relies on s.o., it; depends on s.o., it
	tepatohachikaniwiwa	is emulated and relied on
reluctantly	**kekishashîpye**	reluctantly, without wanting to, dragging one's feet (particle)
	kekishashîpita (Jones)	reluctantly, without wanting to, dragging one's feet (particle)
remain	**ayêshishinwa, ayêshisenwi**	(animate, inanimate) is still lying there, remains behind
remake	**âchihtôwa**	remakes it, makes it anew
remember	**mehkwênemêwa, mehkwênetamwa**	thinks of, remembers s.o., it
	mehkwênemâsowa	is remembered
	mehkwênetamawêwa	thinks of, remembers (it) for s.o.
	mehkwênetîwaki	they remember each other
	mehkwinawêmêwa	reminds s.o. by speech
	mehkwitêhêwa	remembers, calls to mind
	=iyo=kêhi	now, remember; now, bear in mind
remind	**nenehkinawêmêwa**	makes s.o. mindful by speech; stirs up memories or feelings in s.o. by speech
	mîhkwinawêhêwa	reminds s.o., makes s.o. remember, put s.o. in mind of someone
remote	**nanawi**	off in some isolated place; in vain (particle)
	nanawêhkami	in or to a remote area
remove	**mîwenamwa**	removes it
	mîwenamawêwa	removes (it) for s.o.
	pahkwâpowênikêwa	takes the kettle of soup off the fire
	pahkwihkamênowa	removes one's pipe from one's mouth
	pahkwanâshinwa	is blown off
	pahkwaneshamwa	cuts it off (as, a scalp or braid)
	pahkonêwa	removes s.o. (kettle) from fire
	pâpakonamwa	takes it (a covering) off; takes the covering off of it (as, a winter lodge)
	pâpakonapahkwêwa	takes the covering off a winter lodge
	pâpakwakoshêshkawêwa	strips the covers off s.o. by bodily movement
	pâpakwisahêwa, pâpakwisahtôwa	whips the covering off s.o., it
renew	**pîshihtôwa**	renews it
	pîshihtâtêwi	it is renewed
	nôhkihtôwa	creates it anew
	âyâtawinâkwihtôwa owîyâwi	(the Earth) repeatedly renews the appearance of her body (ritual)
repeat	**nanâhpinohtawêwa**	repeats what s.o. says, mocks s.o. by imitating

	nâpâchimowa	repeats what has been said by another; (spiritual intercessor) repeats people's prayers (to convey them to the deities)
repeatedly	**kwêhchipa**	repeatedly (particle)
	nânâpi	the same repeatedly or successively (particle)
	pêpyêchi	coming repeatedly (preverb)
repel	**âchihkâhkênêwa**	puts one's hands on s.o.'s chest to stop them or push them back
replace	**nâpisetawêwa**	replaces (it) for s.o.
	nâpênemowa	regards (s.o.) as a replacement
	nâpenêwa	is a replacement spouse for s.o. (after the death of their spouse)
report	**pyêtâchimowa**	brings a report
	pyêtâchimohêwa	comes and tells s.o.
	tanâchimowa	talks, reports, tells one's story {somewhere} or about {somewhere}; is telling one's story
	peshikwâchimwihtawêwa	reports accurately on s.o.'s behalf
resent	**kekyêshkatawênemêwa**	resents, begrudges s.o.
	metawêwitêhêwa	feels resentful
	otênemêwa	resents s.o. or holds something against s.o. for {some} reason
	menêwihêwa	makes s.o. resentful of being left out or not treated the same
	menêwimêwa	complains that s.o. left one out or did not treat one the same
resist	**âshkâtesiwa**	is opposed, resists
	âshkâtahkasowa	braces oneself in resistance
resound	**papâmwêwêsenwi**	it resounds about
respect	**kosetawêwa, kosetamwa**	avoids s.o., it out of reserve or respect, respects or defers to s.o.
	kosetâtîwaki	they avoid each other out of reserve or respect
	kosetâkaniwiwa	is treated with reserve or respect
respectively	**ayâwi**	respectively, correspondingly (preverb)
respond	**wîkehtawêwa**	(with negative:) does not respond to, heed s.o.
	wîkeshêwa	(with negative:) does not respond, reply
rest	**âkwapiwa**	sits to rest; takes a break
restless	**wîkawi**	restlessly (preverb)
	wîkawapiwa	fidgets, moves restlessly in one's seat
rest on	**sêsishinwa, sêsisenwi**	(animate, inanimate) lies or leans on top
	sêsisetôwa	rests it on {somewhere}
	sêsisechikêwa	lays down a layer (of it) on top
	sêsikâhiwa	rests one's leg or legs on {somewhere}
	sêsikâtêkâpâwa	stands with one's foot resting {somewhere}
	sêsitiyêpiwa	sits perched on {somewhere}
retarded	**kêkyêpêha**	mentally retarded person
reveal	**mehtôchinawîhtawêwa**	reveals oneself to s.o.
reverse	**kohkisêwa**	quickly reverses direction
reversed	**âyâpôchîkwêshkamwa**	wears them (footwear) on the wrong feet
rhythmic	**têhtêpanwi**	there is rhythmic movement, undulation
rib	**ohpikayi**	one's rib; a rib
	pôhkwihpikêshinwa	falls and breaks one's rib
	nanânishkwihpikêshkêwa	one's ribs slip out of joint
ribbon	**sênipâhi**	ribbon
	sênipâhikwâsôni	ribbonwork

	êkwikwâtêhi	ribbonwork appliqué
	êkwikwâtêhi-manetôwêkenwi	broadcloth blanket with ribbonwork appliqué
rice	manômini	wild rice; rice
rich	manâtesiwa	is rich
ride horse	nômekowa	rides on horseback
	nômekwiwa	rides on horseback
	inômekowa	rides on horseback to {somewhere}
	kîyômekowa	rides about on horseback
	nahômekowa	knows how to ride a horse
	nahômekwiwa	knows how to ride a horse
	wêpômekwiwa	rides (as, a horse), starts riding
	kîhkâpahônekwiwa	circles around on horseback at a gallop
ridge	ahkwitâhkîki	on top of a hill, bank, ridge (locative noun)
right	kwîyena	exactly, just happen to; right
	tepikiwaki, tepikenwi	they are the right number; it is the right amount, correct
	tepinehki	for the right length of time, for quite a while (particle)
	tepinehkîhi	for the right length of time, for quite a while (dimin.) (particle)
	wâwanikenwi	it does not work right, turns out bad
right (side)	nemayâwîneki	on my right (locative noun)
	wêchi-mayâwîchi	on one's right (oblique participle)
right one	mehkochêmêwa	asks, names, or calls s.o. who is just the right one
ring	tetepîhi	ring
ring-and-pin	nîpikwêhaki	the ring-and-pin game (nested cup-shaped bones, attached to a stick by a buckskin string, which are thrown up and caught on the end)
	nîpikwêhiwaki	they play the ring-and-pin game
rinse	kôkawisahtôwa	rinses it
ripe	ahtesowa, ahtehtêwi	(animate, inanimate) is ripe, ripening
ripple	mamâtâpôsêwi	it (water) moves, has ripples
rise	nîmêshkêwa, nîmêshkêwi	(animate, inanimate) rises up in the air
	kechîwa	(sun) rises; emerges, goes out
rise and fall	têhtêpechânâmowa	one's stomach rises and falls as one breathes
	têhtêpipiwêsêwi	the pile on it (as, a bearskin) undulates
rival	nîtôsha	my (man's) rival; my (woman's) co-wife
river	sîpôwi	river
road	myêwi	road, path
	myêwiwi	it is a road
	omyêmiwa	has a road
roack	wâwiyêpenwâni	roach (worn on head)
roar	nanamahkwêwi	it roars, there is a roar
	nîsehkwêwi	there is a roar from the crowd (as it speaks in chorus), a rumble of assent
	wîsakowêmikatwi (Jones)	there is "a mighty roar"
roast	apwânêwa, apwâtamwa	roasts s.o., it
	apônêwa	roasts for s.o.
	apôsowa	roasts for oneself
	apwâchikani	grill, rack for roasting and drying meat
	nasâhkohwêwa, nasâhkohamwa	roasts s.o., it on a roasting stick set in the ground
	nasâhkohikêwa	roasts on a roasting stick
	nekohwêwa, nekohamwa	roasts s.o., it in ashes
	nekwahwêwa, nekwahamwa	roasts s.o., it in ashes
roasting stick	nasâhkohikani	roasting stick (set in the ground)
	nasikani	roasting stick; roasting stick of meat (archaic)

327

rob	**manihêwa**	robs s.o. of (it)
	manihetîwaki	they rob each other
robin	**chîhchîkahkwahâha**	robin
rock (noun)	**aseni**	rock, stone
	ahkwichi-asenye	on top of the rock or stone (particle compound)
	nâmi-asenye	under the rock or rocks (particle compound)
	asenihkihkîki	on the rocks, in a rocky place (locative noun)
	kohkoseni	granite rock
	kohkoseniwiwa	is a granite rock
rock (verb)	**nânômahamwa**	makes it rock back and forth by hitting it
	nânômeshkêwi	it rocks back and forth, it sways
rod	**pîwâpehkwi, pîyâpehkwi**	iron rod
roll	**tetepechêhiwa**	rolls
	tetepechêsahtôwa	sets it rolling
	tetepechêsêwa	falls rolling
	tetepechêshkêwi	it goes rolling
	shashahkechêhiwa	(horse, dog) rolls in something
Rolling Skull	**wêwîshêha**	Rolling Skull (in story)
	wêwîshêhihkwêwa	Rolling Skull Woman (in story)
roll over	**kohkishinwa**	rolls over, turns over as one lies
roof	**apahkwêwa**	makes a roof or lodge-covering (of it)
	apahkwêweni	roofing material, lodge-covering
	ahkwitapahkwe	on top of the roof (particle)
	âpehtawapahkwe	halfway up to the roof (particle)
	mîsâhkoniwipehkwanêyâwi	its roof is covered with moss
	papakâshkipehkwanêyâwi	it has a flat roof
	wâsikînipehkwanêyâwi	it has a sharp-pointed roof
room	**memênawi**	enough room, space, time (particle, preverb)
	memênawâwi	there is room
	memênawichinwa	has enough room to fit in
	têpapiwa	has enough room to sit, fits in one's seat
root	**ochêpihki**	root
	ochêpihkiwiwi	it is a root
	pîsichêpihkakatôhiwi	it has small roots
rope	**nenoswayêyâpi**	buffalo-hide rope
rot	**anenwa, anetwi**	(animate, inanimate) rots
	shekwanenwa	rots to pieces
	ashkipakanenwa, ashkipakanetwi	(animate, inanimate) is green with rot
rough	**kâwesiwa, kâwâwi**	(animate, inanimate) is rough
round	**wâwiyêyâwi**	it is round
row	**pemâkwapiwaki** (plural)	they sit together in a row (or rows) or in a bunch
	tepikîshkâkwapiwaki (plural)	they sit in a row
	tepikîshkâkwasowaki (plural)	they lie on the ground in a row
	tepikîshkikâpâwaki (plural)	they stand side-by-side in a row
	tepikîshkishinôki (plural)	they lie side-by-side in a row
	tepichîkwanêshkâtîwaki (plural)	they are in a row sitting knee-to-knee
rub	**shashawenêwa**	rubs s.o. down, loosens s.o. (person, hide) by rubbing
	shîshîhkenêwa	rubs s.o., gives s.o. a rub
	shîshîhkyêwakenêwa	rubs s.o. down, rubs s.o.'s muscles
	memekwinîkwênowa	rubs one's eyes
	peshepâhkoshkâtîmikatôni (plural)	they (as, trees) rub against each other
	peshepâpitênamwa	rubs the blade of it (as, a hatchet)
ruffle	**sayâwi**	so as to ruffle or upset (preverb)
	sayâwihêwa	makes s.o. tingle, shudder, or be ruffled

	opisêwitepêwa	one's head is ruffled
ruin	memyêshkîhkamwa	ruins it
	neshiwanâchihêwa, neshiwanâchihtôwa	ruins s.o., it, makes s.o. miserable
	neshiwanâtahwêwa, neshiwanâtahamwa	ruins s.o. (as, a drum), it by striking
	neshiwanâtehkawêwa	ruin s.o. (as, by getting s.o. drunk), ruins s.o.'s reputation
	neshiwanâtenêwa, neshiwanâtenamwa	ruins s.o. (as, a watch), it by handling
	neshiwanâteswêwa, neshiwanâtesamwa	ruins s.o. (as, corn, beans, potatoes), it by heating
	neshiwanâteshkawêwa, neshiwanâteshkamwa	ruins s.o. (as, corn or beans), it by trampling
	neshiwanâteshwêwa, neshiwanâteshamwa	ruins s.o. (as, s.o.'s hair), it by cutting
	panâchâwi	it is ruined
	panâchihêwa, panâchihtôwa	ruins s.o., it; bewitches or puts a spell on s.o.
rule	ishisenwi	it is a rule {so}, it lies or is set {so}
	inâhkonamawêwa	makes {such} a rule for s.o.
	inâhkonâsowa	is subject to {such} a rule or law
	inâhkonikêwa	makes {such} a rule or law
	kîshâhkonamawêwa	has laid down the rule for (it) for s.o.
	menwâhkonikêwa	has a good rule, law
	sanakâhkonamawêwa	sets difficult rules for s.o.
	sanakâhkonikêwa	sets difficult rules
	wêchinowâhkonikêhêwa	makes easy rules for s.o.
rump	chîkitiyêkâpâwa	stands with rump out
	chîkitiyêshinwa	lies with rump out
run	pemipahowa, pemipahôtêwi	runs by, along; it (as, a train) runs by, along
	pemipenowa	speeds off, starts running
	kehchipenowa	runs at top speed
	aniwisêwa	runs fast
	ihpahowa	runs to {somewhere}
	anemipahowa	runs off, on, away
	anemwêwêpahowa	runs with noise
	chêchêkipahowa	runs crying
	kekômyêpahowa	runs with (it) on one's back
	ketâsîpahowa	runs climbing
	akôsîpahômikatwi	it runs climbing
	kîwipahowa	runs about
	nahipahowa	can run
	nakashkipahowa	runs bent forward
	nakipahowa	stops in one's run
	nênekîwiwa	runs with a rolling gait
	nowipahowa	runs out, goes out on the run
	nowipahônêwa	runs out carrying s.o.
	pahkihtêpahowa	passes out from running
	pakamipahowa	arrives running
	pashkichipahowa	runs over the top
	pyêhpahowa	runs this way
	tetepipahowa	runs in a circle
	wêpipahowa	starts to run
	wêpôtêpahowa	starts on a crouching run
	akwâpyêsêwa	runs out of the water

	kechisêwa	runs out
	nakisêwa	stops running
	nowisêwa	runs out
	pîchisêwa, pîchisêwi	(animate, inanimate) runs, flies in
	natwipahwânêwa	runs to look for s.o.
	nâchipahônêwa, nâchipahôtôwa	runs after s.o., it; runs to get s.o., it
	ahkwimâchîwa	gives out in running, becomes exhausted
	kochimâchîwa	tries to see how fast one can run
run along	**nâkatôsêwa**	runs following (s.o., it)
run away	**pemâmoshkêwa**	proceeds to run away
run into	**pâpakisehkâtîwaki**	they keep running into each other
	tahkoshkawêwa, tahkoshkamwa	meets, encounters s.o., it, accidentally runs into it
	tahkoshkâtîwaki	they ran into each other (colliding or encountering)
run off with	**awachipahônêwa, awachipahôtôwa**	runs off, over with s.o., it
	awachipahôtâkêwa	runs off with (it) of others
run out	**nôtêsêwa, nôtêsêwi**	runs out of food, gets no food when it runs out; it runs out, time runs out
	ahkwamowa	runs out of food
run up to	**mawinanêwa**	attacks s.o., runs up to s.o.
runner	**ashkâpêwa**	ceremonial runner
nunny nose	**wînikomêwa**	has a runny nose
rush	**pyêtâshkêwa, pyêtâshkêwi**	comes rushing, falls or speeds this way; it falls or speeds this way
	pônâshkêwa	stops falling, stops rushing
rush out	**ketâshkêwi**	it falls out, rushes out
	nowâshkêwa, nowâshkêwi	(animate, inanimate) falls, rushes out
	môhkîhtawêwa	rushes out to attack s.o.

S

sacrifice	**wâhtenamwa**	offers it, sacrifices it; bets it
	wâhtenikêwa	sacrifices (it), makes a sacrifice of (it)
sad	**kîwâchinawêmêwa**	makes s.o. feel sad or lonely by what one says
saddle	**ahtômyâkani**	saddle
saddlebag	**pashkichimotêhi**	saddlebag
salamander	**kahkâhkachîha**	salamander
sail	**awatâsowa**	sails on the wind
saliva	**nesîsepetonâkani**	my saliva, my drool
Salt Creek	**wîshkopanôheki**	at Salt Creek (locative noun)
same	**awiyâtoke**	still the same, still the case (particle)
	âyêniwe, êyêniwe	steadily, in one place, staying the same (particle)
	nêyâpi	back (to its former state), the same as before (particle, preverb)
	âhpene	both or all alike, regularly the same (particle)
	âyâhpene	each the same, each kind separate (particle)
	îni=meko	the same one (inanimate)
	chêwi	equally, the same (preverb, preparticle)
	chêchêwi	alike, the same as each other (preverb)
	chêwinâhi	at the same time (particle)
	chêchêwinâhi	both or all at the same time; at equal distances apart (particle)

	nahpi	at the same time (preverb)
	nanâhpi	along with that, also at the same time (particle, preverb)
	nêyâpimêwa	says the same thing to s.o. as was said before
	nêyâpisenwi	it is the same as it was, it is back to the same place or amount as before
	nâpikêwa	builds in the same spot
sand	**nêkawi**	sand
sand-bar	**nêkawahkiwi**	sand-bar, sandy place
sap	**wîshkopâpowi**	sap; wine
satisfied	**têpênemowa**	is satisfied, has had enough
satisfy	**kîhpochêshkawêwa**	(having eaten) satisfies s.o.
Sauk	**asâkîwa**	Sauk
	asâkînâki	in Sauk country (locative noun)
	nîmahâha	Missouri River Sauk
	nîmahâhinâki	in Missouri River Sauk country, in Nebraska (locative noun)
save	**ashkonêwa, ashkonamwa**	saves s.o., it
	ashkonamâtisowa	saves (it) for oneself
	ashkwatamawêwa	saves (it, food) for s.o.
	ashkwi	saving, leaving (preverb)
savor	**sôpihkesowa**	savors one's smoking, enjoys a smoke
say	**inêwa, itamwa**	says {so} to s.o., it; calls s.o., it {so}
	ishiwêwa	says {so} to people
	ihkyêwa	says {so}, says {so} to someone
	itâtêwi	{such} is said of it
	itamawêwa	says {so} of (it) to s.o., means {so} in saying (it) to s.o.
	itîwaki	they say {so} to each other, one says to the other
	iwa	says {so}
	iyômikatwi	it says {so}
	iyoweni	thing said
	mayakimêwa	says strange things to s.o.
	nêyâpimêwa	says the same thing to s.o. as was said before
	=ipi (=ipihi)	they say, it is said, supposedly, you're supposed to
saying	**inowâkani**	saying, word
scales	**onahakayani**	scales (as, of a fish)
	mamâkinahakêwa	has large scales
scalp	**nîshehkwayi**	my scalp
	owîshehkwayi	a scalp; one's scalp
	mîshehkwayi	a scalp
	omîshehkwayi	one's scalp
	meshahkwânêwa	scalps s.o.
	mashahkwânêwa	scalps s.o.
	mashahkwânâsowa	is scalped
	meshahkwâshwêwa, meshahkwâshamwa	scalps s.o., it
	mashahkwâshwêwa	scalps s.o.
	pyêshiwêwa	(warrior) brings home a prisoner or scalp
	wâhkanakitepêshwêwa	cuts the scalp from s.o.'s head
	wâshkêtepêshinwa	lies with one's head scalped
scalp-lock	**môshôni**	scalp-lock
	omôshôniwa	he has a scalp-lock
scalp-stick	**meshkwâhkonikani**	scalp-stick (for a warrior's niece to carry with an attached scalp in the Scalp Dance)
scar	**wîsikiwa**	has a scar

scare up	ashihkawêwa	flushes s.o. (bird, animal) up, scares s.o. up
scarify	pêhpêshwêwa	scarifies s.o., makes small cuts in s.o.'s skin
scatter	kwâpâshkêwa, kwâpâshkêwi	(animate, inanimate) flies or falls scattering
	kwâpisêwaki (plural)	they fly in all directions
	kwâpinehkâtîwaki (plural)	they chase each other to scatter
	kwâhkwâpâhkêwa	throws (it, them) in different directions
	seswêsêwa, seswêsêwi	(animate, inanimate) scatters, splatters
	seswêhtêwi	it explodes and scatters in pieces from the heat
	seswêyâhkêwa	scatters (it)
	seswêyâmowaki	they scattered in flight
scissors	môshowâkani	pair of scissors
scold	neshkimêwa	scolds, forbids, admonishes s.o.
	pyêtwêwêmêwa	comes scolding behind s.o.
scorch	kâhkesowa, kâhketêwi	(animate, inanimate) dries up, gets scorched
	panakeswêwa, panakesamwa	scorches s.o., it; parches s.o., it
scrape	kâshkâshkahwêwa, kâshkâshkahamwa	scrapes, files s.o., it
	kâshkatahamawêwa	scrapes (it) for s.o.
	pashkwahwêwa	scrapes the hair off s.o. (a hide)
	pashkohwêwa	scrapes the hair off s.o. (a hide)
scraper	pashkwahikani	beaming tool, scraper for removing hair from hide
	nâshêkihikani	wooden hide-scraper (for softening a stretched hide)
scratch	keshîpenowa	scratches (an itch)
	keshîpenêwa	scratches s.o.
	keshîpitepênowa	scratches one's head
	âwahkîkwêsahêwa	scratches s.o.'s face
	kâhkâhkenowa	scratches oneself hard
	kâhkihkenêwa	scratches s.o. deeply (with the hand or hands)
	kâhkihkichinwa	gets scratched on something
	mechiminehkênâtêwi	it is scratched by claws, has scratch marks
scratch up	pâpahkyênêwa	scratches s.o. up, tears s.o. up
	pâpahkyêsahêwa	clawed s.o. to pieces
scream	chêchêkwa	screams, cries out
	chêchêkihêwa	makes s.o. scream
	chêchêkechênêwa	hugs s.o. making them scream
	wîshkwêwêkesiwa	screams
	wîshikowêwa	speaks, sings, screams loudly
	nepâtwêwêkesiwa	screams bloody murder
	kokowêwa	lets out a sudden, loud scream
	wêpwêwêkesiwa	starts to yell loudly, scream
	kîshâkotwêwêkesiwa	wails terribly, screams as loudly as possible
	wîyatâwêwêkesiwa	screams in terror, screams bloody murder
scum	mîsâhkoni	pond scum; moss
sea	kehchikamîwi	sea
search for: → seek		
seasons	kokwêhkâpiweni	change of seasons
seat	nanâhapiwa	seats oneself
second	nîshônameki	second, the second time (particle)
second thought	ketê='nahi	with second thoughts, with changed attitude, with fortunes reversed; too bad!, what a pity!
secret	kîmôchi	stealthily, secretly (particle, preverb)
	kîmôtesiwa	is stealthy, secretive
	kîmôchâwi	it is secret
	kîmôtanohkyêwa	does things in secret

	kîmôtâyêniwa	laughs secretly
	kîmôsehtawêwa	hears s.o. say things they do not know are being heard
	kyâsowa	keeps (it) a secret
	kyâtamwa	keeps it a secret
	kyâtamawêwa	keeps (it) a secret from s.o.
	kyâtamâtîwaki	they keep (it) a secret from each other
secure	wîshikeshkamwa	makes it secure by one's step, by dwelling there
	wîshikishinwa	lies secure
securely	âyachîtapinêwa, âyachîtapitôwa	ties s.o., it securely
	âyachîtapisowa, âyachîtapitêwi	is tied securely, it is tied securely
see	nêwêwa, nêtamwa	sees s.o., it
	nêtamawêwa	sees it of s.o.
	nêtamâtisowa	sees (it) for oneself
	nêwotisowa	sees oneself
	nêwotîwaki (plural)	they see each other, they meet, they are together
	nêwowêwa	sees people, sees
	ahkwâpiwa	sees {so far}
	châkâpiwa	sees everywhere
	ênâpatamwa	fails to see it
	inâpamêwa, inâpatamwa	sees s.o., it {so}, looks at s.o., it {so}
	kîwâpamêwa, kîwâpatamwa	goes about seeing s.o., it
	kîmâhêwa, kîmâhtôwa	sees, approaches s.o., it unobserved
	kokwêhkâpatamwa	sees it changing
	menwâpamêwa	likes to see s.o.
	menwâpatîwaki	they like to see each other
	menwâpiwa	sees well
	nahkwâpamêwa	sees s.o. right off
	nahkwâpatâniwa	is easily noticed, is readily seen
	nâwanwâpamêwa	follows s.o. keeping them in sight
	natawâpiwa	tries to see
	osâpamêwa, osâpatamwa	sees s.o., it from {somewhere}
	pînâpiwa	sees fresh things
	pyêsâpamêwa	sees s.o. coming
	tanâpamêwa	sees s.o. (as being) {somewhere}
	têpâpiwa	sees enough; is able to see (from a distance or clairvoyantly)
	têpâpamêwa, têpâpatamwa	is able to see s.o., it (in the distance or clairvoyantly)
	têpâpatamâkêwa	is able to see (it) in the distance for people
	têpâpatâniwi	it can be seen in the distance
	wâsêyâpiwa	sees as if in daytime
	=mâhi	you see, I mean, obviously
	=kîna	there you go; (you) see!
	kahkinôhi	we shall see! (particle)
seed	ihkwêwimini	seed
seek	natawi	seek to, try to, expect to, plan to; it's time to (preverb)
	natawâpamêwa, natawâpatamwa	looks for s.o., it
	natonêhwêwa, natonêhamwa	seeks s.o., it
	natonêhamawêwa	seeks (it) for s.o.
	natawênetâkosiwa	is sought
	natochêhwêwa, natochêhamwa	pokes around searching for s.o., it, pokes around in it
	natochênikêwa	tries to find or get hold of something by hand, rummages around
	natochêshkamwa	seeks to come to it

333

	natwihkawêhêwa	looks for s.o.'s tracks
	natwipahwânêwa	runs to look for s.o.
	natwipekwêhamwa	pokes through the ashes searching for it
	nâchiyâmêwa, nâchiyâtamwa	seek out s.o., it by smell, follows the odor of s.o., it
	nâchiyêwa	follows an odor, is attracted by an odor
	mesatonêhwêwaki (plural)	they all looked for s.o.
	pematonêhwêwa	goes by looking for s.o.
	wêpatonêhwêwa	starts to seek s.o.
	ânawâpamêwa	looks for s.o. and doesn't see them
	kwînatonêhwêwa, kwînatonêhamwa	fails to find s.o., it
	nâtâhkwêshinwa	seeks help, goes after help
see off	pechinôshkawêwa	sees s.o. off, sees s.o. on their way
see through	tahpâpiwa	sees through
	tahpâpatâniwi	it can be seen through
seize	sakânowênêwa	seizes s.o. by the tail
	sakikânêwa	seizes s.o. by the leg
	asamonamwa	grabs a handful of it (as, cloth, hair, skin, or flesh)
	asamwisahêwa	grabs a handful of s.o.'s skin
	asamwitepênêwa	seizes s.o. by the hair
select	wâwâpamêwa, wâwâpatamwa	selects s.o., it
selectively	pahkitîwi	selectively, as the ceremonial assignment to selected ones (preverb)
sell	atâwêwa	sells, sells (it)
	atâmêwa	sells (it) to s.o.
send	awatâhêwa	makes s.o. take (it), sends (it) by s.o.
	awatâhiwêwa	sends (it) along
	awatâsetawêwa	sends (it) to s.o. on the wind
	penôhêwa	sends s.o. back, home
	penohêwa	sends s.o. back, home
	pôsihêwa, pôsihtôwa	sends s.o., it; puts s.o., it into a boat, a vehicle, or a container with an upward-oriented opening (as, a cauldron or mortar);
	pyêmikihtôwa	causes it to come
	pyêmikihtawêwa	sends (it) to s.o. through the mail
separate	âteseshkêwaki	they divide into two groups
	âteshikêwa	builds a separate house
	nêhtôsetôwa	places them (inanimate) separately by themselves
	nênêhtôsetôwa	sorts them (inanimate) out
	pahkêwa	separates, goes off a different way, turns aside, gets off the road
	shîkônêwa, shîkônamwa	sorts s.o., it out, separates s.o., it
	kahkenamwa	strips it (fiber), separates it (inner bark) from the outer bark
separately	âteshi	separately (particle, preverb)
	âteshîmêhi	separately (dimin.) (particle, preverb)
	âyâteshi	separately from each other (particle)
	âteshisetôwa	places it separately, by itself
	âyatehchi	away from each other, each by oneself, separately (particle)
	chachâtapi	discretely, each separately, each dealing with one's own (particle)
	chachâtepi	discretely, each separately, each dealing with one's own (particle)
	chachâtapinawe	each separately (particle)

	chachâtapinowe	each separately (particle)
	chachâtepinowi	each separately (particle)
	nêhtawi	separately, in a separate group of their kind (particle, preverb)
	nênêhtawi	in separate groups (each of one kind) (particle)
	nêhtawâkwapiwaki (plural)	they sit together in a separate group (of one kind)
	nêhtawihetîwaki (plural)	they get together by themselves
	shîkôwi	separately; only those particular ones (preverb)
	shîkôsetôwa	puts it by itself, places it separately
sequence	pemi	in sequence (preverb)
	pemeshkawêwa	goes to them in sequence
serious	kekyêhtenâmi	seriously (preverb)
	kekyêhtenâmehtawêwa	takes what s.o. says seriously
	kekyêhtenâmênetamwa	thinks seriously about it
	kekyêhtenâmimêwa	means what one says to s.o.
	kekyêhtenâminâkosiwa	has a serious expression on one's face
	kekyêhtenâmitêhêwa	is serious-minded
serve	sîkahikêwa	serves food
	sîkahikawêwa	serves food for s.o., dishes out food to s.o.
	sîkahamawêwa	serves, pours (it) for s.o.
	sîkahamâtisowa	serves oneself, dishes out food to oneself
	sîkahamâtîwaki	they serve (it) for each other
	pakisahamwa	serves it out
set	ahkwisetawêwa	sets it {so far, so long} for s.o.
	ahkwâhkonamawêwa	sets it {so far, so long} for s.o.
	ahkwâhkonâtêwi	it is set {so far, so long}
	nanâhahkanêwa, nanâhahkatôwa	sets, fixes s.o., it into the ground, etc.; hangs it (kettle) over fire
	nanâhâhkwisetôwa	set it (as, a log) in position
	nîshôhkatôwa	sets them (inan.) in the ground as a pair
	nehkîwa	(sun) sets, goes out of sight
set about	pemi	past, by, in the course, along, in sequence; go ahead and, start to, set about, directly, right (preverb)
set down	pakinêwa, pakitamwa	sets s.o., it down; throws s.o., it away; divorces s.o.
	pakishiwenêwa, pakishiwetôwa	conducts s.o., it to freedom; sets s.o., it down
set loose	pakisapinêwa	sets s.o. loose from their bonds
set out	nâkwêwa	sets out, goes away
set up	nemanêwa, nematôwa	sets s.o., it up
seven	nôhika	seven (particle)
	nôhika tashiwaki, nôhika tasenôni	they (animate, inanimate) are seven, there are seven of them
seventeen	nôhikanesiwe	seventeen (particle)
	nôhikanîsiwe	seventeen (particle)
	nôhikanesiwe taswipepônwêwa	is seventeen years old
	nôhikanîsiwe taswipepônwêwa	is seventeen years old
	nôhikanesiwa	is seventeen years old
seventh	nôhikânameki	seventh (particle)
seventy	nôhikâpitaki	seventy (particle)
sever	pahkahâtêwi	it (stringlike) is severed by tool, chopped through
	pahkahwêwa, pahkahamwa	chops through the rope holding s.o.; chops it (stringlike) through
several	nâhtaswi	several
severe	kwêhtânihêwa	gives s.o. a terrible beating, inflicts a terrible death on s.o.
	kwêhtânamêwa	bites s.o. severely

	kwêhtânimêwa	hits s.o. hard by what one says
	mamîkwâchi	severely, rigorously (preverb)
sew	achikwânêwa, achikwâtamwa	sews s.o., it
	achikwâsowa	sews, is sewing
	nahikwamwa	knows how to sew it
	nahikwâsowa	knows how to sew
	kîshikwâtêwi	it (as, a blanket) has ribbonwork sewn on it
	kepôkwâtamwa	sews it shut
	kochikwamwa	tries to sew it
	kokwêchikwâsowa	tries to sew
	kokwêchikwâsikawêwa	tries to sew for s.o.
	mêchimôkwâtêwi	it is sewed together permanently
	patashkikwamwa	sews it on
	pîwâhikwâsowa	sews beadwork
	sênipâhikwâsowa	sews ribbon-appliqué
	tahtakwikwamwa	sews them (inanimate) together, sews (it) to it
	tahtakwikwâtêwani	they (inanimate) are sewn together
	wêpikwamwa	begins to sew it
sex	nepôtêwi	sexual, sexually; extremely (preverb, particle)
	nêpôtêwâki	sex, sexual matters (participle)
	nepôtêwesiwa	has strong sexual desires
	nêpôtêha	man with a great sexual appetite
	âmanôneniwa	man with a great sexual appetite
	âmanêha	sexually promiscuous woman, whore
	nepôtêwimêwa	speaks to s.o. about sex or with off-color remarks
	wâwanâtâmanwa	engages in sex with wild abandon
sex (have sex)	kêkôhi tôtawêwa	does something to s.o.; he has sex with her
	manêwa, matamwa	he copulates with her, it (Note: this word is used in winter stories but is generally avoided.)
	manetîwaki (plural)	they copulate
	mênetîha	fornicator; screw-up
	âmanwa	has sexual inclinations, has sex, (deer) is rutting
	âmanohkatawêwa	engages in sexual activity with s.o.
	mâhkwiwa	he copulates
	nanâheshkawêwa	he positions himself on her (for intercourse)
	shîkwatahwêwa	he abandons her after having enough of copulating with her
shadow	onôkênawiwa	has a soul, reflection, or shadow
	tahkâhkoshkamwa, tahkâhkoshkamômikatwi	(animate, inanimate) casts a shadow
shake	memekwisahêwa	shakes s.o. hard
	memekohkwêsêwa	shakes one's head
	nânômehkwêsêwa	shakes one's head
	nenekisêwi	it shakes, it (as, the earth) quakes
	nenekikanêwa	shakes from weakness, becomes weak and shaky
	pawenamwa	shakes it out, shakes it clean
	pawinehkêsahowa	shakes one's hand off
	pawisahêwa, pawisahtôwa	shakes s.o. (as a pipe), it out
	pahpawisahêwa	shakes s.o. violently
	pawihkeshêwêsahêwa	shakes the ashes out of s.o. (pipe)
	pahpawihkeshêwêhwêwa	knocks the ashes out of s.o. (a pipe)
	sakinechênêwa	shakes s.o.'s hand
	sakinechênetîwaki (plural)	they shake hands
	wîshikâhkêwa	shakes (it) hard

shallow	**chahkwîtemyâhiwi**	it is shallow
shame	**mêneshi**	so as to cause shame (preverb)
	mêneshâwi	it is shameful
	mêneshîhkânowa	does something that brings shame and ridicule
	mêneshitêhêwa	is ashamed
	mêneshitêhâkani	shame
	mêneshimêwa, mêneshotamwa	shames s.o., it by speech
	mêneshikêmowa	shames people
	mêneshîhtawêwa	is ashamed before s.o.
	mêneshîhtamwa	is ashamed to do it, is ashamed of it
	mêneshîkwêkâpâwa	stands shamefaced
shape	**aneshkêwa, aneshkêwi**	(animate, inanimate) takes shape, forms up
	ashikahamwa	cuts it to shape by chopping
	aneshamwa	cuts it out, cuts it to shape
	aneshamawêwa	cuts (it) out for s.o., cuts (it) to shape for s.o.
share	**anâkwashiwa**	has or gets a share of game (to keep or distribute)
	nakwâhtakwi	missing one's sharing of food (particle)
sharp	**kînesiwa, kînyâwi**	(animate, inanimate) is sharp
	âhkwi	sharply, dangerously, (of perception) plainly (preverb)
	wâsikînikomêyâwi	it is sharp at the point
sharpen	**kînihêwa, kînihtôwa**	sharpens s.o., it
	wâsikînikomêhamwa	sharpens it to a point by chopping
	wâsikînikomêshamwa	sharpens it to a point by cutting
sharply	**âhkwi**	sharply, (of perception) plainly (preverb)
shatter	**sheshekotêwi**	it is shattered by gunshot
shave	**kâshkahowa**	gets a shave, shaves
shawl	**môshwêhi**	shawl
	kêkânôhkwêsîhi	long-fringed shawl
Shawnee	**shâwanôwa**	Shawnee
	shâwanôwekêwa	dances the Shawnee dance
	shâwanôwiwa	dances the Shawnee dance
she	**wîna**	he or she (emphatic or contrastive); (by) himself or herself
shed	**shîkwîwa**	sheds one's clothes, skin, horns
	pahkwiwinêwa	sheds one's horns
	pepeshkochêshkêwa	is shedding
sheep	**mêmehtânesha**	sheep
shell	**mîkesa**	wampum bead (Jones: "cowrie shell")
	onahakayi	shell of nut, rind of melon
shell (verb)	**pekenêwa**	shell s.o. (corn) (i.e., removes dried kernels from cob)
sheltered	**wîhkwêyâhkiwiwi**	there is an area sheltered by high ground
shield	**pemitenikana**	shield
	wâwiyêshâtêhi	round shield
shin	**nekahkwani**	my shin, my lower leg, my leg
	okahkwani	his or her shin; a shin
shine	**wawâsetêwi**	it sparkles, shines
	wawâsehkêwi	it is shiny, glistens, sparkles
	wâsanosowa	has something shining or sparkling on one
	wawâsanosowa	has something shining or sparkling on one
	wâsanôtêwi	it glows, it shines with a bright light
	wawâsanôtêwi	it glows, it shines with a bright light
	aniwâpehkesowa, aniwâpehketêwi	(animate, inanimate) shines brightly (stone, metal, or the like)
	apâsetêwi	there is sunshine, the sun shines

337

shinny (game)	**kônanôhaki** (plural)	double ball used in shinny
	kônanôhiwa	plays the double-ball game, shinny
ship	**nâpehkwâni**	ship, sailing vessel
shirt	**pîsehkâhi**	garment, shirt, blouse ("waist")
	opîsehkâhiwa	wears a shirt
	opîsehkâhihêwa	makes a shirt for s.o.
shoe	**shôshîhani**	shoes
	neshôshani	my shoes
	oshôshiwa	wears shoes
	kekishôshîhêpiwa	sits with shoes on
shoot	**pemwêwa, pemotamwa**	shoots s.o., it; shoots at s.o., it
	pemotamawêwa	shoots (it) for s.o.
	pemotîwaki	they shoot at each other
	pemowêwa	shoots
	pîpemowêwa	shoots repeatedly
	meshwêwa, meshotamwa	shoots s.o., it, hits s.o., it with a shot
	anemwêwêsikêwa	goes on firing, shooting a firearm
	aniwâshohwêwa	is a good shot with a bow or gun
	kokwêtâshohwêwa	practices shooting with a bow or gun
	myânâshohwêwa	is a bad shot with a bow or gun
	anwêwêsikêwa	fires a shot, shoots
	châkechênawêwa, châkechênamwa	hits all of s.o., it with a shot
	kashkenawêwa, kashkenamwa	is able to shoot s.o., it
	kawenawêwa	knocks s.o. down by shooting
	kâhkihkenawêwa	scratches s.o. with a shot
	kâhkihkinameshkênawêwa	scratches s.o.'s skin with a shot
	kêsôchênawêwa	how many of s.o. does one hit with one's shot?
	kotâhkohikêwa	practices shooting
	myâhkenawêwa	cripples s.o. by shot
	myâhkesowa	is crippled by gunshot
	nasahtêwa	releases the bow, pulls the trigger
	nânôhkenawêwa	finishes s.o. off with a shot
	otenawêwa	shoots s.o. {somewhere} (on the body)
	otesowa	is shot {somewhere} (with a firearm)
	pahkihtênawêwa	knocks s.o. unconscious with a shot
	paseshênawêwa	grazes s.o.'s ear with a shot
	pâsikenamwa	splits it in two with a shot
	pâshkesikêwa	shoots a firearm
	pâshkeswêwa	shoots s.o. with a firearm, strikes s.o. with lightning
	pehtenawêwa	accidentally shoots s.o.
	pôhkesowa	has a hole shot in one by a firearm
	sîsenawêwa	grazes s.o. with a shot
	sheshekotêwi	it is shattered by gunshot
	tasôchênawêwa	shoots {so many} of them (animate) with one shot
	ashwahtêwa	takes aim to shoot (with a bow)
	kokwêtahtêwa	practices shooting with a bow
	wêpahtêwa	shoots (with a bow), shoots (it, an arrow)
	wîshikahtêwa	shoots hard (with a bow)
	ayâwihchîhiwa	shoots with the bow, contests at archery
	shâpatênawêwa and **shâshâpatênawêwa**	pierces s.o.'s body with a shot (song word; uncertain)
shoot out	**môhkâshkêwa**	shoots out of the water
short	**chahkwi**	short (prenoun)

	chachâhkwi	short (plural) (prenoun)
	chahkwîhiwa, chahkonôhiwi	is short
	chahkwâhkonamawêwa	shortens (it) for s.o.
short cut	kahkamîwa	goes by a short cut
short time	nômake, nômakêhe	for a short time, for a little while (particle)
	nômakêwe	for a short time, for a little while (particle)
	nômakêwi	for a short time (preverb)
shotgun	nîshôtâkani	double-barreled shotgun
	nîshôtâkani-chahkwipâhi	sawed-off shotgun
should not	nanâhi	(idiom; for example, with first person subject): I should not have; I regret; why did I? (preverb)
	mâmahkâchi	(with sarcastic intonation:) it is not necessary, should not have, why did (they)? (particle)
shoulder	otenya	shoulder
	mamâkitenyêwa	is big-shouldered
	pahkwitenyêsahêwa	pulls s.o.'s shoulder out of joint
	pâkitenyêhwêwa	slaps s.o. on the shoulder
shout	kwâkohômêwa, kwâkohôtamwa	shouts to s.o., shouts
	anemwêkesiwa, anemwêwêkesiwa	goes off, along shouting or wailing
	anwêwêkihêwa, anwêwêkihtôwa	makes s.o., it shout, cry out, resonate
	inwêwêkihêwa	makes s.o. shout, cry out {so}
	menipyâkahkiwiwi	there is a shout from the crowd
	menwipyâkahkiwiwi	there is a shout from the crowd
	menipyâkimêwaki	they raise a shout at s.o.
	menwipyâkimêwaki	they raise a shout at s.o.
	menwipyâkôki	they all shout in unison
shove	kâhkâchisahêwa	keeps shoving s.o.
show	wâpatônêwa	shows (it) to s.o.
	wâpatahêwa	shows (it) to s.o., lets s.o. see it
	kehkinôwenêwa	shows s.o. how, shows s.o. the way
	mâchiwenêwa	shows s.o. the way
show up	nâkosiwa	shows up, appears or is seen in public
shred	kîshkîshkeshkêwi	it gets torn to shreds
	nîsîkyâwi	it is all torn, shredded
shrink	ochêkishkêwa, ochêkishkêwi	(animate, inanimate) shrinks
shrivel	achisowa, achihtêwi	(animate, inanimate) shrivels, shrinks from heat
shut	keposhkêwi	it goes shut
	kepanoshkêwi	its opening closes
sibling	netôtêma	my brother or sister; my clan totem
	otôtêmiwa	has a sibling, has (him or her) as a sibling
	otôtêmetîwaki (plural)	they are siblings
	otôtêmetîhaki (plural)	the siblings
	otôtêmâkômêwa	addresses s.o. and treats them as if they were one's sibling
sick	âhkwamatamwa	is sick, indisposed, injured
	âhkwamatamôhiwa	is sick, indisposed, injured (dimin.)
	âhkwamatamôweni	sickness
	âhkwamatamôhkêwa	has sickness in one's family
	âhkwamachihêwa	makes s.o. sick
	êshkamesiwa	gets sicker and sicker
side	neshehki	my side
	meshehki	side (of someone's body)

339

	akâmêheki	on the other shore, on the other side of the stream or lake (particle)
	ashikani	on one side (of two), on the other side (particle)
	ochinawe	on {such} side (particle)
	otakâme	on {such} side of the lodge, river (particle)
	otâhkwe	in {some} direction, on {such} side (particle)
	otâkwapiwaki (plural)	they sit as a group on {such} side
	tâpôwi	on opposite sides, on both sides (preverb)
	wâwîtawi	on both sides (particle)
side by side	**tâhtâpôpiwaki**	they sit side by side
	tâhtâpôhkasowaki, tâhtâpôhkatêwani	they (animate, inanimate) are stuck in the ground side by side
	tâhtâpôkâpâwaki	they (animate) stand side by side
	tâhtâpôkêwaki	they (animate) dance side by side
	tâhtâpôpahowaki	they (animate) run side by side
	tâhtâpôshinôki	they (animate) lie side by side
	tâhtâpôwâshkêwani	they (inanimate) fall side by side
	tâhtâpôwosêwaki	they (animate) walk side by side
	tâhtâpôshimêwa, tâhtâpôsetôwa	places them (animate, inanimate) side by side
side to side	**ashahashawêhkwênwa**	moves one's head from side to side
	papâmitekêwa	dances facing to one side and then the other
sift	**nôshkâsêwa, nôshkâsêwi**	(animate, inanimate) is sifted, winnowed
	nôshkânêwa, nôshkânamwa	winnows s.o. (as, corn), sifts it (as, flour)
sigh	**achikwitêhêshkêwa**	sighs from the heart
sign	**inenikêwa**	makes signs {so}
	ayâwi-'nenikêwa	makes signs, gestures
	inenikawêwa	makes signs to s.o. {so}
	kehkinawâchi	indicatively, distinctively, significantly, as a sign, you can tell (particle)
	kekyêhkinawâchi	as a repeated sign (particle)
	kehkikenwi	there is a sign or trace of it
	kehkisenwi	there is a mark, a trace, or signs where it was
	kehkishinwa	there is a mark, a trace, or signs where one lay
	sakanahkenikêwa	touches the tip of the pen, signs one's name
signal	**ishîkwêhtawêwa**	signals s.o. {so} by the expression on one's face
signify	**ishiwêpi**	for, standing for, signifying {so} (particle, preverb)
	ishiwêpikenwi	it is, signifies {so}
	êshiwêpikeki	what it is all about, what it represents or corresponds to, what the matter with it is (oblique participle)
	ishiwêpawiwa	how one is or does has {such} a reason, significance
	ishiwêpesiwa	how one is has {such} significance
	êshiwêpesikwêni	what might be the matter with him, why he was so (oblique interrogative participle)
	êshiwêpesiwânêni	I wonder what is or was the matter with me (oblique interrogative participle)
silver	**shôniyâhi**	silver, money
	shôniyâhâpehkwi	silver
silversmith	**wîhtwiyâha**	smith, silversmith
	wîhtwîyâha	smith, silversmith
similar	**âwêwi**	somewhat like (it)
	âwêkenwi	it is similar (to it); (with negative) there is no sign if it
simultaneously	**tepikîshki**	simultaneously (particle)
since	**atânahka='shi**	since then; this way, towards here; come over here
	nôchi	since (as, with 'long ago', 'that time') (preverb)

sinew	**ochêhchi**	sinew, tendon
	ochêhtêhi	sinew, tendon (dimin.)
sing	**nakamowa**	sings
	nakamwihêwa, nakamwihtôwa	sings over s.o., it
	nakamwihtawêwa	sings for s.o.
	memyênwa	sings a non-religious song (archaic)
	memyênôwinâkêwa	sings a non-religious song
	ahpahamêwa	sings about (s.o., it)
	âtawinâkêwa	sings over again
	âtawahâtêwi	it is sung over again
	ahpîhchinâkêwa	sings {so long}
	aneminâkêwa	goes singing
	inahamwa	sings the songs {so}
	ishinâkêwa	sings {so}
	kâchipitôwa	leads it as a song
	kâtahamwa	starts singing it
	kîshinâkêwa	finishes singing
	mîshâchinâkêwa	sings sportively
	nahinâkêwa	knows how to sing
	nahkohamawêwa	assists s.o. in singing
	nîkâninâkêwa	leads in singing
	nîmiwahamwa	sings for dancing
	nîmiwahamawêwa	sings for s.o. to dance
	nîpenêhamwa	sings them (inanimate) in order
	pehkîninâkêwa	sings differently
	peminâkêwa	goes by singing
	pôninâkêwa	stops singing
	shêshkinâkêwa	sings unaccompanied
	tashinâkêwa	sings {somewhere}
	tetepinâkêwa	circles singing
	wâwaninâkêwa	does not know how to sing correctly
	wêpinâkêwa	starts to sing
	wîkêchinâkêwa	sings carefully
	wîshikinâkêwa	sings loud
	wîshikowêwa	speaks, sings, screams loudly
singe	**wâwîswêwa**	singes the hair off s.o.
	patahkwêwa	singes (an animal)
sink	**kosâpyêwi**	it sinks
	kosâpyêshkawêwa	sinks s.o. by one's weight
	kotawâmehkîwa	sinks into the ground
	nêkwichishkiwêsêwa	sinks into mud or quicksand
Sioux	**ashâha**	a Sioux person
	ashâhihkwêwa	Sioux woman
	ashâhâtowêwa	speaks the Sioux language
	ashâhikâni	a Sioux lodge
	ashâhinâki	in the Sioux country (locative noun)
sister	**nemisêha**	my elder sister; also applied to a father's brother's daughter and a mother's sister's daughter
	netehkwêma	my sister (of a man)
	otehkwêmiwa	he has a sister, he has (her) as his sister
	otehkwêmemêwa	he has her as his sister
	otehkwêmâkômêwa	he addresses her and treats her as if she were his sister
	nesîma	my younger brother or sister; also applied to a father's brother's daughter and a mother's sister's daughter

	nesîmêha	my younger brother or sister; also applied to a father's brother's daughter and a mother's sister's daughter
	osîmemâwa, osîmêhemâwa	the younger brother or sister
sister-in-law	**netâkwa**	my sister-in-law (of a woman; husband's sister or brother's wife)
	otâkwani	her sister-in-law
	otâkwiwa	she has a sister-in-law, has (her) as a sister-in-law
	otâkwatîhaki	the sisters-in-law
	nînemwa	my sister-in-law (of a man), my brother-in-law (of a woman)
	owînemôni	his sister-in-law, her brother-in-law
	owînemwiwa	has a sibling-in-law of the opposite sex, he has (her) as his sister-in-law, she has (him) as her brother-in-law
sit	**chîtapiwa**	sits upright
	chîtapîhiwa	sits upright (dimin.)
	chîtapihêwa	makes s.o. sit upright
	chîtapenêwa	sits s.o. up, sits s.o. down
	ahkwitapiwa	sits on top
	ahpapiwa	sits on (it)
	anemapiwa	sits riding away
	apîhtawêwa, apîhtamwa	sits (as, in ceremony) for s.o., it ({somewhere}), stays in it
	atamêwapiwa	sits smoking
	âhchîpiwa	sits leaning
	âkwapiwa	sits to rest
	inâkwapiwa	sits assembled {so}
	inâsamapiwa	sits facing {some way}
	inapiwa	sits {so}
	inehpapiwa	sits {so} high
	kehkinechêpiwa	s.o.'s handprints show where one sat
	kekapiwa	sits having (it)
	kekapihêwa	makes s.o. sit having (it)
	kekômyêpiwa	sits with (it) on one's back
	kîhkapiwa	sits closer
	kîshâkwapiwaki (plural)	they have already sat as a group
	kotapiwa	tries to sit
	matakôhkwêpiwa	sits with covered head
	mâtapiwa	moves one's seat, moves from one's place
	mâwatâkwapiwaki (plural)	they sit assembled
	memyêshkâkwapiwaki (plural)	they sit in scattered, disordered groups
	menwapiwa	sits well, has a comfortable seat, has a nice place to sit
	nahehkwêpiwa	can sit up
	nanâhapîhtawêwa	takes a seat by s.o.
	nanâhâkwapiwaki (plural)	they seat themselves in a group or in groups
	nanâhônakapiwa	sits down inside (as, a canoe)
	nematapiwa	sits upright
	nenyêhpapiwa	is weak and has trouble moving from sitting too long
	nenyêmatôkanêpiwa	sits with one's knees up
	nêhtôpiwa	sits in a separate group
	nîmihkamêpiwa	sits smoking
	nômakêpihêwa	makes s.o. sit for a while
	otapiwa	sits in {such} direction
	pemâkwapiwa	sits along in a group
	peshikwapiwa	sits straight

	pyêchipehkwanêpiwa	sits with one's back this way
	shôshkâhkwapiwa	sits erect
	shôshkikâpiwa	sits with one's legs stretched out
	taswâkwapiwaki (plural)	they sit as a group of {so many}
	tashitiyêpiwa	is sitting, perching on (the edge of) {somewhere}
	tetepâkwapiwaki (plural)	they sit around (it) in a circle
	wawîhkwanapiwa	sits on one's knees (with feet together to one side)
	wâpanâtapiwa	sits as one pleases (ritual)
	wâwâtâsamapiwaki (plural)	they sit facing each other
	wêwêpikâpiwa	sits with one's legs dangling
	wîkawikâpiwa	sits moving one's feet
	wîshikapiwa	sits firmly, sits unbudging
	wîtapîmêwa	sits with s.o.
	wîtapîkêwa	sits with people
six	**kotwâshika**	six (particle)
	nekotwâshika	six (older form; also Sauk dialect) (particle)
	kotwâshika tashiwaki	they (animate) are six, there are six of them
	kotwâshika tasenôni	they (inanimate) are six, there are six of them
	kotwâshikenwi	six times
sixteen	**kotwâshikanesiwe**	sixteen (particle)
	kotwâshikanîsiwe	sixteen (particle)
	metâswi-kotwâshika	sixteen (particle compound)
sixth	**kotwâshikânameki**	sixth, the sixth time (particle)
	nekotwâshikânameki (Jones)	sixth, the sixth time (particle)
sixty	**kotwâshikâpitaki**	sixty (particle)
	nekotwâshikâpitaki (Jones)	sixty (particle)
skeleton	**chîkonwâwa**	living skeleton
skillful	**nahêwîwa**	is a good hand at the job, works skillfully
skim	**pasisahêwa**	skims, swishes s.o.
skin	**onameshkaya**	skin
	onamashkaya	skin
	onameshkayiwiwa	has skin
	onamashkayiwiwa	has skin
	ishinameshkêwa	has {such} skin, is of {such} race
	kôkinameshkênowa	washes one's skin
	papakwinameshkêwa	one's skin is loose
	pîninameshkêwa	is clean of skin
	wâpeshkinameshkêwa	is white-skinned
	pyêmishkwashayêhowa	twists one's own skin
	owiyêhêhayi	small animal skins
	amehkwaya	beaver skin
	apenôhêhaya	baby skin
	kekawêwaya	skin with the hair on
	manetôwaya	manitou-skin
	penêsiwaya	raptor skin (in a sacred bundle)
	penêsiwâha	raptor skin (in a sacred bundle) (dimin.)
	peshînâwa	animal or bird skin (in a sacred bundle)
	peshînâhêha	animal or bird skin (in a sacred bundle) (dimin.)
	wâpi-kohpichi-nenoswayi	white buffalo skin
	wîtekôwaya	owl-skin
skin (hide): → hide		
skin (verb)	**peshînêwa**	skins s.o.
	pashîshkenêwa	pulls the skin off s.o. (as, a rabbit)
	pashôshkenêwa	pulls the skin off s.o. (as, a rabbit)

	pashîshkinameshkênêwa	pulls s.o.'s skin off
skip	âyâhchîhtanâhiwa	is skipping (along)
	papasanasitêpahowa	runs with one's feet barely touching the ground
skirt	okôtêhi	her dress, her skirt
	okôtêhêhi	her little dress, her little skirt
	okôtêhiwa	she has on a dress or skirt
	okôtêhêhiwa	she has on a dress or skirt (dimin.)
	okôtêhihêwa	makes a dress or skirt (of it) for her
	okôtêpisowa	she puts on a skirt
	nanâhapisowa	girds oneself; puts on one's skirt
	sâsâkisâhi	underskirt
	pîhtôpisôni	underskirt
skull	chîpayi-owîshi	skull
skunk	shekâkwa	skunk
	shekâkôhêha	skunk (dimin.)
sky	kîshekwi	sky; day
	okîshekomiwa	has (it) as sky
	êh=okîshekomiyani	in your heaven
	inânahkwatwi	it is {such} sky
	ashkipakânahkwakôtêwi	it hangs as blue ("green") sky
	ashkipakânahkwakôtôwa	hangs it as blue ("green") sky
	ashkipakânahkwisetôwa	makes it blue ("green") sky
	meshkwânahkwatwi	it is red sky
	meshahkwatwi	it is clear sky
	nanawahkwi	in the middle of the sky (song word)
	wahkwi	sky (song word)
slack	kêwapenêwa	one's hunger begins to slack off
	kêwapisowa	one's bonds are loosened a bit
	kêwâshkêwa, kêwâshkêwi	(animate, inanimate) starts to slow down, slacks off
slap	pasîkwêhwêwa	slaps s.o. in the face
	pasetonêhwêwa	slaps s.o. on the mouth
	pâkitenyêhwêwa	slaps s.o. on the shoulder
	pâkechêshimêwa, pâkechêsetôwa	slaps s.o., it down or against something
slave	otawahkyânemêwa	has s.o. as a slave, makes s.o. their slave
sleep	nepêwa	sleeps, sleeps {somewhere}
	nepêwêwa	sleeps at s.o.'s house
	nepêwowêwa	sleeps at someone else's house, spends the night
	nepêwotîwaki (plural)	they sleep at each other's houses
	nepahêwa	puts s.o. to bed, gives s.o. a place to sleep, puts s.o. up for the night
	nepêhêwa	puts s.o. to sleep, lets s.o. sleep
	nepêwêwêkahwêwa	puts s.o. to sleep by drumming
	nepêhkânowa	pretends to sleep
	kawekwashiwa	falls asleep
	kîshâkotekwâmwa	sleeps soundly
	tanekwâmwa	is sleeping {somewhere}; is (still) sleeping
	menishkîkwêkwâmwa	sleeps with mattery eyes
	sîsepetonêkwâmwa	drools in one's sleep
	shahkosiwa	is drowsy
	shahkokwâmwa	is drowsy or weak from sleep
	showinekwêkwâmwa	sleeps with one's arms flung out
	wîshasokwâmwa	sweats in one's sleep
	wîhpêwa	sleeps double, sleeps with someone
	wîhpêmêwa, wîhpêtamwa	sleeps with s.o., it

	wîhpêtîwaki	they sleep together
	wîhpêtenowa	gets into someone's bed
sleepwalk	**omatekwashiwa**	gets up while still sleeping, sleepwalks
sleepy	**wîkowiwa**	is sleepy
slender	**shâshôpesiwa, shâshôpyâwi**	(animate, inanimate) is slender
	shâshôpikiwa	is slender, slim
slice	**pahkwêshwêwa**	cuts a slice from s.o.
	pahkwêshamawêwa	cuts a slice of (it) from s.o.
	papahkwêshwêwa, papahkwêshamwa	cut slices or chunks off s.o., it
	chîkâpyêshwêwa, chîkâpyêshamwa	cuts a thin strip or slice off s.o. (as, hide or fat), it
slide	**nîsinawîwa**	slides down
	mîwinawîwa	slides away, moves off
	shôshkwisenwi	it slides and falls
slim	**chakâhkosîhiwa**	is slim-waisted
slip	**shôshkwishinwa**	slips, slips and falls
	shôshkonêwa, shôshkonamwa	has s.o., it slip from one's grasp
	shôshkwanahamîwa	slips as one tries to get one's footing
	shashôshkwanahamîwa	keeps slipping as one tries to get traction
slip in	**nêkwisetôwa**	slips it in, on, under
	nêkwâhkwisetôwa	slips it in, slips it into a space between
	nêkonamawêwa	slides (it) into s.o.
slip out	**nânishkonamwa**	slips it out, off, loose
	nanânishkwinehkêwa	pulls one's hands loose
	nanânishkwihpikêshkêwa	one's ribs slip out of joint
slippery	**ashâshesiwa, ashâshâwi**	(animate, inanimate) is slippery, slick
	ashâshinehkêwa	one's hands are very slippery
	shashôshkwâwi	it is slippery
	shashôshkwikanwi	it (as, a tree or pole) is slippery
	shashôshkwâhkosiwa	(tree) is slippery
slow	**opyêni**	slowly, taking one's time (particle)
	kenâchi	slowly, carefully (particle)
	oshihoshi	slowly, as a slow process (particle)
	opyênesiwa	is slow
	opyêneshkêwi	it goes slowly, is slow, is a slow process
	kêwâshkêwa, kêwâshkêwi	(animate, inanimate) starts to slow down, slacks off
small	**chaki**	small (prenoun or preverb)
	pîsi	small (prenoun, preverb)
	papîwi	small (plural) (prenoun)
	ahkanêhi	small bone (with diminutive suffix)
	chakeshîhiwa, chakâhenôhiwi	(animate, inanimate) is small
	chakâhenwi	(with negative:) it is not small
	chakênetamôhiwa	thinks it to be small (dimin.)
	chakênetisôhiwa	thinks oneself to be small (dimin.)
	papîweshîhiwaki	they (animate) are small, tiny
	papîwâhenôni	they (inanimate) are small, tiny
	papîwâhenôhiwani	they (inanimate) are small, tiny
	pêpîwikenôhiki	any little thing
	pîsenamwa	makes it into small pieces
	pîsikâwosêhiwa	walks taking short steps
	chakâhkosîhiwa	is small-bodied
	chakâpêwesiwa	is small in bodily build
smallpox	**mamahkâpyêwa**	has smallpox

smart	**nepwâhkâwa**	is wise, smart, clever, bright
	nepwâhkêwa	is wise, smart, clever, bright (younger variant)
	otehchi-nepwêwa	catches on
	tahpi-nepwêwa	begins to realize things, gets smarter
smash	**pâhpâshkitepêshimêwa**	smashes s.o.'s head against something
	shâkwisetôwa	smashes it by hitting it against something
	shâshâkwitepêwa	one's head is smashed, one's skull is fractured
	shâshâkwitepêshinwa	lies with one's head smashed
smear	**sheshônêwa**	smears s.o. (with it) using the hand
smell	**menâmêwa, menâtamwa**	smells s.o., it
	menâkosiwa, menâkwatwi	(animate, inanimate) smells bad, stinks
	kochiyâmêwa, kochiyâtamwa	sniffs at s.o., it, tries the smell of s.o., it
	kochiyâtahêwa	makes s.o. try the smell of (it)
	aniwiyâmêwa, aniwiyâtamwa	can smell s.o., it at a distance
	âhkwiyâmêwa	has a keen sense of smell for s.o. (as, tobacco)
	menwiyâmêwa, menwiyâtamwa	likes the smell of s.o., it
	menwiyâkosiwa, menwiyâkwatwi	(animate, inanimate) smells nice
	myâshiyâmêwa, myâshiyâtamwa	smells s.o., it as bad
	myâshiyâkosiwa, myâshiyâkwatwi	(animate, inanimate) smells bad
	ishiyâkosiwa, ishiyâkwatwi	smells {so}
	mayakiyâkwatwi	it smells strange
	nemêsiyâkwatwi	it smells like a fish
	ishiyâsikêwa	makes {such} an odor by burning, cooking, or smoking something
	menwiyâsikêwa	makes or has nice smells of cooking or burning
	menwiyâsowa, menwiyâhtêwi	(animate, inanimate) smells good in cooking, burning
	nanâtwiyêwa	sniffs at an odor, takes a whiff
	nâchiyêwa	follows an odor, is attracted by an odor
	nâchiyâmêwa, nâchiyâtamwa	seek out s.o., it by smell, follows the odor of s.o., it
	nenwiyêwa	has a sense of smell, can smell
	nenwiyâmêwa, nenwiyâtamwa	recognizes the smell of s.o., it
	nenwiyâkosiwa, nenwiyâkwatwi	the odor of (animate, inanimate) is recognizable
	neshiwiyâkosiwa, neshiwiyâkwatwi	(animate, inanimate) stinks, smells awful
	menwiyâkotonwa	one's mouth smells nice
	pyêchiyâhtêwi	the smell of cooking wafts this way
	têpiyâkosiwa, têpiyâkwatwi	the smell of (animate, inanimate) reaches
	wîsakanêshinwa	smells strong
smile	**apanêniwa**	smiles
	apanênemêwa	smiles at s.o.
	apanênetîwaki	they smile at each other
	ênikîkwêhtawêwa	smiles at s.o.
	ênikîkwêkâpâwa	stands with smiling face
	ênikîkwêwosêwa	walks with smiling face
smitten	**meshotîwa**	is smitten (with s.o.)
	meshotîwaki (plural)	they fall in love with each other
smoke (1)	**pekeshêwi**	it smokes, it is smoky, it is foggy
	pêkeshêki	smoke, its smoke; fog
	pêkeshêhiki	smoke (dimin.) (participle)
	pekeshawêwa	makes a cloud of smoke (as, a smoker); has a fire going
	pekeshawanêwa, pekeshawatôwa	"smokes" s.o., it, fumigates s.o., it ceremonially; smokes it up (as, a house)
	pahkîkwasowa	one's eyes are bothered by smoke
	pahkîkwahtêwi	it is so smoky it bothers the eyes

	nâwipekeshe	in the smoke (particle)
	asâwêkiswêwa	smoke-cures s.o. (rawhide) into yellow leather
smoke (2)	nôswêwa, nôsamwa	smokes s.o., it (ceremonially)
	nôsamawêwa	smokes (it) for s.o. (ceremonially)
	nôsowa	smokes oneself (ceremonially)
	nôsikêwa	fumigates things ceremonially, smokes things
	pekeshawanêwa, pekeshawatôwa	smokes s.o., it, fumigates s.o., it ceremonially
smoke (3)	atamêwa	smokes a pipe
	atamêhêwa	gives s.o. a smoke
	atamêhetîwaki	they give each other a smoke
	ashkachihkamêwa	is impatient for a smoke
	nîmihkamêpiwa	sits smoking
	ochihkamêhiwa	smokes from {somewhere}
	nîmihkamêkêwa	dances smoking
	panihkamêwa	misses out on smoking
	sîkâhpwêwa	smokes s.o. (a pipe) completely out
	sôpihkesowa	savors one's smoking, enjoys a smoke
	tepihkamêwa	has a complete smoke, the full amount of smoking
	tepihkesowa	has a complete smoke, the full amount of smoking
	têpihkamêwa	gets enough smoking, is satisfied smoking
	têpihkesowa	gets enough smoking, is satisfied smoking
smokehole	anenêwi	smokehole
	matakwinenêwêhamwa	covers the smokehole of it
smoke out	peswêwa	smokes s.o. out (as, bees or bears)
smooth	shôshkwâwi	it is smooth
	shôshkwânehkwêyâshinwa	one's hair is blown back smooth
	shôshkwâwakeshkâtêwi	the dirt on it (a road) was trodden smooth
smother	ashkanâmowa	is out of breath, is smothering
	kepanâmoshkawêwa	smothers s.o. by pressing
	wâwananâmosowa	is smothered by the heat
snag	inâhkwichinwa	is {so} snagged
snail	pyêmishkwinêha	snail
Snail Dance	pyêmishkwinêhekêwa	dances the Snail Dance
snake	manetôwa	snake, spirit, god, monster
	manetôwi	(of) manitou, (of) snake (prenoun, preverb)
	manetôhêha	little snake
	kîyôtêneniwa	snake
	nânôkechêha	water moccasin
	nêwa	hog-nosed snake, "puff adder"
	shâshâkêha	garter-snake
	shîshîkwêwa	rattlesnake
snakeroot	wâwiyêpenwâneki êshikeki	seneca snakeroot
snare	nekwâpinêwa	snares s.o.
	nekwâpisowa	is snared
	nekwâpichikani	snare
	peshkwahtêpisowa	is caught by the springing of a snare
sneak	kîmîwa	sneaks away
	anawinêwa, anawitamwa	sneaks up on s.o., it
sneaky	kîmôchikenwi	it is sneaky, underhanded
sneeze	châhchâmowa	sneezes
snicker	nanawâtâyêniwa	snickers, chuckles, laughs to oneself
sniff	nanâtwiyêwa	sniffs at an odor, takes a whiff
	pîchikomêwa	sniffs (it) into one's nose (as, medicine or snuff)
snore	kâshkikôhiwa	snores

	têpwêwêkomêwa	can be heard (from a distance) snoring
snot	**meshkikoma**	snot
	oshkikoma	snot
snow	**akôna**	snow
	mehpowi	it snows
	inehpowi	it snows {so}
	akwishkehpowi	it is snowing wet snow
	pehkwehpowi	it snows in clumps
	akwanwîwi	the snow is sticking to the trees
	ashkanwîwi	the first snow (of the season) is on the ground
	ahkwitâkone	on top of the snow (particle)
	ahkwitakône	on top of the snow (particle)
	nâmâkone	under the snow (particle)
	nâmakône	under the snow (particle)
	matakwâkonêwa	is covered with snow
	tawâkonêshkânawêwa	clears a space in the snow with one's feet
	ânwâkoníwa	is barely able to get through the deep snow
	pyêtwêwêyâkonîwa	comes crunching through the snow
	mehchihkatwi	the ground is bare of snow
snowshoe	**âkema**	snowshoe
so	**=châhi**	so, for (idiomatic)
soak	**akwîchinwa, akwîtêwi**	is in the water, is soaking, is floating
	akwîchimêwa, akwîtôwa	soaks s.o., it, has s.o., it in water
	akwînêwa	soaks s.o., it, has s.o., it in water (archaic)
	akwîtawêwa	soaks (it) for s.o.
	nahpawisenwi	it soaked through, is soaking wet
	nahpawishimêwa	gets s.o. soaking wet
	nehkepyêhtêwi	it soaks into what is cooking
soap	**sîpyêhikani**	soap
sober	**anesâchi**	sober, being sober (particle)
so far	**ahkwi**	{so} far, to {such a} point (preverb); until (particle)
	ahkohtâkosiwa, ahkohtâkwatwi	(animate, inanimate) is heard from {so far} away
	ahkomîwa	is {so far} in the water
	ahkopyêwi	the water comes {so far}
	ahpîhchîwa	goes {so} far
soft	**shahkyâwi**	it is soft
	shahkapiwa	sits in a soft place, it is soft where one sits
	shahkâtowêwa	is soft-spoken
	pîhpîshkesiwa, pîhpîshkyâwi	(animate, inanimate) is soft, cushiony
	pîhpîshkapiwa	sits on something soft, cushiony
	nôshkânematôhiwi	there is a soft breeze (dimin.)
	shîshîhkanehkîwa	steps softly
soften	**nâshêkihikêwa**	softens a hide with a wooden hide-scraper
soil	**môwesiwa, môwâwi**	(animate, inanimate) is soiled
soldier	**shamâkanesha**	soldier
	shamahtîha	soldier
solicitous	**kîhkîchi**	tenderly, solicitously, indulgently; sensitive, requiring solicitude (preverb)
so long	**ahkwiwa, ahkonwi**	(animate, inanimate) is {so} long, tall
	îni êhkwichi	that is as far as one's story goes
	ahkoshamawêwa	cuts (it) {so} long for s.o.
	ahkôtêwi	it (house) is {so long}
	âyahkwi	{so} long each, {so} far each (preverb, particle)

	âyahkôhkwêwa	one's hair is {so} long
	âyahkwinîsîpinechêwa	one's fingers are {so} long
	âyahkwiwinêwa	one's horns are {so} long
	ahpîhchinehki	for {so} long
	ahpîhtêtwa	is gone {so long}
so many	taswi	{so many}, {so much} (particle)
	âyâtaswi	{so many} each, {so much} each (particle)
	tashiwa, tasenwi	(animate, inanimate) is {so many, so much}
	âyâtashiwaki (plural)	there are {so many} of them (animate) each
	âyâtasenwi	there is {so much} of it each
	âyâtasenôni (plural)	there are {so many} of them (inanimate) each
	tasônameki	number {so many} (ordinal number) (particle)
	tasôchênamwa	grabs {so many} of them (inanimate) at once
some	âneta	some (of it, of them); partly (particle)
	kêkôhi-'shi	in some or any way; (with negative:) not at all, not under any circumstances
	nekotahi	to some degree, about (particle)
some kind	owiyêhi	some kind of (prenoun)
someone	owiyêha	someone, anyone; someone else, anyone else
	owiyêhiwa	is someone, is some kind of animal
	êwiyêhikwêna	someone or other, some unidentified creature
	wêwiyêhikwêna	someone or other, some unidentified creature
somehow	mamâkôchi	somehow, by some chance (particle)
something	kêkôhi	something, anything
	kêkôhêhi	something, anything (dimin.)
sometimes	âyakwami	intermittently (particle)
	chachawîhi	sometimes (particle)
somewhere	nekotahi	somewhere, anywhere; somewhere else (particle)
so much	taswi	{so much}, {so many} (particle)
	âyâtaswi	{so much} each (particle)
	tasôchêhtamwa	bites of {so much} of it at once
	ahpîhchîwa	does {so much}
son	nekwisa	my son; (of a man) the son of my brother or anyone else I call "brother"; (of a woman) the son of my sister or anyone else I call "sister," or of my father's sister
	okwisiwa	has a son; has (him) as a son
	okwisemêwa	has him as a son
	okwisemâwa	the son
	wêyôsita	the son or daughter (of a man), his son or daughter
song	nakamôni	song
	nakamôniwiwi	it is a song
	onakamôniwa	has a song
	shêshkinâkâkâhani (plural)	songs unaccompanied by a drum
	mêyôwisekini	wailing songs (plural participle)
	nîmiwahikani	dancing song
	nîmiwisekini	dancing songs (plural participle)
	wîseniwisekini	eating songs (plural participle)
son-in-law	nenekwana	my son-in-law (onekwanani his or her son-in-law)
	onekwaniwa	has a son-in-law, has (him) as a son-in-law
	onekwanemêwa	has him as a son-in-law
	nêhâkapita	son-in-law living with his in-laws (participle)
	owîtâkapîhani	his fellow son-in-law in their in-laws' house
	oshinekêwa	the son-in-law
	oshinetamwa	he is the son-in-law (wêshinetaka the son-in-law)

soon	kapôtwe	at some point, some time later, soon, in time, as time went by (particle)
	kayêchîhi	soon, soon after; recently, a short while ago (particle)
	kayêchîhe	soon, soon after; recently, a short while ago (particle)
	keyêchîhi	soon, soon after; recently, a short while ago (particle)
	keyêchîhe	soon, soon after; recently, a short while ago (particle)
	kêyêhchine	pretty soon, shortly, in a short time (particle)
	menwinâhi	soon; some distance away, not far away (particle)
	mêsi	too soon (preverb)
	mâmaya	soon, in the near future; early (particle)
	nôta	too soon, before the time, before completion (particle)
	nânôta	repeatedly too soon (particle)
soothe	wawîkimêwa	soothes or calms s.o. with words
sore	omekîwa	has a sore or sores
	omekiwa (probable variant)	has a sore or sores
	omekihkwêkanwa	has sores on one's neck
	omekikâtêwa	has sores on one's feet
	omekisikiwêwa	has sores on one's back
	omekishîkanwa	has a sore in the small of one's back
	omekîkwêwa	has sores on one's face
	kâshanasitêshinwa	has sore feet
sort	shîkônêwa, shîkônamwa	sorts s.o., it out, separates s.o., it
sort of	tâtaki	sort of, as it were, in a way (particle)
	myâshi	badly; sort of (preverb)
soul	nôkênawa	soul
	menôkênawa	soul
	onôkênawiwa	has a soul, reflection, or shadow
sound	inehtâkosiwa	sounds {so}, is heard {so}
	inwêwa, inwêwi	sounds {so}
	takwêwêkesiwa	sounds together
	tanwêwêkesiwa	is making loud noise (as, wailing, [drum] being drummed on, [bird] calling) ({somewhere})
	kotowêwa	tries to make a sound
soup	nepôpi	soup
	keki-nepôpe	along with the broth (particle)
	ashkâpowi	fresh soup
sour	peshkipanwi	it is sour, puckery to the taste
	wîshkopishinwa	(corn) turns sour
source	ahkwanahkisenwi	it begins, has its source
south	wêchi-nâwahkwêki	south (oblique participle)
	shâwanoki	in the south (ritual) (particle)
so wide	inekihkwatêkiwi	it (as, a river) is {so} wide
space	tawâwi	there is a space, a gap
	tawihtôwa	leaves a space
spank	pasitiyêhwêwa	spanks s.o.
spare	ashkwihêwa	spares s.o., leaves s.o.
	memênawênemêwa	spares s.o. out of fondness or high regard
spark	pakenêshêwi	it (fire) sends out a spark
	sesekeshêwi	it sparks, sparks come out of it
sparkle	wawâsesowa, wawâsetêwi	(animate, inanimate) sparkles, shines (by reflected light)
	wawâsehkêwi	it is shiny, glistens, sparkles
spawn	pâshkâwesiwa	(a fish) spawns
speak	kanawiwa	speaks
	kanônêwa, kanôtamwa	speaks to s.o., it

	kanôtamawêwa	speaks to (s.o.) for s.o.
	kanônetîwaki (plural)	they speak to each other
	kanônetisowa	speaks to oneself
	kanôhkyêwa, kanôhkyêmowa	speaks
	ishimêwa	speaks {so} to s.o.
	ishitîwaki	they speak to each other {so}
	menwâtotamawêwa	speaks well of (it) to s.o.
	menwâtotamâtîwaki	they speak well of (it) to each other
	pemetonêmonohkatawêwa	speaks for s.o.
	ihketowa	speaks {so}
	ihketômikatwi	it speaks {so}
	inâchimêwa, inâtotamwa	speaks {so} of s.o., it
	inekihkwimêwa	speaks to {such} a number of them
	kîshetonêmowa	finishes speaking
	mayâwimêwa	speaks mainly to s.o.
	mayômêwa	makes s.o. weep by speaking, singing, weeping
	mayômowa	weeps as one speaks
	menwâchimowa	speaks well
	menwâchimêwa, menwâtotamwa	speaks well of s.o., it
	menwâtotamawêwa	speaks well of (it) to s.o.
	kokwimêwa	speaks sharply to s.o.
	menwimêwa	speaks nicely to s.o.; gives s.o. good advice; says something nice about s.o.
	myâshimêwa	speaks crossly to s.o.
	myânowêwa	speaks crossly
	pehkînowêwa	speaks differently
	shahkâtowêwa	is soft-spoken
	tahitanetonêmowa	is speaking at length
	wâwaneshkâhowêwa	speaks evil, wickedly
	wîshikowêwa	speaks, sings, screams loudly
speak language	inâtowêwa	speaks {some} language
	pehkînâtowêwa	speaks a different language
	pêpehkînâtowêwaki	they speak different languages
	meshkwahkîhâtowêwa	speaks the Meskwaki language
	nenôtêwâtowêwa	speaks "Indian," speaks Meskwaki
	ashâhâtowêwa	speaks the Sioux language
spear	shamâkani	spear
	sîkomêhikani	three-pronged fish spear, leister
speech	kanakanawîni	speech, formal speech
	kanawiwenl	speech, speaking, form of speech
	tasotone	{so much} speech (particle)
speed	ishisêwa	speeds, flies to {somewhere}
	pyêtâshkêwa, pyêtâshkêwi	comes rushing, falls or speeds this way; it falls, flies, or speeds this way
spider	êsapîhkêha	spider (Jones: spiderweb)
	êhêpikwa	tarantula; water spider
	nepîki tashi-êhêpikwa	water spider
spiderweb	êsapîhkêhêyâpi	spiderweb
spile	nêkamêhkwâni	maple-sap spile (collecting spout)
spill	sîkisêwa, sîkisêwi	spills; it spills, flows out
	sîkahanwi	it spills (from being overfilled or pushed over)
	sîkisahtôwa	empties it out, pours it out, spills it out, dumps it out
	sîkishinwa	falls spilling (it)
	sîkanwishinwa	lets something spill out of one's mouth; spills the beans

	sîkihkamêsêwa	jumps spilling one's pipe
spine	netahtakâkwani	my spine
	otahtakâkwani	his or her spine; a backbone
	wâkisikiwêwa	has a crooked spine
spirit	manetôwa	spirit, god; snake, monster
	kehchi-manetôwa	Great Spirit
	machi-manetôha	evil spirit; Devil
	ashkotênêsiwa	the Spirit of Fire
	papîwi-manetôhêhiwaki	they are small spirits
	keshê-manetôwa	the Gentle Spirit
spirit land	manetônâki	in the land of the spirits (locative noun)
spit	sehkwiwa	spits
	sehkwânêwa, sehkwâtamwa	spits on s.o., it
spit (to roast)	nasâhkohikani	roasting spit, roasting stick
spittle	sehkwiweni	spittle
splash	kwâshkopyêkîwa	(fish) makes a splash in the water
	kwâshkopyêhamwa	splashes it, makes it splash
	anwêwêyâpôshinwa	lands in the water with an audible splash
	patashkepyêhokowa	is splashed by a mass of water
	sîkenîkwêhwêwa	throws (it, liquid) in s.o.'s face
	tanwêwêyâpônikêwa	is noisily splashing water on things
splatter	seswêhamwa	splatters it with a blow
	seswêhokowa, seswêhanwi	(animate, inanimate) is splattered by the impact
	seswêsêwa, seswêsêwi	(animate, inanimate) scatters, splatters
spleen	oteshkîha	spleen
splendid	kîshâkochinâkosiwa	looks splendid
split	pâsikenamwa	splits it (in two) with a shot
	pâsikahwêwa, pâsikahamwa	chops s.o., it in two
	papâsikahwêwa, papâsikahamwa	chops s.o., it into pieces
	papâsikâsenôni	they (inanimate) are blown down and split apart
spoil	panâtesiwa	is spoiled, ruined
	panâtesîmikatwi	it is spoiled, ruined
	myâshishinwa, myâshisenwi	(animate, inanimate) spoils, goes bad
spontaneously	pîneshi	spontaneously, of one's own accord, acting on one's own, unprovoked (particle)
	pîneshihêwa	attacks s.o. unprovoked, approaches s.o. spontaneously
	pînesênetisowa	thinks of oneself spontaneously
spoon	êmehkwâhi	spoon
	êmehkwânahikêwa	uses a spoon
sportive	mîshâchi	sportively (preverb); sporty (prenoun)
	matâkwineniwiwa	is jovial, sportive
spotted	ketakesiwa, ketakyâwi	(animate, inanimate) is striped, spotted
sprawl	showishinwa	lies sprawled out
	showekwâmwa	sleeps sprawled out
spray	seswamêwa, seswatamwa	sprays (it, medicine) on s.o., it with the mouth
	seswamowa	sprays (it) on oneself with the mouth
spread	neneshkishimêwa, neneshkisetôwa	spreads s.o., it out
	neneshkisahtôwa	throws it (as, a blanket) over a surface, spreads it with a flick of the wrists
	meshkisetôwa	spreads it out
	meshkisetawêwa	spreads (it) out for s.o.
	anâhkahêwa	spreads something, (it) down for s.o. to sit or lie on
	anâhkahowa	spreads something, (it) down to sit or lie on
	anâhkahamwa	spreads it down for sitting, lying

	anâhkahamawêwa	spreads (it) for s.o., spreads mats or blankets for s.o.
	anâhkahikêwa	spreads mats or carpeting
	shekenêwa, shekenamwa	spreads s.o. (as, corn), it out to dry
	shekenikêwa	spreads food items out to dry
	showêkinamwa	holds it (as, a blanket) spread out
	showihkechêshkêwa	spreads one's tail-feathers
	showikâtêwa	has one's feet apart
	showinekwêwa	has one's wings spread
	showinekwêshkêwa	spreads one's arms or wings
	showinekwêkwâmwa	sleeps with one's arms flung out
spread open	**tôkapiwa**	sits with one's legs spread apart
	tôkanoshkêwi	its opening spreads open
	tôkishêsetawêwa	has it (as, a bag) open for s.o.
	tôkitiyêwosêwa	walks with legs spread apart
	tatôkikâpiwa	sits with one's legs spread apart
	tatôkikomêwa	one's nostrils spread open
sprinkle	**pâhpiwênêwa, pâhpiwênamwa**	crumbles and sprinkles s.o. (as, tobacco), it
	sîkenitepêhwêwa	sprinkles (it, liquid) on s.o.'s head
spring (season)	**menôhkamîwi**	it is springtime
spring (verb)	**kâtanahamîwa**	springs, bolts off, leaps up (to fly), shoves off with the feet
spring (water)	**tahkepi**	spring (of cool water), well
spur	**patahkechêshkawêwa**	spurs s.o.
squash	**wâpikoni**	squash, pumpkin
	kâtenikanani (plural)	dried pumpkin slices
squash (verb)	**shekonêwa, shekonamwa**	pushes s.o. down; crushes it, squashes it, flattens it
squat	**tashitiyêpiwa**	squats {somewhere} (Jones)
squeak	**kashkîpâhkwi**	tree that squeaks in the wind
	kashkîpeshkâtîmikatôni (plural)	they (as, trees) squeak from rubbing against each other
	kashkîpwêwêshkêwi	it makes a squeaking noise (as, by rubbing)
squirrel	**anikwa**	squirrel (generic)
	achitamôha	redsquirrel
	asâwanikwa	fox squirrel
	kwakwinôha	chipmunk
	môsênikwa	groundsquirrel
	papakanikwa	flying squirrel
St. Louis	**pêkôneki**	at St. Louis (locative noun) (from the early French name "Paincourt")
stab	**keshihkahwêwa**	stabs s.o.
stable	**nêkatôkashêhikâni**	stable
staff	**ahtawâni**	chief's staff of office
stagger	**âyâshôkâsêwa**	staggers
stand	**nemasowa, nematêwi**	(animate, inanimate) stands
	nenyêmasowa, nenyêmatêwi	(animate, inanimate) stands there, is standing there
	nemaswi	standing (preverb)
	nemaswisêwa	lands on one's feet
	ahpanasitêkâpâwa	stands with one's feet on (it)
	asipehkwêkâpâwaki (plural)	they stand with heads together
	ashkwêyawikâpâwa	stands at the end
	chîkitiyêkâpâwa	stands with rump out
	inâsamikâpâwa	stands facing {some way}
	ishikâpawihêwa	makes stand {so}
	ishîkwêkâpâwa	stands facing {so}
	kekinechêkâpâwa	stands with (it) in hand
	kîshikâpawihêwa	has made s.o. stand

	kîshikâpâwa	has taken one's position standing
	kîwikâpâwa	stands around
	makikâpâwaki (plural)	they stand in a large group
	mesiwêhkatêwani (plural)	they (inanimate, as trees) stand all over
	mesiwêkâpâwani (plural)	they (inanimate) stand all over
	nakikâpâwa	stops and stands
	nanâhahkanêwa, nanâhahkatôwa	sets, fixes s.o., it (as, into the ground) to stand
	nîshôkâpâwaki	the two of them stand together
	nyêwôkâpâwaki	the four of them stand together
	ochikâpâwa	stands on {such} side
	pakamikâpâwa	stands arrived
	pakamikâpawîhtawêwa	arrives and stands before s.o.
	pakamikâpawînotawêwa	arrives and stands before s.o.
	pakamikâpawinohkatawêwa	arrives and stands before s.o.
	pehkwikâpâwaki (plural)	they stand close together
	pemikâpâwaki (plural)	they stand in a row
	pônikâpâwa	quits standing
	pyêtanahkikâpâwa	stands with branches this way
	wâwâtâsamikâpâwaki (plural)	they stand facing each other
stand aside	**mîwikâpâwa**	stands aside
	mîwîhtamawêwa	stands aside from (it) for s.o., gives s.o. a chance
stand on end	**nîshkahtakawêshkêwa**	(animal's) hair stands up on end
stand up	**pasekwîwa**	stands up, arises, gets to one's feet
	pasekwîtenêwa	stand s.o. up, lifts s.o. to their feet
	pasekwîchisêwa	jumps to one's feet
	pasekwîchisahêwa	jerks s.o. to one's feet
stand up for	**otowêwa**	stands up for (s.o.), defends (s.o.) verbally
star	**anâkwa**	star
	chaki-anâkôha	little star
	wâpananâkwa	the morning star
stare	**ayînâpiwa**	remains with a fixed stare on one's face
	âhpetâpiwa	freezes staring, has a frozen expression of astonishment
	mechimâpiwa	stares fixedly
	mechimâpamêwa, mechimâpatamwa	looks closely, fixedly at s.o., it, stares at s.o., it
	myânowâpamêwa	stares s.o. down, overpowers s.o. by staring
	myânawâpamêwa	stares s.o. down, overpowers s.o. by staring
start	**wêpi**	start to, begin to, set about (preverb)
	ashkiwêpi	at the start (particle)
	wêpahîwa	starts things (as, a fight), gets started (as, misbehaving)
	wêpahinotawêwa	starts in on s.o.
	wêpîhkawêwa, wêpîhkamwa	starts on s.o., it, takes it up
	wêpyêkiwa, wêpyêkenwi	(animate, inanimate) is starting to grow
	wêpikawiwa	they started off in a group
	wêpahkiwihtôwa	starts (a general activity)
	wêpatahwêwa	starts to beat s.o.
	mâchihêwa	gets s.o. started
	kehkihtôwa	starts it (to show how)
	kehkihtawêwa	starts (it) for s.o. (to show how)
starve	**ânemapenêwa**	is starving
	pahkihtêpenêwa	starves to death
	pîkêpenêwa	starves to death
	wîshâpenêhtôwa owîyawi	starves oneself
	ahpîhtapenêhtôwa owîyawi	makes oneself starve {so long}

	inapenêhtôwa owîyawi	starves oneself {so}
stay	**kîwitêwa**	stays, stays around ({somewhere})
	kîwitêmikatwi	it stays around
	kîwitênotamwa	stays on it, has it as home or homeland
	ashkwîwa	stays behind (when others leave)
	ashkwîhiwa	stays behind (when others leave) (dimin.)
	ashkohkêwa	stays back (when others go on)
stay home	**nesapiwa**	stays home (when others leave)
	nesapiwi	(used for) staying at home (prenoun)
	wîchi-nesapîmêwa	stays home with s.o.
steadily	**âyêniwe, êyêniwe**	steadily, in one place
steal	**kemôtwa**	steals; steals (it)
	kemôtemêwa	steals (it) from s.o.
steal up	**kîmâshkawêwa**	steals up on s.o.
stealthy	**kîmôtesiwa**	is stealthy, secretive
	kîmôtosêwa	walks stealthily
steep	**kîshkâhkiwiwi**	it is a steep hill or mountain
step	**ahpanehkîwa**	steps
	-ahpanehkîwene	(at) a distance of (so many) paces
	âshowanehkîwa	steps over
	âyâwasanehkîwa	goes with bounding strides
	mêmenwikâwosêwa	steps gracefully
	pîsikâwosêhiwa	walks taking short steps
	sesêsikâwosêwa	walks with hurried steps
	wêpikâwosêwa	takes a step, starts walking
	myânanahamîwa	one's step falters
	shîshîhkanahamîwa	walks on tiptoes
	shîshîhkanehkîwa	steps softly
stepchild	**nahpenêwa**	has s.o. as a stepchild
	nahpenâsowa	is a stepchild
	nehpenâsowa	is a stepchild
step on	**ahpishkawêwa, ahpishkamwa**	steps on s.o., it
	ahpishkamawêwa	steps on (it) for s.o.
stick (noun)	**mehtekwi**	tree, wood, stick
	wîkopimishi	basswood tree, stick
	makâhkwatwi	it is a big tree, stick
	mamâkâhkwatôni (plural)	they are big trees, sticks
	peshikwâhkwatwi	it is a straight stick
	pîwêhkenesêwa	picks up small sticks
stick (verb)	**akwamowa, akwamowi**	sticks, sticks on, sticks shut
	kehchîhkawêwa	sticks to s.o., sticks with s.o.
	pasakwishinwa	sticks to {somewhere}, is or gets up against {somewhere} (as, a wall)
	patahkichinwa	is stuck by something sharp
	patashkisêwa, patashkisêwi	(animate, inanimate) falls and sticks
	patashkisahtôwa	throws or slaps it against something to stick
	patashkisetôwa	makes it stick on something
stick in	**pîtehkwênwa**	sticks one's head in
stick out	**sâkishinwa, sâkisenwi**	(animate, inanimate) is sticking out, showing
	keteshkwênwa	sticks out one's head
	keteshkwênotawêwa	sticks out one's head to see s.o.
	sâkinehkêshkêwa	sticks one's arm out into view
	sâkikâshinwa	lies with a foot sticking out
	sâsâkikâshinwa	lies with one's feet sticking out

	sâkikomêshkêwa	sticks one's nose out
	sâkitepêshkêwa	sticks one's head into view
	chîkihtâhpêwa	the nape of one's neck sticks out
	chîkikâpâwa	stands sticking out (as, from the water)
stiff	chîpatesiwa	is stiff
	chîpachisenwi	it is stiff
still	mahkwâchishinwa	lies still
	kehchikâpâwa	stands still
	awiyâtoke	still the same, still the case (particle)
sting	sakahwêwa	stings s.o.
	kâshenamwa	makes it sting or burn by touching it
	kâshamatamwa	has a stinging or burning sensation
	sîsîsi	stingingly, tinglingly (preverb)
stir	anâhamwa	stirs it
	natâhamwa	stirs it up
	natâshêwêhamwa	stirs the coals of the fire
	natâyâpôhamwa	stirs it (as, medicine) together
	ânwishkiwêhamwa	is unable to stir it as a thick mass
	wîkêchihkeshêwênikêwa	carefully stirs the fire
stockade	wâhkâhikani	stockade
stocking	ashikasôni	stocking
stomach	nâmeche	in the stomach (particle)
	papakâshkatêshinwa	lies flat on the stomach
	wîyashkitêhêwa	has an upset stomach
stomp	têhtêweshkamwa	stomps repeatedly (causing vibration)
	têhtêwahkyêshkamwa	is shaking the earth with one's stomping
stone	aseni	stone, rock
	asenya	stone used in sweatbath; rocky precipice
	aseniwiwa, aseniwiwi	(animate, inanimate) is stone
	asenikâni	stone house
	ashkipakâpehkatwi	it is a green stone
	mahkatêwâpehkatwi	it is black stone
stop	nakîwa	stops
	nakîmikatwi	it stops
	nanakîwa	keeps stopping (while walking)
	nakeshkêwa	stops walking, stops changing
	nakisêwa, nakisêwi	stops running; (animate, inanimate) halts suddenly
	nakishinwa	stops, halts
	nakâmowa	stops in flight
	nakinotawêwa	stops for or because of s.o.
	nakenêwa, nakenamwa	stops s.o. (as, to talk to a woman), it
	nakimêwa	stops s.o. by speaking
	pôni	stop, cease, no longer (preverb)
	pônâchimowa	stops talking, stops one's telling or account
	pônâshkêwa	stops falling, stops rushing
	pônenetîwa	stops fighting
	pônenetîhkiwiwi	the fighting stops
	pônepyêwa	quits drinking; no longer drinks
	pônesiwa	stops misbehaving
	pônetonêmowa	stops talking
	pônihtôwa	ceases from it
	pônikahesêwa	stops chopping wood
	pôninechâmêwa	stops taking care of s.o.
	pônitêhêwa	stops worrying, stops being concerned or mentally agitated

	pônwêwêhikêwa	stops drumming
	nahkohwêwa	stops s.o. with a blow
stopper	kepachihikani	stopper, cork (for bottle)
story	âchimôni	story, historical or traditional account
	otâchimôniwa	has a story
	âtesôhkâkana	sacred story, "winter story" (âtesôhkâkâha dimin.)
	âtesôhkêwa	tells a sacred story
	âtesôhkawêwa	tells a sacred story to s.o.
	âtesôhkânêwa	tells a sacred story of s.o.
	âtesôhkâsowa	sacred stories are told of one
	êhkwâchimekosichi	the end of the story about one
	kîshâchimowa	finishes one's story
	sêkâchimowenakatwi	it is a terrifying tale
straddle	pânêshkapihamwa	straddles it
straight	peshikwi	uprightly, honestly, straight (particle, preverb)
	mayâwi	straight, directly, mainly; right in (preverb, prenoun)
	shôshkîwa	goes straight
	êshkamîwa	goes straight (to {somewhere})
	peshikwâchimowa	tells the truth, tells it straight
	pêshikwâpyêwi	it is straight (as, a road or path)
	peshikwênemêwa	thinks s.o. straight
	peshikwisetawêwa	sets (it) straight for s.o.
	shôshkyâwi	it is straight; it is easy, straightforward
	shôshkikiwa, shôshkikenwi	is straight, grows straight; it is straight
	shôshkâhkwapiwa	sits up straight
	shôshkâhkwikâpâwa	stands up straight
	shôshkâmowa	flees on a straight line
	shôshkenêwa, shôshkenamwa	straightens s.o., it
	shôshkikâtêwa	straightens one's leg or legs
	shôshkikâsahowa	kicks one's legs out straight
	shashôshkikâsahowa	kicks one's legs out straight
	shôshkwahâhkwêwa	combs one's hair straight
	shôshkohâhkwêwa	combs one's hair straight
stranded	âtesehkwêshinwa	is stranded on the wrong side of the river or lake
strands	taswâpyêshka	{so many} strands (as, of strung beads) (particle)
strange	mayakikiwa, mayakikenwi	(animate, inanimate) is strange, odd
	mayakihtôwa	does, makes it in a strange way
	mayakechênêwa	finds s.o. strange to the touch
	mayakahômowa	gives a strange cry
	mayakowêwa	says something strange, asks a strange question
	pehkîninâkwatwi	it looks strange
	menâni	strangely, in a weird, unexpected, or inexplicable way; how strange! (particle, preverb)
	menânawiwa	has a strange experience
	namâne	it is strange, unparalleled, unprecedented (particle)
	namânike	it is strange, unprecedented (that) (particle)
strangle	kepinêwênêwa	chokes s.o. with the hands, strangles s.o.
strap	kenahôchikani	prisoner-tie (braided strap for securing war captives)
	kenahôchikanêyâpi	prisoner-tie
	otâpihkâtawêwa	puts a strap on s.o. from {somewhere}
strawberry	ahtêhimini	strawberry
	ahtêhiminehkêwa	picks strawberries
	ahtêhimishi	strawberry vine
stream	anemyâka	downstream, down the line, east (particle)

	âsami	upstream, up the line, west (particle)
	mâtâyâwi	it (a river or stream) joins another river or stream
	nâwakâme	in the middle of the stream or lake (particle)
strength	**nâpyêwêsêwa**	gets one's strength back
stretch	**menesêwa, menehtôwa**	stretches s.o. (as, a hide), it (as, a scalp)
	shîpinawîwa	stretches, stretches out
	shôshkehkêwa	stretches out
strike	**inahamwa**	strikes it {so}
	anematahwêwa	strikes, hits s.o. as one goes along
	nanâtochêhwêwa, **nanâtochêhamwa**	strikes blindly at s.o., it
	pakisatahwêwa	strikes s.o. down, clubs s.o. down
	pakishinwa, pakisenwi	(animate, inanimate) alights, jumps, falls, strikes
	pakatamwa	strikes the post (gives a ritual account of the killing of an enemy)
string	**asapâpi**	string, thread, cord
	asapâpîhi	string, thread, cord (dimin.)
	sôkihchikani	cordage, string, rope
	pîminihkwâni	cordage, string, yarn (collectively)
	pehkochâni	ball of twine
	anemâpyêwi	it (stringlike) extends away
	chahkwâpyêwi	it (stringlike) is short
	shôshkâpyêwi	it (stringlike) is straight
	kîshâpyêsetawêwa	has it strung out for s.o.
	anâhkwênêwa	strings s.o. (a bow)
	anâhkwêsahêwa	quickly strings s.o. (a bow)
striped	**ketakesiwa, ketakyâwi**	(animate, inanimate) is striped, spotted
	ketakikanwi	it (stick, arrow, tail) is striped
	kîshkâpachîkwêwi-mahkatêwesiwa	has black stripes on one's face
stroke	**nâshitepênêwa**	strokes s.o.'s head (once)
	nanâshenêwa	strokes s.o. (repeatedly) on the head, shoulder
	nâshîkwênêwa	strokes s.o.'s face (once)
strong	**mîshkawesiwa, mîshkawâwi**	(animate, inanimate) is strong, has great power or ability
	mîshkawi	powerfully, forcefully, strongly (preverb)
	wîshikesiwa, wîshikyâwi	(animate, inanimate) is strong, has physical strength
	kîkesiwa	has a strong constitution, endurance, stamina
	kîkesîmikatwi	it is strong
	kîkikanêsamwa	makes it strong by heat (as, medicine)
	tôtôwâwi	it is large and strong, massive, sturdy
	mîshkawinâkwatwi	it looks strong
	wîshikanâmowa	breathes hard, pushes hard with one's breath
	wîshikênetamwa	thinks of it strongly, earnestly
	wîshikihtôwa	makes it strong
	wîshikikanêwa	has strength in one's body
	wîshikinawêshkawêwa	(blessing, ceremonial feast) hardens or strengthens s.o.'s bodily constitution or life
	wîshikinawîwa	uses one's strength, makes a powerful effort to move
struggle	**mâkwinawîwa**	struggles hard, puts up a strong resistance
stuck	**anôkîwa**	gets stuck in the mud
	kashkitenwi	it is stuck (in a tight place)
	keshihkisenwi	it is stuck in (as, a knife)
	kîsâchisahtôwa	rams it in and gets it stuck, wedged in
	sanakishinwa	is or gets stuck (as, when unable to proceed or go back while climbing)

stuck in the ground:→ anchored		
stumble	**mehkawishinwa**	stumble
stump	**kîshkitepêhikani**	stump, tree-stump
sturgeon	**namêwa**	sturgeon (archaic)
	nemêwa	sturgeon
substitute	**nâpishinwa**	is a substitute
succeed	**têpi**	succeed in, achieve; sufficiently, as long as (particle, preverb)
	kashkihowa	succeeds (for oneself), is able; succeeds in getting (s.o., it)
	kashkîhkawêwa	manages to deal with s.o., succeeds with s.o.
	kashkitêhamêwa, kashkitêhatamwa	succeeds with s.o., it, succeeds against s.o., is able to persuade s.o.
	têyêpesiwa	leads a completely successful warparty (with scalps or prisoners but no casualties)
	têyêpênemêwa	succeeds in one's desires against s.o.
	têyêpimêwa, têyêpotamwa	succeeds in one's plans against s.o., it
successfully	**pêhki**	really, fully, successfully, easily, earnestly (particle)
suck	**nônôshkatamwa**	sucks it
	sôsôpatamwa	is sucking at it, on it
	ashkâhtamwa	sucks it (water) all up
	sîpwâtamwa	sucks on it (a cupping horn for blood-letting)
sucker	**mêshkwâshakwêha**	red sucker
	mêshkwâshekwêha	red sucker
suddenly	**kokwi**	suddenly (preverb)
suffer	**sîhpwêwa**	suffers
	sîhpwêhêwa	makes s.o. suffer, makes it bad for s.o.
	sîhpwênetamwa	suffers, endures suffering, is in misery
	shîpeshkihêwa	makes s.o. suffer a long time
	kotakesowa	suffers from heat
	kotakênemêwa, kotakênetamwa	knows s.o. to suffer; suffers
	kotakihêwa, kotakihtôwa	makes s.o., it suffer; suffers, has a hard time
	kotakênetamwihêwa	causes s.o. to suffer, is the cause of s.o.'s suffering
	kotakapenêhtôwa owîyawi	makes oneself suffer with hunger
	wîsakamatamwa	suffers pain
	wîsakamachihêwa	causes s.o. pain
sufficiently	**têpi**	sufficiently, as long as; achieve, succeed in (particle, preverb)
sugar	**sîsepâhkwi**	sugar
	sîsepâhkohkêwa	makes maple sugar
	nêkâhikêwa	makes maple syrup into sugar (by heating it and working it with a paddle)
sulk	**metawêwa**	sulks, is resentful
sullen	**âhkwitêhêwa**	is sullen
sumach	**mahkomishi**	sumach
summer	**penâni**	summer, of summer (prenoun)
	penâwi	summer, of summer (prenoun)
	penâwiwi	it is summer, the warm months of the year
	nehkanipenâwe	all summer long (particle)
	nahkanipenâwe	all summer long (particle)
	nekotipenâwe	for one summer (particle)
	penâte	last summer (song word) (particle)
	penâneshiwa	goes on a summer hunt
	pênâneshîhaki (plural)	summer hunting party

	nîpenwi	it is the time when the garden crops are ripe, the middle of summer
sun	**kîsheswa**	sun; moon, month
	kîsheswiwa	is the sun
	kîshesowiwi	it is sunny, the sun is up; it gets the sun
	apâsesowa, apâsiwasowa	suns oneself
	pêmâsikâta	the Sun (participle)
sunfish	**mahkohtawakâha**	sunfish
sunrise	**môhkahanwi**	it is sunrise
sunset	**pakishimowi**	it is sunset
supernatural	**manetôwênemêwa, manetôwênetamwa**	thinks s.o., it supernatural
	manetôwênetâkaniwiwa	is thought a supernatural being
support	**âsônêwa**	supports s.o., helps s.o. stand or walk
	âtâkahâtêwi	it is propped up, held up by a support
	atâhpenamâhkwîwa	pulls on (it) for support
	kehtenamâhkwîwa	holds on tight (for support)
	kekyênenamâhkwîwa	holds on (to it) (for support)
	wîshikenamâhkwîwa	holds on tight (for support)
	pashkonamâhkwîwa	loses one's hold, loses the grip that is supporting one's weight
	nêsawâhi	forked support post of a platform
sure	**mêmêchiki**	I'm sure, one is sure, being sure, positively (particle)
	mêmêchikênemêwa, mêmêchikênetamwa	is sure about s.o., it
	mêmêchikihêwa, mêmêchikihtôwa	makes sure about s.o., it, gets the facts from s.o.
sure enough	**kêhtena**	sure enough (as stated or predicted) (particle)
surface	**môshkakwisêwa, môshkakwisêwi**	(animate, inanimate) comes to the surface
surround	**keposhkawêwa**	surrounds, besieges s.o.
survive	**nêsêwa**	gets well, survives, lives after brush with death, is alive
suspect	**mônênemêwa**	suspects s.o., thinks s.o. likely, thinks one knows about s.o.
	môswênemêwa	is suspicious of s.o., suspects something bad of s.o.
suspenders	**âsôwânakwêpisôni**	suspenders
suspicious	**môshitêhêwa**	is suspicious, suspects something
	masakôchitêhêwa	is suspicious
swallow	**komêwa, kotamwa**	swallows s.o., it
	mesisahêwa, mesisahtôwa	swallows s.o., it whole
swan	**êhêwa**	swan
	êhêwekêwa	dances the Swan Dance
Swan Clan	**wâpesiwisowa**	is a member of the Swan Clan
	êhêwisowa	is a member of the Swan Clan (Jones)
sway	**nânômeshkêwi**	it sways, it rocks back and forth
	nanômâsenwi	it sways in the wind
	nânômâsenwi	it sways in the wind
sweat	**wîshasowa**	feels hot, sweats
	sâkepyêsowa	breaks out into a sweat
	sînepyêkêwa	drips from the effects of dancing
	wîshasokwâmwa	sweats in one's sleep
sweat-bath	**matôteshêwa**	takes a sweat-bath
	matôteshawanêwa	gives s.o. a sweat-bath, treats s.o. with a sweat-bath
sweat-lodge	**matôteshêwikâni**	sweat-lodge
sweep	**chîkakohamwa**	sweeps it
	chîkakohikêwa	sweeps
sweet	**wîshkopenwa, wîshkopanwi**	(animate, inanimate) is sweet, tastes sweet

	wîshkopi	sweet (prenoun)
	wîshkopanohikêwa	sweetens food, uses sugar
	wîshkopanosowa	eats sweet food, has something sweet
	wîshkopisenyâkani	sweet food
sweet flag	**meshinepisôni**	sweet flag, calamus
swell	**makwîtamwa**	has a swelling
	makochêshkêwi	it swells up
	pâseshkêwa, pâseshkêwi	(animate, inanimate) swells up
swim	**pemichimêwa**	swims by
	âshowichimêwa	swims across
	nahichimêwa	knows how to swim
	nôtêchimêwa	gives out in swimming
	anemahokowa	(fish, bird) swims away, off, on
	kîwahokowa	(fish, bird) swims about
	pyêtahokowa	(fish, bird) swims this way
	pemi-tepikîshkahokowaki (plural)	they (fish, birds) swim abreast in an even line
	tashichimêwa	is swimming ({somewhere})
swim underwater	**ahkwanâmowa**	swims {so far} under water
	âshowanâmowa	swims across underwater
	pemanâmowa	swims along or by underwater
	wêpanâmowa	starts swimming underwater
swing	**wêwêpinêwa**	swings s.o. in a swing
	wêwêpisowa	swings, swings oneself
	wêwêpisôni	swing; baby hammock ("baby swing")
	wêwêpakôtêwi	it hangs swinging
	wêpinekwêsêwa	swings one's arm quickly
swing at	**nemahwêwa, nemahamwa**	swings at s.o., it with something as if to strike
swish	**pemisahêwa**	swishes s.o. (as, a skin) in or on the water
sycamore	**kîshowâhkwa**	sycamore
	kîshowâhkowiwa	is a sycamore
syrup	**menêshishi**	maple syrup
	ashkesikêwa	makes maple syrup

t

taboo	**sasâhkwêwa**	is restricted by a taboo, strictly observant; it is taboo for one
	sasâhkwêweniwiwa, sasâhkwêweniwiwi	(animate, inanimate) is subject to taboo, forbidden
tablecloth	**atôhposôni**	feast blanket (used when placing a meal on the ground); tablecloth
	otatôhposôniwetamwa	has it as one's feast blanket or tablecloth
tail	**osowânowi**	a tail; his or her tail
	mesowânowi	a tail
	osowânakwi	a tail; his or her tail
	ahkwânowêwa	has a tail that is {so} long
	chîkânowêwa	holds up one's tail
	kenwânowêwa	has a long tail
	ketakânowêwa	has a striped tail
	kîshkânowêshwêwa	cuts off s.o.'s tail
	kîshkitiyêwa	one's tail is cut off
	sakânowêsahêwa	grabs s.o. by the tail

	sâkânowêkâpâwa	stands with tail in sight
	shôniyâhânowâkani	silver tail
tail-feather	ochiti	tail-feather
	ohkechi	bird's tail, set of tail-feathers
	ketiwikona	golden eagle tail-feather
	ketiwi-ochityêni	golden eagle tail-feathers
	showihkechêshkêwa	spreads one's tail-feathers
take	awanêwa, awatôwa	takes s.o., it away, home
	awahkyêwa	takes someone away, escorts someone to one's home
	awatawêwa	takes (it) away for s.o., takes (it) to s.o.
	awatâkêwa	takes it over (as, to another house)
	atâhpenêwa, atâhpenamwa	takes (hold of) s.o., it, picks s.o., it up
	atâhpehkwênêwa	takes s.o.'s head in one's hands
	atâhpinehkênêwa	takes s.o. by the hand, takes s.o.'s hand
	ishiwenêwa, ishiwetôwa	takes s.o., it to {somewhere}
	ishiwehkyêwa	takes someone to {somewhere}
	anemiwenêwa, anemiwetôwa	takes s.o., it away, leads s.o. off
	anemiwetawêwa	takes (it) away for s.o.
	châkiwetawêwa	takes all of (it) away from s.o.
	têpiwetôwa	takes it all the way
	ketenêwa, ketenamwa	takes s.o., it out, off; doffs it
	ketenamawêwa	takes (it) out for s.o.
	mamenamwa	takes off some of it, takes off a bit of it
	nômenamwa	takes part of it off
	nahkonêwa, nahkonamwa	takes s.o., it in one's hand; accepts s.o., it; catches s.o., it
	nahkonamawêwa	takes (it) in one's hand, accepts (it), catches (it) for s.o.
	nowâwatôwa	takes it outside
	pîtâwanêwa, pîtâwatôwa	takes, puts s.o., it in
	sakinekwênêwa	takes s.o. by the arm
take and leave	pakishiwenêwa, pakishiwetôwa	takes s.o., it {somewhere}; takes s.o., it {somewhere} and leaves them, it, lets them go
take back	petekênemêwa	takes back one's thought, plan, blessing for s.o.
	petekênetamawêwa	takes (it) back for s.o.
	petekyêshihêwa	takes (it) back from s.o.
take care of	pemenêwa, pemenamwa	takes care of s.o., it
	pemenamawêwa	takes care of (it) for s.o.
	pemenetîwaki	they take care of each other
	pemenetisowa	takes care of oneself
	pemeniwêwa	takes care of people
	pemenêweniwiwa	is taken care of
	pemenêweniwêhiwa	is taken care of (dimin.)
	pemenâkaniwiwa	is taken care of
	pemenôshêwa	takes care of a baby, is minding a baby
	nanâhinechâmêwa	takes care of s.o.
	peminechâmêwa	takes care of s.o. on the way
	pôninechâmêwa	stops taking care of s.o.
	tashinechâmêwa	is taking care of s.o.
	nanâhîhkâtisowa	takes care of oneself
	kehchîhkawêwa	takes good care of s.o.
	menwîhkamwa	takes good care of it
take charge	nanâhênemêwa, nanâhênetamwa	tends, controls, takes charge of s.o., it; does as one sees fit with s.o., settles things for s.o.; is in control
take from	ketômyênêwa	takes (it) from s.o.'s back
	ochiwenêwa, ochiwetôwa	takes s.o., it from {somewhere}, from there

take inside	pîtôchâmowa	takes (it) inside of oneself, conceals (it) in one's body
	pîtôchâmêwa	takes s.o. inside of oneself
take out	akwâhwêwa, akwâhamwa	fishes s.o., it out of water, fire (as, with a stick)
	akwâhesowa	ladles some food from the pot for oneself
	akwâpyêhamwa	fishes it out of the water with something, ladles it out of the kettle
	akwâpyêhesowa	ladles some food from the pot for oneself
	môhkenêwa, môhkenamwa	brings or takes s.o., it out, takes s.o., it from a place of concealment or burial
	keteshkinechênêwa	takes (it) out of s.o.'s hands
take part	wîtôhkamwa	takes part in it
take place of	tepishkawêwa	takes s.o.'s place
	nâpishkamawêwa	takes s.o.'s place, stands in for s.o.
take time	otami	taking time, spending time, being busy, occupied, preoccupied (preverb)
	wâwotami	taking the time to, wasting one's time (preverb)
take up	wêpîhkamwihêwa	gets s.o. to take (it) up
	wêpîhkawêwa, wêpîhkamwa	starts on s.o., it, takes it up
talk (relate)	ashkâchimowa	first talks, gives one's first talk
	âmanôwâchimowa	talks about sex
	kenwâchimowa	talks long, gives a long talk
talk (speak)	ahkwânaketonêmowa	ends one's talk or speech
	ahpîhtetonêmowa	talks {so long}
	aniwetonêmowa	talks a lot, speaks well; is a big talker, a good speaker
	inânaketonêmowa	says {so} in talk or speech
	inetonêmowa	talks {so}
	nahânaketonêmowa	is an accomplished speaker
	nahetonêmowa	knows how to talk
	pemetonêmowa	talks going by
	pônetonêmowa	stops talking
	tanânaketonêmowa	engages in talk, is talking
	tanetonêmowa	engages in talk, is talking ({somewhere})
	wêpetonêmowa	starts talking
talk (state)	chachâtapowêwaki	each of them says words
	ênikimêwa	says something funny to s.o., gives s.o. a funny answer
	ênikowêwa	says funny things to people
	inowêwa	speaks to people {so}, talks, declares, states, answers {so}
	menowêwa	says something pleasing
	meshkwîkitêwowêwa	talks annoyingly
	pônimêwa	stops talking to s.o., stops questioning or urging s.o.
	pônowêwa	stops talking, stops discussing
	tashimêwa	talks about s.o., gossips about s.o.
	tanotamwa	talks about it ({somewhere}); says (bad) things about it
	wêpimêwa	begins to talk to s.o.
talk back	nanâhkomêwa	talks back to s.o.
tall	kenôsiwa	is long, tall
	kakânôsiwaki	they (animate) are long, tall
	ahkwanahkesiwa, ahkwanahkatwi	is {so} tall
tallow	ashihkanwi, oshihkanwi	tallow; wax
tame	keshâchinotawêwa	(animal or bird) is tame towards s.o.
	keshâchinohkatawêwa	(animal or bird) is tame towards s.o.
tangled	sasakyâwani	they are tangled (as, the hair [plural])
	sasakânehkwêwa	has curly, kinky, or tangled hair

tan hides	**asêhkêwa**	tans, prepares hides; tans (s.o., as a deerskin)
	asêhkêhtôwa	tans it (as, a bearskin)
	asâwêkisowa	(rawhide) is smoke-cured, tanned
tap	**tâkyênihwêwa**	taps s.o. (as, a drum)
	tâkyênihikêwa	taps the drum
	têhtêwahamwa	taps or thumps repeatedly on it
	têhtêwahikêwa	gives several taps or thumps (with it)
	têhtêwâhkohamwa	taps or thumps repeatedly on it
target of bark	**atôwâha**	wad of bark thrown in the air as a target
	atôwâhiwaki	they have a contest shooting at wads of bark thrown in the air
task	**kîshîhkâtisowa**	finishes doing the task for oneself
	ahpîhchîhkâtisowa	takes {so long} to do the task for oneself
tassel	**atâmini-mîsetonâkanani**	corn tassels
taste	**kotamêwa, kotatamwa**	tastes s.o., it, tries the taste of s.o., it
	ihpokosiwa, ihpokwatwi	(animate, inanimate) tastes {so}
	âhkwihpokwatwi	it tastes sour, strong
	âhkwihpokwatôhiwi	it tastes sour, strong (dimin.)
	myâhpokosiwa, myâhpokwatwi	(animate, inanimate) tastes bad
	myâhpamêwa, myâhpetamwa	dislikes the taste of s.o., it
	nenohpamêwa, nenohpetamwa	recognizes, makes out the taste of s.o., it
	wîkihpwêwa, wîkihpetamwa	likes s.o.'s, its taste
	tâkamêwa, tâkatamwa	tastes s.o., it, gets a taste of s.o., it, gets to eat s.o., it
	wîkamêwa, wîkatamwa	likes s.o.'s, its taste
	wîkenwa, wîkanwi	is good, tastes good
	wîshkopenwa, wîshkopanwi	is sweet, tastes sweet
	nenochêhtamwa	perceives its taste
	tâkamônêwa	allows s.o. a taste of (it)
tasty	**wîkisenyêwa**	finds one's food tasty
tattle-tale	**aniwâchimowa**	says too much, blabs, tells tales, is a tattle-tale
tea	**mashishkiwâpowi**	tea
teach	**kekyêhkimêwa**	teaches s.o.
	kehkinôhamawêwa	teaches s.o., demonstrates (it) to s.o., points (it) out to s.o., shows s.o. how
tear	**tâtwâwi**	it is torn
	tâtonêwa, tâtonamwa	tears s.o., it
	tatâtonêwa, tatâtonamwa	tears s.o. (as, skin), it up, shreds it
	tâtwisahtôwa	tears it quickly
	tâtwikashâtamwa	tears it with one's nail or claw
	châkyâwi	it is all torn, all in tatters
	châkisahtôwa	tears it to pieces
	kîshkenamwa	tears it
	sheshekonêwa, sheshekonamwa	tears s.o., it up
	tâtwineshiwêshinwa	he falls and tears his testicles
tear off	**mamâwakâsenwi**	a chunk of earth is torn off by the wind
	mamamamâwakâsenwi	chunks of earth are torn off by the wind
	mamâwakeshkêwi	a chunk of earth tears away
tears	**nesîsepinîkwâkanani**	my tears
	pâhpakinîkwêkâpâwa	stands shedding tears
	sîsepinîkwêwa	one's eyes are watering, has tears in one's eyes
	sîsepinîkwêkâpâwa	stands with tears in the eyes
	sîkîkwâtamwa	has tears pour from the eyes
tease	**kakâchihêwa**	plays a joke or trick on s.o., teases s.o.
	kakâtwêwa	jokes, teases

	ishawiwêwa	teases s.o. {so}
teasing	kakâchi	"teasing" (of certain relatives) (prenoun)
	nekakâchi-nesekwisa	my "teasing" aunt; my mother's brother's wife
	nekakâchi-nemeshôha	my "teasing" grandfather; my mother's mother's brother and the son of anyone I call this
	kakâtâkômêwa	has s.o. as a "teasing" relative
teenage girl	shêshkesîha	teenage girl, unmarried young woman
	shêshkesîhêha	young teenage girl
	shêshkesîhiwa	is an unmarried teenage girl
	shêshkesîhiwiwa	is an unmarried teenage girl
	oshêshkesîhemiwa	has an unmarried daughter
tell	âchimowa	narrates, reports, tells one's story
	kîwâchimowa	goes around telling, reporting
	âchimohêwa	tells, informs, instructs s.o.
	kashkâchimohêwa	is able to tell s.o., manages to tell s.o.
	âchimohetîwaki	they inform each other
	âchimwihtawêwa	tells (it) for, speaks for s.o.
	âchimêwa, âtotamwa	tells about s.o., it
	âchimekosiwa	is told about
	âchimetisowa	tells about oneself
	âtotâtêwi	it is told of
	inotâtêwi	it is told {so}, it is mentioned {so}, it is planned {so}
	âtotamawêwa	tells of (it) to s.o.
	âtotamâtîwaki	they tell of (it) to each other
	inêwa	tells s.o. (to do) {so}
	inâsowa	is told (to do) {so}
	wîtamawêwa	tells s.o.
	wîtamâtîwaki	they tell each other
	nanâhimêwa	tells s.o. what to do, advises s.o., gives s.o. instructions
	nanâhowêwa	gives instructions, directs others
	ahkwâchimowa	narrates {so far}
	ahkwâchimohêwa	stops telling s.o.
	ahkwâchimêwa, ahkwâtotamwa	tell of s.o., it {so far}
	âhpechimêwa	tells s.o. all the time
	inâchimêweniwiwa	is told of {so}
	inâchimekosiwa, inâchimekwatwi	is told of {so}
	inâchimohêwa	tells, informs s.o. {so}
	inâchimohetîwaki	they inform each other {so}
	âyâhkwâchimêwa	tells on s.o.
	âyâhkwâchimowa	goes and tells everything
	kehtâchimowa	tells everything
	mehtâchimowa	tells plainly, tells the real truth
	matâkwâchimowa	tells an enjoyable, entertaining, or interesting tale
	nîshwâchimowa	tells (of being) as (one of) a pair
	ochimêwa	tells s.o. because of {something}
	pônâchimowa	stops talking, stops one's telling or account
	sâkâchimowa	tells just a little
	sâkâtotamwa	talks about it just a little
	sêkâchimowa	tells a terrifying tale
	tanâchimowa	talks, reports, tells one's story {somewhere} or about what happened {somewhere}; is telling one's story
	tanâchimêwa, tanâtotamwa	tells of s.o., it being {somewhere}
	tanâtotamawêwa	tells s.o. of (it) {somewhere}
temple	otêhtêkwayi	temple (of the head)

	netêhtêkwâki	on my temple
tempt	**âshimêwa**	coaxes, urges, tempts s.o.
	kâchinawêhêwa	tempts or induces s.o. to act
	neshiwanâchitêhêmêwa	tempts to do wrong
	mesawinawêwa, mesawinamwa	is tempted by hunger or desire for s.o., it
	mesawinâkosiwa	looks tempting
ten	**metâswi**	ten (particle)
	metâshiwaki	they are ten, there are ten of them (animate)
	kwichi	ten ("in counting hurriedly"–Jones)
	metâsenwi	ten times (particle)
tenth	**metâsônameki**	tenth, the tenth time (particle)
tend	**menwîhkâtêwi**	it is well taken care of, tended
	nanâhênemêwa, nanâhênetamwa	tends, controls s.o., it
tendon	**ochêpihkyêwâkanani** (plural)	tendons
tent	**papakiwayânikâni**	tent
	pakiwayânikâni	tent
terrain	**inâhkiwiwi**	(elevated land) extends or slopes {so}
terrible	**kîshâkotesiwa**	is in a terrible state (of grief, fear), is excited, is desperate; it's hard on one
	kîshâkochihtôwa	does terrible things to it
	kîshâkochinawêhêwa	makes s.o. feel terrible
	neshiwi	terribly, to an extreme degree (particle, preverb)
	neshîwi	terribly, to an extreme degree (particle, preverb) (younger form)
	neshiwinâkosiwa, neshiwinâkwatwi	(animate, inanimate) looks terrible, awful, fierce
	neshiwâpamêwa	sees s.o. as something terrible
	neshiwanâchîhkâsowa	does something terrible, wicked, destructive
terrier	**wîsakitîha**	terrier
	wîsakitîhêha	terrier (dimin.)
terrific	**ananeshiwi**	terrific; awful (particle)
	aneneshiwi	terrific; awful (particle)
	naneshiwi	terrific; awful (particle)
	neneshiwi	terrific; awful (particle)
terror	**wîyatâwêwêkesiwa**	screams in terror, screams bloody murder
test	**kochihêwa, kochihtôwa**	tries to make, tries, tests s.o., it
testicle	**oneshiwahi**	his testicles
	meneshiwaki	testicles
	keki-oneshiwe	including the testicles (particle compound)
	tâtwineshiwêshinwa	he falls and tears his testicles
that	**îna, îni**	that, that one (animate, inanimate)
	îni ishi	that way, like that
	îniya, îniye	that (past, absent, previous, going away; animate, inanimate)
	înâka, înâmani	that (yonder, invisible; animate, inanimate)
	mâhiya, mâhiye	that (recently present, recently mentioned, going away; animate, inanimate)
	anikânâka, anikâne	that (further away; animate, inanimate)
that way	**kwayêshi**	that way, if that is done (particle)
thaw	**shahkanwi**	there is a thaw
	âpaweshkêwa	thaws out
the idea	**napahki**	the very idea of it! the idea (that)! (particle)
then	**îni**	then, now
	ôni	and, then

	kahôni	and then, so then (particle)
	kôni	and then, so then (younger form) (particle)
	achâhmeko	then, only then, for the first time, for the first time in a long time (particle)
	châhmeko	then, only then, for the first time (in a long time) (particle)
	nahi!	well then!, listen up!
there	înahi	there
	îtepi	(to) there (goal), thither (particle)
	îyâhi	(to) there (ending point) (particle)
	îyâmâhi	over there, at that other place or future time
	înâmâhi	way over there, at that distant place or time
	anikânâhi	yonder, there (further away, further on)
they	wînwâwa	they (emphatic or contrastive)
they say	=ipi (=ipihi)	they say, it is said, supposedly, you're supposed to, let's say
thick	kehpakesiwa	is thick of skin
	kehpakyâwi	it is thick
	makinehpâkwêkiwa	(ice) is thick
	makinehpâkwêkenwi	it has thick walls
thicket	sasakanwi	it is a thicket, thick underbrush
	nâwi-sasakanwe	in the middle of the thicket (particle compound)
	sêsakaki	a thicket (participle)
	pîkwâwi	there is a thicket
	nâwi-pîkwâwe	in the middle of a thicket (particle compound)
thigh	nepwâmi	my thigh
	mepwâmi	a thigh
	âpehtawipwâme	halfway up the thigh (or thighs) (particle)
	mamâkipwâmêwa	has big thighs
	wâwâkapayêwa	is bow-legged (literally, has bent thigh-bones)
thimble	kêpyâhi	thimble
thin	papakêhenwi	it is thin
	papakêhimotêwa	one's belly has thin skin
	papakêhimotêshinwa	one's belly has thin skin as one lies
	papakêhinechêwa	one's hands have thin skin
think	nenehkitêhêwa	thinks
	ishitêhêwa	thinks {so}
	ahkwênemêwa	thinks of s.o. {so far}
	ahpîhtênemêwa, ahpîhtênetamwa	thinks {so much} of s.o., it
	aniwênemêwa	thinks much of s.o.
	atenâwênemêwa	thinks less of s.o.
	ânawênetamwa	thinks it is not enough, gives up on it; gives up hope
	âhkwênemêwa, âhkwênetamwa	thinks a great deal of s.o., it
	ânawênemêwa	thinks s.o. is inadequate, assumes s.o. is not up to it, gives up on s.o., does not have faith in s.o., purposely leaves s.o. out
	âwênemêwa	thinks it is s.o., thinks s.o. is it
	inênekêmowa	has {such} thoughts or feelings towards people
	inênemêwa, inênetamwa	thinks {so} of s.o., it
	inênetamawêwa	thinks of (it) for s.o. {so}
	inênetâkosiwa	is thought of {so}
	inênetîwaki	they think {so} of each other
	inênetisowa	thinks {so} of oneself
	ishitêhâtamwa, ishitêhatamwa	thinks of it {so}
	ishitêhênawêsiwa	it comes into one's heart to think {so}
	ishitêhêpiwa	sits thinking {so}

	keshâtênetîwaki	they think kindly of each other
	kêkôhênemêwa	(with negative:) thinks nothing of s.o., thinks s.o. worth nothing
	kêkôhênetâkosiwa	(with negative:) is considered nothing, is not respected
	mîhkemehkwêwêwitêhêwa	he thinks of courting a woman
	mîhketîwitêhêwa	he thinks of courting
	mînâwênetâkwatwi	it is thought of seriously, given close consideration
	nehtômapiwa	sits pensively, sits alone with one's thoughts
	nepôwênemêwa	thinks s.o. is dead
	neshiwanâtênetâkosiwa	is considered worthless, good-for-nothing
	nîsênetamwa	imagines it descending
	pakamênemêwa	thinks s.o. has arrived
	pâsitawênemêwa, pâsitawênetamwa	is thinking about s.o., it all the time
	peshekênemêwa, peshekênetamwa	thinks s.o., it cute
	peshikênetamwa	thinks it cute
	pînesênetisowa	thinks of oneself spontaneously
	pînênemêwa, pînênetamwa	thinks s.o., it clean
	pônênemêwa, pônênetamwa	stops thinking of s.o., it
	sanakênemêwa, sanakênetamwa	thinks s.o., it difficult, hard to get; gives s.o. a difficult blessing
	sanakênemâsowa	is thought hard to get
	tanênemêwa, tanênetamwa	expects s.o., it; thinks s.o., it is {somewhere}
	tashitêhêwa	expects, is expecting; is thinking; one's thoughts are {somewhere}
	wâpasênemêwa, wâpasênetamwa	thinks lightly, sportively of s.o., it
	wapasênetamwa	thinks lightly, sportively of it
	wâpanwitêhêshinwa	lies thinking until dawn
	wâwaneshkâhênemêwa	thinks s.o. wicked
	wâwaneshkâhênetâkaniwiwa	is thought wicked
	wînênetamwa	thinks it dirty
	wîshâpenêwênemêwa	thinks s.o. is hungry
think about	nenehkênemêwa, nenehkênetamwa	thinks of s.o., it, about s.o., it
	nenehkênetamawêwa	thinks about (it) for s.o.
	nenehkênetamâtisowa	thinks about (it) for oneself
	nenehkênetâkosiwa	is thought about
	nenehkênetîwaki	they think about each other
	nenehkênetisowa	about oneself
think back	wâpanênemêwa	(departing soul) thinks back about s.o. (ritual)
think ill of	ânwênemêwa	thinks ill of s.o., disapproves of s.o., dislikes what s.o. does
	ânwênetâkosiwa	is thought ill of, disapproved of
third	nêsônameki	third, the third time (particle)
thirsty	pêkwitêhêwa	is thirsty
thirteen	neswinesiwe	thirteen (particle)
	neswinîsiwe	thirteen (particle)
	metâswi-neswi	thirteen (particle compound)
	metâswi-neswinesiwe	thirteen (particle compound)
	metâswi-neswinîsiwe	thirteen (particle compound)
thirty	neswâpitaki	thirty (particle)
this	mana	this (animate) (plural **mâhaki**)
	mani	this (inanimate) (plural **mâhani**); consider this (as follows)
	îyâka, îyâmani	this other one (visible; animate, inanimate)

this side	**atâhi-'shi**	on this side; since then, after that
this way	**atânahka**	over this way; come over this way (particle)
	atânahka='shi	this way, towards here; since then; come over here
thong	**pîshâkâhi**	buckskin thong
thorn	**âhkwikomâchiki** (plural participle)	sharp thorns
though	**kakatâni**	even though, even in that case, the reverse of what would be expected; it will be good (particle)
	mehtôchi	like, as it were, as though (particle)
	=wîna	however, but, though you may not think so
thought	**ishitêhâkani**	thought, plan
	oteshitêhâkaniwa	has a thought
	ishitêhêweni	thought, desire
	inênechikani	thought, blessing
	menwitêhâkani	good thoughts
	wâwaneshkâhitêhâkani	wicked thought
	ahkwitêhêwa	one's thought goes {so far}
	inênemêweniwiwa	is the subject of {such} thought
	inênetâkaniwiwa	is the subject of {such} thought
	nahkwitêhamêwa	readily accepts s.o.'s opinion, wish, or blessing
	nahkwitêhêmêwa	readily accepts s.o.'s opinion, wish, or blessing
	nanâhitêhênêwa	directs s.o.'s thoughts
	wîchitêhamêwa	is with s.o. in thought, helps s.o. with their plan or intention
	wîchitêhêmêwa	is with s.o. in thought, helps s.o. with their plan or intention
thousand	**metâswâhkwe**	one thousand (literally, ten hundred) (particle)
	-mahkahkwe	(so many) thousand (in particle compounds)
	nyêwi-mahkahkwe	four thousand (particle compound)
thrash around	**tanenekowa**	thrashes around, fools around, is occupied doing something ({somewhere})
three	**neswi**	three (particle, preparticle)
	neswi	all three together (preverb)
	chêyêneswi	all three (particle)
	neswihêwa, neswihtôwa	has, gets three of them (animate, inanimate)
	nesiwaki, nesenôni	they (animate, inanimate) are three, there are three of them
	nesokoni	three days (particle)
	nesokonakesiwa, nesokonakatwi	is three days old; it is three days
	nesôpiwaki	they sit three together
	nesôshinôki	they lie three together
	nesôhokowaki	they (as, fish) swim three together
	neswawahîme, neswawahîne	three years (particle)
	neswayaki	three kinds, ways, sets, pairs (particle)
	neswâhkwe	three hundred (particle)
	neswâpitaki	thirty (particle)
	neswâpyêki	three portions (particle)
throat	**okotâkani**	his or her throat; throat
	nenakahkwi	the back of my mouth
	wîsakinakahkwêwachiwa	one's throat aches from being cold
through	**shîpâyôtêwa**	crawls through and out the other side
	tahpi	through (preverb) (see **-nepwêwa, -wâsêyâpôkatwi**)
	tahpâpatâniwi	it can be seen through; (with negative:) there is no visibility (as, in a snowstorm)
	tahpehkwamye	through the ice surface (particle)
	tahpinawapahkwe	through the wall of the lodge (particle)
throw	**wêpâhkêwa**	throws (it)

	inâhkêwa	throws (it) to {somewhere}
	awatâhkawêwa	throws (it) over to s.o.
	pyêtâhkawêwa	throws (it) to s.o.
	nenyêshkwâhkêwa	throws (it) in every direction
	nîmêyâhkêwa	throws (it) aloft
	nîsâhkêwa	throws (it) down
	nowâhkêwa	throws (it) out
	chapôkisahêwa, chapôkisahtôwa	throws s.o., it into the water
	pôchisahêwa, pôchisahtôwa	throws s.o., it into a container or vertical hole
	shekisahowa	throws oneself down
throw away	pakinêwa, pakitamwa	sets s.o., it down; throws s.o., it away; divorces s.o.
	pakitamawêwa	throws (it) down for s.o.
	pakisahwêwa, pakisahamwa	throws s.o., it out, headlong
throwing-stick	meshkwêhpîha	throwing-stick (thrown on the ground or snow in a distance contest)
thumb	kehchinechi	thumb
thump	anwêwêtepêhwêwa	thumps s.o. on the head
	têhtêwahamwa	taps or thumps repeatedly on it
thunder	wêpwêwêkesiwaki nenemehkiwaki	there is thunder ("the thunderers begin to be heard")
	pyêtwêwêkatwi nenemehkiwaki	there is thunder ("the sound of the thunderers is coming")
	pâhpâhketonôki nenemehkiwaki	there is thunder and lightning ("the thunderers are opening their mouths")
Thunder Clan	wêmîkôha	member of the Thunder Clan
	wêmîkôhisowa	is a member of the Thunder Clan
	wêmîkôhisota	member of the Thunder Clan
	chîkwêsota	member of the Thunder Clan
thunderer	nenemehkiwa	thunderer, thunder being
	chîkwêwa	thunderer, thunder being
tickle	kenîkesiwa	is ticklish
	kenîkihpanêshkawêwa	tickles s.o.'s throat
tidy (verb)	wîkêtenêwa, wîkêtenamwa	tidies it up
	wîkêchinâkwihtôwa	fixes it up to look better
tie	sôkihêwa, sôkihtôwa	ties, binds s.o., it
	sôkihchikêwa	ties things
	sôkihtawêwa	ties (it) for s.o.
	sôkisowa, sôkihtêwi	(animate, inanimate) is tied
	akwâhkwapinêwa, akwâhkwapitôwa	ties s.o., it to, against
	akwâhkwapisowa, akwâhkwapitêwi	is tied to, against
	asipapitôwa	ties them (inanimate) in a bunch
	asipôhkwêpinêwa	ties their necks together
	ashitâhkwapisowa	is tied to something (as, a tree or post)
	âtesapitêwi	it is tied separately
	âyachîtapinêwa, âyachîtapitôwa	ties s.o., it securely
	âyachîtapisowa, âyachîtapitêwi	(animate, inanimate) is tied securely
	ihpinêwa, ihpitôwa	ties s.o., it {so}
	ihpisowa, ihpitêwi	(animate, inanimate) is tied {so}
	inapinêwa, inapitôwa	ties s.o., it {so}
	kehkichikenêpinêwa	ties (it) around s.o.'s forehead
	kehkichitepêpinêwa	ties (it) around s.o.'s head
	kekyênapinêwa	ties s.o. fast
	kîshapinêwa, kîshapitôwa	finishes tying s.o., it
	kîshâkotapisowa, kîshâkotapitêwi	(animate, inanimate) is very tightly bound

370

	matakwapitôwa	ties it covering
	nanâhapinêwa, nanâhapitôwa	ties s.o., it up
	nanâhapitawêwa	ties (it) for s.o.
	nanâhâpyênamwa	gets it ready to tie, loops it
	nîshôpinêwa, nîshôpitôwa	ties the two of them (animate, inanimate) together
	nyêwôpitêwani	they (inanimate) are tied four together
	patashkapitêwi	it is tied on, it is tied to the outside
	pehkwapinêwa, pehkwapitôwa	ties s.o., it in a bundle; has s.o., it tied in a bundle
	pehkwapitawêwa	ties (it) into a bundle for s.o.
	pehkwapisowa, pehkwapitêwi	(animate, inanimate) is tied in a bundle
	pepyêtekwapinêwa	hogties s.o.
	sakapinêwa, sakapitôwa	ties s.o., it fast
	sakapisowa, sakapitêwi	(animate, inanimate) is tied securely, is tied up
	sakapichikêwa	ties up one's horse
	sakikâpinêwa, sakikâpitôwa	ties s.o., it by the leg
	sakikwêpinêwa	ties s.o. by the neck
	sakikwêpisowa	is tied by or around the neck; ties oneself by the neck
	shâshâshakinekwêpinêwa	ties s.o.'s arms together behind them
	takwapitôwa	ties it together
	tahtakwapinêwa, tahtakwapitôwa	ties them (animate, inanimate) together
	wîkêtapinêwa, wîkêtapitôwa	ties s.o., it carefully
	wîshikapinêwa, wîshikapitôwa	ties s.o., it tight
	pyêmachinowa	she has (it, as a blanket or shawl) folded up and tied around her waist
tiers	**pîhtôkenwi**	it is in tiers, layers
tight	**sanakishinwa**	is in a tight place
tighten	**anahôtâsowa**	(drum) has its drumhead tightened
time	**nâhinâhi**	(at) the time, distance; (it is) the first time (particle)
	îninâhi	at that time; by now (particle)
	îninâhiwiwi	it is that time
	menwinâhi	(it is) the right time, a good time (particle)
	mêmechinêhi	for the last time (particle)
	âhpechi	all the time, permanently, for good (particle, preverb)
	âyashkachi	at long intervals, not too often (particle)
	nêsônameki	third, the third time (particle)
	nehki	for {so} long a time, as long as {such time} (particle)
	îni-nehki	for that long a time
	tepinehki	for the right length of time, for quite a while (particle)
	tepinehkîhi	for the right length of time, for quite a while (dimin.) (particle)
	têpi-nâhinâhi	for long enough, far enough (particle compound)
	ashitahi	(with negative:) not for a long time (particle)
	mêh-otehchîkwe	in no time at all (prioritive verb)
	mêh-otehtahkiwikwe	in no time at all (prioritive verb)
	ahtêwi	there is a time (when), there are times (when)
	memênawishinwa	has time
	tanahwêwesiwa	spends one's time {somewhere}
	pyêsehkêwi	the time (for it) comes
	îye	once upon a time, in the past (particle)
	îyêmêhi	a little while back (particle)
	wêwîtepi	for a while (particle)
	nesenwi	three times (particle)
	nyêwenwi	four times (particle)
	metâsenwi	ten times (particle)

	nîshwâpitakenwi	twenty times (particle)
	kêsenwi	how many times? (particle)
	nâhtasenwi	a few times (particle)
tingle	sayâwihêwa	makes s.o. tingle, shudder, or be ruffled
	sayâwinawêhêwa	makes s.o. tingle (as, with fear or pleasure)
	sayâwinawêshkêwa	a tingling sensation comes over one
	sayâwamatamwa	feels a tingling sensation, has chills up one's spine
	sayasayâwanasitêwa	feels a tingling in the soles of one's feet
	sayâwinechêshkêwa	gets a tingling sensation in one's hand or hands
tiny	papîweshîhiwaki	they (animate) are tiny
	papîwâhenôhiwi	it is tiny
	papîsikashêwi	(of) tiny hoof (prenoun)
tip (noun)	tashikomêsetôwa	dips its tip (as, of an arrow) {somewhere}
tip (verb)	achitawenamwa	tips it up (as, to drink from it)
tip over	kôhkâhanwi	it tipped over (in the water), was overset
	kôhkâsahêwa	tips s.o. over
	kîpeshkamwa	tips it over by foot
tiptoe	shîshîhkanahamîwa	walks on tiptoes
tired	ayîhkwiwa	is tired, weary
	ayîhkwihêwa	tires s.o.
	ayîhkwapiwa	is tired of sitting
	ashkapiwa	is tired of sitting
	ayîhkwinehkêhokowa	one's arms get tired from one's load
	pîshkyêwêwa	one's muscles become tired, cramped
tired of	pîshkênemêwa, pîshkênetamwa	is or gets tired of s.o., it
	pîshkatamwa	is or gets tired of eating or drinking it
toad	mamahkêha	toad
tobacco	asêmâwa, nesêmâwa	tobacco
	onesêmâwiwa	has tobacco
	nenôtêwîha	Indian tobacco
	anenôtêwîha	Indian tobacco (archaic)
	âhkonêwa	Indian tobacco
	wâhkonêwa	Indian tobacco (less common)
	pahkinesêmâwêwa	plucks tobacco leaves
tobacco pouch	ahpwâkanimôha	tobacco pouch
	ahpwâkanimotêha	tobacco pouch
	otôhpwâkanimotêhiwa	has a tobacco pouch, has (it) as a tobacco pouch
toe	nîsîpanasitâkani	toe (**kenîsîpanasitâkanani** your toes)
	ashkwênasichi	little toe
	kehtanasichi	big toe
together	takwi	both or all together, at the same time, along with (it, etc.) (particle, preverb)
	tahtakwi	all together, collectively (particle, preverb); collective (prenoun)
	têyêhtakwi	all together, in general (particle)
	tahtakoshkêwaki	they (animate) flock together
	tahtakôhpowaki	they all eat together
	tahtakwapinêwa, tahtakwapitôwa	ties them (animate, inanimate) together
	tahtakwihtôwaki	they make it together
	tahtakwikwamwa	sews them (inanimate) together, sews (it) to it
	tahtakwikwâtêwani	they (inanimate) are sewn together
	tahtakwisahêwa	shoves them (animate) together
	tahtakwisetôwa	places it, them (inanimate) together
	tahtakwîwaki	they (animate) go together

	mesôtêwi	all together, universally (particle, preverb)
	asipi	all together (preverb)
	tâpônamwa	puts it or them together double (as, folding a blanket)
	tâpôpinêwa	wraps the two of them (animate, as hides) together
together with	wîchi	together with, joining with (preverb, particle)
	wîchi-nesapîmêwa	stays home with s.o.
Tohkan	tohkâna	Tohkan, member of the Tohkan division
	tohkâniwiwa	is a Tohkan
	tohkânihkwêwa	Tohkan woman
	oshkasha	Tohkan (archaic; also Sauk dialect)
	oshkashiwiwa	is a Tohkan (archaic; also Sauk dialect)
toilet	sâkichîwa	goes out; goes to the toilet
tomorrow	wâpake	tomorrow (subjunctive verb)
	wâpaki	the next day (in the past) (changed conjunct verb)
	âwasi-wâpake	the day after tomorrow (subjunctive verb)
tongue	nînaniwi	my tongue
	owînaniwi	his or her tongue; a tongue
	sâkinaniwêsêwa	sticks out one's tongue
	sâkinaniwêhtawêwa	sticks out one's tongue at s.o.
too	êyîki	and, also, too (particle)
	nêhi, =nêhi	too (particle and enclitic)
too far	kwêhkwêwi	going too far (particle, preverb)
	wênôchinawêmêwa	(with or without negative:) goes too far and upsets s.o. with what one says
	kwayânâhkêwa	throws (it) too far
too much	asâmi	too much (preverb, particle); certainly! (particle)
	asâmehkâchi	too much (preverb)
	nônenamwa	picks it up and has nowhere to put it
tool	ayôweni	tool
	otayôweniwa	has a tool
tooth	owîpichi	his or her tooth; a tooth
	owîpichiwa	has teeth
	kakânwâpitêwa	has long teeth
	mamâkâpitêwa	has big teeth
	mehtâpitêwa	bares one's teeth, one's teeth are exposed
	memyêshkâpitêwa	has irregular teeth
	meshkwanwîwa	has no teeth, has only bare gums
	pînâpitêwa	has a good set of teeth
	pîsâpitêhiwa	has little teeth
	nîshkâpitêshkêwa	bares one's teeth
	papahkwâpitêhwêwa	knocks s.o.'s teeth out
	pyêtwêyâpitêsêwa	the snapping of one's teeth can be heard approaching
toothache	môsêhkêwa	has a toothache
top (on top)	ahkwichi	on top (particle, preparticle)
	ahkwichitasane	on top of the platform (particle)
	ahkwichitepe	on top of the head (particle)
	âyâpyêchi	on top of everything else, going so fas as to (particle)
top (toy)	tôpahiyâha	top (spun as a toy)
	nîmihchîha	whip top (spun with a small whip)
top end	pyêtanahkeshkamwa	comes out the top end of it
	pyêtanahkikâpâwi	it (tree) stands with its top inclined this way
torment	pekishkihêwa	pesters s.o., torments s.o.
	pekishkimêwa	pesters s.o., troubles s.o. by speech
touch	mêshenêwa, mêshenamwa	touches s.o., it

	mêshehkawêwa, mêshehkamwa	touches s.o., it by foot or body; infects s.o., it
	mêsheshkawêwa	touches s.o. by foot or body
	mêshinawâtîwaki	they come into contact with each other, their bodies touch
	mêshinehkênêwa	touches s.o.'s hand
	mêshisêwi	it touches
	mêshîsêwi	it touches the ground
	mehkochênamwa	finds it by touch
	sahkenamwa	touches the tip to it; puts pen to paper
	tâkahwêwa	touches s.o., taps s.o.
	tâkatamwa	touches it in eating
	tâkenêwa	touches s.o.
	tâkeshkamwa	touches it with one's foot
	tâkichinwa	is touched or brushed by something (as one passes)
	tâkitepênêwa	touches s.o. on the head
	tâkâhkwêhamwa	touches it with a stick
town: → village		
toy	**tashîhkânoweni**	toy
tracks	**pemihkawêwa**	has left tracks, footprints
	ahkwihkawêwa	one's tracks go {so far}, one's tracks end
	anemikâshinwa	one's footprints can be seen continuing on
	kehkanasitêkâpâwa	there are marks from s.o.'s feet where they stood
	keshihkihkawêwa	one's tracks are deep, clear
	pîchihkawêwa	one's tracks go in
	wêpihkawêwa	one's tracks begin
	ahkawihêwa	is on s.o.'s tracks, comes upon s.o.'s tracks
	natwihkawêhêwa	looks for s.o.'s tracks
	wâpachihkawêhêwa	looks for s.o.'s tracks, follows s.o.'s tracks
	wâpachihkawêhchikêwa	looks for tracks
trade	**âshitônikêwa**	trades
	âshitônikawêwa	trades with s.o.
	atâwêneniwa	trader
train (noun)	**êshkotêwîhi**	railroad train; steam boat
	kênwâpihkâtêhi	freight train
	kîweshkêwîhi	passenger train
train (verb)	**nakachihêwa**	trains s.o. (an animal) to follow commands
trample	**châkeshkâtêwi**	it is trampled up
transform	**kohkikiwa**	is transformed, changes one's bodily form
	kohkinâkwihowa	transforms oneself
	kohkikihônowa	transforms oneself
	kênwâsowêwikihônowa	transforms oneself into a mountain lion
	mehtosêneniwikihônowa	transforms oneself into a human being
trap	**takwahônêwa**	traps s.o., catches s.o. in a deadfall, runs s.o. over
	takwahôtôwa	is trapping
	takwahôtawêwa	is trapping for s.o.
	takwahôchîhi	trap
	takwahôsowa	is caught in a trap or deadfall; is run over, crushed
	nekwâpichikêwa	catches something in a trap, snare, spiderweb
	tesôtawêwa	sets a trap for s.o. (archaic; /t/ rather than /ht/ conjectured)
	tesôsowa	is caught in a trap (archaic)
	tesôchîhi	trap (archaic)
	pîyâpehkwîhi	metal trap
	nîsamôhi	deadfall trap
	nâtahâpyêwa	he checks his traps

	kepânakwêshkawêwa	gets s.o. trapped, has s.o. trapped in a hole
travel	kîweshkêwa	travels, goes on a journey
	keshikîwa	travels rapidly, goes without delay
	otehkêwa	travels for {some} reason
tread	ahpanasitêwosêwa	treads on (it) as one walks
tree	mehtekwi	tree, wood, stick
	mehtekôhi	little tree
	meshiwâhkwa	dead fallen tree
	makâhkwatwi	it is a large tree
	mamâkâhkwatôni (plural)	they are large trees or sticks
	inâhkowiwa, inâhkowiwi	(animate, inanimate) is {such} a tree
	ketowênêhâhkowi	what kind of tree are you? (see: **owênêhâhkowiwa**)
	pehkwâhkwâwi	grove of trees
	âpehtawâhkwe	half the height of a tree (particle)
	chîkâhkwe	next to a tree (particle)
tremble	nenekesiwa	is trembling
	nenekeshkêwi	it trembles, quakes
	nenekapisowa	trembles, is shaking
	nenekashkahamwa	one's voice trembles
	nenekitêhêshkêwa	one's heart trembles
	nenekyêwêshkêwa	is trembling all over
	nenekâpôshkêwi	its water trembles
	nenekepyêyâwi	its water trembles
	pahkihtêshkêwa	vomits and retches to death; trembles to death
	pîkêshkêwa	vomits and retches to death; trembles to death
trick	pâhpiweni	trick
	ishiwêpiyôhkawêwa	tricks s.o. into doing {so}
trigger	nasenamwa	pulls its trigger
	nasahtêwa	releases the bow, pulls the trigger
trim	shâshâkwikiwa	has a trim body
trip	pechikâchinwa	trips on something
	pechikâshinwa	trips and falls
trouble	memyêshkihêwa	makes trouble for s.o.
	memyêshkênemêwa	plans trouble for s.o., makes things rough for s.o.
	meshihtâwihêwa	gets s.o. in trouble, causes trouble for s.o.
	meshihtâwimêwa	gets s.o. in trouble by what one says'
	pekishkyâwi	it is troublesome, tiresome
	pekishkinawêhêwa	makes s.o. feel troubled
	pekishkênetamwa	thinks it troublesome, too much trouble
	pekishkitêhêwa	is troubled
	pekishkîhkâtîwaki	they quarrel, make trouble for each other
true	kêhtena	truly, sure enough (as stated or predicted); it is true (particle)
	kêhtenâhiwi	it is true
	kêhtenâhênetamwa	thinks it true
	têpimêwa	says what is true about s.o.
	têpwêwa	speaks the truth; one's prayer or request is granted
	têpwêmikatwi	it is true
trust	ahpênemowa	relies on (it), places trust in (it)
try	kochi	try to, try and (preverb)
	kokwêchi	try to, practice (preverb)
	kochawiwa	tries
	kochîhkawêwa	tries to consort with s.o., tries to persuade s.o., tries to help s.o.
	kochisahowa	tries to jump; ventures to ask (to court or marry)

	kokwêchisêwa	tries to fly
	natawi	seek to, try to, expect to, plan to; it's time to (preverb)
	natawihêwa	tries to get s.o. (to), sounds s.o. out (for something)
	ayîkwâmi	with best effort, trying one's best (preverb)
	ayîkwâmîwa	does one's utmost, tries one's best
	wîshâshinwa	tries one's level best (to), is anxious (to)
try (in court)	**tepitîwa**	stands trial
	tepitîhêwa	tries s.o. (in court)
tuberculosis	**ashihpanêwa**	has tuberculosis ("consumption")
tuck	**peshkikwâtamwa**	takes a tuck in it (sewing)
turkey	**penêwa**	turkey
	penêhkêwa	hunts turkeys
	penêhkawêwa	hunts turkeys for s.o.
	penêmowa	imitates the call of a turkey
turkey vulture	**wînâkêwa**	turkey vulture ("buzzard")
	tahowêha	turkey vulture ("buzzard") (archaic)
turn (in turn)	**pyêteshitêwi**	it comes in its turn
	âshita, âshitami	in turn, in return (particle)
turn around	**kohkîwa**	turns around
	kohkapiwa	turns around in one's seat
	kohkikâpâwa	turns around standing
	kohkinawîwa	turns around
	kokwênepechêhamwa	turns it around and around or over and over with something
turn aside	**pahkêwa**	separates, goes off a different way, turns aside, gets off the road
turn back	**kîwêwa**	turns back
	kîwêpahowa	runs back
turn loose	**pakisâhkwimêwa**	declares s.o. free, turns s.o. loose
turn off	**wâkîwa**	turns off, turns in, veers off (does not keep going straight)
turn out	**=chîhi**	it turned out, was seen, was discovered
	keyêhapa	in fact, as it turns out (particle)
	=yêhapa	in fact, as it turns out
turn over	**kohkenamwa**	turns it over
	kohkahamwa	turns it over by tool
	âpôshkechênamwa	turns it over
	âpôshkechêsahêwa	flips s.o. over
turtle	**mahkwâhkêha**	mud turtle
	meshihkêha	snapping-turtle
	meshihkenâhkwa	snapping-turtle (archaic)
	papahkîha	soft-shell turtle
	ohkenâhkwaya, ohkenâhkwa	turtle-shell
twang	**anwêwêhwêwa**	twangs s.o. (bow)
twelve	**nîshwinîsiwe**	twelve (particle)
	nîshwinîsiwi	twelve (particle)
	nîshwinîsiwa	is twelve years old
twenty	**nîshwâpitaki**	twenty (particle)
twice	**nîshenwi**	twice (particle)
twig	**kepiwi**	twig, small piece of brushwood (Jones also "osier stem")
	kepîhi	little twig
twins	**nîshôtêhaki**	twins
	nîshôtêhehkêwa	she has, gives birth to twins
	nîshôtêhiwa	is a twin
twist	**pyêmenamawêwa**	twists (it) sideways for s.o.

	pyêmîkwêwa	one's face is twisted
	pyêmikopyêhamwa	twists and tightens it (as, a rope) with a stick
	pyêmishkwikanwi	it is twisted (as, a vine)
	pyêmishkwisêwa	runs twisting and turning
	pyêmishkwâshkêwa	runs twisting and turning
	pyêmishkwitôtanêsêwa	sprains the ankle (literally, twists the heel)
	tetepishkenamwa	twists it, makes a twist of it
two	**nîshwi**	two (particle, preparticle)
	nîshwi	as a pair, both together (preverb)
	nîshiwaki, nîshenôni	they (animate, inanimate) are two, there are two of them; they join up together
	nîshîhiwaki, nîshenôhiwani	they (animate, inanimate) are two, there are two of them (dimin.)
	nîshwihêwa, nîshwihtôwa	has, gets two of them (anim., inan.)
	nîshokonakatwi	it is two days
	nîshôchêhpwêwa	holds or carries two of them together in one's mouth
	nîshôkenôni	they (inanimate) grow together, as a pair
	nîshôkêwa (1)	dances together, dances with (s.o.) as a couple
	nîshôkêwaki (2) (plural)	they dwell together as a pair
	nîshôkêhiwaki	just the two of them dwell together (dimin.)
	nîshônêwaki, nîshônamôki	the two of them together picked s.o., it up, carried s.o., it
	nîshôsetôwa	places two of them (inanimate) together, jointly places it
	nîshôkâpawihêwa	makes the two of them (anim.) stand together
	nîshwêwêmêwa	scolds them both together
	nîshwimêwa	includes them both in what one says
two (in two)	**pâsikahwêwa, pâsikahamwa**	chops s.o., it in two
	pâsikenêwa, pâsikenamwa	divides s.o., it in two, tears s.o., it in two
	pâsikenamwa	splits it in two with a shot
	pâsikâkachiwa	(bow) snaps in two from the cold
	pôhkonêwa, pôhkonamwa	breaks s.o., it, snaps s.o., it in two

u

ugly	**myânesiwa**	is ugly
	myâshinâkosiwa	looks ugly
	machinâkosiwa	is ugly, is not good-looking
	nakahkawikiwa	is ugly, is a weird creature
umbilical cord	**pahkinwiyêwa**	one's umbilical cord separates off
unable	**wâwani**	be unable to, be poor at (preverb)
	wâwani-ishawiwa	is unable to do it right, is at a loss
	wâwanâhpenanêwa, wâwanâhpenatôwa	is unable to deal with or get at s.o., it; has no chance with s.o.
	ânonêwa, ânonamwa	is unable to lift s.o., it
	ânôhpenanêwa	is unable to kill s.o., fails to get s.o.
	ânônamêwa	is unable to get around
	ânwikanêwa	is too exhausted or weak to move
unaffected	**pashkwi**	(with **âkwi nekotahi:**) there is no place not affected (in the specified way)
unburnt	**ashkosowa, ashkotêwi**	(animate, inanimate) is left unburnt or uncooked
unbreakable	**mêchimônêwa**	has an unbreakable grip on s.o.

uncle	**neshisêha**	my maternal uncle, my mother's brother; the son of any man I call "mother's brother"
	oshisêhemâkômêwa	addresses him and treats him as if he were one's mother's brother
	wêshisêhemâkômaka	my mother's brother's son (for example) (participle)
	onekwâhetîhaki	the uncle and nephew (a man and his sister's son)
	nôsa	my father's brother (also, my father)
	ôsâkômêwa	addresses him and treats him as if he were one's father
	wêyôsâkômaka	my father's brother (participle)
uncomfortable	**myâshishinwa**	lies uncomfortably
	wâwanâkômêwa, wâwanâkôtamwa	is uncomfortable with s.o., it, is not used to s.o.'s ways
unconcernedly	**wânatohka**	unconcernedly, as if nothing were wrong or unusual (particle)
unconscious	**pahkihtêshinwa**	falls unconscious
uncontrollably	**ânemeshkêwa, ânemeshkêwi**	vomits and retches uncontrollably, trembles uncontrollably, darts around at random; it moves or rolls about rapidly and confusedly
unconvincing	**mêmênesowêwa**	speaks unbelievably, unconvincingly
uncover	**pâhkenamawêwa**	uncovers, opens (it) for s.o.; opens the door for s.o.
	pâhkakonêwa	takes the covers off s.o.
	pâhkakoshênowa	throws off the covers
	pâhkîkwênêwa	uncovers s.o.'s face
	pâhkîkwêshimêwa	uncovers s.o.'s face
	mehchitiyênêwa	uncovers s.o.'s bottom
	pâpakonamwa	takes the covering off of it (a winter lodge)
	pâpakonapahkwêwa	takes the covering off a winter lodge
	pâpakwisahêwa, pâpakwisahtôwa	whips the covering off s.o., it
under	**nâmi**	under (preparticle)
	nâminekwe	under the arm (particle)
	nâmitasane	under the platform (particle)
	nâmi-tâhtapakwe	under a leaf (particle) (see **tâhtapakwi**)
underdone	**nôtêhtêwi**	it is underdone
underground	**nâmahkamiki**	underground (particle)
	nâmahkîki	underground, under the earth, down in the ground (particle)
	nâmahkîmêhi	underground, under the earth, down in the ground (dimin.) (particle)
underneath	**nâmeki**	underneath, inside (particle)
understand	**nenohtawêwa, nenohtamwa**	understands s.o., it, believes s.o., it
	ishiwêpehtawêwa	understands s.o. to be saying {so}, to mean {so}
	nanânehtawêwa	follows and understands what s.o. says
	tahpehtawêwa	finally understands s.o.
	tahpi-nepwêwa	begins to realize things, gets smarter
	wâwanehtawêwa	fails to hear, understand s.o.
under water	**nâmepyêki**	under the water (particle)
	nâmepyêkîmêhi	under the water (dimin.) (particle)
	nâmâpyêki	under the water (less common) (particle)
	kotawîwa	goes under the water
	kokwêtawîwaki	they (animate) go under the water
	kotawîhtawêwa	dives in after s.o.
	kotawepyêhwêwa	pushes s.o. under the water with something
undisturbed	**wânisetôwa**	leaves it undisturbed, unused
undo	**peneshkenamwa**	takes it (hair) down, undoes it

	peneshkenamawêwa	takes it (hair) down, undoes (it) for s.o.
	peneshkânehkwênowa	undoes one's hair
	peneshkehkêwi	it comes unfastened
undress	mehchinawênowa	undresses
	mehchinawênêwa	undresses s.o.
	mehchinawêwa	is undressed
	peninawîwa	takes one's clothes off
	penenowa	takes one's clothes off
	penîhtêwa	gets undressed
	penîhtêhêwa	undresses s.o., has s.o. undress
uneasy	ashkinawêhêwa	makes s.o. feel uneasy
uneven	ashahashawêkikanwi	it (tree or wood) is uneven
unfriendly	nasatâwikenwi	it is unfriendly
unhappy	ânemitêhêwa	is ill at ease
unharmed	pînôsowiwa	is unharmed
uniform sky	nekotwânahkwatwi	the sky is uniformly cloudless or overcast
unprovoked	pîneshihêwa	attacks s.o. unprovoked, approaches s.o. spontaneously
unseemly	payâhkichinâkosiwa	has an unseemly expression on one's face
unsuccessful	ânawihowa	is unsuccessful
unsurprisingly	wâwosâhi	unsurprisingly, expectably; even, going so far as to; (with a negative:) it is not to be expected, not going so far as to (particle). Also used with a negative meaning even without a negative present.
	wâwasâhi	unsurprisingly, etc. (younger variant of **wâwosâhi**)
untie	âpihwêwa, âpihamwa	unties s.o., it
	âpishkonêwa, âpishkonamwa	unties s.o., it
	âpihamawêwa	unties it for s.o.
	âpihiwanehkêwa	unties a pack
	âpinahwêwa, âpinahamwa	unties s.o., it, unties bag containing s.o., it
	âpishkwâkwatawêwa	unties and lays (it) out for s.o.
	âpishkwisahtôwa	rapidly unties it
until	pâshi	until, continuing until (particle)
	pânôhi	not until then (particle)
untruth	ishitîweni:	**ashe ishitîweni** untruth
unwilling	shâkwênemowa	is unwilling
	shâkwênemêwa	is unwilling for s.o. to, does not want s.o. to, gets tired of s.o.
	kashkatesiwa	is unwilling, holds back
	kîhkîhkiwenêwa	takes s.o. against their will
unworried	wânapiwa	is peaceable, at peace, unconcerned
	wânahkyêwa	is without worries, paying no attention, undisturbed, at ease
unwrap	mehtenêwa, mehtenamwa	unwraps s.o., it, exposing them, it to view
up	ahpemeki	up, aloft (particle)
	ahpemêheki	up, aloft (dimin.) (particle)
	akôsîhtawêwa	climbs up after s.o.
	ketâsîwa	climbs up (a hill)
	ketâsîyôtêwa	crawls up, crawls uphill
	nîmêwenêwa	carries s.o. up
	nîmêyâshkêwa, nîmêyâshkêwi	jumps up in the air, it flies up in the air
uproot	pahkwachiwêshkêwi	becomes uprooted
	papahkwachiwêpokôtêwani	they are uprooted by the flood
upset	neshkitêhêwa	feels angry, offended, upset, disheartened
	sayâwi	so as to ruffle or upset (preverb)

upside-down	**achitawenamwa**	turns it upside-down
	achitawânakwakôchinwa	hangs upside-down
	achitawânowakôchinwa	hangs upside-down
upstream	**âsami**	upstream, up the (railroad) line, west (particle)
up to it	**tepâtesiwa**	is up to it
urge	**âshimêwa, âshotamwa**	coaxes, urges, tempts s.o., eggs s.o., it on; urges (it) on s.o.; urges it, advises it
	kakâtônêwa	urges s.o.
	kâchinehkawêwa	urges s.o., drives s.o. on
	wîshikimêwa	urges s.o. strongly
urinate	**shekiwa**	urinates
	shekinêwa, shekitamwa	urinates on s.o., it
	shekikwâmwa	wets one's bed
	nîshkishêwa	urinates in a large stream
	pônishêwa	stops urinating
	nâpishâmêwa	urinates on the same spot as s.o.
	chîkâshkahwêwa	shoots one's urine out
urine	**shekiweni**	urine
	mîshâmiyâkwatwi	it smells of urine
use	**awêwa, ayôwa**	uses s.o., it; puts s.o. to work; wears (it, clothing), sings (it, song)
	awâsowa	is used, is put to work
	ayôtêwi, ayôtâtêwi	it is used
	ayôhetîwaki	they make each other use (it)
	ayôtîwaki	they use (it) on each other
	otayôweniwa	has (it) as something to use (song word)
used to	**anehkawêwa, anehkamwa**	is or gets used to s.o., it, is or gets acquainted with s.o.
	nakachi	get used to (preverb)
	nahi	know how to, used to, subject to, given to, keep, frequently (preverb)
	wâwanîwesiwa	cannot get used to it
uselessly	**nanawi**	uselessly, for nothing, in vain; off in some isolated place (particle)
	nanawâtesiwa	he is useless as a hunter, never kills anything
	nanawênemêwa	wastes one's thoughts on s.o.
use up	**châkahwêwa**	uses up the supply of (it)
utter	**pakanâmowa**	(with negative:) utters no sound

V

vagina	**ohketenani**	her vagina
	mehketena	a vagina
	meshiketenêwa (Jones)	she has a large vagina
	meshihketenêwa	she has a large vagina
vain	**nanawi**	off in some isolated place; in vain (particle)
valley	**pîhtawâhkîki**	in a narrow valley between high hills (locative noun)
various	**nanayêna**	in various places, in various directions (particle)
	wîyaki	various, of various kinds (particle, prenoun)
very	**pôsi**	very, much, more so (particle, preverb, preparticle)
	kwêhtâni	so very much (particle, preverb)
	nanôpehka	a great deal, many, considerable, very (particle)
	=kena=wîna	very much (enclitics)

vex	kîhkîhkinawêhêwa	vexes s.o. by acting contrary to their wishes
	kîhkîhkinawêhtôwa	vexes it by acting contrary to its wishes
	mîhtamênemêwa	vexes s.o. by thought; is vexed thinking about s.o. (archaic)
victory	pyêchineniwêwa	(member of a warparty) returns victorious (with prisoners or scalps)
	pyêchineniwêwisekini	victory songs (plural participle)
view	anemâpatâniwi	there is a view, one can see some distance
	môhkisêwa	runs into view
village	ôtêweni	village, town
	otôtêweniwa	has a village, town
	chîkôtêwene	at or along the edge of the village
	mâwâkâni	village
	menôtani	enemy village (archaic)
	mâwâsenwi	there is a village, a group of lodges ({somewhere})
	mâwâsetôwaki	they have a village, they have their houses all together
	wîchi-mâwâsetôkêwa	lives in a village with others
	wîkiyâpihkîki	in the village, among houses (locative noun)
vine	kîwâpyêhi	crawling vine (Huron Smith: climbing bittersweet)
	showanakeshi	grapevine
visible	mehtôsâpatâniwi	it is visible
	wâsapahkwêsenwi	its roof stands out clearly against the darker background (in the distance)
	tahpâpatâniwi	(with negative:) there is no visibility (as, in a snowstorm)
vision	môshihêwa, môshihtôwa	has a vision of s.o., it
visit	nawihêwa	visits s.o.
	nawihetîwaki	they visit each other
	pîtikawêwa	enters s.o.'s house to visit them, visits s.o.
	pîtikâtîwaki	they visit to each other
voice	aniwishimowa	uses a loud voice
	ishishimowa	speaks with {such} voice
	inekihkwishimowa	one's voice is {so} big, {so} low
	kâshkehtâkosiwa	one's voice is heard (speaking, singing, or weeping)
	makishimowa	talks with a deep voice
	menohtâkosiwa	one's voice sounds nice
	menwishimowa	has a nice-sounding voice, has a sweet or pretty voice
	nâsâwishimowa	one's voice is weak
	nehkwêtamwa	one's voice grows faint as one moves away
	nênehkowêwa	the sound of one's voice dies away
	nenekashkahamwa	one's voice trembles
	nenekishimowa	speaks with a quivering voice (as if about to cry)
	panâchishimowa	loses one's voice
	masâchi tahpishimôhiwa	one's voice can barely be heard
	sakâki tahpishimôhiwa	one's voice can barely be heard
	tepasishimôhiwa	speaks in a low voice
vomit	mêmenatamwa	vomits
	mêmenachâtamwa	vomits it up
	mêmenatêhwêwa	administers an emetic to s.o.
	mêmenatêhowa	induces vomiting, takes an emetic
	mêmenatêsowa	is made to vomit (by it)
	mêmenachâkani	vomit
	châkisahtôwa	vomits it all up
	pahkihtêshkêwa	vomits and retches to death; trembles to death
	pîkêshkêwa	vomits and retches to death; trembles to death

381

W

Wabano	**wâpanôwiweni**	Wabano Rite
wade	**âshowîwa**	wades, wades across
	akwâyâshowîwa	wades out of the water
	pakâyâshowîwa	wades into the water
	wêpâshowîwa	begins to wade
waft	**awatâshimêwa**	sends s.o. wafting
	awatâsetawêwa	sends it wafting to s.o. on the wind
wag	**wêwêpânowêsêwa**	wags one's tail, swings one's tail
	kokwênepitepêsahêwa	wags s.o.'s head from side to side
wagon	**atâpyâna**	wagon
wail	**anemwêkesiwa, anemwêwêkesiwa**	goes off, along shouting or wailing
	inwêwêkesiwa, inwêwêkatwi	wails {so}, there is {such} sound
	pemwêkesiwa	goes along wailing
	wêpwêkesiwa	starts to wail
	wîshâwêwêkesiwa	wails loudly
	kîwêtamwa	goes about wailing (song word)
	tanwêtamwa	is wailing, shouting, making one's voice sound ({somewhere})
	nanâtwêwêmêwa, nanâtwêwêtamwa	wails for s.o., it; tries to make s.o. come by calling or wailing
	mêyôwisekini	wailing songs (plural participle)
waist	**âpehtaweche**	up to the waist
	êh=okehchîpîhichi	at one's belt line, at one's waist
	opishkwêchêwa	is big around the waist
wait	**ahkamawêwa**	lies in wait for s.o.
	tanahkamawêwa	lies in wait for s.o. {somewhere}
	apwîhêwa, apwîhtôwa	waits for s.o., it
	tanapwîhêwa, tanapwîhtôwa	is waiting for s.o., it ({somewhere})
	ashkachipwîhêwa	impatiently awaits s.o.
	ânawapwîhêwa	gives up waiting for s.o.
	pyêhêwa	waits to accost s.o.
	ahkapîhtamwa	stakes it out; lies in wait
	kêwaki	Wait a bit! (particle)
	nah=penani!	Wait up! Hang on!
wake up	**tôhki**	wake up (doing whatever) (preverb)
	tôhkîwa	wakes up
	tôhkisêwa	wakes up abruptly
	tôhkenêwa	wakes s.o. up by touching
	tôhkeshkawêwa	wakes s.o. up by bodily contact
	tôhkihêwa	wakes s.o. up
	tôhkimêwa	wakes s.o. up by voice
	tôhkikêmowa	wakes people up by calling out
	tôhkinehkawêwa	rousts s.o., rouses s.o. from sleep
	tôhkwêwêhpwêwa	wakes s.o. up by blowing (as, on a whistle)
	tôhkwêwêhwêwa	wakes s.o. up by knocking, pounding, or drumming
	tôhkwêwêshkawêwa	wakes s.o. up by stomping (as, by dancing)
	tôhkikomasowa	is awakened by heat in one's nose
	pânekwashiwa	emerges fully from sleep, becomes wide awake
wake for dead	**nîpâshimêwa**	holds or attends a wake for s.o.
walk	**pemosêwa**	walks along
	pemosahêwa	makes s.o. walk
	pemehkêwa	walks, walks along, walks on, walks by, goes by

	ahpîhtosêwa	walks {so far}
	aniweshkamwa	walks much on it
	âhpetosêwa	walks all the time
	âtamosêwa	walks briskly
	inosêwa	walks {so}, to {somewhere}
	ishitêhêwosêwa	walks with {such} thought
	kekinechêwosahêwa	makes s.o. walk with (it) in hand
	kîhkâwosêwa	walks in a circle
	kîsâtosêwa	has the bother of walking
	kîyosêwa	walks about
	kîyosênotamwa	walks about on it
	nahosêwa	can walk
	nakeshkêwa	stops walking
	nômakêwosêwa	walks a while: **nômakêwosêchi** when he had walked a little way
	nôtenosêwa	he walks in the wind (song word)
	pakôsosêwa	walks on ahead
	pyêtosêwa	comes walking
	shîshêwosêwa	hunts as one walks
	shôshkâhkosêwa	walks erect
	tahkamosêwa	walks across an open space
	tanosêwa	walks {somewhere, in some position or location}
	tepikîshkosêwaki	they walk in an even line abreast
	teteposêwa	walks in a circle
	teteposahêwa	makes s.o. walk in a circle
	wanawosêwa	walks forgetting one's worries
	wêposêwa	starts walking
	wêposahêwa	makes s.o. start walking
	wêwêpânehkwêwosahêwa	makes s.o. walk with swaying mane (song word)
	wîhkowêwosêwa	walks inviting people
walkingstick	mehtekwapenôha	walkingstick (insect)
wall	tahpinawapahkwe	through the wall of the lodge
	pakapahkwêhamwa	knocks on the side of it with something
	pakapahkwêhikêwa	knocks on the side of the lodge with something
	anwêwêpahkwênikêwa	raps on the side of the lodge
walleye	okâwa	walleye
	akâwa	walleye
wallow	kôkîwa	mires, wallows
walnut	pakâni	nut (generic); hickory nut; black walnut
	mahkwi-pakâni	black walnut (literally, bear nut)
walnut tree	pakânâhkwi	walnut tree
	pakânâhkowiwa	is a walnut tree
wampum	mîkesa	wampum bead
	mîkesiwiwi	it is decorated with wampum
	mîkesâtepêwa	has wampum in one's hair
	mîkesêtepêwa	has wampum in one's hair
	pîsimîkaki (plural)	wampum beads
	pîsimîki	of wampum beads (prenoun)
	pîsimîkiwinêwa	has braids decorated with wampum
	pîsimîkiwiwa, pîsimîkiwiwi	is decked with wampum; it is decorated with wampum
want	natawênemêwa, natawênetamwa	wants s.o., it; seeks to know about, find, get s.o., it; expects s.o. to come
	natawênetamawêwa	wants (it) for s.o.

	natawênetamâtisowa	wants (it) for oneself
war	manesenôhi	war
	manesenôwehkwêsetôwa	sets war on it (the earth)
	manesenôwinêwa	dies in war
	meshihkatwi	war
	natopaniwa	goes on the war-path
	nêtopâha	man on the war-path
	natopanihkatawêwa	goes to war against s.o.
	natopaniwenahkiwiwi	a warparty is organized to go out
	mayâwosêwa	leads a warparty
War Chief Clan	manesenôkimâwa	member of the War Chief Clan (the highest lineage of the Fox Clan)
	manesenôkimâwisowa	is a member of the War Chief Clan
	mênesenôkimâwisota	member of the War Chief Clan
war honors	panesihêwa	he beats s.o. in winning war honors (by killing an enemy first)
	panesihtôwa	he wins top war honors
warm	apeswêwa, apesamwa	warms s.o., it, heats s.o., it up
	apesowa, apetêwi	(animate, inanimate) is warm, gets warm
	apanôtêwi	it (as, a house) is warm
	awasowa	warms oneself
	apesokowêhiwa	warms one's back
	apesokowêpiwa	sits warming one's back
	apesokowêshinwa	lies warming one's back
	apesôwêhiwa	warms one's back
	apisikiwêhiwa	warms one's back
	apikâsowa	warms one's feet
	apimotêsowa	warms one's belly
	kîshowihowa	puts on or wears warm clothing
	kîshowishinwa, kîshowisenwi	lies warm
	tahitanawasowa	stays warming oneself by the fire
warm water	keshôpyêhtêwi	water is heated, getting warm
	kêshôpyêhtêki	warm water
	keshôpyêhtêwi	warm water
	keshôpyêsamwa	warms it (as, water)
	keshôpyêyâwi	it (as, a river) has warm water
warn	neshkimâwasowa	gives a direct warning not to do something
	shîkahamawêwa	disparages (it) to s.o., warns s.o. sternly against (it)
warparty head	mêyâwosâta	the leader of the warparty (see: **mayâwosêwa**)
	mêyâwosêha (only possessed:)	**omêyâwosêhemwâwani** the leader of their warparty
warrior	wêtâsêwa	warrior
	wêtâsêwiwa	is a warrior
	wêtâsêwihêwa	makes s.o. a warrior
wart	chîhchîkoma	wart
	nechîhchîkoma	my wart
wash	kôkenêwa, kôkenamwa	washes s.o., it, cleans s.o., it
	kôkenamawêwa	washes (it) for s.o.
	kôkenikêwa	washes, does washing
	kesîkwêwa	washes one's face
	kesînechêwa	washes one's hands
	kôkâhkonowa	washes oneself all over
	kôkikenênowa	washes one's forehead
	kôkitepênowa	washes one's head

	mîwawisetôwa	washes it away
waste	wâpashihêwa, wâpashihtôwa	mocks, wastes s.o., it
	wâpashihtawêwa	mocks, wastes (it) for him
watch	ahkawâpiwa	watches, guards, oversees
	êhkawâpîha	guard, sentry
	êhkawâpîhi	thing that watches
	ahkawâpihêwa, ahkawâpihtôwa	makes s.o., it watch, places s.o., it as a guard
	ahkawâpamêwa, ahkawâpatamwa	watches over s.o., it; watches over s.o., it, guards s.o., it
	ahkawâpamâsowa	is watched over
	ahkawâpamêweniwiwa	is watched over
	ahkawâpatâtêwi	it is watched over
	ahkawâpakêmowa	guards people, protects people
	ahkawâpatahêwa	has s.o. watch over (it)
	ahkawâpatahiwêwa	has people watch over (it)
	nâkatawênemêwa, nâkatawênetamwa	keeps s.o., it in mind, keeps track of s.o., it, watches s.o., it, pays close attention to it
	nâkatawênetisowa	watches oneself, watches out for oneself
	nâkasawâpamêwa	keeps one's eye on s.o.
	nâsâpatamwa	keeps one's eye on it as one approaches it
	wâwosâpamêwa	is watching s.o. (at length or intently) from {somewhere}
watch over	nâkatawênechikêwa	watches over things, keeps track of things
	nâkatawênekêmowa	watches over, keeps track
water	nepi	water
	ahkopyêwi	the water comes {so far}
	akwâpyêhônêwa	drags s.o. out of the water
	chapôkenêwa, chapôkenamwa	dips s.o., it in water
	chapôkâhkwisenwi	it lies extending into the water
	chapôkâsenwi	it blows into the water
	chapôkâshowîwa	wades into the water
	chapôkôtêpahowa	crawls rapidly into the water
	kekôpyêshinwa	lies in the water
	kîshôpyêhtêwi	it is hot water
	kotawîwa	goes under the water
	kotawiwenêwa	drags s.o. under the water
	mahkwâtâpôsenwi	the water is calm, quiet
	mâchikamîwi	it is moving water, the spring was swollen with water
	môshkâpowêwa	adds (it as) water to the cooking
	nepinâtwa	goes after water
	pâhpâkepyêhamwa	pats it (water) repeatedly
	shêpyêyâwi	there is unfrozen water
	tahkikâwawishinwa	cools one's feet in water
	ahkwitepyêki	on top of the water (particle)
	chîkepyêki	close to the water (particle)
	nâmepyêki	under the water (particle)
	nâmepyêkîmêhi	under the water (dimin.) (particle)
Water Clan	nêpiwisota	member of the Water Clan
	kêhchikamîwisota	member of the Water Clan (literally, Sea or Ocean)
waterhole	mônepyâni	waterhole in the ice
watermelon	wêshkihtâhi	watermelon
water moccasin	nânôkechêha	water moccasin
water monster	meshikenêpikwa	underwater bear (a bearlike water monster)
wave (noun)	atekôwa	large wave

	atekôwâshkêwi	there are large waves, it has large waves
	atakôwâshkêwi	there are large waves, it has large waves
wave hand	**wêwêpinehkêhtawêwa**	waves one's hand at s.o.
wax	**nemêhkwâni**	wax; glue
	ashihkanwi	wax; tallow
	oshihkanwi	wax; tallow
way (1)	**ishi**	{some} way, {so}, {thus}, to {somewhere} (particle, preverb, prenoun)
way (2)	**nîshkeshkawêwa**	gets in s.o.'s way
	nîshkênetamwa	thinks it a bother, in the way
we	**nînâna**	we (exclusive, excluding "you") (emphatic or contrastive); (by) ourselves
	kînâna	we (inclusive, including "you") (emphatic or contrastive); (by) ourselves
weak	**nînawi**	weakly (preverb)
	nînawesiwa, nînawâwi	is weak
	nînawihêwa, nînawihtôwa	weakens s.o., it
	nâsâwishimowa	one's voice is weak
	nenyêhpachiwa	is numb and weak from the cold
	nenyêhpapiwa	is weak and has trouble moving from sitting too long
	nenyêhpesiwa	is weak, has trouble moving or doing anything; is crippled
	nenyêhpinehkêwachiwa	one's fingers are numb from the cold
	nenyêhpishinwa	is weak and has trouble moving from lying too long
	nôhkyâhenôhiwi	it is weak, it is not strong (dimin.)
	pîshkyâwi	it is weak (metaphorically, as from disuse or neglect)
	shahkosiwa	is drowsy, listless, weak, down-hearted
	shahkokwâmwa	is weak from sleep
	shahkwikanêwa	is weak in one's limbs
weapon	**âhkwahki**	weaponry (participle)
	otâhkwatomiwa	has (it) as a weapon
wear	**akwiwa**	wears, puts on, or wraps oneself in (it, a blanket or robe)
	akwihêwa	puts (it, a blanket or robe) on s.o. to wear
	oshehkîmêwa, oshehkîtamwa	wears s.o. (as, a hide), it
	ishishehkîtamwa	wears {such} clothing, is dressed {so}
	myâshishehkîtamwa	wears shabby clothing
wear out	**ahkoshkamwa**	wears it out
	ahkoshkânawêwa	wears out clothes
	shîkoshkamwa	discards it after wearing it out (as, clothing)
	châkahôtêwi	it is worn out by being dragged
	châkeshkamwa	wears it out
	châkeshkânawêwa	wears out one's clothing
	pekoshkamwa	wears it out (as, a moccasin)
	pîkênanêwa	completely wears s.o. out, wears s.o. down to nothing
weasel	**shekosa**	weasel
weather	**wîshatêwi**	it is warm weather
	kesîyâwi	it is very cold weather
	-kîshekatwi	it is a day (of such weather) (with preverb)
	nahâwinwi	it is warm weather
weave	**kochipanîwa**	tries to weave
	nahipanîwa	knows how to weave
	pemipanîwa	weaves
	nîpitawêwa	weaves (it) for s.o.
weeds	**pîkwashkatwi**	the grass and weeds have grown up tall

	nâwi-pîkwashki	in the middle of thick weeds (particle compound)
	mônashkahikêwa	digs weeds
weed (verb)	**tatakohamwa**	weeds it
weep	**mayôwa**	weeps
	mayôwi	it weeps (song word)
	mayôhêwa	makes s.o. weep
	mayôhiwêwi	that makes people weep (prenoun)
	mayôhtâkêwa	makes (s.o.) weep for people
	mayôshinwa	lies weeping
	pônwêwêkesiwa, pônwêkesiwa	stops weeping
weep for	**mawimêwa, mawitamwa**	weeps for s.o., it, mourns s.o.
	mawitisowa	weeps for oneself
	mayôhkatamwa	weeps over it, bewails it
weigh	**ahpîhchiwanakesiwa**	(animate, inanimate) weighs {so much}
	ahpîhchiwanakatwi	
	ishiwanakesiwa	weighs {so much}
	tepâhkoshkamwa	weighs it, balances them
weight	**nâwisêwa**	loses weight
weird	**nakahkawikiwa**	is ugly, is a weird creature
well	**wîkêchihêwa, wîkêchihtôwa**	makes s.o., it well, fixes it up right
well!	**kashinâkwa**	Gosh! Why! Well! Well now! Well?
	kashinâhi	Gosh! Why! Well! Well now! Well?
	kashinâ!	Gosh! Why! Well! Well now! Well?
	shinâkwa	Gosh! Why! Well! Well now!
	shinâ!	Gosh! Why! Well! Well now!
well along	**mêkwêtanekowa**	is advanced in one's work or activity
	mêkwêwowêwa	he is well into his speech, has talked for some time
well cooked	**nepisowa, nepihtêwi**	(animate, inanimate) is well cooked
well, spring	**tahkepi**	spring (of cool water), well
west	**êh=pakishimoki**	west (locative participle)
	wêchi-pakishimoki	west (oblique participle)
	âsami	west, upstream, up the (railroad) line (particle)
wet	**nepiwiwi**	it is wet
	nepiwâhkosiwa	is wet (all over)
	nepiwinameshkênêwa	wets s.o.'s skin
whale	**meshînamêwa**	whale
	meshînamêkwa	whale
what	**wêkonêhi**	what? (inanimate interrogative pronoun)
	wêkonêhi	what? what kind of? (prenoun)
	wênêhetôwa	what manitou?
	wâh	what? what did you say?
	wâyi	what? what did you say? (older form)
	awahîna, awahîma	what's-his-name; the one called (so-and-so)
	awahîni, awahîmi	what-you-may-call-it; the thing called (so-and-so)
what else?	**tâninapâchi**	what else can be done (but)? all one can do (is) (particle)
wheel	**têtepisâha**	wheel
	konepâshkêwi	it wheels around
when	**tâninâhi**	when? at what distance? (particle)
where	**tânahi**	where?
	tâtepi	whither? where to? where from? (particle)
	tâna, tâni	where is? which one is?
whetstone	**shîkona**	whetstone, grindstone; cliff
which	**tâna, tâni**	which one is? where is? (animate, inanimate)

while	**menwinehki**	for a good while, for some time, for not very long (particle)
	wêwîtepi	for a while (particle)
	ayôwenehki	it takes or took a while (particle)
	mâmanîninâhi	every little while, at short intervals of time (particle)
whimper	**sîsîkwa**	whimpers
	sîsîkimêwa	whimpers before s.o.
whip	**kîshkatahwêwa**	whips s.o.
	pasitiyêhikani	quirt (riding whip), switch
whippoorwill	**kokowêha**	whippoorwill
whirl	**tetepipokôtêwi**	it floats whirling
	tetepisêwa	whirls around, flies in a circle
whiskey	**ashkotêwâpowi**	whiskey
	wîshkîhi	whiskey
whisper	**kâshkanasowa**	whispers
	kâshkanachîhtawêwa	whispers to s.o.
whistle (noun)	**pepikwêshkwi**	whistle (held in the mouth by a dancer)
	pepikwêshkowiwi	it is a whistle
whistle (verb)	**shâshôkwa**	whistles
	shâshôkimêwa	whistles at s.o., for s.o.
	shâshôkinâkêwa	whistles a tune
white	**wâpeshkesiwa, wâpeshkyâwi**	(animate, inanimate) is white
	wâpeshkâhkonowa	paints oneself white, has one's body painted white
	wâpeshkinameshkêwa	is white-skinned
	wâpeshkipehkwanwa	has a white back
	wâpeshkitepêwa	has a white head
	wâpeshkîkwêwa	has a white face; (ear of corn) has white kernels
	wâpeshkyêkiwa	(buckskin) is white
	wâpitepêwa	one's head is white
	wâpahtakawêwa	(animal) has a white coat
	wâwâpimatetêwa	is wearing white leggins
	wâpinôha	white person (song word); a species of bird ("snow-bird")
	wâpinôhi	white thing (song word)
white ash	**wîsakâhkwa**	white ash (tree)
white man	**wâpeshkinameshkâta**	white man
	môhkomâna	American; white man
whither	**tâtepi**	where to? where from? (particle)
whittle	**tahitanehkomêwa**	is whittling
whizz loudly	**aniwêwêyâkêposowa, aniwêwêyâkêpotêwi**	(animate, inanimate) whizzes loudly through the air
	kîshâkotwêwêyâkêposowa	goes whizzing through the air with tremendous noise
	nehkwêwêyâkêposowa	goes whizzing out of sight
	pyêtwêwêyâkêposowa	comes whizzing through the air
	pyêtwêwêyâkêpotêwi	it comes whizzing through the air
	pyêtwêyâkêpotêwi	it comes whizzing through the air
who	**wênêha**	who? what creature or animal?
	kewênêhi	who are you?
	ketowênêhi	who are you? (archaic)
whole	**mesikiwa, mesikenwi**	(animate, inanimate) is whole, survives in one piece
whoop (verb)	**wâwâkahamwa**	whoops
why	**wêchi-**	the reason why (preverb with initial change [see **ochi**])
	wêkonêhi wêchi-	why? (interrogative pronoun + preverb with initial change [see **ochi**])
	kashi=châhi êh=teki.	Why? How come? What for?

388

why then?	**peshkwichâhi, peshkochâhi**	Why then ..? So, how do you explain ..? (particle)
wicked	**wâwaneshkâhawiwa**	is wicked
	wâwaneshkâhanohkyêwa	does something wicked
	wâwaneshkâhitêhêwa	is wicked at heart
	wâwaneshkâhîhtêwa	does something wicked, acts wickedly
wide	**makahtakatwi**	it is wide (as, a belt)
	makâkamîyâwi	it is a wide stream
	makatêkiwi	it is a wide stream
	makatêkîhiwi	it is a wide stream (dimin.)
widow,	**shîkâwa**	widow, widower
widower	**shîkâwiwa**	is a widow, widower
	keki-shîkâwe	(while still) in unreleased widowhood, widower-hood (particle compound)
	shîkâwiweni	widowhood, widower-hood
	pânîwa	is a widow or widower no longer under strict mourning restrictions
	pânîhêwa	frees s.o. (widow or widower) from strict mourning restrictions
wife	**nîwa**	my wife (**owîwani** his wife)
	ometemosemêhani	his wife
	nîshôhkwêwêwa	he has two wives
	nyêwôhkwêwêwa	he has four wives
	mânôhkwêwêwa	he has many wives
	awatehkwêwêwa	he takes home a wife
	wêpîhkwêwêwa	he beats his (own) wife
	nîtôsha	my (woman's) co-wife; my (man's) rival
wild	**nênôchîha**	wild animal, wild horse
	nênôchîhi	wild plants
	nênôchîhêhi	wild plants (dimin.)
	nenôtêwi	Indian, native, wild (prenoun, preverb)
	pakwachi	wild (prenoun)
	wâwanâtâmanwa	engages in sex with wild abandon
wildcat	**peshiwa**	wildcat (lynx or bobcat)
will	**wîh=**	will, shall, is going to, must; (in subordinate clauses) to, so that, in order to; (with subjunctive, iterative, plain interrogative, changed interrogative, prohibitive, potential, or imperative modes) wish to, dare to, be about to, be inclined to, was going to (future proclitic preverb or prefix)
	îh=	will, etc. (younger variant of **wîh=**)
	wîhi- (also wîh-)	(like **wîh=** will, etc. [future] but may be preceded by **êh=** [aorist] and may be followed by an enclitic) (preverb)
willing	**anwâchîwa**	consents, is willing
	anwâchînohkatâtîwaki	they are willing towards each other
	anwâchinawêmêwa	makes s.o. willing by speech
willow	**sasapihkâha**	willow
	sasapihkâhimishihkiwiwi	there are willows
	meshkwâpîmishi	"red willow" (red-osier dogwood)
win	**anihêwa, anihtôwa**	defeats s.o., wins it
	anihiwêwa	wins
	nawasohkyêwa	wins the race
wind	**nôtenwi**	the wind blows

	nôteki	wind (participle)
	nôtenwi	wind (noun)
	aniwânematwi	it blows hard, there is a wind storm
	êniwânemahki	wind storm (participle)
	inânematwi	the wind blows {so}
	pônânematwi	the wind stops
	pyêtânematwi	the wind blows this way
	âpenôyâwi	it is sheltered from the wind
wine	**wîshkopâpowi**	wine; sap
	shôminâpowi	wine
wing	**onekwîkani**	s.o.'s (as, a bird's) wing; a wing
	onekwîkaniwa	has wings
	sakinekwêhpwêwa	bites s.o. on the wing
	showinekwêwa	has one's wings spread
	showinekwêshkêwa	spreads one's arms or wings
	showinekwêsêwa	falls with spread wings
	inâkêwa	has {such} wings
	châk-ênâkâchiki	all the kinds of birds, (literally) those of every wing
	papahkwâkênêwa	plucks s.o.'s wing-feathers
Winnebago	**wînepyêkôhkwêwa**	Winnebago woman
	wînepyêkônâki	(in) Winnebago country
	wînepyêkôwa	Winnebago
winter	**pepôwi**	it is winter
	pepôni	winter, in winter (prenoun, preverb)
	pepôwi	winter (preverb)
	pepônoki	last winter
	pepônatesiwa	Spirit of Winter
	nehkanipepônwe	all winter long
	mânwipepônakatwi	it is many winters
wipe	**kâsînamwa**	wipes it off with one's hand
	kâsîkâshinwa	wipes one's foot (on something)
	kâsîkwêhowa	wipes one's face
	kâsîmitiyêhowa	wipes one's bottom
	kâsînechêhowa	wipes one's hands, wipes one's hands on (it)
	kâsîtepêhowa	wipes one's head
	kâsîtonêhowa	wipes one's mouth, wipes one's mouth with (it)
	wâhkamahamwa	wipes it clean
wisdom	**nepwâhkâweni, nepwâhkêweni**	wisdom, intelligence, (piece of) knowledge, cleverness
wise	**nepwâhkâwa**	is wise, smart, clever, bright
	nepwâhkêwa	is wise, smart, clever, bright (younger form)
	nepwâhkâhêwa	makes s.o. wise
wish	**tânî='nahi**	I wish
	tayânahi, tawânahi	would that! (archaic) (particle)
with	**wîchi**	with (preverb)
	keki	having, provided with (preverb, prenoun, preparticle)
	nanâhpi	with something else at the same time (particle, preverb)
	ahpi	along with it all (preverb)
	takwi	both or all together, at the same time, along with (it, etc.) (particle, preverb)
	takoswêwa, takosamwa	cooks s.o., it along with (it)
	takosowa	is cooked with (it)
witchcraft	**nanâhkawesiweni**	witchcraft
withdraw	**nêkwîwa**	slips away, withdraws

without	**ashenowihtôwa**	is without it
	mehtâhkwi	without anything, without doing anything, without a weapon (particle, preverb)
	mehtâhkwe (Jones)	without anything (particle)
	kâhki	barehanded, without anything (particle)
	mehchi	by hand, without a weapon (particle)
wolf	**mahwêwa**	wolf
	mahwêwiwa	is a wolf
Wolf Clan	**mahwêwisowa**	is a member of the Wolf Clan
	mêhwêwisota	member of the Wolf Clan
	mêhwêwisôha	member of the Wolf Clan
wolverine	**wâpikaya**	wolverine
woman	**ihkwêwa**	woman
	ihkwêhêha	young woman
	ihkwêwiwa	she is a woman
	ihkwêwiweni	womanhood
	ihkwêwanohkyâni	women's products; women's equipment and supplies
	netehkwêyôma	my woman, female member of my group
	netôhkwêyôma	my woman, female member of my group
	kehchihkwêwiwa	she is a grown woman
	kekihkwêwe	including the women
	keshâchihkwêwiwa	she is a kind woman
	keshâchi-metemôhiwa	she is a kind old woman
	manetôhkwêwa	manitou woman
	manetôhkwêwiwa	she is a manitou woman
	natonehkwêwêwa	seeks a woman
	nawênihkwêhêha	pretty young woman
	ênowênihkwêhêha	pretty young woman (archaic)
	nawênihkwêhêhiwa	she is a pretty young woman
	ênowênihkwêhêhiwa	she is a pretty young woman (archaic)
	pyêtehkwêwêwa	brings a woman
womanly	**menwihkwêwiwa**	she has a nice womanly shape
wonder	**kênemâpi='h=wêna**	I wonder whether; it might be that
wood	**mehtekwi**	tree, wood, stick
woodchuck	**mônânêha**	woodchuck
woodcock	**wîkocha**	woodcock; white grub
	kwîkocha	woodcock; white grub
woodpecker	**mêmêwa**	pileated woodpecker
	mêshkwitepâta (masahkwêha)	red-headed woodpecker
	masahkwêha	hairy or downy woodpecker
woods	**mehtekwahkihkiwi**	woods, wooded area
	mehtekwahkihkiwiwi	there is a wooded area
	mehtekwihkîki	in the woods (locative noun)
	mehtekwahkîki	in the woods (locative noun)
	pîtêyâhkwîwa	enters the woods
word	**inowâkani**	saying, word
	kanawîni	speech, word
	sahkowêwa	one's words reach
work	**mîhkechêwîwa**	works
	mîhkechêwîweni	work
	ishîhtêwa	works so, dresses {so}
	mayôtanekowa	weeps as one works
	mêkwêtanekowa	is advanced in one's work or activity

	nahîhkânowa	knows how to work, make things
	nahîhtêwa	knows how to do work
	nanawitanekowa	works for naught
	wêpitanekowa	begins to work
work at	**mîhkemêwa, mîhketamwa**	works at s.o., it; courts s.o.; picks it; mines it
work into	**pepyêsakonamwa**	works it into patties
worker	**mîhkechêwîha**	worker, hired hand
worm	**manetôsêha**	insect, worm
	mêmeshkwatayêha	earthworm
	môsêwa	wood worm, borer
worry	**ashkitêhêwa**	worries
	pîkêtêhêwa	worries too much, worries or grieves to death
	ashkênemêwa	worries about s.o.
	ânemênemêwa	is worried about s.o., thinks s.o. is in danger
	otehtênemêwa	worries about s.o., is concerned about s.o.
	aniwîhkawêwa, aniwîhkamwa	concerns oneself much with s.o., it
worse, worst	**pôsawiwa**	is worse, gets worse
	anikêmêhiwa	is worse (than the other), is moreso, overdoes it
	pôsenekôha	worst one, one that does the worst
	âyakwîchihêwa	makes things still worse for s.o.
worship	**mamâtomowa**	worships, prays
	mamâtomôni	worship, religion
	mamâtomoweni	worship, religion
	mamâtomohêwa	makes s.o. worship
would	**âmi**	would, should, could (preverb)
	âmihtahi	would (particle) (usually after **îni, ôni** then)
wound	**kîsâtesowa**	is badly wounded by gunshot
	pâhtâsowa	is seriously wounded by gunshot
wrap	**wîwenêwa, wîwenamwa**	wraps s.o., it up
	wîwapinêwa, wîwapitôwa	wraps (and ties) s.o., it
	wîwikâpisowa	wraps one's feet (with it)
	wîwisenwi	it is wrapped (in it)
	wîhkwêpitawêwa	wraps (it) (as, in a buckskin) for s.o.
	kahkîwishinwa	is lying well wrapped up
wrap around	**pyêmâhkohwêwa**	wraps oneself around s.o.
	tetepâhkwisetawêwa	wraps (it) around for s.o.
	tetepâhkwisêwa, tetepâhkwisêwi	(animate, inanimate) wraps around
	tetepâhkwishinwa	lies or is placed to wrap around
wren	**nânômasakîha**	wren
wrestle	**anâsowa**	wrestles, horses around, tussles amorously
wretched	**ketemâki**	wretchedly (preverb)
	ketemâkênemêwa, ketemâkênetamwa	has compassion for s.o., it, thinks s.o., it is wretched
	ketemâkênetisowa	feels himself wretched
	ketemâkihêwa, ketemâkihtôwa	ill-treats s.o., it, makes s.o., it wretched, brings ruin, ill fate upon s.o., it
	ketemâkinâkêwa	sings wretchedly
	ketemâkitêhêwa	feels wretched
	ketemâkitêhâkani	a feeling of wretchedness
	ketemâkitêhêwênemêwa	thinks s.o. feels wretched
wring	**sînepyênikêwa**	wrings out the washed clothes
wrinkle	**nîshkikomêshkêwa**	wrinkles up one's nose
wrinkled	**osîkîkwêhiwa**	has a wrinkled face (dimin.)

	osîkawishinwa	is wrinkled from being in water
	osîkinameshkêwawishinwa	has wrinkled skin from being in water
	osîkashayêshinwa	has wrinkled skin
	nîshkikomêshkêwa	wrinkles up one's nose
write	anepyêhamwa	writes it
	anepyêhikêwa	writes
	anepyêhikawêwa	writes to s.o.
	anepyêhotîwaki	they write each other down, enroll each other
wrong	myâshêwîwa	does the wrong thing, does the work poorly
	nanôtênemêwa	has the wrong idea about s.o.
	nanôchimêwa	says something bad about s.o. that is false
	neshiwanâchitanekowa	does something wrong, destructive
	neshiwanâchitêhêmêwa	tempts to do wrong
	memyêshkyâwi	it is wrong, bad, wicked, ruinous
wrong time	kwîchi	at just the wrong time; just had to be (ironic) (particle)
wrong way	âpôchîwa	goes backwards, the wrong way
	âpôtakôtôwa	hangs it the wrong way around
	payâhkichi	in another way or direction, in the wrong way or direction (particle)
	payâhkitâchimowa	gets on the wrong track in what one says, says something out of the way

y

yank	keteshkanwisahêwa	yanks s.o. off breaking their bite
yard	tatakwanwi	yard, area around summer house kept free of grass and litter
yard (measure)	-yâche	(so many) yards (in particle compounds) (**nîshwi-yâche** two yards)
yawn	âyamâsowa	yawns
year	kehkatwi	year
	âyakwami-kehkatwe	year by year (particle compound)
	âpehtawawahîne	half a year (particle)
	nekotawahîne	one year (particle)
	nekotawahînakatwi	it is one year
	nîshwawahîne	two years (particle)
	nîshwawahîmakatwi	it is two years
	nîshwipepônwe	two years (particle)
	nyêwawahîne	four years (particle)
	nyêwawahîmakatwi	it is four years
	metâswawahîne	ten years (particle)
	mânwawahîne	many years (particle)
	mânwawahîmakatwi	it is many years
	nâhtaswawahîme	several years (particle)
	nâhtaswawahîmêhe	several years (dimin.) (particle)
	taswawahîme, taswawahîne	{so many} years (particle)
	taswawahîmakatwi	it is {so many} years
	taswipepônwe	{so many} years (particle)
	mânwipepônwêwa	is many years old
	mamânwipepônwêwaki (plural)	they are each many years old
	metâswipepônwêwa	is ten years old

	taswipepônwêwa	is {so many} years old
	nîshwâpitakesiwa	is twenty years old
yell	**wêpwêwêkesiwa**	starts to yell loudly, scream
yellow	**asâwesiwa, asâwâwi**	(animate, inanimate) is yellow
	asâwi	yellow; brown (archaic) (prenoun)
yes	**ehêhe**	yes (answering a question)
	hao	hello; alright, yes (agreeing to a suggestion or request)
yesterday	**anâkowe**	yesterday (particle)
yet	**kêwaki**	as yet; still; yet a while; wait a bit
	mêhi	yet; (with prioritive modes) before (preverb)
yielding	**shashawâwi**	it is pliant, yielding
yoke	**ahtômepyâni**	yoke for carrying two buckets of sap
you	**kîna**	you (singular) (emphatic or contrastive); (by) yourself
you (plural)	**kînwâwa**	you (plural) (emphatic or contrastive); (by) yourselves
young	**ashkikiwa, ashkikenwi**	is young, new, fresh
	êshkikîha	young person
	oshkinawêha	unmarried young man
	oshkinawêhiwa	he is, becomes a young man
	oshkinawêhiwiwa	he is, becomes a young man
	ashkanamîkwêha	young man (endearing; archaic)
	panashâha	young (of animal or bird)
	mêmeshkomêhaki	young buffaloes, young horses

Appendixes

1. Animals   396

2. Birds   400

3. Bodyparts   403

4. Calendar   408

5. Numbers and Counting   409

6. Relatives   412

1. Animals

The names of living creatures are listed here in the conventional order of their scientific families, except for birds, which are given in Appendix 2.

MAMMALS

Marsupials	**âyênîha, êyênîha**	possum
Elephants	**wêwêpikôha**	elephant
Primates	**nêtonamâshîha**	monkey
Hares and rabbits	**wâpôsôha**	snowshoe hare
	meshwêha	rabbit (cottontail)
Shrews and moles	**mahkwâshôpa**	shrew
	kêchichikwêha	mole
Bats	**pîshâkaninekwêha**	bat
Bears	**mahkwa**	bear (black bear)
	kâkânwikashêwa,	grizzly bear
	kêkânwikashêha	
Raccoons	**êsepana, êsepâha**	raccoon
Weasels, etc.	**ochêka**	fisher
(Mustelidae)	**shekosa**	weasel
	mîka	mink
	anapishkwêha	mink (archaic)
	ketatêwa	otter
	wâpikaya	wolverine
	masakahkwa	badger
	shekâkwa	skunk
Wolves, etc.	**mahwêwa**	wolf
(Canidae)	**anemôha**	dog
	wîsakitîha	terrier
	wâkoshêha	fox
Cats	**kênwâsowêwa**	mountain lion
	peshiwa	wildcat (lynx or bobcat)
	kâshôha	domestic cat
	onâyina	African lion
Squirrels, etc.	**mônânêha**	woodchuck
(Sciuridae)	**wêtôtêwâha**	prairie dog
	anikwa	squirrel (generic)

Appendix 1. Animals

	môsênikwa	groundsquirrel
	kwakwinôha	chipmunk
	asâwanikwa	fox squirrel
	achitamôha	redsquirrel
	papakanikwa	flying squirrel
Pocket gophers	**pîhtôshketôha**	pocket gopher
Beavers	**amehkwa**	beaver
Mice	**wâpikonôha**	mouse
Muskrats	**ashashkwa**	muskrat
Porcupines	**akâkwa**	porcupine
Horses, etc.	**nêkatôkashêha,** **nêkatôshkashêha,** **nêkatôshkashâha,** **katôshkashâha**	horse, pony
	mâmâkeshêha	mule
Camels	**mêkwisikîha**	camel
Swine	**kôhkôsha**	pig, hog
Deer (Cervidae)	**meshêwêwa**	elk (wapiti)
	peshekesiwa, **peshekisiwa**	deer (whitetail)
	kêtakenêha	fawn
	ayâpêwa	male deer, buck (also: buffalo bull)
	mâkinîha	young male deer
	môswa	moose
Buffalos, etc, (Bovidae)	**nenoswa** (1)	buffalo (ceremonial, older usage)
	inenoswa, **anenoswa**	buffalo (archaic)
	kohpichi-nenoswa, **kohpichîha**	buffalo
	ayâpêwa	buffalo bull (also: male deer, buck)
	nenoswa (2)	head of domestic cattle, cow
	anetehkwa	domestic goat
	mêmehtânesha	domestic sheep
Antelopes	**wâpitîha**	antelope (pronghorn)
Hippopotamuses	**êkwîchika,** **êkwîchîha**	hippopotamus
Whales	**meshînamêwa,** **meshînamêkwa**	whale

FISHES, AMPHIBIANS, AND REPTILES

Fishes	**nemêsa**	fish
	namêsa	fish (archaic)
	nemêwa	sturgeon
	myânamêkwa, **myânahîwa**	catfish
	wâsesîha	bullhead
	ashikana	bass
	kenôshêwa	pike
	okâwa, akâwa	walleye
	mêshkwâshakwêha, **mêshkwâshekwêha**	red sucker
	wîshôka	large fish species (perhaps garfish)
	mahkohtawakâha	sunfish
	kenêpikwamêkwa	eel
Frogs and toads	**konwâshkêha**	frog
	tôtôwa	bullfrog
	mamahkêha	toad
	kwananachîha	tree frog
Turtles	**mahkwâhkêha**	mud turtle
	meshihkêha	snapping-turtle
	meshihkenâhkwa	snapping-turtle (archaic)
	papahkîha	soft-shell turtle
Lizards	**shôkesîha**	lizard
	kahkâhkachîha	salamander
	mânêshêha	mud puppy
Snakes	**manetôwa**	snake (also: spirit, god, monster)
	kîyôtêneniwa	snake
	nêwa	hog-nosed snake ("puff adder")
	shâshâkêha	garter-snake
	nânôkechêha	water moccasin
	shîshîkwêwa	timber rattlesnake
	nâtowêwa	massasauga rattlesnake
Crocodilians	**kôhkôtenîha**	alligator

ARTHROPODS AND MISCELLANEOUS

Insects	**manetôsêha**	insect, worm (insect larva)
	pîshkinâniwa, **pîshkinânîha**	dragonfly
	kwâhkwâtêha	grasshopper
	papakesa	grasshopper (variety)
	čîniškatamôha	katydid
	tôtôsiwa	cricket
	êhtesikêha	locust
	mehtekwapenôha	walkingstick

398

Appendix 1. Animals

ahkwa	louse
mêškwihkenôha	bedbug
âčikašîwa	beetle
môwečîhkêha	dung beetle
pêpôhkoškâha	click beetle
môsêwa	woodworm (wood-boring beetle larva)
wâwâsêsîha, wêwâsêsîha	firefly
mêmêkêha	butterfly
kâhkâwahowêha	fuzzy caterpillar, woollybear
ôčêwa	fly
ôhkwêwa	maggot
masasâhkwa	horsefly
pepikwa	flea
âsiyahkâha	gnat
sakimêwa	mosquito
âmôwa	bee, wasp, hornet
mahkwâmôwa	bumblebee
wâwâpičitîha	white-tailed hornet
ênikonôsa	ant

Other arthropods	**ashâhkîwa**	crayfish
	êsapîhkêha	spider
	êhêpikwa	tarantula
	mênâkočêha	daddy-longlegs
	ašikwa	tick
	mâmânwikâtêha	centipede

Other invertebrates	**pyêmishkwinêha**	snail
	êsîha	mussel, shellfish (also: bivalve shell)
	mêmeshkwatayêha	earthworm
	akashkwâha	bloodsucker

2. Birds

The names of birds are listed here in the conventional order of their scientific families.

Loons
    mâkwa   loon
Grebes
    shekahôha   pied-billed grebe (locally, "hell-diver")
Pelicans
    shêtêwa   pelican
Herons
    sakiwa   great blue heron
Bitterns
    kîshekwi-wâpatâha   least bittern (lit., "sky-watcher")
    wîkamosiwa   American bittern
Swans
    êhêwa   swan
Geese
    anehka   Canada goose
    peshishkesa   brant
    kênakîha   snow goose (including blue goose)
    wâpi-kênakîha   white morph of snow goose (lit., "white snow goose")
    kênakîha kêtakihkâhkâta   blue morph of snow goose (lit., "snow goose with
                                      mottled-breast")
Ducks
    shîshîpa   duck (generic)
    kâkânwichitîha   pintail (lit., "long tail")
    meshishipa   mallard (lit., "big duck")
    myânâhkwi-meshishipa   black duck
    wîkîkwêha   wood duck
    wâwîpekwâkêha   teal (lit., "one with blue wings")
    shâshôkôha   goldeneye (lit., "whistler")
    âhâwêwa   oldsquaw, long-tailed duck
    mêhkatêwesita shîshîpa   white-winged scoter (lit., "black duck")
Vultures
    wînâkêwa   turkey vulture, buzzard
Hawks
    kêhkêhkwa   duck hawk, peregrine falcon
    nâmêyâhkwisâha   large forest-dwelling hawk, probably goshawk
    sîkiminêwa   buteo, "chickenhawk"
    pâkahâhkwâhehkêha   chickenhawk
Eagles
    ketiwa   eagle (generic); golden eagle (specific)
    mekesiwa   bald eagle
Osprey
    meshinowêwa   osprey
Grouse and Quail
    kîwânîha   prairie chicken
    pahkiwa   ruffed grouse, partridge (locally, "pheasant")
    pahkiwa ênwêwêhota   ruffed grouse (lit., "partridge that drums")
    pôhkwîha   quail
Turkey
    penêwa   turkey

Appendix 2. Birds

Cranes
        atechâhkwa   crane (perhaps generic, but especially sandhill crane)
        wâpitenâhkwa   crane species (probably whooping crane)
        wêtepîwa   crane (perhaps specifically sandhill crane)
Gallinules
        shêkâtêha   moorhen, gallinule
Woodcock, Snipe, and Sandpipers
        kwîkocha   woodcock (also, 'white grub')
        chêkîha   jack snipe (from English)
        mashkotêwêtowêha   curlew
Gulls and Terns
        akayâshkwa   gull or tern (generic)
Pigeons and Doves
        omîmîwa   passenger pigeon (extinct), pigeon
        pêhkomîmîwa   passenger pigeon (lit, "real pigeon")
        manetômîmîwa   mourning dove (lit., "spirit pigeon")
Parrots
        pâshkatamôha   Carolina parakeet (extinct; now used for 'parrot')
Cuckoos
        penêhtôwa   cuckoo (locally, "rain crow")
Owls
        wîtekôwa   owl (generic)
        mashkotêwîtekôwa   burrowing owl (lit., "prairie owl")
        nenekapenôha   screech owl
        pônopônôha   saw-whet owl
        wîhkonemîwa   great horned owl (locally, "hoot owl")
Goatsuckers
        kokowêha   whippoorwill
        pêshkwêha   nighthawk
Hummingbirds
        nônôhkâha   hummingbird
Kingfishers
        ateshkâha, atashkâha   kingfisher
Woodpeckers
        mêmêwa   pileated woodpecker
        mêshkwitepâta masahkwêha   red-headed woodpecker
        masahkwêha   hairy or downy woodpecker
        meshêwêmonêha   yellow-shafted flicker
Flycatchers
        meshkwichitôwa   great-crested flycatcher
Crows and Jays
        kâkâkiwa   crow
        tîtîwa   bluejay
Titmice
        kehchikânânâha   chickadee
Nuthatches
        âhâmêha   nuthatch
Wrens
        nânômasakîha   wren
Mockingbirds and Thrashers
        mâmâtwêha, mêmâtwêha   catbird (lit., "moaner")
        kêkyêhkwêha   brown thrasher (lit., "teacher")
Thrushes and Bluebirds
        chîhchîkahkwahâha   robin

chîkitiyêkâpâha	bluebird (imitative, as if "stands with the butt up")

Meadowlarks, Blackbirds, and Orioles

asâwîshkenôha	oriole ("yellow bird")
mâmahkatêwihkâhkâta	bobolink (lit., "black-breasted prairie-dweller")
mashkotêki kîwitâta	
owînenwi-mîchîha	meadowlark (imitative, as if "fat-eater")
sakenâhkwa	blackbird (generic)
sakenâhkwa êsâwitepâta	yellow-headed blackbird
sakenâhkwa mêshkwitenyâta	redwinged blackbird (lit., "red-shouldered blackbird")
sakenâhkwa kênwichitiyâta	grackle (lit., "long-tailed blackbird")
sakenâhkwa	cowbird (lit., "blackbird that eats back sores")
meniwisikiwâkani mâmîchita	

Tanagers

meshkwîshkenôha	scarlet tanager (lit., "black-winged redbird")
mâmahkatêwinekwâta	

Finches and Buntings

meshkwîshkenôha	cardinal (lit., "redbird that says in winter")
pêpôni-kîwitâta	
wîpekwîshkenôha	indigo bunting (lit., "blue bird")

Domestic and Introduced Birds

kînîha	guinea fowl
môhkomâni-peshishkesa	domestic goose (lit., "American's brant")
môhkomâni-shîshîpa	domestic duck (lit., "American's duck")
môhkomânîshkenôha	house sparrow (lit., "American's bird")
môhkomânomîmîwa	domestic pigeon (lit., "American's pigeon")
pahkiwa kênwihkechâta	ring-necked pheasant (lit., "long-tailed partridge")
pâkahâhkwâha	chicken, rooster
pâkahâtîha, pâkahâtîhêha	chicken

3. Parts of the Body
(Including a selection of inflected forms.)

Additional words referring to bodyparts can be found in the two sections of the dictionary.

arm (1)	**nenekwîkani**	my arm, my wing
arm (2)	**nehchiwa**	my upper arm, my biceps
	ohchiwani	s.o.'s upper arm
back (1)	**nepehkwani, nehpehkwani**	my back
	opehkwani	s.o.'s back; a back
	opehkwaneki	on s.o.'s back
back (2)	**neshîkani**	the small of my back, my lower back, my hindquarters
	oshîkaneki	at the small of s.o.'s back, on s.o.'s hindquarters
backbone	**netahtakâkwani**	my backbone, my spine
	otahtakâkwani	s.o.'s spine; a backbone
body	**owîyawi**	his or her body
brain	**nînêtepi**	my brain
	nînêtepîki	in my brain
	owînêtepi	s.o.'s brain
calf	**nenâna**	the calf of my leg
	onânani	his or her calf
	onâneki	on his or her calf
	menâna	a calf
cheek	**nenowayi**	my cheek
	onowayi	his or her cheek
	onowâki	on his or her cheek
chest	**nehkâhki**	my chest
	ohkâhkeki	on his or her chest
chin	**nîhkwi**	my chin
	kîhkwîki	on your chin
	owîhkwi	his or her chin
ear	**nehtawakayi**	my ear
	kehtawakâwâki	in your (pl.) ears
	ohtawakayi	s.o.'s ear; an ear
	ohtawakâki	in s.o.'s ear or ears
elbow	**netôshkwani**	my elbow
	otôshkwaneki	on his or her elbow

	metôshkwani	an elbow
eye	**neshkîshekwi**	my eye
	neshkîshekôni	my eyes
	keshkîshekonânani	our (inc.) eyes
	oshkîshekôni	s.o.'s eyes
	oshkîshekoki	in or on s.o.'s eyes
	oshkîshekowâwani	their eyes
	meshkîshekôni	eyes
finger	**nîsîpinechâkani**	finger
	onîsîpinečâkanani	s.o.'s fingers
	âwinôhikanechi	forefinger, index finger
	netâwinôhikanechi	my forefinger
	otâwinôhikanechîki	on s.o.'s forefinger
	ashkwênechi	little finger, endclaw
	otashkwênechîki	on s.o.'s little finger
	oteshkwênechîki	on s.o.'s little finger
foot	**nehkâchi**	my foot
	nehkâtani	my feet
	ohkâchi	s.o.'s foot; a foot
	ohkâteki	on s.o.'s foot
	ohkâtwâki	on their feet
	mehkâchi	a foot
foreleg	**nîkân-ohkâteki** (Jones)	on the forelegs
forearm	**onepâkayi**	his or her forearm
	onepâkayani	his forearms
hair (1)	**nînesani**	my hair (on my head)
	owînesi	a hair of his or her head
	mînesi	a head hair
hair (2)	**owîsayani** (plural)	fur, hair (of an animal or of the human body)
hair (3)	**mîshikwâkani**	a pubic hair
	omîshikwâkanani	his or her pubic hair
hand	**nenehki**	my hand
	onehkeki	in s.o.'s hand or hands
	menehki	a hand
head	**nîshi**	my head
	nîsheki	on my head
	newîshemeki (preferred by some)	on my head
	owîsheki	on s.o.'s head
	owîshi	s.o.'s head; a head

heart	**netêhi**	my heart
	otêhi	s.o.'s heart
	metêhi	a (human or animal) heart
	otêheki	in s.o.'s heart
horn	**owîwîna**	horn, antler
	owîwînahi	s.o.'s horns
intestine	**onakeshi**	s.o.'s intestines; an intestine
	onakeshêni (pl. form)	intestines, entrails
	onakeshiwâwani (Jones)	their entrails
jaw	**netâmihkani**	my jaw
	netâmihkaneki	on my jaw, chin
	otâmihkani	s.o.'s jaw; a jaw, jawbone
knee	**nechîkwaneki**	at my knee, knees
	ochîkwani	his or her knee; knee
leg		See 'calf', 'shin', 'thigh'.
liver	**ohkoni**	s.o.'s liver; a liver
marrow	**owîpikani**	marrow
mouth	**netôni**	my mouth
	ketôni	your mouth
	otôni	s.o.'s mouth
	otôneki	on s.o.'s mouth
	otônwâwani	their mouths
	otônwâki	in their mouths
	metôni	a mouth
nail	**neshkasha**	my nail, my claw, my hoof
	keshkashêki	your nails, claws
	keshkashyêki	your nails, claws
	oshkashîki	on s.o.'s nail, claw
nape	**nehtâhpi**	the nape of my neck
	ohtâhpeki	at his or her nape
navel (1)	**nînwîshi**	my navel
	owînwi	his or her navel
	owînwîki	on his or her navel
navel (2)	**owînwîshi**	his or her navel
	kînwîshîki	at your navel
neck	**nehkwêkani**	my neck
	ohkwêkaneki	on s.o.'s neck

nose	**nehkiwani**	my nose
	ohkiwani	s.o.'s nose, beak
	ohkiwaneki	on s.o.'s nose
	mehkiwani	a nose
paw	**onechi**	a paw; s.o.'s (an animal's) paw
	nîkâninehkâkani	front hoof, front paw
penis (1)	**nînakayi**	my penis
	owînakayi	his penis
	owînakâwâwani	their penises
	mînakayi	a penis
penis (2)	**wêchi-neniwichi**	his penis (lit., what makes him a man)
phlegm	**netakikwâha**	my phlegm
scalp	**nîshehkwayi**	my scalp
	mîshehkwayi	scalp
	mîshehkwayani	scalps
	owîshehkwayi	scalp
shin	**nekahkwani**	my shin, my lower leg, my leg
	okahkwani	s.o.'s shin; a shin
	okahkwaneki	on s.o.'s shin
side	**neshehki**	my side
	oshehkeki	on his or her side
	meshehki	side (of someone's body)
skin	**onameshkaya**	skin
	onameshkayani	s.o.'s skin
	onamashkaya	skin
	onamashkayani	s.o.'s skin
	onemashkayani (Jones)	s.o.'s skin
soul	**nôkênawa**	a soul
	nenôkênawa	my soul
	onôkênawani	his or her soul
	kenôkênawâwaki	your souls
	menôkênawa	a soul
spleen	**oteshkîha**	a spleen
	oteshkîhani	s.o.'s spleen
tail (1)	**nesowânowi**	my tail
	kesowânowi	your tail
	osowânowi	s.o.'s tail; a tail
	mesowânowi	a tail

tail (2)	**nesowânakwi**	my tail
	osowânakwi	s.o.'s tail; a tail
tail-feather	**ochiti**	tail-feather
	ochityêni	tail-feathers
testicles	**neneshiwaki**	my testicles
	oneshiwahi	his testicles
	meneshiwaki	testicles
thigh	**nepwâmi**	my thigh
	opwâmi	s.o.'s thigh; a thigh, upper leg
	opwâmani	s.o.'s thighs
throat (1)	**kekotâkaneki**	in your throat
	okotâkani	s.o.'s throat; a throat
	okotâkaneki	in s.o.'s throat
throat (2)	**nenakahkwi**	the back of my mouth
thumb	**kehchinechi**	thumb
toe	**onîsîpanasitâkanani**	s.o.'s toes
tongue	**nînaniwi**	my tongue
	owînaniwi	s.o.'s tongue
tooth	**nîpichi**	my tooth
	nîpitani	my teeth
	owîpichi	s.o.'s tooth; a tooth
	owîpitani	s.o.'s teeth; teeth
	owîpiteki	on s.o.'s teeth
	owîpitwâwani	their teeth
	owîpichinawani	one's teeth
vagina (1)	**ohketenani**	her vagina
	mehketena	a vagina
vagina (2)	**wêchi-ihkwêwichi**	her private parts (lit., what makes her a woman)
wing	**nenekwîkani**	my arm, my wing
	nenekwîkaneki	on my wing
	onekwîkani	s.o.'s (e.g., a bird's) wing; a wing

4. Calendar

NOTE: The words for the days of the week and the calendar months are borrowed from English.   There is often a tendency to pronounce them more like English than the conventional spellings would imply.

Days of the week

Sunday	**sânitîhi**
Monday	**mânitîhi**
Tuesday	**tôshtîhi**
Wednesday	**wênishtîhi**
Thursday	**sêshtîhi**
Friday	**panâyitîhi** (older **pâyitîhi**)
Saturday	**sâtitîhi**

Calendar months

January	**chênawêha, chêniwêha**
February	**sepowêha**
March	**mâcha**
April	**îpana**
May	**mîha**
June	**chôna**
July	**chônâya**
August	**âkishta**
September	**sepitênopêha, sepitêmipêha**
October	**âkihtôpêha**
November	**nôpênopêha**
December	**tîsênopêha, tîsêmipêha**

5. Numbers and Counting

Basic numbers

1	**nekoti**	one
2	**nîshwi**	two
3	**neswi**	three
4	**nyêwi**	four
5	**nyânanwi**	five
6	**kotwâshika**, **nekotwâshika**	six
7	**nôhika**	seven
8	**shwâshika**, **neshwâshika**	eight
9	**shâka**	nine
10	**metâswi**	ten
11	**nekotinesiwe, nekotinîsiwe, nekotinesiwi, nekotinîsiwi**	eleven (1)
	metâswi-nekotinîsiwe	eleven (2)
	metâswi-nekoti	eleven (3)
12	**nîshwinîsiwe, nîshwinîsiwi**	twelve (1)
	metâswi-nîshwi	twelve (2)
13	**neswinesiwe, neswinîsiwe**	thirteen (1)
	metâswi-neswinesiwe, metâswi-neswinîsiwe	thirteen (2)
	metâswi-neswi	thirteen (3)
14	**nyêwinesiwe, nyêwinîsiwe**	fourteen (1)
	metâswi-nyêwi	fourteen (2)
15	**nyânanwinesiwe, nyânanwinîsiwe, nyânanwinîsiwi**	fifteen (1)
	metâswi-nyânanwi	fifteen (2)
16	**kotwâshikanesiwe, kotwâshikanîsiwe**	sixteen
17	**nôhikanesiwe, nôhikanîsiwe**	seventeen
18	**shwâshikanesiwe, shwâshikanîsiwi**	eighteen
19	**shâkanesiwe**	nineteen
20	**nîshwâpitaki**	twenty
25	**nîshwâpitaki nyânanwinesiwe**	twenty-five
30	**neswâpitaki**	thirty
40	**nyêwâpitaki**	forty
50	**shekihkanawe**	fifty (1)
	nyânanwâpitaki	fifty (2) (Jones)
60	**nekotwâshikâpitaki**	sixty
70	**nôhikâpitaki, nôhika taswâpitaki**	seventy
80	**shwâshikâpitaki, neshwâshikâpitaki**	eighty
90	**shâkâpitaki**	ninety

100	**nekotwâhkwe**	one hundred
200	**nîshwâhkwe**	two hundred
300	**neswâhkwe**	three hundred
400	**nyêwâhkwe**	four hundred
500	**nyânanwâhkwe**	five hundred
600	**kotwâshika taswâhkwe**	six hundred
700	**nôhika taswâhkwe**	seven hundred
800	**shwâshika taswâhkwe**	eight hundred
1,000	**metâswâhkwe**	ten hundred, a thousand

Be so many

	animate	inanimate	
1	**nekotîhiwa**	**nekotenôhiwi**	there is (only) one
2	**nîshiwaki**	**nîshenôni**	there are two of them
3	**nesiwaki**	**nesenôni**	there are three of them
4	**nyêwiwak**	**nyêwenôni**	there are four of them
5	**nyânaniwaki**	**nyânanenôni**	there are five of them
6	**kotwâshika tashiwaki**	**kotwâshika tasenôni**	there are six of them
7	**nôhika tashiwaki**	**nôhika tasenôni**	there are seven of them
8	**shwâshika tashiwaki**	**shwâshika tasenôni**	there are eight of them
9	**shâka tashiwaki**	**shâka tasenôni**	there are nine of them
10	**metâshiwaki**		there are ten of them

Days (1)

1	**nekotokoni**	one day
2	**nesokoni**	three days
3	**nîshokoni**	two days
4	**nyêwokoni**	four days
5	**nyânanokoni**	five days
6	**kotwâshika tasokoni**	six days
7	**nôhika tasokoni**	seven days
8	**shwâshika tasokoni**	eight days
9	**shâka tasokoni**	nine days
10	**metâsokoni**	ten days

Days (2)

1	**nekotokonakatwi**	it is one day
2	**nîshokonakatwi**	it is two days
3	**nesokonakatwi**	it is three days
4	**nyêwokonakatwi**	it is four days
5	**nyânanokonakatwi**	it is five days
8	**shwâshika tasokonakatwi**	it is eight days

Days (3)

1	**nekoti-wâsêyâwe**	for one day, in one day
2	**nîshwi-wâsêyâwe**	for two days
4	**nyêwi-wâsêyâwe**	for four days
8	**shwâshika taswi-wâsêyâwe**	for eight days
10	**metâswi-wâsêyâwe**	for ten days

Groups, kinds

1	**nekotayaki**	one group, set, pair, couple, kind
2	**nîshwayaki**	two groups, sets, pairs, kinds
3	**neswayaki**	three groups, sets, pairs, kinds
4	**nyêwayaki**	four groups, sets, pairs, kinds

Nights

1	**nekoti-tepehkwe,**	for one night
	nekotitepehkwe	
2	**nîshwitepehkwe**	for two nights
4	**nyêwitepehkwe**	for four nights
8	**shwâshika taswitepehkwe**	for eight nights

Ordinals

2	**nîshônameki**	second, the second time, number two
3	**nêsônameki**	third, the third time
4	**nyêwônameki**	fourth, the fourth time
5	**nyânanônameki**	fifth, the fifth time
6	**kotwâshikânameki,**	sixth, the sixth time
	nekotwâshikânameki	
7	**nôhikânameki**	seventh, the seventh time
8	**shwâshikânameki,**	eighth, the eighth time
	neshwâshikânameki	
9	**shâkânameki**	ninth, the ninth time
10	**metâsônameki**	tenth, the tenth time

Times

1	**nekotenwi**	once
2	**nîshenwi**	twice
3	**nesenwi**	three times
4	**nyêwenwi**	four times
5	**nyânanenwi**	five times
6	**kotwâshikenwi**	six times
8	**shwâshikenwi**	eight times
10	**metâsenwi**	ten times
15	**metâsenwi nyânanenwi**	fifteen times
20	**nîshwâpitakenwi**	twenty times

Years (1)

1	**nekotawahîme, nekotawahîne**	one year
2	**nîshwawahîme, nîshwawahîne**	two years
3	**neswawahîme, neswawahîne**	three years
4	**nyêwawahîme, nyêwawahîne**	four years
5	**nyânanwawahîme**	five years
10	**metâswawahîme,**	ten years
	metâswawahîne	

Years (2)

1	**nîshwipepônwe**	two years

6. Relatives

This appendix has the Meskwaki kinship terminology. It gives the words for different relatives, and also verbs and nouns derived from these, which are an integral part of total system. The words for 'friend' and 'enemy' are included, as they are inflected like kinship terms.

Inflections. The inflection of kinship terms for possessor can be illustrated by the word **nekwisa** 'my son'. This is the regular set of inflections for any possessed noun of the animate gender. (Note that as a term of grammar "possession" includes other relationships besides literal ownership, as in this case.)

nekwisa my son		**nekwisaki** my sons	
kekwisa your (singular) son		**kekwisaki** your (singular) sons	
okwisani his or her son		**okwisahi** his or her sons	
nekwisenâna our (exclusive) son		**nekwisenânaki** our (exclusive) sons	
kekwisenâna our (inclusive) son		**kekwisenânaki** our (inclusive) sons	
kekwiswâwa your (plural) son		**kekwiswâwaki** your (plural) sons	
okwiswâwani their son		**okwiswâwahi** their sons	
okwisinawa one's son			
okwisemâwa the son			

A singular possessor is indicated by a prefix: first person **ne-** ('my'), second person **ke-** ('your'), third person **o-** ('his' or 'her'). A plural possessor is marked by one of these prefixes together with a suffix: **-enân-** for first person plural ('our'), **-wâw-** for second person plural ('your') or third person plural ('their'). The first plural suffix is used together with the first person prefix (**ne-...-enân-**) to indicate first plural EXCLUSIVE: 'we, us, our' in the sense that *excludes* 'you'. The first plural suffix is used together with the second person prefix (**ke-...-enân-**) to indicate first plural INCLUSIVE: 'we, us, our' in the sense that *includes* 'you'.

In kinship terms that have **-î-** in the first syllable the prefixes combine with this to give first person **nî-**, second person **kî-**, third person **owî-**. In kinship terms that have **-ô-** in the first syllable the prefixes combine with this to give first person **nô-**, second person **kô-**, third person **ô-**.

Two forms do not specify a possessor: the inflection **o-...-inaw-** indicates that the possessor is indefinite, and the inflection **o-...-emâw-** provides an abstract term for the relative that makes no direct reference to anyone else.

Each inflected form ends with a suffix that indicates if the possessed relative is singular or plural. If the possessor is a first or second person ('my', 'your', 'our') or unspecified, the singular suffix is **-a** and the plural suffix is **-aki**. If the possessor is third person ('his', 'her', 'their') the singular suffix is **-ani** and the plural suffix is **-ahi**. (The suffixes **-ani** and **-ahi** are the OBVIATIVE suffixes, which the rules of Meskwaki grammar require to be used on any animate noun under certain conditions. Terms with non–third person possessors also have obviative forms, but if the possessor is third person only obviative forms are used.)

Vocative (address) forms. A word followed by a translation with an exclamation mark (!) is the term of address used in speaking directly to the relative. The usual suffixes are **-e** for the singular and **-etike** for the plural, but as the vocative singulars of kinship terms are often irregular the forms are given where they are available.

Extensional uses. It is highly characteristic of Meskwaki kinship terminology that in addition to a basic meaning most terms have extensional uses. Extending the use of a basic term to a more distant relative amounts to equating that relative with the closer one for terminological purposes.

Two pervasive rules or principles operate to bring this about. One rule equates siblings of the same sex. For example, a father's brother is called **nôsa** 'my father', and his children are called "brother" and "sister." A mother's sister's children are also called "brother" and "sister," but **nekya** 'my mother' is distinct from **nekîha** 'my mother's sister', the term used also for all more distant "maternal aunts." Otherwise, the equation of brothers and of sisters works the same way. For example, a man calls his brother's children **nekwisa** 'my son' or **netânesa** 'my daughter', and these same terms are used by a woman for her sister's children.

The second rule equates relatives in different generations: as a link to more distant relatives, a man's sister is treated like his daughter. For example, father's sister's son is called the same as sister's son, which for a man is **nenekwâha** 'my nephew' and for a woman (by the first rule) is **nekwisa** 'my son'. The reciprocal relationship is consistent with this: a person's mother's brother's son is also called **neshisêha** 'my mother's brother'.

It is important to note, however, that when a more distant relative is terminologically equated with a closer relative, the two are not collapsed into a single, undifferentiated category. The language has ways of making it clear which kind of relative is being referred to. For example, although the usual way to refer to a father's brother is as **nôsa** (the same word as for 'my father'), to make the reference to an uncle unambiguous one can say, for example, **nôsa tâtaki** 'my sort-of father' or explicitly **nôsa otôtêmani** 'my father's brother'.

Diminutives. Meskwaki nouns quite commonly make a diminutive form, most often with a suffix **-êh**. (Sometimes the vowel is different and there may be other irregularities, but there is always an **-h** preceded by a long vowel.) Many kinship terms thus have diminutive forms; for example, the term **nôhkomesa** 'my grandmother' has a diminutive form **nôhkomesêha** 'my grandmother'. (But some kinship terms have no diminutive, notably those for parents and in-laws.) A diminutive may refer to smallness (of a child) or may imply affection ('the dear one') or pity ('the poor thing'), but sometimes a variant with the shape of a diminutive is used interchangeably with the non-diminutive or is even the preferred expression. Diminutive forms that seem especially common are given separately in the list below, but in most cases no attempt is made to define their various idiomatic uses.

Verbs of possession. Reference is often made to relatives and relationships using verbs of possession. These are made from the form of the basic kinship term with a third person singular possessor ('his' or 'her'). For example, the verb **ôsiwa** 'he or she has a father' is derived from **ôsani** 'his or her father' by adding **-i** to **ôs-**, which is **ôsani** minus the obviative singular noun suffix **-ani**. (The **-wa** is the verb ending for third person singular, 'he' or 'she'.) This can mean 'his or her father is living' and also 'he or she has (the man referred to) as father', or equivalently 'he is his son' or 'she is his daughter', as the case may be.

A second kind of verb of possession adds **-em** instead of **-i**. For example, in addition to **ôsiwa** 'he or she has a father' or 'has him as a father' there is **ôsemêwa**, which only means 'he or she has him as a father'. These verbs are always transitive (having an object). They are listed in the form that would be used for a third person singular ('he' or 'she') possessing another third person ('him', 'her', 'them'), which has the ending **-êwa**, but they are rare in this basic shape. Rather, they are typically used in expressions like **âkwi=mâh=nîna ôsemenânini.** 'You are not my father.' (literally, 'I do not have you as my father.').

Verbs of the type **ôsiwa** 'he or she has (him as) a father' and those of the type **ôsemêwa** 'he or she has him as a father' can both be used in both literal and extended senses. To specify that the extended use of a kinship term is meant, a third type of verb of possession can be used, one made by adding **-âkôm** instead of **-i** or **-em**. For example, there is a verb **ôsâkômêwa** 'he or she addresses him and treats him as if he were a father', which is used to say things like **wêyôsâkômaka** 'my father's brother'.

Participles. In addition to the use of the basic kinship terms, kin relationships may also be referred to by participles made from the derived verbs of possession. Participles are verb forms that mean things like 'the one who ...' ('the ones who ...'). For example, the singular participle made from the verb **ôsiwa** 'he or she has a father' is **wêyôsita**, literally 'the one who has a father' or 'the one who has him as a father'. In the same way that the verb can also be used to mean 'he is his son' or 'she is his daughter' the participle can be used for 'the son (of the man)' or 'the daughter (of the man)'.

Reciprocal verbs. The verbs of possession made with **-em** may make derived reciprocal verbs (as is generally the case with transitive verbs that take animate objects). These verbs describe two people (or more, if appropriate) as having a particular kin relationship. They are characterized by **-etî-**, the regular reciprocal marker, which usually replaces the **-em** but is occasionally found added after it. For example, from **otehkwêmemêwa** 'he has her as his sister' is derived **otehkwêmetîwaki** 'they are brother and sister'.

Terms for pairs of relatives. From many of the reciprocal verbs there are made plural nouns that denote pairs of relatives (or sometimes a set of more than two). These are characterized by **-tîh-** (reciprocal **-tî-** plus noun-forming **-h**). For example, from **otehkwêmetîwaki** 'they are brother and sister' is derived **otehkwêmetîhaki** 'the brother and sister'.

List of terms, arranged by generations.

Grandparents

grandfather (1)	**nemeshôha** my grandfather. By extension, anyone my father or mother calls **nôsa** 'my father's brother' or **neshisêha** 'my mother's brother'.
	omeshôhani his or her grandfather
	nemesho (my) grandfather!
	nemeshôhetike (my) grandfathers!
	omeshôhiwa he or she has a grandfather, has him as a grandfather
	omeshôhemêwa he or she has him as a grandfather
	wêmeshôhâkômaka my grandfather's brother, or a more distant relative I call "grandfather"
grandfather (2)	**nemeshômesa** my grandfather
	omeshômesani his or her grandfather
	nemeshômese (my) grandfather!
	nemeshômesetike (my) grandfathers!
	omeshômesiwa he or she has a grandfather, has him as a grandfather, is his grandchild

	omeshômesemêwa he or she has him as a grandfather, is his grandchild
	omeshômesâkômêwa he or she addresses him and treats him as if he were a grandfather
	omeshômesiwâkômêwa he or she addresses him and treats him as if he were a grandfather
teasing grandfather	**nekakâchi-nemeshôha** my "teasing" grandfather (my mother's mother's brother or the son of anyone I call this)
grandmother (1)	**nôhkomesa** my grandmother. By extension, anyone my father or mother calls **nekîha** 'my mother's sister', anyone my father calls **nesekwisa** 'father's sister', and (for some speakers) anyone my mother calls **nesekwisa** 'father's sister'.
	ôhkomesani his or her grandmother
	ôhkomeswâwani their grandmother
	anôhko (my) grandmother!
	nôhkomesenâte (our) grandmother!
	ôhkomesiwa he or she has a grandmother, has her as a grandmother, is her grandchild
	ôhkomesemêwa he or she has her as a grandmother, is her grandchild
grandmother (2)	**nôhkomesêha** my grandmother
	ôhkomesêhani his or her grandmother
grandparent	**wêyôshisemita** his, her, or their grandparent
	wêyôshisemichiki his, her, or their grandparents
	ôshisemetîhaki the grandparent and grandchild
great-grandmother	**ânehkêwi-nôhkomesa** my great-grandmother

Parents

father	**nôsa** my father; my stepfather. By extension, my father's brother; the son of anyone my father calls **nôsa** 'my father's brother' or **nekîha** 'my mother's sister'; the husband of anyone I call **nekîha** 'my mother's sister', including my mother's father's sister (regardless of what I call her).
	ôsani his or her father; his or her father's brother
	anôse (my) father! (my) uncle (father's brother)!
	nôsenâte (our) father!
	ôsiwa he or she has a father, has him as father, is his child
	wêyôsiyâna my (own) father (not someone else I call **nôsa**)
	ôsemêwa he or she has him as father, is his son or daughter
	ôsâkômêwa he or she addresses him and treats him as if he were a father
	wêyôsâkômaka my father's brother

mother	**nekya** my mother
	okyêni his or her mother
	anêhe (my) mother!
	okiki at his or her mother's; like his or her mother
	nekinâna our mother (ours but not yours)

okiwâwani their mother

okiwa he or she has a mother, has her as mother, is her child

okimêwa he or she has her as a mother

parent (1)   **nemesôtânaki** my parents (only plural)

omesôtânahi his or her parents

omesôtâniwa he or she has parents

parent (2)   **wênîchânesita** his or her parent, the parent of a child or children

wênîchânesêhita his or her parent, the parent of a child or children

parent (3)   **wêkwisita** his mother or his father; the man or boy's parent

neniwa wêkwisita or **wêkwisita neniwa** the man or boy's father

ihkwêwa wêkwisita or **wêkwisita ihkwêwa** the man or boy's mother

wêkwisichiki his mother and father; the man or boy's parents

parent (4)   **wêtânesita** her mother or her father; the girl or woman's parent

pashitôha wêtânesita or **neniwa wêtânesita** her father; the woman or
    girl's father

metemôha wêtânesita or **ihkwêwa wêtânesita** her mother; the woman or
    girl's mother

wêtânesichiki her mother and father; the woman or girl's parents

Aunts and Uncles

uncle (1)   **neshisêha** my mother's brother (technically, my cross-uncle). By extension,
    the son of anyone I call **neshisêha**, anyone my mother calls "brother" by
    extension, and the son of anyone my mother calls **nôsa** or **nekîha**.

oshisêhani his or her mother's brother

oshisani (archaic and rare) = **oshisêhani**

neshise (my) uncle!

neshisêhetike (my) uncles!

oshisêhiwa he or she has an uncle (mother's brother), has him as an uncle

oshisêhemêwa he or she has him as an uncle (mother's brother)

oshisêhemâkômêwa he or she addresses him and treats him as if he were
    a mother's brother

wêshisêhemâkômaka my mother's brother's son; also, the son of anyone
    else referred to this way

uncle (2)   (for father's brother, see 'father')

aunt (1)   **nekîha** my mother's sister (technically, my parallel aunt); also, my
    stepmother. By extension, the daughter of anyone I call **neshisêha** 'my
    mother's brother', the daughter of anyone my mother calls **nôsa** or
    nekîha, the wife of my father's brother (or of anyone else I call **nôsa** by
    extension), and (for some speakers) my mother's father's sister.

okîhani his or her mother's sister or stepmother

nekîhe (my) aunt (mother's sister)! (my) stepmother!

okîhiwa he or she has a mother's sister, has her as a mother's sister; he's her
    nephew (sister's son), she's her niece (sister's daughter)

aunt (2)	**nesekwisa** my father's sister (technically, my cross-aunt). By extension, the daughter of anyone my father calls **nôsa** 'my father's brother' or **nekîha** 'my mother's sister'; also, the wife of my mother's brother (and see "teasing aunt").
	nesekwi (less commonly **nesekwise**) (my) father's sister!
	osekwisiwa he or she has a father's sister, has her as a father's sister; he's her nephew (brother's son), she's her niece (brother's daughter)
teasing aunt	**nekakâchi-nesekwisa** my "teasing" aunt (my mother's brother's wife)

Brothers and Sisters

older brother	**nesesêha** my older brother; my older half brother or stepbrother. By extension, a boy or man older than I am who is my father's brother's son, my mother's sister's son, or the son of anyone I call **nôsa** 'my father's brother' or **nekîha** 'my mother's sister' by extension.
	osesêhani his or her older brother
	osesani (older, less common) = **osesêhani**
	nesese (my) older brother!
	nesesêhetike (my) older brothers!
	nesesêhenâte (our) older brother!
	osesêhiwa he or she has an older brother, has him as an older brother
older sister	**nemisêha** my older sister; my older half sister or stepsister. By extension, a girl or woman older than I am who is my father's brother's daughter, my mother's sister's daughter, or the daughter of anyone I call **nôsa** 'my father's brother' or **nekîha** 'my mother's sister' by extension.
	omisêhani his or her older sister
	omisani (archaic; rare) = **omisêhani**
	nemise (my) older sister!
younger sibling (1)	**nesîma** my younger brother, my younger sister; my younger half brother or stepbrother, my younger half sister or stepsister. By extension, a younger person who is my father's brother's child, my mother's sister's child, or the child of anyone I call **nôsa** 'my father's brother' or **nekîha** 'my mother's sister' by extension (archaic or ritual).
	osîmani his or her younger brother or sister (archaic or ritual)
	nesîhi, nesîhe, nesîme (my) younger brother! (my) younger sister!
	osîmemâwa the younger brother or sister
	osîmetîwaki they are brothers, they are siblings
	osîmetîhaki the brothers
	osîmâkôtîwaki they address and treat each other as siblings
younger sibling (2)	**nesîmêha** my younger brother, my younger sister; my younger half brother or stepbrother, my younger half sister or stepsister. By extension, a younger person who is my father's brother's child, my mother's sister's child, or the child of anyone I call **nekîha** 'my mother's sister' by extension.
	osîmêhiwa he or she has a younger brother or sister, has him as a younger brother, has her as a younger sister

osîmêhemêwa he or she has him as a younger brother, has her as a younger sister

osîmêhemâwa the younger brother or sister

woman's brother

netawêmâwa my brother (of a woman); my clan brother (of a woman)

otawêmâwani her brother

netawêmâwe (my) brother! (woman speaking)

otawêmâwiwa she has a brother, has him as a brother

otawêmâwitêhêwa she thinks of him as her real brother

man's sister

netehkwêma my sister (of a man); my clan sister (of a man)

otehkwêmani his sister

netehkwême (my) sister! (man speaking)

otehkwêmiwa he has a sister, has her as a sister

otehkwêmemêwa he has her as his sister

otehkwêmâkômêwa he addresses her and treats her as if she were his sister

otehkwêmetîwaki they are brother and sister

otehkwêmetîhaki the brother and sister

sibling

netôtêma my brother or sister, my clan brother or sister, my clan totem (animal or spirit; also used reciprocally)

netôtêmaki my brothers, my sisters, my brothers and sisters

otôtêmani his or her sibling; (especially) his brother, her sister

netôtême (my) clan brother! (my) clan totem!

otôtêmiwa he or she has a sibling, has him or her as a sibling or clan totem

otôtêmetîwaki they are siblings

otôtêmetîhaki the siblings

Cousins

(There is no separate word for 'cousin'; cousins are classed with various other relatives depending on the specific relationship. The child of a parent's same-sex sibling (father's brother or mother's sister) is called "brother" or "sister." The children of a father's sister are called the same as the children of one's own sister: a man calls them "nephew" and "niece," and a woman calls them "son" and "daughter." A mother's brother's son and daughter are called the same as a mother's brother and sister.)

parallel cousin

The son of a father's brother or of a mother's sister is called a brother.

The daughter of a father's brother or of a mother's sister is called a sister.

cross-cousin

A man calls the son of his father's sister "nephew" (**nenekwâha**).

A man calls the daughter his father's sister "niece" (**neshemîha**).

A woman calls the son of her father's sister "son" (**nekwisa**).

A woman calls the daughter of her father's sister "daughter" (**netânesa**).

The son of a mother's brother is called "mother's brother" (**neshisêha**).

The daughter of a mother's brother is called "mother's sister" (**nekîha**).

Sons and Daughters

son (1)   **nekwisa** my son; my stepson. By extension, (of a man) my brother's son, (of a woman) my sister's son, and the son of anyone else a man calls "brother" or a woman calls "sister"; also (of a man) the son of my wife's sister, father's sister, or brother's daughter, and (of a woman) the son of my husband's brother.

         okwisani his or her son

         nekwîhi (less commonly **nekwise**) (my) son!

         okwisiwa he or she has a son, has him as a son

         okwisemêwa he or she has him as a son

         okwisemâwa the son (of the family)

         okwisetîhaki the parent and son

son (2)   **nekwisêha** my (dear, little, pitiful) son

         okwisêhani his or her (dear, little, pitiful) son

daughter (1)   **netânesa** my daughter; my stepdaughter. By extension, my brother's daughter (of a man), my sister's daughter (of a woman), and the daughter of anyone else a man calls "brother" or a woman calls "sister"; also (of a man) the daughter of my wife's sister, father's sister, or brother's daughter, and (of a woman) the daughter of my husband's brother.

         otânesani his or her daughter

         netâha or **netâhe** (less commonly **netânese**) (my) daughter!

         otânesiwa he or she has a daughter, has her as a daughter

         otânesemâwa the daughter (of the family)

         otânesemêwa has her as a daughter

         otânesetîhaki the mother and daughter

daughter (2)   **netânesêha** my (dear, little, pitiful) daughter

         otânesêhani his or her (dear, little, pitiful) daughter

child (1)   **nenîchânesa** my child; my stepchild. By extension, the child of anyone I call "brother" or "sister."

         nenîchânesetike (my) children!

         onîchânesani his or her child

         onîchânesiwa he or she has a child, has him or her as a child

         onîčânesemâwaki the children (of the family), other people's children

         onîchânesemêwa he or she has him or her as a child

         onîchânesetîhaki the parent and child or children

child (2)   **nenîchânesêha** my child

         onîchânesêhani his or her child

         onîchânesêhiwa he or she has a child, has him or her as a child

child (3)   **apenôha** child

         apenôhêha (little, young) child; baby

         keki-apenôhe, kek-apenôhe along with his, her, or their children

         netapenôhema my own child (not someone else I call "son" or "daughter")

child (4)   **wêyôsita** the man's son or daughter

         wêyôsichiki the man's children

child (5) **wêkita** the woman's son or daughter
  wêkichiki the woman's children

Nephews and Nieces

nephew (1) **nenekwâha** my nephew; specifically, the son of a man's sister or of a woman's brother (technically, my cross-nephew). By extension, the son of anyone a man calls "sister" or of his father's sister or his father's father's sister, and the son of anyone a woman calls "brother"; also (of a woman) the son of my husband's sister or his father's sister.
  nenêhe (less commonly **nenekwa**) (my) nephew!
  onekwâhani his or her nephew
  onekwâhiwa he or she has a nephew, has him as a nephew
  onekwâhemêwa he or she has him as a nephew
  onekwâhetîhaki the uncle and nephew (a man and his sister's son)

nephew (2) **nenekwanesa** my cross-nephew (archaic; ceremonial)

niece (1) **neshemîha** my niece; specifically, the daughter of a man's sister or of a woman's brother (technically, my cross-niece). By extension, the daughter of anyone a man calls "sister" or of his father's sister or his father's father's sister, and the daughter of anyone a woman calls "brother"; also (of a woman) the daughter of my husband's sister or his father's sister.
  oshemîhani his or her niece
  neshemi (my) niece!
  oshemîhiwa he or she has a niece, has her as a niece

niece (2) **keshemisa** your niece (i.e., cross-niece) (archaic and rare)
  oshemisani his or her niece (i.e., cross-niece) (archaic and rare)

Grandchildren

grandchild (1) **nôshisema** my grandchild. By extension, the child of anyone I call "son" or "daughter," or that I call "nephew" or "niece," or that I call "grandchild."
  ôshisemani his or her grandchild
  noshîhi or **noshîhe** (my) grandchild!
  nôshiseme, nôshise, nôshisemêwe (my) grandchild! (less common)
  nôshisemetike (my) grandchildren!
  ôshisemiwa he or she has a grandchild, has him or her as a grandchild
  ôshisememêwa he or she has him or her as a grandchild
  ôshisemetîhaki the grandparent and grandchild

grandchild (2) **nôshisemêha** my grandchild (especially if little, dear, or pitiful)
  ôshisemêhani his or her grandchild
  ôchisemêhani his or her dear grandchild
  nôshisemêhetike (my) grandchildren!

grandchild (3) **nôshisemêhkôha** my dear grandchild
  nôshisemêhko (my) dear grandchild!
  atemêhkôha my dear grandchild

grandchild (4) **wêmeshôhita** his grandchild, the grandchild of the man
  wêmeshômesita his grandchild, the grandchild of the man

grandchild (5)	**wêyôhkomesita** her grandchild, the grandchild of the woman
	wêyôhkomesêhita her grandchild, the grandchild of the woman
	wêyôhkomesêhichiki her grandchildren, the grandchildren of the woman
great-grandchild (1)	**ânehkêwi nôshisemaki** my great-grandchildren
	otânehkêwi-ôshisemani his or her great-grandchild
great-grandchild (2)	**ketânehkôchi-kôshisemêha** your great-grandchild
great-grandchild (3)	**nîshônameki ôshisemani** his or her great-grandchild

Spouses

husband (1)	**nenâpêma** my husband
	nenâpêmêha my (pitiful or deceased) husband
	onâpêmani, onâpêmêhani her husband
	onâpêmwâwahi their husbands
	nenâpême (my) husband!
	onâpêmiwa, onâpêmêhiwa she marries or is married, has or gets a husband; she marries him or is married to him; she is his wife
	onâpêmemêwa she has him as her husband
husband (2)	**wêwîwita** the husband (of the couple); her husband
wife (1)	**nîwa** my wife
	owîwani his wife
	owîwêhani his wife (less common)
	owîwâwahi their wives
	owîweki at his wife's
	nîwe (my) wife!
	owîwiwa, owîwêhiwa he marries or is married, has or gets a wife; he marries her or is married to her; he is her husband
	owîwemêwa he has her as his wife
	owîwetîwaki they are married (to each other), they are husband and wife
	owîwetîhaki married couple, husband and wife
wife (2)	**wênâpêmita** the wife (of the couple); his wife
wife (3)	**metemo** wife! (literally, old lady!) ("A gentle term of address to a wife, whether she is old or young." [William Jones])
spouse	**wîchawiwaka** my husband; my wife (literally, my companion)
	wîchawiwata your husband; your wife
	wîchawiwâchini her husband; his wife

In-Laws

father-in-law	**nemeshôma** my father-in-law. By extension, anyone my husband (or my wife) calls **nôsa** 'my father's brother' or **neshisêha** 'my mother's brother'.
	omeshômani his or her father-in-law
	nemeshôme (my) father-in-law!
	omeshômiwa he or she has a father-in-law, has him as a father-in-law

mother-in-law	**nôhkoma** my mother-in-law. By extension, anyone my husband (or my wife) calls **nesekwisa** 'my father's sister' or **nekîha** 'my mother's sister'. **ôhkomani** his or her mother-in-law **nôhkome** (my) mother-in-law!
parent-in-law (1)	**wêsemita** the woman's father-in-law or mother-in-law **wêsemichiki** the woman's parents-in-law
parent-in-law (2)	**wênekwanita** the man's father-in-law or mother-in-law **wênekwanichiki** the man's parents-in-law
brother-in-law (1)	**nîhtâwa** my brother-in-law (of a man; wife's brother or sister's husband). By extension, anyone my wife calls "brother," or the husband of my father's sister or of my father's father's sister, and also anyone else that a child of mine would call **neshisêha** 'my mother's brother'. **owîhtâwani** his brother-in-law **owîhtâwâwani** their brother-in-law **nîhta** (my) brother-in-law! (man speaking) **owîhtâwiwa** he has a brother-in-law, has him as a brother-in-law **owîhtâwemêwa** he has him as a brother-in-law **owîhtâtîwaki** they are brothers-in-law **owîhtâtîhaki, owîhtâwetîhaki** the brothers-in-law
brother-in-law (2)	**nemêshâhema** my brother-in-law (of a man). Extensional uses are not attested. **omêshâhemani** his brother-in-law **mêsha** brother-in-law! (man speaking)
brother-in-law (3)	see 'sibling-in-law'
sister-in-law (1)	**netâkwa** my sister-in-law (of a woman; husband's sister or brother's wife). By extension, anyone my husband calls "sister," and also anyone else that a child of mine would call **nekîha** 'my mother's sister'. **otâkwani** her sister-in-law **otâkwiwa** she has a sister-in-law, has her as a sister-in-law **otâkwatîhaki** the sisters-in-law
sister-in-law (2)	see 'sibling-in-law'
sibling-in-law	**nînemwa** my sister-in-law (of a man; wife's sister or brother's wife), my brother-in-law (of a woman; husband's brother or sister's husband). By extension (as used by a man), anyone my wife calls "sister" or anyone else that a child of mine would call **nekîha** 'my mother's sister', and (as used by a woman) anyone my husband calls "brother," or the husband of my father's sister or of my father's father's sister, and also anyone else that a child of mine would call **neshisêha** 'my mother's brother'. **owînemôni** his sister-in-law, her brother-in-law **nînemwe** (my) sister-in-law! (man speaking) **owînemwiwa** has a sibling-in-law of the opposite sex, he has her as his sister-in-law, she has him as her brother-in-law **owînemotîwaki** they are brother-in-law and sister-in-law

co-wife	**nîtôsha** my co-wife (of a woman); my rival (of a man)
	owîtôshani, **owîtôshêni** her co-wife; his rival
	owîtôshiwa she has a co-wife, has her as a co-wife
	owîtôshetîwaki they are co-wives
	owîtôshetîhaki the co-wives
son-in-law (1)	**nenekwana** my son-in-law. By extension, the husband of anyone I call "daughter" or "niece."
	onekwanani his or her son-in-law
	nenekwane (my) son-in-law!
	onekwaniwa he or she has a son-in-law, has him as a son-in-law
	onekwanemêwa he or she has him as a son-in-law
son-in-law (2)	**oshinekêwa** the son-in-law (in the family)
	oshineke son-in-law!
son-in-law (3)	**oshinetamwa** he is the son-in-law; he or she has in-laws, is married in
	wêshinetaka the son-in-law
	wêshinetake son-in-law!
son-in-law (4)	**nêhâkapita** son-in-law living with his in-laws
	nahâkapiwa he lives with his in-laws
	tanahâkapiwa he lives {someplace} with his in-laws
son-in-law (5)	**owîtâkapîhani** his fellow son-in-law living in their in-laws' house
daughter-in-law (1)	**nesemya** my daughter-in-law. By extension, the wife of anyone I call "son" or "nephew."
	osemyêni his or her daughter-in-law
	keseminâna our daughter-in-law
	nesemye (my) daughter-in-law!
	osemiwa he or she has a daughter-in-law, has her as a daughter-in-law
daughter-in-law (2)	**nahâkanihkwêwa** daughter-in-law living with her in-laws
	nahâkanihkwe daughter-in-law!
Friend and enemy	
friend	**nîhkâna** my friend (in general); my close male friend (of a man or boy)
	owîhkânani his or her friend; his close male friend
	nîhkâne (my) friend!
	nîhkânetike (my) friends!
	owîhkâniwa he or she has a friend, has him or her as a friend
	owîhkânemêwa he or she has him or her as a friend
	owîhkânetîwaki they are friends
	owîhkânetîhaki the friends
enemy	**nîchîshkwêha** my enemy
	owîchîshkwêhani his enemy
	owîchîshkwêhwâwahi their enemies
	owîchîshkwêhiwa he or she has an enemy, has him or her as an enemy
	owîchîshkwêhetîwaki they are enemies

www.ingramcontent.com/pod-product-compliance
Lightning Source LLC
Chambersburg PA
CBHW080242030426
42334CB00023BA/2673